THE ATLAS OF
AMERICAN
ARCHITECTURE

THE ATLAS OF
AMERICAN ARCHITECTURE

TOM MARTINSON

FOREWORD BY RICHARD MEIER

**2000 Years of Architecture, City Planning,
Landscape Architecture and Civil Engineering**

RIZZOLI
NEW YORK

First published in the United States of America in 2009 by
RIZZOLI INTERNATIONAL PUBLICATIONS, INC.
300 Park Avenue South, New York, NY 10010
www.rizzoliusa.com

ISBN-13: 978-0-8478-3257-6

Library of Congress Control Number: 2009924743

Martinson, Tom, 1944–

The Atlas of American Architecture / Tom Martinson; foreword by Richard Meier

Distributed to the U. S. Trade by Random House, New York

Endpapers The Rookery lobby, Chicago, Illinois (Fig. 659)
Page 1 Mickey's Diner, St. Paul, Minnesota (Fig. 883)
Pages 2–3 Buckingham Memorial Fountain, Chicago, Illinois (Fig. 1046)

Designed by Abigail Sturges

Edited by John Morris Dixon

Printed and bound in China

2009 2010 2011 2012 2013 2014/ 10 9 8 7 6 5 4 3 2 1

To Joyce
Whose idea this was

And to Malcolm
Who insisted that it be published

CONTENTS

FOREWORD

RICHARD MEIER

t is hard to disagree with Ada Louise Huxtable on most of her architectural criticism, and reading her words in a piece for *The New York Times* more than thirty years after its publication, once again I realize most of us are a few paces behind her. "A great deal has happened outside the conventional centers of power and culture and there is a whole world of architecture between New York and San Francisco and beyond Charleston and Savannah, lost in the shadow of the Chicago skyscraper," she wrote in 1978. "It has been there all along, but the tendency has been to write it off and out of the history books." At last we have a volume that celebrates the architecture of our nation with the inclusive spirit that is quintessentially American, featuring everything from the simplicity of the white picket fence to the astonishing feats of civil engineering that mark our cities' highest towers.

The individuality of American architecture defies any one descriptive label, as the diversity of the works represented in this atlas attests. The works here are united by their qualities of imagination, innovation, and integration of a variety of influences. The boldness of the American dream, so completely embodied in the act of building a home of one's own, has made residential work the foundation of America's particular commitment to the art of architecture in a way that is unique in the world. The daring experimentation that charges the work of Thomas Jefferson, H. H. Richardson, Louis Henri Sullivan, Bernard Maybeck, Frank Lloyd Wright, and Mies van der Rohe led naturally to the development of a singularly American ideal expressed through architecture for our places of work and the strong silhouette of the corporate headquarters that emerged during the twentieth century. The expansion upon these ideals by Eero Saarinen, Kevin Roche, and John Dinkeloo made the interiors of corporate architecture part of the whole, bringing every fixture and piece of furniture into the design in a manner that was revolutionary. So too has the American take on the planned community, first evinced in the design for Llewelyn Park in 1852, proven distinctive given the advantage of landmass in the United States. It is in this realm especially that our responsibility weighs most vitally in moving the continuum of architecture forward in this century; we must create more works of quality for the community, executed more painstakingly than they have been in the past.

During my first project abroad in the 1970s, the Museum for the Decorative Arts in Frankfurt, I noticed that a brief introductory description often followed my name, meant to encapsulate anything you might need to know about my involvement with the project—"the American." As I have traveled the world to work since then I have come to recognize this moniker as something more than just a statement of nationality, and it is one that I wear with pride. Openness and clarity are characteristics that represent American architecture at its best, and they are the principles that I hope to bring to every design endeavor. Our nation's best buildings offer a gratifying spatial experience wherein the occupant experience the larger place while moving through the immediate space. America's finest buildings possess an extroverted sense of what they are and how they relate to their surroundings. To reach out to the landscape with the confidence of Schindler, Neutra, Rudolph, Breuer, and Kahn, as the best of our architects do today, is to be an American architect. I have said before that I would rather build a project in the United States than anywhere else in the world. America is the place where freedom, productivity, experimentation, and innovation meet.

PREFACE

This book started out innocently enough, not really meant to be a book at all. One fine May day in 2002, I made a passing comment to my wife that when I was in college, our syllabus for American architecture was pitiful.

"So do one yourself," Joyce replied. A good-natured challenge.

Trouble was, it sounded like a cool idea. An engaging quest for the summer. After all, an architectural syllabus is usually little more than a listing of significant entries by name, date, designer,

and locality. Sometimes with a couple of background sentences.

As you can see all too well, my simple listing soon got out of hand. Given the wonders of the Internet, it was easy to confirm addresses. With addresses, the syllabus imperceptibly evolved into tour notes.

At that point—the summer of 2002 by now long gone, of course—one might as well add background information, in case friends ask for recommendations of what to see (and why) in, say, Virginia or New Mexico, or LA. Illustration was inevitable.

As this allée at Shirley Plantation in Virginia (Fig. 1) and townscape in Bennington, Vermont (Fig. 2) illustrate, a sense of design can transform ordinary settings into memorable places. In addition to architecture, the best of built America reflects exceptional creativity in planning, landscapes, and engineering.

A Hybrid Guide

In effect, then, my recreational syllabus evolved into a guide. Yet this is obviously not a conventional architectural field guidebook, physically compact and ordered by location. Rather, you can better think of it as a guide to appreciating what has been built in the United States. Site entries, background information, and illustrations describe telling examples of significant design innovations and prominent fashions. Distinct sensibilities—attitudes, technologies, and styles—are grouped wherever possible for comparison, so that you can more easily follow how ideas about planning and design developed across the United States.

While architecture is central to the story of built America, it is not the entire story (Figs. 1, 2). Accordingly, you will also find extensive sections that focus on the concurrent development of American city planning, landscape architecture, and civil engineering.

You will also notice that a number of the entries no longer exist, or have been altered beyond recognition. These works were highly influential, some of them quite controversial in their time, and help to explain a given school or era.

Because chapters are not organized around touring routes, with maps, design historians would characterize this book as a survey, not accurately a guide. Even so, don't let that deter you from using entry addresses and the places index to visit sites that appeal to you. Mapquest ® and Google Maps ® provide detailed maps at multiple scales in minutes for any sites you might wish to visit.

One of Many Possible Viewpoints

It should go without saying, although I'll say it anyway, that this book adopts merely one of numerous possible ways of discussing what has been built in the United States. Since everyone works from a personal perspective, anyone else would organize this material differently. Naturally, regardless of approach, every book is colored by its author's interpretations. As with any subject, everyone knows something, no one knows everything. So please think of this book simply as a resource to assist in establishing your own canon of favorite works.

Organization

The United States is, of course, geographically large, physically diverse, and culturally varied. Its development history spans thousands of years. These attributes easily defeat any attempt to devise a single, ideal format that works elegantly across such vast dimensions of time, space, and human intent. Since I'm necessarily telling many very different stories, these are told in what seems to be the most effective way in each situation. That is why the book's sections are variously organized around cultural eras, colonial influences, regions, design disciplines, schools, personalities, and illustrative building types.

What is Missing

You might rightly wonder why I do not address the architectural treasures of Puerto Rico. Notwithstanding its United States commonwealth status, Puerto Rico's rich cultural traditions have for the most part developed independently of mainland American influences, even since the 1898 cession by Spain (Fig. 3).

As another missing aspect, for practical reasons—this is a general survey, after all—many prominent American building tradi-

FIG. 3 Independent Culture Puerto Rico has been a U.S. possession since 1898, a commonwealth since 1952. Even so, its rich cultural heritage developed largely outside of mainland American influences. Consequently, marvelous Puerto Rican designs like this spectacularly colorful 1882 Parque de Bombas (fire station) in Ponce are not included in this survey. *Library of Congress, Prints & Photographs, Historic American Buildings Survey*

FIGS. 4, 5, 6 Highly Engaging. Not Included. Among several interesting design categories not systematically cited in this book are environmental art like Christo and Jeanne-Claude's 1991 *Umbrellas* installation, which was located next to I-5 at Tejon Pass in Southern California (Fig. 4); semi-permanent structures like this now-demolished Michigan drive-in theater (Fig. 5); and ephemeral constructions such as the St. Paul, Minnesota, Winter Carnival ice palaces (Fig. 6).

tions are virtually unmentioned here. Omissions include well-known regional expressions like New Mexico adobes, Shotgun houses of New Orleans, Dogtrot houses of the South, and "Painted Lady" Victorians of San Francisco.

Neither will you find more than sporadic mention of temporary constructions like large-scale environmental art (Fig. 4), drive-in theaters (Fig. 5), and ephemeral structures like ice palaces, notably the series built since 1886 for the St. Paul Winter Carnival (Fig. 6).

Representative Examples

That addresses the basics. Of course, the specific choices of entries are the central decisions for any book like this. Which examples are most effective in *representing* the best and most interesting of what Americans have built?

In response, I offer a broad sampling from American architecture, city planning, landscape architecture, and civil engineering. Together, these entries illustrate a wide range of creative effort, from high art to popular culture. Specialized sources are cited in Sources by Chapter at the end of the book, if you are interested in a detailed treatment of a particular building, designer, or school.

As you can surely imagine, despite more than a thousand entries, plus several hundred additional supporting citations, numerous structures and sites of national significance are not included. Scores of imaginative, important designers are not specifically identified.

Selections ultimately come down to personal judgment. Understandably, the sites and structures included are weighted toward those I have experienced. My choices of entries were also tempered (although not strictly determined, as noted above) by current physical condition of examples and by their reasonable public accessibility.

Several Interest Levels

You can read through this book at any of several levels of detail. If you look only at the images and headlines, you should be able to gain a good sense of the diverse visual richness of American built environments. Images, headlines, and captions together provide a storyboard overview of major themes. Of course, please feel free to read the full text. (My deepest gratitude to those of you who do!)

And you can easily extract basic touring information from the underlying syllabus: the name, date, designer(s), and address at the head of each individual entry. Combined with indexes for places and creators, and Internet mapping, the book can function as a custom field guide, self-tailored to your specific interests.

Technical Notes

NAME I have used the original name for most entries, unless something is conventionally known by a later name. Especially over the past couple of decades, numerous American entities have reconstituted themselves, merged, or devised quirky new names, and who knows whether they'll be the same by the time you read this?

DATE Ideally, I've accurately determined the span from beginning of design to opening of the building or use of the site. If only a single date is given, it should mark opening-initial use. I stress "ideally" because commonly accepted dates for a given building or development might be based on different project benchmarks from those I'm using. Also, on occasion, fresh research proves that dates everyone thinks are accurate are actually way off.

DESIGNERS I have sought to identify individuals, firms, and public agencies that made material *creative* contributions to a structure or site. Unfortunately, this information is not always realistically available, and some works are by now irretrievably anonymous. Moreover, it is not unusual for traditional attributions of a designer or builder to be eventually found mistaken.

ADDRESS Given that I highly recommend site visits, I consider the addresses to be an important feature. *Two caveats*: Many of these entries are private homes, and inclusion here does not imply any right to intrude on an owner's everyday life. While I have indicated which houses are open to the public at the time of writing—some by reservation only—readers should confirm current schedules on the houses' websites.

Also, I have visited more than 90 percent these sites sometime over the past 40 years, and have not gotten back recently to check the current conditions of every one. Inevitably, a few by now have been razed or materially altered even when not so noted.

EMPHASIS For individual sites and structures, you will find no reliable correlation between the text length of any given entry and its qualitative significance to the built environment. As an example, a landmark design like the Chrysler Building in Manhattan (see the Moderne chapter) is so well known, its superior visual qualities so evident, that there is no need to go into a detailed exposition. At the other extreme, some very modest designs do require more text, often to provide necessary background, as does the Gaffney Peach water tower in South Carolina (Fig. 7, see the Popular Culture chapter).

ADJUNCTS A section of nine *selected* building types follows the architecture chapters. To me, these particular categories usefully highlight how American architecture reflects American culture. Beyond that, be sure not to read too much into my choices of these particular categories, as opposed to others that could have been included instead.

Even so, these particular types are not arbitrary examples. For instance, a colleague questioned my inclusion of a chapter on follies rather than one on hospital design, a field in which American architects were technical innovators throughout the twentieth century. Nevertheless, modern hospital design is largely a specialists' exercise in continuously refining functional efficiencies. Because of this overriding emphasis on technical details over environmental experiences, there are few modern U.S. hospitals I would recommend that you visit to experience as memorable creative works.

However, I'm confident that you will *love* the follies.

BUILDING PERFORMANCE As we all understand, improving a project's environmental impact is increasingly critical in architecture and—more important—to the world. Even so, it is not feasible within the scope of a general survey to systematically showcase innovative environmental responses, although I do occasionally refer to representative historic passive approaches like the side-balcony and center-hall house plans of Charleston.

Since the 1973 oil embargo, mainstream American architecture has evolved through super insulation and efficient mechanical sys-

FIG. 7 Text Length Verses Importance No correlation is implied between text length and intrinsic design significance. An offbeat entry like this "Peachy" water tower in Gaffney, South Carolina, may require more text explanation (see the Popular Culture chapter) than does a superior work with evident visual qualities.

tems, has revisited traditional passive approaches, and is now at the Green Building stage (especially visible in green roofs). Concerns have widened beyond energy use to encompass lower-impact construction materials and finishes. Leadership in Energy and Environmental Design (LEED) certification is now routinely required by non-residential clients, with a platinum LEED rating coveted.

Still, this is mostly about achieving better technical standards—valuable, of course—while continuing to design buildings with the primary creative attention lavished on style (Postmodernism) or art (Deconstruction). Surprisingly, more than three decades after the first world energy shock, there still seems to be very little comprehensive environmental design underway, that is design that seamlessly integrates site and building with respect to energy use, climate-biome, health, and functional innovations reflecting today's lifestyles.

The current cutting edge of environmental-focused planning seems to be the Eco-Effectiveness of American architect William McDonough and German chemist Michael Braungart, as presented in their 2002 book, *Cradle to Cradle: Remaking the Way We Make Things*. The authors propose a complete revision of our production metabolism, aimed at designing products (and ultimately, built environments) as components of a sustaining biology, rather than to simply consume energy and materials that eventually become waste, even if they can be recycled.

Ultimately, perhaps, the currently way-out field of synthetic biology will provide us with the capacity to literally grow ecologically efficient buildings and communities.

INCLUDING CONTEMPORARY WORK Finally, a word about recent works. The prudent approach for any author is to limit entries to those built no later than about a lifetime before the present. That provides plenty of time for studied reflection. Despite the practical wisdom of a cut-off date set safely in the past, there is, as always, really interesting contemporary work.

Without a doubt, some of the recent entries I've cited here will not seem significant in a couple of decades. And from the informed perspective gained by distance, anyone glancing through these pages in the 2020s might marvel at how I could possibly have overlooked *this* building or *that* designer!

If you have a casual interest in American building, I hope that paging through this book leaves you with a sense of the remarkable design achievements that have occurred over the past three millennia in what is now the United States of America.

For anyone with an ongoing, active interest in built America, this material is intended to assist you in forming additional insights about American creativity and identifying memorable places to visit.

If design is your passion, as it is for me, I expect that you will strongly disagree with at least some of my choices (and omissions) of entries, not to mention, with my interpretations. Compiling this "simple listing," my original intention, has been an absorbing and immensely rewarding exercise for me—as it would doubtless be for you. I hope, then, that you will consider this effort in need of considerable improvement, like my college syllabus.

So do one yourself!

Tom Martinson
Minneapolis, March 2009

INTRODUCTION

To me, and probably to you, built America is endlessly fascinating. Anyone traveling widely throughout the United States soon appreciates a fundamental national quality: with respect to its people and places, America is diverse. That diversity can result in apparent contradictions, where "American" constructions are characteristically both practical *and* fashion-conscious, both innovative *and* imitative. From its natural landscapes to its design expressions, the United States is a land of extreme variety.

People and Settings

Some Americans, like the Hopi, trace their heritage back into the mists of prehistory. Others have just arrived, from everywhere on the planet. No matter when they came, for each generation of immigrants, America has traditionally offered an opportunity to start afresh, comparatively free of the limiting customs they left behind.

Reflecting its human diversity, the United States contains innu-

merable physical environments and dozens of distinct climates. The resulting combinations of national origin, locality, and climate produced a myriad of American built settings, most of them quite different from the Old World.

So not only did many emigrants to America fully intend to start afresh, they really had to—beginning with the ways they constructed their homes and laid out their communities.

FIGS. 8, 9 Towns Looked Different Because Daily Life Was Different. The outsized scale of trans-Appalachian farming ensured that nineteenth-century rural settlements in the United States would have little in common, visually, with the European communes where their founding citizens were born. Midwestern "Ag" towns functioned as regional commercial centers, laid out to ease the delivery of produce to rail-side grain elevators. Hence, American farm towns like Appleton, Minnesota (Fig. 8) looked very different from, for instance, close-grained German market towns like Nordlingen (Fig. 9) on Germany's Romantic Road, which also functioned as social centers, physically organized around a town hall square.

FIG. 10 Shelter First Rarely did settler on the frontier initially build more than huts constructed of locally available materials like sod and branches. This 1929 photo shows a home-shelter along the Selewik River in Alaska. *Library of Congress, Prints & Photographs*

FIGS. 11, 12 Ever-changing Fashion The American notion of stylish evolved continuously. In the nineteenth century, for instance, architectural fashion changed sharply with each generation. This pristine, white-clapboard Connecticut church (Fig. 11) would have been the paragon of good taste while Enlightenment ideals remained strong, well into the 1800s. As Romanticism began to color the national mood by the 1830s, a design like this would have come to have seemed "old-fashioned." By then, a weathered (or warmly painted) board-and-batten design like this Bluffton, South Carolina, church attributed to Richard Upjohn (Fig. 12) would have been mainstream, though soon to be displaced as contemporary by the Eastlake style. And before the end of the century Eastlake would be replaced as the current fashion by the American Colonial Revivals.

American Communities

You can see how this came about, for example, in the widely dispersed, nineteeth-century farm towns of the American Midwest. Both visually and in the experiences of everyday life, these were markedly unlike the European villages where their founders were born. Compared to ancestral plots in Europe, a typical 160-acre American farm homestead was enormous, requiring new agricultural techniques in order to farm the land efficiently. The considerable distance between neighboring Midwestern farmhouses, much less to the nearest town, meant that a Continental, village lifestyle could not prevail in much of rural, trans-Appalachian United States.

As late as 1930, well over 40 percent of Americans lived a rural existence, half of them as farmers. And while Midwestern farm towns offered Saturday evening socialization for rural families such rural towns functioned more as service centers, and less as cultural hearths, than did European villages of similar size. So for example, if German towns (Fig. 9) commonly focused on a masonry *Rathaus*, the community's council building, the most-prominent structure in a typical Midwestern farm town populated by German (and other) emigrants was a frame-construction grain elevator (Fig. 8).

American Houses

Housing also differed between Old World and New. Naturally, the earliest settlers' housing in any part of the United States had to be quickly built shelter, constructed of available local materials. These were often barely more than huts, usually built of thatch, logs, sod (Fig. 10), or mud adobe.

Better houses were constructed as soon as time and money allowed. But only a handful of houses, like Virginia Tidewater mansions (Fig. 69), in any colonial or pioneer era were built as enduring housing, expected to be passed down through future generations in the manner of English estates. Among several reasons why this was so, probably the most significant was opportunity.

The Influence of Opportunity

Living in the Land of Opportunity, Americans expected upward change in their lives as a matter of course. It was always possible that one might build a still-better house in the future. American-style opportunity also meant that adult children were not necessarily attached financially or by social norms to family lands, and might instead choose to move elsewhere. Nor was it uncommon for an entire family to uproot and move on to another part of the country in search of improved fortune.

The Prominence of Architectural Fashion

This "rootless" trait in American culture has long been noted by observers, especially by those who contend that American culture is inherently shallow because it is not strongly tied to rich, comparatively timeless traditions like, say, those of Tuscany or Provence.

Less noted, with respect to rootlessness, is the consequent prominence of fashion in American housing. Compared to historic, long-lasting housing conventions of Europe, Asia, and Latin America, housing in the United States has been widely affected by passing fashions.

As we will see, for instance, in the 1800s a succession of architectural fashions swept throughout the United States. For the first three decades, reflecting the lasting influence of Enlightenment sensibilities, a straightforward, white clapboard box with green shutters remained as the standard for the tasteful contemporary American house and other structures (Fig. 11).

FIG. 13 **Ethnic Expressions**
The national building
heritages of European
immigrants were rarely
expressed faithfully in
American architecture. To be
sure, some communities with
prominent ethnic
backgrounds built structures
intended to evoke the Old
Country, like the arresting
Flemish imagery employed
for the New Ulm, Minnesota,
post office (1909, John Knox
Taylor, official architect),
which was meant to recall
the town pioneers'
Germanic ancestry.
Notwithstanding, the United
States was so different from
Europe that even such
intentional nods to ethnicity
were inevitably synthesized
into novel architectural
expressions.

With the rise of romanticism by the 1830s, contemporary architectural fashion shifted to irregular board-and-batten cottages, villas, and churches (Fig. 12), perhaps painted in a dusky red or chocolate brown, which were intended to nestle romantically into their natural surroundings. In the next sharp break, occurring during the social unrest right around the Civil War, energetic imageries like Eastlake (Fig. 158), meant to stand out aggressively, emerged as the height of fashion.

These overwrought expressions increasingly seemed dated after the 1876 Centennial, when American Colonial Revival imageries gained wide popularity, in large part because they were thought to reflect that the United States was maturing as a nation (Fig. 177).

In the twentieth century, American housing largely followed three familiar approaches. Inexpensive developers' tract houses were commonly based on inherently efficient historic types like the Cape Cod. Design innovations like the Craftsman Bungalow and the California Ranch House reflected national social changes, offering new forms of housing that accommodated changing lifestyles.

In a third common approach, a historic style was applied cosmetically to a generic plan. Such designs could be quite suave, like many houses and commercial buildings of the 1920s and 1930s; or flat and cartoon-like, as was more typical in the 1990s and early 2000s for both housing and commercial structures. Appliqué houses of any era were rarely functionally innovative, although their mechanical systems were technologically up-to-date.

Ethnic Influences

Irrespective of these characteristically "American" approaches to designing homes and planning communities, many Americans initially retained strong ties to their ancestral national cultures. Some ethnic groups had little choice, as their emigrants were pressed by market forces and social pressures into Chinatowns, barrios, and other segregated enclaves on the wrong side of the tracks. These districts were typically built to higher densities, manifested in urban wards as tenement flats rather than as detached houses, for instance.

Many immigrants unsurprisingly chose, in the past and still today, to begin their lives in America by living close to family or to those from their home villages who had already settled in the United States. Inevitably, sections of big American cities became known as Little Italy, Greektown, and dozens of other international references. These were initially mostly European, although in recent decades, prominently Asian and African. Out on the developing, nineteenth-century frontier, residents of a new rural settlement might be predominantly German, or Swedish, or primarily of another common ancestry.

Especially up to about 1950, these urban wards and ethnic towns could be vibrant centers of their national culture, as expressed in almost anything from religion to restaurant cuisine. Well into the 1920s, for example, residents of a medium-sized city like Minneapolis could choose from among dozens of locally produced foreign-language newspapers. In larger cities like Chicago, it was not unusual for impressive Irish Catholic, German Catholic, and Polish Catholic parish churches to be built almost within sight of each other.

Even so, despite sometimes-pervasive cultural self-identity, rarely did these communities or their buildings (Fig. 13) *look* anything like the cities and villages of their national origins. That is partly because American culture tends to synthesize outside cultural exemplars into characteristically "American" expressions. For built America, this characteristic synthesis of outside influences often reflects three prominent and persistent qualities. These are locality, innovation, and common sense.

Locality

The significance of locality to built America is apparent in several respects. As just noted, ethnic groups did not physically replicate their homeland communities. Neither did they replicate their native architecture, beyond isolated examples like Chinatown imageries. Nevertheless, subtle ethnic predilections influenced decisions about how and where to build in the new country. These could be as obscure to outsiders as the propensity for German Catholics to build imposing stone or brick churches in the center of town, while Scandinavian Lutherans from the same community commonly built simple white frame churches outside of town, on rural hilltops wherever possible. Both approaches established visual prominence, though in characteristic ways.

Necessarily, locality in the forms of climate, weather, and available building materials influenced what Americans built. A cold climate with heavy snows required sturdier roof construction than would a more temperate climate. Because of severe winter weather, some New England farm buildings were physically interconnected (Fig. 14). Raised main floors made eminent sense in New Orleans (Fig. 57), always at risk of flooding. Log cabins were built in wooded frontiers, but sod or mud-brick adobe were the original building materials of choice in the largely treeless Great Plains and the Southwest.

In the post–World War II era, these traditional regional distinctions have almost completely disappeared. Nationwide, recent

FIG. 14 Climate and Weather Influenced What Americans Built. The Benjamin Abbot farmhouse in Andover, Massachusetts, built after 1685, illustrates a functional response to harsh New England winters. House, utility shed, main barn, and an add-on were all internally interconnected, so that routine chores and daily animal care would not require going out into blizzards. *Library of Congress, Prints & Photographs, Historic American Buildings Survey*

FIG. 15 Innovation Can Transcend Mere Utility Buckminster Fuller's Geodesic domes have been employed all over the world as efficient, inexpensive shelter. Nevertheless, this intrinsic functionality did not prevent United States Pavilion, by Fuller with Cambridge Seven, Architects, from becoming the visual centerpiece at Expo '67 in Montreal.

designs of both housing and commercial buildings featured applied style, with little emphasis on functional innovations in plan. Given today's near-universal access to advanced technologies and building materials, some of the earlier, locality-related concerns are no longer as vital, technically. Still, if only from the perspectives of energy use and livability among dissimilar climates, this current national prominence of generic planning approaches and cosmetic designs in so diverse a country should be a matter of concern.

Innovation

This present-day (though hopefully temporary) relative indifference to innovation is all the more disappointing when compared to traditional levels of innovation in American building. At their best, Americans have innovated brilliantly in organizing and transferring land, in laying out towns efficiently, and in creatively adapting Old World building conventions to accommodate New World settlement conditions.

As one eminent exemplar, Richard Buckminster Fuller (1895–1983) was the Leonardo of American innovators-inventers. "Bucky" Fuller was a true polymath, a U.S. Navy officer as a young adult and a professor of poetry at Harvard in mid-life, all the while pursuing an astonishing array of interests before and after. His famous self-assessment, "I seem to be a verb," seemed entirely accurate.

Fuller applied mathematics, especially solid geometry, to devise a revolutionary three-wheeled "Dymaxion" car in 1933, and a Dymaxion house (designed in 1927–1928, on display at the Henry Ford Museum-Greenfield Village in suburban Detroit). His "Geodesic" domes were employed all over the world as highly efficient enclosures which could be erected quickly in difficult locales. The American Pavilion at Expo '67 in Montreal was Fuller's most spectacular Geodesic design (Fig. 15).

While few Americans approached Fuller's stature as an inventor, it was largely through practical innovations that communities and individual structures acquired their memorable, indigenous flavor—their sense of being *American*.

Historically, because millions of immigrants spread out across immense expanses of the North American hinterlands, they were effectively on their own with respect to solving a myriad of novel daily problems. As a consequence, especially throughout the nineteenth century, an American tradition of local innovation emerged in response to these unique functional problems. Hence, American ingenuity has been typified by straightforward, efficient solutions, ideally achieved through what was popularly called an economy of means.

National innovation also occurred in direct response to social changes. As one very simplified illustration, up through the late 1800s, even middle-class families commonly retained young women as domestic servants. Victorian-era American houses were replete with elaborate, dust-catching woodwork (Fig. 16); cooking took place in a dim, utilitarian space tucked away at the back

With the rapid growth of American business corporations by the late 1800s, increasing numbers of females chose to work as clerks. As a result, fewer young women were available as domestics. Consequently, many the "housewife" was forced to take over cleaning and meal preparation. Predictably, easier-to-clean houses soon became popular, featuring simplified woodwork, with far fewer nooks and crannies (Fig. 17). About the same time, Frank Lloyd Wright devised innovative new house plans organized around a modern, light-filled kitchen overlooking the children's play area, sometimes also providing a view of street activity.

FIG. 16, 17 **Practicality Shaped Architectural Innovation.** Prior to the late-nineteenth-century rise of business corporations, even middle-class American families could readily secure domestic help, since the alternative for many young women was grueling factory work. As a consequence, the elaborate woodwork and cavernous volumes of Victorian-era houses, illustrated here by the 1886 Carson House (Fig. 16) in Eureka, California, architects Samuel and Joseph C. Newsom (see the Romantic Revivals and Eclecticism chapter), were of little practical concern to homeowners. By the turn of the twentieth century, the era of plentiful domestics was ending. Now, as growing corporations needed endless ranks of clerks, young women increasingly chose office work, thus contributing to a permanent shortage of domestics. Houses were soon trimmed down to adapt to the new realities of maintenance. The architectural response is apparent in this comparison of the Carson interior with an interior of the 1910 Carter House in Evanston, Illinois (Fig. 17) designed by Prairie School architect Walter Burley Griffin. *Library of Congress, Prints & Photographs, Historic American Buildings Survey*

Common Sense

These kinds of practical innovations highlight a third enduring quality influencing built America: common sense. Especially through the early decades of the twentieth century , a visitor from a visually opulent city like Paris or Buenos Aires traveling around the United States might well have been shocked by the comparative inelegance of much American building. Among several reasons for this were a continuous, rapid pace of growth and the pragmatic goal of recent arrivals simply to survive. Too, American social values have famously seemed to many observers to emphasize making money over cultural attainment.

Whatever the explanation, while ornate forms of architectural adornment common in Europe are certainly not unknown in the United States (see the Beaux Arts chapter), they are not typical of what Americans have built. Instead, practical, simplified house types like the Cape Cod (see the New England Colonial Architecture chapter) evolved out of innovative responses to functional requirements, climate, weather conditions, and available building materials. Such designs were honest expressions of their time and place. That gave them an indigenous flavor, a native quality which rendered them fresh and authentic.

Indeed, significant American building innovations have largely been technical. Compared to, say, the grandeur of public Paris, the glorious Baroque churches and palaces of Germany, and the Renaissance treasures of Italy, American architecture is not renowned for *style*, as opposed to mere fashion.

Rather, many American design advances are functional innovations. These include such straightforward accommodations as high ceilings in hot climates and radiant floor heating in cold climates.

Practical construction innovations have been prominent throughout American history. As one celebrated example, the balloon frame made possible the rapid, economical construction of housing and small commercial buildings in boom cities like Chicago and San Francisco (see the Industrial Structures chapter).

Similarly, development of the radical Chicago skyscraper accurately mirrored the no-nonsense, commercial values of those "titans of industry" who devised the modern American corporate state in the late 1800s (see The Chicago School chapter).

The Endless Variety of Built America

None of this talk about practicality should suggest that built America is boring! Quite the opposite, as you will see. Despite (or perhaps, because of) the fact that the United States is influenced by every culture on Earth, its overall built environment is unlike that of any other nation across the globe. American building is uniquely diverse.

Highlighting these familiar American qualities of locality, innovation, and common sense can help to explain *why* a given design was approached as it was, though of course this does not explain every design cited here, or in any broad survey. Like the way I've organized this book and my choices of works to include, my emphasis on these particular qualities is simply one way of presenting the material.

Many other insights will probably occur to you, as you consider the remarkable panorama of built America.

PRE-COLUMBIAN

ENVIRONMENTS

10,000 BCE—1900 CE

Aboriginal Cultures

10,000 BCE–1300 CE

FIG. 18 Living With the Natural Landscape As a practical matter, aboriginal Americans had to live in harmony with nature in order to survive. More than just accommodating climate and weather and understanding the habits of prey, ancient North American societies sought to harmonize with the universe through ritual.

Personal rituals would be a routine part of daily life. Community rituals might center around a sacred object like this monolith at Second Mesa in northern Arizona. Some civilizations held seasonal ceremonies at national ritual centers like Chaco Canyon (Figs. 21, 22).

People have lived in the Americas for a very long time, at least 10,000 years and perhaps as many as 30,000. Carbon dating confirms vestiges of human settlement from about 10,000 BCE in Brazil and 10,500 BCE in Chile. Debris of everyday life at the Meadowcroft Rockshelter near Pittsburgh may date from as early as about 12,000 BCE.

Much aboriginal American habitation appears to trace back to three distinct migrations across the Bering Strait, with waves occurring about 9000 BCE, 7000 BCE, and 2000 BCE. These early dates imply six distinct fonts of civilization, globally: Mesoamerica and Peru along with Sumer, Egypt, the Indus Valley, and the Yellow River Valley.

Whatever are the precise origins of American civilization, the story of built America begins when our nomadic predecessors decided to take root, someplace. The precise nature of how this settling-in occurred varied by time and by culture, as we will see. But taking root would have occurred in a typical sequence. This started with agriculture, which of course required farmers to stay put, to live near their crops. Eventually, neighboring farmers might form villages, small clusters of rude shelters, for socialization and protection.

In time, successful societies built cities like Poverty Point, which had to be more ordered than villages because of larger populations and a consequent need to distinguish among residential quarters, ritual areas, and worksites. A small number of these cities developed according to a pre-determined pattern—a city plan.

Ultimately, a very few cities-regions, like Teotihuacán and Chaco Canyon, functioned as national ritual-ceremonial centers. These were distinguished by monumental public architecture, and by axial-geometric city (or even regional) plan patterns.

We should begin the story of built America with a word about rituals. Living directly from the land requires continuous accommodations with the natural world. For some aboriginal Americans, these accommodations went well beyond merely recognizing seasonal patterns of Nature and understanding the habits of prey. These first Americans would surely have perceived a serene, eternal harmony in the heavens, and must have compared it to the routine turmoil of life on Earth: dealing with violent storms, flooding, drought, sweltering heat, bone-chilling cold. In apparent response, Aboriginals developed intricate rituals intended to harmonize with the universe, in order to bring balance and order to Earth and, consequently, safety and stability to human life.

Today, most of us probably think of these ceremonies as "Native American religion," just another among a worldwide multitude of beliefs. That would be a fundamental misreading.

One cannot understand stupendous ritual constructions like Chaco Canyon simply as building. To these Americans, ritual centers were integral parts of the universe, without which human life would inevitably falter. Hence, to their nations, ritual settings were the most important works of society.

Second Mesa FIG. 18
Cosmic Prehistory
Hwy. 264, NE of Hwy. 87, Navajo County, Arizona

In the Hopi creation story, Second Mesa is the navel of the universe. Because of a traditional belief that Hopis are to serve as protectors of Creation, Hopi sacred custom requires endless observance of ceremonial laws in order to maintain the harmony of the universe. So to Hopis, Second Mesa is the most important place in the world. Oraibi, on nearby Third Mesa, dating from about 1150 CE, is among the oldest continuously occupied settlements in the continental United States.

ANTECEDENTS IN THE AMERICAS

Valley of Tehuacán
7000 BCE
Mesoamerica/South-central Mexico

North American agricultural cultivation in this region may date from as far back as 9000 years ago, with the planting and harvesting of maize. Cultivation in fixed locales implies the need for seasonal territorial habitation in order to tend crops. Hence, farmers would likely have settled, at least semi-permanently, near their fields.

Norte Chico
3200 BCE
North Coastal Peru

Inevitably, settlers formed villages. Urbanization seems to have emerged in the Americas around 3200 BCE, perhaps a few centuries earlier at Norte Chico, which Charles C. Mann identified as "the Americas' first urban complex," located near present-day Lima. Elsewhere in Peru, major public buildings were constructed c. 3200–2500 BCE, an era mostly prior to the traditional dating of the Great Pyramid of Giza around 2600 BCE.

By then, Sumer, the world's first great civilization, had been developing for about 6000 years.

FIG. 19 **Monumental City Building** Several great North American nations built monumental centers for government, ritual, and commerce. Teotihuacán near Mexico City is one of the supreme works among aboriginal civilizations in the Americas. Avenue of the Dead once extended for more than two miles from the base of the Pyramid of the Moon, visible in the distance.

Monte Albán
500 BCE –750 CE
Oaxaca de Juárez, Mexico, vic.

Monte Albán was the first monumental Mesoamerican urban center, an aggressive state which forcibly incorporated dozens of independent communities in the process of establishing a domain of about 10,000 square miles. A peak local population of about 30,000 was attained in 500 CE. Monte Albán's constructions were organized around a grand ceremonial plaza.

By today's standards, this society engaged in city planning and architecture. Monte Albán is among the greatest of pre-Columbian works.

Teotihuacán FIG. 19
0–750 CE
Mexico City, Mexico, vic.

Teotihuacán represents the last of four critical cultural landmarks in Mesoamerican civilization: (1) Agricultural cultivation began in the Valley of Tehuacán about 7000 BCE. (2) Settlers had established a regional group of villages by about 3200 BCE at Norte Chico. (3) Architectural pretense emerged with Monte Albán. (4) At Teotihuacán, truly epic city building is evident. This was a center of government, ritual, and commerce, with two great pyramidal temples and dozens of smaller stepped pyramids set in a precise grid plan organized around an immense axial boulevard. Teotihuacán occupied eight square miles in area, with a peak population of 125,000. Today, even reduced to just its core ceremonial area, Teotihuacán is awesome.

EARLY HABITATIONS IN THE UNITED STATES

Hohokam Salt River Irrigation Canals
0 –1450 CE
Southern Arizona; Pueblo Grande interpretive site at 4619 E. Washington St., Phoenix, Arizona

Almost from the beginnings of Hohokam culture, its people began building what eventually grew into a 1000-mile canal system, regulating the flow of water from the Salt River in the vicinity of present-day Phoenix. Canals were maintained for more than 1000 years, requiring a large, stable population in the region. According to some estimates, peak area population may have reached 50,000.

While the Phoenix-area canals are best known, ancient agriculture was apparently widespread across the Sonoran Desert. Irrigation canals dating from as early as 1000 BCE have recently been discovered along the Santa Cruz River in Tucson. Hohokam culture died out by about 1450 CE.

Mississippi River Valley Settlements
800 CE
Louisiana

The influence of Mesoamerican culture appears to have spread into what is now the southerly mid-section of the United States. Here, local cultures employed advanced practices in agriculture, also constructing truncated pyramids similar to those built earlier in central Mexico.

This suggests that the Lower Mississippi Valley might have been populated by a diaspora from Teotihuacán and other societies, which had fallen into sharp decline less than a lifetime earlier.

PUEBLO CULTURE

Canyon de Chelly
350–1300 CE
3 mi. SE of Chinle, Navajo County, Arizona; from I-40, N 70 mi. on Hwy. 191 to Chinle

The deep, narrow Canyon de Chelly contains the ruins of a complex settlement constructed near the bases of massive cliffs. White House (1066–1275), a cliff dwelling sited beneath a sheer, 600-foot rock face, is the architectural highlight. Still, this bravura construction, seemingly carved right out of the natural rock, is hardly more than a speck within its stunning natural setting.

Mesa Verde FIG. 20
550–1300 CE
Hwy. 160, 10 mi. SE of Cortez, Colorado

The earliest settlers to this area were nomadic hunter-gatherers, who began to farm on the mesas, living nearby in pit dwellings. By about 750 CE pit houses were replaced by adobe surface dwellings, while pit structures were given over to ceremonial functions, eventually evolving into kivas.

By about 1000 CE, the mesas-uplands had become devoted to agriculture, while people lived in stone houses in the canyons at the bases of cliffs. Some of these houses were grouped together, in effect forming multi-family structures.

The years 1100–1300 CE were a classic age for Mesa Verde, as small, individual pueblos were abandoned in favor of large communal dwellings-villages set into natural recesses in cliff walls: the famous cliff dwellings. Individual rooms were extremely small, at about 50 square feet. Understandably, everyday social life took place primarily in nearby outdoor courtyards.

Many of the Mesa Verde cliff dwellings were constructed between the late 1190s and the late 1270s. Cliff Palace is the architectural landmark from this era, with 217 rooms and 23 kivas. The larger structures were of a comparatively sophisticated sandstone-masonry construction. Architecturally, American apartment living dates from the last two inhabited eras at Mesa Verde.

Chaco Canyon FIGS. 21, 22
Mid-800s–mid-1200s CE
SE of Farmington, New Mexico
Warning: 17 mi. of the 21 mi. access road from Hwy. 550 is an indescribably rutted, pothole-infested washboard when dry, and practically impassable when wet.

Chaco Culture was a semi-urban society developed by predecessors of today's Pueblo Indians. Chaco Canyon apparently served as a national ceremonial center for Ancestral Puebloans. The area

FIG. 20 **Early Apartment Living** Cliff Palace in Mesa Verde National Park in Colorado is the best-known Pueblo construction, engagingly photogenic. It was built as an innovative functional response to its setting and use.

FIGS. 21, 22 **Cosmic Architecture** Like the Hopi civilization at Second Mesa, Chaco Culture envisioned primordial cosmic connections to the universe, accessed ritually through this vast construction. Ceremonies took place within the circular kivas (Fig. 21). Pueblo Bonito formed the nexus of an immense ceremonial domain centered on Chaco Canyon (Fig. 22) in northern New Mexico.

included the primary physical components of a vast, partly invisible regional structure of a type which Marko Pogačnik refers to as a landscape temple.

Chaco Canyon's planning and construction evidence advanced architecture and engineering, including 400 miles of 30-foot-wide roads interconnecting a 60,000-square-mile Chaco region extending into Colorado and Arizona. These roads seem to have been built primarily to serve as ritual, spirit connections to the universe, reflecting the Ancestral Puebloans' sacred worldview.

Pueblo Bonito (919–1067) formed the heart of the Chaco world (Fig. 22). This four-story ceremonial structure contained more than 600 rooms, most of them uninhabitable volumes, along with 40 kivas. Chaco building plans were laid out in half-moon or "D" patterns, which enclosed the circular kiva chambers (Fig. 21). In their general form, these "D" shapes superficially resemble the semi-circular layout of the much earlier Poverty Point community (following entry).

Like Second Mesa (cited above), Chaco Canyon would have been understood by its society as a vital hub of the universe. However, it appears that Chaco Canyon served more as a seasonal ritual center, rather than as an everyday, working city. Its ceremonial district included several outlying, aligned constructions, located up to 15 miles distant. Some of these sites are not visible from the ceremonial core around Pueblo Bonito. In the extreme, the Chaco nation's lunar observatory at Chimney Rock in Colorado (1076) is located 90 miles from Pueblo Bonito.

The entire complex followed master astronomical interrelationships, ultimately focusing back on Pueblo Bonito. In effect, two layers of cosmic ritual systems engaged with the natural landscape: "solar" buildings and "lunar" buildings, the latter functioning in 18.6-year cycles.

After more than two centuries of use, the purpose of the immense sacred network centered on Chaco Canyon was apparently concluded. Structures were then ritually closed: wall open-

ings were carefully infilled with stone, kiva timbers were removed, the kivas burned.

Its builders departed, and Chaco Canyon was returned to Mother Earth.

MOUND BUILDERS

Poverty Point Community FIG. 23
1500–700 BCE
Epps, Louisiana vic. I-20 to Delhi exit, N on Hwy. 17, E on Hwy. 134, N on Rt. 577

Countless thousands of mounds were constructed in the eastern United States and Canada. The earliest yet discovered date from about 3400 BCE, in northeastern Louisiana near Poverty Point. These 11 irregular Ouachita Mounds are arranged in a circle.

Poverty Point Community was a major development in mound building, a remarkably advanced society for its era and its remote locale. The inhabitants were traders who obtained supplies and materials by way of a far-flung trading network linked by rivers. While much of the community's commerce occurred within a few

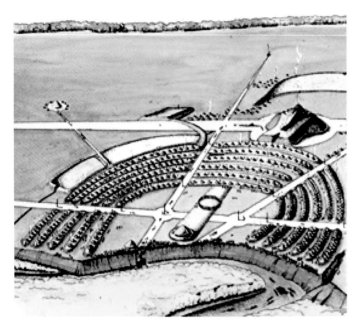

FIG. 23 City Planning Poverty Point Community flourished in the mists of North American prehistory, three millennia ago. The community's expansive, ordered earthworks mark the first geometric city plan in what is now the United States. *El Camino College*

hundred miles of this location, copper was sourced from the south shore of Lake Superior, 1000 miles distant.

Poverty Point developed as a large, geometric earthworks construction, defined by an expanding semi-circle of six concentric rings, the outer ring three-quarters of a mile in diameter. Radial pathways converged on a central plaza, which overlooked the immense Mississippi River floodplain below. The middle radial connected with the largest mound, which was located just beyond the outer ring. This bird-shaped construction measured an impressive 700 feet by 640 feet at its base, rising to 70 feet in height. Poverty Point's ordered layout marks the first known appearance of a geometric city plan in the United States.

Great Serpent Mound FIG. 24

800 BCE–400 CE? 950–1200 CE?
Hwy. 73, 4 mi. NE of Locust Grove, Adams County, Ohio

Possibly during the first millennium BCE, an "Adena-Hopewell" culture emerged in what is now south-central Ohio, spreading out-

ward as far as northwestern Wisconsin, the Louisiana Delta, and present-day Toronto. More than 5,000 effigy mounds associated with this culture have been identified in southern Wisconsin alone. Most of these mounds were plowed under by homesteaders in the 1800s.

Great Serpent Mound, which writhes for about one-quarter of a mile in length, is the most striking of the few remaining earth constructions. The dating of Serpent Mound is uncertain—some experts now think it may have been built long after the Adena-Hopewell era, perhaps after 1000 CE—as is its exact purpose, though some of the Adena-Hopewell constructions were employed as burial mounds.

Regardless of dating, these mounds may illustrate how Adena-Hopewell culture approached the ceremonial aspects of life from a very different perspective from the Chaco Culture's. Where Chaco ritual was cosmic and national, Adena-Hopewell seems comparatively practical and local. It may be that some of these mounds functioned simply as community idols, intended to capture the presumed powers and attributes of the animals they replicated, thereby protecting and enhancing the lives of the mound builders and their clans.

Cahokia FIG. 25

700–1400 CE
Collinsville Rd., S of I-55, 1.5 mi. W of I-255, Collinsville, Illinois

Cahokia is the largest Mesoamerican-like urban complex in the United States, visually dominated by 19 platform mounds arranged around a large central plaza. Cahokia's peak population, c. 1050 –1200 CE, was probably between 10,000 and 20,000, constituting a major city.

More than 100 tributary mounds were located in a five-square-mile suburban area outside of a central palisade, within which a 200-acre sacred precinct developed. Five circular "woodhenges" were built between 900 and 1100 CE, possibly functioning as astronomical calendars.

At its zenith of activity, Cahokia traded from the Atlantic to Oklahoma, but around 1200 the city slipped into decline, to be completely abandoned by about 1400.

Sixty-nine of the more than 120 aboriginal Cahokia mounds are preserved within today's historic site area, including the 14-acre, 100-foot-high Monks Mound (Fig. 25). These earth constructions are visually quite impressive, and a site visit is enhanced by excellent interpretive exhibits.

FIG. 24 Seriously Sinuous Earthworks Among thousands of effigy mounds built in the American Midwest, Great Serpent Mound in Ohio is the most arresting among those still extant. *Ohio Department of Natural Resources*

FIG. 25 Epic Midwestern City Building Located only a few miles from St. Louis, Cahokia offers monumental earthworks rivaling the great Mesoamerican cities (for scale, note the truck in the photo). Monk's Mound, illustrated here, marked the center of a highly ordered urban region with as many as 20,000 inhabitants.

Indigenous Cultures

1300–1900

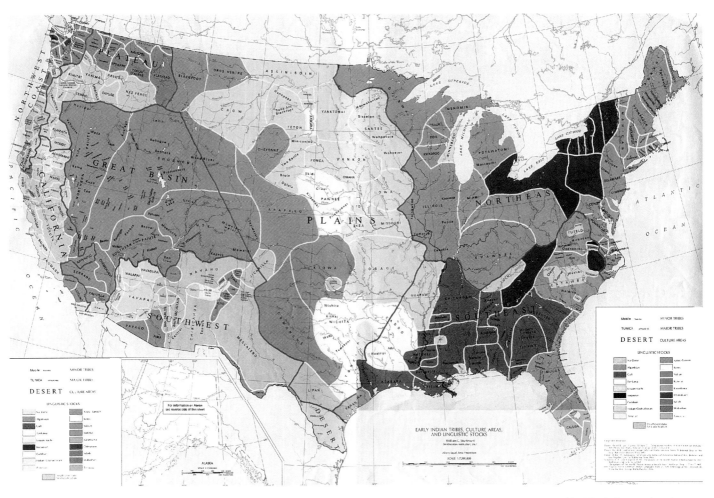

FIG. 26 Indigenous Americans By the standards and values of European pioneers, North America was virtually empty. In reality, as these U.S. maps imply, at the time of the Columbian voyages, 10 million to as many as 100 million indigenous Americans lived border-to-border, coast-to-coast. *University of Texas Libraries*

Around 1300 CE, North American aboriginal culture underwent abrupt, widespread changes among the nations living in what are now the United States, Canada, and Mexico. This turmoil was concurrent with the abandonment of communities like Canyon de Chelly and Mesa Verde and the Chaco Canyon ritual area (see the Aboriginal Cultures chapter).

Francis Jennings speculated that sometime around 1300 a new wave of immigrants from Alaska and the Canadian Northwest poured into what is now the United States, possibly causing mass dislocations among existing nations in the American West. Charles C. Mann noted multiple negative impacts at Cahokia as well as in southern Mayan regions, including intense social-political conflicts, natural disasters (perhaps on the scale of the 1930s Dust Bowl), environmental mismanagement, and local population growth beyond the environmental capacities available to sustain such growth.

Some or all of these could explain the widespread abandonment of ancestral lands, cities, and settlements that occurred around 1300. As a result, especially residents of larger communities were apparently forced to disperse, scattering to distant locales.

FIGS. 28, 29 **Rural Urbanism** Two adobe apartment blocks facing each other across a small stream establish the architectural character of Taos Pueblo in northern New Mexico. Functional adobe construction fortuitously resulted in memorable visual character, seemingly replicating the mountains beyond.

Whatever the reasons for this abandonment and apparent diaspora, 1300 is a useful date to distinguish a break between ancient, aboriginal North American cultures and the indigenous cultures encountered two centuries later by European explorers (Figs. 26).

As American "manifest destiny" expansion progressed, these indigenous nations were pressed into reservations during the late 1800s. Ironically and shamefully, *Native* Americans were not granted citizenship as U.S. nationals until 1924. Understandably, design advances declined in indigenous cultures by the mid-1800s.

The following examples provide a generalized overview of indigenous shelters devised by Americans. These especially illustrate innovative responses to climate and to local availability of materials.

PERMANENT STRUCTURES

Taos Pueblo FIGS. 28, 29
1300s, rebuilt c. 1700
3 mi. N of Taos, New Mexico, via Paseo Del Pueblo Norte

Architecturally, this communal village is expressed almost as modern apartments. Two blocky, mud-adobe masses, the *Hlauuma* (North House, Fig. 28) and *Hlaukwima* (South House), separated by a small stream, are visually prominent within the central, traditional area of Taos Pueblo.

Originally, inhabitants entered their separate living spaces by way of ladders through holes in the roof, but by now conventional exterior doors have been opened into each unit. Dramatic visual interest is generated by the contrast of strong sunlight against shadows cast across cascades of unadorned forms, played off against mountains in the background.

Acoma Pueblo, "Sky City" FIG. 30
rebuilt after 1599
60 mi. W of Albuquerque, New Mexico, on I-40 to Exit 108, S 12 mi. on Rt. 23

Like several other indigenous communities, including Taos (above) and Oraibi (Aboriginal Cultures chapter), the Pueblo of Acoma asserts that it is the oldest continuously occupied settlement in North America, citing a possible date of 1150 CE for initial occupation of its 70-acre mesa. Regardless of its founding date, Acoma Pueblo existed as a cluster of adobe buildings centuries prior to its "discovery" by the Spanish in 1540. It was burned down in a fit of pique by other Spaniards in 1599. The pueblo that we visit today was rebuilt after 1599.

Compared to Taos, the indigenous Acoma pueblo is less remarkable, architecturally. That is of little matter, since Acoma commands surely the most spectacular townsite in the American West. One approaches the site across an immense desert landscape, punctuated by a towering formation, Enchanted Mesa. Eventually one arrives at Acoma, which is perched nearly 400 feet above the desert floor, atop another mesa. The community is built adjacent to the sheer cliff edge, offering breathtaking views to the distant horizon. Rarely has architecture so fully exploited the visual potentials of its natural setting as at Acoma. Be sure to experience the overall natural and built setting from the uphill overlook to the west, which is magnificent in late-afternoon sunlight.

Zuni Pueblo
rebuilt after 1705
Zuni, New Mexico; I-40 to Gallup, S on Rt. 602, W on Rt. 53

Zuni Pueblo was built atop the foundations of the pre-Columbian community of Halona, which was one of the legendary Seven Cities of Cibola.

Zuni housing is "apartment-style," similar to Taos Pueblo, though not as architecturally striking. The rebuilt village was developed around an irregular central plaza-courtyard. Eight dense clusters of apartment-like blocks established a primary defensive enclosure. Periodic construction over three centuries has unavoidably altered Zuni's earlier visual qualities.

SEMI-PERMANENT STRUCTURES

Iroquois Longhouse
indeterminate dates
Northeastern United States

Longhouses were organic structures—no stone or mud brick used in their construction—supported by a rhythmic spacing of side posts and covered in hide or bark. Typically, longhouses were about 120 feet in length, but at least one was 400 feet long.

Seminole Chickee FIG. 31
indeterminate dates
South Florida

Especially for housing located near wetlands like the Everglades, the Seminole elevated thatched huts above the ground on poles to protect against flooding and snakes. Chickees are still constructed today.

Mandan Earth Lodges FIG. 32
indeterminate dates
Great Plains, especially North Dakota

Plains earth lodges were house-sized structures with any of a variety of roof shapes. Earth lodges were often grouped into dense village clusters.

Chinook Lodge
indeterminate dates
Pacific Northwest

Chinook lodges were similar in interior volume to Mandan earth lodges. However, these structures were characterized by a pitched roof supported by joists and purlins.

TEMPORARY-MOVABLE STRUCTURES

Tepee (Tipi) FIG. 33
indeterminate dates
Great Plains

A remarkable innovation, the ubiquitous tepee was a quickly assembled conical shelter supported on branches and covered by animal hides or bark. The plains tepee provided efficient, reliable shelter for nomadic tribes.

FIG. 30 **Nature as Master Architect** Acoma Pueblo's "Sky City" occupies an awesome natural setting which ensures that any human construction will pretty much fade into insignificance. From this perspective near the cliff-top village, the colonial-era church of St. Esteban (see the Spanish Colonial Architecture chapter) seems to visually equal the distant mesas. As experienced, however, mere building cannot compare to these spectacular natural surroundings. *Library of Congress, Prints & Photographs, Historic American Buildings Survey*

FIG. 31 **The Essence of Shelter** Seminole Chickees are functional in the extreme, providing a thatched roof for shade and a raised platform for protection from flooding and snakes. This time-honored construction is still employed today in South Florida, here modified for tourism-oriented retail.

FIG. 32 **Efficient Utility** Plains nations like the North Dakota Mandan built their earth lodges with abundant local materials, primarily sod, just as would later European homesteaders on the same lands. *Library of Congress, Prints & Photographs*

FIG. 33 **Housing Innovation** Tepees offered remarkably efficient housing, easy to put up and to take down. Portability was essential for hunters who roamed endlessly across great distances. *Library of Congress, Prints & Photographs*

FIG. 34 The Most American of Indigenous Housing As the American republic formed its founding myths in the 1800s, the Log Cabin grew into a powerful symbol of simple virtue. Countless contemporary paintings depicted cheerful families living in noble simplicity in their spotless log houses. In reality, most American log buildings were rude affairs like the spectacularly wretched Siverly and Bowker log saloon in Wiseman, Alaska, built before 1913. *Library of Congress, Prints & Photographs, Historic American Buildings Survey*

FIG. 35 The Visual Power of Simplicity "Architecture" was probably the last thing on the minds of the builders of this garrison/blockhouse in Maine. Yet like many utilitarian structures, the handsome ruggedness of this building is appealing. *Library of Congress, Prints & Photographs, Historic American Buildings Survey*

FIG. 36 Totally Successful Sham. Abraham Lincoln's "official" log cabin is a fake, a replica built nearly a century after Lincoln's birth. But since it is reverently and impressively ensconced within this monumental stone temple in Kentucky, it seems reasonable to simply overlook the cabin's complete lack of authenticity. *Library of Congress, Prints & Photographs, Historic American Buildings Survey*

Igloo
indeterminate dates
Mackenzie Delta

The fabeled igloo or snow house was a practical response to climate and available building materials; they were constructed out of blocks of ice, with a water-snow-mixture as binding mortar. Summer shelters were constructed of wood, whale bone, hides, or tundra sod, similar to the later "soddies" of European settlers on the Great Plains.

Hale
indeterminate dates
Hawai'i

Indigenous Hawaiians lived in simple huts supported by a pole-and-purlin structure, which was covered by thatching. Dry-laid stone walls were a prominent construction feature of some hales, though for most the structure-thatching formed a continuous, wall-roof enclosure. Size and height of a hale were directly proportional to the social status of its inhabitant, ranging from as low as 4 feet in height to as much as 20 feet high. The largest hales, for chiefs and shamans, could be as large as 15 feet wide and 30 feet long.

LOG CONSTRUCTION / LOG CABINS

European immigrants settling in frontier territories in effect became indigenous residents of the United States. They were largely on their own, and living with nature to a much greater extent than were those residing in towns or farmers living in well-populated regions.

Necessarily working with the land and ever conscious of climate and weather, frontier settlers adapted quickly to local conditions and available materials. Shelter was constructed from wood, stone, even sod—whatever was readily available locally.

Among all of these available materials, log construction—especially the celebrated Log Cabin—eventually came to be considered as the most *American* of indigenous architecture, not only because log construction was widely employed in wooded frontier areas, but also because the log cabin, in romanticized retrospect, took on a righteous image, a symbol of simple virtue.

For this reason, throughout much of the 1800s, up to the Civil War, it was almost a requirement for American politicians to establish a log cabin somewhere in their background, as did Abraham Lincoln, whose family had already built five log cabins by the time they settled in Illinois.

There is a marvelous irony to all this, because log cabins were not indigenous to North America. Log construction was first introduced in the Delaware River Valley by Swedish and Finnish emigrants, and separately by Russians in Alaska (Fig. 34) and along the Pacific Coast above San Francisco.

Most historic U.S. log cabins trace their lineage back to log construction initially introduced around Philadelphia.

Garrison/Blockhouse FIG. 35
1754
Fort Halifax, Winslow, Maine

A powerful, blocky mass with a second-floor overhang; construction is of squared logs. Early in the colonial era, the term "garrison" described a square fort with an overhanging second floor, which exactly describes this structure. "Blockhouse" was used to describe a sturdy building that could be used as a refuge from attacks.

However, over more than two centuries, these meanings have evolved in common usage. Today, we would describe this as a blockhouse. Meanwhile, "garrison" is now commonly applied to an ordinary colonial-looking house with a slightly projecting second floor, like the McIntire garrison house, also located in Maine (Fig. 85).

Abraham Lincoln Birthplace Cabin FIG. 36
1809; replicated in 1897, 1906, 1909
Lincoln Birthplace Historical Site, 2995 Lincoln Farm Rd., Hodgenville, Kentucky; W of S. Hwy. 31, N of Rt. 61

Several log cabins authentically associated with Lincoln's life have been restored in Kentucky and Illinois, but this "official" cabin is historically preposterous. The actual cabin of Lincoln's birth was disassembled shortly after he was born in 1809. Three separate imitations were built between 1897 and 1909, three to four decades after Lincoln's assassination. The last replica was enshrined in this monumental stone temple designed by the noted classicist architect John Russell Pope. So much for the notion of the humble log cabin as representing simple virtue!

FIGS. 37, 38 Russian Log Construction Swedes and Finns introduced log construction to the eastern United States. Russians constructed log buildings in Alaska and southward, nearly all the way down to San Francisco. Alas, few remain. The marvelous Holy Assumption Russian Orthodox Church in Kenai, Alaska, whose log walls were sheathed over soon after construction, is among the best remaining Russian log structures in the United States. *Library of Congress, Prints & Photographs, Historic American Buildings Survey*

Holy Assumption Russian Orthodox Church FIGS. 37, 38
1894–1895; bell tower, 1900
Fr. Alexander Yaroshevich, "builder-priest"
Mission & Overland Sts., Kenai (city), Alaska

This modest, gabled-roofed building with a small onion-dome cupola is a rare remaining example of Russian log construction in the United States. Its exterior log walls were sheathed over in the twentieth century. It is marvelous to come upon, now set within its own square, defined by a picket fence.

COLONIAL

ARCHITECTURE

1565–1850

Spanish Colonial Architecture

1565–1850

FIGS. 39, 40 **New Spain** Spanish expansion across North America was directed from Mexico City, capital of New Spain. Colonial authorities intended to efficiently standardize colonization across the continent, encompassing everything from military encampments to great cities. In reality, of course, an endless diversity of local situations guaranteed that architecture and urbanism varied in the extreme. That is evident in this comparison of the National Cathedral enfronting the *Zócalo*, the monumental central plaza in Mexico City (Fig. 39), with the simple gateway of San Francisco de Asís at Ranchos de Taos in remote northern New Mexico (Fig. 40).

The Spanish were the first Europeans to settle permanently in the New World, initially in the Caribbean. Spanish North American colonization was eventually directed from the capital of New Spain, Mexico City (Fig. 39). Hence, Spanish presence in the United States emerged in two distant centers: first in Florida, when early Spanish colonization focused on the Caribbean; and then in the American Southwest (Fig. 40), reflecting the colonial-era primacy of Mexico City.

Spanish exploration in the 1500s extended over immense areas of the United States. Soldier-explorers like Hernando de Soto and Francisco de Coronado ranged from Florida north nearly to Ohio and west to San Francisco. They were followed in due course by Franciscan and Dominican friars, who founded missions to convert indigenous peoples to the True Faith. In so doing, religious orders effectively founded cities.

These missionary-colonization efforts from the 1600s into the early 1800s occurred primarily in four areas of the American Southwest: the Upper Rio Grande Valley and ancestral Pueblo lands west and north of Albuquerque into northeastern Arizona; Texas, especially at San Antonio; the Sonoran Desert south of Tucson into Mexico; and Alta California, from San Diego north to Sonoma.

It should be noted that even the finest works of Spanish colonial architecture in what is now the United States were not in the same league as numerous Iberian-influenced buildings in Mexico. This is not meant in any way to denigrate colonial designs in the United States, which are certainly visually satisfying.

But there can be no comparison with great works of the Renaissance period (c. 1550–1630) nor, especially, the Baroque (c. 1630–1730) in Mexico City (Fig. 39), Guanajuato, Puebla, Tepoztlán, and elsewhere. If you are interested, Manuel Toussaint's *Colonial Art in Mexico* provides background.

FLORIDA 1565–1821

As early as the 1520s, Spain attempted to colonize the U.S. Eastern Seaboard between South Carolina and Florida, but these outposts were soon abandoned. However, when the French built a fort near Jacksonville in 1564, Spain established a fort at nearby St. Augustine the following year in order to hinder French expansion.

Castillo San Marcos FIG. 41
1672–1695; structurally enhanced and modernized, 1738–1762
Ignacio Daza, designer-military engineer
Mantanzas River, St. Augustine, Florida

The *Castillo* was nicely described by G. E. Kidder Smith as "massive, businesslike, yet strangely elegant." Built of a local shell stone, the fort is straightforward and symmetrical in its ordered plan, its direct geometry clearly inspired by Renaissance ideals. A central plaza is ringed by rooms, which are enclosed by walls a dozen feet thick at the base. Bastions project from each corner; the entire fort is set within a wide moat.

UPPER RIO GRANDE VALLEY 1598–1834

Governor's Palace
1610–1612; modified 1860s, 1909–1913
The Plaza, Santa Fe, New Mexico

Governor's Palace was constructed as part of the first presidio built after Santa Fe was founded in 1609 or 1610—two to three years after the English arrived at Jamestown. While the building we see today is generally similar to the initial 1600s design, significant modifications have occurred over its long life. As one example, the projecting *vigas* creating a sidewalk arcade are not original.

Naturally, Santa Fe has changed over nearly four centuries, especially after the onset of significant Anglo tourism in the 1920s. Indeed, the entire feeling of this once-sleepy town has radically changed over the past two decades. Still, if you frame your view across the Plaza toward the Governor's Palace, you can still appreciate the pleasant human scale of colonial Santa Fe (Fig. 768).

FIG. 41 Changes in Perception Over Time When built in a far-off wilderness more than three centuries ago, Castillo San Marcos in Florida, would have been understood by European military engineers as an unremarkable, off-the-shelf design. Time and rarity have transformed our perception. Today, we appreciate this utterly functional structure as an outstanding architectural landmark. *Library of Congress, Prints & Photographs, Historic American Buildings Survey*

San Esteban
1629–1644; periodic later modifications
Acoma, New Mexico; 60 mi. W of Albuquerque on I-40 to Exit 108, S 12 mi. on Rt. 23

In its plainness—adobe-plaster exterior and whitewashed interior walls and natural wood ceiling within an immense nave volume—San Esteban demonstrates the timeless power of architectural simplicity. Compared to most of its contemporaries, San Esteban is massive and seems even more so because the exterior is unbroken by projecting transepts: Marc Treib aptly described it as "boatlike."

However, the stunning setting on a 400-foot-high mesa is the pueblo's greatest visual feature (Fig. 30 and Acoma Pueblo text, Indigenous Cultures chapter). When the Spanish built their church in the pre-existing indigenous village, they located it right at a precipitous escarpment. Perhaps this was a symbolic decision, so the church would visually stand by itself. For whatever reason, this decision created one of the most dramatic building sites in the United States.

San José de la Laguna FIG. 42
1699–1706; later rebuilding
Laguna Pueblo, New Mexico; 45 mi. W of Albuquerque on I-40 to Rt. 124

San José provides the visual highlight for its surrounding commune. An earth-colored village constructed of stone and adobe

FIG. 42 The Architectural Power of Color San José de la Laguna church in New Mexico gains its visual prominence primarily from color. Its brilliantly whitewashed exterior stands out from the darker mud adobe of its surrounding pueblo.

FIG. 43 **Landmark Rear** The massive adobe buttress of San Francisco de Asís, "Ranchos de Taos," in northern New Mexico is surely the best-known visual image among Spanish colonial churches in the United States. This signature feature changes with periodic replastering, so on your next visit, it will look a little different from this view. *Library of Congress, Prints & Photographs, Historic American Buildings Survey*

FIG. 44 **"Remember the Alamo!"** The restored Alamo façade of Mission San Antonio de Valero in San Antonio is certainly handsome. But that is probably less important to Texans, for whom this conserved battle site–ruin is practically sacred. *Library of Congress, Prints & Photographs, Historic American Buildings Survey*

clusters haphazardly around a small rise, atop which the bright, whitewashed church stands—seemingly almost in a spotlight. Marc Treib described the vibrant interior as "animated by color and ornamentation."

San Francisco de Asís, "Ranchos de Taos" FIG. 43

1813–1815; rebuilt 1967, 1979–1981
SE side of Hwy. 68, Ranchos de Taos, New Mexico

"Ranchos de Taos" is the iconic New Mexico mission church, primarily on account of its massive rear adobe buttress, which faces the passing highway to Taos, four miles farther up the road. The church was made famous by painter Georgia O'Keeffe, who commented, "That piece of the back said all I needed to say about the church."

Because of its bulky, unembellished exterior, this rear view was probably among of the most memorable images for architectural-history students during the High Modern era of the 1950s and 1960s. "Stubby" front towers establish a strong formal personality (Fig. 40). The interior is architecturally less notable.

TEXAS 1659–1795

Franciscans established five missions along a short stretch of the San Antonio River between 1718 and 1731. These have been incorporated by the National Park Service into a San Antonio Missions National Historical Park and symbolically interconnected by a "Mission Trail" extending south out of downtown San Antonio.

Mission San Antonio de Valero, The Alamo FIG. 44

1724 ff. 1744–1757; 1761; 1849; 1920–1921; 1930s
John Fries, architect-builder for 1849 stabilization
N. Alamo St. at Houston St., San Antonio, Texas

The twin towers, nave vaulting, and dome of the original church collapsed in 1761 because of poor construction techniques, never to be fully rebuilt. In this semi-ruined structure, the celebrated Battle of the Alamo took place during the 1836 Texas War of Independence. The Alamo was stabilized more than a decade later, deeded to the State of Texas in 1905, and now functions as a carefully maintained shrine.

FIG. 45 **Successful Background Architecture** Judged by its separate parts, San Antonio's Neustra Señora de la Purísima Concepción de Acuña mission is visually austere, in ways bordering on crudeness. Compare, for instance, its rudimentary entrance pediment with that of Mission Santa Barbara (Fig. 53). Even so, the overall effect is certainly engaging. Architecturally, a plainness of the main body of the church enhances the prominence of its slightly ornamented towers.

FIGS . 46, 47, 48 More Authentically Baroque San José y San Miguel de Aguayo is one of America's great colonial monuments, visually arresting due to its powerful massing (Fig. 46), handsome textured stone walls, and exceptional stone carving, especially its rose window (Fig. 47). The nave is subdued by comparison, though still visually impressive, its ceiling vaults leading the eye upwards to a domed space marking what would be the transept crossing in a conventional Latin plan (Fig. 48). *Figs. 47, 48: Library of Congress, Prints & Photographs, Historic American Buildings Survey*

Nuestra Señora de la Purísima Concepción de Acuña
FIG. 45
1731–1754
807 Mission Rd. at Felisa St., San Antonio, Texas

Unlike the Alamo, this mission, including its church, is largely intact, although the original colorful geometric painted wall patterns have faded. Purísima is not as architecturally impressive as the nearby San José y San Miguel (next entry). Nonetheless, this is a solidly handsome design.

San José y San Miguel de Aguayo **FIGS. 46, 47, 48**
1768–1781
Fr. Pedro Ramirez de Arellano, builder; **Pedro Huizar**, sculptor
Mission Rd. at Roosevelt Rd., San Antonio, Texas

San José y San Miguel stands on the site of an earlier mission church. Along with San Xavier del Bac, near Tucson (next entry), San José is considered to be one of the two finest Spanish Colonial

Baroque designs in the United States. Huizar (or Huisar) was sent by King Philip V of Spain expressly to adorn this structure; clearly, the sculptor's long journey was worthwhile (Fig. 47).

SONORAN DESERT SOUTHWEST 1700s

San Xavier del Bac **FIGS. 49, 50, 51**
1783–1797
Ignacio Gaona, architect; **Pedro Bojourquez**, builder
W of I-19 Exit 92, 10 mi. S of Tucson, Arizona

The remarkable Jesuit Eusebio Francisco Kino founded a number of so-called Kino Missions in the Mexican Sonoran Desert in the late 1600s and early 1700s. San Xavier, which was built by Franciscans long after Fr. Kino's death, is the architectural star of this group, a singularly sophisticated and creative expression of American Spanish Colonial Baroque, inside (Fig. 51) and out. San

FIGS. 49, 50, 51 **White Dove of the Desert** The extraordinary San Xavier del Bac near Tucson excels at each level of design, from siting to the rich decoration of its interiors. Magnificent still today, this brilliant white construction must have seemed a dreamlike apparition to travelers approaching across the arid Sonoran landscape two centuries ago. *Fig. 49: Library of Congress, Prints & Photographs, Historic American Buildings Survey*

Xavier's intrinsic architectural impact is intensified by its austere desert setting, against which the precise, brilliant whiteness of the exterior plays off effectively against the rough-and-dusty surrounding landscape. Unfortunately, this once-magical scene is now diminished by a large surface parking lot located directly in front of the church. At one time, a visitor would have appreciated a magnificent visual tension between built and natural. Today, one is more likely to experience a wall of idling tour busses.

ALTA CALIFORNIA 1769–c. 1850

Another extraordinary friar, Fr. Junipero Serra, founded nine missions along El Camino Real, the Royal Highway of New Spain which connected Upper California as far north as San Francisco Bay with Mexico City. Twelve more missions were founded after Fr. Serra's death. These churches are architecturally diverse, some freestanding, others with ancillaries. San Fernando and Purisima are horizontal, almost barracks-like, in contrast to neoclassical colonial imagery at Santa Barbara.

By the 1830s, a broad mix of cultural influences was evident in California architecture. Following its independence from Spain in 1821, Mexico declared Alta (Upper) California a territory in 1825. In 1833, the Mexican Republic reduced the political power of the Church over the provinces, opening mission lands to settlers. Not only did this increase the prominence of private landholders, especially holders of vast ranchos similar to the Mexican Haciendas, but it brought increasing numbers of Anglo settlers, who brought along U.S. cultural references and new architectural traditions.

Mission San Francisco de Asís, "Mission Dolores" FIG. 52

1782–1791; restored, 1916–1918
Willis Polk, restoration architect
Dolores at 16th St., San Francisco, California

Compact and dignified, with rounded pilasters, the mission has almost the sense of a Swiss Chalet in its massing. Even this early, California architecture was already individualistic and expressive.

Mission San Diego de Alcala

1811–1813
N of Mission Valley Rd. off I-15 and Friars Rd., San Diego, California

San Diego, founded in 1769, was the first of Fr. Serra's missions; it moved to its present location in 1774. Gebhard and Winter described the style of this later mission church as "neo-Classic, with hints toward the Baroque." They noted that "its posterns, scalloped parapets, arches, its single-wall bell tower were motifs" that came to characterize the Mission Revival of c. 1895–1915. By the end of the 1800s, the church was in ruins, but it was reconstructed in 1931 and again in 1946.

Mission Santa Barbara FIG. 53

1812–1820; seminary block 1899–1901; reconstructed 1926–1927
Laguna N of Los Olivos, Santa Barbara, California

David Gebhard identified the refined church façade, with its six engaged Ionic columns and enclosed pediment, as taken from a plate in the Spanish edition of Vitruvius, which served as *the* authority on classical architecture for Renaissance-era (and as here, much later) designers. In its architectural qualities, with a marvelous site nestled into the foothills just above town, and with a long view over the Pacific Ocean, Mission Santa Barbara offers the ultimate Spanish Colonial setting in present-day California.

FIG. 52 Variety of Imageries Like other California Camino Real missions, Mission San Francisco de Asis, "Mission Dolores," was given a distinctive architectural imagery. Possibly because of the effectiveness of the Church's symbolic uses of architecture and art during the Counter Reformation of the late 1500s, several of California's early missions were endowed with architectural pretense, despite their out-of-the-way locations and tiny populations. *Library of Congress, Prints & Photographs, Historic American Buildings Survey*

FIG. 53 The Ultimate California Mission A lifetime before Santa Barbara became a wintering spot for cultured elites, this architecturally refined California mission was built in the foothills just above town. Today, nestled among posh neighborhoods, Mission Santa Barbara stands literally a world apart from other Camino Real missions.

Casa de la Guerra FIG. 54

1819–1826; restored and incorporated into El Paseo, 1922–1923
Jose de la Guerra, builder; **James Osborne Craig**, restoration architect
11-19 E. De La Guerra St., Santa Barbara, California

The California adobe was typically very different from the bulky, closed adobe of the Desert Southwest. Here is a feeling of opening to rather than protecting from the natural environment. Yet with an "L" or "U"-shaped plan, such adobes would also establish a zone of privacy for their inhabitants. This combination of openness to nature while maintaining family privacy would emerge as the design basis of the postwar California ranch house as developed by Cliff May (see American Colonial Revivals chapter).

Craig's restoration coincided with the adobe's incorporation into his suave El Paseo shopping arcade, accessed alongside Casa de la Guerra by the Street of Spain (see Period Revivals chapter).

Larkin House FIG. 55

1834–1837; south balcony added, 1905; house restored, 1922
Thomas Oliver Larkin, owner-builder
464 Calle Principal, SW cor. Jefferson St., Monterey, California (open)

Anglo settlers to Mexican California adapted American architectural imageries to local conditions, often, as here, resulting in distinctive regional architecture. This so-called Monterey Style, which was actually first realized, although almost simultaneously, in Santa Barbara, developed from the widespread regional use of adobe. The resulting designs were also colored by both the straightforward, well-established Federal style and also the romantic Greek Revival style then sweeping the United States. A mild local climate was another major design influence.

The resulting architecture is characterized as a simple, rectangular, two-story adobe building protected by a low-pitched, overhanging roof and featuring a cantilevered second-floor balcony or wrap-around porch. The Larkin House is a prime example of the Monterey Style, visually impressive in its directness.

FIG. 54 The California Adobe Casa de la Guerra in Santa Barbara was built around a patio, which provided a degree of privacy for everyday family activities, while still opening up the rooms to the outdoors. A century later, Cliff May's California Ranch House (see the American Colonial Revivals chapter) would be inspired by these traditional attributes of family privacy and connections to nature. *Library of Congress, Prints & Photographs, Historic American Buildings Survey*

Casa Amesti

mid-1830s–c. 1850; addition and restoration, 1919; "Moorish" Garden, 1919
Frances Adler Elkins, architect for 1919 changes; **Worth, Adler & Milleken**, garden architects
516 Polk St., Monterey, California

Along with the Larkin House, Casa Amesti is a standout among several handsome "Monterey" houses on the residential edge of downtown Monterey. Two-foot-thick adobe walls result in deep window and door reveals that are especially prominent in the main, first-floor room. The Moorish Garden was historically incongruous when devised, but by now is historic in its own right.

FIG. 55 Regional Expressions The basic adobe was adapted into many regional variations, depending on local conditions and lifestyles. For the Larkin House, located just blocks from the temperate Pacific Ocean, an outside balcony allowed residents to take full advantage of Monterey's mild climate. Symmetry enhances a general sense of formality, reflecting its location on a main street.

French Colonial Architecture

1600–1820

FIG. 56 French Characteristics Cahokia Courthouse in Illinois follows a common French Mississippi River Valley housing formula: a primary living level, the main floor, is surrounded by an exterior gallery. Located well away from potential flooding, the building has been set just above grade. In situations where flooding was more likely, the main floor might be raised several feet above grade, and in extreme situations like New Orleans, a full story (next figure).

By the early 1700s, the French nominally controlled more land in North America than did the Spanish. Hugh Morrison noted that French landholdings extended from the Alleghenies to the Rockies, from the Gulf of Mexico north and east to Hudson's Bay and Labrador. These immense holdings had spread from the initial French settlement on the St. Lawrence, Tadoussac, founded in 1600.

Such a vast land area did not result in a commensurate number of settlements. Rather, the French acted primarily as traders. French nationals established few permanent towns within this immense titular area, and most of what they did build was subsequently lost to floods, fires, or development.

As a consequence, the primary remaining French artifacts in the United States are concentrated in Louisiana, effectively the last U.S. colonial holding relinquished by the French, and the region of densest French settlement.

France lost its territories in 1763, with lands east of the Mississippi ceded to England, and those to the west taken over,

FIG. 57 **New Orleans "Raised Cottage"** Built on the site of the early Jean Pascal House, "Madam John's Legacy" illustrates characteristic French residential construction in low-lying New Orleans, where even in the relatively elevated French Quarter the main floor was raised a full story above grade as a wise precaution against flooding.

FIG. 58 **French Construction** Builders of Cahokia Courthouse employed an advanced eighteenth-century construction technique, *poteaux-sur-sole*, utilizing plaster-filled log walls resting on a stone sill.

technically at least, by Spain. However, Morrison noted that these territories remained "culturally French" until eventually absorbed by American western expansion. In the meantime, French social influence in the lower Mississippi valley actually increased between 1760 and 1790, as Acadians expelled from Nova Scotia by the British emigrated to the bayou districts of southern Louisiana.

Jean Pascal House, "Madam John's Legacy" FIG. 57
1728–1731; rebuilt, 1788–1789
Robert Jones, rebuilder
632 Dumaine St., Vieux Carré, New Orleans, Louisiana (open)

Pascal constructed a house on this site in the late 1720s, only a decade after the founding of *Nouvelle Orléans*. His house was finished by 1731. It burned down in 1788, after which the present house was constructed in its place by Jones. The main floor was set atop a masonry-enclosed basement story as protection against flooding, which occurred in parts of the city on average of once each decade until an extensive system of levees was built in the twentieth century. Later New Orleans houses retained this characteristic as the "raised cottage" style. An exterior gallery protected by a wide roof overhang extends along the street front.

Cahokia Courthouse FIGS. 56, 58
c. 1737; conversion 1793; moved to the 1904 St. Louis fair and later to Jackson Park in Chicago before being re-erected on the original site in 1939
First & Elm Sts., Cahokia, Illinois

Originally built as a residence, known at the Le Poincet House, the building was converted for use as a courthouse and jail in 1793. This is an archetypical rural French pioneer house: one story, vertical log walls with a plaster infill, all resting on a *poteaux-sur-sole* stone foundation that was then a superior form of construction (Fig. 58). A double-pitch hip roof with wide overhangs provides protection from sun and weather. Because it was located on what was originally an open, rural site, not routinely susceptible to flooding, a grade-level gallery extends around the house, providing access to the rooms, which are nonetheless interconnected within.

There is a rustic stateliness to this building, which is larger than it appears to be in photos without human figures. The courtroom emanates a sense of simple dignity despite, or perhaps on account of, its rough bench seating. Like many Illinois historic sites, Cahokia Courthouse is beautifully maintained, with admirable interpretive facilities.

Parlange FIG. 59
c. 1750, remodeled and expanded c. 1820
Hwy. 1, 6 mi. S of New Roads, Louisiana (private residence, visits by appointment)

This large plantation house foreshadows, in its scale and presence, the grand Antebellum plantation mansions that would be built in the mid-1800s. As at Cahokia (previous entry), a large overhanging roof shelters a wrap-around exterior gallery, although here in perpetually soggy Louisiana, it is raised to the second story. The ground-floor exterior walls are of brick, while the upper floor is enclosed in cypress timbers chinked with a clay-moss mixture. Morrison called Parlange "in every respect a classic example of the French Colonial style as it developed in the lower [Mississippi valley]."

Great Hall

c.1778; destroyed by 20C fire after restoration; reconstructed, 1971–1973
Grand Portage National Monument, off Hwy. 61, NE of Grand Portage, Minnesota

French cultural influence was surprisingly widespread if often subtle, extending well beyond Louisiana. This fur-trading outpost was built by a British-Scots company, hard against the Canadian border in a wilderness earlier frequented by French trappers.

Despite growing British political influence over the region and, of course, the British client, the Great Hall's architecture is more French than English, from its exterior gallery to its *poteaux-sur-sole* construction. It may be that the actual builders were local descendants of earlier French trappers, who naturally adopted traditional French building conventions.

Maison Olivier (Acadian House) FIG. 60

1815; improvements, 1840s
Charles DuClozel Olivier, builder
1200 N. Main St./Hwy. 31, on the N outskirts of St. Martinville, Louisiana, within the Longfellow-Evangeline State Historic Site (open)

Constructed more than a decade after the United States took possession of Louisiana, this "Raised Creole Cottage" design retains its French Colonial architectural sensibilities as expressed in a raised cottage imagery, a descendant of earlier colonial designs like the Pascal House. This relatively small house is romantically sited by a large clearing, set amid live oaks draped in garlands of Spanish moss.

FIG. 59 Country French In effect, Parlange is a plantation-scale version of Cahokia Courthouse. It is much larger and, reflecting its location along the Mississippi River flood plain, the main floor has been raised a full story above grade. *Library of Congress, Prints & Photographs, Historic American Buildings Survey*

FIG. 60 A(r)cadian Everyday Life Maison Oliver (Acadian House) offers another variation on French residential construction, locally called a "Raised Creole Cottage." Because of its small size, casual siting, and informal design, the house feels especially authentic as an idyllic representation of Cajun (derived from Acadian) life in the early 1800s.

Southern Colonial Architecture

1607–1780

FIG. 61 Culture in the Colonies Contemporary English culture spread rapidly in the Southern Colonies, especially in Virginia. Within the same century as the rude settlement at Jamestown, the College of William and Mary constructed its landmark Wren Building in nearby Williamsburg, which was soon to develop around the nearly mile-long axis of a monumental town plan (see the European New World Town Plans chapter). Within another generation, great Georgian mansions with formal gardens began to appear throughout Virginia's Tidewater region (see the Formalism chapter).

The early appearance and rapid spread of pretension and cultural refinement are among the noteworthy traits of Southern Colonial architecture. Less than a century after the settlement of Jamestown in 1607, a monumental, architecturally ambitious colonial capital was underway in nearby Williamsburg (see the European New World Town Plans chapter). Within another generation, imposing Georgian plantation houses had been constructed along tidewater rivers from the Potomac in Northern Virginia to the Ashley in South Carolina.

Throughout the 1600s, colonists built in a functional variant of the traditional medieval English manner. By the early 1700s, however, Virginia had adopted Renaissance design sensibilities (Fig. 62), by way of the great Christopher Wren. As Richard Bushman noted, gracious eighteenth-century Virginia plantations included formal gardens with their estate houses. Virginia planters were already aspiring English country gentlemen.

This chapter is heavy on Virginia plantation houses, with good reason: these buildings well represent architectural aspirations in the Southern colonies. A greater number of outstanding buildings can be found in the vicinity than can be included here; be sure to consult Morrison and Pierson to identify and locate them before heading off for a highly recommended tour of Virginia's architectural treasures.

VIRGINIA

FIG. 62 Renaissance Design Sensibilities In the late 1600s and early 1700s, the superior architecture of Christopher Wren, as in his Royal Hospital in London, provided an ultimate design benchmark for English colonial builders in America. Still, English models were only superficially translated in most New World designs. Compare, for example, the sheer visual command of the hospital with William & Mary's mild-mannered Wren Building (Fig. 61), which has traditionally been attributed to the very hand of the great Wren. Not a chance!

College of William and Mary, "Wren Building" FIG. 61
1695–1700; 1709–1723; 1729–1739; 1859–1861; restored 1927–1931
"Modeled by" **Christopher Wren**; **Thomas Hadley**, master builder
W end of Duke of Gloucester St., Williamsburg, Virginia

The Wren Building serves as a simple, dignified terminus to the town end of this monumental street, facing the Capitol, nearly a mile distant. It should be noted that this building pre-dated the celebrated 1699 Plan of Williamsburg (see the European New Word Town Plans chapter) which was developed in relation to the college building, then essentially complete. The Wren Building design was surely not from Wren's hand. Rather, the imagery reflects the general manner of Wren. This is a pure Renaissance expression, with nary a trace of medieval Gothicism.

Arthur Allen House, "Bacon's Castle" FIG. 63
c. 1665; numerous later alterations; restored, 1973
Arthur Allen, owner-builder
Hwy. 617 off Hwy. 10, Surry County, Virginia (open)

Overall, this early "High Jacobean" house is ungainly, especially an awkward addition by William Hankins. But any such deficiencies

are compensated by the distinctive end chimneys made up of three brick stacks set diagonally.

Capitol FIG. 64
1699–1705; rebuilt, 1748–1753; conjecturally reconstructed 1931–1934
Henry Cary, master builder; **Perry, Shaw & Hepburn**, reconstruction architects
E end of Duke of Gloucester St., Williamsburg, Virginia

Familiar icon of Colonial Williamsburg, this H-shaped building was reconstructed based on the best available evidence at the time. Subsequent discoveries of historic documents indicate the original was slightly different from what we see, but that is of little practical consequence except, perhaps, to antiquarians, in that the essence of this building's importance is its civic location and monumental image, and the great historical events and personalities identified with this premier colonial site.

Governor's Palace FIG. 65
1706–1722; ballroom addition, 1752
Office of **Christopher Wren**, attributed designer; **Henry Cary**, master builder
N end of Duke of Gloucester St. cross axis, Williamsburg, Virginia (open)

Governor's Palace is the third architectural luminary of monumental Williamsburg, the grandest colonial residence when built.

FIG. 64 It's in the Details Williamsburg's sturdy Capitol is saved from heaviness by the small-scale texture of its brickwork. The attenuated cupola is marked by a delicacy that seems out of character with the rest of the design. Though by now, of course, the entire composition is so familiar that we no longer question its proportions.

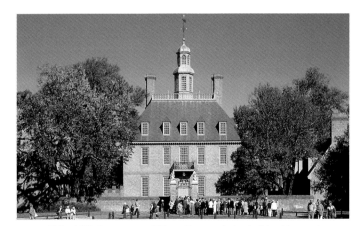

FIG. 63 Colonial Pretense Architectural pretension in Virginia dates from no later than the mid-1600s, with the Arthur Allen House, "Bacon's Castle," and its distinctive medieval end gables with clustered chimney stacks. *Library of Congress, Prints & Photographs, Historic American Buildings Survey*

FIG. 65 Colonial Refinement, and More The grandest colonial residence when built, Williamsburg's Governor's Palace was gloriously enhanced through restoration which went well beyond strict historical accuracy. That is of little concern to those of us who are completely charmed by these creative indulgences, and today, a lifetime after restoration, the current ahistorically polished state of Governor's Palace is authentically "historical" in its own right.

FIG. 66 American Synthesis Shirley illustrates how Tradition is synthesized into unexpected expressions in the United States. A simplified Georgian design over a cubic form is topped by a French mansard punctuated by a dense array of dormers. The exterior was embellished a century after initial construction with a boldly projecting porch.

FIGS. 67, 68 Nascent Modernity The Lee Mansion, "Stratford Hall," was a highly advanced design, proto-modern in its blocky massing and in the virtual absence of exterior ornament. Inside, formal entrances open directly into the spacious Great Hall. The property is also significant for the distinguished Lee family history and superb reconstructed gardens (see the Garden Restorations chapter). *Interior: Library of Congress, Prints & Photographs, Historic American Buildings Survey*

It occupies a critical terminus on the short-cross axis, marked at the Duke of Gloucester Street by Bruton Parish Church. Refined taste is expressed here in a total designed environment: (1) location on a formal axis; (2) high architectural pretense; (3) designed interiors; and (4) extensive formal gardens.

Shirley FIG. 66

1723–1738; porches c. 1831
20 mi. SE of Richmond off Hwy. 5, Charles City County, Virginia (open)

This cube-like house, with its later two-story projecting porch, is among the most singular of Southern Colonial mansions. A three-story, suspended interior staircase provides the memorable architectural feature.

Lee Mansion, "Stratford Hall" FIGS. 67, 68

1730–1738; remodeled, 1800; restored, 1929–1940
Thomas Lee, owner-builder; **Sidney Fiske Kimball**, architect for the 1929–1940 restoration
40 mi. E of Fredericksburg, off Hwy. 3, Westmoreland County, Virginia (open)

With its bold floor plan and almost complete lack of exterior ornament, Stratford Hall is a unique exercise in New World Palladianism. The house is visually powerful, though not especially heavy. In its remarkable directness and unexpected freshness of imagery, Stratford is in effect, one of America's earliest modern designs.

Stratford's elaborate reconstructed gardens (see the Garden Restorations chapter) are twentieth-century design landmarks in their own right.

Westover FIG. 69

1730–1734; house renovated and dependencies attached, 1898–1905
William Byrd II, owner-builder
25 mi. SE of Richmond off Hwy. 5, Charles City County, Virginia (open)

If you could visit only one Early Georgian Virginia plantation house, this magnificent mansion would be it. William Pierson described Westover as "serene, gracious, and thoughtfully conceived . . . one of the most thoroughly English houses extant from eighteenth-century America."

Christ Church FIG. 70

1730–1735

Robert Carter, owner-builder

Starting from Kilmarnock, Lancaster County, Virginia: 2.5 mi. SW on Rt. 3, right on Rt. 222; first left on Rt. 646, straight ahead

Carter's superb design is atypical for the period in its austere, bulky, vertical massing, primarily reflecting a straightforward Greek Cross plan. The design is understated, subtly developed. In the estimation of William O'Neal, Christ Church ranks as a nationally significant masterpiece of the early Georgian period.

Wilton FIGS. 71, 72

1750–1753; rebuilt on new site, 1933–1935

William Randolph, III, owner-builder; design attributed to **Richard Taliaferro**; **Claiborne & Taylor**, reconstruction architects
215 S. Wilton Rd., S of Cary Street Rd., Richmond, Virginia (open)

Comparatively modest in size, this Early Georgian "town house," originally located along the James River about 15 miles outside of Richmond, is exquisitely restored and furnished. The interior is singular in its floor-to-ceiling paneling in every room (Fig. 72). A must visit.

FIG. 69 Early Georgian Archetype Westover is the most complete example of an Early Georgian American estate, including: the estimable qualities of its builder, William Byrd II; the fine proportions and handsome detailing of the house itself; commodious interior spaces; superb wrought-iron gates by a noted London smith, Thomas Robinson; and a heavily wooded site overlooking the James River.

FIG. 70 Elegant Geometry The simple, cubic forms of Christ Church reflect its unembellished Greek Cross plan. While the exterior envelope is direct, its ornament understated, this does not reflect thrift. Rather, the building was carefully crafted with taste and restraint.

FIG. 71, 72 Surpassing Qualities Wilton has been immaculately restored to a state of perfection. Its well-proportioned façade is more than matched by handsome

interiors, each room paneled floor to ceiling. *Library of Congress, Prints & Photographs, Historic American Buildings Survey*

FIGS. 73, 74 Late Georgian Touchstone Mt. Airy is especially engaging because of its fine proportions, attention to details, and the arresting color and tactility of its stonework.

FIG. 75 Engaging Informality Mount Vernon is America's best-known colonial house, its attraction transcending the historical association with George Washington. Architecturally, Mount Vernon has it both ways: despite imposing size, formal siting, and a creatively reconstructed landscape, the property conveys an overall sense of ease, a lack of ceremony that is very *American* in its feeling.

Mount Airy FIGS. 73, 74

1754–1764; 1844; 1965

John Ariss?, attributed architect for owner **John Tayloe**

From Tappahannock, 4 mi. N on Rt. 360, left on Rt. 624; gate is directly ahead; Richmond County, Virginia. (private residence, occasionally open for tours)

Mount Airy is a Late Georgian–Palladian design, described by the Historic American Buildings Survey as "the most outstanding 18th C. stone house erected in Virginia." In its proportions and composition, expressive use of materials, and detailing, Mount Airy is indeed a superior work of architecture.

Mount Vernon FIG. 75

1757–1759 expansion of mid-1730s house; additions and enhancements, 1774–1799

Lawrence Washington, original builder; **William Fairfax**, expansion builder

15 mi. S of Washington, D.C., at the end of George Washington Memorial Pkwy., Fairfax County, Virginia (open)

Noble in its seeming straightforwardness, Mount Vernon has inspired countless imitations as everything from the fictional J. R.

Ewing's Southfork to suburban banks. Few if any have captured Mount Vernon's simple monumentality, which stems from a design based on practical functionality. George Washington's elaborate Palladian window (or serliana) on the north elevation is all the more visually effective as an ornate counterpoint. Everyday life on a colonial plantation-estate is suggested through the beautifully maintained grounds and outbuildings.

THE CAROLINAS / SOUTHEAST

Drayton Hall FIG. 76
1738–1742
John Drayton, owner-attributed builder
3380 Ashley River Rd., Charleston, South Carolina (open)

An early exercise in English-influenced Palladianism in the colonies, suggesting the cultural sophistication of colonial Charleston. Morrison stated that when built, Drayton Hall was "far in advance, architecturally, of contemporary great houses in Virginia." High architectural qualities carry into the interiors, including a "majestic" paneled entrance hall and stairs. This plantation house enjoys a beautiful site overlooking the Ashley River, several miles outside of town.

St. Michael's Episcopal Church FIGS. 77, 78
1752–1753, essentially completed, 1761
Samuel Cardy, master builder
78 Meeting St., Charleston, South Carolina

Morrison and Pierson concur that this is "one of the great Georgian churches in the colonies." Like other "important [colonial] city churches" built after 1750, St. Michael's was patterned after James Gibbs's St. Martin-in-the-Fields in London. More so than for St. Martin, the tower here is deliberately overscaled for effect, compared to the church itself.

Slave Market FIG. 79
1758
Public Square, Louisville, Georgia

Architectural history in general and this book in particular tend to focus on great works, which often means buildings for elites, as especially throughout this chapter. Nevertheless, up through 1863, slavery was an everyday fact of life in much of colonial America/the United States.

This is not something we like to think about, but as this market illustrates, slavery was not a hidden, parallel world, but rather functioned right out in front of society: this regional market for the sale of humans is prominently sited in the center of town, located at a crossroads along U.S. Highway 1, the original north-south national highway along the East Coast. Befitting its civic location, the structure offers a bit of architectural pretense, far more than housing destined for the people sold here. The cupola with stylistically later pointed-arch openings probably dates from the nineteenth-century Romantic era.

CHARLESTON URBAN HOUSES

Robert Pringle "Single" House FIG. 80
70 Tradd St., Charleston, South Carolina

Miles Brewton "Double" House FIGS. 81, 82
1765–1769
Ezra Waite, builder
27 King St., Charleston, South Carolina

Charleston's compact urban core is one of America's great architectural treasures, with far too many splendid individual buildings to cite in this overview.

The so-called "Single House" is a local plan innovation, in which a single line of rooms on both levels extends from front to back, served by a side veranda-porch, the "piazza." The house is raised to further capture sea breezes, which together with extra-high ceilings, made it possible to live a tiny bit more comfortably in this intensely humid climate, before air conditioning. The Judge Robert Pringle

House is a prime example of the Charleston Single House.

The Charleston Double House looks like a typical Georgian–English Palladian house though its plan is organized around a wide, full-length hall-corridor which provides enhanced air circulation on the interior The Miles Brewton House (confusingly sometimes also called the Pringle House) is the finest of Charleston's Double Houses. Its elegant hall-corridor extends from front to back (Fig. 82), though in some Double Houses, the hall extends from side to side.

Tryon Palace

1767–1770; destroyed by fire, 1798; reconstructed, 1952–1959
John Hawks, architect; **Claude Sauthier** garden designer; **Perry, Shaw, Hepburn & Dean**, reconstruction architects; **Morley Williams**, landscape architect for reconstructed gardens
610 Pollock St., New Bern, North Carolina (open)

Along with Mt. Airy and Mount Vernon, Tryon Palace was one of a few colonial Georgian designs with a complete Palladian villa layout, with planned dependencies. By the time of its construction, refinement was widespread among great Southern houses, and Tryon Palace's architectural design included integral formal gardens, along with a kitchen garden.

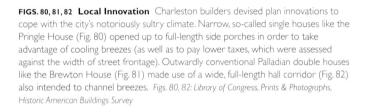

FIGS. 80, 81, 82 Local Innovation Charleston builders devised plan innovations to cope with the city's notoriously sultry climate. Narrow, so-called single houses like the Pringle House (Fig. 80) opened up to full-length side porches in order to take advantage of cooling breezes (as well as to pay lower taxes, which were assessed against the width of street frontage). Outwardly conventional Palladian double houses like the Brewton House (Fig. 81) made use of a wide, full-length hall corridor (Fig. 82) also intended to channel breezes. *Figs. 80, 82: Library of Congress, Prints & Photographs, Historic American Buildings Survey*

New England Colonial Architecture

1620–1800

FIG. 83 The Village Green Colonial New England towns like Lexington, Massachusetts, developed compactly, with houses loosely clustered outwardly from a common open area, a "green." This focused civic layout was conceptually similar to Spanish colonial towns, although the New England common rarely matched the geometrical regularity of the ideal Spanish plaza, and in New England a meeting house replaced the mission church as the prominent building overlooking the public area.

Seven New England colonies were established by the English between 1620 and 1639. Geographically, these extended from New Haven to Maine. The most prominent of these was the Massachusetts Bay Colony, centered in Boston. As colonial Boston grew, outlying settlements were founded in order to disperse the population: towns such as Salem, Cambridge, Lexington, Concord, and Ipswich.

These communities initially developed compactly—physically and socially organized around a meeting house which typically faced a village common or green (Fig. 83). Private landholdings clustered loosely outward from the common. Hugh Morrison noted that public conventions made assemblage of large parcels difficult, so "New England became a region of small land parcels and compact settlements (usually no more than about a mile in greatest extent) very different from the feudal patroonships of the Dutch along the Hudson or the lordly plantations of Virginia and Maryland."

At the outset of settlement, New England colonial construction was necessarily rude, largely made up of mud huts and tents, though wood-frame structures soon appeared. Morrison stated that only eight brick and four stone houses are known to have been built before 1700, although there were probably a few more. By contrast, thousands of frame houses were constructed in the 1600s, dozens of which survive today in some form.

FIG. 84 Functional Practicality
Some Americans, like the plantation lords of Virginia, were fashion-conscious. Others, such as the builder of the Whipple House, illustrated here, ignored current fashion in favor of familiar medieval building conventions which lent themselves to efficient construction and ease of remodeling and expansion.

FIGS. 85, 86 Enduring Imagery The popularity of colonial-era garrison houses like the McIntire House (Fig. 85) has endured across three centuries. Abridged versions remain ubiquitous in American tract subdivisions (Fig. 86). *Fig. 85: Library of Congress, Prints & Photographs, Historic American Buildings Survey*

John Whipple House FIG. 84

c. 1655, additions 1670, 1700; restored, 1898, 1953–1954; relocated, 1927
Arthur A. Shurcliff, landscape architect for the 1950s gardens
1 S. Village Green, Ipswich, Massachusetts (open)

One of the oldest surviving New England colonial houses, the Whipple House illustrates a delay in the arrival of European styles, as well as the pragmatic nature of New England colonial architecture. Its design following traditional medieval English rural houses, the Whipple House lagged well behind contemporary continental fashion, given that in London, Inigo Jones and Renaissance architecture had been in vogue for well more than a generation when this house was built in the mid-1600s.

Over the ensuing years, needs for more space were satisfied by purely functional expansions, with little apparent consideration of architectural esthetics. This emphasis on functional practicality over formal beauty is an enduring characteristic of the American vernacular.

McIntire Garrison House FIG. 85

c. 1660–1692
Alexander Maxwell, builder
Hwy. 91, 5 mi. W of York, Maine.

Some kind of fortified retreat was often necessary for early colonists. Ideally, this was a blockhouse (see the Indigenous Cultures chapter), but at least a building of unusually sturdy construction. According to Morrison, in early times colonists used the term "blockhouse" to refer to a square fort building with second-floor overhangs; "garrison" meant only a structure with heavy protective walls. However, over the years, New England houses with second-floor overhangs like the McIntire House came to be known as garrison houses. During the colonial era these usually had overhangs on the front and both sides, as here; but eventually only the front overhang was retained. This simplified, front-over-hang garrison expression has been ubiquitous almost up to the present, in subdivisions throughout the Northeast and Midwest (Fig. 86).

Parson Capen House

1683

1 Howlett St., Topsfield, Massachusetts (open)

Like the Whipple House, the design is medieval (Tudor era in reference) in its vocabulary, and as restored to an unaltered state, it is the most architecturally pure of the early New England frame houses. There is undeniable visual presence in its straightforwardness, which along with functional practicality, is a quintessential American architectural quality.

Old Ship Meeting House FIG. 87

1681, modified 1729–1731, 1755, 1791

90 Main St., Hingham, Massachusetts

The Meeting House fulfilled a central civic role in each New England town. Since the Puritan faith was a reaction to established Anglicanism, these buildings were not based on the Gothic design traditions of the established Church of England. Rather, the New England Meeting House developed as a fresh American architectural expression—square and unadorned, with bench seating focused on a lectern in the absence of an altar. Here, again, we see the functional emphasis that would become an enduring American building convention.

CLASSICAL INFLUENCES

By around 1700, Renaissance ideas and ideals increasingly influenced American colonial architecture. Of course, changes in style did not occur overnight. This transition commenced in 1695, with the College of William and Mary's Wren Building in Williamsburg (see the Southern Colonial Architecture chapter), a precursor of Renaissance-inspired classicism in the colonies.

By about 1720, important American houses and public buildings showed obvious classicist sensibilities. These designs were reasonably correct, as codified by ancient writers like Vitruvius, and by Renaissance and Baroque master architects like Palladio (Fig. 88) and, of course, Wren. The new classicist buildings were formal, usually symmetrical in plan and elevation.

MacPhaedris-Warner House

1718–1723

John Drew, builder

150 Daniel St., Portsmouth, New Hampshire (open)

One of the very first of what William Pierson described as a New England Wren-Baroque house. Although these were typically wood-frame structures, here the construction is of Flemish-bond brick walls, similar to Virginia's Early Georgian houses of a decade later.

Christ "Old North" Church FIG. 89

1723

William Price, designer

193 Salem St., Boston, Massachusetts

Trinity Church FIG. 90

1725-1726

Richard Munday, architect

Queen Anne Square, Newport, Rhode Island

Old North is an early colonial example of Christopher Wren's church imageries, only a few decades later than Wren's celebrated London churches (Fig. 89). In the Colonies, it follows only Williamsburg's Bruton Parish Church (1711–1715). Pierson identified Christ Church as "the first church in the English colonies to

FIG. 87 Community Center While the Green may have provided a physical focus for early Massachusetts Bay Colony towns, the meeting house functioned as the social center of these communities. Since Puritans were by definition against many English traditions, including historical architectural expressions, meeting houses like Old Ship attained architectural eminence through prominent siting, clarity of form, and restrained detailing.

FIG. 88 Fountainhead of Classicism The matchless works of Italian Renaissance architect Andrea Palladio (1508–1580), like his 1559–1560 Villa Foscari near Venice, inspired leading European designers like Christopher Wren. Palladianism was a major influence on colonial architecture as classicist sensibilities spread across the New World. See, for example, Figs. 94, 105, and following chapter on Neoclassicism.

FIGS. 89, 90 **New England Wrenesque** Likenesses of Christopher Wren's late-seventeenth-century London churches began appearing in New England by the 1720s. First among these were the masonry Christ "Old North" Church in Boston

(Fig. 89) and the wood-frame Trinity Church in Newport (Fig. 90). *Library of Congress, Prints & Photographs, Historic American Buildings Survey*

FIG. 91 **Public Landmark** Old Colony House occupies the uphill end of Newport's colonial public center, where Washington Street slopes gently downhill toward Brick Market (Fig. 97) and the harbor. It is nicely scaled for its setting: large enough to provide a genuine civic presence, but not so big as to overwhelm its neighbors.

assume the fully developed character of a Wren church," principally on account of its tower and spire. Richard Munday's 1725–1726 Trinity Church in Newport is a near-contemporary wood-frame version of the masonry Christ Church (Fig. 90).

Old Colony House FIG. 91
1739–1741
Richard Munday, architect-builder
Washington Square, Newport, Rhode Island

Wren's design influence extended to public buildings, as at Williamsburg. Old Colony House is not at all correct, or even as serious as, say, Independence Hall in Philadelphia (see the Mid-Atlantic Colonial Architecture chapter). Rather, this is a "delightful...boisterous provincial" design, in Pierson's knowing estimation.

Isaac Royall House FIGS. 92, 93
East façade, 1733–1737; West façade 1747–1750
Isaac Royall, Sr., 1733–1737 rebuilder of existing late-1600s brick residence;
Isaac Royall, Jr., remodeler of 1747–1750
Main between George and Royall Sts., Medford, Massachusetts (open)

Architecturally, Royall is expressed as a freestanding townhouse, with blank brick side walls. The highly articulated east elevation

FIGS. 92, 93 Superior Remodeling The Isaac Royall House we see today is the result of two separate remodeling campaigns, by father (Fig. 92) and by son (Fig. 93). Remodeling often diminishes a design, and more than one hand usually dilutes the guiding architectural concept. The Royalls confounded both wisdoms; while the principal elevations substantially differ, they are nonetheless tied together by similar high levels of design sensibility and quality of detailing.

FIGS. 94, 95 The Sum Transcends its Parts. No less an authority than Hugh Morrison criticized Redwood Library at length for several formal shortcomings. In actual experience, it would be hard for most of us to fault this humane and engaging building, especially its later, light-filled reading room (Fig. 95). *Fig. 95: Library of Congress, Prints & Photographs, Historic American Buildings Survey*

FIG. 96 A National Treasure In visually extravagant Newport, one might hardly look twice at the chaste exterior of Touro Synagogue, even though the building is located on a prominent site between the town's superb Colonial and Gilded Age districts. Within, however, visitors experience one of the great American interiors, a symphony of classicist detail, brilliantly adapted by Peter Harrison to the needs of Jewish worship. *Photograph © John T. Hopf published through the courtesy of the Touro Synagogue Foundation*

(Fig. 92) is especially vigorous, unusually vertical in composition, while the west elevation (Fig. 93) introduces three-story pilasters . The significant difference between the two principal façades is atypical, reflecting separate rebuilding campaigns by father and by son. The main house and adjacent slave quarters have been beautifully restored, with a park-like setting. A highly recommended visit.

Redwood Library FIGS. 94, 95
1748–1750; 1858, Reading Room; 1875, Delivery Room & Wings; 1912, 1939, 1986
Peter Harrison, architect; **George Snell**, Reading Room architect; **George Champlin Mason**, Delivery Room & Wings architect
50 Bellevue Ave. at Redwood St., Newport, Rhode Island

The estimable Harrison was America's first professional architect. This handsomely proportioned, carefully detailed design was, remarkably, his first building. Historians have suggested several possible English models for parts of the design, but it seems to be primarily based on a 1736 publication of Palladio's work. Additions by Snell and Mason, especially Snell's light-filled Reading Room (Fig. 95), enhance the appealing character of this marvelous small-scaled library.

Vassall (Longfellow) House
1759
John Vassall, builder
105 Brattle St., Cambridge, Massachusetts (open)

The Vassall House is a historic landmark on account of its longtime resident (1837–1882), poet Henry Wadsworth Longfellow. However, this is a very handsome, archetypical Late Georgian frame design, apart from any historical associations. The house has been nicely restored.

Touro Synagogue FIG. 96
1759–1763
Peter Harrison, architect; **Isaac Hart & Company**, builder
72 Touro St., Newport, Rhode Island

Touro Synagogue is historically significant as the first Jewish house of worship built in the colonies. Architecturally, the interior is superbly detailed, in Pierson's judgment, "one of the masterpieces of the colonial eighteenth century."

Brick Market FIG. 97
1760–1763; restored, 1928–1930
Peter Harrison, architect
Thames St. at Washington, Newport, Rhode Island

Harrison's final design for this building was probably based on Inigo Jones's Somerset House in London. If so, the brick base is less textured than that of its model, with less ornament, the pilaster capitals toned down from Corinthian to Ionic. As so simplified, it is a very "American" design, solid without appearing stolid, visually anchoring this important public corner.

Stephen Salisbury Mansion
1772
40 Highland St., Worcester, Massachusetts (moved from Lincoln Square in 1929) (open)

A sumptuous Late Georgian manse, an advertisement for the restrained good taste of it owner, one of the area's wealthiest citizens. The house is compositionally a bit more horizontal than is typical of this style, which only adds to its visual grounding. Now restored and open to the public.

FIG. 97 Precedent Simplified Peter Harrison's Brick Market was based on a London building by Inigo Jones. Like many American buildings guided by European designs, Brick Market was simplified as compared to its European model.

VERNACULAR HOUSES

Buildings cited in this chapter, and most of the entries in other chapters, are exceptional, either as precursors or because of their significant design qualities. However, these entries of course comprise only a tiny fraction of built America. For one thing, there were many similar structures, built later and/or with more modest design qualities. Also, there is always a much larger group of vernacular structures in any period, which usually do not show up in surveys of significant architecture.

Some vernacular types have proved to be especially prominent and enduring. The New England Saltbox and the Cape Cod are two of these. Both types were ubiquitous in New England before the Revolution, and both developed in response to climate, weather, available construction materials, and the need for economy and functional flexibility, including easy expansion.

Both of these house types appeared in the 1600s, and were built well into the 1800s. They passed out of popularity by the Civil War, but with the onset of the American Colonial Revivals (see that chapter) after the 1876 Centennial Exposition in Philadelphia (see the Fairs & Exhibitions chapter), they regained popularity nationwide, though from then on employed as styles, rather than built as contemporary vernacular types.

SALTBOX AND CATSLIDE

Two-story "Saltbox" and "Catslide" houses evolved from medieval English vernacular houses. As the Saltbox name suggests, this was a plain, gabled house, in which the rear portion of the roof gable extended out over an addition, or "lean-to." In a catslide variation, the roof slope broke at the addition, extending less steeply out over the addition.

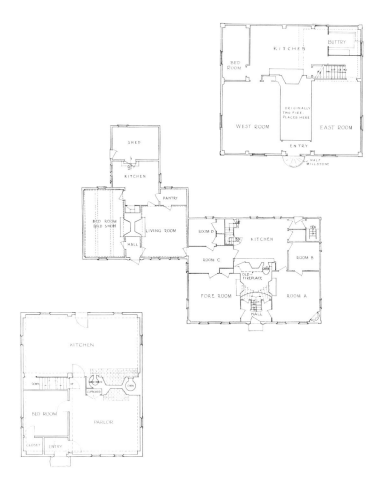

FIG. 98 Classic Saltbox Resplendent in its barn-red color, the restored Hyland House illustrates classic saltbox form.

FIG. 99 Endless Variations By common classification, Cape Cods appear in any of three configurations; six, if "doubled." Even so, few houses on Cape Cod are pure examples. Here, the complex Jabez Wilder plan is illustrated between a Double Full Cape (top) and a Double Three-Quarters Cape (bottom). All three of these plans exhibit idiosyncrasies. *Library of Congress, Prints & Photographs, Historic American Buildings Survey*

FIG. 100 Cape Cod Variant The simple Cape Cod type adapts to a seemingly endless number of variations. Here, as one example, the Jabez Wilder House is distinguished by a graceful bow roof, which like the Dutch gambrel, offers a bit of additional headroom on the upper floor.

FIGS. 101, 102 **Down-to-earth Sophistication** For all of their inherent economies, Cape Cods can be quite impressive, architecturally. The Elisha Cobb Double Full Cape is deceptively large and primly handsome, notably its interior woodwork and detailing. *Library of Congress, Prints & Photographs, Historic American Buildings Survey*

Jethro Coffin House

1686; restored, 1927
Alfred F. Shurrocks, restoration architect
Sunset Hill Rd., off W. Chester St., Nantucket, Massachusetts (open)

The Coffin House provides a pure example of the New England Saltbox; from the sides and rear it seems almost abstractly modern, excepting the tiny, medieval-sized windows. The exterior mass reads as seamless, which is atypical for most saltboxes, as the addition is usually apparent, whether the roof pitch remains constant or is broken in a catslide. The Coffin House is owned by the Nantucket Historical Association and is open to the public.

Hyland House FIG. 98

c. 1690–1710
84 Boston St., Guilford, Connecticut (open)

A classic saltbox, with the addition clearly expressed. The house has been restored and is well maintained.

CAPE COD

The Cape Cod is an indigenous American type, evolving out of single-room shelters built within a decade after the Pilgrims arrived near the future site of Boston in 1620. Despite the name, and the numbers of these houses found on the Cape Cod peninsula, it is uncertain whether the Cape Cod house, so named in 1800, actually originated on Cape Cod. That is because the type evolved gradually, and there seems to be no single house that can be identified as the first pure Cape.

The characteristic Cape Cod is one story, with a knee-wall attic space used for small sleeping areas. The Cape Cod was traditionally built around a massive central fireplace chimney, covered by a simple gable with low eaves, and sided in painted clapboards or weathered shingles.

In effect, the Cape Cod type offered a modular plan (Fig. 99). The classic Cape, or "Full Cape," had two equal-sized main rooms, called the Hall and the Parlor. The former served as a living space and the latter as the main bedroom.

A more basic version, called the "Half-Cape," included only one main room. A larger, intermediate version provided a sec-ond main room, smaller than the other room. This was sometimes called a "Three-quarters Cape."

Eventually, a kitchen and additional bedrooms were added at the back in all three versions. When this occurred, the Cape would be known as a "Double House." The ultimate house would be described as a "Double Full Cape."

As noted above, the economy and architectural flexibility of the Cape Cod type assured its enduring popularity.

In the twentieth century, well into the postwar era, the Cape Cod was employed widely, serving as the basis of inexpensive starter houses at Levittown (see the Community Development chapter), as models for the upper-middle-class homes of Royal Barry Wills (see the American Colonial Revival chapter), and the starting basis for some of the top-end estate homes designed by Edwin Lundie (see his Sweatt House in the Period Revivals chapter, Fig. 336).

Jabez Wilder House FIGS. 99, 100

1690; later addition
557 S. Main St./Rt 228, 1.5 mi. S of central Hingham, Massachusetts

An expansive, mature Double Full Cape, with large Hall and Parlor, plus kitchen and rooms behind. The graceful bow roof is not common, although neither is it rare. Corner quoins and other trim, plus the white paint, illustrate the tastes of the much later American Colonial Revival era. If you visit Hingham, be sure to take note of the numerous colonial and Federal houses, including Cape Cods of all varieties, that line Rt. 228 extending south out of central Hingham, almost all the way to Rt. 53.

Elisha Cobb House FIGS. 101, 102

c. 1800; later additions and remodeling
Prince Valley Rd., 1 mi. W of Hwy. 6, Truro, Cape Cod, Massachusetts (not visible from the road)

This polished Double Full Cape was apparently expanded from an earlier Half Cape. A catslide flat-gable roof with a slight break in slope covers later additions, which extend off the back (Fig. 101). The west elevation especially illustrates how well the Cape Cod type accommodates additions and remodeling, without loss of basic design integrity. The painted front clapboard seems additionally refined, as played off visually against the weathered shingled sides and rear. Subtle refinement continues into the interiors.

Mid-Atlantic Colonial Architecture

1626–1783

FIG. 103 Quality Architecture Colonial architecture in both major Mid-Atlantic centers—New Amsterdam/New York City and Philadelphia—was rarely avant-garde or ostentatious. Rather, the best of Mid-Atlantic colonial design is attractive because of careful attention to details and for the use of handsome materials, as here, at Cliveden in Philadelphia.

Early European settlement of the middle colonies was initially dominated by the Dutch, for whom the English explorer Henry Hudson had sailed up the Hudson River as far as Albany in 1609. A Dutch West India Company was organized in 1621 to abet Dutch explorers and traders who had established a New Netherlands colony in the Hudson River Valley, the northeastern part of what is now New Jersey, and the western third of Long Island. Military control of this region was established with the 1626 construction of Fort Amsterdam on the southern tip of Manhattan Island.

The Dutch governed this region for only four decades, building little of any architectural significance, as was typical in a frontier situation. Still, a Dutch influence lingers on well more than three centuries after cession of political control. New York City's cosmopolitan tolerance is rooted in Dutch sensibilities, and vestiges of the great Dutch patroonships are still in evidence in the Hudson Valley (see the Ordering the Land chapter).

Morrison noted that a distinct Dutch and Flemish architectural influence—manifested for instance, in a predilection for stone in houses, or Flemish bond brickwork and Dutch cross-bond masonry walls, stepped gables, and a distinctive gambrel roof—"maintained a remarkable isolation from the ebb and flow" of Eastern stylistic development. He attributed this to the "insularity" of Dutch New World communities.

Continental architectural fashion was more closely followed in and around Philadelphia, where English Georgian attitudes were well understood. By 1700, upwards of two-thirds of Philadelphia's houses were of brick; some of these were proto-Georgian architectural expressions.

State House, "Independence Hall"
1731–1736, finished 1745; tower, 1750–1753; 1828
Andrew Hamilton, initial scheme; **William Strickland**, architect of the 1828 tower
Chestnut St., between 5th and 6th Sts., Philadelphia, Pennsylvania

Given the old adage about the esthetic perils of committee design, it is a miracle that Independence Hall is architecturally as coherent as it is. Between the initial design of 1730 and its periodic restorations after the mid-1950s, dozens of architects, builders, craftsmen,

and administrators made significant design and planning decisions for this structure and its setting.

Van Cortlandt House FIG. 104
1748–1749; renovated, 1913–1918
Frederick van Cortlandt, owner-builder; **Norman Isham**, renovation architect
Van Cortlandt Park, Broadway at 244th St., The Bronx, New York (open)

Unlike, for instance, many of the eighteenth-century Virginia gentry, Dutch landholders in the mid-Atlantic region were not known for cultural pretentiousness. This large, ruggedly attractive fieldstone house is architecturally plain almost to the point of dowdiness, compared to contemporaries like Mount Pleasant and Cliveden (following).

Mount Pleasant FIGS. 105, 106
1761–1762
John MacPherson, builder
Fairmount Park, Philadelphia, Pennsylvania (open)

Mount Pleasant is architecturally similar to Cliveden (next entry) in scale and imagery, though agreeably almost grand in its stand-alone siting and for the use of contrasting exterior materials to achieve a striking visual effect, which continues into the interiors.

Cliveden FIGS. 103, 107
1763–1767; colonnade, 1776
Benjamin Chew, owner-architect; **Jacob Knor**, master builder
6401 Germantown Ave., Philadelphia, Pennsylvania (open)

A projecting central bay and pediment identifies this design as Late Georgian (Fig. 103). However, architectural style is not as important as Cliveden's handsome rubble-stone walls, careful detailing, and beautiful interiors, especially its fine entrance hall (Fig. 107).

FIG. 104 Rugged Appeal
Compared to pretentious contemporary designs elsewhere in the colonies, the Van Cortlandt House is awkwardly proportioned and indifferently detailed. Such shortcomings are largely overshadowed by its textured fieldstone walls. *Library of Congress, Prints & Photographs, Historic American Buildings Survey*

FIGS. 105, 106 **Architecture as Texture** Mount Pleasant is agreeably tactile, from its tasteful exterior to the elegant interior woodwork. *Fig. 106: Library of Congress, Prints & Photographs, Historic American Buildings Survey*

FIG. 107 **Conservative Consistency** OPPOSITE At first glance, Cliveden may seem to be just another handsome Late Georgian House (Fig. 103). Visitors soon appreciate that conventionality is not necessarily a shortcoming, as the property transcends the ordinary through an overall consistency in the execution of siting, landscape, proportions, detailing, use of materials, interior spaces, and finishes. The resulting sense of architectural wholeness is why Cliveden is considered to be one of the finest landmarks of Mid-Atlantic colonial architecture. *Library of Congress, Prints & Photographs, Historic American Buildings Survey*

Dyckman House FIG. 108

1783; later additions; restored 1915–1916
William Dyckman, builder
Broadway at 204th St., New York, New York (open)

The Dutch had been out of power on Manhattan Island for well more than a century by 1783, so this simple farmhouse illustrates how Dutch residential design attributes lingered, stereotypically featuring, in Morrison's words, "…wide clapboards, broad gambrel roof with flaring eaves, and fieldstone masonry [here, in the foundations and part side walls] to taste."

Of course like any school, Dutch Colonial architecture in the Hudson River Valley was actually more nuanced than this common stereotype. But, indeed, these very characteristics remain prominent when we think about American "Dutch Colonial" houses. Morrison warmly praised the Dyckman house for the "splendid sweep [of the roof] over the generous porch."

FIG. 108 **A Satisfying Home** Beyond its distinctive sweeping roofline, the Dyckman House is noteworthy for how it fits into the community, with its visual informality and human scale, its warm stone textures, and a sense of connection with its neighbors suggested by the broad front porch. *Library of Congress, Prints & Photographs, Historic American Buildings Survey*

AMERICAN

ARCHITECTURE

1780 – 2004

Neoclassicism

1780–1860

FIG. 109 American Neoclassicism Four distinct versions of Neoclassicism were prominent in American architecture. Collectively, they comprised a wide emotional range, from the rational to the romantic. Within this rich architectural tradition, Thomas Jefferson was *the* design luminary. His creative interpretations of classical models, represented here by the Rotunda at his University of Virginia Academical Village, were meant to symbolically connect timeless political ideals then associated with the democracies of Antiquity to the seemingly unlimited potentials of the new nation.

Neoclassicism in America is traditionally classified by architectural historians into two stylistic modes. One of these is the austere Federal Style, buildings reflecting Enlightenment ideals. Federal was fashionable between the late 1700s and about 1820, then gradually passing from use as the influence of Enlightenment thought diminished.

The second Neoclassical style is the Greek Revival, which was based on romanticized ancient Greek building idioms. It was widely employed from the early 1800s on up to the Civil War, reflecting the concurrent Western cultural prominence of Romanticism.

Architectural historian William Pierson, Jr., demonstrated that this familiar canon is not a nuanced description of Neoclassicism from the late 1700s to the mid 1800s. According to Pierson, American Neoclassicism occurred in four distinct forms. He labeled these as Federal, Republican, Rational, and Greek Revival. Indicating meaningful distinctions, these categories are used on the following pages.

FEDERAL STYLE

As the new nation coalesced in the 1780s, American Neoclassicism emerged gradually and tentatively through slight design modifications to the prevailing expressions of English Neoclassicism–Georgian.

Refinement of detail and proportion leading to what Pierson described as restrained elegance characterized this Federal style, notably in the designs of Boston architect Charles Bulfinch and Salem woodcarver Samuel McIntire.

First Harrison Gray Otis House FIG. 110
1795–1796
Charles Bulfinch, architect
141 Cambridge St., Boston, Massachusetts (open)

An ultramodern design, both architecturally pure and also idiosyncratic. Bulfinch abstracted a conventional Georgian *parti* to the point of austerity. With deep reveals, especially at the Palladian window, the flat façade comes off as substantial, rather than thin, as it might have. At the third floor, the architect resorted to a kind of Mannerism, in which openings are abruptly cut off at the sill by a stone string course.

Massachusetts State House
1795–1798; remodeled, 1895; expanded, 1917
Charles Bulfinch, architect
Beacon at Park Sts., Boston, Massachusetts

A spirited play of visual elements apparently intended as much for effect as to achieve any proportional correctness. Especially on a sunny day, it is satisfyingly grand.

Samuel Sloan "President's" House, Williams College FIG. 111
1801
936 Main St., Williamstown, Massachusetts (open for college events)

An exquisitely fragile façade, with the delicacy of an interior by the influential British architect Robert Adam, if lacking Adam's characteristic richness. Sloan was designed by a Boston architect whose name has subsequently been lost; woodwork was shipped in from Boston. While the house is beautiful in and of itself, it additionally gains from a prominent site on the glorious Williams College campus

Gardner-Pingree House
1804–1805
Samuel McIntire, architect
128 Essex St., Salem, Massachusetts (open)

Unlike Bulfinch in his first Otis House, here McIntire played it straight. The result is near perfection in image, proportion, and detail. Gardner-Pingree is one of those rare completely lucid designs that is so beautiful in its visual harmony as to evoke an emotional response.

First Church of Christ
1815–1817; slightly altered, 1881
Charles Bulfinch, design architect; **Thomas Hearsey**, supervising architect
Main St. at Village Green, Lancaster, Massachusetts

FIG. 110 Federal Minimalism Charles Bulfinch's First Harrison Gray Otis House illustrates the characteristic unfussiness of the Federal style, the earliest version of American Neoclassicism. Bulfinch designed three houses for Otis, each so abstracted that they read almost as modern expressions.

FIG. 111 Fragile Beauty The extreme delicacy of the Samuel Sloan "President's" House façade seems to anticipate the often-fragile designs of the mid-century Romantic Revivals.

First Church reflects the interplay of two different design approaches: Bulfinch's predilection toward abstraction and Hearsey's responsibility to necessarily adjust. Hence Bulfinch's bold conceptual design was softened during construction, as Hearsey added volutes to the tower sides, reduced the cupola in size, and balanced the entrance portico with three equal arched openings. While the employment of two designers in sequence could well have resulted in a visual debacle, First Church benefited from the best of each architect.

FIG. 112 **Rome as the Model** Jefferson was enamored with the dynamic buildings of imperial Rome such as the Pantheon, whose bold inventions spoke to him in ways that the æsthetic restraint of classical Greek architecture did not.

FIG. 113 **Modern Expressions of Antiquity** In its commanding siting alone, the Virginia State Capitol confirms the powerful influence of French Neoclassicism on Jefferson, an appreciation reinforced by the architect's esteem for ancient Roman monuments.
Library of Congress, Prints & Photographs, Historic American Buildings Survey

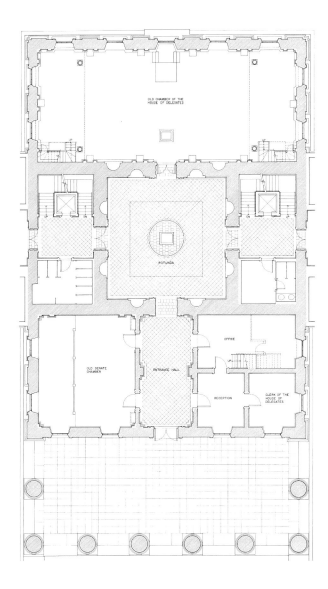

FIGS. 114, 115 The Essence of Democracy Jefferson's Virginia State Capitol plan symbolized the importance of balance in his democratic ideal for government. The main floor was apportioned into three equal modules, with the House occupying the space at the back, the Senate and administrators on either side of the formal entrance hall in front, and a beautifully proportioned public rotunda in the center. Heavy brackets under the rotunda balcony mask modern ventilation ducts. *Library of Congress, Prints & Photographs, Historic American Buildings Survey*

REPUBLICAN

Thomas Jefferson created a personal version of Neoclassicism which Pierson labeled Republican. Jefferson intended to express timeless political ideals in his architecture, and took the monuments of Imperial Rome like the Pantheon (Fig. 112) —not, as one might think, of "democratic" Classical Greece— as his stylistic models. Jefferson was also influenced by the pure architectural forms of his near-contemporaries, French architects Claude-Nicholas Ledoux (1736–1806) (see Fig. 571), and Etienne-Louis Boullée (1728–1799). Jefferson's brilliant, creative, and idiosyncratic designs stand alone in his era, among the greatest works of American architecture.

Virginia State Capitol FIGS. 113, 114, 115
1785–1798; wings added, 1904–1906; renovation and expansion 2003–2006
Thomas Jefferson, architect; **Charles-Louis Clérisseau**, collaborator;
Maximilian Godefroy (1816), **John Notman** (1850), landscape designers
Between 9th and Governor Sts., Richmond, Virginia

Jefferson introduced classical tradition for American public buildings. This temple-front scheme was subsequently altered (the latest revision, by Hillier Architecture, completed in 2006) and the magnificent original overlook to the James River has by now been largely masked by downtown construction. Regardless, the intrinsic power and dignity of Jefferson's design remain intact. Be sure to experience the interior rotunda when you visit.

Godefroy's 1816 Capitol Square plan established a commensurate setting for the Capitol, which up until then had been only superficially improved. This area was rendered as a romantic landscape by Notman's 1850 plan, a character which largely prevails today.

Monticello FIGS. 116, 117, 118
1768–1782; 1796–1817
Thomas Jefferson, architect
5 mi. SE of Charlottesville, Virginia, off Hwy. 53. (open)

Pierson described Monticello as "the experimental laboratory in which Jefferson put all his ideas and theories to the test." Jefferson's original 1770s house on the site was radically rebuilt into what we now recognize as Monticello. This house is the culmination of an ever-evolving, mature design of 1793 onward, which

FIGS. 116, 117, 118 **Jefferson's Singular Monticello** Save, perhaps, only Frank Lloyd Wright's Taliesin, Monticello is America's most intriguing and inventive residence. Inside and out, Jefferson's creative genius offers a visual banquet for anyone attracted to architecture. *Library of Congress, Prints & Photographs, Historic American Buildings Survey*

seems to have initially been based on the 1782–1786 Hôtel de Salm in Paris. Though by the time Jefferson got through personalizing his home, it was singular and unprecedented, on either continent.

Monticello can be appreciated for several aspects: its association with a president; its beautiful, mountaintop site; the everyday workings of the estate; Jefferson's experiments in agriculture, notably with grapes and winemaking; the formal site layout; the house itself as a visual environment; the library, basis of the Library of Congress; memorable solutions like the pass-through bed (Fig. 118) and two-story clock; and numerous stylistic and design innovations.

As Pierson further observed, Jefferson "was one of the most extraordinary minds of his time, he left few facets of life unexplored, and the diversity and scope of his accomplishments were prodigious." In this respect, Monticello is a faithful reflection of its creator.

University of Virginia "Academical Village" FIGS. 109, 119

1814–1826; rotunda rebuilt, 1898–1902, restored to its original state, 1973–1976

Thomas Jefferson, architect; **Benjamin Henry Latrobe**, design consultant "The Lawn," S of University Ave. at Rugby Rd., Charlottesville, Virginia

The Academical Village established an American design paradigm for an ordered campus (Fig. 119). Jefferson's *parti* has been copied for everything from college campuses to suburban office parks, though never equaled as a visual environment.

FIG. 119 **The Academical Village** Jefferson's University of Virginia marked a radical break from the past in important ways, ranging from democratic self-government by the faculty to the orderly arrangement of structures around the great Lawn (Figs. 109, 119). As a glorious architectural expression, and in its imaginative variations in detail, the Academical Village is one of the supreme works of built America.

After an 1895 fire in the Rotunda (Fig. 109), its interior was redesigned by Stanford White, 1898–1902. The McKim, Mead & White building closing off Jefferson's unlimited vista to the south was constructed at this time. In terms of planning, design, and symbolism, the Academical Village is one of the supreme achievements of American architecture.

Bremo FIG. 120
1817–1820
George Hartwell Cocke, builder; **John Neilson**, attributed master carpenter
N bank of James River, 2.4 mi. W of Hwy. 15, Fluvanna County, Virginia
private residence

Radical in the very best sense, Bremo has Jefferson's design genius written all over, from the extraordinary, ultramodern purity of the central house to the flanking temple wings.

RATIONAL

Neoclassical design was based on an architectural system of Renaissance rules governing symmetry, proportion, and detail. The very idea of a system of design is highly rational and, unsur-

FIG. 120 **Nascent Modernism** The pure, essentially modern forms of Bremo reflect the ideal of clarity in Enlightenment thought. *Library of Congress, Prints & Photographs, Historic American Buildings Survey*

prisingly, a third form of American Neoclassicism emerged as Rational, in Pierson's expanded classification.

This phase of Neoclassicism is characterized by clarity, directness, and monumental presence. Benjamin Latrobe, William Strickland, and Robert Mills were the most prominent national practitioners of this genre.

Since the rationalism of the early 1800s was grounded in Enlightenment thought – that is, in Modernism – this rational-

FIG. 121 Residential Monumentality Remarkably direct on account of its solid proportion and minimum of ornament, the Custis-Lee Mansion stands out on its overlook above the immense spaces and imposing monuments of the Federal City.
Library of Congress, Prints & Photographs, Historic American Buildings Survey

FIG. 122 Radical Break With Tradition Rather than relying on the conventional, century-and-a-half-old English Baroque expressions still in vogue, Benjamin Latrobe looked to the forms of imperial Rome as inspiration for his Neoclassical Cathedral of Baltimore.

FIG. 123 Functional Beauty Robert Mills's Fireproof Building in Charleston (foreground, left) has straightforward vaulted, masonry rooms enclosed by a simple exterior envelope. Despite the structure's utilitarian purpose, it is graceful and dignified, inside and out.

ist phase of Neoclassicism may be understood as the beginnings of modern American architecture.

United States Capitol

1793–1865 ff.
William Thornton, **Benjamin Henry Latrobe**, **Charles Bulfinch**, **Robert Mills**, **Thomas Ustick Walter**, architects; **Frederick Law Olmsted**, landscape architect for Capitol grounds (1874–1892);
Thomas Wisedell, architect for the west stairways and terraces
Capitol Hill, Washington, D.C.

A singular building in so many ways, from details like Latrobe's celebrated "corncob" column capitals to the overriding fact that as the seat of federal government, the Capitol is symbolically the most important building in the United States. Thornton's relatively austere 1792 design established the general design concept: a dignified, symmetrical building visually characterized by an encolumned temple front and dome.

The Capitol gradually morphed into its current sprawling state through a continuing sequence of additions and remodelings. These were initially undertaken by true architectural heavyweights, up through the Civil War. But that early tradition of design excellence was turned on its head with the mediocre East Front expansion undertaken in the late 1950s by the (non) Architect of the Capitol, J. George Stewart. Despite this aesthetic affront, the Capitol from the west has developed into a fascinating, idiosyncratic building (see The Mall chapter).

Custis-Lee Mansion FIG. 121

1802–1804, wings; 1817, center section
George Washington Parke Custis, builder
Arlington National Cemetery, Virginia (open)

A dense, powerful composition, Greek in imagery, but fully American in its simplified directness.

Cathedral of Baltimore FIG. 122

1804–1821; South Tower, 1831; North Tower, 1837; Portico, 1841–1863; Additions, 1879, 1890
Benjamin Henry Latrobe, architect
Cathedral St., between Franklin and Mulberry, Baltimore, Maryland

Latrobe devised both a traditional design and a modern, Neoclassical scheme. The client, Bishop John Carroll, chose modernity, and so, as Pierson noted, Baltimore's Roman Catholic cathedral became "the first [prominent] church in America to break completely with the Wren-Gibbs type."

This was also the first major American church since Bruton Parish in Williamsburg to be based on a cruciform plan—with a crossing, transepts, and choir. That offered the potential for a truly monumental interior, which Latrobe achieved with a large dome set over the crossing. Rather than employing pendentives to support the dome, Latrobe used a cylinder, which, as Pierson observed, changed the traditional spatial relationships, so that the crossing became the primary space, from which nave, transepts, and choir radiate, as secondary spaces.

Second Bank of the United States

1818–1824
William Strickland, architect
420 Chestnut St., Philadelphia, Pennsylvania

Given that Strickland's design was based on the Parthenon, the Second Bank must be recognized as a progenitor of the fourth, Greek Revival, phase of American Neoclassicism. Yet in its stark directness and monumentality, the Second Bank still very much reflects the norms of the rational phase.

FIG. 124 **Playing on Antiquity** Fairmount Water Works was very early for such a picturesque expression, bordering on folly, for Philadelphia's municipal utility.

Fireproof Building FIG. 123
1822–1827
Robert Mills, architect; **John George Spidle**, construction supervisor
100 Meeting St., Charleston, South Carolina

Rarely if ever has a lowly public records-storage program resulted in a building of such architectural quality. The cubic form of the structure is massive though not visually heavy, nor weighted down with superfluous decoration. All in all, this is a design of powerful dignity, if not of outright elegance. Mills's original design was supposedly even better, softened somewhat by Spidle's modifications during construction.

Custom House, now Federal Hall National Memorial
1834–1842; restored 2004–2006
Alexander Jackson Davis, **Town & Davis**; **John Frazee**, architects
26 Wall St., New York, New York

The Custom House is a transitional design between rationality and romanticism, both employing a Greek vocabulary, no longer abstracted, as was the Second Bank and especially the Fireproof Building. Here the designers sought to create a literal Greek temple, in a nod toward to the romanticism that was beginning to sweep the nation.

GREEK REVIVAL

Architectural rationalism reflected Enlightenment thought. Indeed, the Revolutionary generation's agenda of reason, scientific discovery, social progress—of course the constitutionally derived nation itself—could not have existed without the underlying principles of Enlightenment thought.

Inevitably, a reaction to rationalism set in among younger generations, both in Europe and in the United States. This reaction drew from romanticism, which emphasized feeling over thinking, and prized the mythologized past over Modernity. The Greek Revival mode of Neoclassicism emerged as an architectural reflection of romanticism. For the most part, the Greek Revival in the United States was an architecture of effect, intended to evoke an emotional response from the observer. Greek design idioms were manipulated in ways that resulted in architectural expressions that Pierson described as irrational and sentimental.

FIGS. 125, 126 More than Initially Meets the Eye Shadows-on-the-Teche is anything but conventional, offering distinctive, latently modern architectural expressions on each elevation.

FIG. 127 The Noble Home Andalusia is the archetypical American Greek mansion, appropriately stately, inside and out, for the nation's most powerful banker of his time. *Library of Congress, Prints & Photographs, Historic American Buildings Survey*

FIG. 128 Classical Expression One can understand how Greek Revival architecture was valued for its democratic lack of opulence by comparing the chaste North Carolina State Capitol with grand, French-Roman state capitols of the later Gilded Age, like Minnesota's (Figs. 172 & 173).

Fairmount Water Works FIG. 124

1812–1822; decommissioned, 1909

Frederick C. Graff, design engineer; **Benjamin Latrobe**, engineer; 1798–1801 city water system

NE bank of Schuylkill River, Philadelphia, Pennsylvania

Surely this is one of the most picturesque public works facilities of any era. All the hydraulics are hidden under the guise of small temples. This is an extremely early date for a such a theatrical architecture of effect; perhaps the designers intended a serious neoclassical statement and today we react to a perceived romantic charm that was unintended by the designers.

Shadows-on-the-Teche FIGS. 125, 126

1831–1834

James Bedell, **Jotham Bedell**, master builders

317 E. Main St./Hwy. 182, New Iberia, Louisiana (open)

Shadows is set just above the Bayou Teche, on a large, wooded property at the edge of New Iberia's handsome, small-scale downtown.

The southwest, street, elevation (Fig. 125) presents a gracious two-story colonnade of Doric columns. While this was a familiar device in the Antebellum South, here the elevation is expressed with Jeffersonian directness: still gracious but also rather modern in its relative lack of ornament.

As one moves around to the southeast, garden elevation, the effect of the triangular form defined by the end roof gable is exaggerated by a dearth of ornament. Absent the balcony rail and frieze, it could have been designed in the 1970s.

The sense of latent modernity continues on the northeast, river, elevation (Fig. 126), where the expression of mass is especially prominent. Columns have been reduced in size, and in number to just two, which are visually overwhelmed by mass and void. An intriguing design.

Nicholas Biddle Mansion, "Andalusia" FIG. 127

1833–1840

Thomas Ustick Walter, architect

Andalusia, Pennsylvania (open; see website www.andalusiahousemuseum.org for directions and hours)

Andalusia illustrates the archetypical Greek temple-front design. It is beautifully proportioned, and that quality combined with restrained detailing results in a splendid visual effect. The purity of Walter's design contrasts with the rest of Andalusia, a rambling 1806 addition by Benjamin Henry Latrobe to the original 1797 house.

North Carolina State Capitol FIG. 128
1833–1840
William Nichols, Jr., basic plan; **Ithiel Town, Town & Davis**, architects; **David Paton**, construction/supervisory architect
Union Square, Raleigh, North Carolina

Despite individual design contributions by multiple architects, there is an estimable clarity to this building, which is a model of the American Greek Revival. Later Gothic Revival interiors contrast with the restrained Greek imagery.

Bank of Louisville FIG. 129
1835–1837
James Dakin, architect; **Gideon Shryock**, construction supervisor
316 W. Main St., Louisville, Kentucky

An innovative "urban" temple front based on the Greek distyle-in-antis typology; the pylon forms have been splayed enough that the façade reads almost as Egyptian. Yet in its crispness and reticence in decoration, this was also a very modern design. The interior was remodeled by Harry Weese & Associates to accommodate a multi-auditorium performance arts center.

Andrew Hayes House FIG. 130
1837–1838
303 N. Kalamazoo Ave., NW corner Prospect, Marshall, Michigan

The small Greek temple-front house at its best. Two-story Doric columns establish a formal image, while an asymmetrical side elevation serves as the actual front of the house. Everything about this property is ideal for maximum visual effect, from the handsome stone exterior walls, to the spacious landscaped yard, to the human scale of this architecturally rich town.

FIG. 129 Civic Presence Classical forms have been successfully employed since antiquity to project a monumental civic presence, even for modest-sized buildings like the Bank of Louisville. *Library of Congress, Prints & Photographs, Historic American Buildings Survey*

FIG. 130 Symbols of Democracy in the North During the Romantic Era, Greek Revival architecture was widely understood as a reference to classical Athenian democracy. In the 1830s and 1840s, this was an especially popular imagery from central New York State to southern Wisconsin. The Andrew Hayes House in Marshall, Michigan, is a fine example of Greek Revival houses of the era.

FIG. 131 **Diminishing to the West** Like any style, the Greek Revival gradually fell out of favor. A scattering of Greek designs was built as far west as Oregon by the 1850s, though few of any high architectural suignificance were built on the Great Plains, where substantial settlement had not occurred prior to the style's decline in popularity. Iowa's Old State Capitol is one of the westernmost of notable Greek Revival buildings.

Fitch-Gorham-Brooks House

c. 1840, 1921

Jabez Fitch, builder; **Jens Jensen**, landscape architect (1921)
310 N. Kalamazoo Ave., NE corner Prospect, Marshall, Michigan

Another side-entrance plan, like the Hayes House (above) across the street. Set prominently above the street, it is regal in bearing. The 1921 Jensen landscape is north of the house.

Burnside Plantation, "The Houmas"

1840; restored, 1940

John Smith Preston, builder; **Douglass Freret**, restoration architect
Burnside, Louisiana; I-10 exit 179 or 182 S to intersect. of Rts. 44 & 22; S on
Rt. 44 to Rt. 942 (open)

A classic Antebellum Mansion: formal and stately, with a beauty approaching elegance. The house is encircled by two-story Doric columns, from which a balcony extends along the front and both sides. The Houmas represents a significant architectural development of the Southern plantation house: compare to Parlange in the French Colonial Architecture chapter, rebuilt only a generation earlier.

Iowa Old State Capitol FIG. 131

1840–1842

John Francis Rague, architect; **Chauncy Swan**, construction supervisor
Capitol St. between Washington and Jefferson Sts., Iowa City, Iowa

A straightforward rendition of Greek Revival, rendered especially prominent by its formal siting. Although everything was pretty much done by the book, all the pieces came together in a composition of remarkable dignity for a public building of relatively modest scale.

Tennessee State Capitol FIG. 132

1845–1859

William Strickland, architect; completed by **Francis W. Strickland**
Capitol Blvd. at Cedar St., Nashville, Tennessee

Much more picturesque than Strickland's Second Bank of the United States, reflecting a culture that was by now well into the Romantic Era. Strickland eschewed a pure temple expression, instead pushing out side porticoes and employing a tall lantern based on the 4th-century BCE Choragic Monument of Lysicrates in Athens. Interiors are decorative compared to Strickland's earlier Philadelphia bank, especially the ornamental ironwork in the library.

FIG. 132 **The Last Hurrah** William Strickland's Tennessee State Capitol was very late for Greek Revival, not completed until just before the Civil War. Employing a prominent lantern and ornate interiors, Strickland intended a picturesque expression, rather than correctness, which had been his goal for the earlier Second Bank of the United States (previously in this chapter). Hence, the same style could be rendered by the same architect as either rational or romantic. *Library of Congress, Prints & Photographs, Historic American Buildings Survey*

Romantic Revivals and Eclecticism

1830–1900

FIG. 133 The Architecture of Feeling An architecture of emotion flourished in the United States throughout the Romantic Era. In architecture, the picturesque was valued above all else. Gothic imageries, in part because of their spiritual associations, were widely popular. Whatever imagery was employed, architects emphasized striking visual effect, which could be achieved economically with little more than trim and paint, as demonstrated by the attention-grabbing 1871 St. Julien Cox House in St. Peter, Minnesota.

Nineteenth-century American architecture was very different from architecture of the preceding century. This was more than simply a matter of colonial vs. republican values. By the 1830s, our architecture was powerfully influenced by the dramatic shift in Western thought from Enlightenment rationalism, which had been manifested in early phases of Neoclassical architecture, to the romanticism of the Romantic Movement, which was manifested in the Greek Revival, among other vocabularies. Moreover, the new nation was steadily growing culturally more diverse. Americans began developing romantic myths about how their nation differed—for the better, of course!—from all other nations, past and present.

These influences and others came together to establish an architecture of emotional feeling, what we now call picturesque. William Pierson observed that this term came to connote beauty and truth; these were seen as admirable traits for American society, hence to be reflected in American architecture. There was a naïve nobility to this striving for higher values during the early decades of the American republic, almost up to the Civil War. At its extreme, this resulted in a search for

utopian purity, and that is why Gothic imagery, with its spiritual connotations, was widely popular.

Kathleen Mahoney noted that the Gothic architectural imageries imported from England were employed in the United States in a very wide range of applications, from imposing villas like Lyndhurst (Figs. 135, 136) to the rustic cottages championed by Andrew Jackson Downing and Alexander Jackson Davis. Still, no matter how picturesque and appealing it seemed, American Gothic lacked the whimsy of the æsthetic, eighteenth-century English "Gothick," its nominal ancestor (Fig. 134). Even so, the cottages included here under "Carpenter's Gothic" are delightful reminders of the romantic optimism of mid-nineteenth-century America.

FIG. 134 Romantic Whimsy The best English "Gothick" designs were not simply picturesque, but unabashedly fanciful, like Strawberry Hill in suburban London, transformed from 1750 to the 1790s by Horace Walpole. Few American Romantic Revival buildings achieved such forthright emotional expression.

FIGS. 135, 136 Gothic Revival Like No Other Lyndhurst, located on the Hudson River just north of New York City, is the greatest of American Gothic Revival houses, strikingly picturesque on the outside, and even better within. *Library of Congress, Prints & Photographs, Historic American Buildings Survey*

GOTHIC REVIVAL

Lyndhurst FIGS. 135, 136
1838; greatly expanded, 1864–1865
Alexander Jackson Davis, architect for initial design and expansion
635 S. Broadway, Tarrytown, New York (open)

A *highly* recommended tour of the beautifully maintained Lyndhurst offers an encyclopedic example of an American villa estate with two famous owners, a landscaped property overlooking the Hudson River, a renowned architect, a marvelously animated exterior, and superb interiors with period furnishings from three owner families. For visitors, everything comes together with a striking visual consistency. Lyndhurst is a National Trust property.

Trinity Church
1841–1846
Richard Upjohn, architect
Wall St. at Broadway, New York, New York

Trinity Church is a well-known Manhattan icon because of its prominent setting, visually terminating the west end of Wall Street. It is also historically significant as the design that launched Upjohn's stellar career. Until its cleaning in the 1990s, Trinity was covered by a rich coating of black soot, its darkness intensified into pure silhouette throughout much of any sunny day by the deep shadows cast by adjacent skyscrapers.

Grace Church FIG. 137
1843–1846
James Renwick, Jr., architect
802 Broadway at 10th St., New York, New York

One of the great American Gothic Revival churches, Grace Church is more correct (compared to English models) than were the loose interpretations of Gothic typically designed in the United States. Even in densely built-up Manhattan, Grace Church stands out visually because its siting takes advantage of the long Broadway corridor.

Smithsonian Institution, "The Castle"
1847–1855; partly rebuilt 1865–1867
James Renwick, Jr., architect; **Adolph Cluss**, architect for post-fire rebuilding
S side of National Mall between 9th and 12th sts., Washington, D.C.

Renwick's lively potpourri of forms and details establishes a distinctive skyline along the Mall, despite being physically overshadowed by massive neighbors. This is as informal, almost playful, a building as Renwick would design.

CARPENTER'S GOTHIC

Delamater House
1843–1844
Alexander Jackson Davis, architect
44 Montgomery St., W side of Rt. 9, Rhinebeck, New York
(open as Delamater Inn B&B)

The archetypical board & batten cottage, surprisingly larger in presence than it seems to be in photographs. Pierson demonstrated that its design was a refinement of an "English cottage" designed by Andrew Jackson Downing, sent in a letter to Davis in 1842.

Rotch House FIG. 138
1845–1846
Alexander Jackson Davis, design architect; **William R. Emerson**, project architect
19 Irving St. (originally at 103 Orchard St.), New Bedford, Massachusetts

FIG. 137 Renwick's Career Grace Church was the first major commission for the illustrious Gothicist James Renwick, Jr., who went on to design St. Patrick's Cathedral in New York and many other American landmarks. *Library of Congress, Prints & Photographs, Historic American Buildings Survey*

FIG. 138 Gothic Cottage "Cottage" is a wry conceit for large residences like the Rotch House. Architect Davis made the exterior plausibly cottage-like by skilled architectural exaggeration: specifically its outlandishly oversized central section, steep peaks, and overscaled, carved bargeboard. The result is one American design that approaches the whimsy of English "Gothick." *Library of Congress, Prints & Photographs, Historic American Buildings Survey*

Davis expressed Rotch as a "cottage," though it is really quite a large house. He accomplished this by playing creatively with proportions, like enlarging openings above norms, so what would, say, conventionally be an eight-foot dimension might actually be ten feet. The decorative bargeboard, employing a flowing, fleur-de-lis pattern, was overscaled for good effect, and its tracery plays off especially well against the smooth exterior walls.

FIG. 139, 140 **Carpenter's Gothic** The designer of Bowen House, "Roseland," played it fairly straight on the exterior, compared to the Rotch House (Fig. 138), developing a personality through Gothicized details and vivid coloring. Picturesque exaggeration of scale occurs on the inside, with the cathedral window. *Fig. 140: Library of Congress, Prints & Photographs, Historic American Buildings Survey*

Bowen House, "Roseland" FIGS. 139, 140
1846
Joseph Wells, architect
W side Rt. 169, Woodstock, Connecticut (open)

A crisp, board-and-batten design, again expressed as a cottage. Unlike the Rotch House (above), which employed tricks of proportion to appear cottage-like, the Bowen House is set back from the road within a spacious, wooded yard, which tends to diminish its apparent size. Again compared to Davis's Rotch design, Wells's here played pretty much by the rules, so the initial visual attraction is the vivid rose-pink walls and rich brown trim.

The house is located in a tiny village, set well back within its large lot and maintained in perfect condition by the Society for the Preservation of New England Antiquities. It contains Gothic furniture purchased for the house by the original owner. As its interiors attest, there is much more to Roseland than just arresting color.

St. John Chrysostom Church FIG. 141
1851–1853; restored, 1973–1976
Richard Upjohn, architect
1111 Genesee, SW corner Church, St. John's Military Academy, Delafield, Wisconsin

Rarely is Carpenter's Gothic expressed so economically yet with so much visual impact as here. Upjohn's design is remarkably balanced on several visual thresholds: between rough and elegant, simple and interesting, bucolic and knowing.

St. John's relies on massing, deep reveals and full, rich color, a deep brownish red that is characteristic of the era. (Typically, surviving nineteenth-century Carpenter's Gothic structures were painted white in the twentieth century, influenced by American Colonial Revival tastes.) A freestanding, splayed-wall bell tower out front is very effective as a sign and in establishing a sense of procession toward the chapel.

Weed House, "The Gables"
1853
Josiah Walton, architect
1124 Oakland Dr., Muscatine, Iowa

A charming dollhouse with all the requisite Gothic elements and details, including a steeply pitched roof and elaborately carved bargeboards.

EGYPTIAN REVIVAL

Greek Revival and Gothic imageries held explicit connotations for Americans. One was political, a reference to the notion of a pure democracy in Golden Age Greece. The other, as noted above, was religious-spiritual.

Of course not all, surely not even a majority of Americans was preoccupied with overt expressions of government. Nor was everyone particularly attracted to the Awakening-era spirituality that declined after the Millerite debacle in 1844. Indeed, even as Transcendentalists called for simplicity and reflection, American culture was simultaneously marked by commercialization and a growing emphasis on taste and style.

As a consequence, other romantic architectural imageries emerged that reflected this diversity of social values. Some of them, like Egyptian Revival and other exotic expressions, were merely intended to achieve effect. They came and went like any passing fashion.

FIG. 141 An Economy of Means
Richard Upjohn achieved an
architectural statement by modest
means in his chapel-scale St. John
Chrysostom Church. Its red color,
steeply pitched roof, and splayed-wall
bell tower (in the background) are
especially memorable.

FIG. 142 Uncommon Refinement
Egyptian Revival designs are commonly
massive and heavy. By contrast, Whaler's
Church on Long Island expresses
pharaohnic imagery with remarkable
delicacy and lightness.

Whaler's Church FIG. 142

1844

Minard Lafever, architect-builder

Union St., S end of Church St., Sag Harbor, Long Island, New York

Lafever came up with an effective (and unusual for Egyptian Revival) visual play of coarse against fine: a blunt mastaba form is visually softened by delicate siding. The resulting appealing fragility of Lafever's design is the source of its inter-est—that a building which clearly reads as "Egyptian," is yet so un-Egyptian in its lightness. According to Richard Carrott, the central tower was originally "topped by a copy of the Choragic Monument of Lysicrates, which in turn ended in a high pagoda-like spire." While such an almost-unimaginable visual extravaganza would have been right in character for the Romantic era, the comparatively chaste current state seems preferable today.

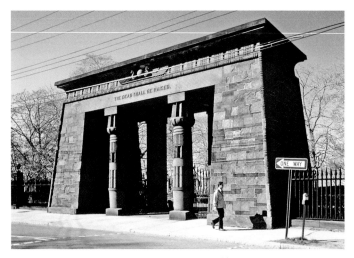

Grove Street Cemetery Gateway FIG. 143
1845–1848
Henry Austin, architect
227 Grove St. at Prospect St., New Haven, Connecticut

Dignified, though not somber, and just a little spooky—a perfect image for a cemetery gateway. There are few Egyptian Revival buildings in the United States, and rarely more than one in any given city. These are marvelous as rare visual counterpoints.

CONTEMPORARY INFLUENCES

Unlike the exotic revivals, the French Second Empire and Italianate imageries reflected the social desire for high-style expressions that made reference to recent, rather than ancient, European buildings. Eastlake, by contrast, was primarily a matter of design-as-contemporary-art.

Corcoran (now Renwick) Gallery FIGS. 144, 145
1859–1861; restored, 1967–1972
James Renwick, Jr., architect; **John Carl Warnecke & Associates**, restoration architects; **Hugh Newell Jacobson & Associates**, interior restoration architects
Pennsylvania Ave. at 17th St. NW., Washington, D.C.

This is a French Second Empire design of extraordinary urbanity and presence, holding its own among neighbors like the massive State, War & Navy building and the White House. The red brick exterior and sandstone is especially glorious in the city's largely color-neutral ceremonial core. The upper gallery volumes (Fig. 144) are wonderful airy spaces for the unhurried view of art, now showcasing crafts and decorative arts.

FIG. 143 The Imagery of Death Perhaps because of fabled immortality rituals in the age of pharaohs, Egyptian imageries were prominent in Romantic-era cemeteries. Few such designs are as beautifully scaled and carefully detailed as the Grove Street Cemetery gateway in New Haven.

FIG. 144, 145 Rare Sophistication James Renwick's Corcoran Gallery in Washington is as urbane a French Second Empire design as can be found in the United States. *Fig. 145: Library of Congress, Prints & Photographs, Historic American Buildings Survey*

Benjamin Allen House, "Terrace Hill" FIG. 146
1867–1869; restored 1972–1983
William W. Boyington, architect; **J.T. Elletson**, landscape architect;
Wagner, Marquardt, Wetherell, Ericsson, restoration architects
2300 Grand Ave., Des Moines, Iowa (open)

Terrace Hill is characterized by a strongly vertical composition of towers, chimneys, and projections. In massing, this is Italianate, but the mansard roof dormers are so prominent that a French Second Empire character dominates.

State, War & Navy Building FIG. 147
1871–1888
Alfred B. Mullett, Thomas Lincoln Casey, Richard von Ezdorf,
architects
Pennsylvania Ave. at 17th St. NW., Washington, D.C.

This extraordinary pile rambles on for an entire block, presenting undoubtedly the most animated and agitated exterior in the capital. In its overdone but endearing excess, State, War & Navy provides a bookend demonstration of the extremes of expression possible with the French Second Empire style. Compare it to the elegant, restrained Corcoran Gallery (Fig. 145) located just across Pennsylvania Avenue.

FIG. 146 French Italianate Terrace Hill in Des Moines is Italianate in form, but its mansard rooflines read strongly as French Second Empire. *Library of Congress, Prints & Photographs, Historic American Buildings Survey*

FIG. 147 Endearing Excess The State, War & Navy Building in Washington was long considered by tastemakers to be an artistic monstrosity. But with age, at long last, comes respectability. *Library of Congress, Prints & Photographs, Historic American Buildings Survey*

FIG. 148 **Monumental Civic Presence** The Old Post Office in St. Louis is appropriately grand without reliance on visual excess. *Library of Congress, Prints & Photographs, Historic American Buildings Survey*

Old Post Office FIG. 148
1872–1884; restored, 1984
Alfred B. Mullett, architect; **Daniel Chester French**, sculptor; **Patty, Berkebile, Nelson**; **Harry Weese & Associates**, adaptive-reuse architects
801 Olive St., St. Louis, Missouri

Unlike his over-the-top design for State, War & Navy (Fig. 147), this Mullet landmark employed a French Second Empire vocabulary to create a building of surpassing civic monumentality—grand and imposing. Once endangered as a surplus property, the Old Post Office has been recycled as an office building.

Cloud State Bank FIG. 149
1881
Reid & Reid, architects
Washington St., McLeansboro, Illinois

A high-spirited confection. Kidder Smith exulted that "half the architectural motifs in the latter part of the nineteenth century were gathered together for this marvelous bank," which under it all is more French Second Empire than anything else.

George Stone House
1852
606 W. 3rd St., Muscatine, Iowa

Dignified and imposing on its hilltop setting, the Stone House is a handsome Italianate design which has not been appreciably compromised by the stucco re-covering of its original brick walls.

Abner Pratt "Honolulu" House FIG. 150
1860
William L. Buck, attributed architect
107 N. Kalamazoo Ave., Marshall, Michigan (open)

Honolulu House provides high drama in this visually engaging Midwestern town, otherwise noted for its handsome Greek Revival houses (see the Neoclassicism chapter). This is an exotic design for the Midwest—really, for anywhere—almost a cartoon of an Italian Villa, with oversized brackets engaging into visually freestanding support columns. Pratt is actually a very large house, deceptive in scale and meant to read as cottage-like. Since the house is so carefully detailed, it is apparent that the design was intended to be taken seriously as architecture, as it surely should be, and not as a mere novelty.

FIG. 149 **American Idol** Cloud State Bank (right) in an Illinois town would be a standout anywhere, a marvelous architectural confection.

FIG. 150 **Well Beyond the Ordinary** Abner Pratt's "Honolulu" House is a delightful, lighthearted architectural adventure. The Iolani Palace (Fig. 154), in Honolulu itself, seems almost reserved by comparison.

Frederick Hall House FIG. 151
1869–1870
Lucius Mills, builder
126 E. Main St., Ionia, Michigan (open)

The Hall House demonstrates the high level of accomplishment in the 1800s by builders employing pattern books. Hall was indeed designed by the book, though with special attention given to the carved eave brackets. Unlike spectacular or exotic designs, houses like this became local civic landmarks because of their attention to detail and the quality of materials and craftsmanship.

EXOTIC IMAGERIES

Frederick Church Mansion, "Olana" FIGS. 152, 153
1870–1874; addition 1888–1890
Frederic Edwin Church, designer; **Calvert Vaux**, consulting architect
Rt. 9G, S of Hudson, New York (open)

Even in an America that seems to enjoy an excess of everything, this estate of the famous landscape painter is unique, the product of a great artist and aesthete who had the opportunity to travel extensively throughout the Near East.

The house was developed organically, though not haphazardly, in a casual Oriental vocabulary, inside and out. This total work of art is enhanced by Olana's stunning site, commanding sublime views over the Hudson River Valley. By the greatest of fortune, the

FIG. 151 **By the (Pattern) Book** Nineteenth-century builders used pattern books to impressive effect, as the Frederick Hall House in Michigan confirms. The county courthouse is visible in the background of this view.

FIG. 152, 153 Exotic Grandeur The Frederick Church mansion, "Olana," is a singular design for a sublime Hudson Valley site by a great artist who was deeply influenced by Orientalism. *Fig. 153: Library of Congress, Prints & Photographs, Historic American Buildings Survey*

property has remained essentially intact, and is under public ownership, open to visitors.

Iolani Palace FIG. 154
1879–1882
T. J. Baker, C. J. Wall, Isaac Moore, architects
King and Richard Sts., Honolulu, Hawaii

Kidder Smith hit it on the head when he described this design as "Suggesting the Renaissance gone tropic, with hints of Second Empire France." Iolani Palace is stately, open, and set in a spacious enclave, appropriate for its original role as Hawaii's seat of state.

EASTLAKE

Emlen Physick House FIG. 155
1879
Frank Furness, attributed architect
1048 Washington St., Cape May, New Jersey (open)

The attribution to Furness (see the Progressives chapter) is based on similarities in the floor plans of the Physick House and the Rhawn House near Philadelphia, designed the same year by Furness. However, the Physick exterior elevations are pretty subdued compared to what we expect from Furness and in comparison to the sumptuous vocabulary of forms and textures employed on the Rhawn House. No matter, the Physick House is a handsome Eastlake design, characteristically thin, with exterior surfaces broken down into panels by flat moldings.

FIG. 154 American Royalty An agreeable mix of Tradition and tropics, Iolani Palace is the only American (former) seat of state with a throne room.

FIG. 155 Archetypical Eastlake The Emlen Physick House in New Jersey epitomizes the agitated, fragile, "sticky" verticality that is characteristic of this style.

William Carson Mansion FIGS. 156, 157
1884–1886
Samuel and **Joseph Newsom**, architects
143 M St. at 2nd St., Eureka, California (private club)

Hands-down, the Carson Mansion is the grandest and greatest Victorian-era house in the United States, an overwhelming visual tour-de-force in everything from its super scale to endless detail and texture. The interiors are every bit as good as the marvelous exterior. The architectural imagery is usually described as Queen Anne, but in its fidgety "stickyness," this is the ultimate Eastlake house. The Carson Mansion is truly worth a trip to out-of-the-way Eureka, which contains several architectural treasures, beginning with another house by the Newsoms, kitty-corner across the street.

FIGS. 156, 157 **The Ultimate Eastlake** The William Carson Mansion is in a class by itself—indeed, in a *world* by itself. Visitors to this (now) private club who are overwhelmed by its exterior should not expect a respite of visual tranquility inside! (For another interior view, see Fig. 16.) *Fig. 157: Library of Congress, Prints & Photographs, Historic American Buildings Survey*

FIG. 158 **Unrestrained by Good Taste** Gaudy Eastlakes like the Charles Hackley House in Michigan were contemporaries with elegant Beaux Arts mansions and refined Shingle Style homes. Well more than a century ago, a broad divergence in taste was already apparent among affluent Americans. Recently re-colored as a Painted Lady, the house now looks a bit less outrageous than in this 1970s view.

FIG. 159 **Refined Eastlake** After the Hackley House (Fig. 158), the beautifully put-together John Ralston House in Oregon restores one's faith in the Eastlake style.

Charles Hackley House FIG. 158
1887–1889
David S. Hopkins, architect
484 W. Webster Ave., Muskegon, Michigan (open, as is Hume House next door)

Hackley is a vigorous Eastlake, far less restrained than the Physick House (Fig. 155) and not nearly as sophisticated as the Ralston House (Fig. 159). You can easily understand why a house like this was considered to be the embodiment of bad taste from the 1890s until quite recently. Safely removed from that era by more than a century, we can now admire its sheer exuberance, overlooking the hodgepodge of ornamentation and the tacked-on projections to the basic house form. If this still leaves you a bit queasy, the Hume House, next door at 472 Webster, built at the same time as the Hackley House by the same architect, is a little less overbearing.

John Ralston House FIG. 159
1889
632 Baker St. SE., Albany, Oregon

A wonderful true cottage which despite a profusion of Eastlake detail and stickwork, maintains its composure. If there is such a thing as a refined Eastlake design, then this is it.

Victorian Gothic

1860–1900

FIG. 160 Architecture Reflects Society Florid Victorian architecture mirrored the supremely confident, almost swashbuckling English ruling class of the mid-to-late 1800s. To be sure, Victorian imageries were also employed outside of the British Empire, including in the United States. Beyond the Commonwealth, however, Victorianism was simply an expression of style, since it did not reflect the social tenor of Commonwealth nations. The magnificent exuberance of designs like London's 1865 St. Pancras Station, by Gilbert Scott, seemed culturally authentic only in *Britannia*.

Victorian Gothic is truly British in more ways than in its association with the reign of a queen. With respect to authentic Victorian expressions in architecture, New York University art historian Carol Herselle Krinsky observed that British power reached a peak by the mid-1800s, when Queen Victoria and a select few of her noble subjects quite literally *owned* a significant part of the world.

British economic and military power were then globally preeminent. Little wonder that William Blake fervently envisioned London as the long-awaited New Jerusalem. Those were heady times for England. Krinsky continued that it would have been implausible in that cultural context to imagine a continuation of restrained Regency Neoclassicism as authentically reflecting Victorian-era values. And so exuberant, aggressive Victorian imageries emerged, mirroring the brash confidence of England (Fig. 160).

Of course this means that Victorian Gothic buildings in the United States were simply expressions of style. They did not authentically depict America's place in the world, nor did they accurately reflect the nation's self-image. Nevertheless, one can surely understand the fascination of American designers with this florid, complex architectural imagery.

FIG. 161 **Almost Authentic** The Upjohns endowed their fantastic Green-Wood Cemetery Gateway with such a profusion of English quotes that it is a wonder they did not receive a "Good Try" commendation from the Queen!

Because of the disruption caused by the American Civil War, and because Victorian Gothic was overshadowed, especially in the nation's explosively growing midsection, by the Richardsonian Romanesque (see the Progressives chapter) throughout the 1880s boom years, relatively few Victorian buildings survive in the United States, and fewer still are of high architectural distinction.

Regardless, the representatives cited here are marvelous visual treasures.

FIG. 162 **A Classic Pile** One can only stand in awe in reflection on the tremendous number of bricks required to build Harvard's massive Memorial Hall. The tower's spectacularly vertical, flamboyantly colorful roof, lost to fire in the 1950s, was rebuilt in 1999, after this view was taken. As a result, Memorial Hall once again dominates the local skyline, as well as its nearby streetscape.

Green-Wood Cemetery Gateway FIG. 161
1861
Richard M. Upjohn & Son, architects
Fifth Ave. at 25th St., Brooklyn, New York

A fabulous stone concoction, drawing confidently on everything English from Wells Cathedral to contemporary London design— probably about as close to a genuine Victorian expression as can be found in the United States. The central, gateway section is fantastically intricate, employing a disciplined mélange of open buttresses, spindles, and crockets. This ornateness is enhanced visually as played off against the comparative simplicity of the flanking gatehouses.

Memorial Hall, Harvard University FIG. 162
1870–1878
Ware and Van Brunt, architects
Cambridge and Quincy Sts., Cambridge, Massachusetts

An arresting exercise in Ruskinian Gothic, this massive, multicolored edifice pretty much defines what is affectionately described by architectural historians as a "brick pile." The building program included a banquet hall and a theater, in addition to a memorial corridor. The resulting visual composition is a bit awkward— which might be considered a plus for Victorians!

Third Judicial District Courthouse,
now **Jefferson Market Library** FIG. 163
1874–1877; restored, 1967
Calvert Vaux, **Frederick C. Withers**, architects; **Giorgio Cavaglieri**, restoration architect
425 Sixth Ave. at W. 10th St., New York, New York

If one wished to understand the American version of High Victorian, then this is the building to study. A profusion of forms, textures, and details, was somehow, if just barely, kept under control by its eminent designer, Vaux. Left abandoned for two decades after the Second World War, the courthouse was, unbelievably to us now, threatened with destruction. Happily, it was eventually preserved as a community branch library. In any role, this is a magnificent building, with a spectacular visual presence.

Mitchell Building FIG. 164
1876–1878

Mackie Building FIG. 164
1879–1880
Edward Townsend Mix, architect; **W. A. Holbrook**, associate architect
207-225 E. Michigan St., Milwaukee, Wisconsin

With such powerful and animated façades, these side-by-side siblings provide textbook examples of Victorian-era visual excess. Mix brashly commandeered just about every trick in the Victorian playbook, especially polychromy, without apparent fear of the disaster he was surely courting, and in the end, it all came out fine.

Smithsonian Institution Arts and Industries Building
1881
Adolph Cluss, **Paul Schulze**, architects
S side of Capitol Mall, between 8th and 10th Sts. SW., Washington, D.C.

While we rightly think of Victorian as English in derivation, Pamela Scott demonstrated that this design was inspired by German precedents expropriated from an earlier Vienna exhibition. Despite a daunting mix of masses, towers, shapes, textures, and polychrome, the building holds together visually, primarily because of a powerful, underlying symmetry established by its Greek Cross plan.

FIG. 164 Heartland Landmarks Out here in the wilds of the American Midwest, the Mitchell and Mackie buildings in Milwaukee (right and left in photo) demonstrate how to vamp-up basic French Second Empire vocabularies into seriously Victorian expressions. *Library of Congress, Prints & Photographs, Historic American Buildings Survey*

FIG. 165 Prairie Victorian The First National Bank in Dawson, Minnesota, is architecturally expressive enough to add a bit of distinction to an otherwise visually unremarkable small town.

First National Bank FIG. 165
1892
E side 6th St. between Chestnut and Pine, Dawson, Minnesota

Not that many truly engaging Victorian expressions were built in the United States outside of big cities, and it is especially rare to find one extant in a tiny prairie town like Dawson. The bank's basic brick envelope still recognizably derives from the Richardsonian Romanesque, although its designer knowingly sculpted the central section in the manner of America's Victorian master, Frank Furness (see the Progressives chapter). While First National Bank would of course look timid if placed right alongside of a Furness building in Philadelphia, just about anywhere in small-town American it would be a standout. The building has been partly boarded up, and one hopes that this treasure will not be lost.

FIG. 163 Victorian Splendor Even those who do not care for Victorian architecture—there are still more than a few around—can surely appreciate the Third Judicial District Courthouse/Jefferson Market Library in New York as a great design without fear of compromising their aesthetic principles. *Library of Congress, Prints & Photographs, Historic American Buildings Survey*

Beaux Arts

1865–1941

FIG. 166 Roman-French Classical Tradition Monumental Paris is the starting (and ending) point for the Beaux Arts. A sense of grandeur suffuses the city's public realm, from the effusive conversations of Parisian society at sidewalk cafés to great, radial boulevards such as Avenue Foch, seen here from atop the Arc de Triomphe. Such axial streets were laid out under Emperor Napoleon III and his prefect, Baron Hausmann, between 1853 and 1870. Like the adoption of Victorian imageries outside of the British Empire, Beaux Arts architecture seldom seemed quite as convincing beyond France, sometimes even beyond Paris. Nevertheless, American Gilded Age tycoons did their level best to build and live according to Beaux Arts ideals. They pretty much succeeded in Newport.

Beaux Arts architectural imageries and cityscapes (Fig. 166) were introduced to American high society largely through the designs of Richard Morris Hunt for the Vanderbilt family (Fig. 167). "Beaux Arts" refers to the *École Nationale et Spéciale des Beaux Arts*, the School of Fine Arts in Paris, where Hunt studied in the 1850s.

The *École* was singularly influential to American architecture from the Gilded Age following the Civil War through the 1930s. Up until the outbreak of World War I, an *École* education was almost essential for any American architect who hoped for major commissions from prominent clients. This applied as well to Progressives like Henry Hobson Richardson and Louis H.

Sullivan (see the Progressives chapter). Moreover, virtually all the American architectural schools followed Beaux Arts training methods before the outbreak of World War II. And even as Bauhaus modernism replaced Beaux Arts traditionalism in postwar architectural education, the *École*-trained professor Jean Labatut at Princeton was highly influential—memorable, really—in the professional education of master architects such as Charles W. Moore and Robert Venturi in the 1950s (see the Modern Masters chapter).

Beaux Arts ateliers emphasized an exhaustive, detailed application of what Paul R. Baker described as an "idealized Roman-French classical tradition [which] strongly opposed the picturesque character of the Gothic." Hunt submitted a Beaux Arts scheme for an 1863 Central Park gateway competition and employed a Beaux Arts architectural vocabulary in an 1869 design for the Lenox Library in New York City. However, Hunt's 1878–1882 William K. Vanderbilt mansion in Manhattan (razed) set the tone for Gilded Age magnates. Châteauesque mansions of varying design quality soon appeared in the best neighborhoods of major American cities.

Given that the owners of these new mansions were the nation's financiers and business leaders, Beaux Arts imageries were widely employed for business offices and civic buildings as well, establishing an "architecture of the imperial age," in Lewis Mumford's disapproving view. This shift in architectural taste to the Beaux Arts accelerated after the 1893 World's Columbian Exposition, although the movement to the Beaux Arts was already well underway, certainly along the East Coast, when the Fair's glittering Beaux Arts "White City" opened (Fig. 739).

In the 1890s, American architects who wished to attract or retain major clients dropped progressive vocabularies like the Richardsonian Romanesque and henceforth designed primarily in the Beaux Arts manner. Major firms associated with Beaux Arts expressions included McKim, Mead & White, Carrère & Hastings, and Delano & Aldrich; and among prominent practitioners were John Russell Pope and Harrie T. Lindeberg.

ACADEMIC TRADITION

The Villard Houses
1881–1886, conversion to restaurant, hotel, retail, and association offices, 1978–1980
McKim, Mead & White, architects
451–455 Madison Ave. at 50th St., New York, New York

Here, the Italian Renaissance palazzo model was transformed and upgraded to satisfy the boundless appetites of the American Gilded Age rich. Four elegant town houses were organized around a formal courtyard, with interior finishes fully worthy of royalty. The Villard-Reid town house interiors by Stanford White were utterly sumptuous. Later incorporated into a hotel development, (see the Retail & Hotels chapter), the complex offers visitors a sense of what the Villard interiors were like.

FIG. 167 Hunt and the Vanderbilts For all intents and purposes, Richard Morris Hunt served (perhaps more accurately, reigned) as official family architect for the Vanderbilts. The Breakers (1892–1895) for Cornelius Vanderbilt II marked a culmination of this relationship: the largest, and arguably most opulent mansion in Newport. This interior view of its "Cottage Porch" suggests the nature of Gilded Age lifestyles. *Library of Congress, Prints & Photographs, Historic American Buildings Survey*

FIG. 168 Newport's Gold Standard William K. Vanderbilt's "Marble House" is extraordinary in every sense, "marvelously beautiful" in its imposing hauteur.

William K. Vanderbilt "Marble House" FIG. 168
1888–1892
Richard Morris Hunt, architect
Bellevue Ave., Newport, Rhode Island (open)

Marble House was very literally the Gold Standard against which other American mansions were judged. It is exceptional and excessive in virtually every important respect, from its perfectly incised marble exterior to the overwhelmingly ornate Gold Room inside.

FIG. 169 **American Versailles** George Washington Vanderbilt's wilderness retreat, "Biltmore," in its immense acreage, if not for its architecture and landscapes, truly rivaled the great European estates.

FIG. 170 **Supreme Refinement** Stanford White's version of grandeur was more subtly ornate than was Richard Morris Hunt's, as can be judged by a comparison of Hunt's Marble House (Fig. 168) with White's nearby design for the Herman Oelrichs House, "Rosecliff," whose front terrace is illustrated here.

George Washington Vanderbilt Estate, "Biltmore" FIG. 169

1888–1895

Richard Morris Hunt, architect; **Frederick Law Olmsted**,
landscape architect
Asheville, North Carolina (open)

Truly "American" at a scale that even Louis XIV could envy: 125,000 acres in the Blue Ridge foothills provided the setting for a 255-room main house. In truth, Biltmore is not the best of either Hunt or, especially, of Olmsted, but that is trifling in the face of the development's stupendous proportions.

Herman Oelrichs House, "Rosecliff" FIG. 170

1897–1902

McKim, Mead & White, architects
Bellevue Ave., Newport, Rhode Island (open)

Stanford White's design was disciplined to perfection. At first glance, the composition seems to be one of classical symmetry, but the offset entrance location subtly animates the façade. An illusion of compactness masks the home's true size and complexity of function. The overall design theme—the Grand Trianon at Versailles its putative model—was executed flawlessly, at several levels of scale.

CITY BEAUTIFUL CLASSICISM

Boston Public Library FIG. 171

1888–1895; annex, 1964–1973

McKim, Mead & White, architects; **Augustus Saint-Gaudens, Bela Pratt, Daniel Chester French**, sculptors; **John Singer Sargent** and numerous other artists; **Philip Johnson**, annex architect
Copley Square, Boston, Massachusetts

FIG. 171 **Surpassing Civic Art** Charles Follen McKim's Boston Public Library is a brilliant integration of architecture, sculpture, and painting.

The Boston library is especially significant as a demonstration of how to enfront a major public space, for its collaborative public art, and as a signature design of the McKim, Mead & White practice. With respect to its architecture, it is difficult to imagine how the building could have been any better.

FIG. 172, 173 **Consummate Achievement** There was really nothing new about Cass Gilbert's design concept for the Minnesota State Capitol. The building's estimable visual qualities derive largely from Gilbert's resolute attention to the countless small esthetic decisions made while the design was being developed—and subsequently throughout construction.

Minnesota State Capitol FIGS. 172, 173
1893–1904
Cass Gilbert, architect; **Daniel Chester French**, sculptor; **John LaFarge**, **Kenyon Cox**, **Frank J. Millet**, **Edward Simmons**, artists
Aurora Ave. at Park St., St. Paul, Minnesota

Gilbert's design is widely appreciated as the finest of the Renaissance-dome state capitols. As David Gebhard pointed out, however, there is nothing really new or daring here. The building succeeds because of the quality of Gilbert's design, his handling of proportions, and, especially on the interior, the richness of materials and integral art, including glass, murals, and sculpture.

New York Public Library
1902–1911
Carrère & Hastings, architects
Fifth Ave. at 42nd St., New York, New York

This flagship is the very image for most of us of what a traditional big-city library would look like, particularly its monumental presence engaged in a highly developed visual interplay with its streetscape, integral art, and sculpture. It offers, as well, the impressive space of its great reading room and the urbane, now-revitalized Bryant Park behind. The library can be appreciated as a textbook demonstration of the public potentials inherent in the American Beaux Arts.

Temple of the Scottish Rite FIG. 174

1910–1916
John Russell Pope, architect
1733 16th St. NW., Washington, D.C.

The Temple is the design that established Pope as a master of monumental buildings. Steven Bedford related that from its opening until well into the 1930s, the Scottish Rite Temple was the subject of constant critical praise, including an assessment by the Architectural Review of London that "this monumental composition may surely be said to have reached the high-water mark of achievement in that newer interpretation of the Classic style."

Lincoln Memorial FIG. 931

1911–1922; Lincoln statue lighted, 1927; building lighted, 1972
Henry Bacon, architect; **Daniel Chester French**, sculptor of the Lincoln statue; **Jules Guerin**, artist for murals; **Frederick Law Olmsted, Jr.**, landscape advisor for the reflecting pool; **James Greenleaf**, landscape advisor for site plantings
W end of the National Mall, Washington, D.C.

FIG. 174 **Forgotten Over Time** John Russell Pope's Temple of the Scottish Rite in Washington, D.C., slighted by modernist tastemakers for decades, was one of the most acclaimed buildings in the United States for a generation after its completion.

There is much more here than initially meets the eye. To begin with, Bacon distilled the classic Greek temple prototype to its bare essence: this is nearly a modernist expression, especially remarkable in view of its date. The building is integral with its district setting, terminating the long axis of the Mall on a large scale, and the forecourt reflecting pool at comparatively smaller scale.

In addition, the watergate on the west side physically integrates an upper surface road and lower limited-access parkway with a formal Potomac edge, establishing a visual base for the Memorial as seen from across the river. Finally, and not at all least, the monumental sculpture of Lincoln is carefully lighted.

All in all, the Lincoln Memorial was a virtuoso performance on the part of Bacon, although the Commission of Fine Arts participated deeply and continuously in Memorial planning and design decisions between Congressional approval in early 1911 and completion. This is a case study in how to exploit dramatic site potential with subtlety and dignity.

Palace of Fine Arts FIG. 175

1913–1915; rebuilt 1965–1967
Bernard Maybeck, architect
Within Hwy. 101, Marina Blvd. and Baker St., San Francisco, California

Maybeck is not easy to pin down, stylistically, and here he based his design on classicism, but it is a classicism overcome with emotion. Maybeck's splendid visual composition, which seems almost to be a romantic ruin, both epitomized and also pretty much closed out Roman opulence in American architecture.

FIG. 175 **Overcome With Emotion** Bernard Maybeck's Palace of Fine Arts is one of the most emotionally charged of American Beaux Arts structures. *Library of Congress, Prints & Photographs, Historic American Buildings Survey*

United States Supreme Court FIG. 176

1925–1935
Cass Gilbert, architect
E. Capitol and 1st Sts. NE., Washington, D.C.

Going by the book can be a successful approach (see the Lincoln Memorial entry in the Civic Design chapter), but here that approach is less satisfying in realization. The Supreme Court program offered all the right ingredients: the highest court in the land, a prominent national site, a master designer, plenty of public art, and a more-than-sufficient budget.

Yet rather than resulting in a triumphant summation of Gilbert's outstanding career, this building is merely impressive, lacking the dynamic visual creativity of his Minnesota Capitol (Fig 172) and many of his subsequent works. It is difficult not to compare this design unfavorably to John Russell Pope's superb contemporary, the National Gallery of Art, located just a few blocks away (Fig. 382).

FIG. 176 **Not Supreme, Alas** Cass Gilbert's United States Supreme Court design is competent and appropriately monumental. Unfortunately, the building lacks the energizing spirit that separates exceptional architecture from the merely respectable. *Library of Congress, Prints & Photographs, Historic American Buildings Survey*

American Colonial Revivals

1870–1962

FIG. 177 Emphasizing American Traditions The 1876 Centennial celebration inspired an upwelling of nativist pride throughout the United States. Architects responded by emphasizing *American* characteristics in their designs: American Georgian and Federal detailing were employed in place of conventional English vocabularies. Some of these new "American" designs were sophisticated transliterations of traditional models. This 1903 house in Duluth, then in effect an economic-cultural suburb of civic powerhouse Cleveland, shows how references to the past could be simplified into fresh, engaging architecture.

Colonial Revivals resulted from an Americanization of European design precedents. They developed from the 1870s onward, spearheaded by American Queen Anne designers who replaced conventional British Queen Anne elements with eighteenth-century American Georgian and Federal detailing and decorative features (Fig. 177).

David Gebhard identified four American Colonial Revival modes, beginning with the Shingle Style, which he noted was "the first major return in architectural styling to the simplicity and Puritanism of America's early years." Because shingling was so prominent, the Shingle Style seemed, then and still now, to be a distinct style.

FIG. 178 **American Expression** Henry Hobson Richardson's robust interpretation of the Queen Anne, the 1874–1876 William Watts Sherman House, opened up a new avenue of expression for American architects.

By 1890, the Queen Anne-Colonial Revival had become popular. Initially, "picturesque Queen Anne designs were simplified" through the use of Georgian and Federal detailing. Just before 1900, highly developed Georgian and Federal Colonial Revival styles appeared throughout much of the United States.

Finally, by about 1915, the notion of correctness had supplanted the earlier, more imaginative phases of the Colonial Revivals, leading to an often impressive, but usually dry, academic rendering of the American past.

Typical American Colonial Revival characteristics included: simplified rectangular forms topped by gabled or hip roofs; balanced, if not actually symmetrical arrangement of openings; shingle, brick, or clapboard exteriors; employment of Classical vocabularies, including columns, cornices, and entablatures; small-paned windows and, often, Palladian windows. Sophisticated interpretations of American Colonial Revivals were built through the 1930s, and indeed, in the output of Royal Barry Wills, until the prominent architect's death in 1962.

SHINGLE STYLE

William Watts Sherman House FIG. 178
1874–1876
Henry Hobson Richardson, **Gambrill & Richardson**, architects;
Stanford White, architect of the 1881 library alteration
2 Shepard Ave., Newport, Rhode Island (limited access; college offices)

The American Shingle Style grew out of this powerful, tactile design. Richardson combined his characteristic interconnected internal spaces with a distinctive Queen Anne imagery. Samuel White stated that Watts Sherman was "unlike any American house that preceded it, [exerting] an immediate impact on late-nineteenth-century architecture."

Newport Casino FIGS. 179, 180
1879–1881, partly restored after a 1953 fire
McKim, Mead & White, architects
194 Bellevue Ave., Newport, Rhode Island

An early urban "mixed-use" development, of a design quality largely unmatched since. Street retail offers no hint of the a large

FIGS. 179, 180 **Separate Worlds** Newport Casino's retail storefronts (left) screen an exclusive private club's inner court (right). This layering of public access and private uses allowed the not-so-high to seemingly mix with High Society.

FIG. 181 **Form By Intent** The powerful simple roof form of McKim, Mead & White's William Low House in Rhode Island was a designed counterpoint, intended to create visual tension against its fine-grained wall textures. *Library of Congress, Prints & Photographs, Historic American Buildings Survey*

FIG. 182 **Polished Shingle Style** The Charles Lang Freer House in Detroit is practically an Arts & Crafts expression, solid without appearing stolid. The stairs and retaining wall are later modifications.

FIG. 183 **Classic Clubhouse** Shinnecock Hills Country Club on Long Island is revered in the world of Golf, its venerable, comfortably rambling clubhouse by Stanford White a Shingle Style classic.

interior court, about which the club's social and athletic activities could be pursued in elegant privacy. The scheme was loosely modeled after an English project by Richard Norman Shaw, but this is a modern, American expression, with little fustiness.

William Low House FIG. 181
1886–1887, razed
McKim, Mead & White, architects
Bristol, Rhode Island

Everything was visually encompassed within a single massive gable form. Thus the façade was subtly animated in detail while visually unified overall. Low was one of the great American houses of the late 1800s. Its destruction was an immense cultural loss.

Charles Lang Freer House FIG. 182
1890–1893
Wilson Eyre, Jr., architect
71 E. Ferry St., Detroit, Michigan (limited access; college offices)

Freer is among the most polished of Shingle Style houses, so carefully detailed as to seem almost more Arts & Crafts than Colonial Revival.

Shinnecock Hills Country Club FIG. 183
1891–1892, 1895
Stanford White, clubhouse architect
200 Tuckahoe Rd., Southampton, New York

Shinnecock Hills is revered in American golf as one of the five incorporators of the United States Golf Association. Its clubhouse was the first to be built in the United States. However the clubhouse requires no historic basis for recognition, as it is clearly significant architecturally. White's suave, almost jaunty design strikes just the right tone for a country club, providing a model for subsequent designs across the nation.

Unitarian Church FIGS. 184, 185
1898
A. C. Schweinfurth, architect
Bancroft Way at Dana, Berkeley, California

There is something transformative about California! In this remarkable building, the Eastern elegance of the Shingle Style has been turned into an organic form that seems to be growing up out of the earth.

3200 Block of Pacific Avenue FIG. 186
1901–1913
Ernest Coxhead, Bernard Maybeck, Willis Polk, William Knowles, architects
3203–3277 Pacific Ave., San Francisco, California

An extraordinarily inventive sequence of shingled townhouses works its way down a steep hill. The architectural star of the group is the Waybur townhouse at 3232 Pacific, a 1902 design of surpassing refinement by Ernest Coxhead.

FIGS. 184, 185 Organic Shingle Style
A. C. Schweinfurth's rustic Unitarian Church in Berkeley seems almost to have grown up out of the soil, especially the trunk-like corner posts.
Photographs © Marc Treib

FIG. 186 Urbane Shingle Style
These townhouses along the 3200 Block of Pacific Avenue in San Francisco are located just across the Bay from the Unitarian Church (Figs. 184 & 185). While the church and these houses are all superior designs, their visual characters—from the rustic church to these refined houses—so differ that together they illustrate bookend expressions of the Shingle Style.

FIG. 187 **The Ubiquitous Queen Anne Porch** Spurred by a national economic recovery in the late 1890s, a flood of home remodeling occurred between about 1900 and the early 'teens. This big front porch grafted onto the French Second Empire Amos Miller House is an example of these Queen Anne modernizations of Romantic-era houses.

FIG. 188 **Classic Queen Anne** Even though it was remodeled with Colonial Revival quotes after 1900, the Carson-Tracy House still provides a checklist of typical Queen Anne attributes.

QUEEN ANNE–COLONIAL REVIVAL

Queen Anne imageries were highly popular around 1900. Few great monuments were rendered in the Queen Anne, a middle-class style of choice, while Shingle Style or the Georgian and Federal imageries were favored by wealthy Americans.

Queen Anne motifs like front porches with big columns were widely employed in house remodelings around 1900. After a gradual national recovery from the Panic of 1893, the combination of economic optimism and the turning of a new

century required up-to-date styles. Thus many post-Civil War Italianate and French Second Empire homes were updated in the Queen Anne style.

Amos Miller House FIG. 187
c. 1873; front porch c. 1910
616 E. 1st St., Mechanicsville, Iowa

Miller is an archetypical Queen Anne remodeling of an earlier house, in this case, one with French Second Empire imagery. A large porch was wrapped around the front and one side, held up by sturdy Ionic columns. Though the new porch is not even slightly

FIG. 189 **Singular Queen Anne Colonial Revival** In a blindfold description, I. Vernon Hill's Cook House would seem to fall squarely into Queen Anne-Colonial

Revival convention: a bit irregular (if formal overall), tactile, classicist references in detail, and so forth. As realized, however, Hill's spectacular design is unique.

"French," any stylistic inconsistency is rendered moot by the fact that both the original house and the porch are visually robust, and by the picturesque qualities of the remodeled house.

Carson-Tracy House FIG. 188
c. 1888; remodeled c. 1906
601 N. 6th St., Burlington, Iowa

A checklist of David Gebhard's Queen Anne taxonomy: irregular in plan; vertical emphasis; surface tactility, especially fish-scale shingles; extensive front porch; corner tower. Colonial Revival remodeling added classical details, especially the Palladian window. To cap it all off, today's Chinese red against pale yellow is certainly an attention-grabbing color combination.

Ward House
1896
804 E. Elm Ave., Waseca, Minnesota

Queen Anne of a very different character from the previous entry. This temple-front design is symmetrical, excepting the later side addition, including a characteristic Palladian window. Especially when sited on a slight eminence, as here, an imagery like this could be imposing without heaviness, grand with seeming ostentatious. Houses of this character were ubiquitous throughout the Midwest in the early 1900s.

House FIG. 177
1903
2219 E. Superior St., Duluth, Minnesota

Most American Queen Anne houses occupy some point on an evolutionary scale, from busy and "sticky" to formal and simplified. A few Queen Anne designs are based on a fresh synthesis of multiple Colonial Revival vocabularies. This house is a sophisticated example of the latter, cohesively blending a range of inspirations from Shingle Style to hints of Georgian into a fresh imagery.

Cook House FIG. 189
1900
I. Vernon Hill, architect
501 W. Skyline Pkwy., Duluth, Minnesota

American architecture has been enriched by brilliantly creative designs by gifted, less-known local and regional architects. Hill died tragically young after only a few years of practice in remote Duluth, but he surely would have been a star in prewar American architecture had he lived longer. In this remarkable design for a spectacular site perched high above Lake Superior, Hill took the American Queen Anne in an unexpected direction, deftly balancing nature and built, symmetry and asymmetry, the rustic and the refined.

GEORGIAN–FEDERAL REVIVAL

From the 'teens into the 1930s, Georgian imageries were favored by wealthy Americans. Steven McLeod Bedford noted the attraction of this vocabulary to society architect John Russell Pope: "Essential components of the style were codified, yet it allowed a certain freedom of composition, since [Pope's] creative strength lay in manipulating styles that permitted . . . reinvention."

FIG. 190 **The Very Picture of Southampton** Drive along Hill Street to the James Breese House, "The Orchard," and you will have no trouble understanding the cachet attached to this fabled summer retreat for the rich and famous.

By the turn of the twentieth century, the American Country House had emerged as a mature building type. Clive Aslet observed that while it held a kinship to English country houses, the American version was clearly understood as a "new type of dwelling."

Among its typical salient attributes were a freestanding location, well beyond developed suburbia; an independent farming operation (see the Rural Structures chapter); formal gardens integral to the house design; and a very large and expensive estate house, "furnished in the richest manner," in Aslet's words.

While not all American country houses were of a Georgian Colonial Revival imagery, this was a popular architectural vocabulary among those wishing to affect the image of landed gentry.

James Breese House, "The Orchard" FIG. 190
1898–1907; subdivided
McKim, Mead & White, architects; **Frederick Law Olmsted**, landscape architect
155 Hill St., Southampton, New York

An early-1800s house was expanded into this immense estate house—more than 250 feet across. It reads as a visually relaxed and much, much larger version of Mount Vernon (Fig. 75). By employing flanking wings, engaged pavilions, and a large vocabulary of window treatments and varying heights and rooflines, the architecture made the house read as if it had been added to informally over decades. However the interiors were beautifully detailed as a piece. Now refurbished and converted into condominiums, the house and its spacious front lawn can be easily seen from gateways at the sidewalk along this grand street.

Richards House
1907; later alterations
Francis Wilson, architect
1731 Santa Barbara St., Santa Barbara, California

The upper-middle-class version of Georgian Colonial Revival. It differs from countless Georgian Colonial Revival builder's houses mainly in its somewhat larger size, better detailing, and in the owner's employment of an architect. Wilson came up with a free interpretation, with references to Early and Late Georgian, and even a hint of the Federal in its relative simplicity.

FIG. 191 Country Life Providing very different settings from the highly public
Southampton scene (The Orchard, Fig. 190), upper-class enclaves like Far Hills offer a
haven from the pressures of public life, ideally in a residence of great quality like John
Russell Pope's Thomas Frothingham House (top).

FIG. 192 The Ultimate Estate The Georgian Revival main house of Marshall Field's
"Caumsett" (bottom) occupies only one small part of a 1,750-acre estate, which also
included a working farm group, polo grounds, and a variety of recreation facilities,
overlooking Long Island Sound. (See Figs. 597, 598 for images of Camusett's farm
group and polo stables.)

ACADEMIC

Thomas Frothingham House FIG. 191
1919–1921; additions, 2005–2008
John Russell Pope, architect
Liberty Corner Rd., Far Hills, New Jersey (I-287 exit 26; E to light, right on Lyons Rd.; right on Liberty Corner; follow USGA signs (open-USGA headquarters-museum)

Pope modified convention in plan and elevation, employing dependencies to accommodate a living room separated from the main body of the house. A traditional Georgian façade was visually energized by a projecting entrance pediment, supported by two-story Corinthian columns.

The quality of detailing, the graceful setting, and an overall restraint result in a property of great dignity. The house and grounds are immaculately maintained by the current owner, the United States Golf Association.

Marshall Field II Estate, "Caumsett" FIG. 192
1920–1930
John Russell Pope, architect; **Alfred Hopkins**, architect for the farm group; **George H. Gillies**, master gardener (exterior accessible; interior used as college offices)
Caumsett State Park, West Neck Rd., Lloyd Neck, Huntington, Long Island, New York

Caumsett is in effect a high-design Georgian Revival village, set on a 1,750-acre site on the North Shore of Long Island. The grounds include a stately red-brick main house, a cluster of white farm buildings (Fig. 597) and brick polo stables (Fig. 598), shingled beach house and barn, and the usual guest cottages, beach cabanas, tennis courts, polo fields, and support buildings.

The entire rolling property is visually organized around an access-road loop, which provides both long vistas and close views of major buildings, which are designed in several "compatible" American Colonial styles, so as not to be monotonous. Bedford stated that this ensemble reflects a culmination of Pope's design techniques developed over the previous quarter century. Caumsett is a remarkably engaging visual environment.

VARIETY OF COLONIAL IMAGERIES

Several American Colonial imageries were widely employed well into the 1930s. The Cape Cod was the most popular among these types, according to David Gebhard, prolific chronicler of the era. This popularity continued on into the 1950s, as basic variations of the Cape Cod were utilized by postwar mass-housing developers like William Levitt.

Simplicity of form and flexibility in accommodating a broad range of programmatic requirements rendered the Cape Cod as suitable for anything from 750-square-foot budget houses for young families to much more gracious homes like those designed for affluent Americans by Royal Barry Wills (1895–1962).

Major American Colonial types included the medieval New England Colonial, the New England Colonial Box, the Georgian Williamsburg or Tidewater Colonial, the gambrel-roofed Dutch Colonial, the wood-sided Early American Farmhouse, the stone Pennsylvania Farmhouse, and Spanish/Hispanic domestic colonial variations in California.

Other American Colonial house imageries were regionally popular. These included the Caribbean or Bermuda Colonial in Florida and along the Gulf of Mexico; the New Orleans Style; territorial Pueblo Revival in New Mexico; the Monterey and Ranch House in California and what Gebhard described as "a picturesque mixture of colonial, earlier Craftsman, and Medieval period-revival designs of the 1920s" in the Pacific Northwest.

In Gebhard's estimation, the relative popularity of American Colonial Revival houses built in the 1930s rank as: (1) the Cape Cod Cottage; (2) Early American Farmhouse; (3) Early New England Colonial; (4) Pennsylvania Colonial; (5) New England Colonial Box; (6) Georgian; (7) Regency/Federal; (8) Dutch Colonial; (9) Williamsburg version of the Georgian (Wrenesque); and (10) Greek Revival.

A brief sampling of these later American Colonial houses follows. If you would like to look a little deeper into imageries of this era, be sure to consult the two Gebhard-Winterthur publications cited in the Sources by Chapter list.

CAPE COD

Blackbourne House FIG. 193
1938–1939, later additions and alterations
Royal Barry Wills, architect
5015 Wooddale Ln., Edina, Minnesota

In 1938, Life magazine commissioned "eight of the most distinguished architects in America" to design a dream house for a typical American family. One family each lived in the East, South, Midwest, and Far West. The families ranged in annual income from about $75,000 to $250,000 in 2008 dollars. Each owner was given the choice between a modern and a traditional design.

The Albert Blackbournes of Minneapolis had to choose between a Usonian design by Frank Lloyd Wright and a traditional Cape Cod by Wills—which they built on this creekside, suburban site.

FIG. 193 "Standing the Test of Time" Royal Barry Wills's Blackbourne design was chosen by its owner for the respectability of its imagery, and for its inherent comfort. In cost, this upper-middle-class version of the Cape Cod lies between Levittown tract houses (see the Community Development chapter) and Cape Cod variations employed for estate houses (see Edwin Lundie's Sweatt House, Fig. 336, in the Period Revivals chapter).

The choice was based on domestic comfort, cost, and the desirability of an architectural imagery that had "stood the test of time," given that Blackbourne was a stockbroker who wished to project a personal image of constancy.

The working drawings and specifications were subsequently made easily available to individuals and builders, and thus the design was constructed across the country. This house, together with media ubiquity, solidified Wills's position as America's premier house architect.

EARLY AMERICAN FARMHOUSE

Brooks House
1936
Royal Barry Wills, architect
300 Adams St., Milton, Massachusetts

The New England clapboard farmhouse is reliably "American" imagery, stylistically unpretentious, even in this unusually fine rendition, and thus able to visually accommodate tacked-on additions better than some other familiar colonial archetypes. The 1636 Fairbanks house (see the New England Colonial Architecture chapter) served as the point of departure for Colonial Revival expressions of the Early American Farmhouse. Given their intrinsic austerity, debased variations on the New England colonial box are still employed for budget housing.

NEW ENGLAND COLONIALS

Ordway House
1929
Royal Barry Wills, architect
90 Warren St., Newton Center, Massachusetts

The classic "New England Colonial" is based on medieval garrison houses like the 1660 McIntyre and the 1683 Capen houses (see the New England Colonial Architecture chapter). This type is functional, inexpensive to build, and physically flexible enough to accommodate a saltbox roof extension at the rear. Postwar New England Colonial variations were distilled down to a wood-sheathed, two-story rectangle with a vestigial second-floor overhang at the front. While these provide economical housing for millions of Americans, the mediocre Post–World War II architectural norm is only superficially comparable to the careful design and setting of Wills's architecturally superior, prewar Ordway House.

FIG. 194 Dutch Colonial In most of the United States, any house with a gambrel roof is automatically considered to be "Dutch." The Schermier House in Santa Barbara is a well-above-average example of Dutch Colonial Revival, despite its decidedly un-Dutch locale, on the "American Riviera."

FIG. 196 Southern Accommodation Neel Reed's comfortably expansive James Dickey House is a thoughtfully devised reference to Mount Vernon. Although the front columns seem proportionately too thin when glimpsed straight-on from the street (as in this view), they read correctly when viewed, foreshortened, from the guest approach alongside the house.

FIG. 195 Differences Between Styles American building is prominently an architecture of synthesis, so thresholds between one style and another are not always significant. Because this postwar house in Litchfield, Connecticut has a gambrel roof, we label it as Dutch. But substitute a gable for the gambrel and it becomes a mainstream Cape Cod.

Fig. 197 Monterey Revival Roland Coates's Pitner House illustrates how styles evolve over time. With an overhanging balcony (at the rear), it superficially reminds one of the Larkin House in the Spanish Colonial Revival chapter. But as can be seen from this view of the front, Pitner is much larger—and far more luxurious in its appointments—than its putative colonial ancestor.

DUTCH COLONIAL

Schermier House FIG. 194
1922
Soule, Hastings & Murphy, architects
1713 Lasuen, Santa Barbara, California

Elsewhere than in the Mid-Atlantic around Philadelphia and in parts of New England, "Dutch Colonial" usually connotes little more than that the house is built with a gambrel roofline. However, this architect's design (Fig. 194) is more sophisticated than were those of most builder's houses, despite the apparent incongruence of its location in Mediterranean Santa Barbara. Concave roof overhangs and varied, seemingly informal window sizing and spacing set this house apart from run-of-the-mill Dutch Colonials.

House FIG. 195
1947–1948; later additions
Harry Wynn, architect
202 North St., Litchfield, Connecticut

A handsome gambrel-roofed design that owes much to Royal Barry Wills. The house is the product of a local architect and local builder who both fully understood what they were doing and were clearly successful. Although the house is fairly large in floor area, its apparent scale is substantially reduced by virtue of the roof, and by placing the house well back on its spacious lot.

GEORGIAN-TIDEWATER-WILLIAMSBURG

James Dickey House FIG. 196
1914–1917
Neel Reid, architect
456 W. Paces Ferry Road, NW., Atlanta, Georgia

Dickey was based on Mount Vernon (Fig. 75), although it was necessarily simplified and brought up to date, functionally. Reid did not favor historical correctness if it had to be accomplished at the expense of gracious contemporary living. Consequently, his Dickey design is a knowing reference to Mount Vernon, rather than a faithful copy.

CALIFORNIA DOMESTIC COLONIAL

Pitner House FIG. 197
1928
Roland Coate, architect
1138 Arden Rd., San Marino, California

The Monterey Style is characterized by almost-rough simplicity and a full-length projecting balcony, hung from an overhanging hip roof by simple poles (see the Larkin House and Casa Amesti in the Spanish Colonial Revival Architecture chapter). While the Pitner House satisfies these attributes, rarely is the style rendered as elegantly as in this sumptuous design.

Cliff May House, "Mandalay" FIG. 199
1938–1939; remodeled, 1949; addition, 1983
Cliff May, architect; **Aurele Vermuelin** (1939), **Douglas Bayliss** (1949), landscape architects
Old Ranch Rd., off Sunset Blvd., Brentwood, Los Angeles, California

Cliff May effectively invented the California ranch house, and as a consequence, the architect was an influential fountainhead of the

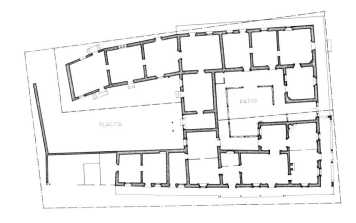

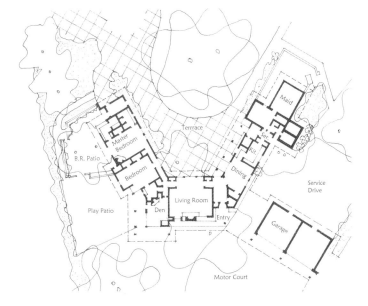

FIGS. 198, 199, 200 California Colonial Cliff May's ranch houses were inspired by Spanish colonial-era lifestyles, for which houses provided secluded family spaces like the transitional *placita* and enclosed *patio* (top). May's splayed floor plans, like the plan of his own house, "Mandalay" (middle), are also organized around family spaces, located out of direct public view. May's designs are intrinsically Spanish-American Colonial in the ways they *function*. That is not to be confused with how a house *looks*, for instance, the Spanish Colonial Revival imageries based on style in the Period Revivals chapter. May's houses typically nestle into their sites, ideally sheltered from public view by abundant landscaping, as in his 1939 Riviera Ranch subdivision in the Brentwood section of Los Angeles (bottom). *Fig 198: Library of Congress, Prints & Photographs, Historic American Buildings Survey; Fig 199: after May, 1958*

FIG. 201 The Most Beautiful Street in America Litchfield's North Street, peer of the town's equally celebrated South Street, gains its alluring beauty from an early twentieth-century Colonial Revival transformation of Litchfield's existing townscape.

post–World War II American Ranch House. May referred to Spanish colonial haciendas, not in terms of direct copying of imageries, but rather as a benchmark of how to live comfortably in a Southern California setting, especially in plan (Fig. 198).

May's houses were comparatively styleless, emphasizing integration of the built into a created landscape and, especially, family privacy. As a result, most of his houses (when visible from a public street at all) are hard to find under masses of luxuriant foliage, as in the subdivision where this house is located (Fig. 200). Since all of the houses except one in this subdivision are by May, a visitor can glimpse enough fragments among several homes to establish a whole in one's mind.

May's own house is an archetype of the California ranch house, with a splayed-U plan (Fig. 199) providing maximum privacy and site engagement. Within this serene subdivision, one can easily imagine being out in rural California, not a block or two from frenetic, urban LA.

COLONIAL REVIVALS IN THE PUBLIC REALM

While American Colonial Revivals are commonly illustrated largely through domestic architecture, as in this book, these vocabularies were widely employed for public and commercial buildings before the Second World War (see, for example, the Greendale Town Hall, Fig. 829), and for new Protestant churches before and well after the war.

Especially in New England and the Southeast (where American Colonial imageries have been continuously popular right up through the present), one still comes across scores of schools, libraries, post offices, town halls, and firehouses in red brick with white trim, the typical Colonial Revival gesture. Nationally, as late as 1968, Standard Oil of Indiana employed an "Early American" imagery for more of its gas stations than of any other style.

That suggests a strong disconnect between national tastemakers and the general public, since for cultural opinion leaders, the 1924 publication of Lewis Mumford's *Sticks and Stones* signaled the end of intellectual respectability for American Colonial Revival architecture, indeed, for tradition.

Other than a perpetual recycling of Independence Hall for everything from city halls to branch banks (Fig. 1042), surviving American Colonial commercial buildings may not be recognized as "Colonial" by present-day Americans, given the lack of well-known commercial buildings dating from the colonial era. Moreover, American Colonial commercial buildings commonly referenced late-1800s British Victorian design as a point of departure.

Probably few of us today fully appreciate the prominence and influence of the Colonial Revivals in twentieth-century American life and culture. This movement has been long-lasting, pervasive, and in some instances, transformative, including not just buildings, but furnishings and decorative arts, fiction, landscapes, and even complete New England towns whose now-familiar regional image was created almost out of whole cloth by revivalists of the late 1800s and early 1900s.

William Butler observed that our present-day picture of a typical New England town "is a nucleated village of white clapboard houses lining elm-shaded streets, with a simple [white] Congregational church, a general store, and a small schoolhouse surrounding a park-like green." In reality, this immensely appealing scene is almost totally a twentieth-century construct.

In reality, colonial-era villages were generally rude environments, and virtually no fully authentic colonial townscape exists—and only a comparatively few individual landmarks, mostly historic houses and churches. After a long decline following a golden age dating from about 1780 to around 1830, some of these towns were rediscovered in the late 1800s by urban elites, who transformed them, as leisure retreats, into the picturesque townscapes that we today appreciate as authentically "colonial." Elm boulevards were planted, open spaces were refashioned and landscaped into Greens. Architecturally unsophisticated existing houses were rebuilt and enlarged with taste. Original colors in red, brown, green, and blue, some simply unpainted, were painted over in white, with dark-colored window shutters added. It should be noted that this American Colonialization was not rigorously historical: architectural references to the post-colonial Federal period were common.

Hence, classic New England colonial towns like Norman Rockwell's Stockbridge, Massachusetts (its main street made up of an engaging visual mix of late-nineteenth-century and Colonial Revival imageries) and the archetype, Litchfield, Connecticut, generally reflect early twentieth-century tastes.

Litchfield, Connecticut FIGS. 201, 202

1719; town transformed after 1913; Congregational church reconstructed as colonial, 1919–1929

A. P. F. Adenaw, LaFarge and Morris, F. B. J. Renshaw, architects of the 1913 colonialization plans; **John Charles Olmsted, Frederick Law Olmsted, Jr.**, landscape architects; **Richard Henry Dana, Jr.**, church reconstruction architect

Sinclair Lewis supposedly contended that "the only street in America more beautiful than North Street in Litchfield (Fig. 201) was South Street in Litchfield." However, as William Butler noted, Litchfield was the first American town to "remodel its historic landscape comprehensively in the colonial style." Beginning in 1913, this undertaking predating Santa Barbara's deliberate transformation into a dream Andalusian town after 1925 (see the Period Revivals chapter).

The glorious townscape that we experience today is a far cry from colonial-era Litchfield, when most residents lived in one- or two-room "unpainted plank structures," excepting three garrison houses. An architecturally undistinguished Congregational meeting house was eventually constructed, painted red. There was no sign of the later parklike Green in the town center; the location was then referred to simply as an "area" or "space." This land contained market stalls, animal pens, garbage heaps, and woodpiles.

Enjoying industrial prosperity after the Revolution, Litchfield was admired for its Federal-era architecture. What became noted residential streets after 1913 were congested commercial streets during the postcolonial years. Only one house was painted white during this era. The town experienced a "rapid depopulation and dismantling of industry" in the 1830s, although it retained its landed aristocracy. The central, pre-Green area was planted in 1835.

Along with numerous other New England towns, Litchfield was a comparative hotbed of beautification improvements though the mid-1800s. These efforts were not intended to evoke the colonial past; rather, improvements were intended as modern and civilizing.

In the Gilded Age, however, New England towns like Litchfield provided an outlet for Antimodernism, offering settings which harked back to an earlier, "better" time. Though as Butler cautioned, this was not back to a "homespun" age, but rather a romanticized "golden age of prosperity."

This civic revision was to be an idealized colonial image, rather than historically accurate: stables, pens, shops, and outbuildings were banished; flower gardens, not vegetable gardens, were planted; houses were painted white instead of red; and citizens installed "regimented rows" of elms along streets, "based on sparse historic references to sporadic tree plantings."

The 1913 revamping of Litchfield was intended to leave "not the slightest vestige of modern design." White wooden cornices, doorways, and other now-correct details were applied to Victorian storefronts. Some brick buildings were oversided with clapboards.

The Olmsteds devised an idealized colonial Green (Fig. 202), which was, of course, necessary, since there had been no civic planted space at all before 1835, much less an authentically colonial civic place. Their newly landscaped space conformed to the contemporary notion of "colonial," right down to the details of lamp posts and benches. One cynic quite accurately observed that Litchfield looked more colonial in 1930 than it ever did in the colonial era.

By now, American Colonial Revival has become as authentic and as historic a style as Colonial, and we can enjoy Litchfield and other Colonial Revival townscapes purely for their visual qualities.

FIG. 202 **Idealized Colonial Green** Litchfield's "colonial" green was constructed in the twentieth century, a landmark American Colonial Revival device.

Progressives

1866–1924

FIG. 203 Inventing an American Architecture From the perspectives of "progressive" architects, the American Colonial Revivals were still overly dependent on European precedents. They were intent on moving beyond Continental architectural conventions in seeking fresh, American expressions. For his Pennsylvania Academy of Fine Arts in Philadelphia, progressive Frank Furness designed with an inventive directness that was startlingly bolder than the florid Victorian buildings of his English contemporaries.

Progressives are American originals. Of course, "progressive" describes many kinds of creative, political, and social activities. As employed in this book, the term refers to architects whose creative syntheses of architectural precedent and U.S. culture established a distinct, "American" architecture.

The progressive movement of American architecture can be efficiently illustrated by the works of three great masters: Frank Furness (1839–1912), Henry Hobson Richardson (1838–1886), and Louis Henri Sullivan (1856–1924). Too often, and unfairly, these three are treated as a kind of warm-up for the incom-

parable Frank Lloyd Wright, who worked for Sullivan, even as Sullivan worked, briefly, for Furness.

For this chapter, progressive design includes this great triumvirate as well as examples of Richardson's stylistic legacy, Richardsonian Romanesque. The chapter's timeframe begins with the first buildings by Furness and by Richardson in 1866, and ends symbolically with Sullivan's lonely death in 1924.

Wright is considered the progenitor of the architecturally progressive Prairie School. Frank Lloyd Wright and the Prairie School are the subjects of two later chapters.

FRANK FURNESS

Frank Furness is the least-known of the great progressive masters, although his Philadelphia-based practice was responsible for more than 600 projects, vastly more than either Richardson or Sullivan, even approaching the career output of Wright, whose work was accomplished over seven decades.

Furness's personal style is difficult to pin down, or even to adequately describe. In a generalized sense, it is Victorian Gothic, but a highly personalized Victorian of astonishing creativity, achieved through exaggeration, employment of decorative motifs, plays of scale, juxtapositions, and bold massing (Fig. 203). In a word, it is mannerism.

Yet the designs of Frank Furness are so singular and unforgettable that even that classification seems incomplete. Fellow Philadelphian Robert Venturi supplied the necessary insight when he confessed "absolute, unrestrained adoration and respect" for the work of Furness, because of its "quality, spirit, diversity, wit, tragic dimension." As these qualities are expressed

in a design, Furness's buildings become "tense with a feeling of life and reality."

Pennsylvania Academy of Fine Arts FIGS. 203, 204, 205
1871–1876; restored 1973
Frank Furness, George W. Hewitt, architects
118 N. Broad St., SW cor. Cherry St., Philadelphia, Pennsylvania

The Academy of Fine Arts is arguably the greatest Furness building. The architect began with relatively straightforward massing, then added an awesome mix of colors, textures, and decoration. Despite this aggressive palette, somehow, the exterior comes off almost as stately. The richly polychromed galleries within are marvelous beyond any description.

FIG. 206 Out of the Ordinary Centennial National Bank may be ordinary in function and in its location, but its subtly arresting architecture is anything but.

FIG. 208 A Symphony of Detail Undine Barge Club in Philadelphia achieves remarkable visual presence through Furness' balanced interplay of materials, colors, rhythms, and textures.

FIG. 207 Classic Furness As usual for Furness designs, his two side-by-side Provident Life and Trust Company buildings virtually defy description. *Library of Congress, Prints & Photographs, Historic American Buildings Survey*

FIG. 209 Almost Impossibly Tactile The University of Pennsylvania's library, now renamed the "Furness Building," defines the extremes of well-mannered tactility. *Library of Congress, Prints & Photographs, Historic American Buildings Survey*

Centennial National Bank FIG. 206

1876, altered
Frank Furness, architect
SE cor. Market and 32nd Sts., Philadelphia, Pennsylvania

Centennial Bank is a typical Furness design in that it is an ordinary commercial program in an ordinary city neighborhood; it was not intended as an elaborate civic statement. Nevertheless, the building occupies its corner with uncommon dignity and presence. The exterior displays only a minimum of ornamentation, instead relying on a subtle employment of understated brick detailing, symbolically befitting a bank. The full-height entrance mass crowned with spiky crockets presses down visually onto the

entrance, thus seemingly accounting for the stubby, impossibly squished columns. Although changes in windows and roofing have diminished the original effect, Centennial Bank is still a treasure.

Provident Life and Trust Company FIG. 207

1876–1879; 1888–1890; razed, 1960
Frank Furness, Furness, Evans & Co., architects
409 Chestnut St., Philadelphia, Pennsylvania

Classic Furness: exaggerations, plays of scale, juxtapositions, bold massing. The original two-story building was visually overshadowed by a ten-story corner addition.

Undine Barge Club FIG. 208
1882–1883
Frank Furness, Furness & Evans, architects
East River Dr. on the Schuylkill River, Philadelphia, Pennsylvania

Although it is one among several side-by-side boat houses, the Undine clubhouse stands out from its neighbors on account of its beautiful stonework, its color, and the skilled employment of projections and clerestories. Furness achieved a personal expression in this structure through atypical (for the architect) restraint, almost delicacy.

University of Pennsylvania Library, "Furness Building"
FIG. 209
1888–1890; additions, 1914–15, 1924, 1931; restored, 1985–1991
Frank Furness, architect; **Venturi, Scott Brown & Associates**, restoration architects
W side of 34th, N of Spruce, University of Pennsylvania campus, Philadelphia, Pennsylvania

A large, rambling brick pile that nevertheless retains its composure. The exterior comes to a visual focus on the entrance tower. Inside, the mildly agitated four-story reading room, now beautifully restored and furnished, is a visual highlight.

HENRY HOBSON RICHARDSON

Henry Hobson Richardson was larger than life in multiple respects, including his ample physical girth, the majestic visual power of his designs, and the widespread influence of his Richardsonian Romanesque architectural imagery, which was imitated, though rarely equaled, in thousands of buildings designed by others from the 1880s into the early 1900s. Remarkably, Richardson's active practice spanned just two decades, and his greatest works, from Trinity Church to the Glessner House, were all designed over little more than a dozen years: 1872–1885.

Trinity Church FIG. 210
1872–1877; front porch, 1894–1897
Henry Hobson Richardson, architect; **John La Farge**, artist;
Shepley, Rutan & Coolidge, architects for porch and front towers
Copley Square, Boston, Massachusetts

As typical of Richardson's designs, Trinity Church is visually robust without seeming ponderous. Even so early in his practice, while still in his 30s, Richardson demonstrated complete mastery in this design, from the visual play of the massive tower above a deeply perforated façade, to the awe-inspiring interior (Fig. 658), at once simple in plan and volume and endlessly rich and varied in experience.

William Watts Sherman House
1874–1876
Henry Hobson Richardson, Gambrill & Richardson,
architects; **Stanford White**, architect of 1881 library alteration
2 Shepard Ave., Newport, Rhode Island

See the American Colonial Revivals chapter.

Oliver Ames Free Library
1877–1879
Henry Hobson Richardson, architect; **Frederick Law Olmsted**,
landscape architect
53 Main St., North Easton, Massachusetts

FIG. 210 Masterpiece Trinity Church in Boston stands among the greatest American designs, visually rich and endlessly varied. See also Fig. 658 in the Interior Spaces chapter.

FIG. 211 Mixed Message Prominent boulders visually strengthening the Ames Gate Lodge signify that an estate guardhouse is serious business ("Do not enter. Really."). But that stern tone is leavened by Richardson's doll-house expression ("Sorry we have to do this.").

Despite its coarse stone exterior and siting set well back, above the street, this building has a welcoming personality, even before one reaches the warm woods of the vaulted stack room.

F. L. Ames Gate Lodge FIG. 211
1880–1881
Henry Hobson Richardson, architect; **Augustus Saint-Gaudens**, sculptor
135 Elm St., North Easton, Massachusetts

A fantastic play of scale and texture, a master synthesis of design sources.

FIG. 212 **As Good as it Gets** Pittsburgh's Allegheny County Courthouse spawned imitations across the United States. None equaled Richardson's potent, seminal design. The tower is especially fine. Note the "Bridge of Sighs" (right, in this view) which, like its precursor in Venice, links the courts to the jail

FIG. 213 **Übermensch** Chicago has always respected open expressions of power. So when Richardson's uncompromisingly masculine John J. Glessner House went up on its block of modish town houses, neighboring Captains of Industry must have experienced acute spasms of palazzo envy. The front of the house is on Prairie Avenue, to the left in this photo; this view includes service portions extending along the side street. Larger windows face the house's private garden. *Library of Congress, Prints & Photographs, Historic American Buildings Survey*

Allegheny County Courthouse FIG. 212
1883–1888
Henry Hobson Richardson, architect; **Frederick Law Olmsted**, landscape architect; completed by **Shepley, Rutan & Coolidge**, architects
Grant St. between 5th and Forbes Aves., Pittsburgh, Pennsylvania

Allegheny is the largest of Richardson's buildings. Hundreds of city halls and court houses mimicked this design, but none approached Allegheny's surpassing architectural qualities.

John J. Glessner House FIG. 213
1885–1887
Henry Hobson Richardson, architect
1800 S. Prairie Ave., Chicago, Illinois (open)

Prairie Avenue was the premier residential thoroughfare in Chicago when Glessner built his radical, rusticated stone house. It was sur-

rounded by architecturally tasteful mansions dressed up in the familiar array of historical styles, not one which could even begin to compete, visually, with Richardson's forceful design.

RICHARDSONIAN ROMANESQUE

Richardson's rusticated-stone designs, especially the Pittsburgh court house and his massive, 1885–1887 Marshall Field Wholesale Store in Chicago (razed), were immensely influential among American architects. That led to widespread employment of a Richardsonian Romanesque style. During the late 1880s national boom, until the deep economic depression beginning in 1893, it

was not uncommon in fast-growing Midwestern cities for several *blocks* of new construction to be designed in the Richardsonian style. By the time the national economy recovered late in the 1890s, Beaux Arts–City Beautiful imageries had become the current fashion, and the expression of Richardsonian imageries plummeted, although watered-down versions persisted in some rural areas up until about 1910.

Mabel Tainter Memorial FIGS. 214, 215
1889–1890
Harvey Ellis, attributed designer; **Leroy S. Buffington**, architect of record
205 Main St., Menomonie, Wisconsin

The peerless Ellis (see the National Romanticism chapter) has traditionally been credited with designing Tainter while working as

FIG. 216 **Technical Adroitness** Buildings are typically laid out on multiple grids, reflecting, for instance, differing modules for masonry and frame construction, which may in turn vary from space-planning and finish modules inside. For the Stanford University Quad, these common disparities are resolved elegantly. Look closely at this seemingly symmetrical cluster of stubby support columns: they do not quite align with the elaborate corbel between the two arches. Also, notice that the widths of the arches differ. Apparently at least three differing grids were resolved at this spot, unnoticed, since most eyes would be attracted to the splendid ornament. Or perhaps to the heart-motif capitals of the outer columns! *Library of Congress, Prints & Photographs, Historic American Buildings Survey*

chief designer in Buffington's office, based on a signed 1891 rendering. However, Ellis scholar Eileen Manning Michels concluded that Ellis probably was not the project designer, based on ambiguities in timing, rendering technique, and Tainter's atypical (for Ellis) symmetrical façade.

As Michels suspects, Tainter's exterior almost certainly also reflects the efforts of other Buffington staff designers, who could have fleshed out Ellis's conceptual scheme, a common process in architectural offices, then and now. Even so, no other local, i.e. Minneapolis or St. Paul, figure but Ellis could have designed Tainter's sensational, carved-oak auditorium (Fig. 214). All of us Ellis aficionados will no doubt go to our graves without knowing the answer to this mystery.

Stanford University Quadrangle FIG. 216
1887–1891
Shepley, Rutan & Coolidge, architects; **Frederick Law Olmsted**, landscape architect
Leland Stanford University, Palm Drive, Palo Alto, California

Richardsonian Romanesque at its most cosmopolitan and mature, employed by the successor firm to Richardson's practice. As befitting an exotic California setting, and its academic program, the architectural imagery moves toward Mediterranean, enhanced by the warm, golden stone. The clustered columns evoke the sense of a sheltered Medieval cloister.

Stanford Memorial Church FIG. 217
1887, 1899–1902; rebuilt after earthquake, 1913; post-earthquake renovations, 1990–1999
Charles Allerton Coolidge, architect; **C. E. Hodges**, architect of 1913 rebuilding; **Hardy Holzman Pfeiffer Associates**, architects of the 1990–1999 renovations
Leland Stanford University, Palm Drive, Palo Alto, California

Memorial Church serves as the Stanford Quadrangle's visual centerpiece, a unique synthesis of Romanesque moving into Mission, expressing an emerging architectural fashion of early twentieth-century California. The fresco on the upper pediment is wonderful, and the polychromed sanctuary is even better, especially now, after the recent renovation.

Ellis County Court House FIG. 218
1894–1897
J. Riely Gordon, architect
Main St. at Square, Waxahachie, Texas

Among the seemingly numberless Richardsonian Romanesque courthouses in the United States, many of which are architecturally quite good, Ellis County is undoubtedly the most memorable. The substantial main building block is visually buttressed by projecting pavilions along each exterior wall, encased in a polychromy of stone and terra cotta. Gordon's massive tower is just about indescribable.

LOUIS HENRI SULLIVAN

Louis Sullivan, his predecessor, Richardson, and his follower, Wright, are traditionally regarded as the patriarchs of modern American architecture (Furness is usually treated as an intriguing precursor). Without a doubt some of Sullivan's buildings, like the National Farmers' Bank, occupy the very top rank of American architecture. Nevertheless, Sullivan's influence on American architecture could not have equaled that of giants like Richardson and Wright. Indeed, Sullivan is probably best remembered in the hoary legends of architecture for his pronouncement that the Beaux-Arts White City (Fig. 739) of the 1893 Chicago World's Fair had set architecture back 50 years; and for the fact that he died alone, a drunk and destitute, in a dingy hotel room.

Moreover, it should be noted that Sullivan was at his best when supported by a strong partner. He was at the peak of his career until Dankmar Adler retired in 1895. Later, the estimable hand of George Grant Elmslie is apparent in designs like that of the National Farmers' Bank. Nevertheless, when he died *The New York Times* hailed Sullivan as the "dean of American architects," a remarkable tribute, considering the exceptional design abilities of several of his contemporaries.

Getty Tomb FIG. 219
1890
Louis H. Sullivan, architect
North central edge of Graceland Cemetery, 4001 N. Clark, Chicago, Illinois

Getty is the essence of timeless beauty. Sullivan's design is restrained and elegant, dignified yet without a trace of somberness. Few structures so flawlessly satisfy their purpose.

FIG. 217 Synthesis of Locality and Fashion Stanford Memorial Church illustrates how nimbly American design follows fashion. Just as the Stanford University Quad signaled the increasing prominence of classicism in its formal planning, so, too, a decade later, did the architects acknowledge the emergent popularity of Mission Revival in California with this fluent exterior. Inside, they devised an impressive of "Richardsonian Baroque." *Library of Congress, Prints & Photographs, Historic American Buildings Survey*

FIG. 218 ABOVE **Texas-style Romanesque** Ellis County Court House is so fantastically over-the-top in its expressiveness—the tower alone is worth the journey to Waxahachie—that it is a required pilgrimage for all Richardsonian mavens.

FIG. 219 Simply Perfect The Getty Tomb in Chicago is architecture at its most exquisite. The photo shows almost the entire front of the cubic structure. *Library of Congress, Prints & Photographs, Historic American Buildings Survey*

FIG. 220 **The Tall Building, Carefully Considered.** The Wainwright in St. Louis was Louis Sullivan's first tall building, a notable artistic success, especially for its rich spandrel ornament.

FIG. 221 **Emotional Engagement** Comparisons between Sullivan's Wainwright (this image) and Getty (Fig. 219) tombs are inevitable. If Getty achieves an almost unapproachable architectural purity, like classical Greek temples, then Wainwright is a Roman building, a bit more accessible to most of us on account of its comparative expressiveness. *Library of Congress, Prints & Photographs, Historic American Buildings Survey*

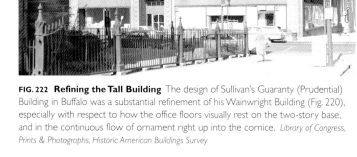

FIG. 222 **Refining the Tall Building** The design of Sullivan's Guaranty (Prudential) Building in Buffalo was a substantial refinement of his Wainwright Building (Fig. 220), especially with respect to how the office floors visually rest on the two-story base, and in the continuous flow of ornament right up into the cornice. *Library of Congress, Prints & Photographs, Historic American Buildings Survey*

Wainwright Building FIG. 220

1890–1891; restored, late 1970s
Adler & Sullivan, architects; **Hastings & Chivetta**, restoration architects
111 N. Seventh St., St. Louis, Missouri

Sullivan's first high-rise building is a fine demonstration of his objectives, if not yet quite soaring in its massing. The design was carefully controlled by virtue of its symmetrical plan and tightly composed façades. Wainwright's intense red coloring and stylized naturalistic ornament combine to create a potent visual effect.

Wainwright Tomb FIG. 221

1892
Louis H. Sullivan, architect
SE section of Bellefontaine Cemetery, reached from W. Florissant Ave., N of I-70, St. Louis, Missouri

This stately, domed cube overlooks a sublime vista from high above the vast Mississippi River floodplain. If one senses just a touch of the Oriental in its dome and ornamentation, Sullivan's design is all-American in its abstracted directness.

Guaranty (Prudential) Building FIG. 222

1894–1896
Louis Sullivan, **Dankmar Adler**, architects
28 Church St., Buffalo, New York

An impressive development of the Wainwright. While only two stories higher, Guaranty reads unambiguously as a vertical building. Its ornament is even more luxuriant than Wainwright's, seemingly applied to every inch of exterior surface. Guaranty and Richard Upjohn's St Paul's Episcopal Cathedral (1849–1851) right across the street are effectively set off by a landscaped square just to the east. Especially in morning sunlight, these two landmarks are prominent even in the context of Buffalo's architecturally rich downtown.

Schlesinger and Mayer (Carson, Pirie, Scott) Department Store FIGS. 223, 224

1898–1899; 1903–1904; 1906; converted to mixed use, 2007
Louis H. Sullivan, architect; 1906 addition, **D. H. Burnham & Company**, architects
1 S. State St., Chicago, Illinois

FIGS. 223, 224 **The Organic Store** Schlesinger and Mayer is a fine Chicago School design from the third floor upward. Few probably notice, since Sullivan's lush ornamentation on the first two levels is what everyone remembers. *Fig 224: Library of Congress, Prints & Photographs, Historic American Buildings Survey*

This design is canonical Chicago School, with a Sullivan twist. The severely modern upper stories, expressed as a skeleton frame, rest on a two-story base entwined in sumptuous, organic, Art Nouveau–like ornament.

National Farmers Bank FIGS. 225, 226
1906–1908; interior renovated, modified, 1957
Louis H. Sullivan, **George Grant Elmslie**, architects;
Harwell H. Harris, renovation architect
101 N. Cedar, Owatonna, Minnesota

National Farmers Bank stands among the supreme achievements in American architecture. Sullivan and Elmslie provided advanced demonstrations in several aspects of planning and design: (1) The bank beautifully enfronts the town's public square (Fig. 226); (2) an authentic sense of dignity is achieved without recourse to then-conventional Beaux Arts imagery; (3) elemental geometries can be employed to establish a modern imagery; (4) simplicity of form effectively counterbalances a profusion of brilliant ornament (Fig. 225);

and (5) genre painting is effectively employed at unexpectedly monumental scale. An absolute must visit for designers and mavens alike.

Merchants National Bank FIG. 227

1913–1915, later alterations
Louis H. Sullivan, **Parker N. Berry**, architects
Cor. 4th Ave. and Broad, Grinnell, Iowa

While the Owatonna bank was Sullivan's last eminent building, Merchants Bank stands out among his subsequent work. An extraordinary terra cotta oculus dominates the main entrance. In itself, the oculus is striking ornament; it gains even more visual effect as played off against the austere brick façade. The interior, which has been remodeled, was a handsome, though artistically lesser, variation on the Owatonna bank.

The Chicago School

1879–1895

FIG. 228 The Modern American City Chicago's Great Fire of 1871 incinerated much of the city's built-up core. Virtually everything in this view up North Michigan Avenue was leveled, save the turreted stone water tower (center in the distance), which had been completed just two years earlier. For all of the human misery and economic loss caused by the fire, it proved to be a critical shaping event in Chicago's history. Over the ensuing two decades, the most advanced standards were increasingly employed in rebuilding. Technical innovation was required to solve dysfunctional conditions that had inevitably built up, piecemeal, since Chicago's founding four decades earlier. In effect, a modern city eventually rose from the ashes. The "Modern," the "innovative," and confidence in the city's capacity for heroic achievement have colored Chicago's civic self-image ever since.

Chicago School describes the illustrious body of early modern architecture built in Chicago and also refers to the constellation of talent practicing in Chicago in the late 1800s: Louis Sullivan, John Wellborn Root, Charles Atwood, Daniel Burnham, Frank Lloyd Wright, and many others. In this chapter, "Chicago School" focuses on exceptional buildings designed by Chicago architects and constructed in Chicago after the fire of 1871 (Fig. 228) and underway by the time of the 1893 World's Fair (see the Fairs & Expositions chapter). Here 1895 is employed as a nominal date for the opening of these final "pre-Columbian" buildings, thus ending the Chicago School era.

Parenthetically, after World War Two, the spirit of the Chicago School era seemed to have returned: innovative architecture prominently featuring structure was once again at the forefront, and several notable local architectural practices gained national and even international attention, just as when the Chicago School flourished. These heady times were widely known as the Second Chicago School. More on this at the end of the chapter.

While the assemblage of such brilliant talent probably cannot be fully explained, the underlying dynamics are widely acknowledged: (1) Chicago's explosive growth provided abundant opportunity; (2) the city was already established, so construction funding was available; (3) Chicago was still too new to have developed limiting traditions; (4) hence, function, more than fashion, was valued in building; (5) the Great Fire of 1871 provided opportunity to experiment prior to the 1880s construction boom, (6) the fire demonstrated an urgent need for fireproof construction techniques; (7) Chicago was grounded in innovation, including the widespread employment of balloon framing in the 1830s onward; and (8) the growth and intensity of downtown business dictated tall, thus necessarily innovative, buildings.

Civil engineer William Le Baron Jenney was a key figure in the Chicago School. Jenney designed the seminal First Leiter Building (1879), demonstrating iron-frame construction, leading to the rapid development of fireproof, steel-frame construction. As an employer, Jenney introduced many Chicago School architects to structural design. Unsurprisingly, the expression of structure was a prominent characteristic of the Chicago School.

Many other noteworthy examples of the Chicago School can be found in and around the Loop. These include the Second Leiter Building by Jenney, 1891, at 403 S. State St., Burnham's Fisher Building, 1896, at 343 S. Dearborn, and Louis Sullivan's Gage Building, 1898–1899, at 18 S. Michigan Avenue (Fig. 234). Sullivan's landmark Schlesinger & Mayer store on State Street, 1898–1904, is cited in the preceding Progressives chapter.

After 1900, traditional imageries were increasingly prominent in Chicago, as elsewhere. However, this architectural conservatism was literally skin-deep, since the technological advances of the Chicago School were universally adopted, and continuously improved upon. The 1922 Chicago Tribune competition marks a culmination of traditional architectural expressions in Chicago (Fig. 346).

First Leiter Building FIG. 229
1879; razed, 1972
William Le Baron Jenney, engineer-architect
200 W. Monroe, corner Wells, Chicago, Illinois

As is common for ground-breaking work, this modest warehouse was designed in a mix of the old and new. Leiter's partially skeletal structure pointed the way to fully framed buildings and the

FIG. 229 **Where it All Began** The First Leiter Building was the first Chicago School building. Its cast-iron skeletal system was not yet fully developed, but once the idea of framed high-rise construction was demonstrated, structurally mature, steel-framed towers would soon be commonplace. *Library of Congress, Prints & Photographs, Historic American Buildings Survey*

dematerialization of the exterior wall. So this was the first Chicago School building, and as such, progenitor of modern American commercial architecture.

Monadnock Block FIGS. 230, 231
1884–1891/1893
Burnham & Root, architects for the north half; **Holabird & Roche**, architects for the south half
53 W. Jackson Blvd. at Dearborn St., Chicago, Illinois

An unexpected design, seemingly rife with contradictions: Monadnock is utterly modern in approach, expressed without ornament. However, it was structured with old-fashioned, exterior brick bearing walls rather than an up-to-date steel frame.

Although designed without reference to traditional architectural imageries, Monadnock's north half is vaguely Egyptian in feeling due to the flared base (Fig. 231). Despite its powerful brick mass with deep window reveals, it nonetheless does not feel ponderously heavy. It was a creative triumph by its designer, the illustrious John Wellborn Root.

Reliance Building FIG. 232
1890–1895
Charles B. Atwood, Burnham & Root / D. H. Burnham & Company, architects; **Edward Shankland**, structural engineer
32 N. State St., Chicago, Illinois

With Reliance, everything finally came together as "Chicago construction," a steel-frame system with glass infill. The façade is animated by projecting bays and three-part windows (fixed central panes flanked by operable sash) now known as "Chicago windows," all subtly articulated and ornamented. Reliance has been recently restored and converted into a boutique hotel, to the great relief of those concerned about its preservation.

Marquette Building FIG. 233
1893–1895, west bay addition, 1905
Holabird & Roche, architects
140 S. Dearborn St., Chicago, Illinois

Marquette illustrates a mature expression of the Chicago School. The design feels straightforward and modern, while employing the ancient three-part organization, in which the exterior walls visually rest on a two-story base, and are topped off by upper stories functioning as a cornice. Clarity is achieved through the open expression of structure, tempered by the use of quoining to achieve texturing beyond that afforded by the window reveals. As in classical Greek temples, the corners are thickened up to add visual stability.

SECOND CHICAGO SCHOOL

Two key events in the 1930s refocused Chicago architecture on modernity.

One of these was the 1933 Century of Progress Exposition (see the Fairs & Expositions chapter). Its physical planners were two young modernist architects, Louis Skidmore and Nathaniel Owings, who would found Skidmore, Owings & Merrill (SOM) in 1936. The fair was remembered for its emphasis on modernity and the future, symbolized for many by the House of Tomorrow designed by Keck & Keck (Fig. 748).

The second key event was the arrival of Ludwig Mies van der Rohe in 1938. Mies became head of the architecture pro-

FIGS. 230, 231 Modernism and Antimodernism The rapid ascent of the corporate state in the late 1800s left some Americans feeling ambivalent about U.S. society. One senses some of this ambivalence in Chicago's Monadnock Block, which is modern in its lack of ornament while almost Medieval, characteristic of Antimodernism, in the massiveness of its flaring exterior walls. *Fig. 230: Library of Congress, Prints & Photographs, Historic American Buildings Survey*

FIG. 232 **Chicago Construction** Charles Atwood's Reliance Building was designed barely a decade after completion of the First Leiter Building. Already, the Chicago School formula had developed in full: steel frame and plate-glass infill, including the characteristic three-part windows and projecting bays.

gram at the Armour Institute of Technology, renamed two years later as the Illinois Institute of Technology. Mies developed a campus master plan and designed several campus buildings in the 1940s and 1950s (see the Postwar Modernism chapter for other Chicago-area buildings by Mies).

Mies as a local teacher and practitioner, indeed, as a *presence*, greatly aided the reemergence of Modernism in Chicago architecture after the World War II. Led by such firms as Skidmore, Owings & Merrill and C. F. Murphy & Associates, what became known as the Second Chicago School dominated downtown architecture from the 1950s though the 1970s. Several of these buildings are identified in the Postwar Modernism and Late Modernism chapters.

S. R. Crown Hall, IIT FIG. 235
1952–1956
Ludwig Mies van der Rohe, architect
3360 S. State St., Chicago, Illinois

Architecture as abstraction: Crown Hall is symmetrical in plan and transparent by virtue of floor-to-ceiling glazing (the lower panels are translucent). Visible roof trusses provide a column-free interior that Mies described as "universal space," endlessly flexible in accommodating inevitable changes in program over time. On the other hand, in Chicago's climate the periphery is chilly in winter, and the entire interior sweltering on hot, sunny days in the spring and fall.

Inland Steel Building
1954–1958
Walter A. Netsch and **Bruce Graham** of **Skidmore, Owings & Merrill**, architects; **Richard Lippold**, sculptor
30 W. Monroe, Chicago, Illinois

Working from a preliminary concept by Netsch, Graham turned this building inside-out. Office space is expressed as a pure, clear-span form; mechanical, stairs, and elevators are placed in a free-standing tower alongside. Inland Steel was a highly influential postwar building, and housed the Chicago office of SOM in the 1960s and early 1970s.

FIG. 233 Mature Chicago School By the 1890s, Chicago School expressions of structure had become the standard approach for the city's commercial architecture. Nevertheless, fashion is rarely to be denied in America, and in the Marquette Building, which was under design when the World's Columbian Exposition opened (see the Fairs & Expositions chapter), one can pick out subtle influences of classicism in its details and its overall formality.

FIG. 234 Chicago School Classics Louis Sullivan's façade of the 1899 Gage Building is one of numerous Chicago School landmarks found in and around Chicago's Loop.

FIG. 235 The Presence of Mies Ludwig Mies van der Rohe revitalized fundamental Chicago School precepts after arriving in the late 1930s, as illustrated here by his Crown Hall at the Illinois Institute of Technology. Mies also re-instilled local expectations of superior design that had been largely lost during the Depression.

Frank Lloyd Wright
1887–1963

FIG. 236 Grounded in America Frank Lloyd Wright is the architect most widely recognized by the American public. There are several reasons why this is so; his singular buildings and unforgettable persona are surely chief among them. Wright's childhood grounding in American life and national myths is symbolized here by his Wisconsin estate, Taliesin, built on his mother's family land. Wright instinctively felt the pulse and promise of America. Unsurprisingly, his designs connected powerfully with many Americans. *Published with the permission of the Frank Lloyd Wright Foundation*

Frank Lloyd Wright (1867–1959) stands alone among American architects. A half-century after his death, Wright is still the most widely recognized architect to the American public. Little wonder. Over the course of his seven-decade career, Wright designed dozens of iconic buildings (Fig. 236), and routinely challenged traditional conventions.

It is hardly a stretch to contend that he invented the modern American house. Wright's Prairie House plans were designed, in part, in response to the radical social changes in women's lives which occurred around 1900. Among his most important advances, he replaced the dark kitchen, tucked away in the back, with a modern, light-filled work space, where the "housewife" could easily keep track of neighborhood goings-on. In addition to numerous functional improvements in plan, Wright devised a constant stream of structural and mechanical innovations.

From the 1930s onward, Wright developed and refined an "American" approach to regional growth, called Broadacre, which remains instructive for its overall insights and technical demonstrations.

Wright the charismatic personality fully matched Wright the brilliant designer. He periodically and no doubt wittingly scandalized a large share of American society. He wrote, lectured, appeared on TV, baited the press; rarely did he pass up an opportunity to advance his views. To his detractors, this proved that he was a shameless self-promoter. Admirers, on the other hand, loved Wright for "telling it like it is." No virtue in false modesty if one is a genius, as Wright himself noted!

The Wright bibliography is vast. Hundreds of books have been written about his life and career, plus thousands of articles and numberless references. This chapter is merely a representative listing, taken from among Wright's best-known buildings.

EARLY WORK 1887–1896

Frank Lloyd Wright House & Studio FIGS. 237, 238
1889–1890, addition-studio, 1895–1898
Frank Lloyd Wright, architect
428 Forest Ave. / 951 Chicago Ave., Oak Park, Illinois (open)

Although shingled, this is hardly a conventional Shingle Style house. Wright's design is abstracted compared to the contemporary Shingle Style. The studio addition is expressed in geometric masses, while ornament is suppressed, employed primarily as background texture. Within, one experiences a memorable succession of spaces and volumes.

James Charnley House FIG. 239
1891–1892
Adler & Sullivan, architects; **Frank Lloyd Wright**, project designer
1365 N. Astor St., Chicago, Illinois (open)

For an urban site that was very different from suburban Oak Park, Wright expressed the detached house as an abstracted brick mass, visually resting on a stone base. In effect, this was a modern reinterpretation of the Florentine palazzo, at a somewhat smaller scale. Even assuming the active critical support of Sullivan, Charnley is a remarkably mature work for a 24-year-old designer.

The house is now the national headquarters of the Society of Architectural Historians.

William Winslow House FIG. 240
1894
Frank Lloyd Wright, architect
515 Auvergne Pl., River Forest, Illinois

An extraordinarily elegant and polished design, done by Wright alone in his mid-20s. The simple building mass is tempered by subtle textures; its horizontal composition prefigures his soon-to-

FIG. 237, 238 Home as Life Home life was fundamental to Wright. His first house and studio were combined, with a barrel-vaulted playroom for his children on the upper floor. To Wright, family and work were *life* – inseparable. Wright later combined family and work at Taliesin and Taliesin West, with a greatly expanded family of associates and apprentices. *Fig 238: Library of Congress, Prints & Photographs, Historic American Buildings Survey*

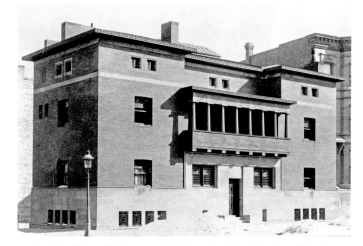

239 Early Brilliance Wright was only 24 when he designed the James Charnley House in Chicago. Even if Louis Sullivan actively oversaw the design, this was still a remarkable achievement for someone so young. *Library of Congress, Prints & Photographs, Historic American Buildings Survey*

FIG. 240 **Swift Rise to Maturity** In practice on his own, Wright displayed exceptional maturity with his impressive design for the Winslow House in River Forest. Its handsomely abstracted character was appreciated at the time as fully modern, although Wright ensured that it wouldn't seem out-of-place in its conventional, affluent neighborhood by emphasizing symmetry, and by grounding the house firmly to its site.

FIG. 241 **Period Architecture** Wright was proficient in period styles, although his designs were altered from traditional practice. Window hooding, slab chimneys, and numerous less-prominent touches guaranteed that Wright's Nathan Moore House would never be understood as conventional Tudor!

FIG. 242 **Romeo & Juliet** Ingenious in its self-reinforcing structure, the Misses Lloyd Jones windmill is a highly popular Taliesin icon. *Published with the permission of the Frank Lloyd Wright Foundation*

emerge Prairie Style. Inside, strong asymmetries play off against a formal plan; rooms are still defined, but space flows freely through the front chambers.

Nathan Moore House FIG. 241

1895; rebuilt after fire, 1923
Frank Lloyd Wright, architect
333 Forest Ave., Oak Park, Illinois

The half-timbered, English Gothic look of this house reminds us that Wright could and did work in reference to historical styles. The Moore House is one of several 1890s houses designed by Wright in traditional imageries (for example, the 1892 Georgian Revival George Blossom House, at 4858 S. Kenwood Ave. in Chicago). The house that we see is today is exaggerated in form and detailing compared to the original design, after remodeling and repairs from a fire. Forest Avenue and nearby streets contain a treasure trove of Wright houses.

Misses Lloyd Jones Windmill, "Romeo & Juliet" FIG. 242

1896–1897; rebuilt, 1938
Frank Lloyd Wright, architect
N of Hillside Home School, Taliesin Estate, Spring Green, Wisconsin

This fanciful utility features an innovative self-reinforcing structure, supposedly based on plant biology. Romeo & Juliet is popular among Taliesin visitors, many of whom eagerly climb the steep hill for a closer look.

PRAIRIE STYLE 1897–1915

Ward Willits House FIG. 243

1902–1903
Frank Lloyd Wright, architect
1445 Sheridan Rd., Highland Park, Illinois

Willits was Wright's first great Prairie house. It is unmistakably modern, if not as radical in character as many of Wright's subsequent designs. As in Robie (Fig. 247), horizontality is emphasized on the exterior. Interior spaces are still defined; this is not yet a completely open, free-flowing plan.

Hillside Home School FIG. 244

1902–1903; 1932–1939; 1952
Frank Lloyd Wright, architect
Taliesin Estate, Spring Green, Wisconsin

Replacing Wright's shingled 1887 building, the 1903 structure eventually formed the foundation of his Wisconsin estate. Wright endlessly revised his own buildings, as he tested new ideas about architecture. This was especially true in the case of Hillside, which operated as the summer base of Wright's architectural atelier-school, the Taliesin Fellowship. A 1930s expansion and remodeling added a drafting wing for the Fellowship, connected to Hillside School by a bridge. The Fellowship continued on for more than four decades after Wright's death with the successor practice, Taliesin (Associated) Architects.

The Theater is not to be missed when visiting (Fig. 666).

Unity Temple FIGS. 245, 246

1904–1908; restored after 1971 fire
Frank Lloyd Wright, architect
875 Lake St. at Kenilworth Ave., Oak Park, Illinois

Built for a Unitarian Universalist congregation, this structure is ingenious in many respects, from the overt expression of poured

FIG. 243 **Proto-Prairie House** Ward Willits (above) is not quite a fully developed Prairie house on the inside, although it was advanced enough to be a landmark in Wright's landmark-rich career.

FIG. 244 **Rural Schooling** Wright initially designed Hillside Home School (on the right in this view (below) of the expanded structure) for a school run by his aunts Nell and Jane. Built at a time when "rural school" connoted a one-room frame structure, monumentality on this scale must have been mind-boggling to neighboring Wisconsin farmers.

FIGS. 245, 246 **Church of the Future** Unity Temple in Oak Park was in some ways even more radical than Wright's Prairie houses. The interior is especially intriguing, for its unexpected colors, its flows of interrelated spaces, and ultimately, irs demonstration of Wright's numerous functional solutions. *Library of Congress, Prints & Photographs, Historic American Buildings Survey*

FIG. 247 Iconic Prairie House The Frederick Robie House in Chicago is understandably the most recognized of Wright's Prairie houses. It is lean and extreme, unforgettable for its daring cantilevers and open plan. *Library of Congress, Prints & Photographs, Historic American Buildings Survey*

concrete to its complex, multilevel passages through the sanctuary space. Despite a low construction budget, Unity Temple is a major civic landmark in upscale Uptown Oak Park. Although Wright employed strong forms, he separated the building program into two distinct masses. As a result, this monumental building is nevertheless in scale with its suburban context.

Frederick Robie House FIG. 247
1908–1910
Frank Lloyd Wright, architect
5757 Woodlawn Ave., Chicago, Illinois (open)

The iconic Prairie house, Robie was a radical exercise in abstract form and the integration of space, both interior and exterior. Although horizontals have been exaggerated in the extreme, this play of structure-sculpture was achieved without sacrificing a feeling of domesticity.

Taliesin FIG. 236
1911–1912; 1914; 1925; 1932–1959
Frank Lloyd Wright, architect
Hwy. 23, S of Spring Green, Wisconsin (open)

Wright always felt connected to the land, especially so to his mother's family farmsteads. Wright instinctively retreated here from Chicago/Oak Park after the scandal of his romance with Mamah Cheney, which broke up both of their families. Construction of the house began in 1911. It was rebuilt and enlarged after a fire in 1915, yet again in 1925, and was continuously modified throughout the ensuing decades.

In addition to its historical importance as Wright's home and domain, Taliesin is a demonstration of the high potentials of interrelating building and site and a reminder that the creative process in architecture is ongoing.

EXOTIC INFLUENCES 1915–1930

Barnsdall "Hollyhock" House FIG. 248
1917–1923
Frank Lloyd Wright, architect
4808 Hollywood Blvd., W of Vermont, Los Angeles, California (open)

Several prominent influences shaped Wright's designs. These included his upbringing and home, meaning the prairie Midwest; his technical ingenuity; a knowing sensitivity to the local setting; and also what

art historian Dimitri Tselos termed "exotic influences," especially Mayan architecure and Japanese culture. Wright's Mayan imagery emerged in the 1915–1921 German Warehouse in Richland Center, Wisconsin. His work on the Imperial Hotel in Tokyo, underway in 1916, re-ignited Wright's passion for all things Japanese.

For personal and professional reasons, these middle years of his career were a time to move beyond the Midwest and the prairie, physically and symbolically, experiencing then-exotic realms like Los Angeles, and responding in new design vocabularies.

While the extended, disciplined Barnsdall plan was reminiscent of Midwestern Prairie designs like that of the Coonley House, its overtly Mayan character signaled a new direction in Wright's complex, ever-evolving and expanding architectural vocabulary.

Mrs. George Millard House, "La Miniatura"
1923–1924
Frank Lloyd Wright, architect; **Lloyd Wright**, landscape designer
645 Prospect Crescent., Pasadena, California

For Millard, Wright eschewed overt Mayan references, responding particularly to climate and the availability of new building materials. Millard is the best of Wright's four Los Angeles–area houses developed in so-called "textile block," perforated concrete block that establishes privacy while admitting a sparkling pattern of light into the interiors. While there is still a sense of the Mayan here, in massing and in some of the interior detailing, Millard is really a fresh expression of its time and setting.

Charles Ennis (Ennis-Brown) House FIG. 249
1923–1924
Frank Lloyd Wright, architect
2655 Glendower Ave., Los Angeles, California

Three of Wright's four textile-block houses (Millard, Storer, and Freeman) are delicate in scale. By contrast, the Ennis House is monumental in the extreme. In character and, especially, in its dramatic, hillside siting, Ennis is more than believable as a literal Mayan temple. The house has been deteriorating for years. Fortunately, in 2005 a consortium of preservation organizations announced plans to stabilize and ultimately restore the house.

REEMERGENCE 1930–1941

The 1920s were years of frustration for Wright and also a time of professional growth. This was an era of national prosperity and excess. Yet, especially in the last half of the decade, Wright had few realized structures, far fewer than before the First World War, and a tiny fraction of his post–World War II output.

Although Wright succeeded in keeping his name in the popular media, and published his *Autobiography* in 1932, he had effectively ceased to be a presence in the American architectural profession. Wright would never forget the Midwest of his upbringing. But by the time of his seemingly miraculous mid-1930s reappearance as *the* dominant American architect, at least to the American public, his interests had broadened.

For one thing, Wright had temporarily moved to the Arizona desert in the mid-1920s. In the following decade he relocated to a desert site 20 miles from Phoenix, as his primary domicile.

FIG. 248 A Fusion of Influences When Wright designed the Barnsdall "Hollyhock" House, Los Angeles was considered an exotic land by most Americans. Unsurprisingly, this complex has an unconventional look. First and foremost, however, climate influenced Wright's design, which offers choices among openness, shelter, and retreat depending on the sun and temperature at any given time. The magnificent living room served as the primary retreat. *Photograph © Alexander Vertikoff*

For another, he initiated an architectural training program called the Taliesin Fellowship, intended as an alternative to collegiate architectural schools and as a much-needed source of revenue.

Third, Wright had begun to seriously contemplate the emerging structure and form of major American regions. His prescient proposals, combined under the heading of "Broadacre City," remain the most comprehensive and farseeing in American city planning.

Broadacre City FIG. 250
1930s; model constructed November, 1934, to April, 1935
Frank Lloyd Wright, planner
Broadacre Model located at Dana Gallery, Hillside Home School, Taliesin Estate, Spring Green, Wisconsin

Wright's vision for an archetypical expanding American region was grounded in a keen appreciation of traditional American values. While not all of Broadacre's housing is freestanding, each family is typically given a personal domain. Reflecting the American celebration of freedom of movement, Wright utilized a hierarchy of roads (see the Roads chapter) to organize Broadacre.

FIG. 249 Southland Mayan The Charles Ennis (Ennis-Brown) House is Wright's most literal Mayan reference, both in its sloping, pyramidal walls and for its ceremonial siting, overlooking Los Angeles below.

FIG. 250 **Broadacre City** Broadacre was Wright's visionary interpretation of traditional American values, in particular of the importance many Americans attach to personal space and mobility. *Copyright © 1994 The Frank Lloyd Wright Foundation, Taliesin West, Scottsdale, Arizona, published with permission*

FIG. 251 **The New Wright** After only a handful of designs realized between 1923 and 1933. The Malcolm Willey house in Minneapolis marked the beginning of what was in effect Wright's second career. In its impressive efficiency, Willey prefigured the Usonian house, which Wright was then developing as integral with his Broadacre planning.

FIG. 252 **The Most Famous House in the World** Wright designed dozens of iconic buildings. The Edgar J. Kaufmann House, "Fallingwater," is the one *everyone* knows. *Library of Congress, Prints & Photographs, Historic American Buildings Survey*

Wright employed a continuous built mosaic to efficiently utilize land. Like ancient cities, Broadacre is mostly low and closely woven, in distinct contrast to the high spot densities and leftover spaces around today's American downtowns.

The effectiveness of Wright's approach was confirmed by the 2000 U.S. census, which revealed that the regional density of the closely woven Los Angeles Southland is one-third greater than the New York City metropolitan area, and that "sprawling" Phoenix has developed into a more land-efficient configuration than Chicagoland.

For all of its far-reaching vision, Broadacre inevitably reflected its time: the plan was developed during the depths of the Great Depression. As one example, Wright's call for an ample plot of land for each family is partly a reaction to those millions who were dispossessed by the collapse of the national economy. If all else failed, inhabitants of Broadacre would have yards large enough to grow their own food.

Malcolm Willey House FIG. 251

1932–1934
Frank Lloyd Wright, architect
255 Bedford St. SE., Minneapolis, Minnesota

Sometimes big things come in small packages. This tiny house is not much larger in floor area than a developer's Cape Cod. Nevertheless, it is immensely significant historically as the threshold to Wright's second career, both as an ur-Usonian house, and also as a demonstration of the nature of Broadacre City housing.

Set on a slight eminence, Willey originally enjoyed a magnificent panoramic view, which was later obscured by a wall screening a freeway built in the 1960s along the edge of the front yard.

Edgar J. Kaufmann House, "Fallingwater" FIG. 252

1934–1937
Frank Lloyd Wright, architect
Rt. 381, Mill Run, Pennsylvania (open)

Probably the most famous private residence in the world. To say the least, this weekend retreat house was unexpected and without precedent, hovering almost unbelievably over a waterfall.

Paul Hanna "Honeycomb" House FIG. 253

1936–1937
Frank Lloyd Wright, architect
737 Frenchman's Rd., Stanford–Palo Alto, California

Hanna was the first of Wright's hexagonal Usonian houses, with internal space flowing around a central chimney in a complex geometric, almost a beehive pattern in plan. Although the steeply sloping lot is relatively small, Wright made the most of it, as the house fits snugly, beautifully, into its lush plantings.

S. C. Johnson & Son Administration Building, "Johnson's Wax" FIGS. 254, 255

1936–1939; Research Tower, 1943–1950
Frank Lloyd Wright, architect
1525 Howe St., Racine, Wisconsin

Johnson's Wax offers one of Wright's most memorable interiors. Located in a visually unremarkable area, the building literally turns inward. Outside light (but no outside view) is admitted through horizontally stacked glass tubes which were replaced later with durable plastic facsimiles.

Architectural focus develops around a two-story central office space, whose ceiling is supported by the famous tapered "lotus" columns (Fig. 255). Wright designed a complete furniture system for

FIG. 253 Hexagonal Usonian Usonian houses were conceived as comparatively modest homes relating organically-ecologically to their setting. Many Usonians were deceptively simple in plan and not much larger in floor area than developers' tract houses. Not all Usonians were tiny or simple, however. The plan of Wright's Paul Hanna House enclosess about four times the interior floor area of Willey.

FIG. 254 Usonian Moderne Curving corners might suggest a similarity between the Johnson & Son Administration Building and contemporary Streamline architecture (see the Moderne chapter). Any such comparisons end at that superficial level, since Wright's design was a sweeping departure from convention.

FIG. 255 The Building Inspector Wright's incomparable career generated innumerable tall tales, many of which were essentially true. The Johnson's Wax Story involved the city of Racine's building inspector, who insisted that Wright's proposed "lotus" columns for the Johnson & Son Administration Building would not be strong enough. In a withering retort, Wright choreographed a public test during which a full-size column was massively overloaded with sand bags. Wright probably didn't win many fans among municipal workers by publicly humiliating the official. But of course widely published photos of the triumphant overloaded column were instantly incorporated into Wright lore. The graceful lotus columns are a signature feature of the main office space. *Library of Congress, Prints & Photographs, Historic American Buildings Survey*

the offices, which itself is now an industrial-design classic. The curved corners are superficially consistent with the contemporary Streamline Moderne, but Johnson's Wax's sweeping, voluptuous curves and circles throughout present nothing less than Space Age imagery.

Taliesin West FIG. 256
1937–1959
Frank Lloyd Wright, architect
12621 N. Frank Lloyd Wright Blvd., NE of Scottsdale Rd. and Shea Blvd., Scottsdale, Arizona (open)

Wright was understandably enchanted by the vivid, ever-changing Sonoran desert, eventually building Taliesin West as his primary residence-studio near Phoenix. Even more so than Wright's employment of his Prairie Style as a design reflection of regional characteristics, here, on a rugged, then-remote site, Wright completely engaged with his setting – not just to build in the desert, but to live a desert-influenced lifestyle.

As late as the 1960s, Taliesin West reigned in magnificent isolation. By today, however, urbanized Phoenix has completely engulfed the property. A good imagination about the undeveloped past is useful when you visit. Or see Neil Levine's *The Architecture of Frank Lloyd Wright*, pp. 261, 293.

Jester-Pfeiffer House
1938, design; 1971–1972, construction
Frank Lloyd Wright, architect
Taliesin West, 12621 N. Frank Lloyd Wright Blvd., NE of Scottsdale Rd and Shea Blvd., Scottsdale, Arizona (opened occasionally for Foundation events)

Frank Lloyd Wright Foundation archivist Bruce Brooks Pfeiffer adapted Wright's unbuilt California project for his home on the Taliesin West property, substituting a patio overlooking a desert

expanse for the original pool overlooking the ocean. Free-standing circular forms define what would be rooms in a conventional plan. Any visit is a spectacular experience, though the house is especially wonderful around twilight.

Lloyd Lewis House FIG. 257
1939–1942
Frank Lloyd Wright, architect
153 Little St. Mary's Rd., Libertyville, Illinois

Lewis is a development of Wright's Usonian house. Twice the interior floor area of Willey, the Lewis main floor is raised a full level above a flood plain on its semi-rural, now exurban site. Natural light infuses the cypress and brick interior, making this an exceptionally warm and pleasant living environment.

POSTWAR 1945–1963

In the post–World War II years, Frank Lloyd Wright was well positioned as "America's architect," and, characteristically, he made the most of it. As Wright neared 80 by war's end, his flamboyant personal demeanor was now widely appreciated throughout American society as endearing—Wright almost as a national treasure—perhaps proving Mark Twain's comment about old age conferring respectability. Wright was the subject of countless media stories and interviews. He made memorable public presentations on visionary projects as dissimilar as Broadacre City and a proposed mile-high skyscraper, "The Illinois."

FIG. 256 Taliesin Goes West Just as Wright built Taliesin *with* its site and in response to its northern climate, so, too, did the architect approach his Arizona desert home design as an environmental response to its natural setting and climate. Naturally, neither looks (or is organized in plan) like the other, and that is a useful insight about the essential singularity of all sites. *Published with the permission of the Frank Lloyd Wright Foundation*

Wright's final decade of practice was best known for major civic buildings, although he designed dozens of houses, most of them variations on his Usonian ideal. Many of these houses were developed by associates in Wright's now-large office, and thus fewer of these designs are as distinctive and unforgettable as his iconic earlier houses. Still, even the least of these homes was in many respects superior to contemporary U.S. housing.

As might be the hope of any architect, Wright died in his 92nd year, still active in the practice of architecture.

Lowell Walter House FIG. 258
1945–1950
Frank Lloyd Wright, architect
Rt. W35, N edge of Quasqueton, Iowa (open)

Walter offers a perfect postwar summation of Wright's Usonian themes, completing a *parti* begun with the Willey House of 1934. Wright took full advantage of a beautiful, rural hilltop site. The property is now owned by the Iowa Conservation Commission.

FIG. 258 Postwar Housing Responding to its beautiful, rural Iowa site, the Lowell Walter House opens up to the outside, especially from its fully glazed (with clerestory) living room.

FIG. 259 **Alley Remodeling** Even located in San Francisco, the V. C. Morris Gift Shop would seem not exactly a prime commission, the remodeling of a tiny existing structure sited in a glorified alley. As usual, Wright rose to the occasion, transforming a commonplace building into spectacular architecture, especially on the interior.
Library of Congress, Prints & Photographs, Historic American Buildings Survey

FIGS. 260, 261 **High Rise** H. C. Price Tower was Wright's tallest realized design. Happily, the building has recently been restored, its interiors brilliantly revitalized by Wendy Evans Joseph as an inn (Fig. 261).

V. C. Morris Gift Shop FIG. 259

1948–1949
Frank Lloyd Wright, architect
140 Maiden Ln., San Francisco, California

Morris was literally Wright's jewel box. His remodeling transformed a non-descript alley storefront into a high-art environment appropriate for the sale of expensive china and art glass. The brick façade walls out the city, offering only an irresistible deep-arched entry into the marvelous interior space. A spiral ramp, offering a preview of his Guggenheim Museum plan, provides the animating interior feature.

H. C. Price Tower FIGS. 260, 261

1952–1956; remodeling, 2002–2003
Frank Lloyd Wright, architect; **Wendy Evans Joseph**, architect
of interior remodeling
510 S. Dewey Ave., Bartlesville, Oklahoma

Wright was famed for the characteristic horizontality of his architecture. But he was not immune to the allure of a soaring design, as his 1896 Romeo & Juliet windmill attests.

Alas for Wright—and for us—the 19-story Price Tower was as tall as he was to build. Wright had developed this basic design in 1925 for an unbuilt tower in Manhattan. He adapted it for a Chicago project in 1930, and then again for yet another project in Washington, D.C., in 1940, both also unbuilt. The scheme was finally realized in a structure ingeniously combining side-by-side office and apartment spaces, overlooking this modest city in the lightly rolling Osage Hills.

Derelict for more than a decade, the tower gained new life with a brilliant transformation by Wendy Evans Joseph into a boutique hotel (Fig. 261), restaurant, and art center.

Solomon R. Guggenheim Museum FIGS. 262, 263

1943; 1956–1959; addition and remodeling, 1992
Frank Lloyd Wright, architect; **Gwathmey Siegel & Associates**,
architects for the addition and remodeling
1071 Fifth Ave. at 89th St., New York, New York

This astonishing building has been widely interpreted from either of two extremes: (a) it was Wright's revenge on the city, which he detested; or (b) The Guggenheim is an energizing counterpoint for the city, which Wright felt merited revitalization.

Either way, the Guggenheim is a supreme work of urban sculpture, even if a continuous, spiral display area is not an ideal venue for showing some art. Wright's original Guggenheim design was undertaken in 1943, but construction was postponed because of a series of delays due to code restrictions, a clash of wills between a strong client and a strong architect, and soaring postwar construction costs.

Marin County Civic Center FIGS. 264, 265

1957–1963; 1966–1970
Frank Lloyd Wright, architect; **Aaron Green**, associate architect;
completed by **Taliesin Associated Architects**
N. San Pedro Rd., E of Hwy. 101, San Rafael, California

Underway when Wright died in 1959, this suburban county government complex is enduringly futuristic, yet also a restatement of Wright's classic concepts, especially in the way a building grows organically from its site. The architecture seems splendidly otherworldly, almost as if set down, fully built, by a highly advanced, slightly hedonistic race of space beings. However, Wright's design was fully grounded to Earth, as the wings span between low hills, engaging into this particular site so logically that one senses that no other approach would have been as desirable.

Clearly, The Master went out in style.

FIGS. 262, 263 Building as Sculpture The Guggenheim must be a startling sight to anyone who comes across it without warning (Fig. 262). Its famous spiral ramp (Fig. 263) has been criticized by some as a poor background for showing art. Most visitors probably leave with the feeling that they've just experienced a great work of art.

FIGS. 264, 265 Public Architecture If Marin County wanted instant fame with its new Civic Center, Wright did not disappoint them. This was a virtuoso demonstration in engaging and shaping a site to establish civic presence.

Prairie School
1895–1920

FIG. 266 Milieu for Everyday Life Prairie exteriors are typically abstracted and horizontal, as in the 1914–1915 Bradley House in Madison, Wisconsin, designed by Purcell & Elmslie. Beyond any characteristic look, Prairie architects were especially interested in enhancing the experiences of everyday life. Innovative accommodations to routine human use were among the most important technical contributions of the Prairie School.

Prairie School design—architecture and landscape architecture—developed in the American Midwest under the potent design influence of Frank Lloyd Wright and the guiding spirit of Louis Sullivan.

As a generalized description, this is typically an architecture of horizontality, meant to emulate, indeed, to celebrate, the wide-open Midwestern natural landscapes. Beyond this superficial definition, Prairie School buildings, especially those designed by major practitioners like Purcell & Elmslie and Walter Burley Griffin, were original and sophisticated designs, comprehensively addressing building-to-site connections, inter-relationships of exterior to interior, the spatial flow though interior spaces, and the employment of materials, textures, and furnishings (Fig. 266).

Prairie School architecture peaked just before the American entry into the First World War. By the 1918 Armistice, everything had changed. America was in so many ways a very different nation. Now more outward-looking, with new international stature and responsibilities, the nation saw regionalism as suddenly passé. As a consequence, the Prairie School lost general currency, seemingly disappearing from architectural practice almost overnight. Regardless, Prairie School innovations were absorbed into the ongoing body of American architecture.

FIG. 267 Classical Prairie George Maher's designs, like that of his John Farson House, employed classicist formality married to strong, prairie-like horizontals. As a result, these houses could fit into progressive communities like Oak Park, as well as into neighborhoods characterized by traditional imageries.

FIG. 268 Urban Prairie Louis Sullivan's Bradley House (for the same client as the Purcell & Elmslie-designed house opening this chapter, Fig. 266) made the most of its city lot, especially in the way light was introduced to the upper floor. Cantilevered screened sleeping porches were enclosed by later owners.

RESIDENTIAL

John Farson House FIG. 267

1897
George W. Maher, architect
217 Home Ave., Oak Park, Illinois (open)

Farson is an early example of the monumental version of Prairie School domestic architecture identified with Maher: Beaux Arts symmetry married to prominent horizontality.

Harold C. Bradley House FIG. 268

1908–1909
Louis H. Sullivan, architect
106 N. Prospect Ave., Madison, Wisconsin

This urban prairie house necessarily provides both light and privacy by emphasizing the second floor, which is encircled by a continuous band of windows. A deep gable overhang and projecting balcony supports provide the architectural drama.

Ricker House FIGS. 269, 270

1911–1912
Walter Burley Griffin, architect; **Barry Byrne**, architect for the later garage
1510 Broad St., Grinnell, Iowa

Creatively idiosyncratic; a visually solid two-story main house is flanked by a one-story entrance porch at the front (Fig. 270) and a breezeway-connected garage at the (conventional) rear (Fig. 269). Inside, the main floor plan is "remarkably open," in David Geb-

FIGS. 269, 270 **Acknowledging the Automobile** At the dawn of the auto age, Walter Burley Griffin's Ricker House expressed the everyday importance of the car, reversing then-traditional conventions of entrance and service on a corner lot. The house and Barry Byrne's later garage (Fig. 269) orient to a well-traveled street, showcasing what was usually treated as a side yard and the back of the lot. Conversely, a formal "front" entrance on the residential side street is treated almost indifferently, as a secondary appendage (Fig. 270).

hard's description. Gebhard also noted that the prominence of the garage–auto court acknowledged the emerging importance of the automobile in everyday American life.

Melson House
1912–1914
Walter Burley Griffin, architect
56 River Heights Dr., Mason City, Iowa

Almost indescribable, this small, rock-faced house seems to grow right out of its site and, despite its size, dominates the subdivision (see the Regionalism and Community Development chapters) through its cliff-top siting and singular visual character. Gebhard identified the Melson house as "one of the half dozen most significant houses of the Prairie movement."

James Blythe House II FIG. 271
1913–1914
Walter Burley Griffin, architect
431 1st St. SE., Mason City, Iowa

Blythe offers a beautiful demonstration of the high potentials of Prairie School architecture. The design builds visually from its site on a rough stone base, opening onto the Rock Glen meadow from a slight eminence. A conventional prairie plan has been imaginatively personalized almost, but not quite, to the point of idiosyncrasy. A marvelous living room fireplace faced in a basket-weave pattern of emerald and gold tiles is a landmark American Arts & Crafts decorative-arts design. All in all, the Blythe House is a wonderful experience, especially on a sunny morning.

Hoyt House FIG. 272
1913
Purcell, Feick & Elmslie, architects
300 Hill St., Red Wing, Minnesota

Truly a house for good living, with spaces carefully zoned but not all compartmentalized. Every room easily accommodates its function, yet it is not oversized. Hoyt is the upper-middle-class version of a thoughtfully designed and comfortable house, as the Gallager House is for the middle class.

William Purcell (Purcell-Cutts) House FIG. 273
1913
Purcell & Elmslie, architects; **Harry Franklin Baker**, landscape architect
2328 Lake Pl., Minneapolis, Minnesota (open by reservation with the Minneapolis Institute of the Arts)

For his own home, Purcell indulged himself, not by excess size or opulence, but through imaginative micro-manipulation of space and levels, inventive detailing, integral art and craft, and an extraordinary demonstration of integration of house and yard on a small urban lot. Gebhard understandably appreciated the design as "one of the great Prairie houses in America." The property was meticulously restored by the Minneapolis Institute of Arts.

Gallager House
1913
Purcell, Feick & Elmslie, architects
451 W. Broadway, Winona, Minnesota

FIG. 271 Classic Prairie House The James Blythe House has it all: a suave exterior, a warm and inviting interior, set on a tranquil, wooded lot overlooking Rock Glen (Fig. 994).

FIG. 272 Upper-Middle-Class Housing In this age of vacuous McMansions, Purcell, Feick & Elmslie's Hoyt House reminds us that true elegance in living can be achieved with relative economy.

FIG. 273 The Architect's House William Purcell's Minneapolis house is a wonder of invention, deftly worked onto a small city lot. The house deferentially steps back from the alignment of its neighbors, thereby minimizing possible visual impacts caused by the contrast of its progressive character with a block of conventional developers' houses.

Purcell and Elmslie were not as avant-garde as Wright, nor were their designs as spatially complex as Walter Burley Griffin's. Their niche was to demonstrate a better kind of conventional house. Houses like this one do not seize one's attention the way, say, Wright's Robie House does. Rather these are thoughtful, economical, and comfortable places in which to live.

Clarke House
1915–1916
Barry Byrne, architect; **Alfonso Iannelli**, artist;
Arthur Seifried, garden designer
500 S. Main St., Fairfield, Iowa

Prairie designs varied widely, as demonstrated in this highly personal expression. The exterior reads as if of solid masonry, out of which openings have been carved. In plan, the entrance at one end connects to the attached garage at the other by way of a flowing, extra-high living-dining space. The artistic interior feature is a fireplace mural by Iannelli, a favorite artist of Wright and other Prairie School architects.

FIG. 274 **Landmark Urban School** Carl Schurz High School projects an appropriately muscular character for its dense urban neighborhood, softened slightly by an intriguing, village-like character, and by warm materials.

FIG. 275 **Crossover Design** Merchants National Bank in Winona is primarily Prairie in its horizontality, ornament, and Roman brick. But the design alludes as well to traditional Beaux Arts banks in its formality and columns with capitals. The architects were clearly successful in having it both ways.

FIG. 276 **Monumental Prairie** For J. R. Watkins Medical Products, Maher introduced an almost-civic character to its modest neighborhood, located on the edge of an industrial district.

COMMERCIAL–INSTITUTIONAL

Carl Schurz High School FIG. 274
1908–1910
Dwight H. Perkins, architect
Addison St. at Milwaukee Ave., Chicago, Illinois

Perkins drew from Sullivan and from German precedents for this design, according to Allen Brooks, though this appropriately robust complex is memorable for its visually rich brick and terra cotta exterior and peaked roofs.

Merchants National Bank FIG. 275
1911–1912; later addition and remodeling
Purcell, Feick & Elmslie, architects
102-104 E. 3rd St., Winona, Minnesota

The scheme owes much to Sullivan's Owatonna bank, completed two years before, although here the exterior is more articulated, and the interior lacks the magnificent terra cotta and metal details—and the murals—of the Owatonna bank.

J. R. Watkins Medical Products Co. FIG. 276
1911, 1913
George W. Maher, architect
150–178 Liberty St., Winona, Minnesota

Watkins Products is example of Maher's characteristic mix of Beaux Arts symmetry and Prairie School horizontality. A very impressive presence, especially in this small-scale neighborhood.

FIG. 277, 278 **Synthesis of Imageries** Winona Savings Bank, located just three blocks from Merchants Nation Bank and only a little farther from J. R. Watkins Medical Products, offers another synthesized Prairie bank imagery, this time intermixed with a trace of Egyptian. The genuine Tiffany windows are superb.

Winona Savings Bank FIGS. 277, 278

1914
George W. Maher, architect
W. 4th at Main sts., Winona, Minnesota

An unusual, facile mix of Egyptian and Prairie imageries produced highly sophisticated architecture. Not many banks have genuine Tiffany windows!

Woodbury County Courthouse FIG. 279

1915–1918
Purcell & Elmslie, **William L. Steele**, architects;
Alfonso Iannelli, sculptor
620 Douglas St., Sioux City, Iowa

Designer George Grant Elmslie began with motifs common to this building type, such as a colonnade, entry pediment, strong visual base and entablature, and exaggerated corners. Then he transformed these elements into a wholly new expression of the American courthouse. The domed interior rotunda is breathtaking (Figs. 663, 664).

POSTSCRIPT

After the First World War, the American architectural scene rapidly moved away from Prairie School, Arts & Crafts, and other progressive design movements which had flourished up until America's entry into the war.

Frank Lloyd Wright would practice for another four decades, although his imageries were already moving through Mayan, and he was working mostly in California and Japan.

Walter Burley Griffin and his wife, the gifted architectural designer and renderer Marion Mahoney Griffin, had moved to Australia upon winning the competition to design a new capital at Canberra.

Barry Byrne developed a highly personal, expressionistic, style. His later practice was primarily devoted to Catholic churches, notably St. Patrick's Church in Racine, Wisconsin

FIG. 280 **Expressionism** Barry Byrne's St. Columba Church in St. Paul (at 1305 Lafond) is a very late Prairie School treasure, though often overlooked even by Prairie aficionados.

FIGS. 281, 282 **A Tale of Two Eras** The Henry Salzer and Argyle Scott houses, located only a block apart and designed by the same architect, illustrate the cultural gulf on either side of the First World War. Built just before the outbreak, Salzer is recognizably Prairie (Fig. 281). With the "return to normalcy" after the Armistice, the Prairie School had become passé by 1920. American Colonial Revival was considered right and proper for new times—and thus for the Scotts (Fig. 282).

FIG. 283 **Apostasy!** On retiring (temporarily, as it turned out) from the practice of architecture, leading Prairie School architect William Purcell built this simplified Voyseyesque cottage for himself in the Portland hills.

(1923), Church of Christ the King in Tulsa, Oklahoma (1926), and St. Columba Church (1949–1951) in St. Paul, Minnesota (Fig. 280).

By 1920, some Prairie School architects were designing in American Colonial and Period Revival imageries, evident in houses by Percy D. Bentley and William Gray Purcell, below. A few Prairie School architects carried on into the 1920s with designs that were still recognizably "Prairie." While most of these were less vital than the best Prairie designs from the early 'teens, some, like Alfred Caldwell's 1934–1936 Eagle Point Park pavilions in Dubuque, Iowa, were significant works (see the Regionalism chapter).

Prairie School architecture was much more than a regional style, however, but primarily an ongoing exploration into how to live better in any given situation. This is demonstrated by the consulting work William Purcell did for the Minneapolis developer Henry Peterson in the late 1920s and early 1930s. With the exception of Peterson's own house, these speculative, developers' houses were carried out in various Period and American Colonial imageries. They were not advanced designs, but rather carefully worked out variations on builder's stock plans, subtly better, inside and out, than typical builder's houses.

Henry Salzer House FIG. 281
1912
Percy D. Bentley, architect
1634 King Street, La Crosse, Wisconsin

Argyle Scott House FIG. 282
1920
Percy D. Bentley, architect
1721 King St., La Crosse, Wisconsin

The abrupt shift in architectural fashion after the war is vividly illustrated by this pair of designs by the same architect, located just a block apart.

The Salzer House (Fig. 281) is a prominent landmark in this visually rich neighborhood, the best of Bentley's several Prairie designs (see also the nearby 1910 Bartl House at 238 S. 17th Street and the 1913 Chase House at 221 S. 11th Street). The self-taught Bentley was a "great admirer" of Wright, and here his exterior is a knowing and confident Prairie expression (Mrs. Salzer insisted on a Colonial floor plan and interior detailing).

Bentley's Scott commission came just after the war. By now, national architectural fashion had strongly shifted away from the Prairie School. Mrs. Scott insisted on a fully Colonial house, which Bentley provided (Fig. 282). Only vestiges of the architect's earlier Prairie design sensibilities remain, chiefly in the retaining wall, extended away from the house, rather than physically attached, and, as Brooks noted, in the Prairie-like detailing of exterior siding and the unconventional rendering of the entry pediment. These minor deviations from American Colonial Revival practice will be overlooked by all except specialists.

The sun was clearly setting on the Prairie School as a distinct and comprehensive architectural expression.

William Purcell House FIG. 283
1920
William Gray Purcell, architect
2649 SW. Georgian Pl., Portland, Oregon

For this, his first retirement home (Purcell was to live another 45 years after it was built, and later moved to Pasadena), Purcell worked in a romantic, Arts & Crafts imagery reminiscent of the English architect C. F. A. Voysey. Although he had employed peaked roofs in his Prairie designs, and although the smooth stucco was a very modern finish—and indeed, in many ways this is a very modern design—the overall feeling of this house is more Period Revival than anything else. No casual visitor would have imagined that this was a design by someone who had been nationally prominent as a Prairie School architect just a couple of years before.

Erwin House FIG. 284
1926
John S. Van Bergen, architect
615 Warwick Rd., Kenilworth, Illinois (SE of Winnetka Ave. and Essex Rd.)

Erwin is a fully mature synthesis of prairie spirit and traditional graciousness, surely welcome in the most architecturally polished of neighborhoods, as this one is. While the Prairie School had largely receded into the past by this late date, Van Bergen was clearly still working at it in this superb house, his career masterpiece.

Henry Peterson House FIG. 285
1927–1928
William G. Purcell, architect
3 Red Cedar Ln., Minneapolis, Minnesota

This is a further development of the cottage, following the architect's own Portland house (Fig. 283). The Peterson House is a fresh, expansive, and unconventional look at the cottage, set romantically on a short, dead-end street lined with towering cedars.

Peterson Speculative Houses FIG. 286
1928
Purcell & Strauel, consulting architects
5312 Vincent Ave. S., Minneapolis, Minnesota

1928
Purcell & Strauel, consulting architects
5319 Upton Ave. S., Minneapolis, Minnesota

1928
Purcell & Strauel, consulting architects
5217 Vincent Ave. S., Minneapolis, Minnesota

1928
Purcell & Strauel, consulting architects
5312 Upton Ave. S., Minneapolis, Minnesota

1932
Purcell & Strauel, consulting architects
5309 Upton Ave. S., Minneapolis, Minnesota

Purcell's American Colonial design at 5312 Vincent (Fig. 286) is the most impressive of this group, which also includes a very late Craftsman bungalow and various English expressions. Unlike Bentley's American Colonial Revival Scott House in La Crosse (Fig. 282), 5312 Vincent is recognizably out of mainstream American Colonial practice; those interested in American architecture will immediately note the combined entrance-bay window, dormers notched into the roofline, raised clapboarding, and an overall simplification.

FIG. 284 **The Last Masterpiece** The Prairie School closed out on a high point, with John Van Bergen's regal Erwin House. Even in its visually impressive neighborhood of Period and American Colonial Revival mansions, the Erwin House is a star.

FIG. 285 **Confident in Maturity** Purcell may have moved away from Prairie School expressions after the First World War, but he was, of course, an accomplished architect, as demonstrated by his serene Henry Peterson House .

FIG. 286 **Prairie Sensibilities** Purcell consulted on several speculative houses built by developer Henry Peterson (Fig. 285). These employed Period and American Colonial imageries, but consistent with a common Prairie School emphasis, Purcell focused on making subtle improvements to conventional plans.

Craftsman
1895–1920

FIGS. 287, 288 Widespread Appeal of Craftsman The Arts & Crafts ideals of the American Craftsman movement appealed to a surprisingly broad range of Americans. Top-end Craftsman mansions like the David Gamble House in Pasadena (Fig. 287) were ultimate designs, built to utter perfection. At the other extreme, economical bungalows like this one in Iowa (Fig. 288) were highly appreciated for their functional efficiency, and for their homey, welcoming feeling.

Craftsman design evolved out of the American Arts & Crafts movement, which itself developed out of the English Arts & Crafts movement popularized by John Ruskin and William Morris. Their ideas about reuniting artist and craftsman—and of "pre-industrial" crafts as an alternative to cheap, mass-produced goods—were taken up in the United States by Elbert Hubbard, Gustav Stickley, and such architects as Charles and Henry Greene and Bernard Maybeck (see the California chapter for Maybeck).

Hubbard founded a craftsman community known as the Roycrofters, in East Aurora, New York, which began as a press, soon expanding into furniture, stained glass, and metalwork.

Founded in 1895, this enterprise lasted until the Depression. Stickley founded *The Craftsman*, which, like the later *Sunset*, was a style magazine targeted at the American upper middle class, to whom Stickley sold furniture and accessories.

The Pasadena practice of the Greenes formed the nucleus of a golden age of Craftsman architecture, especially in California. For every great house by the Greenes (Fig. 287), there were thousands of craftsman bungalows (Fig. 288) nationwide and tens of thousands of ordinary bungalows.

Even so, as America moved into a new era of "normalcy" after the First World War, inevitable changes to society resulted in cultural changes as well. As a result, the wide popularity of Craftsman designs and the Arts & Crafts movement—along with that of Prairie School design—diminished sharply in the 1920s.

CRAFTSMAN "GREAT HOUSES"

David Gamble House FIGS. 287, 289
1907–1908
Greene & Greene, architects
4 Westmoreland Pl., Pasadena, California (open)

Gamble is the supreme Craftsman house (Figs. 287, 289). Really, a supreme house, period! Numerous ideal conditions came together to make this extraordinary design possible. Key ingredients included: clients of substantial wealth with a strong interest in Far Eastern culture; the Arcadian climate and aristocratic social-cultural scene of early 1900s Pasadena; a superb, spacious site overlooking the Arroyo; and, of course, gifted architects commissioned at just the right time in their careers.

The developed property is of-a-piece: everything from site landscaping down to the switch plates is a clearly integral part of the overall design concept. Indeed, it is easy to think of the house itself as a three-story-high piece of exquisitely polished furniture. A visit is highly recommended.

Robert Blacker House FIG. 290
1907
Greene & Greene, architects
1177 Hillcrest Ave., Pasadena, California

Blacker was the first of the Greenes' "ultimate bungalows," as Randell Makinson described them. The two-story house is organized around a fairly straightforward "U" shaped core, from which sweeping, one-story appendages extend out into the spacious yard. Like all of the Greenes' houses of this type and era, the Blacker design was thoroughly worked out in every detail, and beautifully crafted. The expansive grounds were the glory of this property; sadly, the beautiful rear garden was later subdivided.

Ernest Batchelder House FIGS. 291, 292
1909, 1913
Ernest Batchelder, designer
626 S. Arroyo Blvd., Pasadena, California

Much smaller than the other houses in this section, Batchelder could plausibly be considered a bungalow, as its long-time owner, historian Robert Winter wryly insists. But in its many creative idiosyncrasies and integral tilework (Batchelder was a leading producer of decorative glazed tile), one experiences a grandness to this house that is wholly disproportionate to its comparatively modest size.

FIG. 289 Designed as a Piece The Greene brothers' magnificent Gamble House (Fig. 287) was meticulously planned and designed, from its siting down to the smallest detail. (Unfortunately, the same cannot be said about the later railing in this photo.)

FIG. 290 Marriage of Craft and Nature In its visual denseness, the Robert Blacker House seems fully rooted to the land. That attribute was even more prominent before its extensive rear garden was subdivided into housing lots.

FIGS. 291, 292 Creativity Trumps Size The Ernest Batchelder House attains a visual presence well out of proportion to its moderate size largely because of an inventive design and the richness of its integral crafts.

FIG. 293 The Inner Craftsman Craftsman houses did not necessarily look like Gamble or Blacker (previous pages). The architects of these two Craftsman classics also designed the Cordelia Culbertson House, with strongly Chinese overtones, not to mention a Spanish-Italian garden downhill. Such eclecticism aside, in its detailing and integration of art and crafts Culbertson is a mainstream Craftsman design.

FIG. 294 He-Man Bungalow Parsons Bungalow is so rugged and extroverted that it almost seems to have been lifted right out of a National Park.

FIG. 295 Prairie Bungalow Prairie architects Purcell, Feick & Elmslie produced the refined Buxton Bungalow. It differs somewhat in character and plan from typical Craftsman bungalows, but shares Craftsman ideals of modesty and emphasis on materials and details.

FIG. 296 Bungalows Everywhere Economical bungalows of visual distinction were built across the United States. This appealingly tactile house was located in a remote mining town in Northern Minnesota.

Cordelia Culbertson House FIG. 293

1911
Greene & Greene, architects
1188 Hillcrest Ave., Pasadena, California

"U" shaped in plan, like the Blacker House just across the street, the house is otherwise very different. The design is subtle and multifaceted: the public view from Hillcrest reveals little of its full nature. From the street it seems to be a large, low-slung California ranch house with Chinese overtones, on account of the green tile roof. No more than about a third of the entire house is visible from the street, nor were the elaborate rear terraces and Spanish-Italian garden, little of which now remain.

CRAFTSMAN BUNGALOWS

Parsons Bungalow FIG. 294

1910; moved and rebuilt, 1980
Arthur & Alfred Heineman, architects
1605 E. Altadena Dr. at Porter Ave., Altadena, California

Bungalow mandarin Robert Winter called this "simply one of the finest…bungalows to be found anywhere." Even for Southern California, Parsons is advanced well beyond the bungalow norm, with massively tactile boulder columns and powerful roof overhangs.

Keyes Bungalow

1911
1369 E. Boston St., Altadena, California

A so-called "airplane bungalow," on account of its spread-out floor plan and low-pitched roof with wide overhangs. To be effective and authentic, an expansive design like this needs a spacious property, which it once had. Now well-screened by vegetation, Keyes can barely be glimpsed from the street.

Buxton Bungalow FIG. 295

1912
Purcell, Feick & Elmslie, architects
424 E. Main St., Owatonna, Minnesota

As David Gebhard noted, the Buxton design is a radical revision in function, compared to a typical Midwestern bungalow plan, and was further transformed into an artistic expression by virtue of its intrinsic design qualities. Located only a few blocks from Louis Sullivan's famed bank (see the Progressives chapter), Buxton is a must-see for bungalow mavens. Note the delicate, Rest-a-While stencil worked into the front trim.

Bungalow FIG. 296

c. 1912
520 8½ St., Virginia, Minnesota

This modest bungalow is abstracted compared to typical Midwestern bungalows. A sweeping roof overhangs the full-width front porch; everything is simplified. To compensate visually, the mass of the house is covered by river boulders. The resulting composition is marvelous, both in its simplicity and for its countervailing rich texture.

BUNGALOW COURTS

Courtyard housing was especially popular in and around Los Angeles from the early 1900s up into the 1930s. This type was

FIG. 297 **Stylish in Pasadena** Bungalow courts were intended as modest-cost housing. Even so, the restored and updated Gartz Court fits in handsomely at its new location in a fashionable section of Pasadena.

expressed in a full range of imageries, from modern to Hansel-and-Gretel. Naturally, some of these were rendered as Craftsman bungalows. In fact, bungalow courts (not all of which were recognizably Craftsman-like) were even built throughout the Midwest in the 'teens and 1920s.

St. Francis Court in Pasadena (1909), designed by Sylvanus Marston, was the first American bungalow court. Unlike much courtyard housing, which was typically attached or semi-detached in plan, this court was developed from freestanding bungalows set on small lots lined up along a narrow central vehicular drive ending in a cul-de-sac.

St. Francis Court was subsequently razed, but other early Pasadena bungalow courts survive, including the Gartz and Bowen courts (following). Additional nearby bungalow courts can be found in at 567 and 572–574 N. Oakland Avenue.

Gartz Court FIG. 297
1910; moved and restored, 1984–1985
de Bretteville and Polyzoides, restoration architects
745 N. Pasadena Ave., Pasadena, California

Smartly dressed up in stucco and half-timbering, these bungalows seem like dapper English cottages. The de Bretteville and Polyzoides restoration is very successful; not only were the original structures returned to prime condition, but the architects devised new garages and rear patios that Robert Winter assures us, "You would swear were original."

Bowen Court FIG. 298
1910
Arthur & Alfred Heineman, architects
539 Villa St., Pasadena, California

FIG. 298 **Classic Bungalow Court** Bowen Court was an early model for the now-traditional layout with a landscaped inner court, this one now luxuriantly overgrown.

Like St. Francis Court, this development is composed of closely spaced freestanding bungalows. However, these units face onto a sidewalk rather than to a drive, like the earliest courts. This innovation led to the pedestrian-oriented internal courtyard, often lushly landscaped, which became the model for American courtyard housing. Today, Bowen Court's courtyard is romantically overgrown.

California

1900–1941

FIG. 299 California is a State of Mind More than a few Americans still think of California as an exotic, almost mythic place, a notion supported by impossibly beautiful natural features and amazing architecture like the Hearst Castle—this view is of its Neptune Pool. *Published with the permission of Hearst Castle®/California State Parks*

California is different. Because of its location, geography, climate, history, culture, and the fantasy of Hollywood, California seemed to be a distant, exotic land to pre–World War II America (Fig. 299).

Over the past century, California also seemed irresistibly attractive to many who needed somewhere to start over or were burning with unconventional ideas. These two groups shared the expectation that anything was possible in this magnificent state. Not surprisingly, many twentieth-century design innovations emerged in California.

California gradually entered into the mainstream of American life after the outbreak of war in the Pacific in 1941; other

FIG. 300 Synthesis of Sources and Function Bernard Maybeck's First Church of Christ, Scientist is a strikingly original synthesis of traditional visual expressions and contemporary use, especially its auditorium.

key events were the opening of Disneyland in 1955 and airline deregulation in 1978, which made the state more accessible to ordinary Americans. With the growing prominence of Silicon Valley by the 1980s, it became apparent that California was a heavyweight in the national economy.

A similar gradual dawning of appreciation occurred with California architecture. As recently as the 1960s, American college students taking the standard two-year architectural history sequence were offered as little as one or two class hours on California architecture. California was treated almost as a foreign country, efficiently summarized in a single book, Esther McCoy's *Five California Architects*.

We now recognize that California was not on the fringes of twentieth-century American architecture, but rather marked its epicenter. As a consequence, California architecture is prominent in several chapters in this book, including The International Style, Period Revivals, and Frank Lloyd Wright.

This chapter offers an illustrative collection of seminal twentieth-century California architectural designs up until the outbreak of the Second World War. This was a period of prolific creative invention in California architecture.

First Church of Christ, Scientist FIG. 300
1910–1912
Bernard Maybeck, architect
2619 Dwight Way, Berkeley, California

Part of the genius of American architecture is the tendency to synthesize a mix of visual traditions into completely fresh and functional expressions. Nowhere is that better illustrated than in this church, one of the most original designs of the twentieth century. The new Christian Science building program was relatively uncommon, and thus not strongly guided, much less constrained, by design traditions. Significantly for the design solution, the architect was presented with a rock-bottom construction budget.

Maybeck's design incorporated several influences, from Beaux Arts to Byzantine, from Gothic to Japanese. These are synthesized into a strikingly imaginative expression. Even more impressive, Maybeck necessarily achieved effect with the most utilitarian of materials: concrete, dimension lumber, cement board, and out-of-the-catalog steel windows.

The auditorium is simply superb, with an overall clarity of expression achieved through countless small design treatments. The ultimate wonder of Maybeck's design is how a building that is in some ways so moody can feel so exhilarating.

Palace of Fine Arts FIG. 175
1913–1915; rebuilt, 1965–1967
Bernard Maybeck, architect; **Welton Becket & Assoc.**, architects for rebuilding
Within Hwy. 101, Marina Blvd. and Baker St., San Francisco, California

See the Beaux Arts chapter.

La Jolla Women's Club FIG. 301
1913–1914
Irving Gill, architect
715 Silverado, La Jolla-San Diego, California

Gill was a progressive who had worked briefly for Louis Sullivan in the early 1890s. Just as the 1930s PWA Moderne style was a

FIG. 301 **Soft Modernism** Irving Gill's approach to Modernism retained vestiges of the past. As a result, buildings like his La Jolla Women's Club, softened by its rounded arcade openings, could seem comfortably contemporary without the starkness that often characterized International Style Modernism.

FIG. 302 **A View into the Future** The breathtakingly transparent Hallidie Building curtain wall predated postwar curtain walls by more than a generation.

FIG. 303 **Modest-cost Housing** Regardless of its International Style imagery, Horatio West Court is highly "American" in its efficient, functional invention.

kind of stripped-away classicism, so this building (like some others by Gill) reads as a kind of stripped-away Spanish Mission. The resulting smooth, white exterior, without a hint of parapets, still seems very modern.

Panama-California Exposition FIGS. 746, 747
1913–1915
Bertram G. Goodhue, architect
Balboa Park, San Diego, California

See the Fairs & Exhibitions chapter.

Walter Dodge House FIG. 394
1914–1916, razed, 1967
Irving Gill, architect
950 N. Kings Rd., Los Angeles, California

See The International Style chapter.

Hallidie Building FIG. 302
1915–1918
Willis Polk, architect
130 Sutter St., San Francisco, California

Every once in a while a building is so advanced as to be futuristic. Polk employed this full-blown suspended glass curtain wall three decades before Pietro Belluschi's Equitable Building in Portland (Fig. 412). The stunning transparency of the façade is enhanced by a delicate cast-iron filigree: the visual tension between past and future is nowhere more clearly demonstrated than here.

Horatio West Court FIG. 303
1919
Irving Gill, architect
140 Hollister, Santa Monica, California

Brilliantly innovative multi-unit housing, even more so given that it was originally intended for low-income tenants. Amazingly, Gill was able to fit four two-story townhouses onto this tiny lot, providing both community and privacy, plus additional storage, a garage, a tiled fireplace, and an outdoor patio for each unit. All this was accomplished in concrete, at a 2008 construction cost of just over $100,000 per unit.

La Cuesta Encantada, "Hearst Castle" FIGS. 299, 304
1919–1947
Julia Morgan, architect; **Charles Gibbs Adams**, landscape architect
Above Hwy. 1, San Simeon, California

Publisher William Randolph Hearst's "Enchanted Hill" has no equal save, perhaps, for Versailles. One cannot even begin to understand the many qualities of this vast and varied estate from its staggering statistics, or even from a single visit. The "Castle" (Fig. 304) is Morgan's inventive, multi-building assemblage of rooms, art, and furnishings shipped over from Europe. The property extended across 100,000 acres (Fig. 299), ranging in character from level oceanfront to steep foothills, stocked with exotic wild game. Hearst Castle is an essential American cultural destination.

Watts Towers FIG. 305
1921–1954
Simon Rodia, craft builder
1765 E. 107th St., Los Angeles, California

Surely this wondrous construction is one of the greatest works of American folk art. Rodia scavenged iron rebars, shards of tile, bottles, and other discards to construct his breathtaking latticework.

FIG. 304 **Thinking Like an Emperor** William Randolph Hearst thought big. His towering main house, "Casa Grande," at La Cuesta Encantada, "Hearst Castle," and ancillary buildings occupied only a tiny fraction of his 250,000-acre coastal estate. *Published with the permission of Hearst Castle®/California State Parks*

FIG. 305 **Native Creativity** Watts Towers are indigenous in several respects, including the self-acquired artistry of sculptor-builder-resident Rodia, the openness of Southern California culture to the off-beat, use of locally scavenged materials, and a mild climate that has extended the life of this singular work.

FIG. 306 **California In My Mind** Considering that the Aztec Hotel's architect was an educated English gentleman, one must seriously ponder the effect California can have on any of us.

FIG. 307 **Hip Hangout** While LA abounds with memorable hangouts, few were as famous in their day as the Brown Derby Café.

FIG. 308 **Sumptuous Far Beyond its Model** Numerous "Andalusian" mansions were built in prewar Los Angeles, most of them much more luxurious than anything (other than a Caliph's palace) you will come across in Moorish Spain. The Bourne House is among the best of this elite Southland cohort.

FIG. 309 **Studied Rusticity** William Wurster's Gregory Farm Group was devised to appear as if it were an assortment of working ranch structures. Succeeding at such artifice required consummate design skills. *Photograph © Marc Treib*

Lovell Beach House FIG. 396
1922–1926
Rudolph M. Schindler, architect
13th and Beach Walk, Newport Beach, California

See The International Style chapter.

Aztec Hotel FIG. 306
1925
Robert Stacy-Judd, architect
NW corner Foothill and Magnolia, Monrovia, California

California, especially the Los Angeles Southland, has long been considered as kind of crazy by some Americans. A building like this helps to explain why.

Brown Derby Café FIG. 307
1926, razed, 1994
3377 Wilshire Blvd., Los Angeles, California

Perhaps because Hollywood is a stage-set industry, the LA Southland has long been a breeding ground of programmatic architecture. The Brown Derby was probably the most famous of these and, alas, now it is lost.

Bourne House FIG. 308
1927
Wallace Neff, architect; **Katherine Bashford**, landscape architect
2035 Lombardy Rd., San Marino, California

Pre–World War II California was a hotbed of housing innovation, especially noted for the International Style, for Cliff May's ranch houses in the LA Southland, and for the so-called Bay Area Tradition in the north. However, there were also dozens of superb Period houses in both Northern and Southern California. The Andalusian Bourne House is one of the finest, even among its impressive neighbors along and near Lombardy Road in ultra-upscale San Marino.

Gregory Farm Group FIG. 309
1927
William W. Wurster, architect
Canham Rd. off Glenwood Dr., rural Santa Cruz, California (private, not visible from road)

Gregory was probably the most celebrated prewar California house—at least among architects. These structures were meant to evoke an unpretentious rural farmstead, although Wurster's carefully calculated simplicity elevated the ensemble to high art.

Paramount Theatre FIG. 310, 679, 680
1930–1931; converted, restored 1973
Timothy Pflueger, Miller & Pflueger, architects; **John M. Woodbridge, Skidmore, Owings & Merrill**, restoration architects
2025 Broadway, Oakland, California

Pflueger's suave Moderne exterior is just the warm-up for the interior experience, which is simply sensational. Among many striking California movie houses, Oakland's Paramount is arguably the most memorable.

Coca Cola Bottling Plant FIG. 311
1936–1937, altered
Robert V. Derrah, architect
1334 S. Central Ave., Los Angeles, California

The Streamline Moderne was especially prominent in California, with many highly sophisticated designs like the 1939 Maritime

FIG. 310 **Movie Star** California and movies go together like Fred and Ginger, though the state's star movie house was not in Hollywood, as one might expect, but all the way north in Oakland: the pretty much incomparable Paramount Theatre. The marvelous tiled marquee offers only a hint of what awaits inside (see the Movie Theaters chapter, Figs. 679, 680).

Museum on the San Francisco waterfront (Fig. 357). While this bottling plant is not superior architecture, the very idea of remodeling a block-long industrial complex to appear as an ocean liner could, without doubt, occur only in California.

Cliff May House, "Mandalay" FIGS. 198, 199, 200
1938–1939; remodeled, 1949; addition., 1983
Cliff May, architect
Old Ranch Rd., off Sunset Blvd., Brentwood, Los Angeles, California

See the American Colonial Revivals chapter.

FIG. 311 **Only in California** This ocean-going Coca Cola bottling plant offers yet another confirmation that California is indeed a state apart. *Carol M. Highsmith / Library of Congress, Prints & Photographs*

Period Revivals

1890–1972

FIGS. 312, 313 Tradition Twentieth-century Period Revival imageries were inspired by historic architecture, primarily the Gothic and classicist landmarks of Europe. Gothic was associated with high-mindedness and the spiritual, hence widely employed for churches and universities. The 1910–1912 Princeton Graduate College (Fig. 312), the work of leading American Gothicist Ralph Adams Cram, is a nationally significant example. Classicist architecture was understood to connote dignity and probity.

That all but guaranteed it would be the style of choice for civic buildings and banks. Even so, Classicism is not necessarily straight-laced. Creative designers can manipulate ordinary classicist vocabularies to great romantic effect, as in the 1912 Temple of the Wings (Fig. 313), designed by Bernard Maybeck and A. Randolph Monroe for a dramatic site in California's Berkeley Hills. (See also Maybeck's Palace of Fine Arts, Beaux Arts chapter, Fig. 175.)

Period Revival imageries differed from the contemporaneous American Colonial Revivals (see that chapter) in that these period expressions drew primarily from European, rather than from American sources. However, this is not a hard-and-fast taxonomy. For instance, although the garrison house type originally drew from English medieval models, it is universally considered to be "American Colonial."

Conversely, Mission Revival, supposedly based on Spanish colonial building in the Americas, is included here as a Period Revival style. Any classification system has its inconsistencies!

Like American Colonial Revivals styles, the Period Revival imageries cited here were prominently employed in three distinct residential situations. One is the Estate, a comprehensive setting, of which the house itself is only one (if still a major) part. Estates may include stylistically integrated farm groups (see the Rural Structures chapter), designed landscapes, and landscape features such as fountains, terraces, and extensive pergolas. When located on water, as they often are, the estate likely includes a boat house, commonly with a rooftop viewing deck, rather than merely a dock.

The second situation is the Affluent Property. These are also architect-designed, and may be architecturally significant. But they lack the elaborate ancillary facilities of the typical estate.

The third situation is the Custom Home, usually part of a multi-lot development. Some of these are architect-designed. While a step below affluent properties, custom homes can be impressive designs. Compared to affluent properties, a custom home is smaller, set on a much smaller lot, and generally less developed in detail in everything from landscaping to interior trim. Nonetheless, it is often very attractive, typically located in upscale subdivisions.

This chapter closes the Period Revivals with the death of Edwin Lundie in 1972. This date is both symbolic and useful, similar to ending the American Colonial Revivals chapter with the death of Royal Barry Wills in 1962. Of course, the employment of derivative styles has continued right up to the present. But with the deaths of these two master architects, distinct eras had clearly ended.

References to tradition, to past imageries, continued on after Lundie's death, prominently in three different versions.

One of these was Postmodernism, typically characterized in the United States by an unknowing application of traditional imageries (see the Postmodernism chapter).

The second was a knowing restatement of the Past, which can be thought of as Neotraditionalism (see the Neotraditionalism chapter).

The third has been the design of developers' tract houses, which have only rarely been of high architectural interest.

MISSION REVIVAL HOUSES

Crocker Row FIG. 314
1894–1895
A. Page Brown, architect
2010, 2016, 2024, 2044, 2052 Garden, Santa Barbara, California

As befitting Santa Barbara, these speculative houses are grander than the typical Mission Revival house. As an ensemble, they offer a showcase for Mission residential design. Another handsome early mission design, the Hopkins House (1897), is located a block away at the northeast corner of Garden & Pedregosa.

House
1915
515 E. Chapman, Fullerton, California

A very strong mission image, with the requisite sculpted parapet. The Islamic arcade over the front entry suggests that the designer intended for the house to read as exotic.

ENGLISH MEDIEVAL REVIVAL HOUSES

Roos House FIG. 315
1909, 1926
Bernard Maybeck, architect
3500 Jackson St., San Francisco, California

Most American "Tudor" designs are characterized by asymmetri-

FIG. 314 **California Mission Revival** As a rule, Mission buildings tended to look a bit thin, but that is not the case with the substantial houses of Crocker Row (two of the five on this Santa Barbara block illustrated here). In these early expressions of the imagery, Mission features were applied to otherwise conventional houses. As the Mission style proliferated, scalloped parapets would become characteristic.

cal plans and decorative half-timbering. Maybeck went well beyond these basics. Inside and out, Roos is a highly personal interpretation of the Medieval, from massing to spaces to details to materials. The magnificent 30-foot-high Living Hall (see Woodbridge and Barnes, 1992, p. 134) seems like a domestic version of a guild hall, except that guild halls didn't enjoy a glorious view of the Golden Gate.

Frank Seiberling Estate, "Stan Hywet Hall" FIGS. 316, 317
1911–1915
Charles Sumner Schneider, George B. Post & Sons, architects; **Warren H. Manning**, landscape architect; **Ellen Biddle Shipman**, landscape architect for English Garden; **Hugo F. Huber**, interiors; **Samuel Yellin**, ironwork
714 N. Portage Path, Akron, Ohio (open)

If you were a founder of Goodyear Tire Company and your product line showed staggering increases in growth due to the recent auto craze, you'd have some leftover cash available to build a cozy, 65-room house on an ample, 3,000-acre property. Of course, given your social position, this undertaking would have to be a dignified affair, requiring prominent designers, an extensive pre-design study

FIG. 315 **Highly Personal Interpretation** American designs based on European precedents have typically synthesized traditional forms into a new version of the old. Bernard Maybeck took that process one giant step farther for his Roos House design, a fresh and highly personal interpretation of English Medieval architecture.

FIGS. 316, 317 **Tudor Revival—and Then Some** The Frank Seiberling Estate, "Stan Hywet Hall" may be physically located in Ohio, but it is clearly grounded in Medieval England, except that no Tudor mansion was as luxuriously appointed within—or as

meticulously groomed without. *Library of Congress, Prints & Photographs, Historic American Buildings Survey*

tour of Medieval English mansions, and the procurement of authentic period furnishings, stained glass, and other artifacts. The grounds would necessarily include a Japanese garden.

For Frank Seiberling, this was not the pipe dream it would be for the rest of us. He and his wife spent nearly a decade, from initial land acquisition to completion, diligently carrying though on their quest. Now that the estate is open to visitors, you can see for yourself just how successful they were.

Rothman House

1926

Paul R. Williams, architect

541 Rossmore Ave., Los Angeles, California

A more conventional expression of Tudor than Roos or Stan Hywet. It features plenty of half-timbering and an Elizabethan chimney. The image is stately without seeming dull.

Stuart Duncan House, "Bonniecrest"

1912–1914, converted to condos, grounds altered and infilled, gated

John Russell Pope, architect

1111 Harrison Ave., Newport, Rhode Island

FIG. 318 **Architect's Dream House** George Howe's own house, "High Hollow" is a brilliant study. Each design element from its approach to its surface textures is integrated to great effect. *The Work of Mellor Meigs & Howe, 1923*

Compton Wynyates in Wiltshire (1520) was the reputed model for Bonniecrest, although Pope's design was replete with plan and style innovations, including a 200-foot gallery which exploited views and breezes from Newport's harbor, just below. In lesser hands, all of the projections, colors and textures could have led to a visual debacle, but Pope deftly pulled it off, with a design described by Steven McLeod Bedford as "controlled elegance."

Subsequent condominiumization has almost, but not quite, obscured the original house from public view. You can best appreciate Pope's design from an original portion, which is especially prominent in morning sunlight, seen from the west gate along Harrison.

NORMAN REVIVAL HOUSES

George Howe House, "High Hollow" FIG. 318

1914–1917; alterations, 1928–1929

George Howe, architect

101 W. Hampton Rd., Chestnut Hill, Philadelphia, Pennsylvania

George Howe is surely among the most underappreciated American architects of the twentieth century, as one can understand from this design for his own family, set on a pleasantly secluded site within the Philadelphia city limits.

Architect and Howe biographer Robert A. M. Stern noted that although the basic scheme draws from Howe's design thesis at the Ecole des Beaux Arts, and thus is at least nominally French, it has strong Italian sensibilities, reminiscent in some ways of the Villa d'Este at Tivoli, and in others of the Villa Madama. And yet, like Jefferson's Monticello, High Hollow is ultimately an American expression: it is difficult to pin down as of any specific European lineage.

Although from a distance the house seems appropriately restrained for Philadelphia sensibilities, up close it is almost tactile; the rear wall of the main house, overlooking the lower garden terrace is a disciplined riot of stone textures.

Those who know of Howe only through his PSFS tower downtown (see The International Style chapter) might be surprised by the architect's consummate skill as a period designer.

Arthur Newbold Estate FIG. 319, 596

1921–1928; razed

Arthur Meigs, Mellor, Meigs & Howe, architects

Laverock, Whitemarsh Valley, Pennsylvania

Newbold was perhaps the definitive Philadelphia rural estate, developed as a French manor. The house had been built in 1914 by another architect, for another owner, as American Colonial. Transformation of this property into an imaginary French country domain began with the construction of a farm group (Fig. 596), including the requisite prominence of barnyard animals, and an ample kitchen garden. Then the original house was encased in stone to complete the makeover, which was a social success commensurate with its architecture: the Newbold Estate appeared on the cover of *Country Life* while its stylistic transformation was still underway.

Edgar J. Kaufmann House, "La Tourelle" FIG. 320
1923–1925
Benno Janssen, Janssen & Cocken, architects; **Albert D. Taylor**, landscape architect; **Chamberlin Dodds**, interiors; **Samuel Yellin**, ironwork
8 La Tourelle Ln., Fox Chapel (Aspinwall vic.), Pennsylvania

Mention "the Kaufmann House," and most people interested in architecture will think of Frank Lloyd Wright's incomparable Fallingwater (Fig. 252). Mavens will also know that Richard Neutra designed Edgar Kaufmann's "Desert House" in Palm Springs (Fig. 404). Before those two, however, Kaufmann commissioned this house, his domicile in suburban Pittsburgh.

La Tourelle—named after its diminutive, witch's-hat entry tower—shows a passing resemblance to Janssen's Longue Vue Club (later in this chapter), which was under construction as design began on this house. Both have massive end chimneys, unadorned masonry walls of handmade bricks for the house, and steep, "Cotswold" slate roofs. Despite its substantial size and visual solidity, there is an engaging, dollhouse quality to the exterior of La Tourelle. Interiors are fitted out in a rich palette of woods and stone; Yellin's ornamental ironwork provides fanciful counterpoints throughout. While little expense seems to have been spared, the house and especially the interiors are reserved rather than opulent.

Hunt House FIG. 321
1931
Frank Joseph Forster, architect
2600 Spirit Knob Rd., Woodland, Minnesota

This affluent property is in its design and social-economic status one level down from the likes of the Newbold estate. Nevertheless, Hunt is a splendid home on a spacious property overlooking Lake Minnetonka. The house is large though not rambling, with full but understated decoration inside and out, especially in the high-space living room. Many American French-Norman residential designs included a prominent curved element, usually enclosing a stair or entry, and that is indeed a signature element of Forster's design.

ITALIAN RENAISSANCE REVIVAL HOUSES

James Deering Estate, "Vizcaya" FIG. 322
1915–1916
Paul Chalfin, design director; **F. Burrell Hoffman, Jr.**, architect;
Elise de Wolfe, interior designer
3251 S. Miami Ave., Miami, Florida (open)

Italian Renaissance estates in the U.S., like their putative fifteenth-century models, were commonly distinct from other Mediterranean styles in two respects: one was an imaginative, as opposed to academic, employment of design precedent; the other was that house and garden were usually approached as two elements of a single,

FIG. 319 Country Life Arthur Meigs skillfully transformed Arthur Newbold's American Colonial house into a *faux* Norman estate. The result was a great architectural and social success, gracing the cover of the nation's elite publication for the seriously rich. *The Work of Mellor Meigs & Howe, 1923*

FIG. 320 The *First* Kaufmann House On first impression, Benno Janssen's design evokes the almost rude directness of historic Cotswold houses. As fully experienced, the Edgar J. Kaufmann House, "La Tourelle," is even more memorable for the quality of its details.

FIG. 321 The Appeal of Norman "French Norman" imageries were popular among affluent Americans throughout the pre–World War II period. The noble beauty of Frank Joseph Forster's Hunt House illustrates why.

FIG. 322 **Renaissance, in Effect** To a fifteenth-century Florentine aristocrat, the James Deering Estate, "Vizcaya," would be unrecognizable as a Renaissance palazzo. But in Miami, effect is often accomplished through splashy gestures, and that is more than sufficient here. The prow of Vizcaya's marvelous stone barge is visible through the right archway.

FIG. 323 **Scaled-down Palazzo** Frederick Ackerman's Elizabeth Quinlan House provides a grace note of urbanity in its Minneapolis neighborhood of handsome Period Revival homes.

comprehensive scheme. Both of these attributes are apparent at Vizcaya. While the house and its gardens are both handsomely developed, the stone barge/breakwater "floating" just offshore in Biscayne Bay provides Vizcaya's memorable design feature.

Edward Inman "Swan" House
1926–1928
Philip Trammell Shutze, architect
130 W. Paces Ferry Rd. NW., Atlanta, Georgia (open)

Compared to Vizcaya, the Swan House is reticent, graceful as opposed to theatrical. Here also, historical precedents are employed imaginatively more than correctly, and the house is integral with its formal setting on a very ample property. The superior design qualities of this house are even more apparent in comparison to nearby grandiose mansions in this well-heeled Buckhead section of Atlanta.

FIG. 326 Perfection in Paradise Smith's Lindley House is a superior example of the traditional estate houses found in Santa Barbara's ultra-upscale suburb of Montecito. Ensconced behind walls on expansive, magnificently landscaped properties, such houses are often showcased through gateways at the public road.

FIGS. 324, 325 American Andalusian George Washington Smith's abstracted imagery, represented here by his Heberton House (Fig. 324), was realized in Santa Barbara in a far more luxurious state than is typical of farmhouses in Moorish Spain (Fig. 325), inspiration for the Andalusian version of the Spanish Colonial Revival.

Elizabeth Quinlan House FIG. 323

1924

Frederick Ackerman, architect

1711 Emerson Ave. S., Minneapolis, Minnesota

The familiar Italian Renaissance palazzo model was abstracted here to upper-class American sensibilities, and scaled down to fit a tight urban lot. Quinlan is a remarkably refined design, including an unexpected rear exterior *cortile*-courtyard, hidden from public view.

ANDALUSIAN REVIVAL HOUSES

Heberton House FIG. 324

1918

George Washington Smith, architect

240 Middle Rd., Montecito, California

This house by Smith for himself, sold to Craig Heberton in 1920, formed the basis for his reputation as a peerless interpreter of Andalusian imageries (Fig. 325), thus providing a model for American Andalusian expressions in Santa Barbara and elsewhere. The house was placed close to the road in order to provide additional privacy for an extensive formal garden at the back.

Lindley House FIG. 326

1919

George Washington Smith, architect

779 Hot Springs, Montecito, California

Smith's first design commission, Lindley was rendered as "Italian," though similar to his Andalusian formula. The property is dis-

FIGS. 327, 328 Surpassing Quality An extraordinarily sophisticated integration of architecture, landscape, interiors, and its Montecito setting, the George Steedman House, "Casa del Herrero," presents an ultimate expression of the American Andalusian style.

creetly closed off from the road by a high wall and lush landscaping; an intriguing glimpse of the house is provided through the motor court entrance.

George Steedman House, "Casa del Herrero" FIGS. 327, 328

1922–1925

George Washington Smith, architect; **Ralph Stevens, Peter Reidel**, garden designers; **Francis Townsend Underhill**, landscape architect, south lawn; **Lockwood de Forest, Jr.**, later landscape modifications

1387 East Valley Rd., Montecito, California (open by advance appointment; see house website)

Arguably the finest Spanish Colonial Revival residence in America, the Steedman House is an inventive translation of Andalusian precedents. The house is set on an expansive property, backed by mountains to the north while facing toward the ocean off to the south.

FIG. 329 **Palm Beach, South Ocean Boulevard** Mansions of the Palm Beach

FIGS. 330, 331 **Society Counts** Palm Beach and Santa Barbara are the American centers of Spanish/Mediterranean imageries. These styles were expressed very differently in the two communities. For Santa Barbara's Andalusian expressions, architectural sophistication and reticence ruled, inside and out. By contrast, as Marjorie Merriweather Post's Mar-a-Lago demonstrates, not only did Palm Beach Mediterranean houses often ramble across their sites (Compare Fig. 330 to the Heberton, Lindley, and Steedman houses, Figs. 324, 326, 327, 328), but their aggressively showy interiors could put a Venetian palace to shame, as one can see in Mrs. Post-Hutton's living room. *Library of Congress, Prints & Photographs, Historic American Buildings Survey*

Planning developed around the outdoor spaces, producing interconnections between inside and outside. Interiors were furnished as Spanish, with antiques whenever possible and superior reproductions when not. Architecture, interiors, landscaping, and setting achieve a magnificent complete expression that was surely never realized for private houses in Andalusia (Fig. 325).

MEDITERRANEAN REVIVAL HOUSES

Willey Kingsley House, "La Bellucia"
1920
Addison Mizner, architect
1200 S. Ocean Blvd., Palm Beach, Florida

Relatively typical in scale and luxury for Mizner's oceanfront Palm Beach houses, this design is based on a series of plan offsets intended to maximize the capture of cooling breezes. As a result, especially from the landside approach, the house seems a jumble of unrelated stuccoed forms. Yet this ingenious plan provides a memorable sequence of indoor and outdoor spaces.

Marjorie Merriweather Post (Mrs. E. F. Hutton) Mansion, "Mar-a-Lago" FIGS. 330, 331
1923–1927
Marion Sims Wyeth, architect; **Joseph Urban**, interior designer; **Lewis & Valentine**, landscape architects; **Franz Barwig**, sculptor
1100 S. Ocean Blvd., Palm Beach, Florida (now a membership club)

Mar-a-Lago illustrates how Old Money is spent differently from that of the merely super-rich. This begins with the choice of an architect. While Addison Mizner was much more prominent, then and now, Wyeth was a Princeton Man, with Ecole des Beaux Arts training, and of course, a gentleman, not an adventurer-salesman like Mizner. Considering the scarcity and desirability of prime Palm Beach property, the estate is vast, overlooking both the Atlantic Ocean and Lake Worth, with room for a 9-hole golf course amidst all of the building and landscaping.

The house is surely impressive—how could it not be, with construction site dimensions of about 600 x 300 feet?—but not gaudy on the exterior. The grandeur was largely kept inside. Urban was a nationalknown designer of stage sets, interiors, and whole buildings; his interiors here are unsurprisingly a design tour-de-force. An apparently unlimited budget was available for European materials and decorative arts—and newly commissioned artwork—under the gold-leafed ceilings. Mrs. Post-Hutton's extensive collection of antique Spanish tiles was worked into the new construction. She could overlook it all, no doubt with unbounded satisfaction, from her 75-foot-high observation tower.

MISCELLANEOUS REVIVALS IN HOUSES

John Ringling Mansion, "Cà d'Zan" FIG. 332
1924–1926; estate restoration, 1992–2002
Mabel Ringling, design impresaria; **Dwight James Baum**, supervising architect
5401 Bay Shore Rd. / Tamiami Trail / Hwy. 41, Sarasota, Florida (open)

The "House of John" (in Venetian dialect) is a classic owner-asarchitect fantasy: Mrs. Ringling called the shots for this wintering home of the famed circus magnate. Two favorite hotels in Venice served as her inspirational departure point. If the result is not superb architecture, it is nonetheless a marvelous collage of exotic motifs, colors, and textures, now fully restored and awaiting your visit.

FIG. 332 **Florida Fancy** The John Ringling Mansion, "Cà d' Zan," is a sparkling personal fantasy, surely successful largely because of Mrs. Ringling's determined insouciance.

Worrell "Zuni" House FIG. 333
1926
Robert Stacy-Judd, architect
710 Adelaide Dr., Santa Monica, California

Nearly every imaginable past architectural imagery seems to have been employed somewhere in America. Many of these are visual disasters, or worse, simply trite. But the English-born Stacy-Judd was able to work from exotic themes—chiefly Mayan—and transform them into amazing buildings. The Aztec Hotel in Monrovia, California was his most famous design (Fig. 306). This house followed the next year in a kind of Pueblo Revival imagery. Gebhard and Winter commented that it is "more fantastic the longer you look at it."

La Cuesta Encantada, "Hearst Castle"
1919–1947
Julia Morgan, architect; **Charles Gibbs Adams**, landscape architect
Above Hwy. 1, San Simeon, California (open)

See the California chapter.

FIG. 333 **Ostensibly Pueblo Revival** Zuni Pueblo (see Indigenous Cutures chapter) and Santa Monica are physically less than 600 miles apart. Architecturally, the ancient pueblo and the highly stylized Worrell "Zuni" House are clearly a world apart.

FIG. 334 **Edwin Lundie's "Indigenous" Imagery** Lundie began a design with a traditional image in mind, which was inevitably transformed into a personal expression. This utility structure on the North Shore of Lake Superior started in design as "Scandinavian" and ended as "Lundie."

FIG. 335 **Reflecting Site and Client** Edwin Lundie's Norman Slade Retreat is rugged enough to hold its own visually on an awesome Lake Superior site. As a counterbalance, this ruggedness is held in check by an architectural polish which signals the cultural sophistication of the client family.

FIG. 336 **Meticulous Moderation** Lundie and his wealthy clients shared a determination to avoid the appearance of unseemly pretentiousness. Hence, Lundie's estate houses were typically broken down in scale. The architect then worked exhaustively through virtually every detail—like this remarkably refined barbecue for the Harold Sweatt House, "Thistledor"—sometimes taking years to complete a full set of working drawings.

FIG. 337 **Country Life** Even when Modernism achieved dominance in the postwar years, many genteel clients continued to favor traditional architecture. Lundie's 1960 Daniel Gainey Estate house in Minnesota is certainly among the most distinguished late Period Revival homes.

EDWIN H. LUNDIE HOUSES

One occasionally encounters architects who have so personalized their designs that they represent a style in and of themselves. Some of these are universally known: Palladio, Wren, Wright, and LeCorbusier. Others are not well-known because they are regional, or because they are not interested in publicity.

St. Paul architect Edwin Hugh Lundie (1886–1972) designed more than 300 projects throughout his career. Although his clients virtually defined the Upper Midwestern aristocracy, Lundie is still little known, in large part because few of his best buildings are accessible to the public, and also because he respected his clients' desire for privacy.

Lundie worked from Northern European and American Colonial models, but by the time a design was finished, it had acquired a distinct "Lundie" imagery, and the initial historical imagery by then seemed little more than a suggestion (Fig. 334).

Lundie literally studied every square inch of his houses, inside and out. It was not unusual for him to spend several years endlessly designing and redesigning a single projects— sometimes weeks spent on a single piece of furniture. Stories of finally taking drawings right off his boards and building them are common among Lundie clients, who nevertheless speak of his work for them with reverence.

Among architects who knew Lundie, his pencil renderings were legendary.

Norman Slade Retreat FIG. 335
1939–1942
Edwin H. Lundie, architect
Hwy. 61, Little Marais vic., Minnesota (not visible from highway)

A very large stone lakeshore retreat for the descendant family of rail baron James J. Hill. As was typical of Lundie, the perceptual scale was minimized, in this situation by setting the house into a downhill slope, so that on approach the house seems much smaller than it does from the rear, Lake Superior elevation, which is rarely seen by anyone other than ore-boat crews passing well offshore.

Slade's visual imagery is sometimes described as "Scandinavian" or "North Woods," but is ultimately an amalgam distilled into Lundie's singular expressions. Each bedroom follows a subtly unique visual theme, down to the design of light switch plates.

Harold Sweatt House, "Thistledor" FIG. 336

1944–1955; substantial later additions
Edwin H. Lundie, architect
S end of Brackett's Point Rd., Orono, Minnesota (private estate, visible from the lake)

Like the Slade Retreat (above) this large house is broken down in scale, this time by fragmenting the program into multiple-gabled, Cape Cod-like forms (Fig. 336). While designing it over a number of years, Lundie worked through several recognizable Period styles before ending up with this unclassifiable imagery. Sweatt commands a spectacular peninsular setting, surrounded by Lake Minnetonka on three sides.

Daniel Gainey Estate FIG. 337

1960; later conference-center expansion, exterior accessible to the public
Edwin H. Lundie, architect
W side of Cedar St./Cty. 45, S of Hwy. 14, Owatonna, Minnesota

Gainey, like Sweatt (above), is broken down into several engaged masses in order to reduce the structure's apparent scale. Lundie was comparatively parsimonious with interior space: his estate homes were always ample in size and volume but never oversized and grandiose. Extensive use of paneling and wood trim further humanized his interiors.

PERIOD REVIVAL ENCLAVES

Enclaves of Period Revival houses can be found in and around virtually every major American city. In mid-sized cities like Kansas City and Minneapolis, some of these enclaves are located within the city proper.

More typically in older, big cities, the most cohesive Period Revival developments are suburban, a situation dating from 1889 with the founding of Bronxville in Westchester County, just outside of New York City.

Country Club in Kansas City is a classic Period Revival development, though because it extends over several square miles and effectively two states, it is not easy to appreciate in a single visit (see the Community Development chapter).

The most visually cohesive traditional subdivision in Kansas City is an American Colonial Revival development (1901–1910) in the Rockhill neighborhood, defined by 46th, Pierce, and Locusts Streets, and Troost Avenue.

The Country Club development in suburban Minneapolis is cited below as a convenient representative of pre–World War II custom homes, both Period Revival and American Colonial Revival. Edina Country Club was influenced by its namesake in Kansas City, but differs in its much smaller lots, with 550 houses located on a quarter-section of land.

Country Club FIGS. 338, 339

1921–1940s
Liebenberg & Kaplan, primary architects
Within Sunnyside and Country Club Rds., Arden Ave., and Minnehaha Creek, Edina, Minnesota

FIGS. 338, 339 Builders' Houses The pre–World War II American upper middle class valued both Period and American Colonial Revival imageries. These builders' houses in Edina's Country Club subdivision were based on a handful of stock plans, which were personalized through numerous small variations.

Thorpe Brothers Real Estate developed Country Club in two distinct sections. From Wooddale Avenue west, houses were to be at least two stories in height and cost at least $750,000 in 2008 dollars. Along the four "alphabet" streets to the east, houses were to be at least story-and-a-half, and cost at least $500,000 in 2008 dollars to build and landscape. As one step below affluent properties, and two beneath estates, these houses were architecturally less pretentious. That was not necessarily bad. While many of the houses are architecturally unexceptional, others are quite free in interpretation of their putative models, presenting fresh, handsome architectural expressions.

Among the most interesting are a French Norman at 4612 Edgebrook Place; an English Tudor next door at 4610 Browndale; and American Colonial Revivals at 4514 Moorland, 4604 Edina Boulevard, and 4504 Sunnyside Road.

For an insight into the evolution of a given style over the twentieth century, compare the Early Georgian at 4505 Wooddale (2000, Mulfinger & Susanka/SALA architects) with the 1920s house based on the same historical floor plan, next door to the south.

Country Club has been subject to continuous remodelings and, especially since the 1990s, expansive additions. A few of these have been visually quite creative. Perhaps the best transformation has been at 4601 Browndale, where a boxy Spanish house was doubled in size without injury to the neighborhood's scale, and with a definite improvement in its architecture.

FIG. 340 Early Mission Burlingame's railroad station illustrates the appealing informality of the first Mission Revival designs, before the style became ossified by convention. *Library of Congress, Prints & Photographs, Historic American Buildings Survey*

FIGS. 341, 342 Extreme Mission Designed and redesigned over the course of three decades, Glenwood Mission Inn evolved from a fairly straightforward Mission Revival expression into a fabulous visual confection.

NON-RESIDENTIAL MISSION REVIVAL

Southern Pacific Railroad Station FIG. 340

1894; addition, 1909

George B. Howard, J. B. Matthews, architects

Burlingame Ave. at California Dr., Burlingame, California

Burlingame's station is one of the first two permanent Mission Revival buildings in California, inspired by A. Page Brown's Mission-style California Pavilion at the 1893 World's Columbian Exposition in Chicago. In it, we thus see how early Mission, especially as practiced in California, was a loose, creative assortment of references, before the style largely devolved into convention, especially outside of California (as in the Loring Park Pavilion, below).

Glenwood Mission Inn FIGS. 341, 342

1902–1931; essentially completed by 1944

Arthur B. Benton, Myron Hunt, Elmer Grey, G. Stanley Wilson, architects

Main, Orange, 6th & 7th Sts., Riverside, California

This immense, wondrous hotel illustrates the evolution of Hispanic imageries over a three-decade development period. The design began as conventional Mission Revival, then was worked through variations of the Spanish Colonial Revival during later redesigns, ending up on the rooftop (below) as a brilliant fantasy of imaginary Hispanic. If you find yourself anywhere near this part of Southern California, a visit—if not a stay—is absolutely mandatory!

Loring Park Pavilion
1906

W of Willow St., N of 15th Street, Minneapolis, Minnesota

A checklist of archetypical Mission Revival convention: light planar walls, arched openings, scalloped end parapets, and quatrefoil windows. The simplicity and delicate scale of this small building are most authentically Mission: the mature, conventional Mission.

While Mission Revival is culturally plausible in Southern California, it also works as an unexpected (if it is rarely employed) visual counterpoint in northern climes. Still, the Mission style was rarely imaginatively expressed outside of California.

NON-RESIDENTIAL GOTHIC REVIVAL

Woolworth Building
1911–1913

Cass Gilbert, architect

233 Broadway, New York, New York

Dubbed "The Cathedral of Commerce" because of its Gothic imagery, this building resembles its Medieval stylistic ancestors in more than just architectural imagery. In its striking verticality and structural innovations, it is very "Gothic" indeed. At nearly 800 feet in height, the Woolworth Building was until 1930 the tallest building in the world.

St. Thomas Church FIG. 343
1905–1914

Cram, Goodhue & Ferguson, architects; reredos by
Bertram G. Goodhue, Lee Lawrie

NW corner Fifth Ave. and 53rd St., New York, New York

The St. Thomas design generated intense disagreements between Ralph Adams Cram and Bertram Goodhue, leading to the withdrawal of Goodhue from the partnership in 1913, just before the church opened. Although we will never know exactly who did what, the general scheme marked by an asymmetrical plan is Cram's, while Goodhue was mostly responsible for the rich detailing, notably the breathtaking altar screen-reredos—you *must* experience the thrilling nave-chancel space! Despite the regrettable artistic animosities between the two designers over seven years of design and construction (1906–1913), the church as built is superb, impressive even for Manhattan.

Harkness Memorial Quadrangle, now Saybrook and Branford Colleges, Yale University FIGS. 344, 345
1917–1921; reconfigured, 1930–1933

James Gamble Rogers, architect; **Beatrix Jones Ferrand**, landscape architect; **Lee Lawrie**, sculptor

S. of Elm St. between York and High Sts., Yale University, New Haven, Connecticut

Easily located by its soaring, 216-foot tower, Harkness is the ultimate devised Medieval, "Collegiate Gothic" environment in the United States, a suitably pictorial reference to the colleges of Oxford and Cambridge. Katherine Solomonson noted that Rogers (1867–1946) introduced "planned inconsistencies" into his design in order to introduce the illusion that the quadrangle had developed over time.

Chicago Tribune Tower FIG. 346
1922–1925

Howells & Hood, architects

435 N. Michigan Ave., Chicago, Illinois

Then and even still now, the Tribune Tower (right-center, Fig. 346) is more than just a building, wrapped up as it was in the personal-

FIG. 343 The Timeless Power of Gothic St. Thomas Church overshadows much larger nearby Midtown Manhattan buildings through sheer emotive force.

FIGS. 344, 345 James Gamble Rogers at Yale Rogers functioned as Yale's campus architect between the World Wars, developing a campus plan (1920–1922) while building and revising residential quads. Rogers's design skills were not overly constrained by correctness. Here we see two views of his Davenport College (1930–1933), where the streetscape (Fig. 344) is expressed in harmony with the Collegiate Gothic employed for adjacent Yale colleges while the inner quadrangle (Fig. 345) is rendered in the current fashion, American Colonial Revival, an imagery that introduced a timely allusion to Yale's colonial New England history.

FIG. 346 **World's Greatest Competition** Robert McCormick, owner of the self-described "World's Greatest Newspaper," the Chicago Tribune, adroitly hyped his 1922 competition for a new office and printing plant. The Chicago Tribune Tower (center-right) and the Wrigley Building across the street (1920–1924, Graham, Anderson, Probst & White, at left) provide a spectacular gateway to the "Magnificent Mile" of North Michigan Avenue, especially when lit at night.

ity of Chicago Tribune owner "Colonel" Robert McCormick, the hype surrounding the international competition for its design, and a self-proclaimed status as "The World's Greatest Newspaper." The Tribune Company's 1923 publication, *Tribune Tower Competition*, provides a remarkably complete snapshot of European and American design in the post–World War I era. Many observers regret that Eliel Saarinen's superb National Romantic design, which placed second (Fig. 384), was not chosen.

FIG. 347 **Awareness of its Context** Bertram Goodhue's Hartley Office Building design recalls enough English Tudor to appear respectable—but not so much as to seem too pretentious for Duluth.

NON-RESIDENTIAL TUDOR/LATE GOTHIC REVIVAL

Hartley Office Building FIG. 347
1914
Bertram G. Goodhue, architect
740 E. Superior St., Duluth, Minnesota

Hartley generally reads as English Gothic, although Goodhue's design has abstracted away the expected ornamental detail to the point that it is as much Midwestern as it is English. When you visit, be sure to take note of Cram's and Goodhue's 1912 Kitchi Gammi Club, kitty-corner across Superior Street.

Tudor City
1925–1928
Fred B. French Co., H. Douglas Ives, architects
E. 40th to E. 43rd sts, between First and Second Aves., New York, New York

Here is "Tudor" on a scale rarely achieved in England beyond Hampton Court. Medieval quotes were applied to more than a dozen apartment buildings, tall and low, organized around private open spaces.

NON-RESIDENTIAL
NORMAN REVIVAL

Longue Vue Club   FIGS. 348, 349
1921–1925; golf course, 1920
Benno Janssen, Janssen & Cocken, architects; **Ralph E. Griswold**,
landscape architect; **Robert White**, golf course architect
400 Longue Vue Dr., off Nadine-Lincoln Rds. and Oakwood Rd., Verona
(Penn Hills), Pennsylvania

The club is visually sublime. It occupies a high promontory commanding long views across the Allegheny River valley, incorporating nearly twice the property acreage required for a championship-length, 18-hole golf course.

Janssen's biographer Donald Miller categorized the architecture as Norman by way of the English architect Edwin Lutyens. Yet even that rarefied accolade cannot fully convey its visual qualities. Despite functional ingenuity in plan, and a beautifully landscaped property, Janssen's architecture is the star attraction. Massive blunt chimneys provide a memorable arrival image; the exquisite stonework is equally impressive (Fig. 349). Thin slabs of warm gray stone are set off by contrasting white mortar. Strong horizontality of the stone courses is softened by voussoir heads at openings and archways. If Golf were Divine, God would no doubt be a member here.

NON-RESIDENTIAL
ENGLISH GEORGIAN REVIVAL

Music Corporation of America Building   FIG. 350
1940
Paul R. Williams, architect
Burton Way between Crescent and Rexford Drives, Beverly Hills, California

Pretty much what Christopher Wren might have done, had he practiced architecture in Southern California just before the Second World War. In the knowing estimation of Gebhard and Winter, the architect "fully understood the Georgian mode" in developing a design that was "traditional, modern, and California."

NON-RESIDENTIAL
ITALIAN RENAISSANCE

Racquet and Tennis Club   FIG. 351
1918
McKim, Mead & White, architects
370 Park Ave., 52nd to 53rd Sts., New York, New York

Unlike many American Italian Renaissance buildings, this one really seems to have been lifted right out of mid-1400s Florence. Although the firm's eponymous design principals had long been dead by the time of its design, the Racquet Club is consummately composed and detailed, standing among the firm's best work.

FIGS. 348, 349 Totally Beautiful Everything about Longue Vue Club is perfect, from its immaculately maintained grounds to the glorious clubhouse stonework.

FIG. 350 Creative Synthesis The Music Corporation of America Building in Beverly Hills is a disarmingly skillful design. Its overall historic imagery imparts a sense of traditional dignity; yet because it was abstracted in detail, the building seems quite modern compared to its more literal Period Revival and American Colonial Revival contemporaries. MCA's portico and cupola establish a monumentality that is softened by subtle diminutions of scale, employing proportional tricks that would later be used to great effect along Main Street at Disneyland.

FIG. 351 Suitably Imposing A palazzo offered just the right image for New York's Racquet and Tennis Club, which catered to business nobility. Through unanticipated good fortune, Mies van der Rohe's Seagram plaza was later built right across the street, further enhancing the club's already premier setting.

NON-RESIDENTIAL
SPANISH / MEDITERRANEAN REVIVAL

El Pueblo Viejo FIG. 352
1922–23; 1925 ff.
Downtown Santa Barbara, California

Santa Barbara County Courthouse FIG. 353
1929
William Mooser & Co., architects
NE corner Anacapa & Figueroa

Fox Arlington Theater FIG. 354
1929–1930
Edwards & Plunkett, architects
1317 State St.

Downtown Santa Barbara was rebuilt after a devastating 1925 earthquake, employing suave, idealized Andalusian imageries pioneered by gentleman architect George Washington Smith. As such things go, the Hispanic style as practiced in Santa Barbara was far more sophisticated and beautifully landscaped than were the supposed models in arid, southern Spain (Fig. 325).

By social agreement later supplemented by municipal zoning controls, downtown Santa Barbara remains mostly "Spanish" (Fig. 352).

FIG. 352 Community of Dreams Given Santa Barbara's gorgeous situation and ideal climate, the notion of developing the community as a Mediterranean fantasy, "the American Riviera," doesn't seem far-fetched, especially since it was so obviously successful. The El Pueblo Viejo district, a small part of which is illustrated in this photograph, is the central focus of Santa Barbara's Spanish/Andalusian expressions.

FIG. 353 Civic Art Santa Barbara's County Courthouse is a magnificent civic landmark. Be sure to see the interiors, especially the Mural Room, when you visit, which you must.

FIG. 354 Entertainment Art The Fox Arlington's soaring tower is only part of its attraction, which also includes a retail arcade linking the box office with the auditorium, and the Atmospheric auditorium itself.

This overall visual consistency is impressive in itself, and only reinforced by major monuments like the Santa Barbara County Courthouse (Fig. 353), the Fox Arlington Theater (Fig. 354), historic adobes (Fig. 54), and some more recent Andalusian expressions (Fig. 557). Certainly the El Pueblo Viejo historic district is the most impressive concentration of Hispanic imageries in the United States.

Worth Avenue FIG. 355
1923 ff

Via Mizner FIG. 356
1924
Addison Mizner, architect
Downtown Palm Beach, Florida

Like his contemporary, George Washington Smith in Santa Barbara, Addison Mizner was a self-taught architect and a noteworthy designer. However Mizner's bent was more toward the entrepreneurial, and the architect both reaped the rewards and experienced the downside of real estate development.

Before he bankrupted himself, Mizner the architect set the tone and imagery for Palm Beach estate houses, employing Mediterranean imageries that were less austere, more decorative, than the Andalusian expressions of Santa Barbara. In addition, Mizner the real estate developer established then-residential Worth Avenue as "one of the most fashionable shopping thoroughfares in the world," in Donald Curl's estimation. Worth Avenue is certainly an extremely handsome streetscape and believably Mediterranean , though as a total visual environment, downtown Palm Beach is not the architectural equal of downtown Santa Barbara.

FIG. 355 Authentic Feeling Worth Avenue in Palm Beach is instructive as urban design in that its streetscape is agreeably irregular: form, height, and decoration differ, in some places almost abruptly, among street-facing structures. As a result, even though this is an entirely made-up ambiance, Worth Avenue feels much more authentic than the over-planned, embarrassingly superficial "Main Streets" that were fashionable throughout the United States in the 1990s and early 2000s.

FIG. 356 Depth of Field By offering a distinct spatial contrast to the adjacent Worth Avenue streetscape, close passages like Via Mizner enhance a visitor's visual experience within Palm Beach's retail district.

Moderne
1920–1950s

FIG. 357 The Allure of the Moderne Among three distinct expressions of the Moderne, Streamline is probably the most common outside of the largest American cities. Numerous American communities retain at least one white, rounded-corner house as a reminder of two prominent tendencies of the 1930s: *simplification*, a practical response to the Great Depression, and the *notion of modernity – progress –* as a way out of the nation's woes. Today, suave Streamline buildings are attractive to us simply for their architectural qualities. The 1939 San Francisco Maritime Museum, designed by William Mooser Sr. and Jr., was originally a park bathhouse.

The Moderne is conventionally traced back to the forms and ornamentation of the 1925 Paris *Exposition des Arts Décoratif.* Yet that celebrated event was really only one of several stylistic sources for the American Moderne. David Gebhard identified other important influences, including: Bertram Goodhue's Romantic Classicism; the Nordic Gothic National Romanticism of Eliel Saarinen (see the National Romanticism chapter for both); the blocky, "Mayan" designs of Frank Lloyd Wright (see Wright chapter); and the developing International Style (see that chapter).

Gebhard classified the Moderne into three distinct expressions: Zigzag or Art Deco of the 1920s; the Streamline of the 1930s; and the stripped classicism of the PWA Moderne of the 1930s. Each of these expressions differed from the other two with respect to both sources and imagery.

Zigzag/Art Deco is distinguished by angularity and decorative ornament. It was intended especially to function as an architecture of effect. American Deco movie theaters of the late 1920s onward shared this architecture of effect, although as both social and practical responses to the Depression, effect

FIG. 358 **Brilliant Reinvention** Boston Avenue Methodist Church was a fresh interpretation for a modern church, from its aggressively stylish exterior to its innovative semicircular sanctuary. The foreground structure is a 1965 annex.

was usually accomplished through economical means such as color, geometric shapes, and dramatic lighting rather than lush architectural ornamentation (see the Movie Theaters chapter).

In contrast to Zigzag/Art Deco buildings, Streamline designs are simplified, reflecting both Depression-era values and a reaction to the excesses and superficiality of the 1920s that Art Deco so accurately mirrored. Streamline buildings are characteristically rounded at the corners, horizontal in composition, and feature glass block and colored Vitrolite surfacing.

FIG. 359 **Retail Landmark** The Bullocks-Wilshire Department Store's tower literally marked the center of L.A.'s emerging Wilshire retail district when it was constructed in the late 1920s. The building's visual composition emphasizes the verticality characteristic of the Zigzag/Art Deco phase of the American Moderne. The innovative interior featured a collection of high-style boutiques.

The PWA Moderne was derived from Beaux Arts classicism, in which classical elements like columns were simplified, as the Streamline was simplified. Modest amounts of sculptural ornament, paralleling the Art Deco reliance on ornament, were added for contemporary effect. The essential formality of this third Moderne phase explains why the expression was often employed for government and civic buildings and for private buildings for which an image of dignity and rectitude was desired.

Although World War II is a convenient and largely accurate cut-off point for the Moderne, variations of Streamline and WPA Moderne imageries persisted well into the 1950s, mostly in smaller cities and towns.

ZIGZAG MODERNE–ART DECO

Boston Avenue Methodist Church FIG. 358
1926–1929
Bruce Goff, Rush, Endacott & Rush, architects; **Adah M. Robinson**, design consultant; **Robert Garrison**, sculptor
1301 S. Boston Ave., Tulsa, Oklahoma

A brilliant contemporary interpretation of the Gothic; indeed, Boston Avenue Methodist Church was really a fresh interpretation of a modern church. With its insistent angularity, architectural sculpture, and semicircular sanctuary—a refinement of the nineteenth-century curved amphitheater, Akron Plan church—Robinson's concept/Goff's design was considered to be a major innovation in religious architecture when completed.

Bullocks-Wilshire Department Store FIG. 359
1928–1929

John Parkinson & Donald Parkinson, architects; **Jock D. Peters**, interior designer; **Feil & Paradice**, associate architects; **George Stanley**, sculptor; **Herman Sachs**, murals
3050 Wilshire Blvd., Los Angeles, California

Inspired by the Paris of the 1925 decorative arts exposition, Bullocks was in effect designed from the inside out, developed as a collection of distinct, international boutiques, which were then wrapped up in a highly fashionable Art Deco envelope. The exterior is not stone, as it appears to be from a distance, but terra cotta manufactured by the matchless Gladding McBean company. Gebhard and Winter called Bullocks-Wilshire a "treasure-trove of late 1920s Moderne design."

450 Sutter Building
1928–1930

Timothy Pflueger, Miller & Pflueger, architects
450 Sutter St., San Francisco, California

Modern yet also decorative. The wraparound massing is prominent from a distance. Up close, one is engaged by the polychrome detail. 450 Sutter is among the most sophisticated Art Deco skyscrapers outside of New York City.

Chrysler Building
1928–1930

William Van Alen, architect
405 Lexington Ave. at 42nd St., New York, New York

This slender tower tapering to a needle point is surely the most beautiful skyscraper in America. An impressive thousand-foot height is secondary to the building's sheer elegance, and the out-of-this-world ground-floor interior.

Daily News Building FIG. 360
1929–1930

Raymond Hood, John Mead Howells, architects
220 E. 42nd St., New York, New York

Completed before PSFS in Philadelphia (see The International Style chapter), this Moderne landmark could be considered to be the first rationalist skyscraper in the United States. Its stripped imagery is quite a contrast to the architects' earlier, 1922–1925 Chicago Tribune Tower (Fig. 346).

Forum Cafeteria
1929; relocated and restored, 1979–1983
George B. Franklin, architect; **John M. Woodbridge, Herbert Polachek**, restoration architects
40 S. Seventh St., Minneapolis, Minnesota

The Forum was the 1920s equivalent of the post–World War II fast-food restaurant, one of several similar interiors for a Midwestern chain which catered to modest-income patrons. Done up in Vitrolite colored glass and molded plaster, the design incorporated an Art Deco mix of geometric and figurative patterns.

The interior was relocated down the block and restored during a redevelopment, and until 2005 housed an expensive restaurant. The Forum's social-economic makeover, like, for instance, the similar cultural transformation of Miami Beach, illustrates how the marketable image of Art Deco has evolved from middle-class popular culture to its present status as hip and high-style.

Shrine of the Little Flower FIG. 361
1929–1931, tower; 1933–1936, church
Henry J. McGill, architect; **René Chambellan**, relief sculptor; **Corrado Joseph Parducci**, bronzes
Woodward Ave. at Twelve Mile Rd., Royal Oak, Michigan

FIG. 360 Modernistic Largely stripped of exterior ornament, the Daily News Building must have seemed startlingly modern among the traditional imageries of its neighbors. Compare this expression of the Moderne with that of the contemporary Chrysler Building, just behind in this view. *Library of Congress, Prints & Photographs, Historic American Buildings Survey*

FIG. 361 Suburban Moderne The American Moderne, especially its Zigzag/Art Deco phase, is rightly considered to be an urban style. So it is a bit surprising to find such highly developed Art Deco as the Shrine of the Little Flower out in the suburbs.

One of the most expressionistic of American Art Deco buildings, especially the tower-sculpture, which served as the radio studio for the fiery Father Charles Coughlin, an early political evangelist, who built the shrine with listener contributions. That accounts for the stone wall carvings of flowers from all (then) 48 U.S. states. The spacious sanctuary seats 3,000,and is "lavishly finished in buff sandstone, travertine, imported marbles, white oak woodwork, and bronze," in Kathryn Eckert's description.

Rockefeller Center

1931–1940

John R. Todd, executive manager; **Raymond Hood, Hood & Fouilhoux**, principal project designer; **Reinhard & Hofmeister**, space planners, technical architects; **Wallace K. Harrison**, associate design architect; **Paul Manship**, "Prometheus" sculpture; **Donald Deskey, Edward Durell Stone**, Radio City interiors; **Carl Milles, Lee Lawrie, Hildreth Meière, Isamu Noguchi**, sculptors; **Harvey Wiley Corbett**, design consultant
W. 48th to W. 51st Sts., between Fifth and Sixth Aves., New York, New York

Arguably the greatest urban development in America, Rockefeller Center was an Olympian civic and real estate undertaking, especially during the Great Depression. Hood's brilliant composition and massing are complemented by a profusion of art and sculpture, and the extraordinary interiors of Radio City Music Hall (see the Interior Spaces chapter).

FIG. 362 Muscular Moderne If Cincinnati's Union Terminal (Fig. 616) established a public presence through its expansive setting and exceptional designed attributes, the Minneapolis Armory relied primarily on visual power. *Minneapolis Public Library*

FIG. 363 Interplanetary Imagery Pan-Pacific's "Buck Rogers" entrance was something to behold. Sadly, it's now gone.

STREAMLINE MODERNE

Union Terminal FIGS. 616, 617

1929–1933; restoration, 1988–1993

Roland Wank, Fellheimer & Wagner, architects; **Paul Philippe Cret**, consulting architect; **Maxfield Keck**, sculptor; **Winold Reiss**, murals; **Ravenna Tile Works**, mosaic frescoes; **Glaser Associates**, restoration architects
1301 Western Ave., Cincinnati, Ohio

See the Transportation Chapter.

Minneapolis Armory FIG. 362

1935–1936; later additions

P. C. Bettenburg, architect; **Elsa Jemne, Lucia Wiley**, murals
500 S. Sixth St., Minneapolis, Minnesota

Bettenburg skillfully accommodated a diverse program into a muscular, seamless architectural envelope. His design is organized around a sizeable, column-free volume used for both drills and public events. That required functional access for bulky military equipment as well as a polished lobby for civilian crowds. Offices and support spaces were unobtrusively tucked away upstairs. Concrete bleachers serve as ingenious counterweights to the roof, balancing the structural forces and thus, like the exterior flying buttresses of Gothic cathedrals, keep the sidewalls upright.

Pan-Pacific Auditorium FIG. 363

1935–1938, razed

Wurdeman & Becket, architects
7600 Beverly Blvd., Los Angeles, California

Pan-Pacific provided a memorable expression of far-out, "Buck Rogers" Moderne. The architectural flair of this otherwise large and faceless building was concentrated on a semi-detached entrance pavilion that featured four futuristic pylons. The auditorium was demolished years ago—no architectural loss in itself—

FIG. 364 **Impervious to Fire** Mr. Butler wanted a fireproof house. This sturdy, poured-concrete design clearly filled the bill.

but that left the pylons as neglected orphans, which eventually succumbed to fire in 1989. The entry pavilion has been recreated, after a fashion, at the Disney/MGM theme park near Orlando.

Butler House FIG. 364
1935–1937; remodeled 1988–1989
Kraetsch & Kraetsch, architects; **Wells, Woodburn & O'Neil**, architects for the remodeling-restoration
2633 S. Fleur Dr., Des Moines, Iowa (open as a B&B)

Unusually brawny for a residence, Butler's poured concrete walls were exposed as the exterior finish. David Gebhard identified this house as one of a half dozen great domestic monuments in the Streamline style.

Cardozo Hotel FIG. 365
1939
Henry Hohauser, architect
1300 Ocean Dr., Miami Beach, Florida

The classic Miami Beach Moderne hotel, it is not the best, architecturally, among its splendid peers along Ocean Drive. (Certainly the Breakwater, at 940 Ocean Drive, is visually more dynamic.) But the Cardozo served as the early 1980s poster child for the revitalization of Miami Beach, as the district was transformed, first visually and then culturally, from a deteriorating, low-rent retirement haven to its current image as youthful, international, fashionable, and expensive.

PWA MODERNE

Seattle Art Museum FIGS. 366, 367
1932
Charles Bebb, Carl Gould, architects
Lakeview–Volunteer Park, Seattle, Washington

Classical simplicity, abstracted to near austerity. The main elevation presents a blank façade between fluted end projections and the central entry, where vestigial columns are expressed as slender, two-story fins. As one approaches, an exquisite metal filigree (Fig. 367)

FIG. 365 **Oceanfront Fabric** While the Cardozo Hotel (center in photo, with rounded corner) is not the architectural star of Ocean Drive, it serves as a visual anchor for the famous Miami Beach Art Deco oceanfront.

FIGS. 366, 367 **Civic Reserve** Few Moderne designs are as elegantly understated as the Seattle Art Museum. Its exquisite entrance traceries alone are worth a visit.

FIG. 368 **Premier Public Architecture** Master Builder Robert Moses insisted on imaginative design and the finest construction for the Jones Beach Bathhouses on Long Island, which still provide ultimate visual benchmarks for American recreation facilities.

FIG. 369 **Top of the Line** In its appropriately precise monumentality, Washington's Federal Reserve Bank achieves a superlative development of the PWA Moderne.

FIG. 370 **Sunny Monument** Miami Beach's U.S. Post Office successfully balances its fun-in-the-sun neighborhood setting with the projection of a civic image.

becomes more prominent, appropriately introducing a smaller, human scale at the entrance.

With the Seattle Art Museum's move downtown into a 1991 building designed by Venturi, Scott Brown & Associates, this facility now houses Seattle's Asian Art Museum.

Jones Beach Bathhouses FIG. 368

1927–1929; 1932
Herbert Magoon, project designer; **Aymar Embury II**, architect
Jones Beach State Park, Nassau County, Long Island, New York

The Moderne at its best: a brilliant synthesis of design influences, constructed with the finest of materials. Rarely in any project, far less for public recreation, has a design been carried out so consis-

tently, from its overall conception down to the manner in which litter is removed.

Federal Reserve Bank FIG. 369

1937
Paul Cret, architect
Constitution Ave. at Twentieth St. NW., Washington, D.C.

The Fed unquestionably represents the national artistic culmination of this phase of the Moderne. This is a design of supreme, monumental reticence.

U.S. Post Office FIG. 370

1937; restored, 1979
Howard L. Cheney, architect; **Charles Hardman**, murals; **Fraser Knight**, restoration architect
1300 Washington Ave., Miami Beach, Florida

A nearly perfect design for its purpose, era, and place. The exterior is visually restrained but not staid, traditional in its symmetry yet modern in expression. Architecturally, it is among the most successful PWA Moderne post offices, nationally.

Model Tobacco Building FIG. 371

1938–1940
Schmidt, Garden & Erikson, architects
1100 Jefferson Davis Hwy., Richmond, Virginia

This expression is in evolution somewhere between the Moderne and Modernism. The elongated front columns and Broadway font point to the former, while the ribbon windows along the sides suggest the International Style.

FIG. 371 **Transitional Design** Model Tobacco Building in Virginia retains a strong flavor of the Moderne in the abstracted front columns and Broadway typeface, applied to an International Style building with prominent bands of ribbon windows.

National Romanticism

1890–1950

FIG. 372 National Romantic Ideal Cranbrook, built in suburban Detroit after 1925, offered an American counterpoint to its contemporary, the German Bauhaus. The campus of this unique educational/cultural complex was designed by the Finnish National Romantic architect, Eliel Saarinen, head of its graduate program in design. Under National Romantic ideals, applied arts, architecture, and town planning were to jointly express the highest visual potentials of a national culture. In this view toward the northeast, the boys' prep school is in the foreground, the art school and museum are at center. Kingswood School for Girls can be seen just beyond the lake. Buildings and open spaces are carefully integrated into the rolling, wooded landscape. This Arcadian setting is further enhanced by site sculpture, ironwork, tapestries, and furnishings produced by Cranbrook artists and craftsmen. *Photograph © Balthazar Korab*

Beginning around 1900, an optimistic wave of National Romanticism swept through the creative fields of Europe. This movement was more prominent in some cultures than it was in others, sometimes with a descriptive label like Jugendstil or Modernista.

Architectural Romanticism manifested in widely different ways among countries, as local movements sought expressions reflecting the higher promise of their society. These ranged from organic ways of expressing beauty like the Art Nouveau of France and Belgium, to the later dark, 1930s propaganda about cultural "Germanness" by the National Socialists in Germany.

Nowhere was a National Romantic movement more prominent and lasting in positive influence than in Finland, where the search for fresh artistic expressions reflecting an ideal national character strongly influenced monumental figures like composer Jean Sibelius, painter Akseli Gallen-Kallela, and architect Eliel Saarinen (1873–1950).

Finnish National Romantic architecture was comprehensive in its outlook. Ideally, a design undertaking would be a "total work of art in which applied arts, architecture and town planning were integrated to form an environmental whole," according to Finnish architect Markku Komonen.

Finnish architecture was to emphasize indigenous materials like timber and granite wherever possible. In addition to symbolic cultural value, this was a practical choice as well, since local building materials were more accessible and abundant than were imported materials.

Saarinen carried along these ideals to the United States in 1923, and they were reinforced in his integrated-disciplines approach, taught and practiced at Cranbrook (later in this chapter), which functioned as an American counterpoint to the Bauhaus.

FIG. 373 **American Cultural Romanticism** In a youthful United States still lacking deeply rooted cultural traditions, fashionable styles with national-romantic undercurrents were sometimes simply invented, as with the late-1800s romanticization of colonial life in California under Spanish rule. The resultant California Mission Style spread to areas of the United States with no plausible connection to Spanish colonial life, like the Iowa City, Iowa, setting of the 1908 Ford House.

FIG. 374 **High Achievement** Because of his confident balancing of forms and textures, Harvey Ellis's 1887–1888 Pillsbury Hall at the University of Minnesota stands apart from the Richarsonian Romanesque norms of the time.

FIG. 375 **The Public's Castle** Both grand and fanciful, St. Louis City Hall stands out among the public monuments lined up along Gateway Mall.

However, variations of regional, if not truly national, romanticism also touched the United States from the late 1800s well into the twentieth century. Frank Lloyd Wright's forceful populism, which also called for a total environmental design approach and favored the use of local building materials, marked one extreme. Wright's Prairie houses were intended to call attention to authentic societal values of the American Midwest.

The regional romanticization of Spanish Colonial California culture following the 1884 publication Helen Hunt Jackson's novel Ramona marked another extreme. The faddish popularity of the Mission style (see the Period Revivals chapter) in everything from houses (Fig. 373) to railroad stations can largely be traced to this influential novel.

The dreamlike romanticism of two brilliant American designers, Harvey Ellis and Bertram Goodhue, established yet another variation.

HARVEY ELLIS

Harvey Ellis (1852–1904) seemed to be something of a nomad, moving throughout the Midwest during the late 1880s and early 1890s to take advantage of architectural opportunities. His handful of built works, like the 1887–1888 Pillsbury Hall at the University of Minnesota in Minneapolis (Fig. 374), were superb. Ellis's unbuilt 1891 Security Bank of Minneapolis design, for the office of Leroy S. Buffington, anticipated Louis Sullivan's jewel-box banks (see the Progressives chapter) by 15 years.

Ellis's designs for the St. Louis firm of Eckel & Mann reflect a singular, highly personal mix of romantic fantasy and awesome design skills. Castle-like, with steep roofs and attenuated towers, these designs remind one of those classic, 1920s bookplates in which a child contemplates high adventure set amidst distant clouds.

The publication of the exhaustively documented *Reconfiguring Harvey Ellis* by Eileen Manning Michels (2004) makes it possible for the first time to fully appreciate Ellis, especially his works as an artist and his extraordinary architectural drawings.

City Hall FIG. 375
1890–1906
Eckel & Mann, architects; **Harvey Ellis**, principal designer
Market St. at Tucker Blvd., St. Louis, Missouri

Several of Eckel & Mann's staff designers had a hand in this project over a decade and a half of development, but Ellis breathed life into the initial scheme, a competent but unexciting exercise in French Academicism. As built, City Hall is much diminished from Ellis's 1891 competition perspective, notably missing his massive entrance tower (p.183 in the Michels book). Even so, the highly articulated façades and barely restrained verticality introduce a vibrancy rarely encountered in American municipal buildings.

Washington Terrace Gatehouse FIG. 376
1893
George R. Mann, architect; **Harvey Ellis**, principal designer
Washington Terrace at Union, St. Louis, Missouri

FIG. 376 Fanciful Gatehouse The Central West End of St. Louis is distinguished by private streets, some (today only symbolically) guarded by architecturally pretentious gatehouses. By contrast, Washington Terrace residents were daring enough to build this child-like gatehouse that has endeared itself to generations of St. Louisans.

FIG. 377 Municipal Whimsy Few American communities are as adventuresome and self-confident as St. Louis. Its Compton Heights Water Tower is one of several municipal fantasies in this visually marvelous city.

A wonderful play-castle turret squeezed down to pedestrian scale. As occurs routinely in many architectural offices, probably more than one designer was involved in this project over the course of design and construction, but the underlying influence of Ellis, especially in the fantastic play of proportions, is unmistakable.

Compton Heights Water Tower FIG. 377

1893 or 1896–1898
George R. Mann, architect; **Harvey Ellis**, attributed designer
Grand Ave., S of I-44, St. Louis, Missouri

Another eye-catching St. Louis civic fantasy with Ellis written all over it. Michels noted that Ellis no longer lived in St. Louis after 1893, so it is possible that an early Ellis concept was later adapted by others, or that Ellis made a cameo design as a basis for Mann's project in 1896, when he lived in Rochester, New York.

BERTRAM GROSVENOR GOODHUE

FIG. 378 Romanticized Gothic Bertram Goodhue took free license with his Gothic imageries. For the Army's West Point campus, the architect devised a romanticized architectural vocabulary that seemed to have been built up in pieces, over ages. Goodhue, 1925

Like Ellis, Bertram Grosvenor Goodhue was a brilliant designer who drew beautifully. Unlike Ellis, Goodhue maintained a conventional architectural practice, first in partnership with famed Gothicist Ralph Adams Cram until 1914, then on his own for the last decade of his short life (1869–1924).

Goodhue is especially known for three kinds of architectural imageries. One of these is Gothic, principally when in partnership with Cram. While Cram's expression of the Gothic was correct and thus often a little stiff, Goodhue's interpretation of it was more imaginative and dramatic, as illustrated by his designs for West Point (Fig. 378), dating from just after the turn of the twentieth century. (See also St. Thomas Church, fig. 343.)

Goodhue is also acknowledged as the creator of the Spanish Colonial Revival style, introduced by his designs for the 1915 San Diego Exposition (see the Fairs and Expositions chapter).

Goodhue's later works are even more significant, reflecting his search for a design synthesis of form and image, tradition and technology, the exotic and the modern, while also exploring interrelationships among architecture, sculpture, and painting.

The following three seminal buildings by Bertram Goodhue illustrate a progression from Gothic, through the exotic, and into a completely fresh and unexpected interpretation of a well-known building type, the state capitol. For all three, Goodhue seemed to be seeking an American expression that, if lightly grounded in the past, primarily reflected the newness and potential of the United States.

FIG. 379 **Balancing Tradition and Modernity** For St. Bartholomew's Church, Goodhue employed the flavors of past styles to maintain an overall traditional sensibility. Played against tradition, his expression of simple masses was modern for its time, signaling an up-to-date functionality in plan. Strong colors and contrasts allow the church to assert considerable visual presence in a district dominated by large commercial buildings.

FIG. 380 **Public Exotica** Many Americans of the time considered Los Angeles to be an exotic land. So instead of drawing from the obvious well, Spanish Colonial Revival (essentially his own earlier invention), Goodhue chose to synthesize exotic references from legendary world cultures for his Los Angeles Public Library. By mixing this imagery with modern massing, Goodhue conveyed, architecturally, that Los Angeles was indeed singular, and a global city of the future.

FIG. 381 **Monarch of the Prairie** For the Nebraska State Capitol, Goodhue again approached the problem of establishing a public symbol without falling back on historical precedent. In effect, he was creating an American National Romanticism. As he did for the Los Angeles Library, Goodhue achieved a memorable architectural expression through a mixture of hard-to-define references to the past and clean, modern massing. The architect took full advantage of Nebraska's virtually unobstructed horizons, as the soaring tower is visible for miles in every direction.

St. Bartholomew's Church FIG. 379

1914–1918

Bertram Goodhue, architect; **McKim, Mead & White**, entrance portals; **Hildreth Meière**, interior mosaics.

Park Ave. at E. 51st St., New York, New York

The prestigious St. Bart's commission came at a time when Goodhue was pondering the perplexing architectural issue of the era: how to design a modern, functional building while working with treasured vocabularies from the distant past that were still highly valued—indeed expected—by the public. Moreover, the parish was determined to reuse a monumental Romanesque style entrance portico from their previous 1902 church by McKim, Mead & White.

Goodhue's solution synthesized imagery, function, and site context into a dignified, uncluttered design. The entrance portico was set out in front of the nave, almost as a freestanding artifact, encased in a visually neutral envelope of smooth stone.

The church itself could then be expressed without need for an overt reference to the Romanesque. The imagery, inside and out, has a noticeable Byzantine flavor, with just a touch of Tudor in front; but overall, St. Bart's is quite modern in feeling. Goodhue did not replicate his historic references so much as abstract them into their essences.

Los Angeles Public Library FIG. 380

1921–1926; 1983–1993

Bertram Goodhue, Carlton Winslow, architects; **Lee Lawrie**, sculptor; **Hardy Holzman Pfeiffer Associates**, architects for the 1980s–1990s remodeling and expansion

S. Flower and W. 5th Sts., Los Angeles, California

For this prominent civic project in the then-exotic California Southland, Goodhue synthesized references from Babylon to Egypt to Rome into something remarkably fresh. Indeed, this is a truly modern abstraction, in which up-to-date cubist massing overshadows any ornament. Color, sculpture, and interior murals were integral to Goodhue's design.

Nebraska State Capitol FIG. 381
1920–1923, completed 1932
Bertram Goodhue, architect; **Lee Lawrie**, sculptor; **Hildreth Meiere**, interior mosaic floors and vaults
K St. at Centennial Mall, Lincoln, Nebraska

The Nebraska Capitol is Goodhue's masterpiece, a landmark of twentieth-century American architecture. In concept, Goodhue played off an unexpectedly vertical tower form against the limitless flatness of this part of Nebraska: approaching from any direction, a visitor sees the tower, alone above the horizon, from miles. The imagery is only faintly traditional, abstracted even compared to the Los Angeles library. If lightly grounded historically, it is clearly modern, especially the tower, the competition design for which owes much to Eliel Saarinen's 1904–1914 Helsinki Railway Station. As one approaches the building, its sculpture becomes increasingly prominent, especially so in the raking sunlight of summer mornings and evenings.

A domed interior rotunda offers a more traditional visual character, though it, too, is abstracted, and reads more as forms and volumes than as a specific imagery or set of details. Interiors are replete with allegories to past wisdom and virtue, explicit and implicit. By the time the building was completed in the early 1930s, architectural sensation was already gravitating to European International Style Modernism, away from the American nationalism toward which Goodhue had been moving. But the Capitol has aged extremely well, and in the twenty-first century, it has prevailed as a seminal American building.

JOHN RUSSELL POPE

John Russell Pope was a polished designer, confident and skilled in a variety of traditional styles. Whether working in Tudor, French, or Georgian imageries, his residential works were both knowing and robust, standing among the finest of American traditional designs (see the American Colonial Revivals and Period Revivals chapters).

Pope is best remembered for his monumental, classicist-inspired buildings and public memorials, which evoked a sense of timeless grandeur, and serve as unequivocal expressions of an American National Romanticism – even when located well outside of Washington, D.C.

Broad Street Union Station
1913–1919
John Russell Pope, architect
W. Broad at David St., Richmond, Virginia

See the Transportation chapter.

National Gallery of Art FIG. 382
1935–1941
John Russell Pope, architect
N National Mall at 6th St., Washington, D.C.

In its monumental dignity, superior detailing, sumptuous materials, practical functionality, and self-effacing unfussiness, the National Gallery is probably as close to a classic art museum design as it is possible to achieve.

Jefferson Memorial FIG. 383
1935–1938, completed as revised in 1943
John Russell Pope, conceptual architect; **Eggers and Higgins**, executive architects
Tidal Basin at S end of White House cross axis, Washington, D.C.

The memorial was to be classicist expression, specifically based on the Pantheon, in recognition of Jefferson's own architectural vocabulary, and his ardent admiration of the second-century Roman building. Pope's design was predictably vilified by Modernists who contended that it was not reflective of its time.

After Pope's death in 1937, his successor practice, Eggers and Higgins, revised and somewhat downsized Pope's scheme. In comparing the memorial as finally constructed to Pope's initial concept, Steven Bedford concluded that while it evokes the original *parti*, it is inferior in proportions, and is "but a weak shadow of the normally forceful and austere monumentality that was Pope's trademark." Even if it does not fully achieve the presence promised by Pope's magnificent design drawings, the Jefferson Memorial became an essential visual focus for monumental Washington.

FIG. 382 The Nation's Gallery Even monumental buildings can seem diminished against the colossal scale of the National Mall (see The Mall chapter). John Russell Pope's National Gallery of Art, however, is appropriately powerful and supremely refined. None of the subsequent constructions along the Mall has approached the epic qualities of this majestic building.

FIG. 383 Roman Tribute Given Thomas Jefferson's love of Roman antiquity, the Pantheon was a logical starting model for his memorial (see the Neoclassicism chapter). Although Pope's design was watered down after his death, which occurred while the design was underway, the Jefferson Memorial is nevertheless a potent visual presence in monumental Washington. *Library of Congress, Prints & Photographs, Historic American Buildings Survey*

FIG. 384 **Saarinen in America** Eliel Saarinen's National Romantic entry in the 1922 Chicago Tribune competition stood apart among more than 260 competition entries. One can still feel a stab of regret that this surpassingly beautiful design was not realized. The year following this impressive American debut, Saarinen moved to the United States to begin work on the Cranbrook campus. *Tribune Tower Competition, 1923*

FIG. 385 **Integrated Design** For Cranbrook Schools, Saarinen considered each level of design, from the campus plan to textiles. This carved-stone gateway illustrates the nature of creative expressions one encounters throughout the campus.

ELIEL SAARINEN

Scandinavian National Romanticism notably arrived in the United States when Eliel Saarinen and his family moved to Detroit in 1923. Saarinen had placed second in the 1922 Chicago Tribune competition, offering a design which the jury described as of "astonishing merit . . . unusual beauty [and] remarkable understanding of the requirements of an American office building" (Fig. 384). So was Finnish National Romantic imagery appreciated in rough-and-tumble Chicago.

Saarinen set up shop in suburban Bloomfield Hills in 1925 as the architect-in-residence for George Booth's new Cranbrook campus (Fig. 372). Cranbrook was a dedicated community informed by already-historic Arts & Crafts ideals, intended to demonstrate an ethical collective lifestyle by integrating everyday life with high social values and craftsman-like production (Fig. 385).

In addition to planning and designing the campus, Saarinen directed a graduate-level design program under the auspices of the Cranbrook Academy of Art. Among the distinguished graduates of this program were Saarinen's son, Eero, city planner Edmund Bacon, designers Charles and Ray Eames, and architects Edward Charles Bassett, Gyo Obata, Ralph Rapson, and Harry Weese.

Cranbrook's design program was multidisciplinary, led by masters and craftsmen in sculpture, architectural decoration, cabinetry, silver, iron, bookbinding, and weaving. The graduate design program was self-directed, and especially in this way differed from the Bauhaus, at which students were expected to function as compliant apprentices to the studio masters.

Cranbrook Schools FIGS. 372, 385
1925–1943
Eliel Saarinen, architect; **Eero Saarinen**, design collaborator for the Art Museum; **Carl Milles**, sculptor
1221 N. Woodward Ave., Bloomfield Hills, Michigan

Cranbrook School for Boys FIG. 386
1925

Cranbrook Academy of Art
1927–1933

Saarinen House
1928–1930

Kingswood School for Girls FIG. 387
1929–1931

Cranbrook Institute of Science FIG. 389
1931–1933

Orpheus Fountain
1934–1938

Art Museum and Library FIG. 388
1937–1943

Cranbrook is one of the most extraordinary built environments in America, the culmination of European National Romanticism in the United States.

The Cranbrook campus offers valuable demonstrations for design at every scale, from the campus plan to architecture to designed landscapes, the employment of art and sculpture, to fur-

FIG. 386 **Visual Anchor** Cranbrook's School for Boys is marked by its tall astronomy tower. While the school's loosely Gothic imagery is expressed horizontally, this spire reminds us that Medieval Gothic emphasized striking verticality

FIG. 388 **Art & Architecture** As illustrated here by Saarinen's Art Museum, the creative integration of architecture, sculpture, and landscape architecture at Cranbrook ranks among the finest environmental design achievements in the United States.

FIG. 387 **The National Romantic Ideal** For Kingswood School for Girls, Saarinen developed a timeless imagery, *designed*, right down to the door knobs. Among the interior highlights are a barrel-vaulted dining hall and a library with leaded-glass clerestory widows. Loja Saarinen-designed rugs and tapestries were employed throughout the building. As a total work of applied arts and crafts, Kingswood approached perfection of the National Romantic ideal.

FIG. 389 **Art & Architecture** As illustrated here by Saarinen's Art Museum, the creative integration of architecture, sculpture, and landscape architecture at Cranbrook ranks among the finest environmental design achievements in the United States.

FIG. 390 **Symphony of Light** Light is modulated throughout the sanctuary of Christ Church Lutheran, building to a climax on the whitewashed brick wall behind the altar. The longer one remains in this space, the more details and textures one discovers. This small church located in a modest, workingman's neighborhood is architecturally more memorable than some large cathedrals.

nishing and textiles. Among the visual high points are the Kingswood School for Girls, Carl Milles's Orpheus Fountain, and Saarinen's own home, all fully or partly accessible to visitors.

Christ Church Lutheran FIG. 390
1949–1950
Eliel Saarinen, Eero Saarinen, architects; **Victor Gilbertson**, associate architect
3244 34th Ave. S., Minneapolis, Minnesota

Eliel Saarinen designed a much larger church in Columbus, Indiana, 1939–1942, which served as a precursor for this design. However, the interior of Christ Church Lutheran stands among the finest early post–World War II American religious architecture, a wondrous symphony of modulated light, subtle textures, and warm wood tones.

ALVAR AALTO

The prominent cultural position of Scandinavian National Romanticism in the United States changed abruptly after World War II. This occurred for several reasons, among them that times and values were now very different from those before the war and that a Scandinavian idiom was of course not indigenous, so not an authentic national expression for American-born architects.

Most significantly, the International Style was ascendant. Even Frank Lloyd Wright had been marginalized by the American architectural profession, while designing some of his most spectacular works. And with Eliel Saarinen dead in 1950, there was no clear leadership in the further development of European National Romanticism from within the United States.

Despite this, many postwar American architects remained respectfully conscious of Scandinavian designers. In part this was because Saarinen had demonstrated at Cranbrook the kind of *total design* that was talked about but had not been fully achieved by the Modernists. Also, Eliel Saarinen's son Eero emerged at mid-century as a superstar architect, even eclipsing Wright in the 1950s (see the Modern Masters chapter).

However, in the 1950s, a new, light, and colorful vocabulary of Scandinavian design came into prominence, mostly in furnishings, textiles, and industrial design. American architects were also discovering remarkable, humane designs by other Scandinavian moderns, such as the Swedish architect Erik Gunnar Asplund (1885–1940). While created before the war, their designs still seemed fresh and advanced in the postwar period now seemingly in the grip of corporate modernism.

Unfortunately, only a handful of National Romantic designs were constructed here by others than the Saarinens, and the several fountains and sculptural groups by Carl Milles (Fig. 391; see also the Landscape Features chapter).

Probably the most significant of these works were two buildings and three interiors by the Finn Alvar Aalto—the best-known of his works initially being the Finnish Pavilion at the 1939–1940 New York World's Fair (Fig. 749). Aalto (1898–1976) was a generation younger than Eliel Saarinen and a contemporary of Marcel Breuer (see the Postwar Modernism and Brutalism chapters). His work reflected a synthesis of grounding in his national culture and fluency in modernism, an explanation that would also fit Frank Lloyd Wright. Baker House is Aalto's best known American building.

Baker House Dormitory, Massachusetts Institute of Technology FIG. 392
1947–1948
Alvar Aalto, architect
362 Memorial Dr., Cambridge, Massachusetts

Aalto's undulating forms, whether in buildings like Baker House or his famous glass vases, supposedly recalled the lakes around his home in Finland. For this urban dormitory, the rationale for Aalto's signature form was to give residential rooms a better view of the adjacent river. Whatever the explanation, there is something soothing about these graceful curves and the simple brick punched-out envelope which overcome the otherwise functional exterior character of this building (Fig. 392). John Morris Dixon observed that the dining hall (the sharply rectangular, smooth-surfaced structure in the center of Fig. 392) is almost an International Style expression, which Aalto brilliantly played off against the warmth of the undulating brick dormitory block. This occurred both inside and out, "juxtaposing different approaches to design in the same building, same architect, same time."

FIG. 391 Fountain by Carl Milles This splendid water sculpture in St. Louis was completed in 1939, when Milles was resident sculptor at Cranbrook. With the abstractly voluptuous figures and water sprays characteristic of Milles's work, the "Meeting of the Waters" energizes Aloe Plaza, on Gateway Mall directly in front of the St. Louis Union Station.

FIG. 392 Signature Curves Alvar Aalto was known for his undulating forms, from glass vases to buildings like Baker House Dormitory at MIT. Innovative design features here include exterior lights (center of photo) that shine down through skylights in the planted dining hall roof. *Photograph: Ezra Stoller © Esto*

The International Style

1914–1940

FIG. 393 Late International Style Icon Le Corbusier's 1928–1931 Villa Savoye in suburban Paris is still commonly thought of as the model for International Style designs in the United States. While Savoye unquestionably provided a heady advertisement for Modern Movement architecture worldwide, it was preceded by four major International Style houses in the Los Angeles Southland alone.

Contrary to a common assumption, the foundations of Modern American architecture predate the twentieth-century European International Style. Since Modernism is grounded in Enlightenment thought of the 1700s, the rational phase of Neoclassicism (see that chapter) effectively marks the outset of modern American architecture.

Surely, as well, certain stylistic and functional innovations must be recognized as modern, not just the imaginative personalization of ancient forms by Richardson (Fig. 210) and the radical Prairie houses by Wright (Fig. 247), but also cast-iron building evelopes (Fig. 609) and the rational skyscrapers of the First Chicago School (Fig. 232). Equally so engineering marvels like the Eads and Brooklyn Bridges (Figs. 1107, 1108).

All of these examples preceded early International Style buildings in Europe, such as the 1911 Steiner House by Adolph Loos, and the 1911–1913 Fagus factory by Walter Gropius.

Hence the International Style is better understood as one of many phases along an already-century-old timeline of Modernism. This particular version of Modernism came to be characterized not so much by technology as by visual abstraction, expressed in distinctive attributes like the planar wall, ribbon windows, flat roof, and stilts. Only in its adaptation of Wright's open ("free") plan did the International Style espouse functional innovation.

Although the International Style is usually considered to be a European movement, many of its seminal works were accomplished in the United States, chiefly in California (see the California chapter). Significant modern houses by the European émigrés Rudolph Schindler and Richard Neutra preceded iconic International Style houses of Europe such as Le Corbusier's Villa Savoye (Fig. 393), and the Tugendhat House by Mies van der Rohe.

RESIDENTIAL INTERNATIONAL STYLE

Walter Dodge House FIG. 394
1914–1916, razed 1967
Irving Gill, architect
950 N. Kings Rd., West Hollywood, Los Angeles, California

A sumptuous, mature precursor of the International Style in America, a confident assemblage of cube-like boxes, all the more impressive in view of its early date.

Schindler Studio House FIG. 395
1921–1922
Rudolph M. Schindler, architect
833 N. Kings Rd., West Hollywood, Los Angeles, California (open)

A double house–quasi duplex plus working offices, Schindler's design was highly experimental in its rambling plan, construction techniques, and living arrangements. The building and the garden integral to its design have been restored.

Lovell Beach House FIG. 396
1922–1926
Rudolph M. Schindler, architect
13th and Beach Walk, Newport Beach, California

In this astonishing design, Schindler stripped the modern house down to its barest essentials. The resulting house is little more than pure structure, a primal concrete frame that more than holds its own, visually, with the ocean.

Lovell "Health" House FIG. 397
1927–1929
Richard Neutra, architect
4616 Dundee Dr., East Hollywood, Los Angeles, California

David Gebhard and Robert Winter stated that "without question, this house and Schindler's [Lovell Beach House, above] are the greatest monuments of the early International Style Modern in Southern California." Here, Neutra demonstrated the mature potential of Modernism for residential design in its open plan and contemporary use of materials.

Dunsmuir Apartments
1936–1937
Gregory Ain, architect
1281 S. Dunsmuir Ave., Baldwin Hills, Los Angeles, California

Ain's stepped-down concept resulted in an ingenious fourplex design that dealt skillfully with a tight, sloping urban site. All units

FIG. 394 First in the Nation By contemporary standards, Irving Gill's expansive Dodge House was abstracted in the extreme, a preview of what was to become known as the International Style. *Library of Congress, Prints & Photographs, Historic American Buildings Survey*

FIG. 395 Experimental Rudolph Schindler's own duplex was not only visually avant-garde, but also experimental in plan as well as in its everyday living arrangements. Now restored, the structure virtually disappears under its lush landscaping.

FIG. 396 Stripped to the Basics Schindler's Lovell Beach House expresses the modernist view of a house as a "machine for living."

FIG. 397 Light and Open Richard Neutra's bright and open Lovell "Health" House was meant to draw attention to local celebrity Dr. Lovell, and his exhortations about the importance of sunlight and fresh air to one's well-being.

FIGS. 398, 399 Suburban Modern Walter Gropius's own home in suburban Boston is subtly austere: understated on the outside, simple and light-filled within. *Fig 399: Library of Congress, Prints & Photographs, Historic American Buildings Survey*

FIG. 400 Elite Landmark Edward Durell Stone's radically modern A. Conger Goodyear House on Long Island was a shocking departure from nearby Period Revival mansions. The old neighborhood has never been the same. *Photograph: Ezra Stoller © Esto*

are provided with space for small gardens, as well as individual roof decks. In its geometric, highly abstract exterior character, Ain's design still reads as palpably Modern.

Walter Gropius House FIGS. 398, 399
1937
Walter Gropius, architect
68 Baker Bridge Rd., Lincoln, Massachusetts (open)

A modest demonstration of International Style design principles. In some ways, it is quite similar to the Moderne. Light-filled and open, this small two-story house takes full advantage of its leafy suburban property.

A. Conger Goodyear House FIG. 400
1938–1940; endangered
Edward Durell Stone, architect
14 Orchard Lane off Wheatley Rd., Old Westbury, New York

Stone had previously designed several large houses in an almost-International Style vocabulary—with a few Moderne touches. In this design, he fully embraced European, International Style Modernism.

Comparatively small in its once-pastoral neighborhood of 40-room mansions, this two-bedroom house was still large by American standards of its time. Much of the exterior wall is floor-to-ceiling glass, but privacy was assured by virtue of its large property and discreet landscape screening.

The Goodyear estate has recently been subdivided for McMansions. The house narrowly escaped demolition in 2004 and is facing an uncertain future.

FIG. 401 **Pioneer Skyscraper** Philadelphia Saving Fund Society (PSFS) was the first International Style skyscraper, although its curved base and banking floor balconies evoke the contemporary Streamline Moderne. Although now adapted as a Loews hotel, the structure is still crowned by its signature PSFS sign. *Library of Congress, Prints & Photographs, Historic American Buildings Survey*

NON-RESIDENTIAL INTERNATIONAL STYLE

Philadelphia Saving Fund Society FIG. 401
1926–1932
Howe and Lescaze, architects; **Bower, Lewis & Thrower and Daroff Design**, architects/designers for the 2000 remodeling
1212 Market St., Philadelphia, Pennsylvania; remodeled 2000 as a hotel.

As the earliest International Style skyscraper, PSFS was designed gradually over several years without the benefit of precedent. As one would expect, the design is not quite put-together, but perhaps the building is more endearing because of inconsistencies like its curved, Streamline Moderne base.

The New School for Social Research
1930
Joseph Urban, architect
66 W. 12th St., between Fifth and Sixth Aves., New York, New York

The New School is sometimes overlooked in surveys of the International Style in America, probably because, frankly, it seems kind of drab compared to many other landmarks of pre–World War II Modernism. Nonetheless, this is a very early example of a working building in the International Style, and thus of high importance historically, if not necessarily for its visual character.

The Museum of Modern Art, "MoMA" FIG. 402
1936–1939; 1951; 1964; 1984; 2004; 2006
Philip L. Goodwin, **Edward Durell Stone**, architects; later expansions by **Philip Johnson**, **Cesar Pelli**, **Yoshio Taniguchi**
11 W. 53rd St., New York, New York

Appropriately, the original MoMA building was not only avant-garde in its machine-esthetic imagery, but its founding director, Alfred H. Barr, Jr., introduced a new functional approach to showing art in bright, free-flowing, anonymous spaces. Visual interpenetration of inside and outside was enhanced when the celebrated sculpture garden by Johnson opened in 1953. See the Neomodernism chapter for more on the latest expansion by Taniguchi (Fig. 1139).

Crow Island School FIG. 403
1938–1940; addition, 1954
Saarinen & Saarinen, architects for the exterior envelope; **Perkins, Wheeler & Will**, architects and educational planners
1112 Willow Rd., Winnetka, Illinois

This (initially) small suburban grade school is a progenitor of post–World War II American school planning and design. It was organized around an individual classroom module, rather than approached from the basis of the overall school building—within which classrooms are lined up along a hallway. This planning concept resulted in a homelike room environment for children, exceptionally open to natural light and outdoor views.

While Eliel Saarinen's late–National Romantic envelope is appealing, both as a warm, comforting expression for grade-schoolers and also within its immediate neighborhood context, the lasting significance of this project rests in the functional innovations of Philip Will, Jr.

FIG. 402 **Temple of Modernism** The Museum of Modern Art's original, pre–World War II building by Philip Goodwin and Edward Durell Stone (center, with banners) was a breathtaking departure from its traditional contemporaries like the building at the extreme right of this view. Philip Johnson's 1964 MoMA expansion is sited between the two. In conjunction with the museum's 2004 expansion, the entrance centered on the original façade—shown here—was replaced by a restoration of the original off-center opening, with its curved, metal-clad canopy.

FIG. 403 **The Fountainhead** Crow Island School provides light-filled, child-scale classrooms, opening directly to the outdoors. In its functional innovations, the school pointed the way for post–World War II American school planning.

Postwar Modernism

1941–1963

FIG. 404 The Magic of Modernity To postwar American society, "modern" promised
a future of unlimited possibilities. "Ultramodern" was the highest accolade. The
architectural magic of modernity was captured in this famous twilight view of Richard

Neutra's Edgar J. Kaufmann "Desert" House. © J. Paul Getty Trust. Used with permission.
Julius Shulman Photography Archive Research Library at the Getty Research Institute

Modernism reached a creative crest in the United
States during the early post–World War II years. Back
in the 1920s and 1930s, advocates of Modernism promoted their cause largely as an elite art form originating from
well outside of the American mainstream – in architecture, primarily through radical European designs.

Since Modernism, especially as so promoted, did not then
reflect the values of American society, only a scattering of true
International Style buildings was realized in the United States
up through the outbreak of war (see International Style chapter). Few significant International Style structures were built
outside of New York and California.

Of course World War II changed everything. After the
war, American society was unrecognizable, compared to its
prewar values. No longer mired in the Depression, and vic-
torious after a global battle, Americans saw only better
things in the future. Hence, Americans were now more than
ready for Modernism: a bold, inventive, making-the-world-
better, Everyday Modernism (to borrow from Marc Trieb)
had, seemingly almost overnight, become intrinsic to American society.

Thus postwar American design did not need to adapt modern
ideals from elsewhere. Rather, "modern" now squarely reflected
American social values. By the time the classic postwar era had
fully played out in the mid-1960s, Modernism had become conventional. But between the late 1940s and the early 1960s, many
Americans were entranced with the future, and modern architecture seemed just right for the times. New ways of looking at

old problems, new technologies, and new materials—all suggested new design expressions generally characterized by the prominence of unadorned, basic forms and visual clarity in detailing.

This mainstream of Modernism is surveyed in four of the book's chapters. First, the seminal International Style, 1914–1940, in the previous chapter; then key examples of Postwar Modernism, 1941–1963, in this chapter; Late Modernism, 1963–2004, in a third chapter; and Neomodernism, 1980–2004, in a fourth. Of course these periods are merely convenient ways of organizing the work, not hard-and-fast eras.

RESIDENTIAL POSTWAR MODERNISM

Idea House I
1941; razed, 1961
Malcom Lein, Miriam Lein, architects

Idea House II
1947; razed, 1969
Hilde Reiss, William Friedman, architects; **Malcolm Lein**, associate architect
Vineland Place at Bryant Ave S., Minneapolis, Minnesota

These fully functional, inhabitable exhibitions by Walker Art Center anticipated society's post–World War II embrace of Modernism. In 1945, the Walker also opened an Everyday Art Gallery, which focused on industrial design and household utensils.

Both the Idea Houses and the Everyday Art Gallery served as a continuation of everyday life exhibitions such as the Model Street at the 1905 St. Louis fair (see Fairs & Exhibitions chapter). Alexandra Griffith Winton noted that the Walker's primary intent for both venues was not just glorifying modern design in the abstract, as an art form, but demonstrating how one might take up a genuinely modern postwar lifestyle.

Edgar J. Kaufmann "Desert" House FIG. 404
1945–1946; restored 1999
Richard Neutra, architect; **Marmol & Radziner**, restoration architects
470 W. Vista Chino, Palm Springs, California

This was Kaufmann's third great house, following La Tourelle (Benno Janssen, 1923–1925, Fig. 320) and Fallingwater (Frank Lloyd Wright, 1934–1937, Fig. 252), both near Pittsburgh.

Esther McCoy described the Desert House as "weightless space enclosed." There was really nothing new here architecturally: a pinwheel plan and prominent horizontals developed with a sense of disciplined informality. Still, everything from house to furnishings was of a piece. Unlike Wright at Fallingwater, where the house seems to grow directly from nature, Neutra expressed the house here as a precisely built object, in sharp contrast with its natural setting. Both approaches worked brilliantly.

The essence of the Desert House was captured in a single view taken by Julius Shulman at dusk, which has been published endlessly. Even today, this famous scene with a transparent house in the gloaming, treeless mountains rising beyond, is stunning. It must have seemed wondrously surrealistic to the American public in the late 1940s.

Charles and Ray Eames House
1945–1949
Charles and **Ray Eames**, designers
203 Chautauqua Blvd., Pacific Palisades, California (open)

Eames was officially Case Study House #8 in John Entenza's program under the auspices of *Arts & Architecture* magazine. Made up of two metal-framed boxes, the house illustrates the combination of simplicity and boldness that characterized postwar California Modernism at its best. Gebhard and Winter judged Eames to be "one of America's great twentieth-century houses."

Edith Farnsworth House FIG. 405
1946–1951
Ludwig Mies van der Rohe, architect
14520 River Rd., Plano, Illinois (open, National Trust property)

Without a bit of exaggeration, Farnsworth was a completely unexpected solution for a simple weekend retreat. In effect, the glass-enclosed space reads as one floor of multistory modern commercial office building—but magically transparent here, on a sylvan riverside site.

As with all of Mies's structures, the house is exquisitely detailed. Like his 1928–1929 German Pavilion in Barcelona, it is deceptive in scale: both are much larger than they appear to be in photographs without human figures.

FIG. 405 **Steel Cabin** In the early 1920s, Ludwig Mies van der Rohe designed country house projects in brick and in concrete, expressing little domestic feeling. With his Edith Farnsworth House design, built from structural steel, Mies pretty much conceded to a lack of interest in conventional domesticity. *Library of Congress, Prints & Photographs, Historic American Buildings Survey*

Figs. 406, 407, 408 The Wonderland of Canaan The celebrated "Glass House" (Fig. 406) marked the beginning of Philip Johnson's half-century transformation of his suburban New Canaan estate into an architectural Arcadia. Also shown here are the library-study (Fig. 407) and the playfully underscaled pavilion-folly (Fig. 408).

Philip Johnson "Glass House" FIGS. 406, 407, 408

1949; guest house, 1951; pavilion-folly, 1963; underground art gallery, 1965; sculpture gallery, 1970; library-study, 1980; Kirstein Tower, 1985; Ghost House, 1985; Gatehouse, 1995

Philip Johnson, architect

842 Ponus Ridge Rd., New Canaan, Connecticut (open by reservation, National Trust property)

Johnson's celebrated glass house is more facile than the exhaustively studied Farnsworth design—and of much better scale for a weekend retreat. Its machine-like imagery plays off against the rolling landscape of its 47-acre site, beautifully reflecting the ancient visual tension of Man v. Nature.

Over the years, Johnson added a number of happily idiosyncratic structures—eventually totaling 14—including the so-called "windowless" guest house, which paired with the Glass House, and a library-study (Fig .407). This series of non-residential structures began with a pondside, false-scale folly (Fig. 408), and ended with a red free-form gatehouse, which Johnson called "Da Monsta." These additions of course changed fundamental site interrelationships, and now the 1,728-square-foot Glass House reads as one among several objects scattered across a spacious Arcadian landscape.

Walker Guest House, "Cannon Balls" FIG. 409

1952–1953

Paul Rudolph, architect

4143 W. Gulf Dr., Sanibel, Florida (private)

FIG. 409 Ultimate Transparency With tilt-up wood panels for exterior walls, the Walker Guest House on the Florida coast completely opens up to the outdoors. *Photograph: Ezra Stoller © Esto*

FIG. 410 American Bauhaus Marcel Breuer's Starkey House in Duluth illustrates how Walter Gropius and his followers achieved visual tension, here by contrasting irregular materials like rough stone with precise architectural geometry.

While the Farnsworth and Johnson houses are daringly transparent, Rudolph moved beyond both in audacity with this totally open envelope. The exterior is enclosed by plywood panels, which can be flipped up out of the way, transforming the house into a completely open, roofed pavilion. The tiny, 24-foot-square floor is raised slightly above the sand, bisected by a wall separating a sleeping alcove from the living area. The panels are balanced by round iron counterweights, hence the family's affectionate nickname.

Starkey House FIG. 410

1954–1955

Marcel Breuer, architect; **Herbert Beckhard**, **Robert Gatje**, associate architects

2620 Greysolon Rd., Duluth, Minnesota (private)

Among Walter Gropius's colleagues and followers at Harvard after the mid-1930s, a boxy Bauhaus residential aesthetic was widely practiced, mainly in New England. Located 1,000 miles to the west, the Starkey House is one of the most extroverted of these designs, in part because of its breathtaking hillside site, overlooking the limitless expanse of Lake Superior.

The house is visually composed of three semi-detached boxes, placed on a rough-hewn granite base. From uphill and the city street, one sees an agreeably unassuming single-story elevation. At the back, the house dramatically opens up through full-height glass to the lake, its volumes floating above and partly sheltering an outdoor entertainment terrace and children's play area.

FIG. 411 **Relaxed Transparency** Pierre Koenig's Stahl House/Case Study House #22 in the hills above L.A. is comfortably domestic as well as dramatically open. © J. Paul Getty Trust. Used with permission. Julius Shulman Photography Archive Research Library at the Getty Research Institute

Stahl House/Case Study House #22 FIG. 411

1959–1960
Pierre Koenig, architect
1635 Woods Dr., West Hollywood, Los Angeles, California

Architecture mavens know this house from the famous Julius Shulman photograph of its glassed-in living area, overlooking the nighttime glow of Los Angeles, far below. The effect of almost total transparency here is very different from the effect of transparency at Mies's Farnsworth House. The comparative informality of the Stahl House feels inviting and free, unlike the restricting architectural purity of Farnsworth. In the way that it sums up architectural and lifestyle ideals of the classic postwar era of the late 1940s to the early 1960s, the Stahl House closed out the era on a high note.

COMMERCIAL POSTWAR MODERNISM

The relative simplicity and clarity of early Postwar Modernism gradually evolved into complex expressions. Significant changes in expression took place between Skidmore, Owings & Merrill's 1948–1952 Lever House and two 1963 buildings by the same firm.

The 1963 Tenneco Building in Houston is based on a simple, rectangular tower form, like Lever House and the 1954–1958 Seagram. But Tenneco's exterior envelope is deeply recessed behind piers and spandrels, resulting in an expression of thickness—very different from the thin, planar, surface envelopes of earlier Modernist towers. This foreshadows a rising interest among architects in expressing mass and visual complexity in a Modern idiom.

Fully developed complexity emerged in SOM's chapel at the U.S. Air Force Academy (see Late Modernism chapter), completed concurrently with Tenneco. In its rational precision, the chapel is obviously a Modernist design. Yet its angular geometry illustrates how the architectural mainstream was moving beyond statements of simplicity.

Equitable Building FIG. 412

1944–1948; restored 1988
Pietro Belluschi, architect; **Soderstrom Architects**, restoration architects
421 SW. 6th Ave., Portland, Oregon

The first large-scale American expression of Postwar Modernism, Equitable's sleek, elegant curtain-wall exterior is an architectural progression beyond its ancestors, like the 1917 Hallidie Building in San Francisco (see the California chapter) and the 1926–1932 PSFS Building in Philadelphia (see The International Style chapter).

FIG. 412 **Not Quite Fully Modern** Portland's Equitable Building was America's first tall curtain-wall building. Its ultramodern outer skin contrasts with an old-fashioned exterior fire stair; postwar high-rise technical conventions like internal fire stairs were not fully worked out at the time of this pioneering design.

FIG. 413 **The Sheer Curtain Wall** The subtly syncopated curtain wall of S.O.M.'s Lever House in New York illustrates the characteristic simplicity of early postwar Modernist designs.

Lever House FIG. 413

1948–1952; restored 2002

Gordon Bunshaft, Skidmore, Owings & Merrill, architect;
Raymond Loewy, interiors
390 Park Ave. at 53rd St., New York, New York

Although designed and constructed well after Equitable, Lever House was far more influential in popularizing Modernism in the United States as a ubiquitous commercial design vocabulary. This was mainly due to its Manhattan location, on Park Avenue, as well as to the prominence and marketing skills of its architects. Lever House is an essential icon of the Modern Movement in America, thankfully recently restored.

860–880 Lakeshore Drive Apartments FIG. 414

1948–1951

900–910 Lakeshore Drive Apartments FIG. 415

1953–1956

Ludwig Mies van der Rohe, architect
860–880 and 900–910 Lakeshore Dr., Chicago, Illinois

These 26-story apartment towers at 860–880, overlooking Lake Michigan, re-established Chicago as a national center of rational architecture soon after World War II. Today, one can admire the superb precision of these designs, from their geometric siting to the hierarchy of orthogonal traceries set up by piers, spandrels, and mullions. In 1951, this commercial curtain-wall architectural imagery seemed radical compared to Chicago's traditional prewar stone and brick apartment buildings. Mies later added two adjacent apartment towers at 900 and 910 Lakeshore Drive.

Manufacturers Trust Company Bank

1951–1954

Gordon Bunshaft, Charles Hughes, Skidmore, Owings & Merrill, architects; **Weiskopf & Pickworth,** structural engineers; **Elanor LeMaire**, interiors; **Harry Bertoia**, sculptor; **Henry Dreyfus**, safe
510 Fifth Ave. corner of W. 43rd St., New York, New York

The very notion of a glass-walled bank created a sensation when the building was designed. Beyond sensation, this transparent cube lighted within by a luminous ceiling was a key landmark in postwar corporate Modernism.

Seagram Building FIG. 416

1954–1958

Ludwig Mies van der Rohe, architect; **Philip Johnson**, associate architect;
Karl Linn, landscape architect
375 Park Ave., 52nd – 53rd St., New York, New York

Seagram is the architectural culmination of high-art, postwar Modernism: simple perfection in proportion, detailing, and materials. The Racquet and Tennis Club (Fig. 351) across Park Avenue provides a complementary backdrop for its plaza. See also the Four Seasons entry, Interior Spaces chapter.

Connecticut General Life Insurance Company Headquarters

1953–1957; endangered

Gordon Bunshaft, Skidmore, Owings & Merrill, architect; **Joanna Diman**, landscapes; **Isamu Noguchi**, site sculpture and courtyards
900 Cottage Grove Rd., Bloomfield, Connecticut

Many American corporations moved to new suburban campuses in the 1950s and later. This was a new planning-design problem without many precedents. While Lever House served as a model of downtown Modernism, Connecticut General did so for suburbia.

FIGS. 414, 415 Consistency of Expression Completed concurrently with Mies van der Rohe's Farnsworth House (Fig. 405) were his meticulously ordered 860-880 Lakeshore Drive apartments in Chicago (left and center in Fig. 414; 860 is mostly hidden behind the white tower in Fig. 415, which also shows Mies's later 900-910 apartments, left-center). One might think that the visual characters of a country retreat and urban apartments would be very different, but if so one would obviously not be Mies.

FIG. 416 Head of the Class Because of its clarity of form and perfection in detail, Mies's Seagram Building in Manhattan was the benchmark by which postwar skyscrapers were judged. At the extreme right in this photo is a corner of Lever House (Fig. 413). *Photograph: Ezra Stoller © Esto*

FIG. 417 **Literally Out of the Blue** SOM's Chase Manhattan Bank introduced an entirely new character to Lower Manhattan. The tower's visual impact was intensified by expressing structural columns outside of the exterior envelope. *Photograph: Ezra Stoller © Esto*

FIG. 418 **Suburban Ideal** Suburban corporate campuses typically emphasized site and building interrelationships with nature. At Upjohn Company Headquarters by SOM this occurs in part through a sequence of landscaped atriums and courts.

Chase Manhattan Bank FIG. 417

1955–1961

Gordon Bunshaft, Skidmore, Owings & Merrill, architects; **Weiskopf & Pickworth**, structural engineers; **Isamu Noguchi**, sunken court; **Jean Dubuffet**, sculptor

Nassau St. within Pine, Liberty, and William Sts., New York, New York

Chase Bank is often cited as a key private investment in the re-establishment of Lower Manhattan as a preeminent financial center after the war. Its 60-story slab design introduced a sharp visual contrast to the existing downtown skyline. Kidder Smith observed that Chase Bank "injected a hard-edged profile into a mélange of turrets, domes, crockets, and finials [which] bedeck most of its eclectic neighbors." Exterior structural columns were pulled out

FIG. 419 **Evolution of Modern Envelopes** Tenneco Building culminates the postwar evolution from sheer 1950s curtain walls, like those of Lever House (Fig. 413) to deep setbacks in the exterior envelope as in this structure, designed by the same firm only a decade later.

from the building envelope, resulting in a greater expression of visual depth compared to the flush curtain wall of Lever House.

See Modernism chapter for Noguchi's sunken court (Fig. 1030).

Upjohn Company Headquarters FIG. 418

1961

Bruce Graham, Skidmore, Owings & Merrill, architects; **Sasaki Associates**, landscape architects

7000 Portage Rd., Portage, Michigan

On a fast learning curve following Connecticut General (above), the suburban corporate campus planning problem evolved into an overall conceptual emphasis on a building's relationship with nature, often to the deliberate exclusion of developing suburbia just beyond the property line, as here. This site was conceptualized as a sequence of distinct spaces, including open building atriums and courts.

Tenneco Building FIG. 419

1962–1963

Skidmore, Owings & Merrill, architects

1010 Milam St., Houston, Texas

As abstract architectural compositions, Tenneco elevations are extremely handsome, with deep anodized tones, crisply detailed. As noted above, the Tenneco design continued the development of exterior architectural expression of the modern office building from light to heavy. This evolution progressed through buildings cited in this chapter from a sheer envelope on Lever House, to strong window-mullion reveals on Seagram, to the outboard structural frame for Chase, to deep exterior setbacks within a powerful structural cage at Tenneco. At each stage along this progression, the exterior became visually more powerful.

Modern Masters

1929–2004

FIGS. 420, 421, 422, 423 Master Architects Four towering figures, prominent in the second half of the twentieth century, are the subjects of this chapter: Louis I. Kahn, represented here by his powerfully elegant Yale Center for British Art, 1969–1972, in New Haven (Fig. 420, top left); Eero Saarinen, represented by his wondrous MIT Chapel, described in this chapter (Fig. 421, top right; exterior Fig. 429); Charles W.

Moore, centered in the mirror during a charrette at his Sea Ranch Condominium #1 Unit 9, described in this chapter, with his design partner, Arthur Andersson and an unidentified student (Fig. 422, bottom left; exterior Fig. 434); and Robert Venturi, seated in the iconic house the architect designed for his mother, Vanna, described in this chapter (Fig. 423, bottom right; exterior Figs. 443 and 536).

America has been blessed with master architects of supreme talent. All created iconic designs which materially influenced the course of American architecture. Singular figures like Thomas Jefferson and Frank Lloyd Wright come to mind.

This chapter focuses on the works of four great masters: Louis I. Kahn, Eero Saarinen, Charles W. Moore, and Robert Venturi. These architects deeply influenced twentieth-century American architecture through their buildings, teaching, and writing.

LOUIS I. KAHN

Louis I. Kahn (1901–1974) was something of a mystic, known for his oracular aphorisms. His students responded in kind: in the mid 1960s, a graffito in Kahn's Penn design studio declared: *The Lord created light / And Kahn discovered it / Now, we may use it.*

Kahn's practice was only modestly active during its first two decades, 1929–1949, in good part because he began at the onset of the Great Depression. Kahn was 50 before designing his first widely noted building, the Yale Art Gallery (1951–1953).

FIG. 424 Abstract and Personal Louis Kahn's Jewish Community Center Bath House in New Jersey is modern and direct without losing the sense of warmth and human scale that was prized by traditionalists.

FIG. 425 Served and Servant For Richards Medical Research Building at the University of Pennsylvania, Louis Kahn expressed utility chases as separate exterior masses, introducing the notion of "served" and "servant" spaces.

FIG. 426 Monument for the Ages The Salk Institute on the California coast seems almost primordial in the way its powerful concrete forms visually engage with a limitless sea. Kahn's design is one of the great American monuments of our time.

This was followed by a small bathhouse for a Jewish community center near Trenton (Fig. 424). At long last, Kahn was commissioned for his first influential project, Richards Labs (Fig. 425) at the University of Pennsylvania. This design proved to be a prototype for Kahn's subsequent buildings, a tightly disciplined, sculptural expression of program function.

Countless 1960s architecture students and many practicing architects emulated Kahn's powerful forms, though rarely did these designs approach the timeless emotive force of Kahn's architecture. Boston City Hall is among the best of Kahn-influenced buildings (Fig. 486).

Louis Kahn died while working on the design of a new capital complex at Dhaka, Bangladesh.

Jewish Community Center "Trenton" Bath House FIG. 424
1954–1955
Louis I. Kahn, architect
999 Lower Ferry Rd., Ewing, New Jersey

As a modern architect, Louis Kahn never copied the great monuments of history. Yet in exploring fundamental qualities like the play of light and establishing presence, Kahn intuitively connected with the essence of architecture through the ages. We respond with real feeling, without necessarily being able to explain precisely why.

This simple shelter, part of a larger, uncompleted complex, is primordial in two respects. David McDonough related that Kahn felt that he had discovered himself in its design. In a second sense of origins, the design solution has been reduced to utter basics in the spirit of Laugier's Primitive Shelter, achieving perfection in its unadorned appropriateness.

Richards Medical Research Building, University of Pennsylvania FIG. 425
1957–1961
Louis I. Kahn, architect; **August Komendant**, structural engineer
3700 Hamilton Walk, University of Pennsylvania campus, Philadelphia, Pennsylvania

Along with Charles Moore's Sea Ranch condominiums (later in this chapter), Richards Labs was one of the most imitated designs of the 1960s. Here Kahn introduced the terminology of "served" and "ser-

FIGS. 427, 428 Classic Simplicity Mies van der Rohe may have coined the phrase "Less is More," but Louis Kahn surely confirmed its validity with the elegantly understated design of his Kimbell Museum in Fort Worth.

vant" spaces, expressing the servant spaces like ducts, stairs, and utilities in bold forms on the exterior, hence turning the building inside out. Most of the designs by others which sought to emulate Richards labs devolved directly into exercises in abstract form-making, largely devoid of Kahn's subtle intellectual underpinnings (see the Brutalism chapter).

Salk Institute FIG. 426
1959–1966, later additions
Louis I. Kahn, architect; **August Komendant**, structural engineer;
Luis Barragan, courtyard design consultant
10010 N. Torrey Pines Rd., La Jolla, San Diego, California

If Louis Kahn had designed only this one project, he would surely rank among the great twentieth-century American architects. The Salk complex can be appreciated at multiple levels, beginning with its articulated concrete forms. However, the true emotive power of this design derives from its minimalist courtyard, aligned with an infinite visual axis out to sea.

Kimbell Art Museum FIGS. 427, 428
1969–1972
Louis I. Kahn, architect; **August Komendant**, structural engineer;
George Patton, landscape architect
3333 Camp Bowie Blvd., Fort Worth, Texas

Kahn's designs are often described as "timeless" forms, and though overused, this best describes the Kimbell. The basic design seems almost elemental, until one begins to appreciate the nuances employed to create such a serene environment, permeated by light (Fig. 428).

EERO SAARINEN

Eero Saarinen (1910–1961) dominated postwar American architecture through sheer creative achievement, arguably rivaling even Frank Lloyd Wright as *the* creative form-giver of the 1950s. Saarinen was the son of Eliel Saarinen (see National Romanticism chapter). Hence, Eero was intimately a part of the Cranbrook design scene from his teen years until well into his career.

Like Wright's designs, Saarinen's were personal and memorable, but unlike Wright's, his vocabularies differed markedly from one commission to the next. There was no "Saarinen Style" (Figs. 429, 430), as there was, say, a Prairie Style or a Mies building.

After Saarinen's untimely death at the age of 51, his practice was carried on by his partners as Kevin Roche, John Dinkeloo & Associates.

General Motors Technical Center FIGS. 431, 432
1945–1958
Eero Saarinen, Saarinen, Swanson and Saarinen, architects; **Smith, Hinchman & Grylls**, associate architects; **Thomas Church**, **Edward A. Eichstedt**, landscape consultants; **Richard Lippold**, integral sculpture; **Harry Bertoia**, **Alexander Calder**, **Antoine Pevsner**, sculptors
Mound Rd. at Twelve Mile Rd., Warren, Michigan

FIGS. 429, 430 **No Saarinen Style** As apparent from these views of Eero Saarinen's MIT Auditorium and Chapel (left and right in top photo) and Yale University's Stiles and Morse colleges of 1958–1962 at Broadway and Tower Parkway in New Haven (foreground in lower photo), his buildings markedly differ, visually. The architect insisted that every design evolved naturally, in response to its particular situation and potential. It would thus be unlikely that any two would look alike.

Saarinen's campus occupies half of a mile-square property. At this scale, the development must be described as monumental, if not almost imperial. Buildings are organized around an immense 22-acre reflecting pool; a domed auditorium and water tower serve as superscale sculpture; sculpture was also introduced at personal scale (Fig. 432). In its sheer expansiveness, the GM Tech Center is an extraordinary period piece, certainly the most impressive corporate campus in the United States.

Jefferson National Expansion Memorial, "Gateway Arch"
1947–1948; 1959–1967
Eero Saarinen & Associates, planners and architects; **Severud-Elstad-Krueger**, structural engineers; **Dan Kiley**, landscape architect
Mississippi Riverfront, St. Louis, Missouri

See the Civic Design chapter.

Chapel and Kresge Auditorium, Massachusetts Institute of Technology FIGS. 421, 429
1950–1955
Eero Saarinen, architect; **Anderson, Beckworth & Haible**, associate architects; **Amman and Whitney**, structural engineers; **Theodore Roszak**, chapel belfry; **Harry Bertoia**, chapel reredos
MIT Campus, off Massachusetts Ave. and Amherst St., Cambridge, Massachusetts

These side-by-side buildings illustrate how Saarinen approached a design problem. He sought an ideal form to fit the specific program, as well as the specific context. Here the auditorium dome (left in Fig. 429) echoes the form of the school's iconic Classical Revival domes, and the chapel (right in Fig. 429) adapts the curved wall and rough brickwork of Aalto's nearby Baker House (Fig. 392). The tiny chapel interior, with its Bertoia sculpture descending from an oculus, is among the most moving religious spaces of its era, radiantly evoking the wonder of the Unknown (Fig. 421).

David S. Ingalls Hockey Rink, Yale University
1953–1959
Eero Saarinen, architect; **Douglas W. Orr**, associate architect; **Fred Severud, Severud-Elstad-Krueger**, structural engineers
73 Sachem St., New Haven, Connecticut

A marvelous piece of architectural sculpture, which Saarinen insisted derived as a "completely logical consequence of the problem," that is, a directly response to the functional program. The architect's basic design goal was to provide a clear span that was beautiful, and this complex catenary structure promised to be a uniquely soaring expression. Indeed.

TWA Idlewild Airport Terminal
1956–1962; later jetway additions; restoration and alterations under way
Eero Saarinen, architect; **Kevin Roche**, design associate; **Ammann & Whitney**, structural engineers
John F. Kennedy Airport, Queens, New York

See the Transportation chapter.

John Foster Dulles Airport
1958–1963; significant later modifications
Eero Saarinen, architect; **Ammann & Whitney**, engineers; **Charles Landrum**, airport consultant; **Dan Kiley**, landscape architect
Dulles Toll Road, Chantilly, Virginia

See the Transportation chapter.

FIGS. 431, 432 **Postwar Monumentality** Saarinen's General Motors Technical Center near Detroit is America's most impressive American corporate campus, encompassing stupendous scale, monumental architecture (Fig. 431), attention to details, and integral art like sculptor Richard Lippold's suspended stairway (Fig. 432).

FIG. 433 **Beauty in Function** The John Deere Headquarters' handsome exterior derives from Saarinen's intention to open the interiors as much as possible to the landscape. Hence, the signature sun screens, which reduce the need for blinds.

John Deere Headquarters FIG. 433

1957–1964; addition, 1977–1978
Eero Saarinen, Kevin Roche, John Dinkeloo, architects; **Ammann and Whitney**, structural engineers; **Sasaki, Walker and Associates**, landscape architects; later campus buildings by **Kevin Roche/John Dinkeloo & Associates**
John Deere Rd., East Moline, Illinois

An exquisite corporate temple of classical simplicity, set within a 600-acre, wooded suburban site. John Dinkeloo famously specified an exterior framework of Cor-ten, a weathering steel then normally used for railroad cars. The steel's rusty patina works beautifully with the golden glass curtain walls of the main building and flanking wings. Many critics contend, with good reason, that Deere's architecture is unsurpassed among American corporate campuses.

CBS Building

1960–1965
Eero Saarinen, Kevin Roche, John Dinkeloo, architects;
Paul Weidlinger, structural engineer; **Warren Platner**, interiors
51 W. 52nd St., New York, New York

In Saarinen's words, "the simplest conceivable" design, known locally as "Black Rock," CBS is the only postwar office tower in Manhattan which is arguably even more elegant and dignified than Seagram (Fig. 416).

The Saarinen office designed virtually everything as a piece, inside and out, excepting only the traditional furnishings in the Chairman's private office. CBS is a superior period piece of a buttoned-down era, when American corporations cared more about product and permanence than about daily fluctuations in stock price.

FIG. 434 Indigenous Response For their Sea Ranch Condominium #1 in California, Charles Moore and his partners drew on the genius of place, renewing local building traditions with a design that became an instant international landmark.

CHARLES W. MOORE

Charles W. Moore (1925–1993) was a brilliantly creative designer and a singularly memorable person. He traveled ceaselessly to the far corners of the globe, absorbing and apparently retaining every visual image en route. As he designed, technical solutions and visual images literally flowed out onto the drawing almost fully developed.

Peripatetic in the extreme, Moore preferred to work with his clients in participatory workshops, and with fellow team members in charrettes. It is safe to say that those who interacted with him on any undertaking never forgot a treasured experience.

Moore established a series of design partnerships coast-to-coast: the legendary MLTW (Moore Lyndon Turnbull Whitaker) association while at Berkeley; Moore Grover Harper (now Centerbrook) when at Yale; Moore, Ruble, Yudell and Urban Innovations Group while at UCLA; and finally Moore/Andersson in Austin.

Given that Moore habitually, if unintentionally, oversubscribed his time, it was often a bit of a challenge to gain his physical presence. But once underway, the solutions followed, seemingly effortlessly, the architectural equivalent of Mozart composing. A week's work would be accomplished by lunch. Like Henry Hobson Richardson, Moore enjoyed life to its fullest, and always made time for unhurried meals and spontaneous inspections of some nearby building or place that had caught his attention.

During his annual summer retreat at his Sea Ranch condominium in California, colleagues, students, and friends appeared almost instantly on his arrival. The ensuing weeks would unfold as a rich, seamless experience of parallel design charrettes on several current projects, calls from his publishers and media, requests from academia, and joyful socialization.

Moore was a virtuoso at almost every aspect of design, from city planning to book layout. His Princeton doctoral dissertation on water in architecture led to collaboration with Lawrence Halprin, for whom Moore functioned as project designer for the Lovejoy Fountain in Portland (Fig. 1047).

Given that Moore was always ready and eager to participate in any and every project, even informal consulting, probably no one will ever be able to compile a complete list of his work. The following entries barely hint at the nature of Moore's interests and output.

Moore House

1960–1962; massively expanded, totally altered
Charles W. Moore, architect
33 Monte Vista Rd., Orinda, California

Moore and his MLTW partners designed a number of iconic Northern California houses notable for their complexity of plan, and out-

riggings known as saddlebags. For himself, however, Moore employed a simple, hipped-roof form, essentially one large room. This widely published house reposed in an elevated clearing, sited as a tiny if beguiling villa. Sliding barn doors opened the interior to the outside. Within, an "aedicula" designated the seating area; a grand piano and a freestanding shower provided other interior features. Despite its comparatively small floor area, the house had considerable presence, as visitors gradually discovered numerous clever tensions between arcane references and functional expressions.

Sea Ranch Condominium #1 FIGS. 422, 434
1963–1965
MLTW/Moore, Lyndon, Turnbull, Whitaker, architects
Seawalk Dr., S of the general store, The Sea Ranch, Sonoma County, California

Perhaps *the* American architectural icon of the mid-1960s, and certainly one of the most copied for its forms. An inspired assemblage of indigenous shed forms works into the spectacular coastal landscape, both standing out and at the same time fitting in. Each of the ten units has a rough inner structure and weathered plank walls, though each is different in plan.

Faculty Club, University of California, Santa Barbara
1966–1968
MLTW/Moore, Turnbull, architects; **Richard Peters**, lighting designer
University of California, Santa Barbara, Goleta, California

As David Gebhard described it, Moore synthesized "the Spanish Colonial Revival Santa Barbara of the 1920s, the Moderne of the 1930s, plus Piranesi and contemporary forms." A dazzling hanging neon sculpture by Richard Peters that energized the dining

FIGS. 435, 436 **Updating Hoary Tradition** Kresge College at the University of California, Santa Cruz was Charles Moore and William Turnbull's witty, knowing take on traditional, self-contained colleges, in a spot-on reflection of Northern California's late-1960s kaleidoscopic era. The winding passage between houses (Fig. 435) leads to a colorful outdoor café intended to promote socialization (Fig. 436).

room was later wantonly destroyed. Proposed integral landscaping was never installed, so today a visitor must have a good imagination to understand the potentials of Moore's design.

Kresge College, University of California, Santa Cruz
FIGS. 435, 436
1966–1974
MLTW/Moore, Turnbull, architects; **Marc Treib**, colors and graphics
University of California, Santa Cruz

The new Santa Cruz campus was developed as a West Coast version of the traditional Oxford/Cambridge model of self-contained colleges. At Kresge, Moore and Turnbull turned that ancient exem-

FIGS. 437, 438 Neighborhood-scaled Worship St. Matthew's fits comfortably into its suburban L.A. residential setting, its woodsy exterior (Fig. 438) offering a foretaste of the warm, embracing sanctuary (Fig. 437).

plar on its head: on approach, only a featureless brown stucco wall is visible though the dense forest.

Once one passes through a gateway everything changes, as the college is revealed in sequence. Movement is organized along a succession of stage-set cutout building fronts, basically white but liberally accented with primary colors. This internalized pedestrian spine is part fantasy Medieval street and partly a marvelously compressed and fun-loving take on Thomas Jefferson's academical village at the University of Virginia.

Piazza d'Italia
1977–1978
Moore, Grover, Harper, Urban Innovation Group, architects;
Perez Associates, executive architects
Poydras, Tchoupitoulas, Lafayette, and Commerce Sts., New Orleans, Louisiana

See the Landscape Features chapter.

St. Matthew's Episcopal Church FIGS. 437, 438
1979–1983
Moore Ruble Yudell, architects; **Campbell & Campbell**, landscape architects
1030 Bienveneda Ave., Pacific Palisades, California

A creative synthesis of appropriately residential scale and a kind of rural-agrarian imagery, with just a whiff of Italy deftly thrown in as a visual counterpoint in the form of a freestanding campanile. The sanctuary is visually quite agitated, although calmed enough by floor-to-ceiling wood for traditional Episcopalian services.

Beverly Hills Civic Center FIG. 439
1981–1992
Urban Innovations Group, architects; **Albert C. Martin Associates**, associated architects; **Campbell & Campbell**, landscape architects
E Side Crescent Dr. between Santa Monica and Little Santa Monica Blvds., Beverly Hills, California

Really, only Charles Moore could have come up with this solution, much less so successfully pulled it off in execution. Moore's scheme organized in plan around a diagonal, "baroque" axis inspired by a 1770 design by French Neoclassicist Claude-Nicolas Ledoux. This united a disparate assortment of existing structures and leftover spaces with the new program. Somehow, Moore's dynamic scheme asserts a strong character of its own, yet enhances the setting of the adjacent existing Spanish Renaissance City Hall. An amazing, if not miraculous feat.

Moore/Andersson Compound FIG. 440
1985–1988
Charles W. Moore, Arthur Andersson, architects
2102 Quarry Rd., Austin, Texas (open by appointment)

This outwardly compact, inwardly expansive scheme included separate living units for Moore and Andersson, a small guest room, and office space for their practice. A site-scale oval ties all the pieces together in plan, inside and out.

The architecture is almost innocuous on the exterior, in deference to the adjacent single-family neighborhood. However, an extraordinary gallery in the Moore unit is probably the most tactile space of Moore's career. It is easy to read this magically animated space as homage to Moore's most admired architect in history, Sir John Soane.

Gethsemane Episcopal Cathedral FIGS. 441, 442
1991–1993
Moore/Andersson, architects
3600 S. 25th St., Fargo, North Dakota

This structure succeeded a century-old downtown cathedral, which burned to the ground in 1989. Rather than rebuild on the old site, the parish-chapter decided to start afresh in the burgeoning Fargo suburbs, along a developing commercial strip.

The design emphasized verticality on the exterior to assert a strong presence amid the usual visual cacophony of a strip, as well as to establish a kind of Carpenter's Gothic imagery combined with grain elevator massing—a reference to the era, if not the actual setting, of the earlier church. (It no doubt helped that Arthur Andersson is a North Dakota native.)

The interiors somewhat recall St. Matthew's (Fig. 437), which the Gethsemane building committee visited before engaging Moore and Andersson. The north chapel, with its brightly colored, Victorianesque hammer-beam bracketing, is the clear visual tour-de-force within. Gethsemane and Marcel Breuer's Convent of the Assumption (Fig. 483) are the two nationally prominent works of architecture in North Dakota.

FIG. 439 **Virtuoso Expansion** Charles Moore's Beverly Hills Civic Center expansion drew from the architect's encyclopedic mastery of forms and imageries. Space was integrated along a new diagonal axis in a way that created distinctive interior and exterior environments, while reinforcing the monumental presence of the historic City Hall (at left in photo).

FIG. 440 **Amazing Space** Charles Moore's Austin residence provides an unforgettable summation of the astonishing tactility that characterized all the architect's own homes. *Photograph © Timothy Hursley*

FIGS. 441, 442 **Gothic Vocabularies** American Gothicism has occurred in several distinct varieties, across nearly two centuries. Moore and Andersson seem to have referenced many of them in one place or another throughout Gethsemane Cathedral in North Dakota. A strong sense of verticality is the common quality, inside and out. *Fig. 442: © Timothy Hursley*

FIG. 443 **Revolutionary** Robert Venturi's mother's house in Philadelphia, here seen from behind, was a bolt out of the blue, built in an era dominated by the corporate International Style. In addition to infuriating the design establishment, Venturi also seems to have anticipated the soon-to-emerge prominence of ambiguity in an American society which was then still—at least outwardly—conformist. See Fig. 536 for a front view and Fig. 423 for an interior.

FIG. 444 **Homage to the Ordinary** Touted by champions and reviled by foes as "ordinary," Venturi's Guild House design reflects a carefully considered clarity of purpose and economy of means.

FIG. 445 **Indiana Inaugural** The visually modest Fire Station #4 provided fodder for the architecture culture wars of the late 1960s. A Columbus, Indiana, commission effectively confirmed Venturi as a significant national figure.

ROBERT VENTURI

Robert Venturi (b. 1925) is at once one of America's most cosmopolitan architects and also deeply influenced by his home city of Philadelphia. Venturi has been inspired by several local sources and influences, especially the city's historic architecture, the restrained urbanity of Philadelphia and its Main Line suburbs, the designs of Frank Furness, Louis Kahn and the so-called Philadelphia School of the 1950s and 1960s, and city planner Edmund Bacon.

His key design and planning collaborators have been John Rauch, Steven Izenour, and especially his wife, architect and planner Denise Scott Brown.

Venturi's significance spans across several disciplines in addition to his architectural design, especially theory, urban design and planning, industrial and exhibition design, and criticism. His seminal books, *Complexity and Contradiction in Architecture* (1966), and *Learning From Las Vegas* (with co-authors Izenour and Scott Brown, 1972) were profoundly influential in shifting many of the guiding assumptions about modern American architecture and urbanism.

Because Venturi's built work represents only a small part of his achievements, one must really consult the various monographs and read his own writings to gain a reasonably complete idea of his design talents and cultural insights.

Vanna Venturi House FIGS. 423, 443, 536
1959–1964
Robert Venturi, Venturi & Short, architects
8330 Millman St., Philadelphia, Pennsylvania

A true celebrity building, met with both brickbats and raves. Venturi demonstrated many of his Both-Ands in this radical-banal, design, which is now understood as revolutionary in its time.

Guild House FIG. 444
1960–1965
Venturi & Rauch, architects; **Cope & Lippincott**, associate architects
711 Spring Garden St., Philadelphia, Pennsylvania

The client, a Quaker community, was unsurprisingly amenable to what Venturi described as the "ugly and ordinary." The design was loaded with wry symbolism, including a golden rooftop TV antenna centered above the front (missing in Fig. 444), all of which served as fodder for the intelligentsia and was simply overlooked by ordinary people.

Fire Station #4 FIG. 445
1966–1967
Venturi & Rauch, architects
Hwy. 46, E of Taylor Rd., Columbus, Indiana

Station #4 was contemporaneous with the publication of *Complexity and Contradiction*. By then, Columbus was widely recognized as a national showcase of signature architecture, a Columbus commission a signal of an architect's national significance.

This outwardly banal design, a "Bill-Ding-Board," in Venturi's description, took Modernism in a new direction, neither corporate International Style nor Brutalism. Naturally, the architectural establishment was outraged—and younger architects captivated. Hence, this tiny structure became a shaping event on the evolutionary timeline of modern American architecture.

Franklin Court, "Ghost House" FIG. 446
1972–1974
Venturi & Rauch, architects; **George Patton Assoc.**, landscape architects
Market St. between 3rd and 4th Sts., Philadelphia, Pennsylvania

A block associated with Benjamin Franklin was to be restored by the National Park Service in honor of the Bicentennial. The only house Franklin had ever owned had been built in an interior courtyard in 1763–1765. Unfortunately, only fragments of foundation and spotty documentation survived. Rather than devise a wholly speculative reconstruction, the architects erected an open steel frame on the site, a "ghost house," to symbolically mark Franklin's homesite. A museum illuminating Franklin's multifaceted life is under the court.

Allen Art Museum Expansion, Oberlin College FIG. 447
1973–1976
Venturi & Rauch, architects
Cor. N. Main and E. Lorain sts., Oberlin, Ohio

The existing museum was designed by Cass Gilbert in 1917 as a Renaissance palazzo, located on a prominent corner and serving as a visual pivot between town and campus. Its purity of form and architectural distinction made physical connections to a new addition problematical.

Venturi's solution was to set his addition back, and to do what Gilbert did, but in a contemporary vocabulary. Thus both are largely planar, with broad eaves and patterned walls with color highlights. Venturi's addition is respectful of Gilbert, but not deferential, and both buildings are strengthened as a result.

ISI Corporation Headquarters FIG. 448
1978
Venturi & Rauch, architects
3501 Market St., Philadelphia, Pennsylvania

The client wanted a distinctive image on the program and budget of an ordinary speculative office building. The design response was an arresting geometric pattern in colored brick and porcelain, another "Bill-Ding-Board" as sophisticated pop art.

FIG. 446 Imagine Rather than make up a phony design to embody Ben Franklin's long-lost house, the architects marked the site with a steel frame "ghost house."

FIG. 447 Respect without Deference Venturi's Allen Art Museum expansion at Oberlin College (foreground) plays the same urbane game as Cass Gilbert's original museum (rear), while projecting a contemporary character. Both structures are stronger as a result.

FIG. 448 A Little Goes a Long Way Despite its rock-bottom construction budget, ISI Corporation Headquarters in Philadelphia is highly memorable because of its patterning.

FIG. 449 **Urban Entertainment** Minneapolis's Hennepin Avenue streetscape was to have sparkled with light, a declining part of Downtown to develop into a signature entertainment district.

FIG. 450 **Revitalizing Tradition** Gordon Wu Hall is fully sympathetic to Princeton's visual traditions, expressed in contemporary ways, while introducing visual energy and physical focus to its immediate setting.

Hennepin Avenue Streetscape FIG. 449

1980–1981, unrealized
**Denise Scott Brown, James Timberlake, Robert Venturi,
Venturi, Rauch & Scott Brown**, urban designers
Hennepin Ave., Minneapolis, Minnesota

The Venturi-Scott Brown practice has undertaken several urban design commissions, their work for Galveston and Miami Beach probably best known. The imaginative design for this stillborn project set a high creative benchmark for efforts to intensify the visual qualities of medium-size downtowns.

Fanciful aluminum "trees" were to be the primary energizing features along a six-block section of Downtown Minneapolis's entertainment street. Corridor edges would have been treated as a continuous collage of color and light. Classic street furniture like benches and receptacles were chosen both for practical reasons and also because they would have added an anchoring dimension of time to this redevelopment district. Had this scheme been carried out according to the designers' vision, Hennepin Avenue likely would have become a national civic landmark, like Lawrence Halprin's nearby Nicollet Mall (see the Civic Design chapter).

Gordon Wu Hall, Princeton University FIG. 450

1980–1983
Venturi, Rauch & Scott Brown Associates, architects
Butler College, Princeton University, W of Washington Rd., Princeton, New Jersey

Engaged by his alma mater to create a dining-social hall as a focus for a residential college, Venturi responded with a highly polished design fully in the manner of traditional seats of learning. He retained heraldic symbolism, but now inlaid into the masonry at pop scale. As is typical for the Venturi practice, the building plan is simultaneously diagrammatic and ingenious.

Fire Station #1/Reedy Creek Emergency Services Headquarters FIG. 451

1992–1994
Venturi, Scott Brown & Associates, architects
NE cor. Buena Vista Dr. and Victory Way, 1 mi. E of World Dr., Walt Disney World Resort, Bay Lake, Florida

A witty visual play on the traditional firehouse, with Dalmatian spots and Fire House Red "brick" porcelain panels as fresh expressions of familiar firehouse symbols. Direct though nuanced, colorful as well as functional, this is a thoughtful architectural solution that nevertheless more than holds its own among the marvelous soft fantasies of Disney World.

FIG. 451 **One Dalmatian** It's pretty difficult to pass by the Fire Station #1/Reedy Creek Emergency Services Headquarters without breaking into delighted giggles. Of course, that's the whole point of Disney World, where it is located.

Mid-Century Expressionism

1933–1990

FIG. 452 Well Out of the Modernist Canon A number of gifted architects broke free from the esthetic straightjacket imposed by rationalist postwar architecture. Their memorable works are represented here by Minoru Yamasaki's serenely decorative McGregor Memorial Center at Wayne State University in Detroit. While designs like this acknowledged underlying modernist principles, this was a Modernism expressed in highly dramatic ways. The public seemed to love these buildings.

Given the diversity of American culture and its physical settings, a rich variety of American architecture is inevitable. Indeed, over the last half of the twentieth century, several traditional and modern vocabularies coexisted with the International Style/Postwar Modernism mainstream.

This chapter offers an overview of prominent mid-century designs which were in one way or another outside of the conventions of establishment practices like Skidmore, Owings & Merrill, and the influential, Bauhaus-grounded tenets of figures such as Walter Gropius and Ludwig Mies van der Rohe.

Since rationalism characterized the postwar American architectural mainstream, the buildings in this chapter are organized around the idea of expressionism. In the colloquial, these designs had *flair* in some way. As such, they were usually highly admired by the general public, sometimes to the dismay of purists.

FIG. 453 **House and Garden, Inseparable** Alden B. Dow's home and studio in Michigan present a surpassingly picturesque ideal of art and nature as one. © *Alden B. Dow Home and Studio*

ALDEN B. DOW

Alden Dow (1904–1982) was at Frank Lloyd Wright's Taliesin in the summer of 1933, returning home to Midland to open his architectural practice in 1934. Dow's buildings were occasionally outwardly Wrightian, though personalized: Dow was sympathetic to Wright's approaches, while not directly imitating his designs.

Alden B. Dow Home & Studio FIG. 453
1934–1941
Alden B. Dow, architect
315 Post St., Midland, Michigan (open by advance website reservation)

An impossibly picturesque scene: architecture as organic sculpture romantically growing from an enhanced, streamside landscape. "Gardens never end and buildings never begin," in Dow's words. After developing this at the beginning of his career, Dow never again equaled the magical integration of building and site he achieved here, on a cherished family property. An utterly beautiful built environment.

THE ARCHITECTURE OF JOY

Morris Lapidus (1902–2001) began his practice in the late 1920s, designing Manhattan storefronts and commercial interiors. In this highly competitive milieu, it was essential to be different, to create effect. Lapidus thus quickly moved beyond the standard Art Deco language of the times in search of a striking new architectural vocabulary.

His 1933 interior for Armstrong's in Manhattan marked an extreme stylistic departure, introducing the amoeba-like "wog-

gle" shapes, "bean-pole" supports, and "cheese holes" that would make his post–World War II hotels famous as the Miami Beach Style. This showroom was so ultramodern that even high-style, contemporary Moderne interiors instantly seemed dated by comparison.

From then on, Lapidus brashly mixed two distinctly different design languages. One was what could now be described as a "Jetsons" vocabulary, made up of his signature motifs noted above: chevrons, beanpoles, woggles, curving walls and cheesehole ceiling cutouts. The other design vocabulary was based on an aggressive, lavishly ornamented interpretation of European traditions, which Lapidus archly described as "a mélange of quasi-French Provincial and Italian Renaissance elements."

The architect skillfully provoked his high-art critics, who could not restrain themselves from condemning the excesses of his Architecture of Joy, as Lapidus labeled his work. He bril-

FIG. 454 **The Architecture of Joy** Morris Lapidus's signature design vocabularies juxtaposed sweeping, futuristic curves on the outside with lavishly overdone traditional expressions within, as here in his Fontainebleau Hotel in Miami Beach.

liantly played on his self-assumed bad-boy role as an antidote to the emotional austerity of mainstream Modernism. Denied acceptance by elite tastemakers until recently, Lapidus was always a big hit with average Americans. Tellingly, his work was also appreciated by Frank Lloyd Wright.

Fontainebleau Hotel FIG. 454
1952–1954, interiors and site landscapes later altered
Morris Lapidus, architect
4441 Collins Ave., Miami Beach, Florida

Expressed on the exterior in a great, sweeping curve, the Fontainebleau marked Lapidus's comprehensive break away from straight lines, as his interiors had moved beyond straight lines two decades earlier. While the hotel was futuristic on the outside, Lapidus considered the inside to be "modern French Provincial." Meant to be "ornate," the interiors were voluptuous in the extreme.

Among many memorable interior features were the "Stairs to Nowhere" and an astonishingly overdone coffee shop rendered as a kind of layered diorama of bacchanalian figures. Unfortunately, the original public spaces were eventually remodeled, and the initial jovial spirit of upfront hedonism largely lost in the process.

Eden Roc Hotel
1954–1955
Morris Lapidus, architect
4525 Collins Ave., Miami Beach, Florida

Built next door to the Fontainebleau, the Eden Roc was intended to better its neighbor. Lapidus settled on a more conservative massing, which looks as much 1930s Streamline as Postwar. This occurred primarily because the owner wanted the "atmosphere" of the Fontainebleau without incurring the costs of the necessary motifs. As a result, the Eden Roc did not achieve the overall memorable personality of the Fontainebleau.

Americana Hotel
1956
Morris Lapidus, architect
9701 Collins Ave., Bal Harbour, Florida

Here, Lapidus developed yet another postwar resort-hotel imagery: superficially Modern in the open expression of structure, yet so animated in its deep reveals and projections—at a time when the flat-façade Lever House was only four years old—that it could never be mistaken for canonical International Style.

FREE-FORM STRUCTURALISM

Free-form structuralism was another reaction to the emotional austerity of the International Style. This direction was inspired by the Italian master, structural engineer Pier Luigi Nervi (1891–1979) and two Spanish-born engineers, Eduardo Torroja y Miret (1900–1961); and Félix Candela (1910–1997), who emigrated to Mexico in 1939.

Nervi's poetic work was based on a wholeness of architecture and structure, leading to graceful, plastic buildings. By comparison, conventional International Style designs seemed almost brittle.

Torroja and Candela were known as the Shell Builders, in recognition of their thin-shell concrete roofs, which functioned as both enclosure and sculpture.

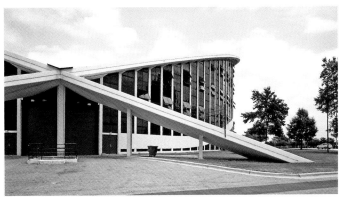

FIG. 455 Structural Gymnastics J. S. Dorton Arena in North Carolina is all about structure, designed from a structural perspective, and so expressed throughout.

FIG. 456 Shell Builders Modernity was expressed in many different ways. In a bold departure from early–World War II norms, Lambert-St. Louis Airport Terminal enclosed its expansive volumes under thin concrete shells.

These two approaches manifested in the United States after the war as expressed structure (Dorton arena, this chapter) and as fluid, sculptural roofs (Priory Chapel of St. Mary and St. Louis, this chapter). Eero Saarinen synthesized Nervi and the shell builders when emphasizing expressed structure in his Dulles Terminal, and with the fluid roofs of his TWA terminal at Idlewild (now JFK) Airport in New York (Transportation chapter).

J. S. Dorton Arena FIG. 455
1950–1952
Matthew Nowicki, William Dietrick, architects; **Fred Severud**, engineer
1025 Blue Ridge Rd. (W side of city on the State Fairgrounds), Raleigh, North Carolina

This stressed-skin roof encloses enough area to seat 10,000 people in a column-free space, sheltering a single room measuring 220 feet by 125 feet.

Lambert-St. Louis Airport Terminal FIG. 456
1956–1957, massive additions
Hellmuth, Yamasaki & Leinweber, architects; **Edgardo Contini, William Becker**, structural engineers
I-70 / Mark Twain Expressway, St. Louis, Missouri

Three sets of thin-shell concrete intersecting vaults were employed as the roof and walls of this terminal. In part because of airport height limitations, the resulting spaces are proportionately low—compared to prewar public volumes like, say, the Grand Central railroad terminal in Manhattan—but they were fresh and uncluttered and seemed, as desired, very modern and functional.

Another entry on this terminal appears in the Transportation chapter.

FIG. 457 **Benedictine Drama** Benedictines are noted for their architecture. The Priory Chapel of St. Mary and St. Louis is striking on the exterior and just as dramatic inside, with a spectacular envelope composed of continuous parabolic arches. photograph © *George Silk, courtesy of HOK*

Priory Chapel of St. Mary and St. Louis FIG. 457
1962
Gyo Obata, Hellmuth, Obata & Kassabaum, architects; **Paul Weidlinger**, structural engineer; **Pier Luigi Nervi**, structural consultant
500 S. Mason Rd. at Conway Rd., Creve Coeur, Missouri

Especially viewed from close up, Obata's shell design is very dramatic. A striking reversal of light-and-dark exterior surfaces occurs at night when the chapel is in use.

NEW FORMALISM

New Formalism was yet another reaction to the perceived sterility and lack of individuality common to postwar Modernism. This direction developed out of the work of Edward Durell Stone (1902–1978), who had designed in the International Style before World War II (see that chapter), but by the 1950s had begun to disassociate himself from the "sparse and cold" vocabulary of the Europeans. For his 1954 design for the American Embassy in New Delhi, State Department program directives provided an essential rationale, requiring a response sympathetic to local conditions. Stone's design embodied that mandate: first, a podium base to hide automobiles; then, a perforated wall and roof overhang—"ancient principles in tropical climates"—in response to climate; and finally, the use of gold color "as a note of oriental opulence."

FIG. 458 **The Lollypop Building** It was not intellectually fashionable to like Edward Durell Stone's Huntington Hartford Gallery of Modern Art in New York – not until 2004, when it was endangered by a full-blown alteration. Unfortunately, outbursts of appreciation were by then way too late, as the building was irreparably defaced the following year. *Photograph: Ezra Stoller © Esto*

FIG. 459 **Ascetic Richness** Minoru Yamasaki's McGregor Memorial Center at Wayne State University effectively plays a Zen-like frontal serenity (Fig. 452) against exotic traceries along the sides and within the atrium (above).

FIG. 460 Decorated Box Orthodox modernist critics routinely derided Yamasaki works such as the Reynolds Metals Company as decorative. That characteristic probably explains why his buildings were so popular with the public.

Both classic and fresh, rational and elegant, the embassy was an immense popular success, reinforced by Stone's 1957 design for a circular version of the embassy for the U.S. Pavilion at the Brussels Exposition. These buildings in effect established a recognizable style, characterized by screen-like, patterned façades, brilliant white or gold color, and simple massing, with an understated expression of structure.

Huntington Hartford Gallery of Modern Art FIG. 458
1958-1965; radically remodeled starting 2005
Edward Durell Stone, architect
2 Columbus Circle, New York, New York

Criticized as an architectural "confection" when it was built, this serene white building was striking in its prominent location, making foils of the darker buildings around it.

National Cultural Center, John F. Kennedy Center for the Performing Arts
1958–1959; revised design, 1962; completed, 1969
Edward Durell Stone, architect
2700 F St., NW., Washington, D.C.

Stone's original, 1959 plan proposed a flamboyant agglomeration of circles and sweeping curves, but budgetary constraints reduced the realized project to a variation on his New Delhi embassy.

McGregor Memorial Center FIGS. 452, 459
1958
Minoru Yamasaki, architect
Wayne State University, 495 Ferry Mall, Detroit, Michigan

A typical Yamasaki modus operandi: decorated simple forms. Two minimal, travertine-covered structures are visually connected by a skylighted interior atrium. The sides are lined with stylized columns in a graceful rhythm. McGregor presents an especially attractive scene as viewed from across the adjacent reflecting pool (Fig. 452).

FIG. 461 Graceful Temple For years after its completion, Northwestern National Life Insurance was consistently cited in local polls as the most beautiful Minneapolis building. NWNL raised the design benchmark downtown with its integration of architecture, landscape, and sculpture.

Reynolds Metals Company FIG. 460
1959
Minoru Yamasaki, architect
16200 Northland Dr., Southfield, Michigan

The underlying architectural *parti* is the International Style villa on raised columns. But Yamasaki hung a perforated, gold-anodized decorative screen in front of the upper floors. Any notion of decoration was strictly *verboten* by modernist orthodoxy in 1960, and thus popular with ordinary people, who were already tiring of bland modernist boxes.

Northwestern National Life Insurance FIG. 461
1963
Minoru Yamasaki, architect; **Sasaki, Walker Associates**, landscape architects; **Harry Bertoia**, sculptor
Washington Ave. at Hennepin Ave., Minneapolis, Minnesota

By the early 1960s Yamasaki had reached maturity in his design approach and imageries. This brilliantly white office building is treated as a Greek temple in massing, enclosed in a continuous screen of vaguely Islamic columns. The design is modern in its min-imalist detailing, yet theatrical in effect. A narrow reflecting pool sets the building off from its surroundings.

Pre-Columbian Wing, Dumbarton Oaks FIG. 462
1960–1963
Philip Johnson, architect; **Massimo Vignelli**, displays
1703 32nd St. N.W. between R and S Sts., Georgetown, Washington, D.C.

Exquisite is not too precious a description for this magnificently refined pavilion, built at a cost of $92 per square foot at a time when typical square-foot building costs were in the teens. When the wing first opened, ladies were required to put rubber tips over their spike heels in order to preserve the teak flooring.

The pavilion is made up of nine circular bays, composed 3 x 3 in plan, the center bay an open atrium. Thick travertine columns support shallow domes; all is enclosed in transparent walls of curv-ing plate glass set in bronze frames. The overall sense of trans-parency and elegance is further enhanced by Vignelli's Lucite display stands.

Amon Carter Museum of Western Art FIG. 463
1961; 1964 and 1977 additions razed
Philip Johnson, architect
3501 Camp Bowie Blvd., Fort Worth, Texas

In plan and site development, Johnson's design is Miesian in its geometric purity. In elevation, stylized front columns introduced a sense of overt decoration that was foreign to orthodox postwar Modernism.

FIG. 462 **Classic Beauty** Philip Johnson's Pre-Columbian Wing at Dumbarton Oaks in Washington, D.C., combines classical purity, elegant materials, restrained detailing, and priceless artifacts. In short, it is simply splendid.

FIG. 464 **Expressive Chicago School** In prominently articulating structure, Bertrand Goldberg's Marina City towers fall squarely within Chicago School traditions. With respect to the project's expressive, non-rectilinear forms, the architect staked out a new local direction.

SCULPTURAL MONUMENTALITY

Several prominent mid-century architects worked in distinc-tive, personal vocabularies. These were expressionistic, more sculptural than decorative, and visually dramatic. The following buildings are representative of a much larger body of impres-sive works.

Marina City FIG. 464
1959–1962
Bertrand Goldberg, architect
300 N. State St., Chicago, Illinois

Marina City became an instant Chicago icon when completed. These highly articulated apartment towers are at once powerful and graceful, structural and rational, as well as sculptural and expressive. The entire development was an early multi-building mixed-use project. In addition to the two signature residential tow-ers, each with parking on the first 19 floors, Marina City included a freestanding auditorium, a hotel, a mid-rise office block later con-verted to a hotel, and a marina on the Chicago River below.

Arthur Milam House FIG. 465
1960–1962
Paul Rudolph, architect
1033 Ponte Vedra Blvd., Ponte Vedra Beach, Florida

Milam was one of the most influential American houses of the 1960s among young architects. The shadow-box exterior was presumed by some observers to be a direct reference to Mondrian paintings, though Rudolph had employed crisp concrete sunshades on previous work, notably his addition to Sarasota's high school. A deeply inset, framed design was a logical solution for a sun-drenched beachfront, without need for De Stijl artists as inspiration.

Rudolph's touch was really remarkable here. Had the framework been any thinner, the façade would have seemed fragile; much thicker and it would have been Brutalist. As designed, the proportions seem just right. The exterior complexity is carried into the interiors, with seven levels, including a living room conversation pit. Built-in seating throughout reduces the need for furniture. Light fully penetrates the house; large sheets of plate glass provide unobstructed views of the ocean.

Tyrone Guthrie Theater FIG. 466
1962–1963, razed, 2006
Ralph Rapson, architect
725 Vineland Pl., Minneapolis, Minnesota

Rapson made the most of a limited construction budget in the design of this thrust-stage theater. A cut-out exterior screen provided visual drama, especially at night, as patrons inside moved through silhouettes produced by the screen.

Philip Pillsbury House FIG. 467
1964, razed 1997
Ralph Rapson, architect
Ferndale Rd., Wayzata, Minnesota

This rambling, animated design is stylistically unclassifiable. Several directions seem to have been skillfully synthesized: one might sense small hints of Louis Kahn, Paul Rudolph, and the modulated rhythms of Le Corbusier. Nevertheless, Pillsbury ultimately read as a personal statement by Rapson alone.

FIG. 466 Architectural Theater Given a tiny construction budget, Ralph Rapson had to improvise brilliantly in order to build an appropriately dramatic home for Tyrone Guthrie Theater performances. His lighthearted building envelope functioned as a magical permanent set created largely out of silhouette and light.

National Center for Atmospheric Research FIG. 468
1961–1967
I. M. Pei & Partners, architects; **Dan Kiley**, landscape architect
W end of Table Mesa Dr., Boulder, Colorado

Magnificent architectural sculpture in concrete, refined beyond any resemblance to Brutalism. Set in the Rocky Mountain foothills, this facility was immensely photogenic and propelled Pei to national prominence among the general public.

Federal Reserve Bank of Minneapolis FIGS. 469, 470
1968–1972; irreparably disfigured, 1990s
Gunnar Birkerts, architect; **Leslie E. Robertson**, structural engineer
250 Marquette Ave., Minneapolis, Minnesota

One of the most original twentieth-century architectural designs and structural-engineering solutions. Office floors were supported by a great catenary (inverted) arch, which required a complex sequence of linked structural accommodations even to build (Fig. 470). The curve of the catenary was expressed in a break in the curtain-wall surface plane. The whole suspension structure floated visually above a minimalist sculpture plaza. All was lost in a thoughtless alteration.

Christian Science Center
1969–1972
I. M. Pei & Partners, architects; **Cossutta & Ponte**, associated architects; **Sasaki, Dawson, DeMay Associates**, landscape architects
175 Huntington Ave., Boston, Massachusetts

A large space program was expressed in a monumental composition which incorporated the nineteenth-century Mother Church with new construction. In its immense area, this development exceeds even Bernini's piazza for St. Peter's in Rome.

National Gallery of Art East Building FIGS. 471, 472
1968–1978
I. M. Pei & Partners, architects; **Weiskopf & Pickworth**, structural engineers; **Kiley, Tyndall, Walker**, landscape architects; **Alexander Calder**, sculptor
N National Mall at 4th St. and Pennsylvania Ave., Washington, D.C.

The building itself is the primary work of art. A triangular site generated the massing, which yields a triangular, light-filled interior atrium. Unlike the original National Gallery next door, designed by John Russell Pope (see the National Romanticism chapter), this building tucks the art galleries themselves into the periphery of the upper building, where they seem almost an afterthought.

FIG. 467 Rapsonian Rapson's singular Philip Pillsbury House in Minnesota was an astonishing composition of animated forms, which miraculously maintained an overall poise.

FIG. 468 Mountain Sculpture On sunny mornings, the National Center for Atmospheric Research is visible from miles away, perched impossibly high in the foothills above Boulder. Closer up, I. M. Pei's abstract sculptural forms interact marvelously with their alpine setting.

FIGS. 469, 470 **Synthesis of Form and Structure** For Birkerts and Robertson's breathtaking Federal Reserve Bank of Minneapolis, spectacular architecture required equally advanced engineering. The office floors were suspended dramatically above a full-block sculpture plaza, which flowed onto Lawrence Halprin's Nicollet Mall (lower left in upper photo, see the Civic Design chapter), with Yamasaki's Northwestern National Life Insurance building (Fig. 461) in the distance.

BRUCE GOFF

Bruce Goff (1904–1982) was a singular figure in twentieth-century American architecture. Deeply influenced by Frank Lloyd Wright, he apprenticed with a Tulsa architectural firm at the age of 12. At age 22, he designed one of the great monuments of the American Moderne, the Boston Avenue Methodist Church (Moderne chapter, Fig. 358). Although his best-known designs, like the Bavinger House in Norman, Oklahoma, are loosely Wrightian, they are so original as to be clearly "Bruce Goff."

FIGS. 471, 472 **The Art of Architecture** I. M. Pei's National Gallery of Art East Building is first and foremost a Mall-scale piece of sculpture (Fig. 471). Conventional artworks are also tucked away in galleries surrounding its central atrium (Fig. 472).

FIG. 473 **This is an American Farm House** Bruce Goff's house for Glen and Luetta Harder in rural Minnesota was at least as functional as conventional farm houses—and a lot more fun to live in!

FIG. 474 **And This is in a Small Midwestern Town** Goff also designed a home in town for Glen Harder's parents (see Fig. 473). Despite what you might think, the Jacob and Anna Harder House fits right into its neighborhood.

Boston Avenue Methodist Church

1926–1929
Bruce Goff, Rush, Endacott & Rush, architects, **Adah M. Robinson**, design consultant; **Robert Garrison**, sculptor
1301 S. Boston Ave., Tulsa, Oklahoma

See Moderne chapter.

Glen and Luetta Harder House FIG. 473

1970–1972; accidentally destroyed by fire
Bruce Goff, architect
Mountain Lake, Minnesota

No first-time visitor could have been truly prepared for this astonishing object. As one approached the Harder farm across a limitless expanse of lightly rolling croplands, the house seemed to change character, finally resolving visually into three immense, semi-engaged stone chimneys and a swooping roof covered in bright orange indoor-outdoor carpeting. One would scarcely have expected all these architectural theatrics from a reading of Goff's apparently straightforward T-plan, though this, too, was filled with nontraditional and eminently functional solutions which made sense for everyday farm life.

Jacob and Anna Harder House FIG. 474
1971–1973
Bruce Goff, architect
W side of 8th St., between 2nd and 3rd Aves., Mountain Lake, Minnesota

This in-town home for Glen Harder's parents is less fantastic only in comparison to Glen's and Luetta's house (preceding entry). Once again, the design builds from apparent simplicity in the central concept, here based on a circle, which is embellished in plan, section, and elevation to an almost impossible extent for such a small house and lot. Despite all the visual gymnastics and texture inside and out, there is a crispness bordering on rectitude to this house, which allows it to blend with its modest, small-scale neighborhood.

E. FAY JONES

Like Bruce Goff, E. Fay Jones (1921–2004) was influenced by the organic architecture of Frank Lloyd Wright but was also a strong designer: there is no sense in his designs that he was merely a Wright acolyte. Thorncrown Chapel, nestled into the Ozark region of Arkansas, far off the beaten path, is his masterpiece.

Thorncrown Chapel FIG. 475
1978–1980
E. Fay Jones & Maurice Jennings, architects
12968 Hwy. 62 West, Eureka Springs, Arkansas

Rarely has such a simple structure been so universally acclaimed as has this timber-lattice shelter enclosing a lofty, Gothic-like space. While the chapel itself is highly photogenic, Jones's design also achieves a close relationship between the building and its natural surroundings.

Pinecote Pavilion
1986–1987
E. Fay Jones & Maurice Jennings, architects; **Andropogon**, site planners, **Edward Blake**, landscape architect
Crosby Arboretum, 370 Ridge Way, Picayune, Mississippi

Jones and Jennings designed several buildings after Thorncrown bearing a strong family resemblance to the chapel. Pinecote Pavilion is perhaps the best of these. It has an interlocking wood lattice framework like that of the chapel, but it differs in its openness, its broadly spreading roof, and its modulated site relationships with piney woods, grasses, and water.

JOHN LAUTNER

John Lautner (1911–1994) may have been the least-recognized great twentieth-century American architect, especially outside of the Los Angeles Southland, where he built most of his 60 houses and a handful of commercial buildings, including the iconic Googies coffee shop (see The Strip chapter).

Lautner biographer Alan Hess groups Lautner along with Frank Furness and Louis Sullivan (see Progressives chapter), Frank Lloyd Wright, and Bruce Goff as proponents of an "American organic modernism" that acknowledged nature as a fundamental design influence. Indeed, some of Lautner's finely crafted wood designs, like his 1941 Bell House in Los Angeles, could easily be mistaken for Usonian houses designed by Wright.

Lautner also worked confidently with powerful, sweeping concrete forms that nearly out-Wrighted Wright in their expressiveness. Of course, the natural and built environments of Los Angeles are very different from those of Wright's Upper Midwest or even of rural Scottsdale during Wright's lifetime. Consequently, Lautner's designs are best understood as direct architectural reflections of the sun-drenched Pacific West, and the often brazen Southland social culture.

Little of Lautner's residential work is fully accessible or even visible to the public. His most published design, the inexpressibly dramatic Arango House (1973) occupies a remote aerie high in the hills overlooking Acapulco Bay, in Mexico.

A few of Lautner's houses, including the sampling listed below, can be glimpsed from public ways. Fortunately, an excellent survey by Hess and photographer Alan Weintraub illustrates Lautner's genius.

Carling House FIG. 476
1947; remodeled, 1991
John Lautner, architect
Hockey Trail Dr., off Pacific View Dr. (from Mulholland), Hollywood Hills, Los Angeles, California

Lautner's design responds creatively to this spectacular mountaintop site. The house was oriented to pick up long views, both into the LA basin to the south, and across the San Fernando Valley to the north.

Here the line between inside and outside was largely eliminated, in that much of the exterior envelope is floor-to-ceiling glass, and an informal sequence of interior spaces flows unobstructed across a concrete interior floor that seamlessly becomes an outdoor terrace, and on out through the native landscape. While the structural

FIG. 475 Ozark Radiance Little wonder that Thorncrown Chapel is a pilgrimage destination, despite its relatively out-of-the-way Arkansas location. *Photograph © Greg Hursley*

FIG. 476 Architecture Fused with Landscape From below, John Lautner's Carling House presents an intriguing suggestion of its intimate and virtually seamless relationship between the built and the natural, inside and outdoors.

FIG. 477 Silver Lake Villa The Reiner House, "Silvertop," reposes regally above a mass of conventional houses facing onto the reservoir.

and textural complexity of the house should be interesting to architecture mavens, the main theme here is dematerialization.

Intense subsequent development has left the house squished between roads; you can practically touch the house while driving by on the upper road, Hockey Trail. It is best appreciated from below, however, when seen from Pacific View about 100 feet east of Hockey Trail (Fig. 476).

Lautner's Bell House is located nearby, just a few minutes west, at 7714 Woodrow Wilson Dr., via Mulholland Drive. Although the Bell House is well hidden by lush landscaping, it is just possible to catch glimpses of it while approaching from the east.

Reiner House, "Silvertop" FIG. 477
1956–1974
John Lautner, architect
2138 Micheltorena St., Silver Lake, Los Angeles, California

Compared to the dematerialized Carling House, Silvertop feels like a formal villa, almost serenely grand, enclosed in great curving walls of sheet glass and brick. Gebhard and Winter awarded the house "a high grade for exotic form," which it surely deserves, even in the company of several nearby houses by the likes of Richard Neutra, R. M. Schindler, Harwell Harris, and Gregory Ain. Sited well above the street, Silvertop is prominent as seen from the east, across the reservoir, especially in morning sunlight.

Malin House, "Chemosphere" FIG. 478
1960–1961
John Lautner, architect
7776 Torreyson Dr., Hollywood Hills, Los Angeles, California

Widely known as the UFO or Flying Saucer House, this eight-sided structure on a pole is less satisfying architecturally than Lautner's other homes. Nevertheless, it is a true LA icon, along with the likes of the Hollywood sign (Fig. 907) and Tail o' the Pup (Fig. 903).

At night, the dazzling, panoramic view from within the house across glittering LA is marvelous. You can walk up the approach drive to look at it from directly below, but Chemosphere is better appreciated from a half block west, uphill on Torreyson (Fig. 478).

FIG. 478 LA Icon Lautner's Malin House, "Chemosphere," became an instant symbol of the Space Age when built nearly a half-century ago. Now mostly masked by trees and brush, it is all the more startling to come upon, close-up.

Brutalism

1953–1980

Brutalism is generally thought of as a British architectural style. The term is commonly applied in the United States to poured-in-place concrete buildings, especially those with strong forms.

As practiced in post–World War II Great Britain, Brutalism was generally pretty direct, even crude. In their *Modern Architecture in Europe*, Dennis and Elizabeth de Witt described Brutalism as a continuation of prewar expressionism, with a tendency to overemphasize and to overexpose in striving for monumental architecture. "The ultimate [Brutalist] expression was the megastructure, that building-as-machine, which like the misunderstood monster in a B-movie, might ... consume an entire city."

Perhaps the two most egregious British examples are the Barbican Center (1959–1981) in London and the truly dreary Cumbernauld Center (1965–1967) in a new town of the same name near Glasgow. Barbican alone encompassed most of the Brutalist era in the British Isles, with many Brutalist buildings designed into the 1970s, well after concrete-based imageries had ceased to be in vogue in the United States.

FIGS. 479, 480 American Brutalism is efficiently showcased by Marcel Breuer's buildings at St. John's University in rural Collegeville, Minnesota. These bold designs emphasize the strength and plasticity of poured concrete, which by Bauhaus tenets was an "honest" material. In these views we see Breuer and Hamilton Smith's dormitories (Fig. 479) from 1968 (foreground) and 1958 (rear) and the structural "trees" in their 1967 Alcuin Library (Fig. 480). There are several Brutalist Breuer works at the side-by-side St. John's university and prep school, including the Abbey Church (Figs. 481, 482).

American Brutalism descends largely from a separate lineage, the postwar designs of Le Corbusier, especially his Unité d'Habitation in Marseille (1947–1952), government buildings in Chandigarh, India (1953–1961), and the La Tourette monastery near Lyon (1957–1960). These powerful designs gain personality from Le Corbusier's confident design idiosyncrasies.

Because Le Corbusier's designs were ultimately so personal, as opposed to a systematic vocabulary like that of Mies van der Rohe, the most successful American Brutalist designs adopted Corbusier's general architectural ethic, without attempting to actually replicate his architecture.

In the United States, Bauhaus émigré Marcel Breuer introduced large-scale, poured concrete architecture with his St.

FIG. 483 Variations on a Theme Following St. John's by a year, Breuer's Convent of the Assumption at the University of Mary in Bismarck shared several elements with the Abbey Church, including a freestanding bell banner and exterior materials.

John's Abbey Church (1953–1961; this chapter). This project was under design concurrently with Breuer's better-known UNESCO Headquarters in Paris, and his University Heights campus for New York University. Powerful, poured concrete forms were prominent in all three designs, and the *pilotis*-piers of the UNESCO secretariat wing are outwardly similar to their Corbusian counterparts in Marseilles. Still, Breuer employed a more polished Brutalist vocabulary than did Le Corbusier.

Boston City Hall is another major American Brutalist monument, based on a winning competition entry by Kallmann, McKinnell & Knowles. Their design superficially resembles Le Corbusier's La Tourette monastery, which was widely admired and widely mimicked by younger American architects. As did Breuer, Kallmann, McKinnell & Knowles refined their design, compared to Corbusier, without much loss of vitality, and in keeping with City Hall's urbane context.

Abbey Church, St. John's University FIGS. 481, 482

1953–1961

Marcel Breuer, architect; **Hamilton Smith, Valarius Michelson**, associate architects

St. John's University, Collegeville, Minnesota

With this powerful, yet nuanced design, Breuer effectively popularized a poured concrete, Corbusian design imagery for a new generation of American architects. Unlike the comparatively restrained contemporary poured-concrete designs of Louis Kahn (see the Modern Masters chapter), Breuer's Abbey Church is bold, if not primal, made up of big, uncomplicated forms, especially the giant, freestanding "bell banner" (Fig. 482). Layers of textures and natural materials are played off visually against these basic building elements, resulting in a surprisingly warm human environment.

Convent of the Assumption, University of Mary FIG. 483

1954–1963

Marcel Breuer, architect; **Hamilton Smith, Traynor & Hermanson**, associate architects

7520 University Dr./Hwy. 1804, S of Bismarck, North Dakota; use the University of Mary south entrance.

A Benedictine campus like St. John's, Convent of the Assumption is a smaller-scale followup of the Abbey Church, sharing basic architectural motifs, although the Assumption bell banner is proportionately more attenuated compared to St. John's. Befitting the barren, windswept Dakota landscape, Breuer's built environment here feels more austere than does the wooded St. John's campus in Minnesota.

Carpenter Center for the Visual Arts, Harvard University

1961–1963

Le Corbusier, architect; **Sert, Jackson & Gourley**, associate architects

Quincy St., Harvard University campus, Cambridge, Massachusetts

Le Corbusier's sole U.S. building, excluding his contributions to the United Nations Headquarters design committee, this structure contains the familiar "Corbu" motifs, but little of the vitality of the architect's buildings abroad.

Art & Architecture Building, Yale University FIG. 484

1958–1964; rebuilt after 1968 fire; restored 2008

Paul Rudolph, architect

York at Chapel Sts., Yale University campus, New Haven, Connecticut

Some buildings literally wring out their stakeholders. The A & A is one of these. The high drama that plagued this building is Shake-

FIG. 484 Cause Célèbre Paul Rudolph's uncompromising Art & Architecture Building at Yale was imposing enough, in multiple respects, to provoke furious student protests during the flaming 1960s. Completed in 1964, the building galvanized a storm of controversy over whether architecture should be appreciated first and foremost as art, or should be a judged on its functional qualities.

FIG. 485 Living in Art In a reprise of the Yale A & A hullabaloo, Rudolph's boldly textured Crawford Manor housing nearby served as a lightning rod for controversy over the role, even the appropriateness, of monumental architecture in everyday life.

spearean in intensity and plot twists. Rudolph's design unintentionally posed a fundamental, quintessentially 1960s question for architects: namely, if a building is an artistic triumph and yet functionally deficient, can it still be great architecture? With this design, Rudolph created a distinctive, personal style characterized by complexly articulated massing and highly textured, hammered concrete surfaces. Considered to be an exceptionally gifted architect well prior to designing this building, Rudolph was famous-infamous forever after.

Crawford Manor FIG. 485

1962–1966

Paul Rudolph, architect

Oak St. Connector at Park St., New Haven, Connecticut

Located just a few blocks from the A & A building (above), this high-rise apartment complex for the elderly revisited the same question: is architecture primarily an art form, or should everyday human needs be paramount to the architect? As public sculpture, Crawford Manor is surely a success. Less certain is whether these high-rise towers are ideal living environments for the elderly.

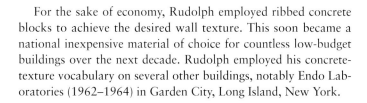

FIGS. 486, 487 Power to the People Boston City Hall was immensely potent, both as a local political symbol and especially as a national muse for architects in the decade after it opened. The moody interiors are worthy of a latter-day Piranesi. *Fig. 487: Library of Congress, Prints & Photographs, Historic American Buildings Survey*

FIG. 489 Solid! By American standards, Manhattan's cityscape is extremely dense. Even so, Breuer's Whitney Museum of American Art visually anchors its surroundings.

For the sake of economy, Rudolph employed ribbed concrete blocks to achieve the desired wall texture. This soon became a national inexpensive material of choice for countless low-budget buildings over the next decade. Rudolph employed his concrete-texture vocabulary on several other buildings, notably Endo Laboratories (1962–1964) in Garden City, Long Island, New York.

Boston City Hall FIGS. 486,487

1962–1968 endangered
Kallmann, McKinnell & Knowles, architects; **Campbell, Aldrich & Nulty**, associate architects; **LeMessurier Associates**, consulting engineers
City Hall Plaza, Boston, Massachusetts

Boston City Hall is an American transliteration of Le Corbusier's La Tourette monastery. It visually revitalized Boston's government core, even as it inspired many imitations, virtually a "Boston School" of architectural imagery.

In the late 1960s, this brawny, complex building seemed to sum up not just the contemporary essence of Boston, but also a vital new direction in American architecture. How quickly that heroic era passed! If many of the 1960s and 1970s Boston School buildings now seem passé, the sheer drama of this seminal building is enduring.

Peabody Terrace, Harvard University FIG. 488

1962–1964
Sert, Jackson & Gourley, architects; **Sasaki Associates**, landscape architects
900 Memorial Dr., Cambridge, Massachusetts

These highly photogenic towers and connected low-rise apartments inspired many sincere imitators, most notably Ralph Rapson's 1968–1973 Cedar Square West housing in Minneapolis.

A filigree of louvers and reveals plays off against the solid concrete of the towers; the designers seem to have gotten the balance exactly right, as the towers are assertive, with nary a trace of heaviness.

Whitney Museum of American Art FIG. 489

1964–1966
Marcel Breuer, Hamilton Smith, architects
945 Madison Ave. at E. 75th St., New York, New York

Breuer's penchant for big, bold forms reached an ultimate consummation with the Whitney; it almost seems to have been carved out of a sold block of stone. Like Frank Lloyd Wright's Guggenheim (Fig. 262), located a short distance away, the Whitney was intended to stand apart from its neighbors. Despite the building's apparent solidity, its column-free galleries are quite flexible; partitions and lighting can be easily moved around to accommodate exhibition requirements.

Design Research Store

1969
Benjamin Thompson, architect
48 Brattle St., Cambridge, Massachusetts

Here, Thompson reduced the Boston School–Brutalist aesthethic to an absolute minimum: a poured concrete structural frame, infilled with plate glass.

THE CUT-INTO BOX

As American society evolved in the 1970s, big, bold, heroic 1960s architecture seemed ever less relevant. Some architects continued to work in variations of Brutalism in the 1970s and later, but most architects moved along with the latest fashions, which after the mid-1970s increasingly favored historical allusions and contextualism. These approaches were philosophically opposite to the values of Brutalism.

In response, many designers who were grounded in the 1960s toned down their designs; while still massive, they were softened through the use of smoother textures and smaller-scale details. This style was labeled the Cut-into Box by David Gebhard. He identified several influences and precedents in addition to Brutalism, including elements of New Formalism (see Mid-Century Expressionism chapter), and the work of Louis Kahn (see Modern Masters chapter).

Gebhard cited typical prominent elements of the Cut-into Box as: multiple rectangular volumes, a horizontal emphasis, brick surface sheathing to hide structure, windows and other openings set into deep reveals, often with slanted sills, and exteriors that are monotone, both in color and material.

This vocabulary was widely embraced across large parts of the United States from the late 1960s into the 1980s. While precursors occurred mostly in the Northeast, especially around Boston, it strengthened around a Harvard-Minnesota axis which was especially prominent during this period. Throughout the 1970s, the Cut-into Box was virtually a Minnesota regional style.

The Architects Collaborative Offices
1966
The Architects Collaborative, architects
46 Brattle St., Boston, Massachusetts

The "TAC" design is on the cusp of the Cut-into Box style: horizontal, made up of several rectilinear volumes, monochromatic in color and material. Only the infill-frame expression of structure is uncharacteristic. This building was especially influential among American architects in the late 1960s, as the designers-tenants were a widely admired architectural practice, including among its founding partners Bauhaus master Walter Gropius, among other teachers at the prestigious Harvard Graduate School of Design.

Cathedral of Christ the King FIG. 490
1966–1969
I .W. Colburn, architect
2600 Vincent Ave., W of Oakland Dr., Kalamazoo (Portage), Michigan

Colburn was perhaps the most expressionistic of those working with Cut-into Box vocabularies. Certainly I-94 motorists must be startled right off their cell phones when coming unexpectedly upon this ultramodern-looking, yet traditional-feeling Episcopal cathedral. Colburn worked from basic brick forms, and that sufficiently softens what might otherwise seem too animated a design for the seat of a bishop.

Bradfield-Emerson Halls/Veterinary Research Laboratory FIG. 491
1968; 1973
Ulrich Franzen, architect
Tower Rd. on the campus of the New York State College of Agriculture/Veterinary Quad at Cornell, Ithaca, New York

Franzen was a master of the Cut-into Box vocabulary. The 13-story, nearly windowless Bradfield Hall can be appreciated as an

FIG. 490 **Cut-into Box Expressionism** I. W. Colburn could *really* work brick, as his Cathedral of Christ the King in Michigan clearly demonstrates.

FIG. 491 **Brick Sheen** Ulrich Franzen designed in a suave variation of the Cut-into Box, distinct from the brawny Boston-Minnesota expression. His Cornell buildings, including Bradford-Emerson Halls/VRL are exceptionally elegant expressions.

FIG. 493 **Quiet Sophistication** It is possible to achieve exceptional bearing through sheer quality of design. Minnetonka's Municipal Building is Exhibit "A."

FIG. 492 **Minimalist Masterpiece** Mass can be expressed architecturally as anything from assertive and bulky to understated and refined. Edward Larrabee Barnes' Walker Art Center falls into the latter category, a supreme work of minimalism.

FIG. 494 **Rural Sculpture** When it opened, Dakota County Government Center in Hastings, Minnesota, stood completely alone, an unexpected presence in the midst of wide-open farmlands.

elegant piece of abstract brick sculpture, much more subtle—its envelope almost a sheen, rather than a mass, of brick—than the typical Harvard-Minnesota rendition.

This structure and his nearby Veterinary Research Tower and adjacent Boyce Thompson Institute at the east end of Tower Road conveniently present a suave demonstration covering a range of Cut-into-Box expressions.

Walker Art Center FIG. 492
1969–1971; later modifications, expansions, and addition
Edward Larrabee Barnes, architect
Vineland Pl. at Lyndale Ave., Minneapolis, Minnesota

Walker Art Center is virtually windowless, with little reveal-generated wall texture. Rather, the brick envelope is almost completely smooth. Like some of its superb art collection, this building represents an outermost expression of minimalism.

The Walker is much more than an elegantly restrained exterior. Its interior is organized around an ingenious spiral plan which provides extreme flexibility in gallery use. Barnes's brilliant, efficient design is even more impressive in comparison to the overbearing 2002-2005 addition directly to the south, by Herzog & de Meuron.

Minnetonka Municipal Building FIG. 493
1970–1971; later additions
Scott R. Berry, Thorsen & Thorshov, architects
14600 Minnetonka Blvd., Minnetonka, Minnesota

The Cut-into Box is essentially monumental abstract sculpture, and as such it is difficult to fully humanize. The Minnetonka Municipal Building is an exceptional demonstration that it is not impossible to do so. Here is a building with both striking abstract visual

qualities and a dignified beauty approaching the best of Scandinavian National Romanticism.

As government has continued to grow, so of course has its space requirements, and Berry's original design has unavoidably been visually diminished by additions at both sides. Only a remnant of the exterior is still visible.

Dakota County Government Center FIG. 494
1973–1974; additions
Wayne Bishop, Ellerbe Associates, architects
1590 W. Hwy. 55, Hastings, Minnesota

Initially, Dakota County Government Center stood completely alone on a slight rise in open farmland. Although the remote site was problematic as a civic location, the original visual solitude intensified the building's sculptural qualities.

Massive subsequent additions have all but subsumed Bishop's original building. Worse, a conventional commercial highway strip has grown out of town to the center, erasing the original sense of splendid visual isolation.

1199 Plaza Apartments
Late 1960s–1975
The Hodne/Stageberg Partners, architects; **Herb Baldwin**, landscape architect
Within First Ave., FDR Dr., 107th and 110th Sts., New York, New York

The design by these Minneapolis architects evolved out of a 1963 national competition. The juxtaposition of towers and horizontal mid-rise wings owes much to Peabody Terrace (Fig. 488), but as built, a brick envelope and interplay of strong projections and deep reveals falls squarely into the Cut-into Box vocabulary.

Late Modernism

1963–2004

FIGS. 495, 496 Increasing Complexity By the mid-1960s, mainstream American Modernism was growing increasingly varied and complex. This evolution is apparent at the U.S. Air Force Academy, where the relative simplicity of the original campus buildings (Fig. 495) contrastss with the intricate chapel design (Fig. 496).

While American architecture was moving in several directions by the mid-1960s, Modernism still dominated the mainstream of American non-residential architecture. The prevailing form of Modernism traced back to the European International Style of the 1920s and 1930s.

Modern American works from those years are identified in The International Style chapter. Early post–World War II Modernism up through the mid-1960s is included in the Postwar Modernism chapter. This chapter picks up with the increasingly complex Modern mainstream after the mid-1960s.

Other schools of Modernism such as the progressive strain of Richardson, Sullivan, and Wright, the contributions of various California Modernists, the Scandinavian-influenced architecture of the Saarinens and Aalto, Mid-century Expressionism, and Brutalism are addressed in several preceding chapters.

As noted previously, the relative simplicity of early Postwar Modernism gradually evolved into increasingly complex expressions. Late Modern residential designs grew especially sculptural. Non-residential designs moved away from visually thin skins to exterior expressions of mass and depth.

EXEMPLARS

The Late Modern period was replete with talent and achievement—thousands of superior buildings were designed by hundreds of exceptionally gifted architects, only a fraction of whom can be cited here, alas. Among this elite cohort are three instructive practices with roots at the beginnings of the period, in the mid-1960s, extending into the twenty-first century. While representative works of Richard Meier are cited in this chapter and in the Deconstruction chapter, buildings of Hardy Holzman Pfeiffer Associates and Frank Gehry are toward the end of this chapter.

RICHARD MEIER

Richard Meier (b. 1934) has served as an influential form giver since the publication of his 1965–1967 Smith House in Darien, Connecticut. Measured by the subsequent proliferation of copies, young American architects seemed enraptured by the design of this pristine white structure, especially by details like a plate glass window passing *behind* a semi-freestanding chimney. A Man verses Nature dialogue with the site, a rocky overlook on Long Island Sound, resulted in an almost impossibly picturesque (and photogenic) scene.

Six years later, Meier outdid his Smith design with the James Douglas House (Fig. 498), surely among the best-known postwar American houses. While the architect continued to attract residential commissions, he concurrently undertook large-scale engagements like the 1970–1977 Bronx Development Center, the 1975–1979 New Harmony Atheneum (Fig. 505), and a 1980–1983 expansion of the High Museum of Art in Atlanta. Of course his 1984–1997 Getty Center commission (Fig. 561) occupied Meier's creative energies over more than a decade.

All of these designs illustrate Meier's explorations of purity of expression. An extremely high level of skill is evident in how the buildings are put together, offering important benchmarks for others. Yet two interrelated qualities, the manipulation of space and the interpenetration of light, are ultimately most impressive, from the earliest to the latest works. The increasing complexity common to the buildings in this chapter is reflected in an increasing, rigorous complexity in the experience of Meier's buildings, which critic Ivor Richards described, in the context of the architect's 2003 Jubilee Church in Rome, as "an instrument of light."

FIG. 497 **Transition** Charles Gwathmey's house and studio for his artist parents served as a bridge between the geometric abstraction of Postwar Modernism and the increasing complexity of Modernist expressions after the early 1960s.

LATE MODERN RESIDENTIAL

Robert Gwathmey House & Studio FIG. 497
1965–1967
Charles Gwathmey and Richard Henderson, architects
122 Bluff Rd., Amagansett, New York

Distinguished by its pure geometries, this 1,200-square-foot weekend house and adjacent studio became an instant landmark of mid-century Modernism. Set in a spacious meadow, now overgrown, house and studio recalled the early modern ideal of a sculptural object in strong contrast to the landscape. In its engaging abstraction, Gwathmey's design established a model for the emphasis on form that became so characteristic of the following era.

James Douglas House FIG. 498
1971–1973
Richard Meier, architect
3490 Lakeshore/Hwy. 119, Harbor Springs, Michigan
(private residence, not visible from road)

Meier's Douglas House is *the* iconic 1970s Late Modern house, an intensely white piece of architectural sculpture, dramatically peeking through dense green forest, high above the Lake Michigan shoreline. Few have been to the house, but one iconic photograph is famous among those interested in architecture.

Spear House FIG. 499
1976–1978
Laurinda Spear, Bernardo Fort-Brescia, architects, **Rem Koolhaas**, design consultant
Bayshore Dr. at NE. 93rd St., Miami Shores, Florida

Just the right design response for its slightly disorderly suburban setting on Biscayne Bay: strong, colorful forms, without a trace of fussiness. The house attracts attention while affording a degree of privacy by virtue of a mostly opaque wall facing the street. A tiny porthole in the front wall offers a mysterious peek into the pool.

FIG. 498 The View Everyone Knows Relatively few have actually visited Richard Meier's Douglas House in an out-of-the-way Michigan locale, but every architecture maven knows this classic Ezra Stoller photo! *Photograph: Ezra Stoller © Esto, published with the permission of Richard Meier & Partners*

FIG. 499 **Tropical Mystique** The Spear House perfectly captured the essence of Miami's narcissistic mythic culture on the threshold of the "Miami Vice" era. Along with the Milam House (Fig. 465), Spear is arguably one of the two most significant modern houses in Florida.

FIG. 500 **Rational v. Intellectual** Because the U.S. Air Force Academy Chapel (Figs. 496 and above) is more arresting than its rationalist neighbors (Fig. 495), it can easily be thought of as a romantic foil. Actually, the design reflects architect Walter Netsch's forays into the nearly impenetrable intellectual denseness of Field Theory. Of course, a towering I.Q. is not required to simply enjoy the Gothic-like main worship space simply for is dazzling visual qualities.

LATE MODERN NON-RESIDENTIAL

U.S. Air Force Academy Chapel FIGS. 496, 500
1956–1963
Walter Netsch, Jr., Skidmore, Owings & Merrill, architects; **Kenneth Naslund**, structural engineer; **Dan Kiley**, landscape architect
W of I-25, N of Colorado Springs, Colorado

The first academy buildings reflected the mainstream International Style of the 1950s: refined and restrained expressions of rationalism. However, Netsch's slightly later chapel design, with its folded plates and stained glass clearly broke free from that mold, providing a transition to the increasingly complex expressions of mainstream modernism in the mid-1960s and later. Despite the chapel's dramatic visual impact, it should be emphasized that this is not in any way a romantic building; indeed, the design proved to be a gateway to Netsch's explorations with his esoteric Field Theory designs at University of Illinois, Chicago Circle, and elsewhere in the late 1960s and 1970s. In its complexity and singular personality, the chapel signals a sharp break with dominant postwar modern idioms.

Chicago Civic Center, "Richard J. Daley Civic Center"
1963–1966
C. F. Murphy Associates, Skidmore, Owings & Merrill, Loebl, Schlossman, Bennett & Dart, architects; **Pablo Picasso**, sculptor
Dearborn, Washington, Clark and Randolph Sts., Chicago, Illinois

Another example of the 1960s movement away from the simplicity of postwar Modernism. Here, the exterior has been visually bulked up, like Tenneco (Fig. 419), by deepening reveals to add strong shadow lines across spandrels and piers. As a result, the building reads as massive, compared to, for instance, Lever House (Fig. 413).

John Hancock Center
1966–1970
Bruce Graham, principal designer; **Fazlur Khan**, chief structural engineer; **Skidmore, Owings & Merrill**, architects and engineers
875 N. Michigan Ave., Chicago, Illinois

FIG. 501 **Consummate Urbanism** When IDS Center opened, its tower predictably drew comments about being out of scale with downtown, as this mid-1970s view illustrates. But as architect Philip Johnson anticipated, similar-sized towers soon sprouted nearby. By now, the IDS tower seems right in scale. Including extensive retail and a hotel, the entire IDS Center is a paradigm of inspired urbanism, drawing a variety of activity to its Crystal Court (Fig. 667).

In designing this super-tall, X-braced trapezoid, the architects took no chances that the project would not be visually prominent, if not the dominant property along North Michigan Avenue. Inevitably dubbed "Big John," the structure encloses a stacked mix of uses: retail, parking, offices, and residential. Everyone seems to have a story about the building, such as the one about waves in upper-floor toilets when the building oscillates in heavy winds.

Weyerhaeuser Headquarters
1968–1971
Edward Charles Bassett, Skidmore, Owings & Merrill, architects; **Sydney Rodgers Associates**, space planners; **Peter Walker, Sasaki Walker Associates**, landscape architects
E side of I-5, off the 320th St. interchange, Federal Way (near Tacoma), Washington

A minimalist, environmental solution for a large facility on an exurban site. From the highway, Weyerhaeuser appears simply as floors spanning between two low hills, somewhat like Frank Lloyd Wright's Marin County center, although much more reticent. By now its spandrels are lushly draped in greenery. The building is set well back into a small clearing, so northbound motorists on I-5 are likely to pass right by without noticing. However, a dramatic view is offered to southbound I-5 motorists, especially when the interiors glow warmly at dusk or on gloomy days.

IDS Center FIG. 501
1968–1972
Philip Johnson & John Burgee, architects; **Edward F. Baker**, associate architect
Nicollet Mall, 7th and 8th Sts., Marquette Ave., Minneapolis, Minnesota

Brilliant architecture and urbanism, a single project that radically transformed a city's self-image and elevated the local architectural benchmark for future downtown office buildings. IDS Center is much more than just a tall tower: its most important component is the Crystal Court (Fig. 667), an enclosed, street-level atrium which serves as a town square, also providing orientation for pedestrians traversing Downtown's second-level skywalk system (Figs. 947–950).

Sears Tower FIG. 502
1968–1974
Bruce Graham, principal designer; **Fazlur Khan**, chief structural engineer; **Skidmore, Owings & Merrill**, architects and engineers
Wacker Drive, Franklin, Adams, and Jackson Sts., Chicago, Illinois

Another super-tall design from Graham and Khan, this one based on nine 75-foot-square "bundled tubes" employed as intrinsic windbracing. The tubes begin to terminate at the 50th floor, until only two extend to the tower's full height of 1,450 feet/110 stories. A precise, elegant enclosure for 4 million square feet of floor area.

Pacific Design Center FIG. 503
1971–1975, 1984–1988; 2007–2009
Cesar Pelli, Gruen Associates, architects
NE corner Melrose Ave. and San Vicente Blvd., Los Angeles, California

The voluminous first building, known locally and not always affectionately as the Blue Whale, visually overwhelmed its small-scale locale. Another scaleless structure, in green, was added a decade later. A third and final increment, sail-like and bright red, was announced in 2006. Built to house large showrooms with little need for windows, these structures seem to exist in a separate dimensional world from their municipal context. Only in LA.

Johns Manville Headquarters FIG. 504
1973–1976
John Sheehy, The Architects Collaborative, architects; **Hubertus Mittman**, landscape architect
SW of Littleton Colorado; from Hwy. 470, S 0.3 mi. on Wadsworth/Hwy. 121; turn right/west at stop lights and follow Deer Creek Canyon Rd. 3.3 mi. (left at stop sign) to entrance road at Deer Creek Facility sign (on the right).

A gorgeous metallic structure has been deftly sited within a small rocky canyon. As one approaches, the building presents a fore-shortened view framed dramatically between two primordial monoliths. The juxtaposition of built with nature is a common

FIG. 502 **Bundled Tubes** For a generation into the postwar era, SOM's Chicago office operated right at the cutting edge of structural-design innovation. Sears Tower is a nearly pure expression of engineering determining form.

FIG. 503 **Separate Realities** With a huge space program on a site bordering a small-scaled neighborhood, there was no possibility that the Pacific Design Center could be "contextual." Rather, "otherworldly" comes to mind.

FIG. 504 Western Sophistication The extraordinary architectural presence of Johns-Manville Headquarters illustrates that "Western" culture involves much more than cowboys and ski resorts. *Photograph © Nick Wheeler*

FIG. 505 Villa of Culture Richard Meier's Atheneum provides a visually extravagant entry image for historic New Harmony, Indiana. Set apart in a corner of town, the large, brilliantly white structure does not detract from the historic visual character of this marvelous, small-scaled community.

architectural theme, but rarely has it been accomplished so spectacularly as in this exquisitely devised example.

Atheneum FIG. 505
1975–1979
Richard Meier, architect
North & Arthur Sts., New Harmony, Indiana

New Harmony is a singular community, marked by successive utopian settlements: Harmonist (1814–1824) and Owenite (1825–1827). Scarcely a quarter section in built-up area, New Harmony offers a treasure trove of historical sites.

Meier was engaged to design this visitors' center right after completing the Douglas House (Fig. 498), and if the client was looking for an arresting monument, the timing was perfect. The Atheneum represents a culmination of Meier's Corbusian-villa explorations, a voluptuous design which does not detract from the small-scale community, since its spacious site is off in one corner of town.

Crystal Cathedral FIGS. 506, 507
1977–1980; Crean Tower-Chapel, 1990
Robert Schuller, founder and impresario; **Philip Johnson, John Burgee**, architects
12141 Lewis St., S of Katella, between Harbor Blvd. and I-5, Garden Grove, California

Truly a cathedral befitting a famous television ministry. The church itself features an enormous, exceedingly photogenic sanctuary volume enclosed in a space-frame tracery. The entire complex (including an earlier church by Richard Neutra, 1959–1961, and Tower of Hope by Dion Neutra, 1967) is visually dazzling anytime, but one should arrive about a half-hour before a Sunday service, as parishioners drive in—and remain for the service itself, of course—to fully appreciate the singular Crystal Cathedral experience. Absent that, you can view the Hour of Power at home, Sunday mornings on TV.

The Atlantis FIG. 508
1978–1982
Arquitectonica, architects
2025 Brickell Ave., Miami, Florida

FIGS. 506, 507 Religious Attraction Robert Schuller's Crystal Cathedral experience is a first-rank attraction for its striking architecture of its extraordinary sanctuary space, its manicured landscapes, and its flawlessly choreographed Sunday services. The legendary Christmas pageant features flying angels and live elephants.

A big, splashy gesture, appropriately mirroring Miami culture. Here is the usual Arquitectonica design formula: beginning with a rational, modern basis that has almost, but not quite, been turned into a cartoon through the employment of primary colors and bold forms. Apparently that was still not enough for the desired visual effect, so the designers introduced a four-story hole part way up this apartment slab to make its exterior even more attention-grabbing. Clearly, it worked.

FIG. 508 The Architecture of Wow! Arquitectonica introduced eye-popping designs like The Atlantis to the Miami area, where the pre-1980s architectural norm had become pretty mundane after 1920s Mediterranean, 1930s Moderne, and 1950s Lapidus hotels.

FIG. 509 **Pure Beauty** 333 Wacker Drive stands out from among its agitated neighbors on account of its serene gracefulness.

333 Wacker Drive FIG. 509
1979–1983
William Pedersen, Kohn Pedersen Fox, architects; **Perkins & Will**, associate architects
333 Wacker Dr., Chicago, Illinois

The bow-shaped, green glass curtain wall of this speculative office tower would be spectacular anywhere, but it seems especially suited for this prominent site along the Chicago River. While Pedersen's design is not mainstream Chicago School, 333 Wacker is nevertheless a great visual resource for Chicago.

James R. Thompson State of Illinois Center FIGS. 510, 511
1979–1985
Helmut Jahn, Murphy/Jahn, architects; **Lester B. Knight**, associate architects
100 W. Randolph St., Chicago, Illinois

State of Illinois is a rarity among public buildings in that it is aggressively non-contextual, both in its relative scalelessness and also because of the massive exterior curvature. It is just barely recognizable as a Chicago School building, primarily in its suggestion of structural rhythms, especially throughout the atrium. State of Illinois has been locally controversial, to say the least. Nevertheless, it is one of the most memorable buildings in Chicago's architecturally super-rich downtown. Be sure to go inside to experience Jahn's awesome soaring atrium.

FIGS. 510, 511 **Not Your Father's Public Building** Helmut Jahn's State of Illinois Center design is a complete departure from our conventional image of a government office building. Its provocative, curving exterior is only a foretaste of the astonishing atrium within.

HARDY HOLZMAN PFEIFFER

The integrated group practice of Hugh Hardy, Malcolm Holzman, and Norman Pfeiffer (Hardy Holzman Pfeiffer Associates—HHPA) bridged almost the entire Late Modernism period of this book and conveniently illustrates the broad range of expression possible under the big tent of Modernism. Their body of work shared the increasing complexity characteristic of Late Modernism, while also responding to context, whether in the use of locally prominent materials or in allusions to historic and regional vernacular construction.

In 1967, Hardy (b. 1932) expanded his five-year-old practice to include Holzman (b. 1940) and Pfeiffer (b. 1940). The firm soon distinguished itself for innovative theaters and institutional designs. HHPA undertook little commercial work. HHPA has been a leader in the design of arts facilities (especially theaters and museums), higher education, and libraries and in the revitalization of historic buildings. Their interiors are legendary, juxtaposing forms, materials, colors, and boldly patterned, custom-designed fabrics and carpeting. HHPA valued a collaboration with artists in building design. The firm separated into three individual practices in 2004.

Mt. Healthy School FIGS. 512, 513
1970–1972; later alterations by others
Hardy Holzman Pfeiffer Associates, architects
Hwy. 58, S of Ogilville, Indiana

Mt. Healthy was one of the prestigious Columbus, Indiana, commissions—in this case to design a then radical, open-plan elementary school in a nearby rural area. HHPA's design solution employed a wondrous mix of locality and sophistication, high design and the ordinary. This was a vibrant environment in which children could be reassured by the familiar while stimulated by a rich visual environment, which was physically broken down in scale inside and out. As educational theories inevitably evolved past the open plan, the building was later substantially modified by others.

FIGS. 516, 517 Resourceful Hybrid The minimal construction budget for Orchestra Hall in Minneapolis meant that visual presence had to be achieved through efficient gestures. For example, the auditorium was shifted off the street grid to signify its civic identity by differing in orientation from nearby commercial buildings (above). Exteriors and the lobby were expressed in an inexpensive, high-tech vocabulary. Acoustical treatment was rendered through a system of clouds rather than the expensive acoustical plasterwork of traditional concert halls. Warmed by wood and color, the concert hall is an acoustical and visual success (below).

FIGS. 514, 515 High Tech The colorful high-tech design vocabulary of the Columbus Occupational Health Association Center seems altogether fitting for an industrial clinic in architecturally cosmopolitan Columbus, Indiana.

Columbus Occupational Health Association Center FIGS. 514, 515
1973–1974
Hardy Holzman Pfeiffer Associates, architects
605 Cottage Ave., Columbus, Indiana

Clinics must be sterile, and unfortunately that often describes their architecture as well. This industrial clinic reads as "clean" in its architectural crispness, although it is anything but sterile visually. During the 1970s, HHPA was known for its brightly colored, High-Tech design vocabulary, which is both symbolically relevant and welcome in this industrial district.

Orchestra Hall FIGS. 516, 517
1973–1974, altered, endangered
Hardy Holzman Pfeiffer Associates, design architects; **Cyril Harris**, acoustical consultant; **Hammel, Green & Abrahamson**, executive architects
11th St. at Marquette Ave., Minneapolis, Minnesota

Something of a miracle. Despite three willful design firms and a modest $7.2 million budget (a little more than $30 million in 2008 dollars), Orchestra Hall opened to rave reviews only 16 months after design began.

The auditorium is a modern transliteration of traditional European concert halls, and is a resounding acoustical success. Audiences passed through a vibrant, High-Tech lobby (redecorated, late 1990s) before entering the auditorium, which is finished in warm woods, brass fixtures, and a soothing, salmon-colored palette.

Best Products Company FIG. 518
1980–1981; 1986; altered
Hardy Holzman Pfeiffer Associates, architects
1400 E. Parham Rd., NE cor. I-95, Richmond, Virginia

An engaging assemblage of forms and details, recovered architectural sculpture and everyday materials. The marvelous contemporary art collection of Sydney and Frances Lewis, company owners, was integral to the building's design. At its high point in the 1980s (the property is now owned by others and has been significantly altered), this was an extraordinary environment, from the road entrance all the way inside to the art hung over secretarial workstations.

WCCO-TV Studio/Headquarters FIGS. 519, 520
1981–1983; altered 2005–2006
Hardy Holzman Pfeiffer Associates, architects
11th St. at Nicollet Mall, Minneapolis, Minnesota

A master's-class demonstration in the use of stone. Located on a prominent downtown site directly across the street from HHPA's earlier Orchestra Hall (above), WCCO is visually rich and urbane, far exceeding the utilitarian norm for this technical building type.

Alaska Center for the Performing Arts FIG. 521
1985–1988
Hardy Holzman Pfeiffer Associates, architects
621 W. Sixth Ave., Anchorage, Alaska

The center's three-auditorium program is inherently bulky, so the elevations are broken down in order to reduce its apparent scale. The resulting assortment of exterior masses, colors, and textures is particularly welcome in the context of bland, low-energy, downtown Anchorage. Interiors are truly "theatrical," especially the exuberantly patterned carpeting, a signature HHPA flourish.

FIG. 518 High Achievement Hardy Holzman Pfeiffer Associates was known for the seamless incorporation of art, craft, and sculpture, as here, at the monumental entrance to Best Products Company headquarters in suburban Richmond, Virginia.

FIGS. 519, 520 Expression through Materials WCCO-TV Studio/Headquarters in Minneapolis is a big departure from the normally utilitarian television studio. Since its site is directly across the street from HHPA's Orchestra Hall (Fig. 517) and M. Paul Friedberg's Peavey Plaza, the client wished to project a civic character. Office spaces are enclosed in warm, golden stone; studios and technical areas are expressed as distinct volumes, clad in copper sheathing.

FIG. 521 Northern Light To reduce the visual impacts of its very large space program, Alaska Center was broken down into a rich assemblage of gables, slopes, and smaller forms. HHPA's characteristically vivid interiors are especially valued during the half-light of the long arctic winter.

FIG. 522 **At Home on the Range** The three-dimensional undulations of the Globe News Center for the Performing Arts in Amarillo refer to cherished local geological formations. *Photograph © Bob Davis courtesy of Holzman Moss Architecture*

The Globe News Center for the Performing Arts FIG. 522
2003–2005
Holzman Moss Architecture, architects
Buchanan St. at SE corner 5th Ave., Amarillo, Texas

With the 2004 separation of HHPA into three independent entities, all three of the former founding partners incorporated their HHPA project teams into their new practices.

Globe News Center was designed around a movable acoustical shell that allows the auditorium to be configured as either a tuned concert hall or as an open, flexible stage for theater or dance. This innovation gets around the usual problem with multi-use cultural venues: technically mediocre space for all events.

Holzman's signature stonework and rich textures are prominent, along with references with special meaning to area residents. Examples include: the undulating exterior envelope, which alludes to a landmark local natural formation; droll cattle-brand carpeting; ceilings-soffits constructed from the sides of livestock trucks, which are ubiquitous in this part of the country. Nuanced reference to locality is another prominent characteristic of Holzman's designs.

FRANK GEHRY

At the outset of the new millennium, Frank Gehry is *the* American signature designer, celebrated today for his flowing, titanium- or stainless steel–clad exteriors the way Philip Johnson was known a generation earlier for his Postmodern skyscrapers. Gehry's designs also illustrate the wide range of Late Modern expressions. Unlike HHPA, in which the three partners jointly commenced project design in a charrette, Gehry functions as the principal designer, while supported by a talented and surely influential staff.

Gehry (b. 1929) is much more than the current "It" architect, however. He was already a highly respected LA Southland design figure by the 1970s, admired for his ability to turn simple forms and inexpensive materials into expressive buildings.

But after his sensational Guggenheim museum in Bilbao, Spain, completed in 1997, one senses that Gehry has almost been trapped by his celebrity, that clients in search of an easy, instant icon engage Gehry to do yet another Bilbao. Given the many vocabularies Gehry has employed during his career, and given his deep interest in everything from city planning to furniture to painting, turning out a extended succession of similar imageries is not what Frank Gehry has been about.

The essence of Gehry's recent design focus is not a specific visual imagery, but rather developing what the architect describes as a personal language of motion. That is a startling direction for architecture, since buildings are thought of as firmly rooted.

Frank Gehry possesses an abundance of the creative instincts and the stellar talent needed to take his idea of movement well beyond its current expressions. Of course, he also needs clients with the vision to move past the now-familiar flowing metal waves.

Davis House / Studio
1972
Frank O. Gehry & Associates, architects
29715 W. Cuthbert Rd., Trancas Beach, Malibu, California
(barely visible from the road)

Painter Ron Davis commissioned Gehry after visiting Gehry's 1968 O'Neill hay barn in San Juan Capistrano. The barn-like interior of the Davis house is highly flexible for a working artist, and its inexpensive sheathing materials evoke a contextual feeling of rural Anglo California that seems especially fitting for this setting.

Functional efficiency and appropriate visual imagery certainly form the basis of Gehry's design solution. Still, this is a creative work above all: as one approaches and moves around the house, the trapezium shape creates illusions of perspective, which are a characteristic of Davis's paintings. Gehry saw the house as a joint and ever-evolving work of art, in which he provided a "beautiful shell," within which Davis would in effect function as an environmental artist while living and working within it.

FIG. 523 Artful Accommodation
Frank Gehry's Gemini G.E.L. building in West Hollywood reused existing structures, inserted a two-story addition (this view), and added an ingenious connective infill. The resulting construction fits so well into to the jumbled Melrose streetscape that one can easily fail to notice, at first, just how inventive this design really was.

Gemini G.E.L. FIG. 523

1976–1979
Frank O. Gehry & Associates, architects
8365 W. Melrose Ave., West Hollywood, Los Angeles, California

In the mid-1970s, Gehry designed several nearly concurrent projects in the form of seemingly ordinary stucco boxes. Gemini is representative of this type, which also includes a student placement center at UCLA (1976–1977). Characteristically for Gehry, there is much more to this design than initially meets the eye: subtle, studied juxtapositions of form, rhythm, and materials.

Gehry House FIG. 524

1977–1978; revised, 1993
Frank O. Gehry & Associates, architects
SW cor. Washington Ave. and 22nd St., Santa Monica, California

Gehry's startling remodeling of his own house in this otherwise fairly conventional neighborhood catapulted him to national attention. The architect offered considered conceptual explanations for his design, but most people probably just saw an ordinary gambrel-roofed house wrapped in chain link, raw plywood, and corrugated metal, the interiors partly gutted and left exposed—not to

FIG. 524 A Sensation, Then and Still Now
Frank Gehry's bewildering remodeling of his Santa Monica home propelled the architect to national attention. Although toned down a bit in a later re-remodeling, this 1970s landmark has not lost its power to shock.

FIG. 525 The Academical Village, Revisited Loyola University Law School is located in a physically undistinguished area of Los Angeles. Gehry responded by breaking out the program into colorful freestanding units, which encouraged human activity while adding visual interest.

FIG. 526 Besting the Boardwalk Thanks to a skilled fusion of colors, textures, and shapes, Gehry's Norton Beach House stands out along the frenzied Venice boardwalk.

FIGS. 527, 528 Late Modern Villa What's *really* weird is not how weird the Winton Guest House in Minnesota might appear to some at first sight, but how good it feels, inside and out, once you've experienced it.

FIG. 529 **The Merchandisers of Venice** Gehry's Chiat/Day Headquarters design required superior creativity—first, to stand out in, yet also be contextual with, messy, vital Venice, and second, to reflect the high qualities of an international advertising agency. Those might seem to be contradictory requirements, but the finished building is certainly a local standout, and as a first-rank work of art, an unforgettable advertisement for its tenant.

mention the asphalt kitchen floor. All the same, if one takes the time to work through everything, this bravura extravaganza comes off as marvelous environmental art.

Loyola University Law School FIG. 525

1981–1984 ff.

Frank O. Gehry & Associates, architects

1441 W. Olympic Blvd., Los Angeles, California

Here, Gehry expressed Loyola's building program as freestanding structures. The resulting architectural village of varied, intriguing forms reads as a three-dimensional collage. A central courtyard offers an animated visual-social environment.

Norton Beach House FIG. 526

1982–1984

Frank O. Gehry & Associates, architects

2509 Ocean Front Walk, Venice, Los Angeles, California

Quite an accomplishment: designing something that really stands out along the tactile Venice boardwalk. Gehry's busy assemblage of seemingly scavenged parts and materials somehow reads as a plausible whole. The freestanding lifeguard tower, a reference to the owner's youth as a lifeguard, provides the signature feature.

Winton Guest House FIGS. 527, 528

1983–1986

Frank Gehry, architect

County Rd. 15, Orono, Minnesota; moved in 2008 to Gainey Conference Center, 2480 S. Country Rd. 45, Owatonna, Minnesota

The Wintons lived in the 1954 Davis House by Philip Johnson, a refined brick and glass rectangle which is not overly large. How-

ever the property is spacious, set well back from the road, high above Lake Minnetonka. Since adding onto the existing house would have been a problematic option, the guest house was set well apart, so that both visually float in the landscape on their own terms. That left Gehry free to design this wondrous collection of volumes.

Chiat/Day Headquarters FIG. 529

1985–1991

Frank Gehry, architect; **Claes Oldenburg, Coosje van Bruggen**, sculptors

Main St., S of Rose St., Venice, Los Angeles, California

A startling design, even for Gehry, and even for LA. Two visually distinct building masses were expressed in a perplexing yet engaging mix of architectural imageries—one seemingly almost conventional and the other much less so—further made memorable by a freestanding entrance portal–sculpture of giant binoculars by Oldenburg and van Bruggen. The building was featured on the cover of Gebhard's and Winter's 1994 LA guidebook, in which they called Chiat/Day "an impressive art object."

Frederick R. Weisman Art Museum, University of Minnesota FIGS. 530, 531

1992–1993; addition, 2007–2009

Frank O. Gehry & Associates, architects; **Meyer, Scherer & Rockcastle**, associate architects

333 E. River Rd., Minneapolis, Minnesota

Weisman was the outcome of Gehry's calculated attempt to visually energize a campus district made up of banal, institutional boxes, and he surely succeeded. In effect, the museum functions as

FIG. 530, 531 **The Flow Begins** Gehry's now-familiar signature flowing-metal imagery was first realized at the Frederick R. Weisman Art Museum at the University of Minnesota. The waves are expressed as distinct from an underlying brick box.

FIG. 532 **The Flow Continues** Peter B. Lewis Building at Case Western Reserve University seems to have benefited from lessons learned on the Weisman. By now the flow has evolved into voluptuous wave-forms which engage—indeed, envelop—the underlying building. This fantastic explosion makes the Weisman seem almost reticent by comparison.

a dynamic, monumental piece of sculpture at a key location, with the non-descript surrounding buildings incorporated into the composition as static foils. Weisman's complex, visual jumble of flowing metal forms has since become a Frank Gehry trademark.

Peter B. Lewis Building, Case Western Reserve University FIG. 532
1999–2002
Frank Gehry, Gehry Partners, architects
Ford Dr. at Bellflower Rd, Cleveland, Ohio

Lewis presents an amazing juxtaposition of architectural forms. The underlying exterior shell appears to be a conventional brick building, with a pleasantly rhythmic pattern of cutout windows. Any sense of conventionality, however, is severed and warped by an explosion of huge metal ribbons. Designed using models, the building's construction required a three-dimensional computer program which located fixed points in space for the building contractor to follow.

Walt Disney Concert Hall FIG. 533
1989–1991; 1998–2003

Frank Gehry, Gehry Partners, architects; **Minoru Nagata, Yasuhisa Toyota** acoustical designers; **Manuel J. Rosales**, organ designer; **Glatter-Götz Orgelbau**, organ builders
Grand Ave. at 1st St., Los Angeles, California

The grandest and most expansive of Frank Gehry's flowing-form envelopes, Disney Hall is a supreme personal triumph for Gehry, and an immense civic success for Los Angeles, which forged a mature civic establishment over the course, and as a direct result, of this daunting undertaking.

Gehry's now-signature flowing vocabulary emerged in the early design stages of the Disney Concert Hall, but due to the length of its development and fund-raising processes, the flowing-form idiom was first realized at the Weisman, climaxed at Bilbao, and seems to have moved into a stunning baroque phase with Disney Hall.

A circuit of elevated, landscaped terraces surrounding the main volumes allows visitors a close-up experience of the exterior forms, and the splendid concert hall interior is enveloped in related swooping surfaces—made of wood.

Jay Pritzker Pavilion FIG. 534
1998–2004
Frank Gehry, Gehry Partners, architects; **Kathryn Gustafson, Gustafson, Guthrie & Nichol**, landscape architects; **Piet Oudolf**, horticultural consultant; **Robert Israel**, lighting designer
Millennium Park, E of Michigan Ave.–Washington St. intersection, Chicago, Illinois

Gehry was engaged to create a signature centerpiece for this half-billion-dollar public environment, and he certainly fulfilled that requirement beyond any possible expectation. This is a "bandshell" like no other. Pritzker stops the visual axis of Washington Street with a bewildering, if intriguing upper fragment; journalist Anne Raver wrote that it "looks like a celestial gateway to another universe"—about as accurate a description as seems possible in mere words.

Gehry's bandshell is adorned with the requisite streaming metal ribbons. These add necessary visual presence to what is actually by program a fairly small structure. The large lawn area for informal seating is criss-crossed—symbolically enclosed—by a 60-foot-high lattice of metal tubes. These further expand the pavilion's apparent scale so that it can really provide a visual focus for a 25-acre park below a wall of looming downtown towers.

FIG. 533 The Flow Reigns Supreme At Walt Disney Concert Hall, Gehry's wave flows have become organic. No longer are the waves applied to the building, as at the Weisman, nor integrated with an underlying form as at Lewis. Now, building and wave read as one. *Carol M. Highsmith / Library of Congress, Prints & Photographs*

FIG. 534 Tantalizing Jay Pritzger Pavilion is surely the most astounding band shell in America, if not in the entire Milky Way galaxy (as is probable). Approaching from the Loop, one first sees the upper fragments above the stage. Even that startling apparition hardly prepares a first-time visitor for what lies ahead.

Postmodernism

1959–2004

FIG. 535 American Postmodernism Postmodern architecture in the United States is typified by superficial references to traditional architectural imageries, chiefly to Classicism. Only rarely, as here in Michael Graves's 1980–1983 library in San Juan Capistrano, California, does a Postmodern design transcend the cardboard-like flatness characteristic of this style.

Postmodernism is used to describe any of several different intellectual and creative movements. British design historian and architect Charles Jencks noted that the term can imply a break with the contemporary orthodoxy, and thus simply connote a negation of reigning Modernism. Alternatively, Postmodernism may be understood as a renewal of and a reconnection with Western humanistic traditions. Jencks favors this view, and has developed a rich interpretation of Postmodern art and architecture emphasizing the canons of Classicism.

Jencks's perspective is impressive and attractive though, sadly, not very relevant to the everyday practice of architecture in the United States. In sharp contrast to his sophisticated point of view, Postmodern American architecture has characteristically been cosmetic, often little more than the style application of historic vocabularies that had been forbidden by the Modern Movement. These designs typically employ Classicist motifs, though they may also, usually indiscriminately, incorporate pieces from other historic imageries.

A primary explanation for this disappointing state of affairs is the lack of background training among post–World War II American architects. In the previous fashion-dominated era, the 1920s–1930s Period Revivals, architects had commonly been educated according to traditional principles, often referred to as Beaux Arts training, after the eminent fine arts ateliers of Paris.

After the war, however, the modernist Bauhaus regimen almost completely expunged traditional design and planning exercises from American architectural schools. Successive generations of architects embraced form-giving rather than mastering the complex and subtle sensibilities of tradition. As a consequence, even many brilliant postwar designers were in effect illiterates when Postmodernism came into fashion.

Notable exceptions, Modern architects proficient at working with tradition, included Princeton graduates of the 1950s influenced by Beaux Arts–trained professor Jean Labatut. Prominent among them are Robert Venturi, Charles W. Moore, and Hugh Hardy. A very few other architects, such as Robert A.M. Stern,

FIG. 536 **Knowing Progenitor** Robert Venturi's house for his mother is compelling because it is as much an intellectual creation as it is architecture. The content informing Venturi's work ensures that his buildings are much more than simply cosmetic expressions of style. (See also Figs. 423, 443)

mastered traditional vocabularies through scholarship and penetrating field study. Postmodern works and historical restorations by these figures are reliably several cuts above the American norm.

VENTURI'S ROLE

Robert Venturi (see the Modern Masters chapter) is widely acknowledged as the progenitor of American Postmodern architecture. Historians now point to Venturi's iconic house of 1959–1964, designed for his mother, as the first Postmodern American building (Figs. 423, 443, 536).

Actually, the house was almost unknown to the profession at first. If Venturi begat Postmodernism, it was on account of his brilliant critique of Modernism in his *Complexity and Contradiction in Architecture* (1966) and his celebration of the exuberant American popular culture in *Learning From Las Vegas* (1972). It should be understood that Venturi did not set out to overturn Modernism, but rather to revitalize a design movement that had become narrow and doctrinaire. Hence his famous play on Mies, "Less is a bore," and a call for inclusiveness in the assertion that "Both/And" is preferable to "Either/Or."

Vanna Venturi House FIGS. 536, 423, 443
1959–1964
Robert Venturi, Venturi & Short, architects
8330 Millman St., Philadelphia, Pennsylvania

In its cardboard-like flatness this house outwardly foreshadows a typical American Postmodern building. But Venturi's design is based on rigorous intellectual analysis and knowing, if subtle, allusions to architecture's grand traditions. There is much more here than initially meets the eye, and that depth is the missing ingredient in so many subsequent Postmodern buildings.

THE GETTY HERESY

It is surely accurate to say that Venturi, along with Charles W. Moore and others, paved the way for American Postmodern architecture. However, three breakthrough events opened the floodgates to a

wider range of imageries in American architectural design.

The first of these was the 1974 opening of the J. Paul Getty Museum (now known as the "Getty Villa") in suburban Los Angeles. This was a studied re-creation based on buildings buried by the eruption of Vesuvius in 79 CE.

Since the museum was intended to display J. Paul Getty's collection of Classical art and sculpture, Getty felt that naturally it would make sense to display the art in a sympathetic setting, within an idealized Roman villa. But more than a few American architects and critics stridently decried the design as "dishonest," for its non-Modernist design approach.

J. Paul Getty Museum, "Getty Villa" FIGS. 537, 549
1970–1974; 1994–2006, renovation and expansion
Norman Neuerberg, historical consultant; **Langdon & Wilson**, architects;
Stephen Garrett, consultant; **Emmet L. Wemple & Associates**,
landscape architects; **Machado and Silvetti**, architects for the renovation
and expansion; **Denis L. Kurutz, Korn Randolph**, landscape architects for
the renovation and expansion
17985 Pacific Coast Hwy., Malibu, California

A true *cause célèbre* among architects, most of them committed Modernists for whom a re-creation of an ancient Roman villa was heresy. As Jencks put it, critics thought it "everything Modernism fought

FIGS. 537, 538 **Worlds Apart** The first Getty Museum in Malibu (Fig. 537; see also Fig. 549) is a learned re-creation from antiquity, intended to display priceless ancient classical art and sculpture. The Getty is of course a world apart from feeble Postmodern gestures like this cosmetic dress-up of a commercial building (Fig. 538). So it is ironic that the exacting Getty design unintentionally paved the way for acceptance of such simplistic references to tradition.

FIG. 539 **Heresy from on High** To architecture mavens at the time, Nixon in China was trivial compared to the shock of the AT&T Building in New York, designed by the high priest of International Style Modernism, Philip Johnson. It should be emphasized that Johnson was an erudite observer of world architecture. Significantly, his AT&T Building is first-class in every respect, enclosed in an elegant stone envelope. Unfortunately, a deep understanding of tradition and unlimited construction budgets would not be the norm for subsequent Postmodern architects and their buildings.

FIG. 540 **Further Adventures in Tradition** After AT&T, Johnson worked facilely through much of Western architectural history. Republic Bank in Houston (1982–1984) is arguably the best of his Postmodern buildings, its spiky, stepped gables referencing rather than literally copying historic Flemish vocabularies. Johnson's earlier, dark-glass-clad, slanted-roof Pennzoil Place (1976) is seen at the immediate right in this foreshortened view. I. M. Pei's five-sided Texas Commerce tower (1978–1982) peeks over the top.

against—luxuriance, vulgar display, cliché." The vehemence of the reaction now seems amazingly overblown, after three decades of pluralism. See additional text in following Neotraditionalism chapter.

REVIVAL OF HISTORICAL ALLUSIONS

Progressive Architecture magazine provided the second breakthrough event. Its April 1975 issue, entitled "Revival of Historical Allusions" featured Robert A.M. Stern's Lang House on the cover, seen far back in its Arcadian setting. The editors knew exactly what they were doing, and minced no words, warning, "So much for the dogma [that style-imageries are bad]; now for the heresy."

The heresy was a selection of houses "designed by some of our most respected architects," which in addition to Stern & Hagmann's Lang House, included the Lee Burns House by Charles W. Moore, two neo-Corbusian additions by Michael Graves, and a delightful cartoon of a Carpenter's Gothic cottage by Lester Walker.

Given that *P/A* then represented the leading edge of architectural design to many architects, and given the lofty professional status of these designers, this exploration of forbidden

imageries was not easily dismissed as an aberration, as the Getty initially was.

The impact of the April 1975 *P/A* issue on the American profession can hardly be overestimated. Although the editors contended that historical allusion was simply one legitimate component of Modern architecture, down in the trenches among architectural designers no one really believed that. Publishing these works represented a big threat to Modernism as the reigning orthodoxy.

CONVERSION OF THE HIGH PRIEST

Philip Johnson's 1978 AT&T design provided the third earth-shaking event for Postmodernism. Although the American architectural profession had by now been softened up, so to speak, no one was prepared for the shock that ensued when Johnson's design was unveiled.

First of all, Johnson was a high priest of Modernism, as curator of the 1932 International Style show at the Museum of Modern Art, and co-author of the influential book, *The International Style*.

Second, Manhattan is the nation's cultural capital.

And third, AT&T was then the nation's flagship corporation. This combination ensured that the design would be a media event; Johnson even appeared on the cover of *Time*, dressed theatrically in a cape, holding a model of AT&T, which quickly became the building most recognized by the general public since Wright's Fallingwater.

AT&T Building FIG. 539
1978–1984
Philip Johnson & John Burgee, architects
550 Madison Ave. at 55th St., New York, New York

Throughout his long career, Johnson was able to slip among fashions with aplomb. Even so, this building was designed only a half dozen years after his Minneapolis IDS Center opened (Fig. 501) and consequently seemed Johnson's most dramatic, if not outrageous act. That said, the "Chippendale" cut-out, and the cardboard flatness so typical of subsequent Postmodern designs are more than balanced here by beautiful stone cladding and high-caliber detailing.

Republic Bank Center FIG. 540
1982–1984
Johnson/Burgee, architects; **Kendall/Heaton**, associate architects
700 Louisiana St., Houston, Texas

Following AT&T, Johnson worked through a wide range of allusions to past architectural imageries. Republic Bank is perhaps the most satisfying design from this period of his career, even if the reference is improbable for a 56-story office tower: seventeenth-century Flemish-Dutch stepped gables. However, Republic Bank is a knowing transformation of the past, and the solid, *bourse*-like base presents a symbolically reassuring image for a financial institution.

DISSEMINATION OF POSTMODERNISM

By 1980 the floodgates of architectural permissiveness were wide open. Even some of the SOM offices eventually began dabbling in historical allusions. Significantly, by the 1980s the historic preservation movement had achieved the political strength in many cities to demand "contextual" buildings in historic districts; that provided a perfect entrée and rationale for Postmodern designs.

These fall into any of three categories.

One of these is Knowing Designs that are contemporary interpretations of precedent. Such designs range from the invention and wit of Charles W. Moore to the exquisite correctness of Allan Greenberg. (More on them in the Modern Masters and Neotraditionalism chapters.)

High-design Postmodernism comprises a second category. These are skilled gestures by very talented designers who do not fully employ, or are uninterested in, the formal conventions of tradition. Examples follow.

Uninspired Postmodernism is the third and by-far-largest category. These are neither especially knowing, nor skilled enough to escape being empty visual gestures. Since such designs are ubiquitous—everything from "contextual" new buildings in historic districts to chain restaurants—examples are not cited here.

Following is a brief sampling of high-design Postmodernism.

FIG. 541 Public Postmodernism Michael Graves's Portland Public Services Building, "The Portland Building," added the knockout punch after Johnson's AT&T body blow to Modernist orthodoxy. Graves made the most of a low budget, employing colors and patterns for striking effect.

Portland Public Services Building, "The Portland Building" FIG. 541
1980–1982
Michael Graves, architect; **Emery Roth & Sons, Edward C. Wundram**, associate architects; **Raymond Kaskey**, sculptor
1120 SW. Fifth Ave., Portland, Oregon

Like AT&T, this was a stunning deed that caught the attention of architects and the public alike. Unlike AT&T, Portland Public Services was a low-budget project, curiously far lower than the budget of a nearby jail built at about the same time. Even so, Graves made a virtue out of low cost, producing a memorable and responsible cartoon of the building he could have done if the project had been budgeted realistically.

River Crest Country Club FIG. 542
1981–1984
Taft Architects; architects; **Geren/CRS Sirrine**, associate architects
1501 Western Ave., Fort Worth, Texas

Faced with a client direction for a Colonial image, the architects rummaged through past Classicist tradition and came up with a design that vaguely, though agreeably, reminds one of the Lee Family Stratford Hall in Virginia (Fig. 67). Unlike the typical, visually thin Postmodern designs, River Crest reads as rock solid. Robert Stern commented that "the result is an unembarrassedly grand setting." A public street runs right in front of the clubhouse, so you

FIG. 542 **Historical Allusion** Taft Architects' River Crest Country Club clubhouse in Texas is a picturesque response to their client's request for a traditional imagery: a reference to the past without resorting to a direct quote. The building's agreeable solidity alludes to River Crest's position as an anchor of Fort Worth society.

FIG. 543 **The Image of Stability** Business is acutely aware of the importance of image. So this stately headquarters for flagship American corporation Procter & Gamble in Cincinnati should seem reassuring to the company's investors. In its monumentality and quality of construction, this office complex is an atypical Postmodern commercial building.

can fully appreciate the exterior, up close. A bright afternoon when sunlight warms the entrance is the best time to visit.

Procter & Gamble Headquarters FIG. 543
1982–1985
Kohn, Pedersen, Fox, architects
E. 5th St., at Broadway, Cincinnati, Ohio

Postmodern architects seemed especially focused on the design of elaborate building tops. This was not a new direction; a visit to Manhattan or Chicago will confirm that fancy tops were a popular conceit among architects in the 1920s and even earlier.

Few 1980s building tops were as visually successful as these, however, as the architects established an enlarged corporate precinct adjacent to their client's bland existing office block. Two massive octagonal towers form the visual centerpiece of the expanded campus. The design seems to be lightly based on the Mausoleum of Halicarnassus, one of the Seven Wonders of the ancient world. This hoary design precedent was synthesized beyond simply a shallow architectural quote, into a fresh expression that combines the bulkiness of mainstream 1960s–1970s American architecture with an elusive flavor of the distant past.

Horton Plaza FIGS. 544, 545
1982–1986
Jon Jerde Partners, design architects
Broadway to G St., between 1st and 4th Aves., San Diego, California

This downtown shoppertainment mall is the Saturday-morning-cartoon version of Italian urbanism—irrepressibly splashy, shallow, almost overbearing, what Jencks described as a "Caesar's Salad of clichés." Regardless, Horton Plaza seems highly popular with the public, including tourists, and it is certainly visually unforgettable despite any formal shortcomings.

FIGS. 544, 545 **Ebullient Scenography** Jon Jerde is nothing if not utterly fearless, as his Horton Plaza retail center in San Diego convincingly demonstrates.

FIGS. 546, 547 **Postmodern Pinnacles** Michael Graves' Dolphin (Fig. 546) and Swan (Fig. 547) hotels at Disney World are the happy result of a rare Postmodern confluence of superior creative abilities, close attention to seemingly every detail, and meticulous, ongoing maintenance by the owner.

Dolphin Hotel FIG. 546
1986–1990
Michael Graves, architect
N of Buena Vista Dr., 2 blocks E of World Dr., Walt Disney World, Bay Lake, Florida

Swan Hotel FIG. 547
1986–1989

The Swan and Dolphin hotels illustrate Postmodernism at its best, as entertainment architecture. Whatever resistance one might have to American Postmodernism is pretty much swept away in the extravangant scale and pure élan of Graves's comprehensive design of site, buildings, and details. Disney's perfection in maintenance assures that these buildings will always seem bright and new. Be sure to experience the unexpectedly human-scaled lobby of the Swan, with its tiny (compared to the overall scale of the hotel) barrel vault and flowered frescos.

Neotraditionalism

1970–2004

FIG. 548 Tradition Neotraditional architects know the past while affirming today's unique place along the endless timeline of history. Allan Greenberg's surpassingly elegant State Department Treaty Ceremony Suite in Washington is a superior contemporary expression of traditional architectural vocabularies.
Photograph © Tim L. Buchman, published with the permission of Allan Greenberg Architect

Quite distinct from Postmodernism, versions of Neotraditionalism emerged at about the same time, also as an alternative to Postwar Modernism. Like distinguished prewar Period architects, American Neotraditionalists have done their homework. Their designs are based on thorough study of historic precedents—of tradition. Hence, Neotraditional buildings read as knowing, contemporary expressions along a stylistic timeline extending onward from antiquity.

Neotraditionalism can be especially appreciated in three variations in the United States. One of these is Correct Expressions. These designs are generally faithful to historic usage, even,

FIG. 549 Idealized Antiquity American architectural takes on the past are often romanticized versions of their putative European models. While the J. Paul Getty Museum or "Getty Villa" in Malibu was based on exhaustive scholarly research, hence about as correct as possible given its use as a late-twentieth-century museum, there is also a marvelous sense of luxuriance to the overall setting that any Pompeian would no doubt envy. See also Fig. 537.

in the case of the Getty, to a specific Classical source. Correct expressions can be thought of as "pure" designs.

Adaptations are a second form of Neotraditional design. Adaptations are creative transformations of past usage that read as knowing, while also clearly contemporary.

The third variation reads as a resumption of the Period and American Colonial Revivals. These buildings—relatively few existing now and most of them substantial houses tucked out of sight on private estates—seem to have restarted the revivals after a postwar interruption.

CORRECT EXPRESSIONS

J. Paul Getty Museum, "Getty Villa" FIGS. 537, 549
1970–1974; 1994–2006, renovation and expansion
Norman Neuerberg, historical consultant; **Langdon & Wilson**, architects; **Stephen Garrett**, consultant; **Emmet L. Wemple & Associates**, landscape architects; **Machado and Silvetti**, architects for renovation and expansion; **Denis L. Kurutz, Korn Randolph**, landscape architects for renovation and expansion
17985 Pacific Coast Hwy., Malibu, California

J. Paul Getty's reasoning was surely logical: Why not display classical art in a classical building? That thought set in motion the decision to base his new museum's design on an excavated villa that had been buried by Vesuvius in 79 CE.

In many respects the 1970–1974 design was faithful to its ancient model, certainly in spirit if not in exact detail. Even so, like Williamsburg (see the Garden Restorations chapter), building and setting were beautifully idealized. As Gebhard and Winter observed, the Getty's lush landscaping "[put] the Old World of the Mediterranean to shame."

Machado and Silvetti's Neotraditional adaptation added depth through knowing references, including bravura architectonic "strata walls" which allude to archeological excavations. In developing the Getty Villa into an irregular "small hill town," in Clifford Pearson's description, the architects remedied the stiff, almost-uncomfortable building-to-site relationship of the original museum. The renovation-expansion has satisfyingly matured the setting by expressing the passage of time between designs: original villa and additions clearly read as from different eras.

For the effect of the Getty Museum on Postmodernism, see that chapter.

Treaty Ceremony Suite, U.S. Department of State FIG. 548
1985–1986
Allan Greenberg, architect
Seventh Floor, Department of State Building, 22nd and C Street, NW., Washington, D.C.

This formal diplomatic setting within the Secretary of State's suite is architecturally superb in every respect. Greenberg's glorious design equals the best American classicist interiors of any era, characterized by a meticulously detailed, refined elegance.

FIG. 550 **Mountaintop Retreat** Dar al-Islam Masjid and Madressa achieves prominence beyond its modest scale on account of its dramatic ridge-top siting and the use of timeless forms like the dome and barrel vaults. In this view, the mosque is to the left and the school is on the right.

FIG. 551 **Standing Out While Fitting In** Robert Stern's deft Neotraditional remodeling of the Observatory Hill Dining Hall, located near Thomas Jefferson's Academical Village, employed familiar forms and materials, expressed with modern straightforwardness.

FIG. 552 **Overcoming Limitations** Legal restrictions and informal constraints may defeat some architects, but not the irrepressible Philip Johnson. His Franklin Square office building in Washington accommodated historic preservation sensibilities without forgoing a distinctive personality.

FIG. 553 **Scandinavian Manners** Architect Dale Mulfinger is Edwin Lundie's biographer (see the Period Revivals chapter), so he knows a thing or two about synthesizing historic sources without copying them. Mulfinger's own house is stylistically indefinable, though comfortably in harmony with the traditional sensibilities of local culture.

ADAPTATIONS

Dar al-Islam Masjid and Madressa FIG. 550
1979–1981
Hassan Fathi, architect
1.3 mi. NW of Abiquiú (Inn), New Mexico on Hwy. 84, right on County 155, 2.4 mi. to main gate

Fathi (1900–1989) was celebrated in Egypt for his work in mud brick, intended to respect locality and the environment. For this Islamic center for understanding, set dramatically along the edge of a high bluff, the architect devised an engaging visual synthesis, including references to unornamented North African mosques. It employs traditional New Mexico adobe construction similar to the mud brick of his best known work, al-Qurna village on the West Bank of the Nile across from Luxor, and it developes an undulating, vaulted roofline which alludes to nearby hills. The overall effect is remarkable, both quietly exotic and yet seemingly indigenous.

Observatory Hill Dining Hall, University of Virginia FIG. 551
1982–1984
Robert A. M. Stern, architect; **Marcellus Wright, Cox & Smith**, associate architects
Charlottesville, Virginia (razed)

A dining hall, especially on this singular, monumental campus planned by Thomas Jefferson, is an ancillary function. Stern nonetheless managed to impart dignity and presence through knowing, imaginative manipulation of classicist forms and details. Even more impressive, Observatory Hill was actually a remodeling of a building constructed a decade earlier.

Franklin Square FIG. 552
1989
John Burgee Architects with Philip Johnson and Richard Fitzgerald & Partners, architects
1300 I (Eye) St. NW., Washington, D.C.

A credible contemporary transliteration of a 1920s academic-classicist office building, responding to historic-preservation sensibilities for this area. The design is both knowing of the earlier period and contemporary—specifically, in the punched-out window openings, which reflect 1970s practice. However, the interior lobby is spot on, almost completely convincing as a 1920s space to all of us save, perhaps, knowledgeable specialists.

Mulfinger House FIG. 553
1995–1996
Dale Mulfinger, architect
4529 Washburn Ave. S., Minneapolis, Minnesota

In the spirit of William Purcell's house a few of miles away (Fig. 272), Mulfinger exercised restraint in this design for his own home, providing, like Purcell, an additional setback from the street. While Mulfinger's house is scaled with its neighbors, acknowledging adjacent rooflines and porches, it also introduces a strong, if indefinable traditional character that is largely missing in this architecturally bland neighborhood. A rich, dark-red exterior ties the house symbolically to colorful traditional Scandinavian villages like Bryggen, a World Heritage site in Norway. In the prominently Scandinavian Upper Midwest, as in Scandinavia itself, warm color is especially welcome against winter snow, and red plays off as a complement to green grass in summer.

Language and Dining Center, Carleton College FIG. 554

1999–2001

Arthur Andersson, Moore/Andersson, Andersson-Wise, architects

SE section of upper campus, Northfield, Minnesota

Carleton's campus is visually characterized by a wide-ranging mixture of architectural imageries: English Gothic, French Second Empire, Richardsonian Romanesque, the cut-into box, even the New Formalism of Minoru Yamasaki. The LDC site is hemmed in by a large, loosely Tudor structure on one side and a bland, International Style building on the other. Andersson synthesized these adjacent references into a new expression which hints at the Medieval while still recognizably contemporary in character, a design that is equally self-effacing and distinctive.

CONTEMPORARY PERIOD AND AMERICAN COLONIAL REVIVALS

Traditional expressions never entirely disappeared from the postwar architectural scene. What did disappear after the retirement, by about 1970, of master architects like Edwin Lundie and Philip Trammell Shutze (see the Period Revivals chapter), was a consistent body of superior quality equal to that of the foremost Period and American Colonial Revival designs between the wars.

In a large part because postwar architectural training shunned traditional Beaux-Arts precepts, and especially downplayed traditional sensibilities. Consequently, architects drawn

FIG. 554 **Cohesive Center** In addition to functionally accommodating, while distinctly expressing, two very different programs, Arthur Andersson's Language and Dining Center at Carleton College was intended to visually harmonize a disparate collection of nearby imageries into a cohesive physical environment—ideally, as a work of architecture in its own right. Andersson's design is successful on all counts.

to tradition usually had to train themselves. That was not easy, and accounts for the feeble character of much of American Postmodernism.

However a few architects born in the 1930s and later have become extremely proficient at designing contemporary Period and American Colonial Revivals. This recent body of superior work dates from Allan Greenberg's 1979–1983 "Farmhouse in Connecticut" in Greenwich (Fig. 555) and continues through the sumptuous designs of such younger firms as Fair-

FIG. 555 **Contemporary Period/Colonial Revivals** Allan Greenberg's "Farmhouse in Connecticut," a splendid homage to the spirit of Mount Vernon, signaled the resumption of traditional residential design at very high levels of proficiency.
Photograph © Peter Mauss/Esto, published with the permission of Allan Greenberg Architect

FIG. 556 **A Puzzlement** The Platt Office Building might well bewilder most first-time observers, beginning with its incongruous setting along a San Fernando Valley strip. Actually, it is a skillful assemblage of historic parts dating from a time before the now-densely built-up Valley was planted in orange groves.

Platt Office Building FIG. 556

1981

T. W. Layman, architect

19725 Sherman Way, Winnetka, San Fernando Valley, Los Angeles, California

This could be a puzzling building to anyone not knowing its background. At first glance it seems, improbably for its setting, to be a late-1880s Victorian, though not exactly Victorian in its somewhat-too-large scale. It is not a contemporary adaptation, because it is a bit too literal, but neither is it Postmodern, as the design is too knowing. Actually, Platt is a skilled assemblage of parts of razed historic houses, concocted into a modern commercial office building.

Chapala Street Office Building FIG. 557

1984

Henry Lenny, Sharpe, Mahan & Assoc., architects

1123 Chapala St., Santa Barbara, California

In-building parking is a contemporary use that was not contemplated in a 1920s building program, when Santa Barbara's transformation into a Mediterranean paradise began. Without historical precedent on how to handle parking, Lenny placed the required spaces on the street level, then built up a kind of acropolis above for the office spaces. While this superstructure is explicitly Hispanic, including a Goodhuesque campanile, it is strongly articulated, well beyond the reserved norms of 1920s Spanish Colonial Revival/Andalusian design, in part reflecting the influence of postwar American architecture.

fax & Sammons. Most of these are private homes inaccessible to the public, and must for now be appreciated through publications like Richard Guy Wilson's *The Colonial Revival House* (2004) and Mary Miers' *American Houses* (2006).

If you are taken with Classicist and Period design, be sure to consult the website of the Institute of Classical Architecture & Classical America, a membership organization dedicated to the promotion of traditional design. Activities range from group tours to builder's design workshops.

FIG. 557 **The Real Thing** Henry Lenny's impressively suave Chapala Street office building in Santa Barbara reads almost as a genuine 1920s Period Revival design, betrayed only by a boldness reflecting American architectural conventions of the late-1960s and 1970s.

Deconstruction

1980–2004

FIG. 558 Ultimate De-construction La Villette cultural park, developed in Paris in the 1980s, illustrates the literal de-construction of a conventional building. Its Swiss/French architect, Bernard Tschumi, based in New York and Paris, dispersed the building program among 35 red sculptural pavilions, two of which are seen here. In a more general sense, the term Deconstruction is used in this chapter to encompass recent American buildings which emphasize sculptural geometries.

O ver the past generation, a number of dramatic, singular designs have been built across the United States. These distinguished buildings are characterized by a knowing mannerism marked by fragmentation and non-rectangular forms—"New Geometries," as the American expatriate critic Philip Jodidio labels them. Because many of these works look like they have been pulled apart, literally deconstructed, I've encompassed them in this chapter under the term Deconstruction as a convenient catch-all for now, until future historians sort out the current era.

Bernard Tschumi's 1982–1987 ff. La Villette cultural park in Paris represents an extreme example of what I've called deconstruction (Fig. 558). Tschumi exploded the building program into 35 freestanding sculptural pieces—*folies*—each painted in the same bright red. These structures were distributed across the site on the basis of a Cartesian grid.

Parenthetically, please let me emphasize that Deconstruction as employed in this chapter is simply descriptive. It does not necessarily imply association of any of these buildings or their architects with the design theory known as Deconstructivism. For those who wish to plumb the arcane depths of this architectural offshoot of 1960s French literary criticism, the writings of the American architect Peter Eisenman will be helpful.

FIGS. 559, 560 Supracontextual Residential remodelings usually strive to smooth over differences between existing and new construction. For the Petal House, Eric Owen Moss tracked way in the other direction. The original tract house is now overwhelmed by artfully exaggerated new forms and surfaces. Not even the garage emerged unscathed (above).

FIG. 561 De-Construction on High Getty Center offers another literal example of de-construction. In the Getty's hilltop cultural village, a massive building program was separated—seemingly pulled apart—in order to minimize visual impacts on the surrounding community, as well as to establish a flow of outdoor spaces throughout the campus. © *John Stephens / J. Paul Getty Trust*

Petal House FIGS. 559, 560
1982
Eric Owen Moss, architect
2828 Midvale Ave., West Los Angeles, California

Like Frank Gehry early in his career, Eric Owen Moss works confidently and expressively with a palette of basic building materials. The Petal House is a remodeling-expansion, located in an unremarkable neighborhood edged by the Santa Monica and San Diego freeways.

Instead of seeking to smooth over any differences, as is typical remodeling practice, Moss exaggerated the changes, visually pulling away new construction from the existing postwar tract house and siding it in different materials, textures, and coloring. The resulting composition is both ordinary and arresting, a marvelous play on the American propensity for functionality.

Getty Center FIG. 561
1984–1997
Richard Meier & Partners, architects; **Robert Irwin**, central garden; **Emmett Wemple & Assoc., Olin Partnership**, landscape architects; **Thierry W. Despont**, galleries
1200 Getty Center Dr., off I-405 N of Sunset Blvd., Brentwood, Los Angeles, California

Meier grouped several buildings to establish an architecture of place on this prominent hilltop, recalling the expansive development of Hadrian's Villa in the hills near Rome. As seen from the air or in model form, Getty Center does indeed appear to be de-constructed, seemingly pulled apart from a now lost primordial state.

Culver City Developments FIGS. 562, 563

8522 National Building
1986–1990
Eric Owen Moss, Architect
8522 National Blvd., Culver City, California

The Box/The Beehive
1990–1994/2000
Eric Owen Moss, Architect
8520-8522 National Blvd., Culver City, California

FIGS. 562, 563 Avant-Garde in LA
For most of its existence, Culver City has been visually forgettable, perhaps known for its oil wells, if anything. Eric Owen Moss transformed the community's image with his astonishing collection of buildings for one developer patron, two of them shown here.

Paramount Laundry Building
1987–1989
Eric Owen Moss, Architect
3960 Ince Blvd., Culver City, California

Lindeblade Tower
1987–1989
Eric Owen Moss, Architect
3962 Ince Blvd., Culver City, California

Gary Group Office Building
1988–1990
Eric Owen Moss, Architect
9046 Lindeblad St., Culver City, California

Samitaur Building
1989–1996
Eric Owen Moss, architect
3457 S. La Cienega, Culver City, California

Stealth/Pterodactyl Buildings
2001
Eric Owen Moss, architect
3528 Hayden Ave., Culver City, California

These eight projects are nearby developments by the same architect for the same client, which have been ongoing for more than two

FIG. 564 **Primal Form on the High Plains** Antoine Predock's American Heritage Center is powerful enough in form to establish visual prominence against the limitless Wyoming natural landscape.

FIG. 565 **Civic Mesa** Will Bruder's copper-sheathed Burton Barr Central Library in Phoenix is outwardly straightforward, an homage to prominent local natural formations, while also reflecting the architect's love of materials. A "flexible box" enclosure provides functionality while accommodating a sequence of compressed and expanded internal spaces, set off by choreographed daily and seasonal progressions of light throughout the interior.

FIG. 566 **Who Needs Art?** Rather than acquire today's egregiously overpriced art, museums may find it more effective to commission signature architecture. That certainly worked for the Milwaukee Art Museum, where Santiago Calatrava's Quadracci Pavilion was instantly better known than the museum's entire collection.

FIG. 567 **Modern Monument, Ancient Roots** The Spanish Architect José Raphael Moneo's Cathedral of Our Lady of the Angels in L.A. is clearly a contemporary expression, though it also seems to draw an essential monumentality from antiquity.

decades. This group is distinguished by imaginative reuses of existing industrial buildings, augmented by new construction. David Gebhard and Robert Winter perfectly described Moss's visually rich and endlessly complex expressions as "serious play."

American Heritage Center FIG. 564

1987–1993
Antoine Predock, architect
University of Wyoming, Willett Dr., one block W of 22nd St., Laramie, Wyoming

A primal, conical form, aligned with two nearby mountains, an apparent literal reference to Native American tepees. Jodidio observed that the building "seems to alternate between a highly futuristic design and an ancient relic." From either perception, this powerful sculptural form seems firmly grounded to its site.

Rock & Roll Hall of Fame

1987–1995
Pei Cobb Freed & Partners, architects; **Leslie E. Robertson**, structural engineer
E. 9th St. on Lake Erie, Cleveland, Ohio

An exercise in pure geometry on a sweeping lakefront site, the building was intended to "express the dynamic music it celebrates." The Hall is a striking piece of architectural sculpture, although it seems a universe away from Graceland!

Burton Barr Central Library FIG. 565

1988–1995
Will Bruder, architect; **Wendell Burnette, DWL Architects**, associate architects
1221 N. Central Ave., Phoenix, Arizona

Bruder approached his design as environmental sculpture, in the architect's words, as a "metaphorical series of abstract canyon walls [within]." Outside, the library stands prominently apart, recalling the signature rocky buttes which punctuate the Phoenix skyline.

Such notions are hardly abstract, since the building is meant to establish a powerful sense of civic presence, acting as a community anchor, in addition to fulfilling its primary functions as an information center. Bruder accomplished this in a remarkably inexpensive building, less than $100 per square foot in construction costs.

LVMH Tower

1994–1999
Christian de Portzamparc, architect
19 E. 57th St., New York, New York

In awarding the French architect Portzamparc a Pritzker Prize, the jury commended him for developing a new esthetic vocabulary bonded neither to Classicism nor to Modernism. The LVMH design employs a free form of folded and creased planes of glass within a sliver site.

Gatehouse, "Da Monsta"

1995
Philip Johnson, architect
Johnson Estate, 842 Ponus Ridge Rd., New Canaan, Connecticut (open by reservation as a National Trust property)

Johnson's designs were always dramatic, regardless of his current favored imagery. This is simply a wonderful piece of environmental sculpture, an architecture "without right angles or verticals." The bright red color is visually effective against either grass or snow. See the Glass House entry in the Postwar Modernism chapter.

Quadracci Pavilion, Milwaukee Art Museum FIG. 566
1993–2001
Santiago Calatrava, architect-engineer
700 N. Art Museum Dr., Milwaukee, Wisconsin

In its free-form structural gymnastics, Calatrava's addition to Eero Saarinen's 1953–1957 Milwaukee War Memorial seems to be a direct descendant of Saarinen's TWA terminal at Idlewild, although even more fantastic and complex. With hardly a straight line anywhere, Quadracci is one of those designs which cannot be adequately described, only experienced. A dramatic lakefront site has been rendered unforgettable.

Cathedral of Our Lady of the Angels FIG. 567
1995–2002
José Rafael Moneo, architect; **Robert Graham**, bronze doors; **John Nava**, tapestries
555 W. Temple St. at N. Grand Ave., Los Angeles, California

The Cathedral is appropriately monumental. An immense interior volume with the floor area of a football field, and more than 40 yards high, seats 2,600. Worshipers are accompanied by a 6,000-pipe Dobson organ. Moneo was directed by his client to reference a California Mission past, although the design seems to draw "more heavily from Iberian Roman forms, as if to suggest a metaphor for New World architecture," in Jodidio's assessment.

National Museum of the American Indian FIG. 568
1993–2004
Douglas J. Cardinal, design architect; **Johnpaul Jones**, associate architect; **CBQC, Polshek Partnership**, executive architects; **Donna House**, ethnobotanist; **EDAW**, landscape architects; **Ramona Sakiestewa**, textiles-interiors
S National Mall between 3rd and 4th Sts. SW., Washington, D.C.

Like the Los Angeles Cathedral (Fig. 567), this design was charged to offer cultural content. Cardinal relied on allegory rather than literal historic references to do so. Nature is the pervasive theme, represented at every level from the curving forms inside and out to warm stone and woods, to native flora in the landscape palette and, of course, in the exhibits. As a result, as a visual expression, this building is unique in monumental Washington.

FIG. 568 One of a Kind In several respects, the National Museum of the American Indian is unique in monumental Washington, notably for its warmly textured, irregularly curvilinear walls.

Seattle Central Library FIGS. 569, 570
1998–2004
Rem Koolhaas, Office of Metropolitan Architecture, LMN, architects; **Arup; Skilling, Ward, Magnusson, Barkshire (Magnusson Klemencic)**, structural engineers; **Inside/Outside**, interiors; **Petra Blaisse, Jones & Jones**, landscape architects
1000 Fourth Ave., Seattle, Washington

Arguably on the cutting edge of library design, and certainly an instant landmark for Seattle, as desired. The architects approached their planning almost as a materials-handling exercise, functionally separating major program elements into distinct "platforms." These masses were then shifted around "to capture light and views," although surely as much or more to achieve avant-garde architectural impact. The result is unconventional, from an immense "Living Room," to monumental flows of interior volume, to a polyhedral, diamond-patterned glass envelope.

FIGS. 569, 570 Library as City Center Not many public libraries truly transform a major downtown, especially a downtown already as full of surprises as Seattle's. In that respect alone, Rem Koolhaas's Seattle Central Library is quite an accomplishment, inside and out.

Neomodernism
1980–2004

FIG. 571 Precursors to Modernism Modern architecture may be traced back to the eighteenth-century French architect Claude-Nicholas Ledoux. As illustrated here by a 1784 Paris tollhouse, Ledoux's designs were radically simplified (compared to contemporary Baroque architecture), emphasizing pure geometric forms like the square and drum of this design. The prominence of simplified, pure forms is shared with recent Neomodernist designs in this chapter. Contemporary American Neomodernism can be understood as the current phase of Modernism along a continuous timeline rooted in Enlightenment thought.

By one practical definition, "modern architecture" has been with us for more than 200 years, since the emergence of Enlightenment thought and the resultant onset of Western modernity. From its beginnings, this modern approach to architecture was characterized by simplification, and by emphasis on pure form. The eighteenth-century French architects Boullée and Ledoux (Fig. 571) are commonly cited as precursors of Modernism.

In the mid-1800s, the expression of structure and the rise of building technology—"new potentialities" in the words of Swiss art historian Sigfried Giedion—were then considered to be the very definition of modern architecture. The nineteenth-century French architect Henri Labrouste was an early leader in emphasizing technology.

Subsequent definitions of modern architecture have variously emphasized the transformation of tradition (Richardson), geometry (Wright), abstraction (The International Style), and rationality (Postwar Modernism). Recently, Modernist inclinations have been prominent in the work of Deconstruction architects like Rem Koolhaas (previous chapter). But when that school veers into the realm of expressionistic sculpture, any underlying Modernist traits are increasingly less central to a design.

Of course conventional versions of Modernist architecture have never disappeared from the nation's drafting boards and computer screens, just from the professional media, which has avidly followed Postmodernism and Deconstruction over the past two decades, until recently. In a large part due to works of Japanese architects, fresh restatements of Modernism are appearing. These stand apart from the devolution of the International Style which dominated the post–World War II era. Like the Ur-Modern designs of the 1700s and 1800s, these *Neo*-modern buildings emphasize form and clarity.

Museum of Contemporary Art, "MOCA" FIG. 572
1983–1987
Arata Isozaki, design architect; **Gruen Associates**, executive architects
250 S. Grand Ave., Los Angeles, California

MOCA is more sculptural than the direct geometry of Boullée and Ledoux, but like these earliest Moderns, the Japanese architect Isozaki skillfully carried out an exercise in pure form. The rich, subtly tactile Indian stone cladding is a glorious touch. Irrespective of any notions about style or imagery, this is undeniably a beautiful building.

Modern Art Museum of Fort Worth FIG. 573
1997–2002
Tadao Ando, architect; **Kendall/Heaton Associates**, associate architects; **SWA Group**, landscape architects
3200 Darnell St., Fort Worth, Texas

Exquisitely detailed, like MOCA (preceding entry), this museum is variously described by the museum itself as "embodying principles of classical Japanese architecture" and "embodying the pure, unadorned elements of a modern work of art."

FIG. 572 Modern Indulgence The intense stone cladding of Arata Isozaki's Museum of Contemporary Art, "MOCA," in L.A. is wonderfully rich, one might think almost impermissibly so for a rationalist architect! Isozaki balanced any emotive effect from the stone with familiar Modernist attributes like bold massing and precise, understated detailing.

FIG. 573 Surpassing Minimalism Tadao Ando's Modern Art Museum of Fort Worth is utterly serene, especially its austere interior spaces. As in the case of Santiago Calatrava's Milwaukee museum pavilion (Fig. 566), you don't have to be an art lover to enjoy a visit to this museum.

In some respects, the building seems to have come right out of a Bauhaus exercise as practiced in American architecture schools during the early 1960s: minimalist, with emphasis on the expression of structure and a focus on the nature of materials. Yet this is a very contemporary building at the turn of the millennium. Indeed, Ando's design is a compelling advertisement for modern architecture in any era.

Rosenthal Center for Contemporary Art FIG. 574
1997–2003
Zaha Hadid, design architect; **KZF**, executive architects
44 E. 6th St. at Walnut, Cincinnati, Ohio

FIG. 574 Assertive Enough Cincinnati's varied and tactile downtown can easily overwhelm a relatively small building like the Rosenthal Center. Zaha Hadid's burly exterior assured that wouldn't happen.

Hadid took a different tack (compared to preceding two entries) in exploring contemporary Modernism. Rather than an expression of pure form in the tradition of Ledoux, like Isozaki's MOCA, this design recalls the De Stijl work of the early twentieth-century Dutch Modernist architect Gerrit Rietveld. Rosenthal Center is more muscular than Rietveld's thin, manipulated planes, and its plan more intricate. Instead of emphasizing the open or free plan of the International Style Modernists, Hadid developed a three-dimensional sequence, beginning at the entrance with an "urban carpet" that resolves into a mezzanine ramp leading to stacked galleries on the upper levels.

Museum of Modern Art, "MoMA"
1997–2006
Yoshio Taniguchi, architect; **Kohn, Pedersen, Fox**, associate architects; **Donald C. Richardson**, **Zion, Breen & Richardson**, restoration architects for sculpture garden; **Ken Smith**, landscape architect of roof garden
11 W. 53rd St., New York, New York

"The Modern" has evolved physically and conceptually since opening in the late 1930s as the epicenter of American Modernism (see Fig. 402 for a view from 53rd Street). For this latest iteration, Taniguchi meticulously crafted an efficient, workable museum which seamlessly interrelates with the museum's superb collections. As a result, MoMA is now, more than ever, an organic whole of building, urbanism, and art.

Taniguchi's plan enhanced the Modern's signature sculpture garden, while doubling gallery space, chiefly through five tiers of new galleries organized around an atrium, which rises from a ground-level lobby connecting 53rd and 54th Streets. In enclosing new structures and stitching together existing architectural fabric, the architect's minimalist aesthethic addressed functional needs to minimize the complexities and inefficiencies which unavoidably built up over decades of periodic remodeling and expansion. Like the earliest Moderns, Taniguchi emphasized clarity, adding an exacting subtlety in detail. The old Modern has been transformed, now with multiple routes through light-filled spaces. See Fig. 1139 for a view of Taniguchi's work taken from 54th Street.

Caltrans District 7 Headquarters FIG. 575
2002–2004
Thom Mayne, Morphosis, architects; **Gruen Assoc.**, associate architects; **John A. Martin & Assoc.**, structural engineers; **Campbell & Campbell**, landscape architects
100 S. Main St., Los Angeles, California

Thom Mayne has always followed his own architectural path, so including any of his buildings in a particular chapter is simply an editorial convenience. Indeed, another Mayne-Morphosis project, the 1993 Diamond Ranch High School in nearby Pomona (100 Diamond Ranch Dr.), would fit easily in the Deconstruction chapter (Fig. 576). While Mayne characterizes his work as problem-solving, there is an undeniable striving for beauty, even effect, to his designs, as is apparent this exquisitely detailed government building.

RE-ENTRY FOR MODERNISM

Postmodernism and the parallel rise of the American historic preservation movement have inadvertently created an intolerance of Modernism in some American cities. Nowhere is this more ironic than in Chicago, where the great triumphs of modern American architecture are ingrained in the City's progressive self-image.

Davis House FIG. 577
1999–2001
John Vinci, Vinci/Hamp Architects
4835 Greenwood Ave., Chicago, Illinois

Although the site is located in the historic Kenwood neighborhood of Queen Anne and Period Revival houses, client and architect decided that the new house "should represent the time in which it's built." Predictably, Vinci's design came as a shock to the neighborhood and to the city's landmarks commission, which, while insisting that—*really*—they actually "encourage contemporary design," found that if contemporary means Modern, then it is "just too different."

Fortunately, owner and architect persevered, and the house was built substantially as proposed. Once it was completed, some of the neighbors found much to appreciate. Even among those who still don't like it, everybody is "dying to be invited there."

Vinci's Davis design falls squarely within classic Chicago progressive tradition. It is organized around function rather than primarily an expression of style, evoking a powerful visual presence, a worthy descendant of the likes of Richardson's Glessner House (Fig. 213). The Davis House is clad in Roman brick, trimmed out in limestone, like Frank Lloyd Wright's nearby Robie House (Fig. 247), an international landmark that also didn't fit deferentially into its setting.

Like Prairie School architects (and Beaux Arts estates), Vinci provided a defined transition between building and yard, by way of a slightly raised outdoor dining terrace overlooking a garden.

The Davis House is especially significant to Chicago, which has been grappling with the inconsistencies of trying to force new buildings to conform to faux-historic imageries, in a city revered worldwide for its radical past departures from the architectural status quo.

FIG. 575 Expressive Functionalism Modernists have emphasized functional elements like stairs and sun screens for a century and more – but rarely so exquisitely as in Thom Mayne's design for Caltrans District 7 Headquarters in L.A.

FIG. 576 Art Over Image Mayne's Diamond Ranch High School (1999–2000) near Pomona, California, looks very different from the architect's Caltrans District 7 design (Fig. 575). What connects them is their sheer quality as art. *Carol M. Highsmith / Library of Congress, Prints & Photographs*

FIG. 577 A Mirror for Society John Vinci's Davis House provided an invaluable mirror for a Chicago community which thought of itself as culturally progressive, but faltered when faced with a progressive design.

SELECTED AMERICAN

BUILDING TYPES

1740–2004

Rural Structures

1740–1950

FIG. 578 **Rural America** The Larson Round Barn and outbuildings vividly illustrate two attributes encountered across rural America. One is a powerful feeling of isolation that is inevitable when individual farms measure in hundreds, if not thousands, of acres. The other is a magnificent accidental monumentality established by the visual play of immense functional structures against a limitless horizon.

Other than pre-Columbian cities like Cahokia (see the Aboriginal Cultures chapter), well into the nineteenth century, most American building was rural. In 1800, for instance, Philadelphia's population was 70,000, New York City's, 60,000, Boston's, 25,000. By contrast—along with millions of Native Americans, of course—more than 500,000 European Americans lived west of the Appalachians, the large majority of them spread across the land on farms, or living in tiny, isolated settlements.

This chapter offers a sampling of American rural structures, with an emphasis on quality of construction, pretense, and picturesqueness. These include farms, freestanding non-agricultural buildings, and visually cohesive settlements.

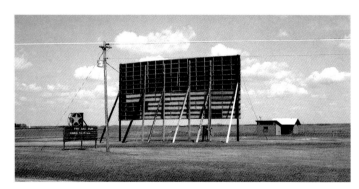

FIG. 579 **Rural Directness** American rural structures are typically functional and unpretentious. This bare-bones drive-in theater located outside of Mahnomen, Minnesota, is a marvel of economy: a screen built on utility poles, with three tiny shacks for projector, concessions, and toilets. There is not even a name, simply a logo, on its attractions signboard. *Library of Congress, Prints & Photographs, Historic American Buildings Survey*

FARM BUILDINGS

Hex Barns FIG. 580
mid–1700s ff.
Berks and Lancaster counties, Pennsylvania

After about 1710, German immigrants streamed into rural South-eastern Pennsylvania. These Germans practiced quality construc-tion which is particularly appreciated today in the area's handsome stone buildings, including barns. Especially in Berks and Lancaster counties, geometric symbols known as *hexenfoos* were often painted on barns.

According to Hugh Morrison, although twentieth-century own-ers commonly contended that these were simply decorative, hex symbols originally were explicitly intended to ward off danger. Whatever the explanation, Pennsylvania hex barns read as dis-tinctive folk art to us.

Round Barn FIG. 581
1826; rebuilt, 1865
Hancock Shaker Village, 5 mi. W of Pittsfield, Massachusetts on Hwy. 20, SW corner Hwy. 41

Handsome, functional simplicity, just what one would expect from buildings of the Shaker sect. Deep-set window and door openings render the barn's massive drum form even stronger, visually. Yet because of the light-colored stone, the structure does not seem pon-derous. As one approaches the barn, its marvelous stonework tex-ture becomes the prominent design element.

Wildesmeier Bank Barn
1859
Hwy. 61, 1.5 mi. NE of Fort Madison, Iowa

The builder took advantage of a steep slope across the building site, so that on-grade access into the barn could be provided on two levels. Bank barns were fairly common throughout much of rural America, wherever a barn site was sufficiently sloped.

Fields Barn FIG. 582
1875
1.5 mi. past Hudson Rd. on University Ave./Old Hwy. 218, NW of Cedar Falls, Iowa

The working barn as architecture. This three-story limestone struc-ture with double cross gables is architecturally pretentious beyond

FIG. 580 Persistence of Old World Traditions Retaining Medieval folk traditions from their Bavarian and Swiss homelands, eighteenth-century Pennsylvania "Dutch" (from non-German-speakers' mispronunciation of *Deutsch*) applied *hexenfoos* to their barns, to guard against farm animals becoming *ferhexed*—bewitched. Such superstitions by now ancient history, hex barns like this one near Oley, Pennsylvania, are maintained as cherished folk art. *Library of Congress, Prints & Photographs, Historic American Buildings Survey*

FIG. 581 Functional Art The characteristic simple beauty of Shaker design is readily apparent in this round barn at the Hancock Shaker Village. *Library of Congress, Prints & Photographs, Historic American Buildings Survey*

FIG. 582 Farm Architecture Architectural pretense is not unknown on working farms, as the ruggedly handsome Fields Barn demonstrates.

FIGS. 583, 584 Enshrinement of Barns The immense, brooding Shelburne Farms Breeding Barn (Fig. 583) and adjacent Old Dairy Barn (Fig. 584) are only part of the Vermont estate's singular collection of monumental barns (see also Webb Farm Barn later in this chapter, Fig. 595).

even the handsome "Pennsylvania Dutch" barns. Gebhard and Mansheim understandably praised Fields as "by far one of the most handsome [Midwestern barns] in its proportions and in its carefully designed fenestration."

Shelburne Farms Barns FIGS. 583, 584
1890–1891
Robert H. Robertson, architect
Shelburne Farms, Harbor Rd. off Rt. 7, SW of Burlington, Vermont

As a rural setting, Shelburne Farms is in a class by itself. Its immense, moody, Breeding Barn (Fig. 583) is visually stunning inside and out. For 40 years after construction, this barn had the largest clear span of any structure in America.

Be sure to note the Old Dairy Barn (Fig. 584), in addition to Shelburne's majestic Farm Barn (Fig. 595) and this Breeding Barn

and the 1902 Coach Barn. Any one of these, alone, would be among the best in the United States. Together, the Shelburne barn collection is architecturally almost supernatural.

Frawley Ranch
1890s ff.
Henry J. Frawley, rancher
Btw. I-90 and Hwy. 85, Spearfish, South Dakota

The combined Frawley spread is an exemplar of a High Plains ranch, assembled from several failed homestead farms. Much of the originally acreage has been sold off, although the remaining stone buildings and the adjacent Anderson Dairy Farm offer visitors a vivid sense of what it was like to ranch in this barren country a century ago.

Larson Round Barn FIG. 578

c. 1900

Ortonville, Minnesota vic., 10 mi. N of town on Hwy. 75, 4 mi. E on County 6, 3 mi. N on County 39

Larson is an immense structure, visually commanding on approach even set out on this scale-less, wide open prairie. Its builder employed a pure 1:1 proportion between drum and roof; the entire composition rests solidly on a stone base. Surely Larson is visually among the most powerful American round barns.

Waller Tobacco Barn

c. 1930

John Waller, designer; **W. S. Penn**, builder

Old Oxford Rd., NE quadrant I-75 and Hwys. 227/460, Georgetown, Kentucky

Waller's five-story, 8,500-square-foot barn is impressive in size, but more significant for its innovative mechanized system, in which tobacco leaves were locked onto a rack right in the field and transferred directly into the barn for curing. This technical innovation reduced handlings per leaf from the usual 6 to 12 down to just two.

NON-AGRICULTURAL STRUCTURES AND SITES

Old Round Church FIG. 585

1812–1814

Bridge St., 0.5 mi. W of Main St./Hwy. 2, Richmond, Vermont

Given the economic subsistence level of pioneer farming, rural and small-town buildings usually had to rely on clarity of form, color, and thoughtful siting to achieve architectural prominence. This 16-sided clapboard structure is sited on a slight eminence above the surrounding fields, nestled visually beneath the Green Mountains. Construction is routine, but its fine form and white color play off elegantly against the surrounding agrarian landscape. The church is well-maintained, now designated a National Landmark.

William B. Ide Adobe FIG. 586

c. 1850

I-5 exit 650, 0.6 mi NE on Adobe Rd., Red Bluff, California

Like the log cabin in Trans-Appalachia (see Indigenous Cultures chapter), the Calfornia adobe was a potent, overly romanticized symbol of past virtue and true Americanism. This restored adobe, charmingly sited near a river under a spreading oak, beautifully fulfills this traditional cultural role.

Buelna's Roadhouse FIG. 587

1852

Felix Buelna, builder

3915 Alpine Rd., Portola Valley, California

Buelna's is a classic single-story false-front, a type that was commonly built as a general store, though here as a tavern. The false-front always seems to appear in movies set in rural towns, yet we hardly ever run across one anymore in real life. Alas, these simple, functional structures are by now charming remnants of a rapidly fading past.

A handsome, two-story twentieth-century false-front can be found in Sonoma, California, on E. Napa St. at 8th St. E. (Fig. 588). In the Midwest, another one-story false front, the Jo Strong General Store, is located along the south side of Cty. J40, in tiny Pittsburg, northwest of Keosauqua, Iowa.

FIG. 585 Setting is Everything Old Round Church is only mildly interesting architecturally. The structure achieves special prominence on account of its dramatic visual contrast with the Vermont landscape.

FIG. 586 Symbol of Virtue The adobe was to California what the log cabin was to Trans-Appalachian America. The William B. Ide Adobe is romantically sited on a wooded rise above the Sacramento River.

FIGS. 587, 588 Fading into History False-front stores like the single-story Buelna's Roadhouse (Fig. 587) and this two-story store outside of Sonoma, California (Fig. 588) were once ubiquitous in small towns throughout the Midwest and West. Alas, old cowboy movies may soon be the only place to see this disappearing building type.
Fig. 587: Library of Congress, Prints & Photographs, Historic American Buildings Survey

Valley Grove Churches FIG. 589

1862, 1880s

Hwy. 246 N, Cty. 29 W, Nerstrand vic., Minnesota

In the Upper Midwest, Protestant churches often achieved visual prominence through their siting. Simple white frame structures were located in open farmlands, on a rise of land wherever possible. Even though these were usually unremarkable in design, churches so sited might be visible for miles.

FIG. 589 Romantic Promontory In and of themselves, the Valley Grove churches are conventional designs of their eras, including utterly plain interiors. However, these two structures engage a picturesque, hilltop setting, site of a pioneer cemetery rich in history. The result is a highly moving cultural landscape, especially for those holding associations with this Minnesota area.

FIGS. 590, 591 Overwhelming Isolation Millions of immigrants began their lives in America on remote farmsteads. Few, if any, lived in such awesome solitude and appalling squalor as did "Yukon Charlie" Yale in these two cabins in the Alaskan wilderness. *Library of Congress, Prints & Photographs, Historic American Buildings Survey*

Here, a stone Greek Revival church faces an austere clapboard Gothic church located only about 100 feet away. This unusually close physical relationship, a hilltop site, and the glorious surrounding woods and steeply rolling farmlands combine to establish one of the most picturesque rural settings in the Midwest. The churchyard cemetery is a Who's Who of prominent pioneer Norwegian-Americans, including the family of economist Thorstein Veblen.

Nauset Coast Guard Station

1871; rebuilt, 1937

Doane Rd., 1 mi. E of Hwy 6, Eastham, Cape Cod, Massachusetts

Nauset is one of nine Coast Guard stations built along the outer shores under a joint federal appropriation. These may have been based on a common design, given that the Menemsha Station on Martha's Vineyard is nearly identical, but lacking Nauset's projecting front porch.

The underlying Early Georgian imagery of both stations would have been a century out of date after the Civil War – or almost impossibly advanced if understood as American Colonial Revival. Whatever the design approach, both buildings are prominent and memorable on account of their larger-than-domestic scale, their clarity of form and, of course, dramatic sites.

Charlie Yale Cabins FIGS. 590, 591

Early 1900s

Charlie Yale, builder

W bank Glacier River, Gates of the Arctic National Park and Preserve, 8 mi. W of Nolan, Alaska

"Hermit prospector" Charlie Yale lived way out here, miles—and days—from anyone else, during the first decade of the twentieth century. His living cabin measured a mere 14 feet square, the adjacent work cabin only 12 by 8 feet.

Today, one can only marvel at the kind of person who could survive, perhaps even thrive, in such isolation, however spectacular the surrounding natural landscape. Still, Yale's chosen lifestyle was really only an extreme situation, not an aberration, in America. In the nineteenth century, the United States was populated by millions of settlers of European ancestry who endured awesome physical and social isolation on their pioneer homesteads in newly opened territories.

COHESIVE SETTLEMENTS

Ephrata Cloister

1740–1746

Johann Konrad Beissel, founder

632 W. Main St., Jct. Hwys. 322 & 222, Ephrata, Pennsylvania

Pietist sects were founded from New England to Iowa. Morrison described the Ephrata settlement as the "Most markedly German and medieval of all Pennsylvania Dutch [that is, German-American] architecture." The three major Ephrata buildings are the *Saal* or great hall, the *Saron*, or Sister House, and the *Bethania*, or Brother House. These steep-roofed Medieval forms are marked by a rugged appeal and clarity of function.

Pleasant Hill FIGS. 592, 593

1815 ff.; Meeting House, 1820

Micajah Burnett, site planner and master builder

3501 Lexington Rd./Hwy. 68, NE of Harrodsburg, Kentucky

FIGS. 592, 593 Shaker Masterpieces Shaker design is understandably considered to be an art form. Due in a large part to the refined sensibilities of its builder Micajah Burnett, Pleasant Hill in Kentucky is architecturally the best of the best. *Fig. 593: Library of Congress, Prints & Photographs, Historic American Buildings Survey*

At its mid-1850s peak, Pleasant Hill ranked among the largest of the 22 U.S. Shaker communities, with a population of about 600 and 250 structures. Pleasant Hill is the best-preserved among these settlements. Burnett was a gifted, self-taught designer. Even compared to the typical elevated norms of Shaker design, his buildings are exceptional, characterized by technical innovations and functional beauty.

Other Shaker settlements of high architectural interest can be found at Sabbathday Lake, Rte. 26, New Gloucester, Maine (1793–present); and Hancock Shaker Village, Hwy. 20, west of Pittsfield, Massachusetts (1790–1960).

Town of Nicodemus FIG. 594

1877 ff.
Graham County, Kansas

Nicodemus is at once atypical, ordinary, and instructive. The town was populated by freedmen, primarily from Kentucky and Tennessee, one of numerous African-American settlements resulting from out-migration from former Confederate and border states during post–Civil War Reconstruction. Its conventional town plat of regular-sized blocks conformed to the U.S. Geological Survey grid.

Nicodemus boomed to 700 citizens within a year of its founding, then lost much of its population when it was bypassed by the railroad. A century after its founding, the town's population had declined to less than 50. Nicodemus today is a poignant reminder that the large majority of nineteenth-century American settlements

FIG. 594 **Betting Against the Odds** Like uncounted thousands of other American settlements, the town of Nicodemus, Kansas, was founded with great hope. But only a small fraction of such hamlets prospered, and once the railroad main line bypassed Nicodemus, the town was effectively doomed. *Library of Congress, Prints & Photographs, Historic American Buildings Survey*

FIG. 596 **American Country French** The farm court on Arthur Newbold's Pennsylvania estate illustrates the meticulously choreographed "rural" lifestyle which was often created for pre–World War II American landed aristocracy. An estate house, outbuildings, kitchen gardens, and the requisite clucking chickens (hissing geese for the truly highbrow) were all integrated into a larger contrived drama of gentrified life. A visitor from Normandy would have been absolutely bewildered by the perfection of it all. *The Work of Mellor Meigs & Howe, 1923*

never attained enough population to sustain a healthy local economy. Its achingly lonely setting on the limitless High Plains of northwestern Kansas provides an unforgettable demonstration that there could be a social cost to America's seemingly inexhaustible supply of land.

FARM GROUPS

By the late 1800s, the American Country House/Estate had emerged as a distinct building type (see the American Colonial Revivals chapter). A working "farm group" was almost necessarily an integral part of such an estate.

Since these expansive, showcase properties were developed by men of immense wealth and social position, it was not uncommon for a farm group, like the estate house itself, of course, to be designed to very high architectural standards. Indeed, skilled architects like Alfred Hopkins specialized in the design of architecturally superior farm groups for country estates.

William Seward Webb Farm Barn FIG. 595
1886–1891 ff.
Robert H. Robertson, architect; **Frederick Law Olmsted**, landscape architect; **Gifford Pinchot**, environmental advisor
Shelburne Farms, Harbor Rd. off Rt. 7, SW of Burlington, Vermont

Lila (Mrs. William) Webb was a Vanderbilt, so it is no surprise that this 3,000-acre farm overlooking Lake Champlain was developed as a grand agricultural estate. Olmsted's 1887 landscape plan called for three physically distinct districts: a park-like, naturalistic landscape around the house; agricultural fields; and forested areas.

FIG. 595 **One of a Kind** No other American estate farm group even approaches the sheer majesty, in scale and in architectural character, of William Seward Webb's farm court, now known as Shelburne's Farm Barn.

FIGS. 597, 598 **Ultimate Gentility** Alfred Hopkins'"Caumsett" Farm Group (Fig. 597) and nearby Polo Stables (Fig. 598) for Marshall Field's Long Island estate attain supreme architectural refinement. These surpassingly picturesque stage settings are obviously located in a parallel universe, not the one with the rude, functional structures typical of rural America.

Along with the Shelburne barns cited earlier in this chapter, the monumental 1888–1889 Farm Barn, enclosing three sides of a two-acre forecourt, completes the estate's farm group. Unlike the other Webb-Shelburne barns, remotely located as agricultural function dictated, this one is part of a devised estate setting, designed for the appreciation of the Webbs' visitors. But like those other barns, this extraordinary construction cannot be pinned down to a precise style, although its general reference seems to be Norman. For anyone interested in barns, Shelburne Farms offers an ultimate experience.

Arthur Newbold Estate Farm Court FIG. 596

1924–1929; razed

Arthur J. Meigs, Mellor, Meigs & Howe, architects

Laverock, Pennsylvania

The Newbold estate was designed as a Norman village by one of the nation's premier Period Revival design firms (Fig. 319). The estate was a great pictorial and social success: while still under reconstruction, it was featured on the cover of *Country Life*, then the gold standard of landed high society in the United States.

The farm court and estate house were closely interrelated, so that farm animals could come up practically to the house and thus heighten the desired rural image. Guests would pass by the farm court, the driveway separated only by a small "goose pond," on the way to the arrival court. This space was defined by the "potager," an ornamental kitchen garden, on one side, and by the estate house and its formal garden setting on the other. Everything was developed in a tightly organized, almost-urban physical composition.

Marshall Field II Estate, "Caumsett" Farm Group

FIGS. 597, 598

1920–1930

Alfred Hopkins, architect

Caumsett State Park, West Neck Rd., Lloyd Neck, Huntington, Long Island, New York

Compared to the tightly sited, European-like stone buildings at the Newbold estate, this "American" farm group is much looser in visual composition, plausibly agricultural in image, and set far distant from the estate house.

For the farm group (Fig. 597), Hopkins began with the basic shapes of American barns, silos, and ancillary buildings, then Georgianized them through signature elements such as a cupola, before

FIG. 599 **Expressiveness on a Tight Budget** Frank Lloyd Wright's Taliesin Midway Farm Group was self-built at infinitessimal cost, compared to Shelburne, Newbold, and Caumsett (earlier in this chapter). Nevertheless, Midway is the most visually imaginative of the four. *Published with the permission of the Frank Lloyd Wright Foundation*

finishing off everything in cedar shingles and sparkling white wood trim. The result is disarmingly beautiful, a studied informality that is plausibly farm-like, if impossibly picturesque for a true working farm.

A quarter mile past the farm group, one encounters the elegant brick Polo Stables (1925, Fig. 598), located just where the entry loop to the main house (Fig. 192) begins and returns. This particular siting is critical, establishing a sense of elite gateway, architecturally and in program, to clearly signal that one is indeed visiting an important estate. Visitors have plenty of time to consider this, as the road works nearly another mile through dense woods before reaching the main house. Everything is very impressive, as it was meant to be.

Taliesin Midway Farm Group FIG. 599

1938; 1947

Frank Lloyd Wright, architect

Taliesin/Lloyd Jones farms, Hwy. 23 S of Spring Green, Wisconsin

Wright began building here on his family farmlands in 1886 with Unity Chapel, and a year later with the first Hillside Home School. After the Taliesin Fellowship took up residence in 1932, a true working farm eventually became necessary. The Milk Tower (1947), a stone structure with a skeletal wood spire-weathervane, provides a signature visual element for this ensemble. The Taliesin farm group includes barns built in 1938 and dairy and machine sheds dating from 1947. (For nearby structures, see Frank Lloyd Wright chapter, Figs. 242 and 244.)

Industrial Structures

1800–1940

FIG. 600 Birthplace of the American Industrial Revolution Large-scale manufacturing began in East Chelmsford, Massachusetts in 1824. Individual mills had operated here, below Pawtucket Falls on the Merrimack River, since 1691. A canal built around the falls opened in 1796; it was purchased in 1821 by Boston entrepreneurs, who formed a manufacturing company and expanded their newly acquired canal into a network capable of powering industrial turbines for large modern factories. In the two decades following the 1824 factory, several more water-powered factories opened. The community was renamed Lowell in 1826, to honor the entrepreneurs' late partner, Francis Cabot Lowell, who had studied the English Industrial Revolution and built a modern mill in Waltham in 1813. Most of the Lowell factories had closed by the late 1920s, derelict (as in this view) until restoration of the city's historic industrial district began in the 1970s.

Landmarks of American industrial construction and engineering can be appreciated in three respects: first, Basic Adaptations, followed by Technological Advances, then Functional Innovations.

This chapter provides only the briefest of overviews. For a traditional perspective on formative international influences, you can consult Sigfried Giedion's classic *Space, Time and Architecture*, especially the section on The Evolution of New Potentialities. Betsy Hunter Bradley surveyed American industrial construction with exceptional thoroughness in *The Works: The Industrial Architecture of the United States*. In addition, you might also wish to read Grant Hildebrand's *Designing for Industry*, an account of assembly-line mass production of autos, to appreciate the countless functional industrial innovations that have been so central to the economic success of the United States and which have so pervasively colored contemporary American culture.

FIG. 601 **Customized Utility** The Hook Windmill is one of a handful of remaining nineteenth-century American windmills. Notably found on the South Fork of Long Island, the surviving mills are admired today for their arresting visual character. Of course they were originally understood simply as labor-saving machines. Each windmill builder devised a distinct technology, so even though all windmills look pretty much alike to most of us, they are actually idiosyncratic in detail. *Library of Congress, Prints & Photographs, Historic American Engineering Record*

FIGS. 602, 603 **Functional Dignity** The adjoining Crown and Eagle mills in Massachusetts were practical constructions, adaptable to changes in manufacturing and to the regional economy while maintaining their inherent visual qualities (Fig. 602). Now somewhat sanitized, architecturally, after conversion to housing (Fig. 603), the combined mills remain visually memorable constructions. *Fig. 602: Library of Congress, Prints & Photographs, Historic American Engineering Record*

BASIC ADAPTATIONS

Infrastructure must be developed soon after settlement of a region or founding of a town. Initially, none of this is very fancy. Trash removal in Litchfield, Connecticut, for example, was simply accommodated at a centralized town dump, which two centuries later was transformed into its "Colonial" town green (see American Colonial Revivals chapter). The covered well below is representative of numberless frontier adaptations, in this case, built of locally produced wood planking, and protected by a slanting cover that both kept out most falling objects, and yet was also efficient for drawing water.

Covered Well
1798
NE quad. Hwys. 68 and 62, Washington, Kentucky

Locally reputed to be the "first water works west of the Alleghenies," this tiny functional construction balances a decided lack of craftsmanship with a ruggedly engaging, frontier visual character.

Hook Windmill FIG. 601
1806; ceased operation in 1908; restored, 1939
Nathaniel Dominy V, builder
N. Main St. at Pantigo Rd., East Hampton, Long Island, New York

Wind-powered grist mills like the Hook Windmill were once common on breezy Long Island. Eleven are still extant, in various states

of repair, including the 1804 Gardiner's Mill, also built by Dominy, a few blocks to the south of Hook, just east of the town pond.

Today, windmills are rare enough that visitors to the area are understandably quite taken with their visual qualities. Of course, windmills were initially appreciated simply as useful machines, a practical way of harnessing an abundant resource—wind—so that residents could enjoy a diet that included more than just fish and vegetables.

While windmills look generally alike to most of us, each builder adopted distinguishing methods of transferring power, holding the grind stone, and solving other arcane technical problems. Such local innovation is a characteristic of American building.

Crown and Eagle Mills FIGS. 602, 603
1825, Crown; 1829–1830, Eagle; 1851, connecting span; 1984, conversion to apartments
Robert Rogerson, architect; **Paul Whitin, Jr.**, architect of 1851 connection; **Bruner/Cott**, architects of 1984 conversion
123 E. Hartford Ave., North Uxbridge, Massachusetts

An ongoing demonstration of American adaptation. The Crown (west) and Eagle (east) mills were built on opposite banks of the Mumford River as cotton textile mills. These were straightforward designs of heavy timber structure and granite exterior walls. Belt-driven textile machinery ran directly off shafts powered by water turbines.

Over the ensuing century, the original mill buildings were linked by a three-story brick infill, additions were constructed and torn down, as markets and products changed. This functional evolution was very pragmatic: clearly there was little thought of style on the parts of the owners. Yet the resulting construction is direct and handsome as an authentic, functional expression (Fig. 602).

By the post–World War II years, the New England textile industry had moved to the lower-wage U.S. Southeast, and the mills stood empty for several decades. After a vandal-set fire in the mid-1970s, the buildings were reconstructed for housing (Fig. 603).

Wapsipinicon Mill FIG. 604
1854; 1867
W. 1st St./Hwy. 20, on the Wapsipinicon River, Independence, Iowa

As another example of industrial adaptation, the original mill on this site processed wool. This structure was rebuilt above its foundation after the Civil War in order to mill grains for feed. Between 1915 and 1940, the mill generated electricity. Like the Crown and Eagle mills, Wapsipinicon Mill is straightforward and functional, of brick above stone foundations, rectilinear in plan. Because of its prominent site at the gateway to downtown Independence, the mill also functions as a visual landmark.

Kennecott Mines FIG. 605
1907–1938; Concentration Mill, 1910, 1914, 1915, 1922
Oscar Rohn, geologist; **Stephen Birch**, mining engineer
Kennicott [sic], McCarthy, vic., Wrangell–St. Elias National Park, Alaska
(Note: Allow at least 2-3 hours, each way, to traverse the 59-mile McCarthy Road from Chitina.)

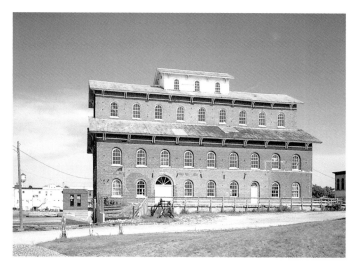

FIG. 604 Industrial Gateway Wapsipinicon Mill in Iowa has proved to be functionally adaptable over a century-and-a-half of change, while handsome enough to serve as a community landmark.

FIG. 605 Astonishing Commercial Exploit One can barely imagine how the remote, almost inaccessible ore fields above Kennecott Mines in Alaska were even explored. That this massive industrial complex was actually constructed is almost beyond comprehension. Functional building fortuitously resulted in a stunning visual cascade down this literally breathtaking slope. *Library of Congress, Prints & Photographs, Historic American Engineering Record*

Befitting Alaska, the Kennecott story is fabulous, marked by stupendous physical and construction feats, as well as by virtually unceasing intrigue among powerful competing syndicates. In 1898, Rohn confirmed massive copper deposits across a precipitous field at 6,000 feet elevation, immediately adjacent to the Kennicott [sic] Glacier. Eight years later, Birch organized the prevailing syndicate, which opened a base camp about three miles away, and nearly 4,000 feet lower, to process the ore. Forty-two buildings and seven structures were constructed between 1908 and 1923. The most prominent of these is the Concentration Mill (Concentrator), which steps dramatically down its steeply pitched mountainside site.

TECHNOLOGICAL ADVANCES

Modern industry and hence, modern society, are possible because of technological advances. In construction, exploiting the potentials of new materials, especially iron and steel, led to radically new ways of building. Advances are apparent in the ability to span space by Abraham Darby's 1775–1779 iron bridge over the Severn at Coalbrookdale in England; and Joseph Paxton's breathtaking Crystal Palace for the 1851 Great Exposition in London (destroyed by fire). Iron, and eventually steel, made high-rise skeletal building construction practical (see The Chicago School chapter).

Balloon Frame Construction
1833
George Washington Snow, engineer and builder
Chicago, Illinois

Sometimes modest innovations have a large cumulative impact. Late in the 1700s, new developments made possible the inexpensive mass production of iron nails, reducing their cost from 25 cents to 3 cents a pound. Shortly thereafter, separate improvements in sawmill technology made mass production of framing lumber practical.

Combining these innovations, Snow devised a rapid method of construction, employing mass-produced nails to fasten slender dimension lumber into a light but rigid frame. Snow's "balloon" or "Chicago" frame made it possible to erect boom cities like Chicago and San Francisco almost literally overnight. Later, ready-cut framed house kits were shipped by rail to towns across the country, including a line of houses offered out of a catalog by Sears, Roebuck & Company.

The first balloon-frame building, Chicago's St. Mary's Roman Catholic Church, was constructed in 1833 and disassembled and reassembled three times during a brief existence.

Skeleton Construction FIG. 606
1848 ff.
James Bogardus, engineer-builder
Lower Manhattan, New York, New York

Bogardus was the first American to exploit the full potential of cast iron for industrial construction. In an 1856 drawing well-known to architectural history students, Bogardus depicted an imaginary four-story factory with no interior columns, supported only by a scattered patchwork skeleton of a cast iron exterior frame. This was not intended as a real proposal—although it is structurally similar to an 1849 design by Bogardus (next entry)—but rather was meant as an arresting demonstration that the thousands-of-

FIG. 606 Skeleton Construction In this startling 1856 drawing, engineer James Bogardus dramatically illustrated how iron framing eliminated any need for load-bearing walls. The era of dematerialization was at hand.

FIG. 607 Iron Framing By the time of his 1856 drawing (Fig. 606), Bogardus had already built a skeleton-frame building, the Edgar Laing Stores in Manhattan. *Library of Congress, Prints & Photographs, Historic American Buildings Survey*

years era of solid bearing walls was now over. And soon, cast iron buildings were constructed across Lower Manhattan.

Edgar Laing Stores FIG. 607
1849; razed, 1971
James Bogardus, engineer-builder
cor. Washington & Murray Sts., New York, New York

A startling design, built when the technological norm required heavy masonry exterior walls to enclose a large commercial building. Bogardus employed cast iron plates only a quarter of an inch thick, bolted to an iron structural framework. According to historian Barksdale Maynard, the building was constructed in just a few weeks, during winter!

Fire Watch Tower FIG. 608
1856
James Bogardus, design engineer; **Julius B. Kroehl**, builder
Marcus Garvey Park, SW of Madison Ave. and E. 121st St., New York, New York

FIG. 608 **Down to the Basics** Bogardus's Fire Watch Tower in New York required a minimum of materials: an iron frame for height, and a stair to get to the watch platform. *Library of Congress, Prints & Photographs, Historic American Engineering Record*

FIG. 609 **The Glory of Iron** Cast iron architecture could be beautiful, especially SoHo structures like the E.V. Haughwout Building. *Library of Congress, Prints & Photographs, Historic American Buildings Survey*

FIG. 610 **Beyond Manhattan** Cast iron was employed here and there throughout the United States. The imposing ZCMI Department Store façade in Salt Lake City is among the best remaining national examples outside of New York City. *Library of Congress, Prints & Photographs, Historic American Engineering Record*

This last remaining New York City fire tower demonstrates how cast iron construction allowed the dematerialization of exterior walls. Masonry walls were no longer necessary to reach substantial heights. Bogardus engineered and constructed two earlier fire watch towers, on 33rd Street (1851) and Macdougal Street (1853). This Harlem project was built by Kroehl, who underbid Bogardus by proposing a shorter tower placed on an elevated site. Despite the skeletal appearance, Bogardus clearly meant to express his design as architecture, as evidenced by the spandrel reveals and delicate fluted Doric columns.

SoHo Cast Iron Historic District
Mid-1800s
Defined by Houston and Canal, Broadway and W. Broadway, New York, New York

According to the City's historic preservation designation, this area encloses the "largest concentration of full and partial cast-iron facades anywhere in the world." For specific addresses and a detailed description, you can consult White and Willensky's *AIA Guide to New York City*.

E. V. Haughwout Building   FIG. 609
1857; restored, 1999
John Gaynor, architect; **Daniel Badger**, manufacturer; **Joseph Pell Lombardi**, restoration architect
488–492 Broadway at Broome St., New York, New York

The elegance of this retail structure is all the more impressive in that the architect achieved it with ready-made panels from Badger's cast iron works. As restored, the Haughwout Building is one of the architectural stars of Manhattan's SoHo cast iron district.

Z.C.M.I. Department Store   FIG. 610
1876–1877; additions in 1880, 1891, 1902, 1910; façade reconstructed, mid-1970s
William Folson & Obert Taylor, architects
15 S. Main St., Salt Lake City, Utah

While New York City's SoHo district is without peer, architectural cast iron was employed elsewhere in the United States. This store in downtown Salt Lake City is surely one of the most handsome remaining cast iron buildings in America. The central section was built first, with later additions to the south also of cast iron; the north addition is enclosed in stamped sheet metal. The entire façade was disassembled in the 1970s and reinstalled as a facing for a new structure.

FUNCTIONAL INNOVATIONS

By all accounts, the industrial revolution began in eighteenth-century England. However, an industrial *production* revolution dates from the early 1900s in Detroit. The industrial visionary Henry Ford is the essential figure in this revolution. Ford was assisted in devising plant innovations by his architect, Albert Kahn.

Ford's key advance was a *better process*. Buildings and materials-handling techniques were developed as integral parts of a whole. In a generalized comparison, the industrial revolution was characterized by many *inventions*. Ford systematized numerous *innovations* into a highly efficient assembly line which made inexpensive automobiles practical for ordinary Americans, and in so doing completely transformed American society.

Ford Motor Company Rouge Plant
1915–1920 ff.
Henry Ford, industrial visionary; **Albert Kahn Associates**, architects and engineers; **William B. Mayo**, Ford's chief facilities planner and construction executive; **Charles E. Sorenson**, Ford's production manager
3001 Miller Rd., Dearborn, Michigan

Albert Kahn's engineering innovations began with the Packard Building 10, completed in 1905, which Wayne Andrews cited as "Detroit's first reinforced concrete factory," with clear-span bays of 32' x 60'. Kahn began working with Henry Ford in 1907 on the new Highland Park plant, which was completed by 1914.

Within a year of Highland Park's completion, Ford decided to built a new "superplant" that would fully reflect his deepening insights about production, which in part were gained from operating experience with the new Highland Park facility. Beginning in 1915, Ford assembled 2,000 acres—more than three square miles—along the River Rouge in then semi-rural Dearborn for this new plant, which can be considered a mature expression of the U.S. industrial production revolution.

Dodge Half-ton Truck Plant FIG. 611
1937; overbuilt and inaccessible to the public
Albert Kahn Associates, architects and engineers
NE cor. of Eight Mile Rd. and Mound Rd., Warren, Michigan

This is the building that architectural history students are shown to represent modern American industrial architecture. In its lightness and distinctive roof profile it still seems ultramodern. Kahn's design is the engaging poster child for Betsy Hunter Bradley's assertion that the century-long development of American industrial engineering up to 1940 "evolved toward a single ideal—the exploitation of natural light and ventilation [with] maximum span. . . ."

Unfortunately, Kahn's landmark structure has long been completely buried among massive later additions to this immense plant, now only to be appreciated in the 1938 photograph provided as Fig. 611.

FIG. 611 The Ultimate Industrial Structure Albert Kahn's Dodge Half-ton Truck Plant near Detroit achieved just about the practical maximum of light-filled, flexible industrial space. *Photograph: Ken Hedrich © Chicago History Museum HB-04803-12*

Transportation

1900–2004

FIG. 612 **Transportation Symbols** Contemporary forms of transportation are always prominent in everyday life, whether the horse, as in this re-created period scene at Colonial Williamsburg, railroads in the 1800s, or autos and airplanes in the twentieth century. That is why transportation facilities like stables, terminals, and garages have been employed to serve as civic symbols, in addition to fulfilling their vital functional roles. A sampling of twentieth-century American transportation landmarks is identified in this chapter.

Transportation is the lifeblood of any city. Visitors arrive at and depart from a city by way of its transportation gateways, especially terminals and garages. As a consequence, as American cities became increasingly self-conscious and competitive by the twentieth century, it was only logical that great transportation facilities were erected which not only satisfied functional needs, but also served as prominent civic symbols.

Initially, these transportation-civic improvements focused on railroad terminals. In post–World War II years, civic focus moved to airline terminals. During the urban renewal era of the 1950s and 1960s, when American downtowns were revitalized, some cities took that opportunity to exploit commuter parking as civic symbols.

(For the impressive St. Louis Union Station, now adapted to other uses, see the following Retail and Hotels Chapter.)

RAILROAD TERMINALS

Washington, D.C., Union Station FIGS. 613, 614
1903–1908; remodeled, 1985–1988
Daniel H. Burnham, architect; **Benjamin Thompson & Associates**, architects for the 1980s remodeling
Directly N of the Capitol, Washington, D.C.

This "Roman" design is the outgrowth of three influences on Burnham. One was the Beaux Arts White City at the 1893 Chicago World's Fair, for which Burnham served as planning director. The second was the report of the 1902 McMillan-Senate Park Commission, of which Burnham was a member. That report called for a restatement of L'Enfant's 1791 alignment for the National Mall. The third influence was Burnham's field studies of European railroad terminals.

As a result, Burnham adopted a Beaux Arts imagery for the facility, the building was sited to reinforce the formal McMillan scheme, and the station was a functional success. Due to its close

FIGS. 613, 614 City Beautiful Monument Designed by the City Beautiful master, Daniel Burnham, who also led the replanning of the national capital, Washington, D.C., Union Station is a national landmark of the City Beautiful movement. Its heroic façade and imperial waiting room are especially impressive. *Library of Congress, Prints & Photographs, Historic American Buildings Survey*

FIGS. 616, 617 Splendid By Any Measure Cincinnati intended its Union Terminal as the be-all, end-all. The main design ingredients included an immense fountain forecourt cut out of an existing industrial district, a semicircular façade of pharaonic scale, and superb interiors featuring panoramic murals. By any measure, Cincinnati's civic quest to build a national icon was a resounding success. *Fig. 617: Library of Congress, Prints & Photographs, Historic American Engineering Record*

the *École des Beaux Arts* training of Whitney Warren. The other is the brilliant functional solution for a program of extreme complexity. This was the contribution of the St. Paul firm of Reed & Stem, which specialized in railroad work, and counted rail baron James J. Hill among its clients.

Broad Street Union Station FIG. 615
1913–1919
John Russell Pope, architect
W. Broad at David St., Richmond, Virginia

Although employing a Roman idiom, a domed pavilion with flanking wings, this design plays down exterior detail to read mainly as four pure masses. This is a very strong design, particularly as played against Richmond's fine-grained physical fabric.

Cincinnati Union Terminal FIGS. 616, 617
1929–1933; restoration, 1988–1993
Roland Wank, Fellheimer & Wagner, architects; **Paul Philippe Cret**, consulting architect; **Maxfield Keck**, sculptor; **Winold Reiss**, murals; **Ravenna Tile Works**, mosaic frescoes; **Glaser Associates**, restoration architects
1301 Western Ave., Cincinnati, Ohio

Cincinnati was the last of the monumental U.S. railroad stations, a consummate expression of the PWA Moderne. The Cincinnati terminal, like the Kansas City station built two decades earlier, occupies its own self-contained environment at the edge of down-

FIG. 615 Civic Monumentality Broad Street Union Station completed a triptych of civic monumentality in Richmond, along with Jefferson's Capitol (Fig. 113) and Monument Avenue (Fig. 1081).

visual relationship with the U.S. Capitol, Union Station effectively symbolized the central national role of transportation

New York Grand Central Terminal
1903–1913
Warren & Wetmore, building architects; **Reed & Stem**, architects for functional interrelationships and circulation
Park Ave. at 42nd St., New York, New York

Grand Central really combines two distinct, if completely integrated, designs. One is its formal architectural character, inside and out, reflecting

FIGS. 618, 619 Human Scale While other major cities sought imposing, monumental terminals, Los Angeles built its romantic, Spanish-flavored Union Terminal, featuring welcoming spaces like a human-scaled arrival patio (Fig. 619).

FIG. 620 Hint of the Future Burlington's Railroad Passenger Station was not only forward-looking in its streamlined visual character, but also in its program, providing an "intermodal" exchange between rail and regional bus lines, a feature that became national planning doctrine a generation later.

FIG. 621 Clippers to the World New York's LaGuardia Marine Air Terminal served the famous Pan Am "flying boats," which interconnected the pre–World War II world at rarefied levels of service. *Library of Congress, Prints & Photographs, Historic American Engineering Record*

town. Beyond its functional role, Union Terminal was intended to convey an important civic statement about Cincinnati, and as such, the project was developed to high design standards with respect to approach, landscape, architectural imagery, integral sculpture, public art, and building materials.

Los Angeles Union Terminal FIGS. 618, 619
1934–1939
John & Donald B. Parkinson, principal architects; **Tommy Tomson**, landscape architect
E of Alameda, between Alison and Macy Sts., Los Angeles, California

The last major metropolitan passenger train depot to be built in the United States, Los Angeles was not monumental, but both urbane and refreshingly humane. The basic imagery reads as Spanish Colonial Revival, while much of the detailing is Moderne. Gebhard and Winter noted that the full landscaping (Fig. 619) conveys an "indoor-outdoor sense of space seldom encountered in large-scale public buildings."

Burlington Railroad Passenger Station FIG. 620
1944
Holabird and Root, architects
300 S. Main St., Burlington, Iowa

Small, when compared to other terminals in this section, although significant. The station was strategically important enough to be

constructed during the World War II, despite rationing. Outwardly, its transitional design looks forward to postwar Modernism while retaining attributes of the Moderne. The facility was planned as what would later be known as an intermodal transportation center, serving trains and buses. That explains the roomy waiting room and fancy restaurant, set behind a curving glass wall. Burlington is sophisticated architecture for a small-city railroad station.

World Trade Center PATH Terminal
2003–20??
Santiago Calatrava, architect and engineer; **DMJM Harris, STV Group**, associate designers and engineers
Fulton St. between Church and Greenwich Sts., New York, New York

Calatrava's PATH Terminal proposal promised to be Manhattan's most stunning piece of architectural sculpture since Frank Lloyd Wright unveiled his Guggenheim Museum design. The soaring roof would have opened up above the interior plaza in good weather, and light would have flooded down to the subterranean rail platforms, uplifting the usual dank commuter experience. In the emotion-wrenching aftermath of the 9/11 attacks, few if any responses received such wide approval among stakeholders as this design. Alas, the complex realities of rebuilding intervened, and the most dramatic features have been scrapped. Even so, the new terminal will be several cuts above the public transportaion norm.

AIRPORT TERMINALS

Marine Air Terminal, La Guardia Airport FIG. 621
1937–1939
Delano & Aldrich, architects; **James Brooks**, artist
La Guardia Airport, off Grand Central Pkwy. at 94th St., Queens, New York

The WPA-funded Marine Air Terminal is a pioneer landmark of scheduled commercial aviation. As its name suggests, the building initially served the famed Pan Am Clipper "flying boats" (following the airline's 1928–31 Dinner Key base in Miami—now City Hall—also designed by Delano & Aldrich). In addition to the building itself, a Moderne landmark (be sure to note the upper frieze of flying fish), the circular hall within contains one of the great remaining Federal Art Project murals, the Cineramic, 12' x 237' "History of Flight," by Brooks.

Passenger Terminal, Santa Barbara Airport FIG. 622
1941, later alterations
Edwards & Plunkett, architects
S. off U.S. 101 on Ward Memorial Blvd. to Sandspit Rd., Goleta, California

A truly civilized commercial airport in terms of an idealized arrival setting. This tiny terminal building, which is smaller than many if not most houses on the "American Riviera," is all decked out in Spanish Colonial Revival garb, a clear sign that one has entered a kind of fantasyland, surely true for Santa Barbara! Ticketing, baggage, and car rentals are all are within steps of one another. Pre-9/11, the open rooftop restaurant, reached via a curving outdoor stairway, offered a splendid place to await arriving flights, which nosed up practically under your table.

Lambert-St. Louis Airport Terminal FIG. 456
1956–1957, massive later expansions
Hellmuth, Yamasaki & Leinweber, architects; **Edgardo Contini, William Becker**, structural engineers
I-70/Mark Twain Expressway, St. Louis, Missouri

The St. Louis terminal inaugurated modern airport design in the United States. Earlier U.S. air terminals had typically been little more been utilitarian shelters, and even the better terminals like Washington National were not innovative airline terminals as much as adaptations from contemporary railroad stations. Presciently, Lambert Terminal was planned for expansion, and in its un-ornamented, sweeping lines, clearly reflected the exhilarating newness of commercial air travel.

TWA Terminal, Idlewild (now JFK) Airport FIGS. 623, 624
1956–1962, later jetway additions
Eero Saarinen, architect; **Kevin Roche**, design associate; **Ammann & Whitney**, engineers
John F. Kennedy Airport, Queens, New York

The idea of sweeping lines first seen at St. Louis is here carried to its sculptural ultimate. Very much a period piece of its time, the terminal, especially its interior, remains plausibly futuristic a half century after its design.

Dulles Airport FIG. 625
1958–1962, significant later modifications
Eero Saarinen, architect; **Ammann & Whitney**, engineers; **Dan Kiley**, landscape architect
Dulles Tollway, Chantilly, Virginia

When Dulles opened, its extraordinarily beautiful and dignified terminal building was visually set out in a meadow with no other structures in sight. Especially at night, this presented a magnificent

FIG. 622 Air Travel as it Should Be As if there weren't so many other reasons why Santa Barbara is paradise, its marvelously scaled airport terminal should alone be persuasive.

FIGS. 623, 624 Enduring Futurism Eero Saarinen's TWA Terminal at Idlewild (now JFK) Airport was genuinely futuristic when opened more than a half-century ago, and has yet to seem less so.

scene. The visual impact of Saarinen's design has been much diminished, though not completely lost, by massive later terminal modifications and adjacent development.

Tampa International Airport
1968–1974; 1987, 1993
Leigh Fisher, concept planner; **Reynolds, Smith & Hills**, architects; **Joseph A. Maxwell Associates**, interiors; **Stresau, Smith & Steward**, landscape architects
I-275 at West Shore, Tampa, Florida

The terminal follows a simple, inspired planning concept, thoroughly worked out in detail. Arrivals park in an integrated garage adjacent to the main terminal building, whose several levels are organized by function. This efficient landside operation is connected by people-movers to remote airside gates. Not only does everything function easily—at least until post-9/11 security—but, with attention to warm tones, materials, and textures, both the central terminal and the remote gate areas are as pleasant as one will find at any major U.S. airport.

United Airlines O'Hare Terminal FIG. 626, 627
1982–1988
Helmut Jahn, Murphy/Jahn, architects; **A. Epstein & Sons**, associate architects; **Michael Hayden**, artist of "Thinking Lightly" in pedestrian tunnel
O'Hare International Airport, Chicago, Illinois

As close to a pure architectural statement as seems possible for working buildings, Jahn's design is characterized by glazed barrel vaults; gate areas are thus flooded with natural light (Fig. 626). Two concourses, B & C, are connected by an underground tunnel offering a computer-assisted sound-and-light show (Fig. 627). It is all very theatrical—and very effective.

PARKING

Miracle Mile
1923 ff.
A. W. Ross, visionary developer
Wilshire Blvd., between La Brea and Fairfax Aves., Los Angeles, California

Ross was among the first to understand that downtowns would be functionally difficult for retailers because of a lack of auto parking,

FIG. 628 **Landmark Garage** Under New Haven's redevelopment director Edward Logue, even a utilitarian program like the Temple Street Parking Garage of 1959–1963 was expressed in *architecture*.

an absolutely essential ingredient in modern American cities like Los Angeles. His solution was to develop a freestanding retail district in the "hypothetical center," in Richard Longstreth's words, of the fast-developing west side of LA. Although Ross was initially ridiculed because the location was initially out in the middle of nowhere, "Miracle Mile" evolved into a successful retail district.

Ross's parking solution was both simple and revolutionary: major buildings were set right up against the Wilshire sidewalk (see the Bullock's image, Fig 359), with sufficient off-street surface parking placed in the rear. Stores could thus be conveniently entered directly from the rear lot, while a traditional streetscape was maintained. The remainder of the block, away from Wilshire, was given over to apartments, which buffered surrounding single-family and duplex neighborhoods, and also provided a relatively inexpensive expansion potential as parking needs grew.

Temple Street Parking Garage FIG. 628

1959–1963
Paul Rudolph, architect
Temple, Church, and George Sts., New Haven, Connecticut

Over 800 feet long, this sculptural, poured-concrete garage was intended as the first phase of a peripheral parking facility that was ultimately to expand above and beyond the Oak Street Connector, to be more than 2,000 feet long. New Haven redevelopment director Edward Logue was the first to act on Victor Gruen's peripheral parking concept developed in 1958 for Fort Worth (see Physical Plans chapter) and demonstrated three decades later in Minneapolis (next entry). Logue was also the leading redevelopment official, in New Haven and later in Boston, to recognize the potentials of design in community renewal.

At this early date, Rudolph understood the program goal as primarily an architectural one, expressed here as a megastructure. Although the facility's planning goal was never fulfilled—no fault of Rudolph's—the Temple Street garage is significant as an early attempt to treat this utilitarian function as architecture.

I-394 Peripheral Parking, "Third Avenue Distributor"

FIGS. 629, 630
1970; construction, 1988–1991
City of Minneapolis, planning and traffic engineering; **Stageberg-Beyer**, architects
NW of 2nd Ave. N. between 3rd and 10th Sts. N., Minneapolis, Minnesota

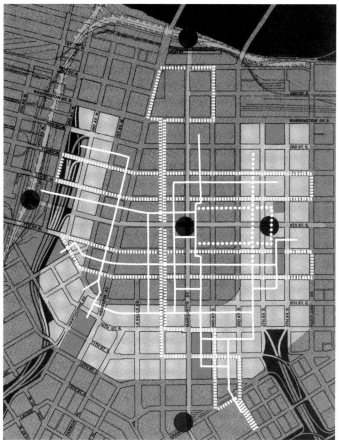

FIGS. 629, 630 **Peripheral Parking** Minneapolis auto commuters can drive off the "Third Avenue Distributor" freeway directly into parking garages (Fig. 629, red on the diagram in Fig. 630), and walk into Downtown through a 70-block network of climate-controlled skywalks (see the Urban Design chapter). *Fig. 630: City of Minneapolis, Metro Center '85, 1970*

Peripheral parking has been talked up by city planners and traffic engineers for decades, but this three-garage facility, which is part of a larger downtown-wide system (Fig. 630), seems to be the only comprehensive integrated working demonstration of the concept in the United States. Vehicles exit the freeway directly into the garages and, when leaving, enter directly back onto the freeway, without using city streets.

After parking their cars, motorists can walk into the city center by way of climate-controlled, second-level pedestrian "skyways," which interconnect a 70-block area of downtown (Fig. 948). As a result, traffic congestion is reduced in the densely built-up downtown core, and large-scale parking in lower-value fringe districts becomes a convenient alternative to costly in-building garages in the developed city center.

Retail and Hotels

1900–2004

FIG. 631   The Timeless Retail Strip The most common retail layout, the simple linear strip, has been employed for at least 2,500 years, since the *stoas* of the Athens *Agora*. Strip commercial prevails because it is inexpensive, functional, and flexible. When the handsom Maltzahn Building in New Ulm, Minnesota, opened in 1890, customers tied up their horse-drawn carriages right out in front. Later, of course, shoppers drove up in automobiles. By the 1920s, a progenitor of the postwar strip retail building, the so-called *taxpayer*, had appeared in Los Angeles. Taxpayers were soon set back from the street in order to provide off-street parking directly in front of the stores. This chapter identifies several retail configurations in American downtowns and suburbs, although in terms of prominence, strip retail continues to dominate.

Since Antiquity, in places like the Athenian agora, retail commerce has functioned as a center of everyday city life. In the United States by around 1900, dry good stores were well established in large American downtowns. These were family businesses like Hudson's in Detroit, Field's in Chicago, and Dayton's in Minneapolis. The most successful of these evolved into department stores (Fig. 632) which served as retail anchors for entire metropolitan areas.

By the 1920s, specialty stores focused on niche markets had clustered around department stores, providing an unparalleled draw: Downtown was *the* place to shop for all but staples like groceries. Largely because of this retail concentration and consequent choices, downtown department stores dominated the regional retail scene well into the post–World War II years, especially for holiday shopping and seasonal attractions, like the fabled multi-floor Christmas tree in Marshall Field's Chicago Loop store.

Yet even at its 1920s peak, the dominance of downtown retail had begun to erode. Key events in outside-of-downtown retail included the development, after 1923, of Miracle Mile in an undeveloped part of Los Angeles (see Transportation chapter);

FIG. 632 **Downtown Department Stores** Local dry goods concerns like John Wanamaker in Philadelphia grew into landmark department stores, signature retailers of their city. In 1909 Wanamaker bought a 10,000-pipe organ, the world's largest, to adorn the interior court of his new store. First played in 1911, the organ was judged not powerful enough for the space, and the instrument was enlarged in stages to a staggering 28,500 pipes. *Library of Congress, Prints & Photographs, Historic American Buildings Survey*

FIG. 633 **Modern Retail** The clean lines of the 1898-1906 Schlesinger and Mayer department store in Chicago (later Carson, Pirie, Scott; see also Figs. 223, 224) visually positioned the store as up-to-date, hence stylish, in Chicago's competitive retail market.

and Country Club Plaza in Kansas City, which opened in 1925 (later in this chapter). This regional dispersion intensified everywhere after the World War II, as retailers addressed the demographic realities of postwar metropolitan expansion.

Hence, several retail subjects are noteworthy. One is the downtown department store, represented architecturally by Louis Sullivan's crisply modern Schlesinger and Mayer/Carson, Pirie, Scott store in the Chicago Loop (Figs. 223, 224, 633). Otherwise few of these stores are nationally significant for their architectural qualities.

Over the past half-century, downtown retail has struggled in many American cities, especially in regions where downtown retail traditions are weaker, as in Denver, or practically non-existent, as in Phoenix. Solutions for addressing the decline in downtown retail have ranged from developing large, suburban-style shopping malls next to department stores, to reducing the traditional scope of products by getting out of intensely competitive markets like major appliances, to closing down completely.

The evolution of regional shopping malls is another important American retail theme. These are to expanding metropolitan areas what the downtown department store was to the central city a lifetime ago. As entries later in the chapter illustrate, regional malls have undergone continuing transformation, from a basic grouping of stores to immense retail-service-entertainment complexes.

FIG. 634 **Urban Entertainment** Universal CityWalk in Los Angeles (1992) is an archetypical urban-entertainment center, an attention-grabbing hybrid mix of venues, including movies, restaurants, and retail.

FIG. 635 **Authentic Center of Activity** Seattle kept its historic working downtown market when other cities demolished theirs, some of them replaced by phony "festival marketplaces." Long after most festival markets have disappeared, Pike Place Market continues to draw crowds attracted to its gritty authenticity.

PREWAR RETAIL

Pike Place Market FIG. 635
1907–1917 ff; Sanitary Public Market, 1910; Corner Market Building, 1912; restored, 1975
Andrew Willartsen, architect of Sanitary Public Market; **Thomas & Grainger**, architects of Corner Market Building; **John Goodwin**, engineer for upper concourse; **George Bartholick**, restoration architect
Between First and Western, Pike and Virginia, Seattle, Washington

A century ago in major cities, public markets were commonly located right in the center of town. But food distribution in most U.S. cities has long been consigned to anonymous warehouses in outlying industrial areas. Fortunately for Seattle, a 1971 citizen initiative saved this downtown market from urban renewal. A cherished local institution, Pike Place Market derives its visual charm from the obviously authentic jumble of structures, a dramatic site overlooking Elliott Bay, and colorful human activity which mixes a working market with the inevitable tourist-oriented retail and restaurants.

FIGS. 636, 637 **Suburban Urbanity** Lake Forest is arguably the classiest of Chicago's splendid North Shore suburbs. There is no argument at all that its Market Square retail center is architecturally without peer.

FIG. 638 **Local Icon** Country Club Plaza is a Kansas City cultural landmark as much as it is a shopping center. Distinctive 1920s Spanish Colonial Revival imageries set this development clearly apart from other area retail districts.

Market Square FIGS. 636, 637

1912–1913, concept; 1915–1916, design and construction
Howard van Doren Shaw, architect
Western Ave., between Deerpath and Westminster, across from the commuter rail station, Lake Forest, Illinois

Lake Forest was founded in 1856, and soon developed into an elite, naturalistic, lakeside enclave. Despite ample local wealth and an exclusive private college, by the early 1900s, the town's commercial area was, in the words of one citizen, a "disgrace to civilization," just possibly a bit of an overreaction! Market Square was the response: an urbane, mixed-use development of 28 stores, a bank, 12 office suites, 30 apartments, a gymnasium, and a clubhouse, laid out in a U shape around a landscaped central court, focused on a central fountain.

Although small—less than 400 feet across—Market Square is important in several respects: (a) for the picturesqueness of its architecture, with a European imagery knowingly synthesized from several sources; (b) the sense of civic presence, which was then virtually absent from American suburbia, especially in the Midwest; (c) the pioneering model of a shopping center "with set boundaries, designed as a unified entity;" (d) a mixed-use program; and (e) "perhaps the first business district to be laid out specifically to accommodate motor vehicles," in the assessment of Richard Longstreth. This combination of attributes assured that Market Square gained national attention and near-universal admiration.

Country Club Plaza FIG. 638

1922–1925; multiple later expansions

Jesse Clyde Nichols, Sr., developer of Country Club; **Edward Buehler Delk**, architect; **Edward W. Tanner**, architect for 1925–1974 expansions and remodelings
SW of 47th St. and Nichols Pkwy., Kansas City, Missouri

County Club Plaza is routinely cited as the first planned U.S. shopping center (despite Market Square, above). Beyond any historical importance, Country Club Plaza is a beloved civic landmark, memorably picturesque, especially as lighted around Christmas. The Spanish Colonial Revival imagery, built around yet another American interpretation of the Giralda tower in Seville, was no doubt influenced by Bertram Goodhue's 1915–1916 San Diego exposition architecture (see Fairs and Expositions chapter).

This seemingly exotic imagery was actually a plausible historical choice: Joan Michalak noted that Kansas City once functioned as the gateway to the American Southwest, along the Santa Fe Trail (see the Roads chapter), so despite its Midwestern location, Kansas City does have a genuine Spanish connection in its heritage, the way St. Louis thinks of itself as a French city.

Four aspects of Country Club Plaza are especially instructive: (a) The visual cohesiveness of the original 1920s imagery; (b) the relative visual discord of architecturally indifferent postwar additions; (c) the effective employment of exterior lighting, especially the outlined buildings during the holday season; and (d) the memorable value of water fountains.

POSTWAR REGIONAL MALLS

Northgate Shopping Center

1946–1950; substantially enlarged and altered
Rex Allison, developer; **John Graham, Jr.**, architect
SE cor. I-5 and NE. Northgate Way, Seattle, Washington

Postwar retail developers recognized that American society was rapidly evolving into something quite different from what it had been before the World War II. Since the 1920s, retailers had observed that people preferred to shop close to their homes, particularly by automobile. For convenience shopping, that preference could be satisfied by neighborhood strip centers which included groceries, hardware, cleaners, a drug store, and basic sundries. But for dry goods, gifts, and larger household products, decentralized retail centers with department stores and specialty shops would be required.

Building from the insights gained from the transitional 1945–1947 Broadway-Crenshaw Center in Los Angeles, Northgate was the original mature suburban regional U.S. shopping mall, defined by easy access, plenty of close-in free parking, multiple entries, a low-rise configuration, a concentration of department and specialty retail, and a self-contained, internal environment.

Southdale FIG. 639
1954–1956; later expansions and remodelings, almost completely altered
Dayton's Department Store, developers; **Victor Gruen & Associates**, architects
SE cor. 66th St. and France Ave., Edina, Minnesota

Southdale was the world's first fully enclosed regional shopping mall. Postwar evolution of the American regional mall can be conveniently illustrated in just three developments. First, Allison and Graham established a general model at Northgate (above). Gruen further clarified the suburban regional mall with refinements, especially outdoor courtyard landscaping, at Northland Shopping Center, which opened in 1954 in suburban Detroit. Finally, at Southdale, the regional shopping mall was fully enclosed and climate-controlled, organized internally around a "Garden Court" in the now-classic dumbbell configuration.

In addition to its historic importance as the world's first fully enclosed regional mall, Southdale was beautifully appointed, with colorful textures in stone, brick, and glazed tile on the outside, chrome, brass, and stone on the interior. The Garden Court featured a three-story golden sculpture by Harry Bertoia and a full-height cage for tropical birds. Southdale was an immediate commercial and social success. The center has been remodeled and expanded periodically over the past half century, so little of the original design remains, although if one knows where to look, it is still just possible to get a sense of what this international retail landmark was like in the 1950s.

Mall of America FIG. 640
1989–1992
The Jerde Partnership, design architects; **HGA, KKE**, executive architects; **Robert E. Bell, Hope Design Group**, Camp Snoopy Architects
S of I-494, between Hwy. 77 and 24th Ave. S., Bloomington, Minnesota

Regional shopping malls have evolved continuously since the 1950s and have grown ever larger in size. While Southdale originally enclosed about 500,000 square feet of floor area, malls like Woodfield, near Chicago's O'Hare airport, are several times as large.

Mall of America opened with about three million square feet of retail, plus more than one million square feet of amusement venues, within an immense interior volume. While important for its sheer size, Mall of America is even more significant as a summation of the ultimate state of the American regional shopping mall at the turn of the twenty-first century. While retail still forms the basis of this mall, its 500+ stores and kiosks are augmented by the Knott's Camp Snoopy amusement park (Fig. 640, now re-branded) at its center, plus 50 restaurants, 7 nightclubs, bowling, a 14-screen multiplex cinema, a wedding chapel, and an aquarium. All venues are cohesively managed and marketed to great effect. While there is nothing unique here, Mall of America is the number one individual attraction in the United States, drawing more visits than Disneyland, the Grand Canyon, and Graceland—combined.

FIG. 639 A World Onto Itself Southdale retail mall was an earthshaking event to its community. The center offered downtown selection with suburban convenience, all in a designed, climate-controlled environment appointed in fine materials. The world's first enclosed shopping mall, Southdale may well also have marked the qualitative peak for this form of retail.

FIG. 640 Retail Evolution Mall of America, located about 15 minutes from Southdale (Fig. 639), highlights the evolution of American retail over four decades. MoA stores are augmented by dozens of restaurants and food vendors, and an array of amusement venues, including an aquarium and the Campy Snoopy rides shown here.

DIVERSIFYING RETAIL

In the later twentieth century, retail both followed earlier practices and splintered off into several new formats. A classic example of this diversification can be found in the Buckhead district of Atlanta, where the upscale Phipps Plaza boutique center is located across the highway from the Lenox Square

FIG. 641 Boutique Retail Freestanding boutique centers like the picturesque Borgata in Scottsdale, Arizona, are especially viable in tourist destinations.

FIGS. 642, 643 Festival Marketplaces Faneuil Hall/Quincy Marketplace remains successful in a large part because it is culturally authentic: located in a highly attractive city and set among landmark buildings with direct associations to the city's history and self-image. In the exterior view (Fig. 642), Faneuil Hall is in the center, the central Quincy Market building is at the right edge. The interior view (Fig. 643) illustrates boutique food vendors in an updated version of the sheds that once flanked the main Quincy Market structure.

regional mall, demonstrating an adjacency, at suburban scale similar to the earlier clustering of specialty retail near the downtown department store.

New forms of retail have emerged in the past two decades. These range from the now-ubiquitous power center, featuring big-box discount stores like Target and Best Buy, to discount malls like the mile-long Sawgrass Mills (12801 W. Sunrise Blvd. at Flamingo Rd., Broward County, Florida), to urban entertainment like Universal CityWalk in the Los Angeles suburb of Universal City (1992, Jon Jerde, Fig. 634) and the glitzy CocoWalk in Miami's Coconut Grove section (3015 Grand Ave.). Many of these are interesting, but few are especially significant architecturally.

Since the 1960s, freestanding boutique retail centers have been built distant from regional malls, especially in tourist destinations like South Florida, Phoenix, and the Los Angeles Southland. The lushly landscaped Bal Harbour Shops (9701 Collins Ave., in northern Miami-Dade County, Florida) was among the first of these. Some of the freestanding centers are architecturally pretentious, but few have achieved more than a shallow theatricality. One of the visually most striking of those few is the Borgata.

The Borgata FIG. 641
1981; later expansion and remodeling
Jones+Mah, architects
6166 N. Scottsdale Rd., Scottsdale, Arizona

Cosmopolitan shoppers of the type who would patronize this center will immediately recognize San Gimignano as the reference. A tiny, impoverished Italian Hill Town would seem to have little relevance for upscale boutique retail in the Desert Southwest, other than both being seasonally overrun with tourists. But these tightly clustered forms, plus indispensable landscaping and fountain, somehow seem appropriate for their purpose and setting.

FESTIVAL MARKETPLACES

Visionary developer James Rouse created a sensation in 1976 with his conversion of a historic site in central Boston into a "*festival marketplace.*" The reused buildings were landmarks dating from the 1740s and 1820s, designed by prominent architects Charles Bulfinch and Alexander Parris. Rouse called on architect Benjamin Thompson to convert the Quincy Market and two structures flanking it into a cheerful tourist attraction.

Rouse's cultural sensitivity, timing, and choice of place were perfect. Historic preservation was rapidly gaining national favor, the Vietnam War had come to a close, the old buildings were visually engaging, and Boston was the historic seat of the American Revolution. His marketplace was a great place for Americans to celebrate their roots during the Bicentennial, after a tumultuous and divisive decade.

Soon, festival marketplaces were underway in cities all over the country. Public officials and developers assumed that if such developments succeeded in reenergizing Boston, then they would do so anywhere. Alas, this assumption proved mistaken, as festival marketplaces failed in quality cities as different as

Richmond and Minneapolis. The ideal qualifications for success are listed below, in the Faneuil Hall Marketplace entry. Only a few of all these festival marketplaces satisfied the majority of these requirements, and remain in operation. Most of the successful ones, including those on the Manhattan, Baltimore, and Miami waterfronts, were developed and operated by Rouse.

Faneuil Hall Marketplace FIGS. 642, 643
1971–1976
The Rouse Company, developers; **Benjamin Thompson Associates**, architects
Between Congress St. and Central Artery, N of State St., Boston, Massachusetts

The complete festival marketplace formula, from its progenitor: (a) a tourist-attractive city; (b) a theme/flavor that reflects the authentic history of that city; (c) a cohesive, visually interesting site; (d) rehabilitation (not necessarily restoration) of landmark structures; (e) simple but graceful modifications, in tune with and also played off against the existing architectural rhythms; (f) skillful employment of colors, textures, and landscaping; (g) quality (though not overpriced) offerings in both products and food; (h) a consistency in theme throughout; (i) attentive maintenance; (j) imaginative programming; and (k) integrated management of facilities, leasing, operations, day-to-day programing, and marketing. This is all much easier said than done!

St. Louis Union Station FIGS. 644, 645, 646
1894; closed 1978; reopened as a festival marketplace, 1985
Theodore Link, architect; **Hellmuth, Obata & Kassabaum**, conversion architects
1820 Market St., St. Louis, Missouri

A few developers other than Rouse also understood the entire formula that was required for success (see the previous entry). Union Station actually went beyond Rouse marketplaces in some ways. For one thing, Union Station itself is an extraordinary structure, far surpassing Faneuil Hall and Quincy Market. For another, train themes resonate strongly at several levels in St. Louis culture. Third, its immense volumes allowed more program, including a high-quality hotel, which offered choices of historic railway-hotel rooms and brand new rooms, both located right within the marketplace. Perhaps most significantly, the railroad theme is pervasive, down to the smallest of details. Union Station is not just an attraction, but an all-encompassing experience.

LIFESTYLE CENTERS

By 2000, "lifestyle centers" had emerged as the latest American specialty retail trend. Precise definitions of lifestyle centers vary, but they generally contain an integral mix of retail and housing, ideally developed in a tight, urban-like form, and often dressed up in some kind of traditional architectural imagery.

Like any fashion, the lifestyle center is typically touted as all-new and up-to-the-minute. In reality, American antecedents with these same attributes date at least as far back as the 1909–1911 planning of the Forest Hills Gardens development in then-suburban Queens, New York (Figs. 821, 822). The direct lifestyle center precedent dates back to the early 1980s: Main Street in the Miami Lakes new town in Florida.

FIGS. 644, 645, 646 Triple Hit As a setting for a festival marketplace, St. Louis Union Station is ideal: fanciful, landmark architecture (Fig. 644), superb historic interiors (Fig. 645), and volumes of space under the train shed available for new construction (Fig. 646).

FIG. 647 **Lifestyle Center** Main Street in the Miami Lakes new town was a 1980s precursor to the recent lifestyle center trend. Typical ingredients include a tight, faux-urban streetscape featuring a mix of retail uses, with apartments on upper floors.

Main Street FIG. 647

1983; 1985; 2004ff.
Lester Collins, community planner, Main Street master planner; **Haynes, Spencer, Richards**, Phase I south architects; **Baldwin & Sackman**, Phase I north architects; **Rowe, Holmes, Hammer, Russell**, Phase II architects; **Forbes Architects**, Phase III architects
W of Ludlam Rd./NW. 67th Ave., 0.5 mi. S of the 826–Palmetto Expwy., Miami Lakes, Miami–Dade County, Florida

Collins laid out the Miami Lakes new town in 1962. By the early 1980s the community had grown enough to support a "downtown." Main Street was the response, taking the form of a narrow, two-block streetscape in the now-familiar retro format of apartments above street-level shop fronts. While most Main Street storefronts are of the nature of gift shops and real estate offices, the development includes a hotel, health club, and multiplex cinema. Grocery and drug stores are located just across a busy arterial.

The multiplex has proved to be a consistent draw, though it appears, anecdotally, that it could have been just as successful located anywhere nearby, given sufficient parking, which here is located behind the theaters, separate from the Main Street streetscape. Housing over storefronts has been successful for a niche market, primarily for those with late-night inclinations or occupations, like waiters.

POSTWAR DESTINATION HOTELS

Like the local department store, the downtown flagship hotel had become an American institution by the 1920s. These are generally well-known in American culture, if not for their architecture, then for social or even literary cachet, like that of the Algonquin Hotel in Manhattan, where the celebrated Roundtable gathered (1919 –). Many of the prewar hotels were quite ornate and visually impressive—the 1907 Plaza Hotel at the southeast corner of New York's Central Park comes to mind—but few of them are essential to understanding American architecture and urbanism. That changed in the mid-1960s, with the exhilarating downtown hotels of architect-developer John Portman.

At the time, convenient, low-rise suburban motels like Holiday Inn (see The Strip chapter) defined the principal postwar directions of the U.S. hospitality industry. If one looked for a newer high-rise hotel, it would most likely be in a vacation-resort setting like Miami Beach or Las Vegas. Downtown hotels were two generations old and more, culturally a lifetime in the past. That was not a desirable attribute in an era that looked eagerly to the future.

Because Portman's hotels were so radical—genuine architectural events—they offered an entirely new lodging experience, neither the stuffy ambiance of the old downtown hotels, nor the mundane convenience of suburban motels. This caused a turnabout from past experience. The Portman hotels were not so much in support of nearby existing attractions, but were instead prime destinations in themselves. It can be argued, for instance, that the first Portman-designed hotel, the Hyatt Regency Atlanta, established that city as a national convention destination.

Hyatt Regency Atlanta FIGS. 648, 649

1964–1967
John Portman & Associates, architects
265 Peachtree St. NE., Atlanta, Georgia

The Hyatt Regency Atlanta is world-famous for its spectacular, full-height internal atrium, the so-called "Jesus Christ space," after a common outburst by first-time visitors. However, the hotel's national significance extends beyond its innovative architecture. As the first postwar downtown destination hotel in the U.S., the Hyatt Regency Atlanta introduced a new benchmark for American commercial hotels, in the process transforming Atlanta's sleepy downtown into a major convention center.

After the opening of this hotel, Portman became something of a celebrity, representing the gold standard for American hotel architects. He subsequently designed numerous hotels across the U.S. for the Hyatt and Western International-Westin chains, and as far away as Shanghai, for the five-star Shangri-La chain.

HOTEL RESTORATIONS AND CONVERSIONS

As American downtowns were revitalized after the late 1960s, hotel capacity was sharply increased, usually by building new hotels, but sometimes refurbishing older ones. While many of the older hotels in downtowns and elsewhere remained distinctly Class B or lower, a few of these revivals resulted in remarkable transformations. The following three examples represent restorations and conversions into superior lodging by contemporary standards.

Changing demands of the office market have encouraged conversion of some older office buildings into hotels. Examples cited in this book include the Reliance Building in Chicago (Fig. 232), the Price Tower in Oklahoma (Figs. 260, 261), and the PSFS Buildling in Philadelphia (Fig. 401).

Biltmore Hotel

1922–23; 1928; restored, 1975–1977; remodeled, 1986
Schultze & Weaver, architects; **Phyllis Lambert**, mid-1970s restoration developer; **Gene Summers**, restoration architect; **Barnett & Schorr**, 1986 remodeling architects; **Giovanni Smeraldi, Anthony B. Heinsbergen, Anthony T. Heinsbergen**, artists, master craftsmen
SW cor. S. Olive and W. 5th Sts., Los Angeles, California

The original Biltmore design reflected a suave mix of sources, especially Beaux Arts, Italian Renaissance, and Spanish Churrigueresque imageries. The resulting architecture was handsome and refined, especially the public interiors.

By the early 1970s, however, the hotel had become a bit run-

down. It was fortunately saved by Lambert, who not only undertook the restoration of the public spaces and renovated the guest rooms, but introduced contemporary art throughout the building. Entire floors were devoted to the art and crafts of a single artist, such as one floor with signed Jim Dine prints and Dine-designed carpeting in each guest room.

The Villard Houses/Helmsley Palace Hotel

1881–1886, partly extant; hotel and restoration, 1977–1981
McKim, Mead & White, architects; **Emery Roth and Sons**, hotel architects; **Tom Lee, Ltd.**, new and restored public interiors
451–455 Madison Ave. at 50th St., New York, New York

By the 1970s, the original residential setting of the magnificent Villard townhouses (see the Beaux Arts chapter) had changed into a dense commercial district. In response to the site's vastly increased value, some less visible and historically significant portions of the townhouse group were demolished and replaced with a new, architecturally undistinguished high-rise hotel tower. Some of the group's most elegant interiors were adapted as public spaces for the hotel, while other, more modest period interiors accommodate offices of design-related organizations and an architecture bookstore. While not an ideal solution for preservationists, the conversion saved the key building exteriors, surrounding a handsome courtyard, and some extraordinary interiors.

La Posada Hotel FIGS. 650, 651

1928–1930; closed 1957–1996; restored and reopened, 1997
Mary Colter, architect
303 E. Second St. (historic Route 66), Winslow, Arizona

For La Posada ("The Lodge"), the matchless Colter exercised total design control, from site planning, landscaping, architecture, and interiors down to the place settings in the dining room. She devised the property as if it had originally been built in 1869, not coincidently the architect's birth year, as the *hacienda* home of a timber baron, then converted to a hotel in 1930, the year it actually opened. Thanks to dozens of visual inventions, the entire chimera seemed eminently plausible.

After 1958, the hotel was carved up for use as offices for the Santa Fe Railroad, and it narrowly escaped demolition in the mid-1990s. Providence in the form of Allan Affeldt, Tina Mion, and Dan Lutzick restored the property, refurnishing it in period, including some of the hotel's original furnishings from 1930. The result is marvelous, a must-stop for travelers along I-40.

Interior Spaces

1827–2004

FIG. 652 Exceptional Interiors Splendid interior spaces have been built across the United States. The Cleveland Arcade remains remarkably intact as one of the great American works of the Victorian era.

Interior spaces are often overlooked in surveys of outstanding architecture. This all-too-common omission occurs in part because architects and the architectural media have traditionally viewed "interior design" as basically cosmetic, a matter of color selection and the ordering of non-structural furnishings, which usually take place while a building is already under construction. From this perspective, interior designers, much less interior decorators, do not function at the conceptual and technical levels of architects, landscape architects, and engineers.

However, many American buildings feature splendid interiors that are intrinsic to the building's design. This chapter identifies several representative interior spaces of exceptional visual quality, among numberless others of note.

FIG. 653 **Sophisticated Passage** Providence's Arcade was quite advanced as a building type for its early nineteenth-century date, following London's famed Burlington Arcade by only a decade.

FIGS. 654, 655, 656 **Gothic Paradise** Louisiana's Old State Capitol is an embarrassment of riches. Beyond the legendary political goings-on associated with this building—truly "Gothic" in their own right—its marvelous, castellated Gothic Revival exterior is only a prelude to the fantastic Victorian Gothic interiors, especially the stained-glass rotunda skylight. *Figs. 655 & 656: Library of Congress, Prints & Photographs, Historic American Buildings Survey*

Arcade FIG. 653

1827–1829

Russell Warren (arcade), **J. C. Bucklin** (exterior), architects

130 Westminster St./65 Weybosset St., Providence, Rhode Island

Providence Arcade is a dignified, carefully ordered interior, quite sophisticated for the young nation of the 1820s. At the exterior entries to the arcade, massive Ionic columns on the street frontages play off visually against the delicate railings just behind.

Old State Capitol Rotunda FIGS. 654, 655, 656

1847–1852; reconstructed 1879–1882; restored, 1982–1994

James H. Dakin, architect; **William A. Freret**, reconstruction architect;

Eean McNaughton, restoration architect

N. Boulevard at St. Philip St., Baton Rouge, Louisiana

This magnificent space is defined by cast iron Gothic tracery, bathed in a rich, multicolored light that filters down from a stained-glass dome. Especially on a sunny day, there is almost a religious feeling to the space, which is especially surprising to encounter in an American government building, much less in the very temple of the bare-knuckle sport of Louisiana politics.

Dakin's building was reduced to ruins after a fire caused by Union troops during the Civil War. Nearly two decades later, Freret was entrusted with its total reconstruction. That accounts for the stylistic differences one notices: while the exterior still reflects Dakin's Romantic Revival Gothic, the interiors are very much Victorian Gothic in character. McNaughton's recent restoration brought everything up to superb condition. An absolute must visit.

Plum Street (Isaac M. Wise) Temple FIG. 657

1865–1866

James Keyes Wilson, architect

Plum and Eighth Sts., Cincinnati, Ohio

Absent strong architectural precedents, early American synagogues were often expressed in exotic, loosely Moorish imageries. This lack of precedent, combined with a total lack of experience with Islamic-Andalusian traditions among American architects was sometimes a plus, as their designs were unconstrained by convention. This dramatic interior is a supreme national example.

Trinity Church FIG. 658

1874–1877

Henry Hobson Richardson, architect; **John La Farge**, polychromy

Copley Square, Boston, Massachusetts

The interiors of this extraordinary church are every bit as good as the exterior (Fig. 210), and that's saying a lot. Like the Plum Street Temple, the basic feel is exotic, though here it seems more Byzantine than Moorish. The interior benefited from consummate talent on the parts of Richardson and La Farge, resulting in a sublime space, certainly among the finest American interiors of its time.

FIG. 657 **Consummate Exoticism** Well into the twentieth century, American synagogues were often expressed in mildly exotic imageries, nowhere more vividly than in Cincinnati's extraordinary mid-nineteenth-century Plum Street Temple. *Library of Congress, Prints & Photographs, Historic American Buildings Survey*

FIG. 658 **Fusion of the Distant Past** The interior of Richardson's Trinity Church in Boston seems to be an adroit blend of several sources, including Early Christian and Byzantine churches.

Cleveland Arcade FIG. 652

1888–1890; restored
John M. Eisenmann, George H. Smith, architects
401 Euclid Ave. connecting to Superior Ave., Cleveland, Ohio

Hands-down, the Cleveland Arcade is the greatest interior arcade in the United States. This magnificent space is flooded with light, which washes over the superb iron filigree. At 300 feet in length and at one point, 100 feet from floor to the underside of its glazed roof, the interior volume can be described as monumental.

While visiting, be sure to see the nearby Colonial Arcade (1898, George H. Smith), which connects Euclid to Prospect Avenue.

The Rookery FIG. 659

1885–1888; lobby and light court remodeled, 1905–1907; later alterations, including painting over roof glazing; restoration, 1988–1993.
Burnham & Root, architects; **Frank Lloyd Wright**, architect for the 1905–1907 remodeling. **Ganny Harboe, McClier Preservation Group**, architects for 1988–1993 restoration.
209 S. LaSalle St., Chicago, Illinois

A brilliant space, both as a design and because it was flooded with natural light. The two-story light court achieves a disciplined ornateness through exuberant expression of structure and a correspondingly relative suppression of ornament. The Rookery light court compares favorably to the illustrious Parisian cast iron interiors of the mid-1800s.

Bradbury Building FIG. 660

1889–1893
Sumner Hunt, George H. Wyman, architects
304 S. Broadway, Los Angeles, California

Unremarkable on the exterior; everything is within. The five-story skylit central court is a fantasy of wrought iron, projecting staircases, and open-cage elevators.

FIG. 659 Symphony of Ironwork Frank Lloyd Wright's "Persian" traceries, introduced with his renovation of The Rookery lobby in Chicago, are uncharacteristic compared to his well-known Prairie imageries, yet fully consistent with his usual daring. *Courtesy Chicago Historical Society/Library of Congress, Prints & Photographs, Historic American Buildings Survey*

FIG. 660 Los Angeles Inner Fantasy One would never guess from the Bradbury Building's unremarkable exterior that its atrium is moody enough to have served as a *noir* movie set. *Library of Congress, Prints & Photographs, Historic American Buildings Survey*

FIGS. 661,662 **Fountain of Dreams** Zaharako's Ice Cream Parlor is the genuine, old-fashioned soda fountain that you knew existed somewhere, but weren't sure exactly where. It's in Columbus, Indiana. But you probably never imagined its graceful Tiffany glass counter lamp! *Library of Congress, Prints & Photographs, Historic American Buildings Survey*

Zaharako's Ice Cream Parlor FIGS. 661,662

1900

329 Washington St., Columbus, Indiana

Columbus is renowned as a mecca of post–World War II American architecture, although the community is not without earlier works of distinction. Family owned and operated for a century, Zaharako's is the classic Victorian-era soda parlor that everyone knew about as a child but probably never actually experienced.

Zaharako's was beautifully fitted out for its role as a social crossroads in Columbus. Carved oak woodwork is found throughout, augmented by a mahogany and Italian marble back bar; soda fountains are of Mexican onyx; a genuine Tiffany lamp stands halfway down the counter. Nor is all of the glitter visual: a pipe organ was installed in 1908. Marvelously, Zaharako's is still in

FIGS. 663,664 **Prairie Space** The Woodbury County Courthouse in Iowa demonstrates that civic grandeur was not restricted to the Beaux Arts. Its magnificent rotunda is enhanced by a profusion of terra cotta Prairie ornamentation. *Library of Congress, Prints & Photographs, Historic American Buildings Survey*

business, right in the center of downtown. If you're reading this book, you'll probably eventually visit Columbus, so be sure to stop in for a sundae, or at least for a look.

Woodbury County Courthouse Rotunda FIGS. 663, 664
1916–1918
Purcell & Elmslie, William L. Steele, architects; **Alfonso Iannelli**, sculptor; **John W. Norton**, murals
620 Douglas St., Sioux City, Iowa

Sioux City is well out of the way for most of us interested in architecture, so, regrettably, few aficionados or professionals have visited this superb late Prairie School building (Fig. 279). For those willing to drive ten hours, each way, from Chicago or five from Minneapolis, a double treat awaits. Architecture mavens will be familiar with the impressive exterior, for which George Grant Elmslie reinterpreted traditional civic design themes in fresh ways.

However, the interior alone is worth a long trip (on weekdays, of course, when it's open), to experience the grand domed rotunda space and to enjoy the profusion of brilliant terra cotta ornamentation, also largely by Elmslie, who a decade earlier was Louis Sullivan's design associate for the Owatonna Farmers National Bank (Figs. 225, 226). Were this building located near a destination city like Chicago, it would attract throngs of design pilgrims.

War Memorial Concourse, St. Paul City Hall/Ramsey County Courthouse FIG. 665
1931–1932
Holabird & Root, Thomas Farr Ellerbe, architects; **Carl Milles**, sculptor
15 W. Kellogg Blvd., St. Paul, Minnesota

It is unexpected to encounter such a highly developed interior design inside a Midwestern government office building. A dramatic visual effect results from the moody darkness, employed as context and counterpoint to the brilliantly lit white onyx Milles sculpture of an Indian God of Peace.

Radio City Music Hall
1931–1932; restored, 1996–1999
Wallace K. Harrison, architect-project designer; **Donald Deskey, Edward Durell Stone**, interior architects; **Stuart Davis**, "Men without Women" mural; **Ezra Winter, Yasuo Kuniyoshi**, murals; **Hardy Holzman Pfeiffer Associates**, restoration architects
1260 Avenue of the Americas at W. 50th St., Rockefeller Center, New York, New York

Splendid beyond any possible description, and now beautifully restored. The great proscenium arch is well known, even to those who have never experienced the auditorium in person. The lobby and even some of the retiring rooms were also major achievements of the Moderne—indeed, among the finest of all American interiors.

Hillside Theater FIG. 666
1952
Frank Lloyd Wright, architect
Hillside Home School, Taliesin Estate, Spring Green, Wisconsin

Wright continuously re-edited his own buildings. This revision, following a fire, came a full half-century after he originally designed Hillside. An extraordinary 90-seat space was carved out of what was at one time a gymnasium. Upon entering, one inevitably focuses on the signature curtain, designed by Wright and constructed by the Fellowship out of canvas, felt, yarn and string. With additional time in the room, it becomes clear that this

FIG. 665 Municipal Environment for Art The War Memorial Concourse in the St. Paul City Hall/Ramsey County Courthouse offers a brilliant interaction of space and light, materials and sculpture. *Library of Congress, Prints & Photographs, Historic American Buildings Survey*

FIG. 666 Vibrant Serenity Despite what could have proved to be an excess of visual variety for such an intimate space, the experience of Frank Lloyd Wright's Hillside Theater is comfortably stimulating. *Published with the permission of Taliesin Associated Architects*

FIG. 667 Commercial Town Square Community socialization can thrive in private spaces, as Johnson and Burgee's IDS Crystal Court in Minneapolis confirms after more than three decades of use.

space is a virtuoso design performance, even for Wright. A steep gradient provides exceptional intimacy, enhanced by good acoustics. Although Wright employed a vibrant mix of dozens of colors, textures, and materials, the overall effect is one of remarkable serenity.

The Four Seasons
1959
Philip Johnson, architect; **Richard Lippold**, sculptor; **Karl Linn**, interior landscapes
99 E. 52nd St., New York, New York

Manhattan naturally abounds with places that reek of power and prestige. Even so, given its premier location in the Seagram Building (Fig. 416), and its "luxury, sophistication, and refinement," the Four Seasons restaurant has few equals, especially for a power lunch in its Grill Room. In addition to the bronze Lippold sculpture over the bar, an appropriate tone is set by a Picasso tapestry and a painting by Joan Miró.

Those of us without sufficient pedigree will be graciously seated in the dining room, probably unaware that this handsome space is considered the secondary location. But no matter, it is impossible not to feel the sheer glamour of New York City from anywhere here.

IDS Crystal Court FIG. 667
1968–1972
Philip Johnson and John Burgee, architects; **Edward F. Baker**, associate architect
Nicollet Mall, between Seventh and Eighth Sts., Minneapolis, Minnesota

IDS Center was a bolt out of the blue for postwar Minneapolis (Fig. 501). This development was stunning to Minneapolitans in several respects, from the 775-foot height of its office tower to the impressive quality of its architectural detailing. Even so, from civic and city planning perspectives, the Crystal Court, the central interior public space, is the most significant part of this development. Unlike enclosed public spaces that sprouted at the bases of many office buildings, this one is integrally related in its forms to the tower above, which is clearly visible through its glazed roof.

Architecturally, this is surely one of the finest mid-century American commercial spaces.

Movie Theaters

1902–1962

FIG. 668 **The Magic of Movies** Movies offer a full range of experiences, from rank escapism to profound insights about life. Movie theaters have been designed in all manners of expressions, from functional boxes to staggeringly ornate palaces. Grauman's Chinese Theater in Hollywood perfectly captures the sense of fantasy that we associate with movies.

FIG. 669 **Ur-Movie Theater** After about 1905, Nickelodeons like the Leader Theater in Washington, D.C., built in 1910, were specifically designed for showing motion pictures. This marked the evolution in entertainment venues away from vaudeville theaters and opera houses, toward a distinct new building type: movie theaters. *Library of Congress, Prints & Photographs*

American movie theaters rapidly evolved into a unique building type early in the twentieth century. Rudimentary projections of moving images date from about 1825, in Paris. Commercial applications of motion pictures were based on processes refined by Thomas Edison in the 1890s. The first showings of a motion picture to paying audiences occurred in Paris in 1895, and in New York City a few months later, in 1896.

At first, motion pictures were treated as curiosities, sometimes included as one act of a vaudeville show, then a dominant form of public entertainment. Since motion pictures required little more than a projector, a flat surface, and seating, screenings could be held in auditoriums, halls, even in large, ordinary rooms.

Films thus enjoyed a cost advantage over vaudeville, which relied on live acts. The first motion picture venue, the Electric Theater, opened in Los Angeles in 1902. By then, peep shows in penny arcades featured films.

FIG. 670 **Movie Palaces** In the Roaring Twenties, movie theaters developed into a grand expression now known as Movie Palaces. Like the Chicago Theatre, these venues featured impressive exterior marquees and opulent, if not fantastic, lobbies and auditoriums.

FIG. 671 **Atmospheric Theaters** John Eberson's dream townscapes were legendary in the movie industry. He devised this fantastic "Italian Garden" with a "deep azure blue sky of the Mediterranean" for the 1924–1925 Grand Riviera Theatre in Detroit. *Library of Congress, Prints & Photographs, Historic American Buildings Survey*

Between 1905 and 1914, motion picture nickelodeons exploded across the nation. While some nickelodeons were buildings converted from other uses, as many as 10,000 of these venues were constructed specifically for the showing of motion pictures, thus were a distinct building type, different from legitimate theater (Fig. 669).

By the time of the landmark *Birth of a Nation* (1915), it was apparent that motion pictures were not a novelty. Films were growing more elaborate, directors and actors were becoming celebrities, and the American public flocked to see the "movies." In response, movie theaters were designed not only to function as such, but were endowed with architectural pretense. Some, like the Saxe in Minneapolis, were dignified. Others, like the Washington in Dallas, were brightly lighted and visually opulent.

Several distinct types of movie theaters were built during the twentieth century. Maggie Valentine identified these, chronologically, as the arcade, the storefront, the nickelodeon, the downtown and neighborhood movie palace, the downtown and neighbor-

hood chain theater, and the multiplex. To this list can be added *free*standing suburban theaters of the post-World War II era. Many variations of these were designed, depending on program and imagery. There was also the air dome, a roofless enclosure dating from the early 1900s, eventually manifested as the drive-in.

This chapter emphasizes the two most pretentious movie theater design characters—the Palace and the Deco—both of which were developed for both single venues and theater chains.

National design leadership of movie theaters can be efficiently illustrated by reference to a handful of architectural practices: those of Thomas Lamb (1871–1942), John Eberson (1875–1954), George (1878–1942) and Cornelius (1861–1927) Rapp, practicing as Rapp & Rapp; plus C. Howard Crane (1885–1952), and the prolific S. Charles Lee (1899–1990). A number of local practices like Liebenberg & Kaplan in Minneapolis designed appealing Art Deco theaters for city neighborhoods and smaller towns.

MOVIE PALACES

Chicago Theatre FIG. 670
1921; converted
Rapp & Rapp, architects
175 N. State St., Chicago, Illinois

Uptown Theatre
1925; vacant
Rapp & Rapp, architects
4814 N. Broadway, Chicago, Illinois

George and Cornelius Rapp were the acknowledged masters of the Movie Baroque, which they typically carried out in an opulent French-Spanish idiom. These two movie palaces are archetypes of the silent-screen era, in their imagery and size and for their Wurlitzer organs, *de rigueur* for a movie palace of any pretense.

The Uptown, vacant since 1981, was the largest American movie theater, at nearly 4,400 seats, and boasted a 28-rank, 10,000-pipe organ. The Chicago is especially admired for its marquee, which was restored in 2003.

Tampa Theatre
1926; restored-converted, 1977
John Eberson, architect
711 N. Franklin St., Tampa, Florida

The earliest American movie palaces, especially those by Rapp & Rapp, were designed in a Neo-Baroque imagery—overdone, to be sure, but then a familiar vocabulary for commercial buildings. Eberson moved movie palaces in two new directions. One of these was the creation of a fantasy visual imagery, employing a free and confident mixture of styles. The Tampa Theatre self-described its architectural imagery as "Florida Mediterranean," made up of a marvelous mixture of Italian Renaissance, Byzantine, Spanish, Greek Revival, Mediterranean, and English Tudor motifs.

Eberson's other style innovation was the so-called "atmospheric theater," introduced in his 1923 Majestic Theater in Houston. He elaborated the auditorium side walls, and in later theaters, often even the lobby, as a dream townscape, above which a night sky held sparkling stars and projected, moving clouds (Fig. 671).

The Tampa Theatre was one of the last movie palaces constructed before "talkies" replaced silent pictures, beginning in 1927. It was also the first air-conditioned theater in the United States.

Indiana Theater FIGS. 672, 673
1926–1927; remodeled, 1958–1960; auditorium subdivided, 1979–1980
Rubush & Hunter, architects; **Alexander Sangernebo**, exterior sculpture;
Joseph Willenborg, interior plasterwork
134 W. Washington St., Indianapolis, Indiana

Major movie palaces were by no means restricted to cosmopolitan cities like Chicago and Los Angeles. In addition to its early proto-palace, the Circle, which opened in 1916, Indianapolis enjoyed this elaborate summation of the silent movie era.

The Indiana was designed by local architects who fully under-stood what was expected of a big-time movie palace. They included a façade in a Spanish Churrigueresque imagery; fine materials, including terrazzo and polished travertine; interiors encrusted with plaster detail and polychrome, right down to the pipe organ con-sole; and, of course, a visually exotic auditorium seating 3,300, done up in a mix of imageries.

Even this was apparently not enough entertainment, so the build-ing also provided an 11,000-square-foot "Indiana Roof Ballroom" on the sixth floor. Its 40-foot-high "atmospheric" space featured an end-grain maple parquet dance floor set on rubber subflooring.

Grauman's Chinese Theater FIG. 668
1927
Raymond Kennedy, Meyer & Holler, architects
6925 Hollywood Blvd., Los Angeles, California

Appropriately for Hollywood, the exterior reads more as a stage set than as permanent "architecture." Despite the name, the visual imagery is more faux-Polynesian than Chinese; one almost expects to see Tiki dolls strewn about. Yet perhaps precisely for its lack of serious architectural pretense, Grauman's is probably America's best-known movie theater.

Ohio Theatre FIG. 674
1928; restoration and Galbreath Pavilion addition, 1978–1984
Thomas Lamb, architect; **Hardy Holzman Pfeiffer Associates**, architects
for the restoration and Galbreath Pavilion
29-39 E. State St., Columbus, Ohio

From the unremarkable Beaux Arts exterior one would never have suspected that such a sumptuous auditorium lay beyond. Among seemingly numberless dazzling architectural effects, the multifac-eted chandelier relief in the auditorium is breathtaking. The restoration-expansion returned the lobby and auditorium to peak condition, and added memorable new environments.

Fox Theatre
1927–1928; converted
C. Howard Crane, architect; **William Kessler and Associates**, restoration
architects; **Ray Shepardson**, consultant
2111 Woodward Ave., Detroit, Michigan

Along with its siblings in Atlanta and St. Louis, which have been restored as performance-arts venues, the Detroit Fox occupied the exotic pinnacle of the 1920s golden age of movie palaces. Although the interior imagery is probably indescribable, Kathryn Bishop Eckert made a game try in identifying it as "Eclectic Hindu-Siamese-Byzantine."

Fox Theatre FIGS. 675, 676
1927–1929; restored, 1981–1982
C. Howard Crane, architect; **Mary Strauss**, director of restoration;
Wurlitzer "Crawford Special" organ restored by **Marlin Mackley**
527 N. Grand Blvd., St. Louis, Missouri

The St. Louis Fox is arguably the ultimate American movie palace. Certainly no expense was spared in a fully successful quest for over-

FIGS. 672, 673 Midwest Fantasy Palaces were built even in medium-sized cities whose self-image tended toward staidness. The Indiana Theater in Indianapolis is a marvelous fantasy, from its elaborate façade to the auditorium and much more. *Fig. 673: Library of Congress, Prints & Photographs, Historic American Buildings Survey*

FIG. 674 Restored Treasure The sumptuous interiors of the Ohio Theatre in Columbus were restored in a conversion to a performing arts center. *Library of Congress, Prints & Photographs, Historic American Buildings Survey*

whelming visual effect. The building cost well more than $60 million in 2008 dollars. Most visitors would probably agree that for this spectacular visual resource, every penny was well spent.

Fox Theatre FIG. 677
1928-1929; converted, restored, 1978
Mayre, Alger & Vinour, architects
660 Peachtree St. NE., Atlanta, Georgia

Atlanta is the third of the great national trinity of ultra-exotic Foxes, along with Detroit and St. Louis (above). Its exterior Orientalism is almost Islamic in feeling, perhaps Islamic Egyptian (not to be confused with the overdone Pharaonic Egyptian).

Los Angeles Theatre
1930–1931; converted
S. Charles Lee, architect
615 S. Broadway, Los Angeles, California

Superb in every way, the theater's French elegance was rendered without a trace of gaudiness. Gebhard and Winter called this "probably the finest theater building in Los Angeles." Surely with respect to its refinement, the Los Angeles represents an architectural culmination of the Movie Baroque palaces, nationally.

DECO THEATERS

By about 1930, a confluence of events redirected the design of American movie theaters. For one thing, it was difficult to imagine how a new design could in any way outdo the Fox theaters at their own game. For another, the Art Deco style had taken hold in American architecture. The Movie Baroque style seemed increasingly outdated: the Great War and all of its cultural baggage were by now—blurred by the frenzied Roaring Twenties—ancient history.

Significantly for movie theaters, emerging Moderne imageries were inherently scenographic, easily manipulated for effect, which could be achieved at a fraction of the exorbitant costs of the earlier Baroque Palaces. Moreover, because of the deepening Depression, the worldly ornateness of the 1920s no longer reflected the new national mood. By the 1930s, then, traditional architectural and ornamental devices were less commonly employed, and visual effect was achieved through economical means like color, geometric shapes, and dramatic lighting.

Pickwick Theater FIG. 678
1929
Zook & McCaughey, architects; **Alfonso Ianelli**, interior decorative arts
5 S. Prospect Ave., Park Ridge, Illinois

Conventionally and impressively Art Deco on the outside, the theater reveals interiors plausibly readable as the insides of a Mayan temple. The auditorium space is tightly defined, architecturally, with a sequence of full-height articulations focusing on the screen. The lobby fountain by Ianelli is a prominent visual feature.

Paramount Theatre FIGS. 310, 679, 680
1930–1931; converted, restored 1973
Timothy Pflueger, Miller & Pflueger, architects; **John M. Woodbridge, Skidmore, Owings & Merrill**, restoration architects
2025 Broadway, Oakland, California

FIGS. 675, 676 Beyond Exotic Movie palaces like the St. Louis Fox Theatre went well beyond "atmospheric" auditoriums and fancy lobbies in their extraordinary degree of ornament. *photographs © Sam Fentress, The Fabulous Fox*

FIG. 677 **Southern Orientalism** Atlanta's Fox Theatre is especially intriguing on the outside, a creative synthesis of Oriental sources. *Library of Congress, Prints & Photographs, Historic American Buildings Survey*

FIG. 678 **Suburban Landmark** Thanks to its monumental exterior and location at a major regional highway intersection, the Pickwick Theater in Park Ridge, Illinois, serves as the primary civic landmark for its community.

FIGS. 679, 680 **Supreme Design Achievement** Oakland's Paramount Theatre, now converted to a performing arts center, is among the greatest American movie theaters. Rather than resorting to overwhelming exoticism, as at the Foxes, Paramount architect Timothy Pflueger showed a consummate attention to decorative detail, the cumulative effect of which is wondrous. See Fig. 310 for an exterior view. *Library of Congress, Prints & Photographs, Historic American Buildings Survey*

The billboard-like, tile mosaic exterior (Fig. 310) only begins to suggest the no-holds-barred Art Deco splendor on the inside. This was arguably the climax of Pflueger's work, and that alone says a lot. Paramount's interiors represent the ultimate in "dream-world escapism," to employ Kidder Smith's description. Certainly the multi-colored, etched-glass sculpture of the lobby, known as the "Canopy of Light," is one of the most remarkable creative design achievements of American movie theaters, among which the Oakland Paramount ranks near, if not at, the very top.

Paramount Theatre FIG. 681
1929–1931; restored, 1976–1978
Rapp & Rapp, architects; **ELS Design Group, Conrad Schmitt Studios**, restoration
23 E. Galena Blvd., Aurora, Illinois

Like its contemporary Oakland Paramount, this theater illustrates the design evolution from 1920s movie palaces into 1930s Deco theaters. There is still more than a little exotica in the auditorium, the side walls of which are developed in Persian-like screen patterns, with lots of red and gold. The brilliant blue ceiling with radiating geometrics is pure Deco. The

FIG. 681 **Mixed Masterpiece** Aurora's Paramount Theatre combines 1920s grandeur and 1930s Deco geometrics with impressive results. *Aurora Paramount Theatre*

rest of the auditorium is restrained compared to 1920s movie palaces, clearly reflecting the changing times after the 1929 stock market crash. Very often, mixing disparate imageries leads to visual catastrophe, but this auditorium is an architectural masterpiece.

Washoe Theater FIGS. 682, 683
1931–1936
B. Marcus Priteca, architect; **Nat Smythe**, artist
305 Main St., Anaconda, Montana

On the exterior, the Washoe is mildly interesting, a modestly ornamented brick box with a marquee similar to those found in hundreds of towns. The interiors are a different story: a totally unexpected splendor of pastels, eight shades of gold leaf, and burnished gold. This palette is softer, almost domestic in feeling compared to the brilliant decoration of the Aurora Paramount.

Smyth was a "Hollywood artist" who supervised a crew of local painters and laborers. Indeed, this is very much a stage set, in that while this is not great architecture, the decoration provides a memorable visual experience. The Washoe would be a noteworthy work anywhere; it is almost miraculous way out here in a rough-and-tumble Western mining town.

Lake Theater FIG. 684
1936
Thomas W. Lamb, architect
1020 Lake St., Oak Park, Illinois

FIGS. 682, 683 **Queen of the Mines** One would not expect such delicate interiors in a rugged Montana mining town. Once you get past a relatively conventional exterior, Anaconda's Washoe Theater sure is a big surprise. *Library of Congress, Prints & Photographs, Historic American Buildings Survey*

Compared to 1920s Palaces, with their signature lobbies and auditoriums, the 1930s Deco Theaters placed a much greater emphasis on their exteriors, especially marquees and pylon signs. The

FIG. 684 **Uptown Center** Oak Park's Lake Theater remains the focus of the community's Uptown area. It is visually animated, but not too animated for this well-mannered Chicago suburb.

FIG. 685 **Visible for Miles** Only a master like S. Charles Lee could so distort conventional rules of proportion in his ultra-exaggerated Academy Theater pylon—and still end up with a landmark design. *Carol M. Highsmith / Library of Congress, Prints & Photographs*

FIGS. 686, 687 **Classic Deco** The Fremont Theater is among the very best remaining American Deco theaters, still virtually intact, from Lee's signature sidewalk terrazzo through the lobby (Fig. 687) into the auditorium.

Lake has a classic Deco exterior-as-sign, especially potent at night, with the intense blue letters of the marquee sign playing off against the pylon, flooded in red.

Academy Theater FIG. 685
1939; converted to a church, 1970s
S. Charles Lee, architect
3100 Manchester Blvd., Inglewood, California

In this design, Lee got past almost-certain architectural disaster unscathed, with his usual aplomb. A nicely proportioned theater building, strongly horizontal in composition, was married to an impossibly tall and slender pylon. Somehow it all came off as plau-

sible, even desirable. Gebhard and Winter understandably assessed the Academy as "a high point of the Streamline Moderne in the United States."

Fremont Theater FIGS. 686, 687
1941–1942
S. Charles Lee, architect
1025 Monterey St., San Luis Obispo, California

Lee was terrific with exterior pylons, and this is one of his best, a gracefully sweeping, conch-shell form. But there is much more to this theater than its spectacular front, which is especially wonderful at night.

The Fremont is rare among remaining American Deco movie theaters as the work of a master designer, basically extant and still showing first-run movies. This happy situation exists because rather than gutting and reordering the historic Fremont venue, the theater's owners tucked in the now-requisite multiplex unobtrusively next door. So the Fremont remains in all its glory, to the benefit of visitors to San Luis Obispo's marvelous, human-scaled downtown.

Maco Theater FIG. 688

c. 1941
Liebenberg & Kaplan, architects
415 Chestnut St., Virginia, Minnesota

The Maco Theater exterior is attractive and not overly fussy, as befits its location in this architecturally unpretentious iron-range town. On the exterior, the stepped marquee-sign is especially fine. In its economy of gesture and visual directness, the Maco street front is one of the best among small-town, Streamline Moderne movie theaters.

DESCENT TO THE MULTIPLEX

Sweeping changes in post–World War II American society meant that movie theater design also changed. At first, movies continued to be shown in prewar theaters, reaching peak national attendance in 1946, as GIs returned home. Some movie theaters were remodeled in the Deco style up into the early 1950s, but 1920s downtown movie palaces began to close down, victims of suburban expansion and high maintenance costs.

Two seismic changes dealt body blows to the postwar American movie industry. One was the 1947 anti-trust breakup of the vertical studio system, under which the major studios also owned the theaters that showed their films. That meant the end of signature movie palaces like the Foxes and Paramounts, with their seemingly unrestrained construction budgets. The second jolt was, of course, television, which began to significantly erode movie audiences by the late 1940s.

Eventually, new movie theaters were built throughout the rapidly expanding U.S. suburbia. But these were rarely architecturally distinguished, as attempts to establish a contemporary style for movie theaters were largely unsatisfying.

Among the few innovative movie theater designs during the classic postwar years were three Cooper Cinerama theaters, located in Denver, Omaha, and suburban Minneapolis (all razed). The Cooper design certainly reflected the feeling of its era, especially American society's postwar fascination with nov-

FIG. 688 The Power of Gesture A small-town venue like the Maco Theater could not economically support architectural grandiosity, so visual effect had to come from efficient use of materials, forms, and colors.

elty. However, freestanding, single-screen movie theaters on increasingly valuable suburban sites ultimately could not compete economically with other commercial uses.

As a consequence, over the past three decades, almost all new movie theaters have been developed in a multiplex format. Most of these have been built in the suburbs, often integrated as part of an entertainment-restaurant component in regional shopping malls. So the great era of American movie houses flourished and then quietly disappeared over barely two generations.

Cooper Cinerama Theater FIG. 689

1961–1962, razed
Richard L. Crowther, architect
Wayzata Boulevard, St. Louis Park, Minnesota

Coopers were freestanding, circular structures intended to both symbolize and exhibit super-wide-screen Cinerama movies on a 105-degree curved screen. Exteriors were enclosed by an orange metal drum, visually floating above a transparent lobby wall. Interiors were at once airily elegant and tinsely, dramatic yet light-hearted, not to be confused with the unemotional corporate International Style Modernism of the same era. These theaters perfectly captured the milieu of Doris Day and the Pink Panther.

FIG. 689 The Last Hurrah Film venues rose from arcades and halls to Palaces and Deco Theaters and then descended back to mundane multiplexes in less than a lifetime. Three Cooper Cinerama Theaters dating from the early 1960s were among the last American movie theaters offering a truly dramatic visual experience.

Resorts

1761–2004

iven the diversity and magnificence of American natural landscapes, resorts are found throughout the United States. In this chapter, resorts are differentiated from other leisure environments: recreational facilities such as golf courses are not addressed in this book; amusement parks are included in the Popular Culture chapter; urban hotels are covered in the Retail and Hotels chapter. This chapter focuses on a sampling of buildings and communities that function as *leisure destinations*, places to stay.

RESORT ARCHITECTURE

Mohonk Mountain House FIG. 691
1869 ff.; 1902; 2005
Albert and Alfred Smiley, developers; **Napoleon LeBrun,**
James E. Ware, architects
1000 Mountain Rest Rd., New Paltz, New York

A seven-story "Victorian Castle" built into a steep cliff overlooking a lake on the edge of the Catskills. Mohonk Mountain House

FIG. 690 Scenic Wonders Because of America's abundance of spectacular physical features, resorts have been built throughout the United States. Awesome natural landmarks such as the Grand Canyon have occasionally inspired extraordinary works like Mary Colter's Lookout Studio, a gift shop/viewing structure dating from 1914. One of several structures she designed for those staying at the canyon, this one seems to have grown right out of the native rock. *photograph © Alexander Vertikoff*

FIG. 691 Old World Reference Mohonk Mountain House was intended to evoke the feeling of historic European resorts. Especially when seen from a distance, it meets that goal with reasonable success. *Library of Congress, Prints & Photographs, Historic American Buildings Survey*

FIG. 692 **Sovereign of the Great Lakes** Set in splendid seclusion on auto-free Mackinac Island, the Grand Hotel offers as close to an authentic Victorian resort experience as is available in the United States.

FIGS. 693, 694 **Western Park Architecture** The characteristic lodge imageries of western national parks largely stem from Yellowstone's Old Faithful Inn. Later park lodges like The Ahwahnee and Timberline (Figs. 697, 699, 700) were much more sophisticated, architecturally, but Old Faithful is as comfortable and authentic as well-worn hunting boots. The Antler Style lobby is the lodge's memorable visual feature. *Library of Congress, Prints & Photographs, Historic American Buildings Survey*

FIG. 695 **Neo-indigenous** Beginning with the intense, pueblo-like Hopi House, architect Mary Colter devised "indigenous" American Southwest regional expressions for a series of structures along the Grand Canyon rim. *Photograph © Alexander Vertikoff*

was meant to emulate Continental grand resorts, though with an American personality. Among the most picturesque of nineteenth-century American resorts, the property remains in the family of the original developers.

Grand Hotel FIG. 692
1887
George Mason, Mason & Rice, architects
West Bluff Rd., Mackinac Island, Michigan

Mackinac Island was designated as a national park in 1875; resort hotels had been built here as early as 1850. On its opening, the majestic Grand Hotel established the island as the premier Great Lakes summer resort destination. The hotel, with its 600-foot veranda colonnade, visually dominates the Island from its blufftop site, providing an enduring iconic image not just for Mackinac Island, but for American resorts.

Old Faithful Inn FIGS. 693, 694
1902–1904
Robert C. Reamer, architect
Yellowstone National Park, Wyoming

An Arts & Crafts structure, with a steeply pitched roof and enclosed in hand-hewn logs and local stone. Such rusticity in the use of native materials and sense of belonging to the site set the tone for subsequent western national park architecture. Inside, an 85-foot-high great hall lobby built of gnarled lodgepoles, with open balconies surrounding a massive stone fireplace, is the principal visual feature. This space is more impressive than the famous geyser just outside.

Hopi House FIG. 695
1902–1905
Mary Colter, architect
Grand Canyon Village, South Rim, Arizona

Mary Elizabeth Jane Colter worked as a staff designer for the ubiquitous Fred Harvey Company between 1902 and 1949. In dozens of hospitality projects, she captured the spirit of the American Southwest in her imageries and in an imaginative use of basic materials. Hopi House, a museum/store located just east of the El Tovar Hotel, was her first of several remarkable designs at the Grand Canyon. Others include Hermit's Rest, the Lookout Studio (Fig. 690) and Watchtower, Phantom Ranch, and Bright Angel Lodge (next entry).

Bright Angel Lodge FIG. 696
1917, preliminary planning; 1933–1936, design and construction
Mary Colter, architect
Grand Canyon Village, South Rim, Arizona

Located at the head of Bright Angel Trail, this facility replaced an earlier hotel. Colter's 1917 design concept envisioned a "cottage village" which, as built in the 1930s, included a main lodge, seven connected cabins, and 15 freestanding structures, some single-unit and others duplex. The architect intended for each structure to offer a distinct personality, yet fit in with other buildings and the natural setting, achieving an overall, "harmony of the environment."

Colter accomplished her design goal through a creative fusion of regional pioneer imageries, authenticity of interior color selections, close attention to construction details, and careful siting of structures among native piñon, juniper, and grasses—all on a strictly limited budget.

FIG. 696 **Mary Colter's Rustic Art** Over a five-decade career, Colter designed imaginative yet economical tourism facilities throughout the American Southwest. For Bright Angel Lodge at Grand Canyon, she blended several strains of regional vernacular, her buildings achieving individual personalities, inside and out, through careful detailing of basic materials like log and stone. *Library of Congress, Prints & Photographs, Historic American Buildings Survey*

FIG. 698 **Northwoods Deco** The ambitious Naniboujou sportsmen's development on Lake Superior was financially wiped out following the 1929 stock market crash, though not before its clubhouse was built. The brilliant main room decoration is painted on inexpensive fiberboard.

FIGS. 699, 700 **Polished Rusticity** Especially magnificent on approach when semi-covered by snow, Timberline Lodge in Oregon is so carefully refined in details and materials that it seems more gracious than rugged. *Exterior by Fred Pflughoft/Oregon Public Broadcasting, Great Lodges of the National Parks; interior: Library of Congress, Prints & Photographs, Historic American Buildings Survey*

FIG. 697 **Nature Exalted** California's Yosemite Valley was surpassingly beautiful before its development as a national park. It is enough to say that The Ahwahnee hotel did not visually detract from the area's natural treasures. *photograph by Fred Pflughoft/Oregon Public Broadcasting, Great Lodges of the National Parks*

The Ahwahnee FIG. 697
1925–1927
Gilbert Stanley Underwood, architect; **Jeannette Dyer Spencer**, murals
Yosemite National Park, California

Beyond splendor: superior architecture, superb interiors, including Spencer's Pueblo Deco murals, a striking natural setting amid massive trees, with a sheer granite backdrop, plus stunning views toward Half Dome and Yosemite Falls. The entire experience is especially marvelous on a bright day after a heavy snowfall. With such an embarrassment of visual riches, the Ahwahnee is certainly among the most unforgettable resorts in the United States.

Naniboujou Resort Clubhouse FIG. 698
1928–1929
Holstead and Sullivan, architects; **Antoine Goufee**, murals
Hwy. 61, 15 mi. NE of Grand Marais, Minnesota

Naniboujou was organized in the late 1920s as an exclusive 3,000-acre sportsman's club. Babe Ruth, Jack Dempsey, Ring Larder, and the governors of New York and Illinois were charter members. The Crash of 1929 put Naniboujou out of business, but not before this clubhouse had been built along the Lake Superior shoreline. Its rustic wood-shingled exterior provides no hint of the spectacular main lodge room, painted in brilliant geometric patterns that might be described as Cree Indians meet Art Deco.

Timberline Lodge FIGS. 699, 700
1935–1938
Tim Turner, architect; **Gilbert Stanley Underwood**, consulting architect; **Ward Gano**, civil engineer; **Emmett Blanchfield**, landscape architect
Mt. Hood National Forest, Oregon

Timberline was designed mainly by U.S. Forest Service staff architects, in what has been called the Cascade style—more polished than the usual rustic park architecture. The tall pointed roof of the "head house" is the signature architectural feature. Set on a spectacular ridgetop, Timberline is one of the most recognized American resort hotels.

Mauna Kea Beach Resort FIG. 701, 702, 1022, 1023, 1024
1965–1968; additions, interiors redecorated
Skidmore, Owings & Merrill, architects; **Eckbo, Dean, Austin & Williams**, landscape architects; **Alexander Girard**, interiors
Kamuela, Kohala Coast, Big Island, Hawaii

An insistently modern hotel looms above lush landscaping (Fig. 701). The opposing imageries work, as built and organic combine to render the architecture and the landscape visually more dramatic with such powerful visual tension. The hotel, organized around a continuous open atrium (Fig. 702), served as a model, in one way or another, for numerous later Hawaiian hotels, and thus for many contemporary resort hotels around the Pacific Rim.

FIGS. 701, 702 Tropical Design Before Mauna Kea Beach Resort, post–World War II Pacific resort hotels were typically egg-crate boxes or, worse, pseudo-Polynesian confections. Mauna Kea's superior design qualities, especially a seamless integration of landscapes, architecture, and interiors sharply raised the benchmark for subsequent luxury resorts. *Photographs © 2005 EDAW/Photography by Dixi Carrillo*

RESORT COMMUNITIES

In the 1800s, resort communities began to appear throughout the United States, serving as refuges from the stresses of everyday life. These places offered visual amenity and seasonal relief from harsh climate, often segregated by economic class or patronized primarily by a single ethnic group. Examples include Pasadena as an upper-class wintering community and Wisconsin Dells as a middle/working-class summer vacation spot. By the early 1900s, resort communities especially attracting Germans, Italians, Irish, Jews, and other ethnic groups were well established in the Catskills, a short trip up and across the Hudson River from New York City.

Covered elsewhere in the book are individual buildings characteristic of other resorts. For landmarks of Newport, Rhode Island, long a summer refuge for the very rich, see the Beaux Art chapter (Figs. 168 and 170) and the American Colonial Revival chapter (Figs. 178, 179, 180). For architecture characteristic of its super-affluent Florida counterpart, Palm Beach, see the Period Revivals chapter (Figs. 330, 355, and 356).

Over the past generation, traditional resort destinations have lost their attraction for a number of reasons, ranging from primitive lodging facilities to competition made possible by inexpensive air fares to once-exotic foreign resorts. In addition, super-resorts like Disney World and Aspen function year-around, and thus are in a stronger economic position to attract visitors than are traditional mom-and-pop resorts in seasonal locales.

Cape May FIG. 703
1761; late 1800s ff.
Cape May County, New Jersey

Cape May is the largest collection of Victorian resort architecture in the nation and claims to be the oldest seashore resort in the U.S., dating its resort foundation from 1761. In 1976, Cape May was one of the first five American communities designated as a National Historic Landmark City.

White Sulphur Springs FIG. 704
After 1778; resort structures, 1810–1989
Greenbrier County, West Virginia

Americans have "taken the waters" for more than two centuries. Towns like Excelsior Springs, Missouri, Hot Springs, Arkansas, and Glenwood Springs and Pagosa Springs, Colorado, grew up around sources of mineral waters celebrated for their healing powers. Many mineral springs are informal affairs, little more than shelter built above locally-known pools.

White Sulphur Springs, now identified with the classic Greenbrier Resort, occupies the other extreme. Here, healing waters bubble up from under a domed Spring House topped by a statue of Hebe, goddess of youth. Gracious cottage rows are scattered across manicured grounds. Guests are requested to honor the resort's dress codes, especially when dining in elegance at the central hotel. Even those of us who are steadfast plebes would agree that the Greenbrier experience is beautifully done.

Oak Bluffs
1835 ff. plan, 1871
Robert Morris Copeland, planner
Martha's Vineyard, Massachusetts

This now-exclusive summer resort town began in the Second Great Awakening era as a simple Wesleyan camp meeting grounds, marked by a handful of pitched tents. By the outset of the Civil War, thousands came to the island to hear services preached by dozens of clergy.

As Oak Bluffs grew into an institution of sorts, temporary tents were replaced by permanent cottages, sited informally along numerous twisty dirt paths. That informal layout was upgraded in 1871 by landscape architect Copeland, whose segmented-grid street plan introduced a pleasant hint of order to the community. The resulting community of tiny "gingerbread" cottages remains as one of the best concentrations of Carpenter's Gothic in the United States.

Pasadena FIG. 705
1874 ff.
Los Angeles County, California

First inhabited by Gabrielino Indians and then by Mexicans, Pasadena was launched as a wintering place with its Anglo incorporation as the "Indiana Colony" in 1874. Good national railway connections allowed the community to flourish in the 1880s and 1890s as a fashionable winter resort catering to affluent Midwesterners. By the early 1900s, civic activity in Midwestern cities like Cincinnati and Minneapolis came to a virtual halt between New Years and mid-April because so many local civic leaders wintered in Pasadena.

Robert Winter noted that many of these elite snowbirds eventually became year-around residents. Hence, Pasadena residents have been well-educated and culturally more aggressive than the general run of Los Angeles immigrants, and many of its citizens have had the wherewithal and ambition to construct homes of architectural distinction (Figs, 287, 290, 291, 293) and commensurate public landscapes.

FIG. 703 Victorian Glory Cape May, New Jersey, is to American Victoriana what Miami Beach is to Art Deco.

FIG. 704 Elite Retreat The Greenbrier Resort at White Sulphur Springs, West Virginia, offers a singular experience in countrified formality. One of the residences is quite accurately named "The President's Cottage," as in *The President. Library of Congress, Prints & Photographs, Historic American Buildings Survey*

FIG. 705 Gracious Winter Haven Pasadena's climate and setting were alluring to many affluent Midwesterners, who would initially winter at a hotel before eventually building second homes in the community like those featured in the Craftsman chapter. Genteel public landscapes like Orange Grove Boulevard (Fig. 705) reflected the sensibilities of these elite snowbirds.

Miami Beach FIG. 706
1920s, 1950s, 1990s
Miami-Dade County, Florida

Completion of a railroad connection to Miami in 1896 made development of South Florida possible. In 1913, inventor Carl Fisher and John Collins began to develop an offshore spit of sand that became Miami Beach. The first wave of development occurred during the Florida real estate bubble in the 1920s, when the Art Deco hotels south of Dade Blvd. were built (Fig. 706). The "MiMo" (Miami Modern) wave of resort development occurred in the early 1950s, fueled by postwar prosperity. High-rise hotels of Morris Lapidus along Collins Avenue (see Mid-century Expressionism chapter) symbolize this era.

FIG. 706 Beyond Substance Miami Beach lifestyles are irresistible to some because the line between real and the illusory can seem blurred. The sense of everyday unreality is heightened by the spectacular visual energy of South Beach.

FIGS. 707, 708 The Relentless Quest for Novelty Destination resort areas like Wisconsin Dells must continuously upgrade their venues if they are to draw repeat visits. Early in the post–World War II years, riding through the scenic river dells in a war-surplus amphibian vehicle, a "Duck," was a signature draw for the Dells. Today, mega-waterparks hold center stage (Fig. 708). Ducks are still running, but now merely as adjuncts to ever-more-extreme constructions, like a super-scale horse that could look down on Troy (Fig. 707).

Since the 1980s, Miami Beach has increasingly attracted working-age families and is less a retirement community than it had been previously. South Beach (the Art Deco district, see the Moderne chapter) experienced a resurgence of popularity in the 1990s as a trendy playground for ultra-fashionable young adults.

Aspen
1945 ff.
Pitkin County, Colorado

Aspen was settled in 1879 as a mining camp, and by 1893 had blossomed into a prosperous city of 12,000. Mining declined after silver was de-monetized in 1893; smelting closed down totally in 1926. In 1936, concurrent with the establishment of Sun Valley, Idaho, as a winter resort, three investors attempted to establish a ski area above Aspen, but World War II eventually halted work. In 1945, Friedl Pfeiffer, who had trained in the Army's mountain

division in nearby Leadville, returned to develop what became Aspen Mountain. Pfeiffer partnered with Chicago industrialist Walter Paepcke, incorporating the Aspen Skiing Corporation in 1946.

While Aspen is a premier winter resort, it is distinct from comparable resorts, like Vail, in two respects. One is that Aspen is a real town, and while it has been overdeveloped, a scattering of authentic structures from the mining era remain. Also, as is more important, Aspen is an established year-around destination. This came about after Paepcke sponsored a Goethe festival in 1949. That led directly to several permanent institutions active during the milder months, including the Aspen Music Festival and School, the International Design Conference, and the Aspen Institute for Humanistic Studies.

Wisconsin Dells FIGS. 707, 708
Post–World War II
Sauk County, Wisconsin

"The Dells" occupies a section of the Wisconsin River noted for its natural beauty and eroded rock formations. The area was popularized in late 1800s through the stereoscope photographs of Henry Hamilton Bennett. Wisconsin Dells took off as a tourist destination in the late 1940s, as war-surplus amphibious vehicles rechristened "Ducks" provided modest-cost vacation outings that were especially accessible from Chicago and Milwaukee.

With the 1952 opening of the Tommy Bartlett Water Ski and Jumping Boat Thrill Show, the Dells gained regional visibility as a destination resort area. By today, a 20-square-mile area has evolved into a visual riot of competing attractions, recently increasingly dominated by extravagant water parks (Fig. 708), including the 70-acre Noah's Ark, and by Kalahari, which encloses 125,000 square feet of water features under one roof. The Dells is the antithesis of the carefully controlled theme park, and thus instructive, good and bad. If you are enthusiastic, after a visit, consider checking out the Circus World museum in nearby Baraboo while you are still in the area.

Wildwood FIGS. 709, 710
Late 1940s through early 1960s
Cape May County, New Jersey

Wildwood and adjacent beachside communities enjoyed a boom in the classic postwar years, with nearly 300 motels built. These were the typical decorated concrete slab/flat roof structures, with themed lobbies known as Populux in Southern California, MiMo in Miami, and Doo Wop here in New Jersey. A few of these hotels and some of their signs are individually distinctive. But the primary visual significance of Wildwood is the overall ensemble of tightly-packed period motels and signs.

Walt Disney World FIG. 711
1960–1964, regional search; 1964–1967, land acquisition and approvals; 1969–1971, site work and initial construction; 1971, opening of Magic Kingdom; 1982, opening of EPCOT–World Showcase
Walter Elias Disney, visionary; **WED Enterprises**, planning and imagineering; **William "Joe" Potter**, director of water management; **Joe Fowler**, senior vice president of engineering and construction; **Bill Evans**, chief landscape architect
Orange and Osceola Counties, Florida

Disney World is a 27,000-acre destination resort organized around a Magic Kingdom (based on the earlier, Anaheim Disneyland; see Popular Culture chapter) and EPCOT-World Showcase, plus supplemental attractions such as Disney–MGM studios, River Country, Discovery Island, the Michael Graves-designed Swan and

FIG. 711 A World Like No Other Walt Disney World achieves its unique sense of convincing fantasy by meticulous planning and flawless maintenance as much as through the cheerful creativity of its "Imagineers." This overview barely suggests the scale and complexity of the 27,000-acre development and the vast interrelated networks of systems required to maintain a sense of perfect order for guests.

FIGS. 709, 710 Postwar Period Pieces Wildwood, located just up the shore from Cape May (early in this chapter), offers a treasure-trove ensemble of Doo-Wop motels. As the El Ray (Fig. 709) illustrates, few of these motels are architecturally distinguished in themselves. While similar buildings elsewhere are likely to be torn down as obsolescent, Wildwood properties maintain their attractiveness because their concentration establishes a distinctive environment, and because contemporary enhancements are encouraged if they are sensitive to the spirit of the original. At the StarLux (Fig. 710), the original motel remains clearly visible, with a recently added fire stair wrapped in a mesh and a wavy canopy added along the roofline. *Fig. 709: Library of Congress, Prints & Photographs, Historic American Buildings Survey*

FIG. 712 Subordinate to the Land The Sea Ranch was planned to preserve its rural character. Coastline was left undeveloped (Figs. 712, 1033), with new buildings set into existing hedgerows (Fig. 1034), leaving intervening meadows completely open. Upland housing was placed back into deep woods, so construction would not compete with the magnificent natural setting.

Dolphin hotels (Figs. 547, 546), and others. The 1990s New Urbanist suburb, Celebration (Figs. 839, 840, 841, 843, 844), is also included within the Disney reserve.

Walt Disney had been upset by the commercial strip which had quickly grown up around Disneyland in California and was determined to assert environmental and visual controls over the new park. This was accomplished in three ways. First, by assembling a huge undeveloped acreage—at nearly 43 square miles—in scale with the largest modern jetports. Second, the Disney organization achieved legislative designation as in effect a self-governing county. Third, the planning and design of the resort itself is meticulous, down to the smallest construction and operational details.

The resulting development is simply stupendous, and hardly anyone seems to hold a neutral opinion about it. When the park first opened, architects and planners hailed Disney World as the leading edge of city building, a limitless fountainhead of advanced technique.

In recent decades, the intelligentsia has reflexively put down Disney World, and, indeed, almost anything "Disney," as plastic and somehow menacing to true American culture. Few must be swayed by these sentiments, however, as Disney World experiences about 30 million admissions annually. Anthropologist and popular-culture expert Stephen Fjellman describes Disney World as "the major middle-class pilgrimage center in the United States." It would be hard to argue otherwise.

The Sea Ranch FIGS. 712, 1033, 1044
1963–1965 ff.
Lawrence Halprin & Associates, planners and landscape architects;
MLTW/Moore, Lyndon, Turnbull & Whitaker, Joseph Esherick, architects; **Barbara Stauffacher**, graphics
Hwy. 1, SE of Gualala, Sonoma County, California

Sea Ranch is celebrated for its master plan (see Environmentalism chapter) and for the iconic Condominium #1 designed by MLTW/Moore, Lyndon, Turnbull, Whitaker (Fig. 434). Halprin in effect invented a new planning approach, which synthesized responses to climate, weather, natural and agricultural landscapes, long and controlled views, privacy requirements, and architectural potential.

Basically, houses were clustered in coastline hedgerows (Fig. 1034) or set back into the upper woods, preserving the existing open feeling of the property (Fig. 712). At the time, this was a radical approach, which unfortunately has been somewhat, though not totally, compromised by successor developers.

The MLTW/ Condominium #1 was instantly famous among American architects on its completion in 1965, widely cribbed for everything from housing to car washes in what was dubbed by some the "Vertical Mine Shaft School." However, the MLTW design derived from a specific combination of creative inspiration and site constraints, the product of superior design abilities. As a consequence, as the old saw goes: "Often imitated, never duplicated."

Seaside FIGS. 713, 714, 715
1982–1985 ff.
Robert Davis, developer; **Andres Duany, Elizabeth Plater-Zyberk**, planners
S of Hwy. 98, Walton County, Florida

Following The Sea Ranch by two decades, Seaside is its opposite in nearly every significant respect. Where the Sea Ranch master plan was innovative and developed from its specific environmental situation, Seaside is derivative and based on romanticized style. Seaside is carried visually by imagery while The Sea Ranch is memorable because of its setting and respect for the pre-existing landscape.

Most important, The Sea Ranch was developed as a personal retreat set in a spacious rural landscape, while Seaside was intended to foster continuous social interaction along a densely built-up streetscape. One can hardly imagine a greater extreme between concepts for an oceanside resort.

FIGS. 713, 714, 715 Highly Stylized Environment Seaside is another nationally prominent oceanfront development, much smaller in land area than The Sea Ranch (above). The resort is a big improvement over the usual wall of condo slabs lined up along countless miles of Florida coastline. Instead, fanciful pavilions are spaced a block apart across Seaside's beachfront (Figs. 713 and 714). This exhilarating openness contrasts with the almost-urban crowding of the resort's residential areas (Fig. 715).

Follies

1848–2004

FIG. 716 The Sheer Delight of Follies Two strains of follies are especially prominent in the United States. One is the earnestly idiosyncratic design, like the octagons
and piously crafted grottoes cited in this chapter. The second version stems from a
heedless quest for commercial attention. As an example of the latter, here we see
the amazing (unfortunately, now-abandoned) Opa-Locka City Hall (Fig. 716), originally
a promotional building for a 1920s Miami real estate development of pioneer aviator
Glenn Curtis. This marvelous pseudo-Arabian confection suggests what was required
of a developer who wished to stand apart from the crowd during the first South
Florida land boom.

An abundance of follies is one of the architectural
delights of America. I use the term to describe idiosyncratic designs that might be anything from well-out-
of-the-ordinary to truly over-the-top. The common thread
among these treasures is an intent to create an arresting, if not
shocking effect (Fig. 716). This differs in intensity from the visual
effect of a romantic design on the senses, or the effect of a
rational design on the intellect.

Of course it is usually not practical to build a folly, so follies did not appear widely in the United States until the
nation (or at least a given region or town) had matured
enough to allow for creative extravagances. Just before the
Civil War, follies in the form of idiosyncratic octagonal
houses began to appear in established regions, mostly east of
the Mississippi River.

Note: Programmatic structures of idiosyncratic design can
be found in the Popular Culture chapter.

OCTAGONS

In 1848, Orson Squire Fowler published a book entitled *A
Home For All, an Octagon Mode of Building*. As the title suggests,

Fowler, a phrenologist, contended that an octagonal shape was ideal for homes. The book must have been convincing to at least some of its readers, because octagon houses began to appear across the United States.

Many of these designs were quite handsome and were clearly intended as serious architecture. A few, certainly including Longwood and the Armour-Stiner House, were also intended by their builders to be unique visual statements.

FIG. 717 Octagon Gone Wild If so desired, an octagonal form could markedly intensify the visual effect. Haller Nutt's Mansion, "Longwood" in Mississippi, once locally referred to as "Nutt's Folly," shows how a respectable octagon can slip over to the wild side.

FIG. 718 Monumental Octagon The Armour-Stiner House's overscaled roof imparts a sense of monumentality, almost of grandeur, to its small-scaled suburban New York State neighborhood. The feeling of monumentally extends within, especially to a voluminous, third-floor reception room. *Library of Congress, Prints & Photographs, Historic American Buildings Survey*

FIG. 719 Just Add Scrollwork... George Bourne's "Wedding Cake" House began as a staid Federal style structure, which was barely altered when encased in a mid-nineteenth-century decorative screen. The barn (at the back), with its jauntily overdone pump canopy, is consistently Gothic Revival.

Haller Nutt Mansion, "Longwood" FIG. 717

1859–1861
Samuel Sloan, architect
140 Lower Woodville Rd., Natchez, Mississippi (open)

An onion dome immediately tips off the visitor that Longwood was not intended as a chaste architectural expression. Construction of this marvelous extravaganza was halted at the outbreak of the Civil War, its interiors uncompleted. G. E. Kidder Smith aptly described Longwood as "Moorish-Tuscan," speculating that it may have been influenced by John Nash's exotic Royal Pavilion in Brighton, England.

Today, visitors find a handsomely restored Longwood; surely house and grounds must be in better condition than ever before. Because the spacious hilltop site has become heavily wooded, one can no longer oversee the vast Mississippi River floodplain, far below. But that is about the only drawback to this treasure.

Armour-Stiner House FIG. 718

1859–1860
45 W. Clinton Ave., Irvington, New York

Nineteenth-century Mannerism: a wonderful play of scale, with a massive French Second Empire roof. It looks as if a giant had removed the cupola from the very top of a large building and plunked it down in this small-scale, suburban setting.

EMBELLISHED HOUSES

As the notion of American follies was established, a seemingly limitless range of wonderfully outrageous houses appeared throughout the United States. This particular strain of American creative expression ranged from crude in conception and construction to quite sophisticated. The following are representative of the latter.

Bourne "Wedding Cake" House FIG. 719

1826; Gothicized, 1855
George W. Bourne, owner-remodeler
104 Summer St. (Rt. 35) Kennebunk, Maine

George Bourne must have felt that his 1826 late-Federal-style house needed a little zip. His architectural solution was to encase it in a fanciful Gothic screen, featuring all manner of crockets and scrollwork. Visual impact is enhanced by the close play of the ornate Carpenter's Gothic tracery against the rather plain original house, which was left pretty much intact, though now painted a delicate pale yellow.

Brown "Spirit" House FIG. 720

1864–1868
Timothy Brown, builder
S. Main St./Rt. 26, 600 ft. S of Rt. 80, Georgetown, New York

The United States is a highly religious country, especially so during periodic Awakenings. Following the collapse of the frenzied Millerite expectation in 1844, some believers turned to Spiritualism. Brown was a self-taught carpenter who claimed to be guided by spirits to build this oddly textured house.

The ubiquitous two-story cube forms the underlying structure. Though this was typically a plain, innocuous design in nineteenth-century America, here Brown created a much stronger expression by employing a coarse pattern of full-height carved projections which read as pilasters. These play off visually against delicate pendant scrollwork that hangs from a cornice made up of three tiers of dentil moldings. Whether or not the Spirit House is an accurate reflection of the Architecture of Heaven, it is probably the only one of its kind on Earth.

John Trube House FIG. 721

1890
Alfred Muller, architect
1621-1627 Sealy Ave., Galveston, Texas

Galveston was the Queen City of this larger-than-life state before a monster hurricane devastated the town in 1900, killing 6,000 of its citizens. The city never regained its preeminent regional standing, although some of its exuberant pre-hurricane fabric has been restored to its previous glory, notably The Strand, a downtown commercial strip.

The Trube House suggests the sense of optimistic, no-holds-barred ostentation that must have prevailed in Galveston in the late 1800s. If this design is at all characteristic, then the city's visual conventions were pretty much unrestrained.

Holt House FIG. 722

1903
Frederick Thomas Harris, designer
405 W. Olive, Redlands, California

The line between a spirited expression of any given imagery and an outright folly can be narrow. However, Harris clearly passed well over that threshold in this voluptuous rendition of the ordinarily staid Mission style.

FIG. 720 **The Architecture of Heaven** The Brown "Spirit" House in New York State was supposedly designed with guidance from a higher plane, so perhaps we now know what to expect when we pass Beyond. *Library of Congress, Prints & Photographs, Historic American Buildings Survey*

FIG. 721 **Clearly Excessive Local Norms** Prior to its devastating 1900 hurricane, Galveston was a swashbuckling city that imagined no limits. In that context, consider that the truly over-the-top John Trube House merely reflected local norms. *Library of Congress, Prints & Photographs, Historic American Buildings Survey*

FIG. 722 **Noble Folly** Follies like the Holt House can be true landmarks, visually energizing even handsome communities like Redlands, California.

FIG. 723 **Spectacular, Even for New Orleans** Notwithstanding the seemingly endless visual wonders of New Orleans, the Doullut "Steamboat" houses easily transcend the city's expressive norms.

FIG. 724 **Wretched in Beverly Hills** With Hollywood just minutes away, visitors should probably be prepared for anything. That's still asking a lot if you unexpectedly come across the Spadena House.

Doullut "Steamboat" Houses FIG. 723
1905, 1913
Milton Paul Doullut, builder
400 & 503 Egania St, at the Mississippi Levee, New Orleans, Louisiana

Despite the devastation wreaked by Hurricane Katrina, New Orleans is probably the most visually arresting city in the United States. Yet even in this rarefied setting, the Doullut Houses stand out. Just one of these twins would be marvelous anywhere. The two of them, sited kitty-corner, are spectacular. These houses would be architectural stars in New Orleans' swanky, architecturally extravagant Garden District; located in this very modest working-man's neighborhood, they seem almost surreal.

Spadena House FIG. 724
1921
Henry Oliver, designer
NE cor. Walden & Carmelita, Beverly Hills, California

A Hansel-and-Gretel fantasy originally built as a movie set, Spadena was later moved to this posh residential neighborhood. The studied wretchedness is fascinating in itself, but the juxtaposition with its architecturally conventional neighbors provides a real jolt for passers-by.

SHAM RUINS AND GROTTOES

English estates of the Romantic Era introduced the notion of sham ruins. These are constructions intended to appear as picturesque remains of ancient monuments.

Although America has not equaled the best English sham ruins, it is not without such constructions. While sham ruins are usually of some pretense, grottoes are usually modest expressions of religious piety.

Romantic Ruins, Tower Grove Park
1868
Henry Shaw, visionary; **James Gurney**, landscape superintendent
NE of the Tower Grove Ave. rotary, S of Magnolia, St. Louis, Missouri

Tower Grove Park was developed after 1868 as a pleasure ground and is home to a delightful assortment of pavilions and gazebos. These ruins were built from leftover stone salvaged from a St. Louis hotel that had burned down the previous year.

Grotto of the Redemption FIG. 725
1912–1996
Frs. Paul M. Dobberson, Matt Szerensce, Louis Greving, builders
N. Broadway, between 2nd and 3rd Sts., West Bend, Iowa

Many grottoes are impressive purely on account of the obvious effort invested in their construction, but this one is notable, as well, as a wonderful work of naïve design. It is set apart from typical American religious grottoes by an extraordinary diversity of textures, not just embedded stone, but a large palette of minerals like quartz and agate. As a result, parts of the grotto glitter, and under some light conditions, entire sections glow. Be sure to go into the Mary With Christ Child grotto on the north side, to experience its unexpected inner-dome volume.

Ave Maria Grotto
1932–1934
Joseph Zoetti, builder
1600 St. Bernard Dr. SE., Cullman, Alabama

Widely known as "Jerusalem in Miniature," this grotto includes hundreds of models of mostly religious landmarks, installed here in the 1930s. In addition to scenes from the Holy Land, these range from St. Peter's and Bernini's piazza to Spanish mission churches of the American Southwest. Numerous secular monuments are also represented, especially from imperial Rome, as are imaginary depictions of legendary objects like the Tower of Babel and Noah's Ark. While the buildings are instantly identifiable, they are not faithful reproductions; rather, features and proportions have been artfully emphasized.

FOLK ART

Watts Towers
1921–1954
Simon Rodia, craft builder
1765 E. 107th St., Los Angeles, California

See the California chapter.

The Wooden Garden FIG. 726
1969–1973
Romano Gabriel, artist-builder
315 2nd St., Eureka, California

A colorful, tactile collage of cut-out images of humans, animals, and flowers. Originally located in a bungalow-scale neighborhood, The Wooden Garden is somewhat diminished by its current, encapsulated installation downtown. Still, Gabriel's inspired work has not been irretrievably lost.

Natchez Street Beach Pavilion
1987; 1992–1993
Jim Adamson, Steve Badanes, Jersey Devil, designers and builders
S end of Natchez St., Seaside, Florida

Jersey Devil is a highly skilled and sophisticated building collective, whose works fall squarely within the best traditions of Folk Art. Their solution for an end-of-street beach pavilion at Seaside (see Resorts chapter) is unlike any of the others. Rather than resting on the dune crest, like the town's other pavilions, this construction flows up and over the dune, marking the crest with a lacy, aluminum umbrella, under which the flaring rail morphs out into seating. A tour-de-force work of craft art.

UNCLASSIFIABLE

Corn Palace FIG. 727
1892, 1921, 1965 ff
604 N. Main St., Mitchell, South Dakota

Despite what its name suggests, this municipal auditorium is not strictly programmatic, in that it is a Decorated Shed, decorated in newly harvested corn and grasses. The underlying imagery is ambiguous; for instance, it isn't clear whether the corner towers are minarets or huge blowups of Fourth-of-July rockets. Given the absence of a prominent Eastern Orthodox influence in the area, one must suppose that the onion domes are intended simply to evoke a sense of exoticism, which surely they do, out here on the Great Plains! Anyway, the main features are the corn murals, which change every year.

Bevo Mill FIG. 728
1917
Klipstein & Rathmann, architects
4749 Gravois Ave., St. Louis, Missouri

St. Louis has been self-confident and fun-loving enough to have built several wonderful follies, including a water tower that appears to be a giant, freestanding Corinthian column, and another expressed visually as a fairy-tale castle turret (Fig. 377).

Bevo Mill was built as a family restaurant intended to serve only near beer, in anticipation of Prohibition. In designing it to appear as a combination windmill–rustic European farm building, the idea was apparently to offer fantasy architecture in case one could not transcend everyday reality through alcohol.

FIG. 725 **Prairie Piety** Grotto of the Redemption can certainly be appreciated as an earnest religious shrine. But its amazingly tactile constructions are pretty much beyond belief.

FIG. 727 **Corn Forever** Many communities attempt to feature locally produced products. Few have been as successful as Mitchell, South Dakota, where the annually renewed Corn Palace murals are big attractions, and effectively eternal.

FIG. 726 **Preserving Folk Art** Folk Art is often lost after its creator is no longer able to care for it. Eureka maintains its priceless Wooden Garden by preserving it behind glass.

FIG. 728 **Enjoy!** St. Louis culture emphasizes the enjoyment of everyday life. That is reflected in a number of exceptional public and private follies, including Bevo Mill.

FIG. 729 **Shameless Self-Promotion** Roaring Twenties tycoon Wilbur Foshay had his name cut in as 10-foot letters around the top of his new tower. Just months after the building's *very* grand opening, Foshay was sent off to federal prison for fraud. That did not prevent his 32-story obelisk from becoming a symbol of Minneapolis.

FIG. 730 **Hand-crafted Masterpiece** Hopperstad Stave Church Replica in Minnesota is a late-twentieth-century tour-de-force construction. One can only marvel that such intricacy was carried off so well. That it was essentially built by volunteers–hobbyists is simply amazing.

Foshay Tower FIG. 729
1926–1929
Magney & Tusler, architects, **Leon Arnal**, design consultant
821 Marquette Ave., Minneapolis, Minnesota

The client's intent was shameless self-promotion, employing the Washington Monument as a dubious design precedent for an office building. Even so, the architects clearly took their task very seriously, and soon after completion, the Foshay Tower was among the most recognized urban icons in the United States.

Hopperstad Stave Church Replica FIG. 730
1997–2001
Gaylord "Guy" Paulson, visionary and wood carver; **Burton Youngs, YHR Partners**, architects; **Dale Ruff**, consulting architect; **Solien & Larson**, structural engineers; **Dean Bowman**, artist
202 1st Ave. N., Hjemkomst Center Park, Moorhead, Minnesota

Medieval Norwegian stave churches once numbered in the hundreds. Today, barely two dozen survive. At least three replicas have been built in the United States. Hopperstad, arguably the best of these, closely follows its namesake landmark in Vik, Norway, which was constructed in 1130.

This bravura facsimile can be especially appreciated in three respects: for its striking visual qualities and craftsmanship, inside and out; for Paulson's marvelous woodcarving, incorporating the traditional Norwegian-Viking mix of pagan and Christian motifs; and for its creation by a handful of ordinary people who not only decided to build such a monumental structure for fun at their own expense, but accomplished it beautifully.

WELL BEYOND UNCLASSIFIABLE

Oral Roberts University FIGS. 731, 732, 733
1961–1963 ff
Oral Roberts, visionary; **Cecil Stanfield**, architect for preliminary design schemes; **Frank Wallace**, campus architect, 1963-1968
7777 S. Lewis Ave., Tulsa, Oklahoma

Praying Hands
1980, relocated to present site, c. 1989
Leonard McMurry, sculptor

Messick Learning Resource Center
1964–1965; 1976–1978
Frank Wallace, architect

Prayer Tower
Ralph L. Reece Memorial Gardens
1966–1967
Frank Wallace, architect

City of Faith Medical Complex
1977–1981; converted to office use, 1989
Oral Roberts, conceptual designer; **Frank Wallace**, architect

Entering along an immaculate "Avenue of Flags" focusing on a 60-foot-high sculpture of praying hands (Fig 731), originally sited at the City of Faith, first-time visitors will instantly realize that ORU is not your typical college campus. Exploration reveals an incomparable collection of "futuristic architecture," of which the reflective golden Messick Center (Fig. 733), which is just too well executed to be dismissed as flashy, serves as the physical centerpiece.

The lifelike sculptural group of Jesus with two children in the Reece Gardens, located directly beneath ORU's iconic Prayer Tower (Fig. 732), offers a personal Rorschach test, separating those who will treasure the scene for its deeply moving piety from those who will consider it saccharine kitsch. The stark, angular City of Faith, its 60-story tower the tallest building in Oklahoma, adds yet another unexpected dimension to the campus.

While the ORU is by now a period piece, reflecting the personal vision and taste of its eponymous founder, one hopes that inevitable future changes will not dilute the cohesive visual impact of this astonishing environment.

FIGS. 731, 732, 733 **Signature Imageries** Many colleges have attempted to establish a singular identity though distinctive architecture. Few have succeeded like Oral Roberts University. These views show the signature Praying Hands entrance (Fig. 731), the iconic Prayer Tower, with Jesus counseling children in the garden below (Fig. 732), and ORU's glittering academic hub, Messick Center (Fig. 733). No matter how you feel about these expressions, you are highly unlikely to confuse ORU with some other campus!

Fairs and Expositions

1876–1984

FIG. 734 Fair Icons
Memorable American expositions are usually identified with signature features like the Court of Honor at the 1893 Chicago fair, Bernard Maybeck's Palace of Fine Arts at San Francisco in 1915, and Charles Moore's 1984 Wonderwall for New Orleans. The Trylon and Perisphere at the 1939–1940 New York World's Fair, illustrated here in a rare period color photograph, are still familiar. *Photograph: Ezra Stoller © Esto*

Fairs have long been employed for economic gain. Indeed, medieval European trade fairs are the direct predecessors of the more-elaborate modern fairs held over the past century and a half. Since the mid-1800s, large "world's fairs" have also been organized as a vehicle to assert leading international status for a host city and nation.

In the United States, fair events extend over a broad range of scale. These range from the ubiquitous county fair (Figs. 735, 736), traditionally held in conjunction with harvest, to the world's fair/international exposition, which, as its name implies, attracts pavilions and exhibits from many nations. According to

Alfred Heller, more than 300 expositions of various grades have occurred worldwide since the 1851 "Great Exposition of the Works of Industry of All Nations" held in Joseph Paxton's Crystal Palace in London.

In between local and world's fairs in scale are themed fairs of varying quality and emphasis, such as the 1898 Trans-Mississippi Exposition in Omaha; Norfolk's 1907 Jamestown Exposition; and the 1915 Negro Historical and Industrial Exposition in Richmond. This chapter identifies major U.S. fairs and expositions which were especially prominent at their time, with a focus on planning, architecture, and landscape design.

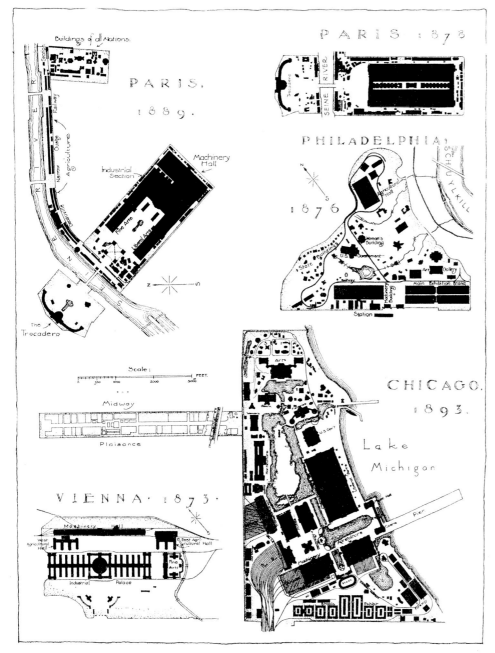

FIGS. 735, 736 **County Fairs** Thousands of local fairs are held annually throughout the United States. At one time these featured agricultural exhibits and the latest in farm machinery, but most of them now revolve around carnival attractions (Fig. 735). Here, at the Dakota County Fair outside of Minneapolis, vestiges of the past linger in an exhibit of historic tractors from as long ago as the . . . 1950s (Fig. 736).

FIG. 737 **Early Expositions** These exposition site plans are drawn to the same scale, illustrating the great increase in size between the Vienna and Chicago fairs, over just two decades. *Werner Hegemann and Elbet Peets,* Civic Art, *1922*

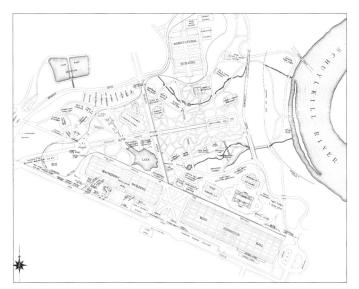

FIG. 738 **Centennial Exposition** The nation's first major exposition, Philadelphia's 1876 fair was developed without benefit of American precedent. That is especially apparent in the abrupt juxtapositions of naturalistic and formal patterns in its site layout. *Library of Congress, Prints & Photographs, Historic American Buildings Survey*

FIG. 739 **World's Columbian Exposition** Without question, Chicago 1893 was the greatest American exposition. The fair was a transformative event for American society. Individual attractions were largely overshadowed by the visually cohesive White City. Its grandeur and pageantry astonished fairgoers at a time when the United States was still predominantly rural, the vast majority of its built environments rude and uninspiring. *Library of Congress, Prints & Photographs*

1876 Centennial Exposition FIG. 738

Hermann J. Schwarzmann, fair planner and architect of Memorial Hall;
Henry Pettit, Joseph M. Wilson, engineers and designers of Main Building and Machinery Hall
Fairmont Park, Philadelphia, Pennsylvania (Memorial Hall is extant.)

Timed to commemorate the U.S. Centenary, the Philadelphia exposition was the first major U.S. fair, serving as a national prototype for such events later. The exposition was set along the Schuylkill River on 285 acres of Fairmount Park. The site was dominated by a 900,000-square-foot Main Exhibition Building and the Machinery Building, which together extended about two-thirds of a mile across the site. At the close of the fair, many of the exhibits were donated to the Smithsonian Institution, ending up in the Arts & Industries Building on the National Mall (see Victorian Gothic chapter). Consistent with honoring American Independence, the fair functioned as an early showcase of American Colonial Revival examples. According to William Rhoads, these were "intended to evoke the [reassuring] colonial past, although their actual forms bore little similarity to their supposed models."

1893 World's Columbian Exposition FIGS. 739, 740, 741

Daniel H. Burnham, chief of construction; **John Wellborn Root, Charles B. Atwood**, supervising architects; **Frederick Law Olmsted**, supervising landscape architect; **Henry "Harry" Codman**, project landscape architect; **Frank Millet**, director of functions; **George Ferris**, inventor and engineer of the Ferris Wheel attraction
Jackson Park, Chicago, Illinois

Timed to mark the 400th anniversary of the discovery voyage by Columbus, the Chicago fair was equally a chauvinistic reaction to the immensely successful 1889 *Exposition Universelle Internationale* in Paris, and to its iconic Eiffel Tower.

The World's Columbian Exposition offered a way to pursue multiple agendas, including asserting the international stature of the United States and demonstrating that Chicago was an upcoming world city. There was as well a professional agenda, especially on the part of Burnham, to prove that Americans were capable of noble artistic feats at least comparable to Eiffel's tower. Overcoming seemingly insurmountable obstacles, the fair miraculously opened to acclaim as an enchanting White City (Fig. 739), and

FIGS. 740, 741 **Artifacts of the Great Fair** Visitors can still experience the general setting of the 1893 Exposition at Chicago's Jackson Park. Olmsted's Lagoon and Island (Fig. 740) are located directly south of the Museum of Science and Industry, originally the Fair's Palace of Fine Arts. The gilded Republic statue has been relocated to just south of the lagoon (Fig. 741). Its previous location, the Court of Honor reflecting pool, was reconfigured into the present yacht harbor. The fair's Midway, sans Ferris Wheel, remains as a landscaped boulevard "Plaisance" extending past the University of Chicago campus to Washington Park.

drew 27.5 million admissions—in just six months of operation, during a year marked by national financial panic, when the country's total population was only 65 million, and long-distance travel was difficult.

From the outset, Burnham planned the fair as a design expression, calling on premier American architects of the period such as Richard Morris Hunt, Charles F. McKim, and Louis Sullivan, and allied professionals like sculptor Augustus Saint-Gaudens. The fair's visual highlights included the Court of Honor, a monumental reflecting pool surrounded by Beaux Arts buildings and focused on a colossal statue, "Republic" (Fig. 741); the Golden Door of Sullivan's Transportation Building; Olmsted's central lagoon and wooded island (Fig. 740); and Ferris's Wheel, which became the fair's popular icon.

Still, the greatest achievement was the grand and cohesive overall visual environment, what Erik Larson described as "an effect of majesty and beauty." As a visitor remarked after experiencing the fair, "Everything [else] will seem small and insignificant."

1901 Pan-American Exposition FIGS. 742, 743
John M. Carrère, master planner and executive architect
Within Delaware, Elmwood, Amherst and Hwy. 198, Buffalo, New York

The Electric Tower/Tower of Light, loosely based on the Giralda in Seville, served as the signature fair structure. Buffalo's exposition was intended to showcase progress over the old nineteenth century and look forward to the new. Its architecture was predominantly Academic Classicism, with an emphasis on Hispanic style references, reflecting recent U.S. possessions of former Spanish colonies.

The exposition site was organized around a carefully ordered

FIGS. 742, 743 **Pan-American Exposition** The stiff formality of Buffalo's 1901 Pan-American Exposition didn't really connect with the core of fairgoers in search of a good time. Visually, only the night lighting, here of the Music Pavilion (Fig. 743), was sufficiently out of the ordinary. *Library of Congress, Prints & Photographs*

FIG. 744 **Louisiana Purchase Exposition** "Meet Me in St. Louis" was another national experience like 1893, this 1904 event emphasizing practical improvements to everyday life. The site layout was much less pretentious than Buffalo's, although at 1,000 acres, St. Louis was the largest fair in land area. *St. Louis Public Library*

Beaux Arts layout, which opened onto a naturalistic landscape and lake to the south. Despite the drama of the brightly lit tower and fully lighted grounds, this high-minded fair was a financial disaster, its attendance falling far below expectations. Those who did attend were largely attracted by its amusement midway. Today, the exposition is primarily associated with the assassination there of President McKinley.

1904 Louisiana Purchase Exposition FIG. 744

Isaac Taylor, director of works; **Emmanuel Masqueray**, director of design; **George Kessler**, director of landscape architecture; **Louis Millet**, chief of mural decoration; **Augustus Saint-Gaudens, Daniel Chester French**, sculptors; **Cass Gilbert**, architect of the Fine Arts Building; **Albert Kelsey**, planner and architect of the Model Street
Forest Park, St. Louis, Missouri

St. Louis had been an also-ran for the world's fair designation won by Chicago for its 1893 exposition (entry above) and a decade later

FIG. 745 **Panama-Pacific International Exposition** San Francisco's 1915 exposition was first and foremost a local morale builder intended as a palliative to the city's disastrous 1906 earthquake/fire. The fair was tightly organized around axial spaces like the Palm Court (Fig. 745). Perhaps because of the exposition's overall cool formality, Bernard Maybeck's intensely romantic Palace of Fine Arts (Fig. 175) became the lasting fair icon. *Library of Congress, Prints & Photographs, Historic American Buildings Survey*

won its own chance to shine. Comparisons are inevitable, and instructive. Unlike Chicago's fair, which reflected Burnham's design vision, the St. Louis exposition was the product of a dense organizational bureaucracy. This was especially manifested in two ways. One is in the physical plan, which was not particularly imaginative, even compared to Carrère's for the 1901 Buffalo fair, much less to Chicago's. Second, St. Louis's focus was practical, compared to the visionary tack taken at Chicago.

Thus if the overriding spirit of the 1893 fair was utopian and experiential, 1904 emphasized what could be done to improve everyday American life. While the 1904 exposition unavoidably reacted to previous fairs, it also struck out in a newly relevant, contemporary direction.

The St. Louis fair did showcase the fine arts to the extent that the only permanent major structure was Cass Gilbert's Fine Arts Building, now the St. Louis Art Museum, which occupied a pivotal site. At the same time, the majority of exhibits focused on education, social work, public health, and housing.

This dichotomy resulted in dual fair icons, the Fine Arts Building and the Model Street. The latter was an assemblage of civic-like buildings arranged along a broad, paved street, meant to demonstrate what the civic core of a typical American town could look like. Mel Scott related that these buildings were accompanied by an assorted examples of designed infrastructure and street furniture, including several styles of drinking fountains and ornamental fountains, signposts, letter boxes, ornamental streetlamps, and more.

William Rhoads observed that American Colonial Revival architecture was again prominent at this fair, perhaps because, like the 1876 and 1893 fairs, the 1904 fair commemorated a shaping event in American history.

1915 Panama-Pacific International Exposition FIG. 745

Willis Polk, chairman of the architectural commission; **John McLaren**, landscape architect-site planner; **Karl Bitter, Stirling Calder**, supervisors of sculpture; **Jules Guerin**, supervisor of color and decoration
Marina District, bounded by the Presidio, the Bay, Van Ness, and Chestnut Sts., San Francisco, California

The San Francisco fair was nominally timed to celebrate the opening of the Panama Canal, although it was equally a much-needed antidote to the city's disastrous 1906 earthquake and fire. The

FIGS. 746, 747 Panama-California Exposition This 1915-1916 fair established San Diego nationally as a unique, romantic destination. From the perspective of advances in architecture and planning, San Diego was second only to the 1893 Chicago fair, as Bertram Goodhue radically redefined how a fair might be laid out, especially taking full advantage of existing site features, while also introducing his Spanish Colonial Revival architectural style. *Fig. 747: San Diego Historical Society*

exposition was a great success in lifting local spirits after nearly a decade of emotionally exhausting rebuilding.

In plan, a sturdy east-west axis extended through the site, punctuated by several north-south cross-axis reflecting pools, called Courts (Fig. 745). Bernard Maybeck's Palace of Fine Arts (Fig. 175) closed one end of the major axis, and is the only surviving structure, carefully rebuilt in the 1960s. Louis Mullgardt's 450-foot "Tower of Jewels," covered in a multicolored envelope of glass, was surely the gaudiest building in a context that was overflowing with visual richness: architecturally, the fair was all dessert, with no main course.

In addition to elaborate visual imageries, light was employed as a central theme, in a broad palette ranging from the outlining of pavilions to powerful searchlights. The stiff, predictable site plan was hardly an advance in fair planning, and most of the fair structures were pleasant ephemera, at best. But Maybeck's moody stage setting captured the affections of San Franciscans, as well as millions of subsequent visitors, right up to the present.

1915–1916 Panama-California Exposition FIGS. 746, 747
Frank P. Allen, Sr., director of works; **Bertram Goodhue**, planner and architect; **Carlton Winslow**, associate architect; **Paul Thiene**, exposition gardener
Balboa Park, San Diego, California

San Diego's fair could be thought of as competing with or complementary to the concurrent San Francisco exposition, in that it also celebrated the opening of the Panama Canal, as well as the 400th anniversary of Balboa's discovery of the Pacific.

In 1910, the local organizing committee engaged John Olmsted and Frederick Law Olmsted, Jr., to plan the exposition. The committee then commissioned Goodhue as supervisory architect. Professional disagreements soon followed, finally to the breaking point. When Goodhue proposed a dramatic new site plan that called for a bridge approach over a deep canyon, the Olmsteds withdrew, leaving Goodhue as effectively the fair planner and architect, assisted primarily by Winslow. Goodhue designed three permanent structures, beginning with the Cabrillo Bridge (1912–1914), and then the California and Fine Arts buildings. Winslow, Allen, and Harrison Albright designed temporary buildings, some of which are extant.

Unlike the contemporaneous San Francisco exhibition, the San Diego fair provided advances in both planning and architecture. These were Goodhue's T-plan (Fig. 747), which broke from the established Beaux Arts site organization of previous fairs; and the brilliant flowering of Goodhue's Spanish Colonial Revival style (Fig. 746). Synthesized from the Mexican Churrigueresque, this style subsequently influenced "Spanish" architectural imageries in Southern California and elsewhere.

1933–1934 A Century of Progress Exposition FIG. 748

Louis Skidmore, Nathaniel Owings, fair site planners; **Harvey Wiley Corbett**, chairman of the architecture commission; **Joseph Urban**, art consultant

Meigs Field area of the Lakefront, between 12th and 39th Sts., Chicago, Illinois

A Century of Progress commemorated the 100th anniversary of Chicago's founding. This implied a modern image. Because the fair took place during the depths of the Great Depression, it was also highly desirable that the event be bright and cheerful. The resulting fair was thus more of a carnival than were previous fairs, whose amusement midways had typically been tucked off in a corner of the fair site.

Built on reclaimed land, the 1933–1934 fair was organized physically around a devised lagoon. But this was not a high-design landscape, as had been Olmsted's lagoon at the 1893 fair, located

FIG. 749 **Fair Architecture** Alvar Aalto's undulating Finnish Pavilion interior was "without doubt the most daring piece of architecture" at the 1939-1940 New York fair, according to historian Sigfried Giedion. (For a permanent Aalto work in America, see Fig. 392.) *Photograph: Ezra Stoller © Esto*

several miles to the south. Architectural imageries were prominently Moderne, not Modern, and brightly colored. If there was a fair icon, it was the Skyride, suspended between two gigantic towers set more than one-third of a mile apart.

For its second year, the exposition was expanded, additions including a fountain in the lagoon and a Foreign Village, a precursor to the World Showcase opened in 1982 at Walt Disney World in Florida. The best Modern design was found on the Street of Tomorrow, where 12 Modernistic houses were built. A polygonal example by Keck & Keck was the most architecturally significant of this group. Five of the Street of Tomorrow houses, including the Keck & Keck, were moved to Beverly Shores, Indiana, after the fair. They are extant.

The fair is historically important among the design professions in that it marks the practical establishment of the firm Skidmore, Owings & Merrill. Nothing of the fair remains on the site, which was initially converted into a small corporate airfield, and now is part of a developing civic landscape undertaken by the City of Chicago beginning in the mid-1990s.

1939–1940 New York World's Fair FIGS. 734, 749

Robert Moses, planner; **Wallace Harrison**, architect of Trylon and Perisphere; **Henry Dreyfus**, designer of Democracity model; **Norman Bel Geddes**, Futurama designer

E side of Grand Central Pkwy., S off Roosevelt Ave., Queens, New York

The hopeful theme of "The World of Tomorrow" was understandable, after nearly a decade of Depression. A slender, 700-foot obelisk (Trylon) and 200-foot sphere (Perisphere) provided the required futuristic image (Fig. 734), although as Robert Hughes remarked, the underlying theme of this thoroughly regimented experience was a corporate demonstration of "industrial design as total social styling." Inside the 180-foot-diameter Perisphere, visitors viewed Democracity, a model of an idealized American environment of 2039, while the GM Futurama offered a comparable urban vision for the year 1960. Despite the popularity of the fair, especially the GM Futurama, the "total design" ideal of course could not be achieved in the diverse American society. Architec-

FIGS. 750, 751 Century 21 Exposition Seattle's agreeable 1962 entry into the international exposition sweepstakes is recalled locally for its monorail; among fair-goers for Minoru Yamasaki's delicate science pavilion (Fig. 750) and delightful traceries (Fig. 751); and nationally for the fair's Space Needle.

turally, Alvar Aalto's Finnish Pavilion interior (Fig. 749) was the highlight. The fair's Flushing Meadows site was reused for the 1964–1965 World's Fair (later in this chapter).

1962 Century 21 Exposition FIGS. 750, 751

Paul Thiry, supervising architect and site planner; **Lawrence Halprin**, exposition landscape architect; **Richard Haag**, reuse planner; **Minoru Yamasaki**, architect of the United States Science Pavilion; **John Graham, Jr.**, **Victor Steinbrueck**, architects of the Space Needle
Seattle Center, between Broad and Mercer Sts., First and Fifth Aves., Seattle, Washington

This pleasant, unassuming expo did not commemorate any specific historic event, other than locally recalling the 1909 Alaska-Yukon-Pacific Exposition, also held in Seattle. A theme and supporting iconic elements slowly came together from a variety of inspirations, including Disneyland's monorail, the USSR's Sputnik satellite, and an aerial restaurant in Stuttgart, Germany. Gradually, the local fair committee fixed on science as the fair theme, and thus the signature national exhibit was Yamasaki's characteristically lacy, crowd-pleasing United States Science Pavilion (Figs. 750, 751).

FIGS. 752, 753 **New York World's Fair** Robert Moses rehashed his 1939–1940 fair with far less success the second time around in 1964-65. A 12-story globe, the Unisphere (Fig. 752), and the New York State Pavilion (Fig. 753) remain.

Despite a tiny 28-acre site, three memorable icons were created. All are still extant. These are the Space Needle tower, the Science Pavilion, now the Pacific Science Center—both genuine period pieces of the early 1960s—and the Swedish Alweg monorail, which was constructed in order to bridge the mile between the expo site and downtown hotels and restaurants. After being shut down awhile, the monorail was restored to service in 2008.

1964-1965 New York World's Fair FIGS. 752, 753

Robert Moses, director; **Andrews & Clark, Clarke & Rapuano**, planners; **Wallace K. Harrison, Edward Durell Stone, Gordon Bunshaft, Henry Dreyfuss, Emil Praeger**, Design Committee; **Peter Muller Munk**, architect of the Unisphere; **Philip Johnson, Richard Foster**, architects. New York State Pavilion; **Lev Zetlin**, structural engineer, New York State Pavilion. E side of Grand Central Pkwy., S of Roosevelt Ave., Queens, New York

Like the 1939–1940 World's Fair on the same site, this fair was all about Robert Moses. Unlike the previous fair, and unlike a typical Moses undertaking, it was disorganized and mediocre. Moses biographer Robert Caro contended that to Moses, the 1964–1965 fair

was little more than a means to an end, seen as a practical way of raising funding to finance the development of a permanent park on the site. Unfortunately for that idea, the fair was so uninteresting that attendance reached only a fraction of Moses's projections. Admissions were boosted slightly by a mishmash of new attractions offered the second year.

The 120-foot Unisphere globe (Fig. 752) served as the nominal fair icon. However, the New York State Pavilion (Fig. 753), loosely suggesting flying saucers alighted on towering stilts, is probably best known to many Americans, as the setting for the climactic scene of the 1997 movie, *Men in Black*. Both structures are extant.

PHASING OUT FAIRS

New York 1964–1965 was the last major fair in the United States. Several reasons can be suggested for this, including a

FIG. 754 **Louisiana World Exposition** Charles Moore's enthusiasm for high-spirited designs was nowhere more evident than in his marvelously playful Wonderwall for the 1984 Louisiana World Exposition in New Orleans. Moore's seemingly limitless reservoir of unexpected, voluptuous expressions is dazzling. *photograph © Marc Treib*

growing social divisiveness in American society exaggerated by the Vietnam War, an ever-increasing proliferation of things to do in the diverse American culture, exponentially higher costs of putting on a fair, and especially the immense popular and artistic successes of Expo '67 in Montreal (Fig. 15)—realistically, a very hard act to top.

World's fair enthusiasm slowly petered out in the United States without much notice, in such forgettable events as HemisFair '68 in San Antonio, Expo '74 in Spokane, and the 1982 Knoxville International Energy Exposition.

The curtain dropped for good after the water-themed 1984 Louisiana World Exposition in New Orleans. True to form for the Big Easy, it was a financial scandal, the only American exposition to have declared bankruptcy during its run. Yet it was quite creative visually and provided long-term physical/economic value to the city that exceeded the negligible lasting effects of many other expositions.

1984 Louisiana World Exposition FIG. 754
Charles W. Moore, William Turnbull, with **August Perez Associates, Kent Bloomer, Leonard Salvato, Arthur Andersson, Urban Innovations Group**, designers of Wonderwall and ancillary structures Mississippi Riverfront, accessible from Poydras, Canal, and Julia Sts., New Orleans, Louisiana

The whole point of New Orleans is to enjoy, and surely Wonderwall, the sensational fair icon, demonstrated the ultimate in visual pleasure, without descending into vulgarity. It was possible to appreciate this astonishing, blocks-long construction in several respects. Among these, Wonderwall offered a way to understand the differences between a Charles Moore design and a typical Postmodern design, principally in its layering, startling freshness of approach, and sheer visual richness and invention, not to mention, for its pure fun. These attributes are missing in the shallower expressions of American Postmodernism.

Sadly—tragically, really—Wonderwall was torn down after the fair closed. In an ideal world, it would have been made permanent, like Maybeck's 1915 Palace of Fine Arts in San Francisco. Still, the exposition district is now probably better off than before. The Riverwalk tourist attraction is the permanent exposition legacy.

CITY PLANNING

1573–2004

Ordering the Land
1573–1796

FIG. 755 A Renaissance Sense of Order The Americas were "discovered" by Europeans just as Renaissance-inspired ideas about rationality and civic order gained prominence. Purely from a city-planning perspective, the timing was ideal, since the New World offered a perceived blank slate on which to test new approaches to city building. In built-up European cities, new Renaissance planning vocabularies like straight avenues and well-proportioned town squares had to be inserted piecemeal into irregular medieval fabric. Even major public improvements like the magnificent *Plaza Mayor* in Salamanca, Spain (Fig. 755) constructed between 1728 and 1755 by Alberto de Churriguera and Andrés Garcia de Quiñones, existed as isolated fragments of Renaissance order within a much larger, unplanned cityscape. No comparable physical restrictions existed in the New World. So entire cities, as well as vast wilderness areas, have been rationally ordered across the United States over the past five centuries.

Starting from zero. Europeans who founded New World settlements began with a blank slate – from their perspective. To them, despite no less than ten million North American inhabitants when Columbus arrived, the seemingly boundless expanse of what is now the United States was wide open, compared to the densely populated Old World of Europe.

Historian Dora Crouch noted that "very few purely Renaissance cities exist in Europe." That is because expressions of Renaissance city building like straight, ceremonial avenues, proportioned public plazas (Fig. 755), and, more basically, general physical order had to be inserted piecemeal into the dense, irregular medieval fabric of existing cities, since there was much less potential to build freestanding new cities in Europe.

So the New World, which was conveniently "discovered" just as Renaissance thought was flourishing, became a demonstration of rational European ideas about city building. These new concepts about ordered communities were codified into land-planning principles to guide the founding of Spanish colonial settlements. The codes were formally issued in 1573 by the Spanish king Philip II as the Laws of the Indies.

Well before that date, however, Renaissance-inspired demonstrations of city planning had inspired settlements throughout New Spain. The idea of rationally ordering the land was introduced in European New World development at monumental scale with Cortés's 1518–1521 reconstruction of Tenochtitlan into Mexico City, following a plan devised by Alonso García Bravo.

Of course Aboriginal Americans had centuries earlier devised epic ordered landscapes like Chaco Canyon, but these systems were not fully perceptible, hence not credible, to Europeans because they referred as well to an unseen cosmic domain (see the Aboriginal Cultures chapter).

A second characteristic of American planning and city building, diversity, is also a direct result of the wide-openness recognized by Europeans (again, purely from the European perspective). The supposition that vast tracts of land were unclaimed attracted European nations with imperial ambitions to North America. Combined with the variety of the conti-

nent's climates and landscapes, this resulted in several distinct approaches to ordering the land.

In regions of North America not controlled by the Spanish, Hildegard Binder Johnson identified four widespread French and English colonial settlement types including systematic patterns with field layouts directly accessible to rivers and roads, like the French long lots or *rangs*; clustered villages with houses and fields in separate locations, as in Massachusetts; irregularly shaped and often large landholdings with private docks and houses located between rivers, as in the Virginia Tidewater; and regular, rectilinear planned town sites like that of Savannah.

Spanish Laws of the Indies FIGS. 756, 757
1573
Council of the Indies; **Juan de Ovando**, president of the Supreme Tribunal (1571–1574); **Diego de Encinas**, compiler (1592–1596)
Seville, Spain/North America–New Spain

This compilation of 148 city planning ordinances was based on previous imperial planning edicts. The 1573 Laws of the Indies was actually the initial step toward the codification of dozens of separate royal edicts issued throughout the 1500s, dating almost from the 1493 Spanish settlement on Hispaniola. These ordinances were intended to ensure not only rational town plans, but to set out guiding standards and everyday procedures for colonial life. Even so, the Laws of the Indies represented only a small part of the royal legislation directed to New World colonization. An ultimate, "complete text" of more than 3,000 laws was published in 1681.

St. Augustine, Florida, founded in 1565, was the first Spanish colonial city founded in what is now the United States. Los Angeles, founded in 1781, was the last major Spanish city. According to Alex Mundigo, Laws-of-the-Indies cities were founded throughout

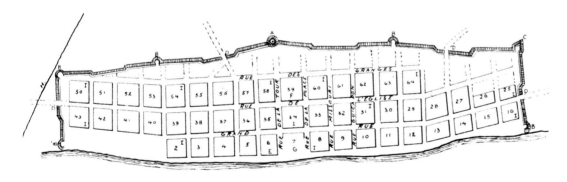

FIGS. 756, 757 Official Planning Ordered Spanish settlements were founded from Florida to California under the Laws of the Indies. The 1764 plan for St. Louis, shown here as the community had developed by 1780 (Fig. 756), is characteristically Spanish in its orthogonal blocks and central plaza. Only a few Spanish plazas remain essentially intact in the United States, notably the spacious *Zócalo* in Sonoma, California (Fig. 757), by now heavily wooded. *Fig. 756: St. Louis Central Public Library*

the New World between 1530 and 1820. However "most of the important cities of Latin America were founded between 1506 and 1570," and 16 of today's 20 largest Spanish cities in America had been founded by 1580, at the very beginning of the period when these laws were being codified. While only a small percentage of the ordinances addressed the physical city plan, Laws-of-the-Indies settlements were characteristically organized around a central plaza —as, for example, in St. Louis (Fig. 756) and Sonoma (Fig. 757)— where government buildings and the church or cathedral were invariably located.

Mundigo traced a conceptual influence back to the Roman city planner Vitruvius, whose *Ten Books on Architecture* had been rediscovered and published at the end of the 1400s, and whose ideas influenced Renaissance architects and planners, particularly in the development of Spanish land planning and city building in the 1500s and later.

French *Rang* Long Lots
Prior to 1745
St. Lawrence Valley, Québec; east of Detroit; near Winnipeg; near Vincennes, Indiana; St. Louis; Louisiana

The St. Lawrence River offered the main access to New France– Québec. Naturally, early land grants fronted the St. Lawrence or its tributaries. These *rangs* were long and narrow parcels, with the shorter dimension along the river, the long dimension extending back into the wilderness typically by a ratio of about 1:10.

Commonly, *rang* lots included a river frontage of less than 200 feet, while extending back nearly 2,000 feet. This configuration offered three benefits: (1) houses in any given commune were lined up close together, ideal for socialization and defense; (2) every

FIG. 758 Modern Patroonship John D. Rockefeller's Westchester County estate, "Kykuit," was developed between 1905 and 1913 on part of an earlier patroonship located above today's Tarrytown, New York. These irregularly shaped Dutch colonial properties were defined by the Hudson River, other physical features, and practical accommodations with neighbors. A patroonship's lowland areas near the river were farmed. Successful farms became centers of human and economic activity, eventually growing into villages like Tarrytown. Estate houses were usually sited upland, like the much later Kykuit, enjoying splendid views across the river valley. *The National Trust for Historic Preservation / Library of Congress, Prints & Photographs, Historic American Buildings Survey*

FIG. 759 Clustered Village New England colonial settlements typically grew out-ward from a central open area, what we now call a green. Some of these, like the central public space in Lexington, Massachusetts, are fairly regular in shape (Fig. 83). However, many were not. This triangle of open space in the center of the small Con-necticut village of South Woodstock was formed by a fork in the road.

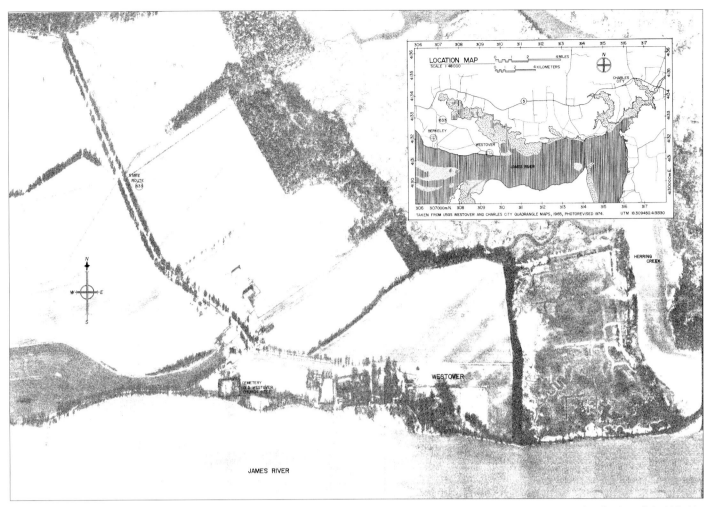

FIG. 760 Irregular Holdings Many colonial properties were irregular in shape, often with loosely defined boundaries. In this aerial view, Westover (see Southern Colonial Architecture chapter) occupies a central position within its plantation. Unlike Dutch patroonships, these properties have the estate house right along the river, adjacent to the fields. *Library of Congress, Prints & Photographs, Historic American Buildings Survey*

landholder enjoyed good transportation access; and (3) lots included a variety of qualities, typically flatlands, slopes, and wooded bluffs.

The *rang* became a cultural unit in Québec, as village social life was associated with the *rang* system. Boundaries were emphasized, usually carefully defined by hedging and fences. Even today, affluent Québecois willingly pay a premium for limestone second homes set on long lots as reflecting authentic, French-Canadian pioneer culture. Long-lot ownership patterns are prominent in Louisiana along the Mississippi River downstream from Baton Rouge.

Dutch Patroonships FIG. 758

1620s–1660s
Dutch West India Company manors along the Hudson River, New York and New Jersey

Patroonships were land grants orienting along the river, like the French *rangs*. They were much larger, however, and not as regular in shape. Parcels might extend twelve miles along the Hudson, or six miles along both sides. No single settlement pattern was typical, although main houses were usually placed upland, with fenced fields located close to the water.

Clustered Massachusetts Villages FIG. 759

After 1641

Bay Colony locations and settlement patterns were determined by law. Towns were to be laid out within one year of a grant, all

houses to be located within a half mile of the meeting house, which was usually located on a central public space, what we call a green or common (Fig. 759). Each farmer was assigned a tract of field, and all citizens shared the woodlands.

As these restrictions were eventually eased, home lots expanded to as much as sixty acres. Johnson observed that these lots "usually fronted winding roads, which resulted in a pleasant blend of the uncertain rectangularity of properties and fields and the adjustment of roads to topography."

Irregular, Scattered Land Holdings FIG. 760

1600s and 1700s
English Middle Colonies, Tidewater areas

Farmsteads in New Jersey, Pennsylvania, Delaware, and the Tidewater Southeast were also located as close to a river as possible. However, the shape and extent of these landholding were pragmatically determined, based primarily on agricultural value. So lots tended to be irregular in shape and scattered in location, with minimal physical-boundary reference to neighboring properties.

Rectangular Town Plats FIGS. 761, 772

1638 and later
New Haven, Philadelphia, Annapolis, Williamsburg, Savannah, and others

In city building, the attraction of geometry is timeless, and geometrics—mainly rectangles, but also squares, circles, and diagonals—established town plan patterns for numerous colonial

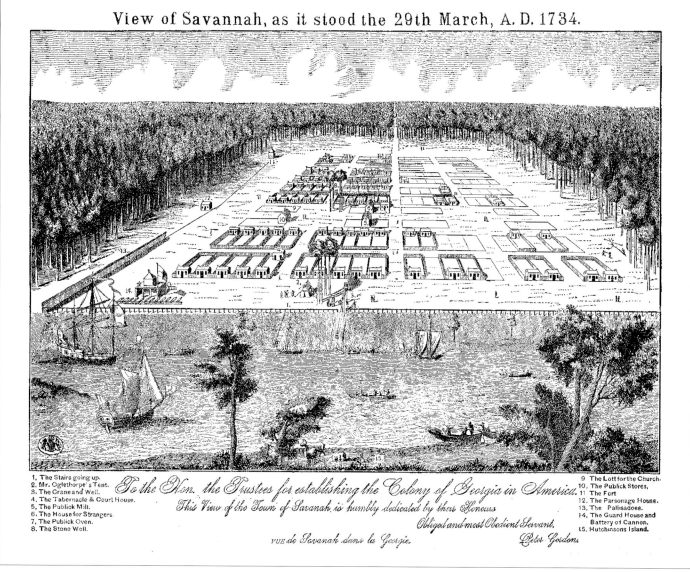

View of Savannah, as it stood the 29th March, A. D. 1734.

1. The Stairs going up.
2. Mr. Oglethorpe's Tent.
3. The Crane and Well.
4. The Tabernacle & Court House.
5. The Publick Mill.
6. The House for Strangers.
7. The Publick Oven.
8. The Stone Well.

9. The Lott for the Church.
10. The Publick Stores,
11. The Fort
12. The Parsonage House.
13. The Pallisadoes.
14. The Guard House and Battery of Cannon.
15. Hutchinsons Island.

To the Hon. the Trustees for establishing the Colony of Georgia in America. This View of the Town of Savanah, is humbly dedicated by their Honours Obliged and most Obedient Servant.

Peter Gordon.

vue de Savanah dans la Georgie.

FIG. 761 Ordering the Wilderness This depiction of Savannah a year after its founding vividly illustrates how rational planning might ignore, indeed might obliterate, the natural environment in the interest of establishing an ordered town. *University of Texas Libraries*

settlements. Among American geometric-plan achievements are the 1638 plan for New Haven based on nine square precincts (Fig. 772), and the brilliant, nuanced 1733 plan for Savannah (Fig. 761).

IMPOSING ORDER ON THE CONTINENT

U.S. Land Ordinance
1785

Thomas Jefferson, Hugh Williamson
Western Territory (U.S. lands between the existing states and Louisiana Territory, generally initially bounded on the west by the Mississippi River)

Jefferson chaired a 1784 committee of the Continental Congress charged with establishing a plan for the sale and governance of western lands. This required a system of land organization. To Jefferson, that meant making individual farmsteads easily available to settlers, to ensure that "as few as possible shall be without [at least] a little portion of land."

Jefferson's idea was distinctly different from earlier ordering approaches like the *rang*, clustered villages, and town plats.

Under the 1785 policy, millions of Americans would live in an evenly decentralized pattern. The political symbolism was certainly clear, for as Phil Patton pointed out, an endless grid did not designate a "privileged center." As Jefferson desired, the basic federal measure would be a rural township, not an urban center, as was characteristic of earlier New World ordering schemes in Latin America.

Jefferson proposed that land surveys and eventual subdivision be based on a decimal system, similar to the Roman centuriation system. He envisioned a ten-mile square as the basic township. Although these provisions were modified in the 1785 act, Johnson noted that Jefferson established two fundamental concepts for ordering U.S. lands: "a non-varying grid, and square subdivisions." However, Hugh Williamson, a member of Jefferson's committee and a mathematician with a doctoral degree from the University of Utrecht, claimed to be the originator of this plan. There is no question of Williamson's ability to independently conceive of such a system. Regardless, many documents establish that Jefferson had been thinking about ordering for years, and personally developed a detailed proposal under the auspices of his committee.

After considering ten- and seven-mile squares, Congress fixed on a six-mile square based on the 66-foot chain devised by the

English mathematician Edmund Gunter. Hence, as a minor irony, the basis for the socially innovative 36-square-mile American township dated back to agricultural practices in feudal, medieval England.

First National Survey
1785–1787
Thomas Hutchins, Geographer of the United States
East Liverpool, Ohio, westward 42 mi.

The national survey under the 1785 Land Ordinance started at a "Point of Beginning" near the present-day location of East Liverpool, where the extension of the southern boundary of Pennsylvania met the Ohio River, to run from that point directly north to Lake Erie. Teams of surveyors headed by Thomas Hutchins laid out seven ranges of six-mile squares, extending southward fifteen ranges, or 90 miles. In multiple respects, much of this work was unacceptably inaccurate, and surveying under the 1785 Ordinance was suspended by Congress.

Land Act FIGS. 762, 763
1796
Rufus Putnam, Jared Mansfield, U.S. surveyors general

As noted above, survey work under the 1785 Ordinance was unacceptably inaccurate, so its provisions were allowed to lapse when the U.S. Congress convened in 1789. Nevertheless, the critical need for survey and land registration persisted. So in 1796 Congress reestablished a rectangular survey system essentially like that established in 1785. Putnam was initially in charge of surveys, but his lack of accuracy caused President Jefferson to appoint Mansfield in his place. Mansfield, a mathematics professor, introduced a culture of meticulousness to the national survey as it extended, eventually, to the West Coast.

The important provisions of the 1796 act included assurance of safe title for individual settlers and, based on a 1792 proposal by Hugh Williamson, of square townships made up of 36 one-mile-square "sections" comprising 640 acres each. These could be easily subdivided into half-sections of 320 acres and quarter sections of 160 acres. As the new nation developed, farms as small as a "quarter-quarter section" of 40 acres would not be uncommon in fertile lands.

Thus was the U.S. Rectangular Survey, what is now referred to as the U.S.G.S. grid (after the United States Geological Survey), established. More than two-thirds of the land area within the 48 contiguous states was ordered according to the U.S.G.S. grid (Fig. 762). As Johnson observed, "the influence of the survey lines on our environment is visible in innumerable ways and runs deep in the living habits of Americans."

As a strong negative, it must be added that since the land survey is an abstract legal framework, unresponsive to the underlying landscape and biomes, the U.S.G.S. grid caused large-scale reordering of existing biology, especially with respect to wetlands (Fig. 763).

LAWS RECOGNIZING REALITIES

From a present-day perspective, we perceive supreme rationality and order in the expansion and development of trans-Appalachian United States in the 1800s. Certainly the intentions of Jefferson and others, and the brilliant intellectual

FIGS. 762, 763 Order Across the Continent After 1796, the U.S.G.S. survey grid was almost universally applied to undeveloped American territories. Today, one can read the ubiquitous section-township grid across California orange groves (Fig. 762) and Minnesota farmlands (Fig. 763), just about anywhere west of the Appalachians. *Fig. 762: Library of Congress, Prints & Photographs, Historic American Engineering Record; Fig. 763: State of Minnesota*

conception of the U.S.G.S. survey grid are monuments of Enlightenment thought.

The reality of westward expansion was often quite different, however, characterized by squatting, claims jumping, and routine disagreements among settlers. In truth, the famed (among American historians and geographers, at least) 1862 Homestead Act, which granted a maximum 160-acre, quarter-section of land free to any "homesteader" who worked the land for five years, was a face-saving mask for the government.

In the words of scholar and land reformer Hernando de Soto, the Homestead Act "was less an act of official generosity than recognition of a fait accompli: Americans had been settling and improving the land extra-legally for decades." The 1862 Homestead Act thus provided a practical way of integrating informal existing ownerships and settlements into the official national legal system.

Once again, the characteristic marriage of innovation and common sense prevailed in built America.

European New World Town Plans

1565–1823

FIGS. 764, 765 Urban Innovations
wo kinds of settlement-founding
approaches were especially prominent
in American colonial town planning.
One of these, noted in the previous
chapter, was the application of universal
ordinances like the Spanish Laws of the
Indies. In a contrasting approach, a custom technical solution was devised in
response to a specific local situation.
 As a supreme national example of
a custom technical solution, James
Oglethorpe, founder of Savannah,
devised a deceptively simple, easily
expandable street-grid pattern (Figs.
764, 780) which allowed efficient movement for commerce while also providing for urbane public spaces as centers
of community life (Fig. 765).

Europeans colonial town planning in what became the
United States was initiated by Spain, primarily in the
American Southwest. The conventions of other European
countries were employed elsewhere. Eventually, English sensibilities gained prominence in colonial-era town planning along
the Eastern Seaboard.

SPANISH SETTLEMENTS

Spanish New World settlements were based on the Laws of
the Indies city planning ordinances issued by King Philip II in
1573. These regulations were intended to set out a standard-

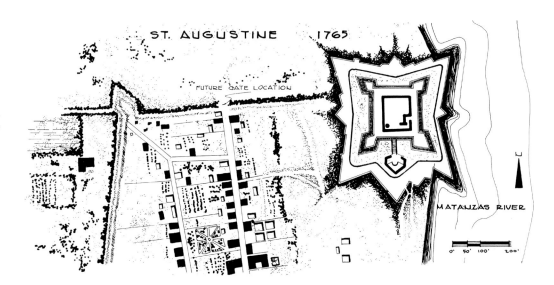

FIGS. 766, 767 Spanish Military Outpost St. Augustine, Florida, was founded as a fort, Castillo San Marcos (Fig. 41). Its star-shaped plan was a common configuration for European military towns of the Renaissance era (Fig. 766). A central court within the fort effectively functioned as a community plaza. Without need for an additional, municipal, plaza, the adjacent town atypically developed along a linear street (Fig. 767). *Library of Congress, Prints & Photographs, Historic American Buildings Survey*

ized, orderly approach to a town's founding and layout, a task usually undertaken by soldiers. The 148 ordinances addressed a wide range of initiatives, from responding to the local physical situation to attracting indigenous peoples to Catholicism.

Laws of the Indies settlements characteristically developed outward from a main plaza, or zócalo, around which principal buildings of church and state were arranged. Dozens of American settlements, like Santa Fe and Sonoma (California), were laid out according to the Laws of the Indies, although this central space was commonly later overbuilt.

Spanish colonial settlements developed around several distinctive components. Government power was based in the presidio, an administrative-military facility. Religious activity was centered in the mission, a cluster of buildings located around the parish church. The settlement itself was known as the pueblo (if Indian) or villa (if Spanish). Wealthy Spanish landowners held haciendas, estates which might cover thousands of acres and include many inhabited villages. Working ranchos were similar in scale and activities to the later Anglo ranches.

Saint Augustine, Florida FIGS. 766, 767
1565, 1702 ff.
Pedro Menéndez de Avilés, governor-founder

St. Augustine is the earliest surviving European settlement in the United States, founded as a frontier military outpost. Its tightly spaced, irregular streetscapes generate an engaging small-scale urbanism, especially St. George Street (Fig. 767), as it extends inward from under the city gate (Fig. 924). Only the spare, physically dominant fort, Castillo de San Marcos (1672–1695, Fig. 41), dates from before 1702, when the early town burned to the ground.

Santa Fe, New Mexico FIG. 768
1609 or 1610
Pedro de Peralta, royal governor-founder

Spain commenced colonizing the upper Rio Grande valley in 1598. This effort was temporarily discontinued in 1607, to be taken up again with the appointment of Peralta in 1609. He started colonization anew, symbolically as well as in fact, by founding a new capital, which he named Santa Fe. Despite the town's many changes over four centuries, one can still appreciate early Spanish colonial

FIG. 768 Spanish Administrative Center Unlike St. Augustine, Santa Fe had no fortifications. The town developed around a classic Laws-of-the-Indies plaza, enfronted by government offices. In this recent view, the one-story Governor's Palace (see Spanish Colonial Architecture chapter) can be glimpsed in the background. The bandstand was relocated in 1868 to make room for the Civil War memorial.

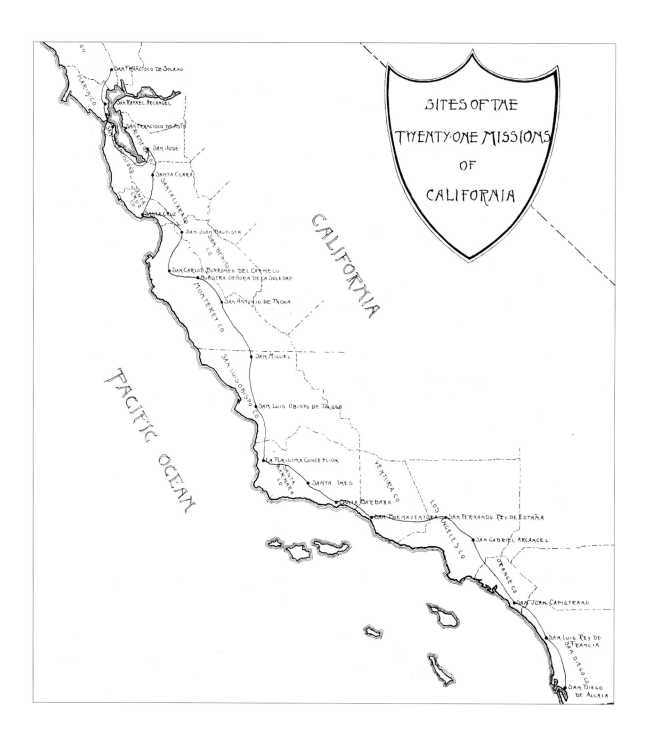

FIGS. 769, 770 Spanish Mission Towns California was colonized by a string of mission settlements, sited a day's ride apart along the Camino Real, or royal road, which extended from San Diego to Sonoma (Fig. 769). A painting of San Carlos Borromeo (Fig. 770)—present-day Carmel—illustrates how Spanish pueblos were built around a mission. *Fig. 769: Edwin Deakin; Fig. 770: Oriane Day, De Young Museum, San Francisco / Library of Congress, Prints & Photographs, Historic American Buildings Survey*

layouts by visiting the Plaza area (Fig. 768), defined along the north by the Governor's Palace (see the Spanish Colonial Architecture chapter).

Camino Real Missions FIGS. 769, 770
1769–1823

Fr. Junipero Serra and others
San Diego (1769); San Antonio (1771); San Gabriel (1771); San Carlos Borromeo [Carmel] (1771); San Luis Obispo (1772); San Francisco [Dolores] (1776); San Juan Capistrano (1776); Santa Clara (1777); San Buenaventura [Ventura] (1782); Santa Barbara (1786); Purisima (1787); Santa Cruz (1791); Soledad (1791); San José (1797) San Juan Bautista (1797); San Miguel (1797); San Fernando (1797); San Luis Rey (1798); Santa Ines [Inez] (1804); San Rafael (1817); Solano (1823).

Fr. Serra oversaw the founding of nine missions located between San Diego and San Francisco. Twelve more were founded after his death in 1784. These missions, all but one of which survive in some form, established the nucleus for later European settlement, and thus of Anglo California.

FIG. 771 **French City Planning** Similar in its orthogonal plan to Laws-of-the-Indies settlements, New Orleans developed around a parade ground, now Jackson Square. Also in line with to Spanish planning conventions, landmarks of Church and State overlook this central space.

FIG. 772 **English Planning** The Spanish organized around plazas, French New Orleans around a parade ground. By the mid-1600s, Renaissance sensibilities had strengthened in England as well. New Haven was laid out in an array of nine large-scale "squares," in a three-by-three layout, the central one reserved as common land. After some early vicissitudes and name changes, this common open space emerged in the early 1800s as the city's Green. The half of the Green shown here is the setting for a line of three churches, a unique arrangement in the United States. The remaining half (to the right of this view) includes no buildings. Yale University structures occupy the upper left in this view.

FRENCH SETTLEMENTS

Nouvelle Orléans FIG. 771
1721
LeBlond de la Tour, Adrien de Pauger engineers and planners
Vieux Carré, New Orleans, Louisiana

New Orleans was founded in 1718 by Jean-Baptiste Le Moyne, Sieur de Bienville. Formal development began three years later, after a basic town plan had been devised.

The original city core, now the Vieux Carré, or French Quarter, was laid out in a regular gridiron pattern. Just as Spanish New World settlements were organized around a central plaza, Nouvelle Orléans was oriented to a *Place d'Armes*, now Jackson Square (Fig. 771), around which were located a church, school, and the governor's administration building.

ENGLISH SETTLEMENTS

Early in their development, cities like Boston and New York seemed as formless and haphazard as medieval English towns. Such first impressions could be deceiving. Richard Bushman noted that strong ideas usually informed the siting and organization of these seemingly unplanned towns. Boston, for instance, was sited on its peninsula to take advantage of the surrounding water for defense.

Like their models in England, English colonial towns in America were often organized around a central market square, although that noun need not be understood to connote geometric regularity. Topography usually ensured that initial settlement layouts were seldom exactly straight, much less perfectly orthogonal, in plan. But by the mid-1600s a new class

of Renaissance-inspired planned towns began to appear in the English colonies. The city plans of these towns were based on an orthogonal grid which was individual both in pattern and in actual experience.

Jamestown, Virginia
1607–1619 ff; reconstructed, 1957 ff.
5 mi. SW of Williamsburg, Virginia

Jamestown was the earliest English settlement in the United States. Its straightforward layout was defined by a functional palisade enclosing wood-framed structures enclosed by wattle-and-daub walls and thatched roofs.

New Haven, Connecticut FIG. 772
1641
John Brockett, town planner

As opposed to the earlier utilitarian layout of Jamestown, for instance, some English colonial towns were laid out with strict geometries around focal spaces: public commons. The nine-square grid for New Haven was developed around an unusually spacious central square, a public common called the Green since the early 1800s. Today, three widely-spaced Protestant churches occupy sites on this Green, a singular architectural-spatial setting in the United States.

Charleston, South Carolina FIGS. 773, 774
1672; original plan expanded, 1739
John Yeamans, governor-founder

The original plan laid out an orthogonal grid within a fortified perimeter (Fig. 774). Two major cross streets served as the basis for later extensions of this grid. John Reps commented that compared to the sophisticated plan geometries of New Haven and Philadelphia, Charleston's was nothing special. Nonetheless, a handsome riverside promenade, the Battery (Fig. 773), eventually emerged from this layout.

Philadelphia, Pennsylvania FIG. 775
1682
Thomas Holme, Surveyor General of Pennsylvania and **William Penn**, planners
Center City

The omnipresent influence of Vitruvius is evident in this balanced grid. The plan is organized into four quadrants by north-south (Broad Street) and east-west (Market Street) axes, which intersect at a central square, the site of City Hall. Blocks on either side of Market Street are twice as deep as other Center City blocks. Each

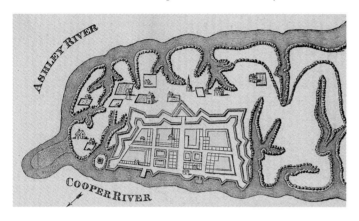

FIGS. 773, 774 Pragmatic Evolution Charleston began as a fort (Fig. 774), which was gradually overbuilt when residential areas grew outward from a main corner at Meeting and Broad streets, marked today by St. Michael's Church (see Southern Colonial Architecture chapter). Along the east and south edges of the old fortifications, the Battery district evolved into an exclusive enclave of distinctive homes (Fig. 773). *Fig. 774: University of Texas Libraries*

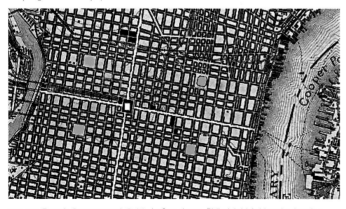

FIG. 775 Penn's Syncopated Grid At first glance, Philadelphia's historic city plan (represented here in its 1898 state) seems to be a simple diagram: two axial streets cross at City Hall; the resulting four quadrants each focus on a green square. A closer look reveals intricate variations in the street grid which provide a wide range of block sizes, thus broad flexibility in uses. *Joyce Martinson after University of Texas Libraries*

quadrant focuses on a smaller, centrally located square; blocks aligned with these squares are half-again longer, north-to-south, than are other blocks. This subtle syncopation provides a variety of block sizes and shapes—development flexibility—while maintaining the overall sense of geometric order implied by an orthogonal grid.

Annapolis, Maryland FIGS. 776, 777
1694–1695
Francis Nicholson, town planner; **Richard Beard**, surveyor

Governor Nicholson's unique, humanely scaled town-plan pattern was organized around two circles which establish prominent settings for the State House-Capitol (Fig. 777) and for the church. Radial streets extend outward from the circles, engaging an irregular rectilinear street grid. Some features of Nicholson's plan, notably his Bloomsbury Square, were not accomplished. See John W. Reps, The Making of Urban America, 1965, pp. 103–108, for more details and insights.

Williamsburg, Virginia FIGS. 778, 779
1699, plan; reconstruction, 1927–1934
Francis Nicholson, town planner; **Theodorick Bland**, surveyor; **Perry, Shaw & Hepburn**, restoration architects; **Arthur Shurcliff**, restoration landscape architect and planner
SW of I-64, between Richmond and Hampton Roads, Virginia

Following his intricate, small-scaled plan for Annapolis, Governor Nicholson totally switched course—after an initial plan characterized by fussy geometrics reminiscent of Annapolis was rejected—and devised a town plan for Williamsburg characterized by monumental simplicity (Fig. 779).

Nicholson's Williamsburg was organized along the expansive, 99-foot-wide Duke of Gloucester Street (Fig. 778), which is nearly a mile long. Grand vistas created by this immense linear space are visually terminated at one end by the Capitol and at the other by the College of William and Mary, which pre-existed, and thus anchored Nicholson's plan (see Southern Colonial Architecture chapter). A cross axis marked by Bruton Parish Church connects Duke of GloucesteStreet to the Governor's Palace. G. E. Kidder Smith noted that this monumental, off-center T-plan anticipated L' Enfant's 1791 conceptually similar plan for Washington, D.C., by nearly a century (see The Mall chapter). For more on Williamburg's plan, see John W. Reps, *The Making of Urban America*, 1965, pp. 108-114.

The 130-acre historic core of Colonial Williamsburg was restored-reconstructed after 1927, and is additionally significant as an American Colonial Revivial landmark in its own right (see the Garden Restorations chapter).

Savannah, Georgia FIGS. 780, 764, 765
1733
James Oglethorpe, town planner
S of the Riverfront

Governor Oglethorpe's exceptionally inventive town plan employed an easily expandable grid of 24 wards, each focused on a public square. Elizabeth Barlow Rogers noted that Oglethorpe followed contemporary private development practice in Georgian London, where it was common to organize plots of speculative housing around a public square.

While this scheme may appear at first glance to be repetitive, the inevitable succession of subtle and not-so-subtle refinements which continuously occur during development assured visual diver-

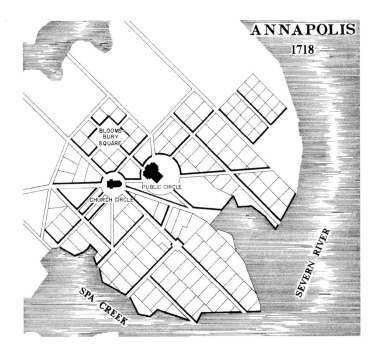

ANNAPOLIS
1718

BLOOMS-
BURY
SQUARE

PUBLIC CIRCLE

CHURCH CIRCLE

SEVERN RIVER

SPA CREEK

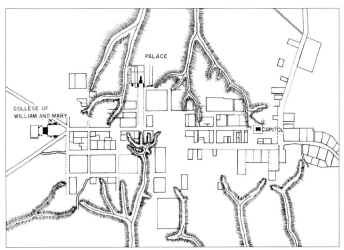

PALACE

COLLEGE OF
WILLIAM AND MARY

CAPITOL

FIGS. 778, 779 Essential Monumentality Governor Nicholson reprised his Annapolis planning achievement with a town plan for his next posting at another colonial capital, Williamsburg. This layout was monumental in the extreme, a complete reversal of Nicholson's Annapolis concept: Williamsburg's principal street extends for nearly a mile, with the Capitol at one end, facing the College of William and Mary (Fig. 61) at the other. Despite heroic vistas which even today seem immense (Fig. 778), here, too, as at Annapolis, the townscape's fine grain maintains an appealing human scale. *Fig. 779: Library of Congress, Prints & Photographs, Historic American Buildings Survey*

FIGS. 776, 777 Humane Urbanity On paper, Governor Nicholson's Annapolis plan might seem a barely harmonized assortment of precincts, squares, geometrics, and axiality (Fig. 776). Quite to the contrary as experienced, however. The circles anchor the townscape with prominent settings for God and State (Fig. 777 shows the State House-Capitol, located on the Public Circle in the plan), while the plan's promiscuous layout offers varied sites for landmark buildings, in the process establishing marvelous human scale and visual interest. *Library of Congress, Prints & Photographs, Historic American Buildings Survey*

sity. Indeed, as Oglethorpe's wards filled out over well more than a century, each square and its surrounding ward took on a distinct visual personality. Some of the wards attracted landmark public and private structures. Together with their human-scale plats, many of these have matured into marvelous civic settings.

But wait. There is more! From a functional perspective, Oglethorpe was either prescient or inspired, probably both. While he surely didn't visualize a Savannah of 130,000 residents when cutting into what was then remote wilderness, and he certainly didn't imagine automobiles, his syncopated street grid provides intrinsic "traffic calming" by today's engineering standards. Through streets alternate with squares, providing efficient movement along what have become commercial ways while preserving residential character on streets connecting with squares, where vehicular traffic must slow down nearly to walking speed in order to navigate the narrow roadways around the squares.

Whether you assess city plans simply on the basis of their grid patterns, as three-dimensional civic environments, or from the technical perspective of modern traffic engineering, you are likely to agree that Oglethorpe's 1733 scheme was a brilliant town plan.

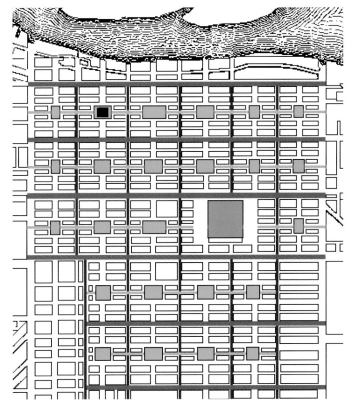

FIG. 780 Diagrammatic Clarity Few American town plans are as easy to comprehend, yet so replete with brilliant subtleties, as Savannah's. *Joyce Martinson*

The Mall

1791–2004

The National Mall, or simply *the Mall*, is an environment without equal in America. Rarely has a truly epic visionary plan been substantially accomplished in the United States, and never at such scale and with such monumental grandeur.

The United States of 1791 was but a fledgling nation, more of an ideal than a functioning state. So the initial, 1791 concept for a monumental federal city focused on an immense, formal public space, the future National Mall, was either foolhardy or astonishingly prescient. Initially slow to attract residents, and

FIGS. 781, 782 Uncommon Grandeur The National Mall in Washington, D.C. is *the* American public space. As a monumental physical-cultural setting, it is without equal in the United States. Today's Mall generally follows the original 1791 axial planning concept of French military engineer, Pierre Charles L'Enfant. Even so, after less than a century of development, L'Enfant's signature axial space had been lost. While axiality was gradually re-emphasized after 1902, in ways subtle and not, the Mall evolved over the twentieth century into a far grander environment then was imagined at its inception. These views are taken from atop the Washington Monument look east toward the Capitol (Fig. 781) and west toward the Lincoln Memorial (Fig. 782) *Library of Congress, Prints & Photographs, Historic American Buildings Survey*

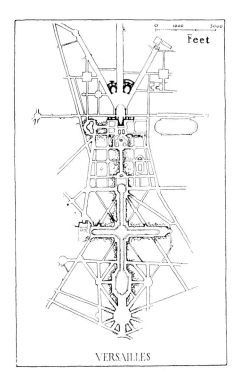

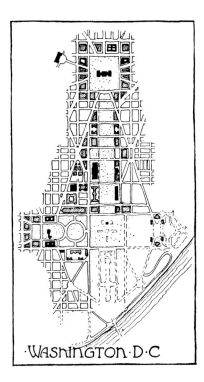

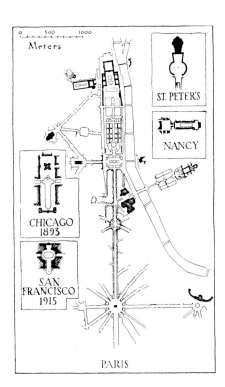

FIG. 783 Monumental Space The National Mall compared with Versailles and the *Louvre-Place de l'Étoile* axis in Paris as monumental spaces. Since the 1920 plan shown here, the Mall has been extended west (down in this drawing) roughly following the dashed lines. *Werner Hegemann and Elbert Peets, Civic Art, 1922*

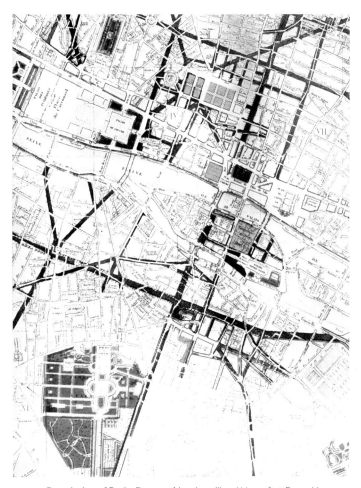

FIG. 784 Reordering of Paris Emperor Napoleon III and his prefect, Baron Hauss-mann, transformed central Paris between 1853 and 1870. Radical modernizing continued on for another generation after the Second Empire was toppled in 1870. New axial boulevards under construction in 1867 are depicted in this drawing. In sharp contrast, the National Mall is the product of numberless interventions over more than two centuries of changing design and planning fashions. *Werner Hegemann and Elbert Peets, Civic Art, 1922*

FIG. 785 Midwestern Monumentality The other great American public mall, Gateway Mall in St. Louis, is much less imposing in scale than is the National Mall.

thus buildings to fill in its vast framework, Washington remained for years "the city of infinite distances."

As a mature axial cityscape, only central Paris is comparable to Washington, D.C (Fig. 783). Yet the great axial boulevards of Paris were set in place during a mere two decades in the mid-1800s, under the powers and direction of a single emperor (Fig. 784). By contrast, the District of Columbia has developed over two centuries, during more than 40 presidencies and 100 congresses. The Mall evolved though numerous changes in design fashion.

In its physical length, Gateway Mall in St. Louis (Figs. 785, 851) is approximately comparable to the National Mall. However, Gateway Mall has always been tightly constrained by the close-grained downtown St. Louis street grid, with neither the potentials nor the pitfalls inherent in the immense land area of the National Mall.

Because the Mall functions as a formal national environment, it has been carefully shaped over the past century by the U.S. Commission of Fine Arts, which must both protect and enhance the Mall. This dual role requires unerring political sensitivity, high conceptual skills, attention to details, and, quite often, infinite patience. Given all this, the Mall is nothing less than a supreme national design achievement.

This chapter provides a synopsis of major planning episodes in the Mall's evolution.

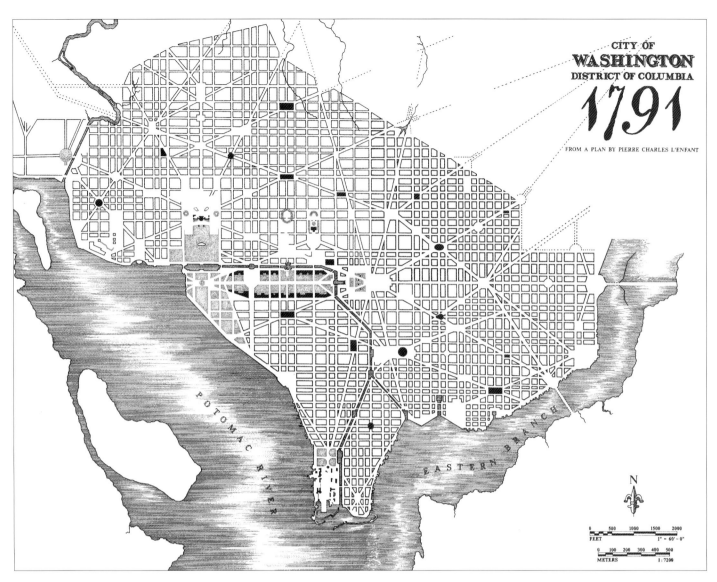

FIG. 786 1791 **L'Enfant Plan** The initial basis for the National Mall. *Library of Congress, Prints & Photographs, Historic American Buildings Survey*

FIG. 787 1815 **Latrobe Scheme** Benjamin Henry Latrobe, the consummate Neo-classicist architect dabbled, unconvincingly, in a naturalistic landscape vocabulary for this proposal, which fortunately was not adopted. The darkened band marks the rise of Capitol Hill. *Library of Congress, Prints & Photographs*

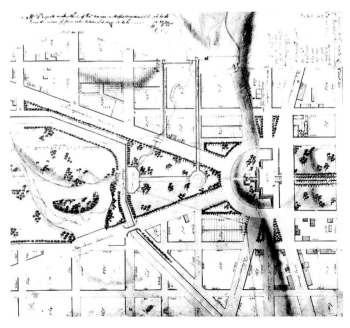

L'Enfant Plan FIG. 786

1791

Pierre Charles L'Enfant, conceptual planner; **Andrew Ellicott**, surveyor-delineator

L'Enfant's concept for the new federal city had to address several important requirements if it was to be fully successful. These included: establishing a unique sense of place through a planning-design aesthetic that would render Washington as a singular national setting; creating an overall perception of order that symbolically reflected the constitutional balance of power between the Presidency and Congress; incorporating existing features as prominent sites for major buildings; and reflecting contemporary Enlightenment thought about Modernity. L'Enfant's planning concept effectively addressed all of these issues.

According to Andro Linklater, L'Enfant was inspired by André Le Nôtre's highly ordered 1663 plan for the gardens at Versailles (Fig. 783), which featured a "goose-foot" pattern of focal points connected by radiating carriageways. Despite its complexity, L'Enfant's monumental grid solution was easy to appreciate in concept: major locations were interconnected by monumental diagonal avenues. A formal space—the Mall—extending from Congress intersected with another formal space extending from the President's house. All was set within an orthogonal framework.

The 1791 plan (Fig. 786), which was fleshed out by Ellicott from a sketch by L'Enfant, was thoroughly nuanced. Subtleties included a syncopated rhythm to city blocks, with several virtues: a hierarchy

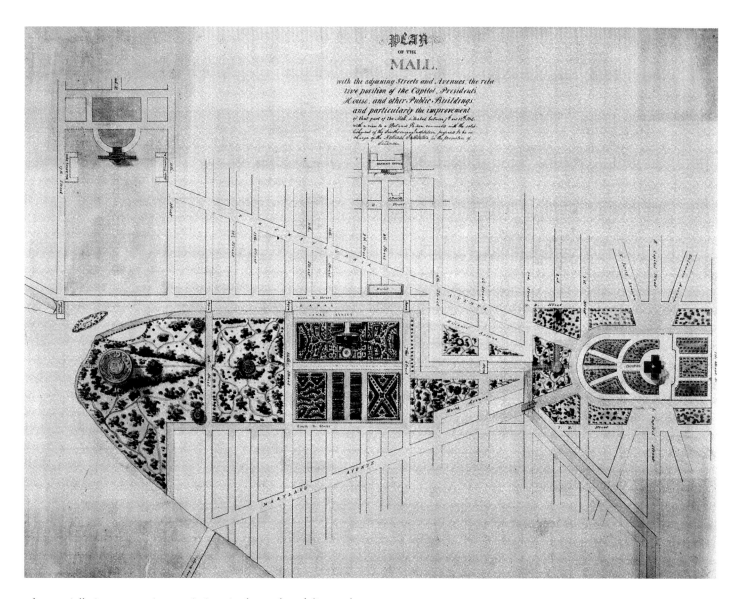

FIG. 788 Mills Plan In this 1841 scheme, Robert Mills retained overall axial alignments while in effecting proposing to turn the Mall into a huge romantic parterre. *National Archives*

of potentially important sites; variations in the angles of diagonals, which enlivened the sequences of movement; and an assortment of odd-shaped parcels, which could add visual interest if creatively developed . All of these provided both functional flexibility and also an experiential balance to the inherent rigidity of a grid layout.

Ellicott Revisions
1792
Andrew Ellicott, Benjamin Banneker, surveyors

Editing of L'Enfant's 1791 conceptual plan began almost immediately. Ellicott and Banneker were highly skilled surveyors – scientists, really – and they further developed the 1791 concepts, some of the changes they made requested by George Washington and Thomas Jefferson. Various engravings of subsequent plan revisions were developed during the 1790s. These retained L'Enfant's overall idea of monumental spaces connected by ceremonial diagonals and the Mall as a large open space, extending westward to the river near 17th Street.

Latrobe Scheme FIG. 787
1815
Benjamin Henry Latrobe, architect-engineer-planner

Reflecting radical changes in aesthetic fashion with the emergence of Romanticism, Latrobe proposed a picturesque landscape scheme for the western forecourt to the Capitol. But his consummate skill

FIG. 788 Mills Plan In this 1841 scheme, Robert Mills retained overall axial alignments while in effecting proposing to turn the Mall into a huge romantic parterre. *National Archives*

as a designer of structures apparently did not extend to landscape planning. His design ignored the formality of L'Enfant's grid, yet did not develop a compensating naturalistic environment approaching the quality of contemporary English landscape design.

Bulfinch Scheme
1822
Charles Bulfinch, architect-planner

Another landscape proposal by another architectural luminary, even less creative than Latrobe's.

Mills Plan FIG. 788
1841
Robert Mills, architect-planner

Mills had been working on Mall schemes for a decade when he was hired to design a building for the new Smithsonian Institution. By this time, Romanticism fully colored the nation's design aesthetic and, unsurprisingly, Mills developed a pleasure-garden Mall plan, for an area that extended all the way from the East Capitol grounds to the Potomac River, which then flowed past 17th Street at the Mall axis.

FIGS. 789, 790 1851 Downing Plan Andrew Jackson Downing's naturalistic plan (the drawing, Fig. 789, is oriented with south to the top, the Capitol is just off the left edge) was far superior as a design to the Latrobe, Bulfinch, and Mills schemes. In minimizing L'Enfant's axiality, Downing moved the Mall in a much different stylistic-environmental direction, as can be seen in this 1871 view (Fig. 790). Note that the not-yet-completed Washington Monument was located well off L'Enfant's original axis, which was shifted to accommodate the monument's placement in the 1901–1902 McMillan Plan. *Fig. 789: National Archives; Fig. 790: Library of Congress, Prints & Photographs*

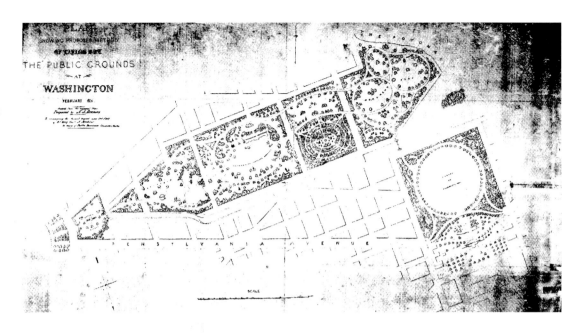

Downing Plan FIGS. 789, 790
1851
Andrew Jackson Downing, "landscape gardener"

Like Mills, Downing employed a current naturalistic landscape imagery for his plan. However, Downing's 1851 plan differed in two significant respects. For one thing, Downing was the leading national figure in landscape architecture, so the design quality of his plan was far superior to previous schemes.

Also, an informed cultural leadership had evolved in the United States, to the point that it was now politically possible, indeed desirable, to improve the Mall for aesthetic purposes, to beautify and to adorn. Downing's picturesque landscape imagery was made up of dense, informal clumps of trees and serpentine walkways, creating "pleasure grounds." This direction, of course, essentially negated L'Enfant's formal order and neoclassic axiality (Fig. 790).

1901-1902 Senate Park Commission "McMillan" Plan
FIGS. 791, 792
James McMillan, Senate sponsor; **Daniel Burnham, Charles McKim, Frederick Law Olmsted, Jr.**, planners; **Augustus Saint-Gaudens**, sculptor; **Charles Moore**, administrator

Due to Romanticism in general, and specifically to the influence of Downing's appealing informality, the essence of L'Enfant's

1791 formal mall space had been lost by the early 1900s. Because of poor soils, Washington's monument had been located off-axis (see Civic Design chapter). Numerous buildings had been constructed right on the Mall itself. Downing-inspired romantic landscapes occupied much of the Mall's remaining open space.

In a visionary undertaking as impressive politically as for its design, the 1901–1902 plan reestablished the Mall as a formal space, indeed, as some said, an imperial space, reflecting the recent American acquisition of Spain's global colonies.

Among its major features, the McMillan Plan slightly realigned the Mall's long axis in order to place the Washington Monument in line with the Capitol and the eventual site of the Lincoln Memorial. To provide a memorial building site, Potomac marshlands were to be filled to extend the Mall all the way to its eventual termination at 23rd Street (Fig. 791).

As part of the landfill process, the Tidal Basin area was to be improved, providing a (future) site for the Jefferson Memorial. The reestablished National Mall was to be lined with Classicist government buildings; a new union train depot was located just north of the Capitol (see Transportation chapter); and several ceremonial avenues, notably Pennsylvania, were widened.

At first glace, this all seemed to be a restatement of L'Enfant's 1791 plan. However, the McMillan Plan is much more a true embodiment of the City Beautiful era than it was a restoration of L'Enfant's Neoclassical sensibilities. Although L'Enfant certainly provided the essential direction for the Mall through his 1791 plan, the Mall as we experience it today owes more to the McMillan Plan than to any other influence.

U.S. Commission of Fine Arts
1910–

The Commission was established by President Taft, charged, among other duties, with protecting monumental Washington, beginning with a decade-long development of the Lincoln Memorial (Fig. 793). The Commission's first chairman was the architect Daniel Burnham, who naturally adopted the 1901–1902 McMillan Plan as the primary Commission benchmark. The Fine Arts Commission has been essential to the successful long-term development of a comprehensive vision of the Mall. Thomas Hines described the Commission as "virtually the executors of the Plan of 1901."

FIGS. 791, 792 McMillan Plan This pivotal plan (Fig. 791) by Daniel Burnham and his gifted colleagues reestablished the National Mall as a formal environment. It should be emphasized that this scheme was not simply a restatement of L'Enfant's original axial concept of a century earlier. Indeed, if the 1791 plan could be understood as ordered, the 1901–1902 concept can only be described as grand, bordering on imperial (Fig. 792). (See also Fig. 846.) *Fig. 791: U.S. Commission of Fine Arts; Fig. 792. Library of Congress, Prints & Photographs, Historic American Buildings Survey*

FIG. 793 The Fine Arts Commission Established within a decade after the McMillan Plan was issued, the U.S. Commission of Fine Arts has been at the center of the National Mall's development over the ensuing century. The Commission devoted ten years to detailed planning and design decisions for the Lincoln Memorial, here depicted in a watercolor from the McMillan Plan (for the memorial as built, see Fig. 795 and Civic Design chapter). *U.S. Commission of Fine Arts, Lee Stalworth photograph*

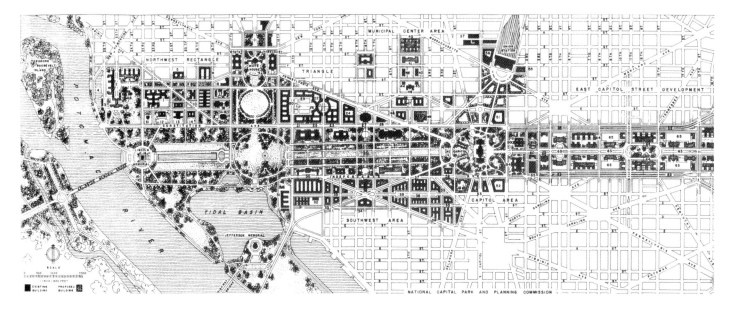

National Capital Park and Planning Commission Plan
1928
Frederick Law Olmsted, Jr., landscape architect; **Charles Eliot II**, commission director

More than a quarter-century of redevelopment was required before, as David Streatfield noted, "a landscape that bore any resemblance to that of the McMillan Plan" was evident. Frederick Law Olmsted, Jr., provided essential continuity over much of the pre–World War II period. Incremental improvements were apparent in the 1928 plan, especially refinements around the White House and Capitol Hill.

National Capital Park and Planning Commission Plan
FIGS. 794, 795
1941
Gilmore Clarke, planning consultant

Clarke's plan simplified the 1901–1902 McMillan Plan, notably the Western–Lincoln Memorial reflecting pool. The geometric formalism previously proposed for the area west of 16th Street was replaced by a forested landscape vocabulary (Fig. 795). That reflected Clarke's key conceptual refinement, that the western section of the Mall would be "distinctly different in character" from the eastern part.

Skidmore, Owings & Merrill Plan FIGS. 796, 797
1964–1965
Skidmore, Owings & Merrill, planners; **Dan Kiley**, landscape consultant

Wartime temporary buildings still occupied much of the western section of the Mall in the 1960; Clarke's 1941 "forest" had therefore not been planted. The 1965 plan reaffirmed the 1901–1902 McMillan Plan by way of simplification and abstraction (Fig. 796). Among the plan's major virtues was its restatement of the completed Mall, thus emphasizing the necessity of removing all of the temporary structures, a goal finally accomplished by 1969 (Fig. 797).

AN ONGOING LEGACY

Along with the planning briefly described above, the Mall has been further shaped by the construction of monuments, and by the occurrence of great social events such as Dr. Martin Luther King Jr.'s 1963 "I Have a Dream" speech (Fig. 798).

Major completed Mall monuments, from Washington to Vietnam, are cited in the Civic Design chapter. The Mall's development-evolution is ongoing. Reflecting its symbolic primacy in Washington, D.C., and the whole United States, the National Mall faces incessant pressure to accommodate additional monuments and memorials, despite being declared a "finished work of civic art" in 2001 by the National Capital Planning Commission.

With respect to location, proposals for national monuments in Washington, D.C., can be addressed in one of three ways. A proposed monument-memorial can be located on a District Site, remote from the National Mall, but still within the Federal City. Or a new monument-memorial may be placed on a

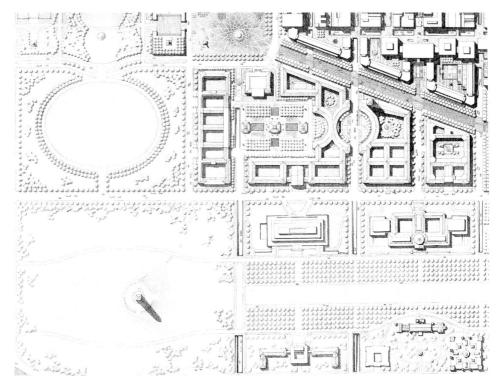

FIG. 796, 797 **Late Twentieth-century Mall Planning** A 1964–1965 Mall scheme grew out of SOM's 1964 Pennsylvania Avenue Plan. As can be seen in this detail (Fig. 796, with the Mall at bottom, the Ellipse and part of the White House lawn at the upper left), this new iteration of the National Mall emphasized simplification and linearity. As part of a 1981 Capitol master plan (Fig. 797), SOM's regimented 1964-1965 planting scheme was extended from just below the Capitol to 14th Street. Gilmore Clarke's 1941 forest concept within the western Mall precinct (Fig. 794) was modified along the Reflecting Pool by a continuation of the regimented planting scheme from the eastern precinct. *Architect of the Capitol*

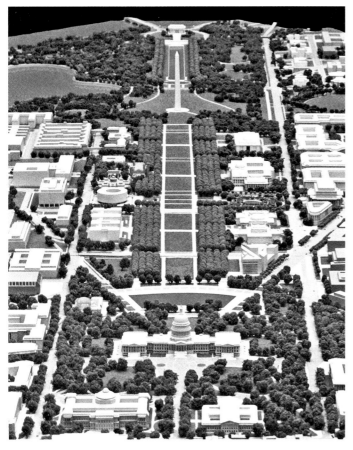

FIG. 798 **"I Have a Dream"** Dr. Martin Luther King's celebrated 1963 speech is the most famous in a succession of significant Mall events. *Library of Congress, Prints & Photographs*

Monumental Site, within the ceremonial district centered on the Mall; The United States Holocaust Memorial Museum (1987–1993, James Ingo Freed, Pei Cobb Freed, architects) is located just off the Mall at 100 Raoul Wallenberg Place SW. Or a proposed monument can be given a Mall Site, located directly on or enfronting the Mall; The National World War II Memorial (1998–2004, Friedrich St. Florian, Leo A Daly, Hartman Cox, architects; Oehme & van Sweden, landscape architects; Ray Kaskey, sculptor) is sited axially on the Mall, just below the

Washington Monument and east of the Reflecting Pool. In 2006, a prominent, cross-axis Mall site was selected for the National Museum of African-American History and Culture.

Brilliant creative contributions over more than two centuries have made the National Mall a singular American environment. Equally brilliant contributions will be required in the future to preserve that priceless legacy without compromising the Mall's unique role of reflecting the distinctive cultural perspective of successive generations of Americans.

National Expansion

1783–1959

FIG. 799 The Omnipresent U.S.G.S. Grid Chicago is an archetypical American city in many ways. It is certainly one of the best places to experience the national land survey (U.S.G.S.) grid which ordered national expansion across most of the trans-Appalachian United States. This view along Chicago's North Avenue illustrates one of the arrow-straight commercial streets that developed along the city's U.S.G.S. section boundaries.

The United States of America was tentatively established in 1783, and expanded in land area primarily through nineteenth-century acquisitions. The present constellation of 50 states dates from 1959, when Alaska and Hawaii were admitted to the Union.

This chapter picks up from the European New World Town Plans chapter. The distinction between the two eras is more than simply political. While both colonial and U.S. cities were developed from regular plan-street grids, the national land survey, later known as the U.S.G.S. grid (see Ordering the Land chapter), radically changed how American settlements were planned.

To generalize, colonial street-grid layouts were individualized for each town—and were usually informal. A few colonial-era town plans, like those for Philadelphia (Fig . 775) and Savannah (Fig. 780), were very sophisticated designs. Most others lacked planning distinction, laid out around local topography, following loosely applied conventions.

This improvised custom approach to laying out new towns completely turned around as the nation was surveyed ahead of settlement, west of the Appalachians. From the early 1800s onward, public lands were transferred into private ownership under the discipline of an endless repetitive grid of townships and sections.

That resulted in four common planning situations.

Where cities were laid out on essentially featureless land, as in Chicago, the plan-street grid easily and almost universally conformed to the underlying U.S.G.S. grid (Fig. 799).

In a second situation, the street grid was superimposed on extreme topographies *as if* they were featureless and flat. As a result, in hilly communities ranging in size from tiny Taylors Falls, Minnesota to San Francisco, the street grid was regular in its plat, and thus unavoidably discontinuous in reality, as street alignments were projected over precipitous drops (Fig. 800). Such breaks could create memorable visual settings.

In a common third situation, the initial town plat aligned with a dominant feature, typically a river, and then subsequent plats conformed to the U.S.G.S. grid. This was the condition in Minneapolis when the initial plat, now the downtown, aligned with the Mississippi River at St. Anthony Falls (the water-power potential of the falls being the reason for settlement at that location). As the settlement grew into a sizable town, new subdivisions were subsequently shifted to align with the U.S.G.S. grid.

The fourth plan-street grid situation was imposed by rail lines. Wherever possible, railroads followed the most direct route between major cities. Diagonal route alignments, as between St. Paul and Fargo, were common. In the 1800s, location on a major rail line was usually essential to a town's prosperity, so communities allowed railroads to do pretty much whatever they wished (Fig. 801). Rail lines frequently disregarded the town grid, even where, as at Columbus, Nebraska, only a slight shift in rail alignment would have been needed to accommodate the grid. Wherever a rail line preceded a settlement, the new town was almost always oriented to the rail line, as at Reno and Billings, whether or not that alignment had any relationship to the national grid.

Even though, because of topography, local features, or railroads, some trans-Appalachian cities did not follow the national grid, rectilinear ordering of the land was pervasive.

Cleveland, Ohio FIG. 802
1796
Seth Pease, Amos Spafford, surveyors
Lake Erie, along the Cuyahoga River

Moses Cleaveland [sic] was charged by the State of Connecticut to found a regional capital of its "Western Reserve." The present-day site of downtown Cleveland was chosen on the basis of its location on Lake Erie and easy communication inland (especially for regional-survey parties) afforded by a river. Initial municipal development was organized around a ten-acre public square, from which extended main streets 90 and 130 feet wide—Euclid Avenue is the latter. Public Square remains the symbolic focus of downtown Cleveland today.

Indianapolis, Indiana FIGS. 803, 804
1821
Alexander Ralston, town planner

Like Washington, D.C., where Ralston had worked with the estimable Andrew Ellicott as a surveyor (see The Mall chapter), Indianapolis was a capital city planned from scratch. Its location in the center of the state was emphasized in Ralston's plan by four diagonal roads which extended outward symbolically to the four corners of Indiana (Fig. 804).

The center of Ralston's mile-square street grid was marked by a circle, originally intended for the governor's house, and since

FIG. 800 **Nature Interruptus** Nature occasionally gets the better of the usually omnipotent national survey grid. Or at least gains a short standoff as here, looking south from Telegraph Hill in San Francisco, where the grid continues heedlessly onward, but the street cannot.

FIG. 801 **Rails Trump Grids** In the 1800s, railroads went pretty much wherever they wished, and the cities they traversed adjusted accordingly, even when such accommodations violated the national survey grid. In rail towns like Mandan, North Dakota, rail yards (Fig. 801) might constitute the community's major built feature. *Library of Congress, Prints & Photographs, Historic American Engineering Record*

FIG. 802 **Public Square** Expressions of public order were useful in attracting settlers to frontier townsites, since order connoted organization, thus implying future prosperity. Cleveland was laid out around its ten-acre Public Square (from the foreground to the monument in Fig. 802, plus two more squares to the north, off the left edge). Cleveland's signature street, Euclid Avenue, extends outward on a diagonal from the upper-right corner of the square.

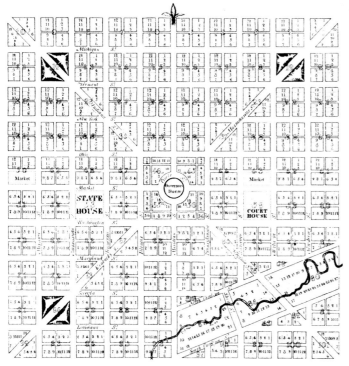

1902 site of the marvelously extravagant Soldiers and Sailors monument (Fig. 803). Two blocks to the west, a square was set aside for the state capitol, with a corresponding square two blocks to the east for the county court house. Following to the pattern of alternating civic and commercial streets like that of Savannah (see European New World Town Plans chapter), the main commercial street, eventually the route of the National Road (see the Roads chapter), ran parallel to the public-civic axis, a block to the south.

Geometric plan patterns were relatively common in the expanding United States. Judge Woodward's 1807 Detroit plan, for instance, street grid employed a cluster of circles with interlocking radial avenues. Ralston's Indianapolis plan was an especially pure expression of geometry, symmetrical about both its north-south and east-west axes.

Chicago, Illinois FIGS. 799, 805

1830

James Thompson, survey engineer

Section 9, Township 39, Range 14, Second Principal Meridian

Thompson was commissioned to lay out a town at the swampy lakehead of a proposed river-canal connecting Lake Michigan—and thus, via the Erie Canal, the Atlantic Ocean—to the Mississippi River. Section 9 would develop as Chicago's downtown core, the most significant square mile between the U.S. East and West Coasts. Thompson's town scheme was laid out with near-absolute regularity according to the U.S.G.S. national survey grid. That is why in Chicago eight long blocks or sixteen short blocks reliably add up to one mile.

Although it was not yet understood in 1830, the river-canal was destined to be obsolete even before its construction began. The first American railroad had opened the year before (see Public Engineering chapter), and by the time the Illinois & Michigan Canal was completed at mid-century railroads had overtaken waterways as the dominant form of long-distance transportation.

Nevertheless, the river-canal (Fig. 805) was immensely consequential to subsequent U.S. transportation routes. By virtue of its leading regional position as an existing water-transportation hub, Chicago's pivotal role was inevitably repeated when rail, highway, and air successively became dominant national transportation modes. As a transportation nexus, Chicago enjoyed an extraordinary commercial advantage over potential Midwestern rivals in everything from meat packing to finance. Chicago O'Hare is today North America's major mid-continent airport in good part because of the fleeting importance, nearly two centuries ago, of a small stream flowing through sparsely inhabited marshlands along the lower Great Lakes shoreline.

San Francisco, California FIGS. 800, 806

1845

Jasper O'Farrell, surveyor

FIG. 806 Unique Visual Tension San Francisco is a singular physical environment, its irregular, hilly terrain, water, and ever-shifting fog playing off dramatically against the city's often colorful buildings, which are sited along a mostly orthogonal street grid.

San Francisco was initially laid out on the basis of the Mexican *vara*: rod, approximately a yard. Among many ways in which San Francisco is unique among American cities is the powerful visual tension that occurred when an orthogonal survey-street grid was superimposed over the city's steeply pitched and varied terrain.

Los Angeles, California FIGS. 807, 808
1849; 1853

Edward Otho Cresap Ord, 1849 surveyor; **Henry Hancock**, 1853 surveyor

After the existing Spanish-Mexican settlement (Fig. 807) was occupied by the American military, signifying its status as a U.S. possession, local officials directed Ord to survey the immediate surroundings in preparation for disposing of municipal lands to private buyers. Ord laid out a regular street grid to the east and to the west of the existing Spanish townsite; neither pattern was aligned true north-south/east-west.

Hancock developed a superblock grid for a much larger regional area which *was* oriented to the compass points. However, it was not based on national land survey measures like the quarter, half, and full mile of 1,320, 2,640, and 5,280 feet. Instead, Hancock worked with governing dimensions of 1,235, 2,470, and 4,940 feet.

Like many American city plans, Hancock's survey grid was simply a starting point for Anglo real estate development. Its precepts were only casually followed in the ensuing decades, as subdivisions generally followed existing market roads and the historic layouts of farm tracts, patterns which can be observed today, slightly rationalized, in central Los Angeles (Fig. 808).

Figs. 807, 808 City of Dazzling Extremes Los Angeles has long bewildered its champions and detractors alike. Striking changes in the physical fabric occur throughout Los Angeles. As a result, the city encompasses an extreme range of physical environments. Up to World War II, much of Los Angeles' land area was still semi-rural in character, like the 1850 Casa Vejar in eastern L.A. County (Fig. 807), today encircled by freeways. Postwar growth has been centered around a dozen-and-a-half dense Southland "urban villages," including Downtown Los Angeles (Fig. 808). Fig. 807: Library of Congress, Prints & Photographs, Historic American Buildings Survey

FIGS. 809, 810 **Gritty City** Butte, Montana is a colorful mining town literally being consumed by its mines (Fig. 810). Parts of the city are visually wretched, though much too vivid to turn away from. *Fig. 810: Library of Congress, Prints & Photographs, Historic American Engineering Record*

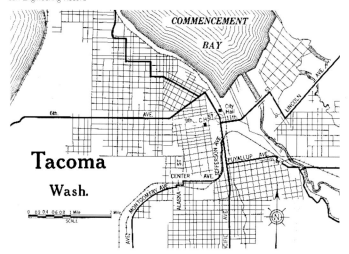

Butte, Montana FIGS. 809, 810
1867, townsite platted; booms in 1875–1879; 1890s; 1906
Historic center bounded by Copper, Arizona, Mercury, and Continental

Butte is one of the most colorful and gritty towns in the United States. It was a gold-prospecting settlement just after the Civil War, made up mostly of tents. Successive strikes of silver and copper led to growth booms.

Within a generation of its founding, Butte's population had exploded to 30,000, a full-fledged city with attractions ranging from a 2,200-seat vaudeville theater, to a prostitution district of "parlor houses." By 1906 Butte boasted an eight-story skyscraper designed by famed New York architect Cass Gilbert. Butte's "Zenith Age" continued until an economic decline following World War I.

Some visitors may find the close juxtaposition of mines and housing to be disconcerting (Fig. 810). In a Faustian arrangement, late-twentieth-century jobs were sustained when more efficient open pit mining was instituted, at the cost of swallowing up entire city neighborhoods.

Tacoma, Washington FIGS. 811, 812
1873
Frederick Law Olmsted, town planner

A fascinating "What-if?" Closely following his Riverside plan (see Community Development chapter) and his Buffalo Parkways planning (see Roads chapter), Olmsted was engaged to devise a city plan for Tacoma by the Northern Pacific Railroad, which had fixed on the location as its western terminus.

Considered purely as an abstract work of design, Olmsted's plan was certainly striking, featuring cascades of curvilinear terraces dropping down to the harbor (Fig. 812). But as John Reps pointed out, the plan lacked community focus or any suggestion of a downtown, did not even identify school sites, and offered only the barest accommodation of the railroad that was the *raison d'être* for the plan, a professional performance Reps understandably assessed as "incomprehensible." Moreover, the plan's intrinsic non-linearity rendered it unacceptable to local landowners who functioned as real-estate promoters. Tacoma actually developed around a grid layout dating from 1880 (Fig. 811).

FIGS. 811, 812 **Dreamscape and Reality** Tacoma developed around a conventional grid plan (Fig. 811). Frederick Law Olmsted's earlier terraced scheme, never adopted, was much more a work of art than it was a functional city plan (Fig. 812). *Fig. 811: University of Texas Libraries; Fig. 812: Tacoma Public Library*

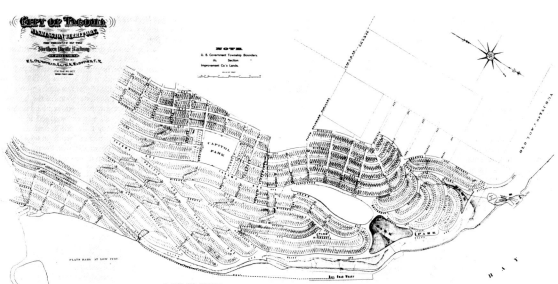

Community Development

1852–2004

FIG. 813 American Planned Communities Coral Gables was developed by George Merrick in suburban Miami after 1921. Characterized by appealing architectural imageries, visual cohesiveness, and lush landscapes (also, of course, by the subtropical South Florida climate), Coral Gables is one of the most distinctive American residential developments.

T he prominent real-estate undertakings in this chapter exemplify the most interesting of American planned developments. While each of these is distinct from the others, often in significant ways, they all share a single characteristic: each follows a visionary idea that was developed consistently, one which has resulted in a distinctive visual environment.

Llewellyn Park FIGS. 814, 815

1852–1858 ff.

Llewellyn S. Haskell, visionary-developer; **Alexander Jackson Davis**, planner and architect

Park Ave. at Main St., 0.5 mi. N of Northfield Ave. exit from WB I-280, West Orange, New Jersey (gated, limited access to visit the Edison mansion)

Llewellyn Park is generally considered to be America's first romantic, naturalistic subdivision. Haskell was influenced by the ideals and designs of landscape architect-theorist Andrew Jackson Downing, who died just as Llewellyn Park's development began. Haskell intended for his hillside community to function as a spiritual utopia, offering residents an elite retreat from the bustle of city life; Manhattan is only a dozen miles away.

Three planning concepts especially shaped Llewellyn Park: (1) part of the site was left romantically wild; (2) a 50-acre section called The Ramble was landscaped as common open space for use

FIGS. 814, 815 Romantic Utopia At Llewellyn Park, villas like the Edison mansion (Fig. 814) were widely spaced on ample lots (labeled PR on plan below) to maintain a sense of rural tranquility. The development was conceived as a haven from the workday rush of nearby Manhattan. Part of its extensive hillside property was left wild, another 50 acres landscaped as a common area, the Ramble. *Fig. 815: Sargent, 1859*

by residents (Fig. 815); and (3) villas were not allowed to visually overpower the landscape. Houses were widely spaced and fences prohibited, so structures appeared to float in nature (Fig. 814). More than a century-and-a-half later, these concepts are still visually effective.

Riverside FIGS. 816, 817

1868–1870 ff.

Olmsted, Vaux & Company, planners and designers
NW of Ogden/Hwy. 43 and Harlem Aves., Cook County, Illinois

In contrast to a beautiful existing setting at Llewellyn Park, here Frederick Law Olmsted and Calvert Vaux began with an unpromis-

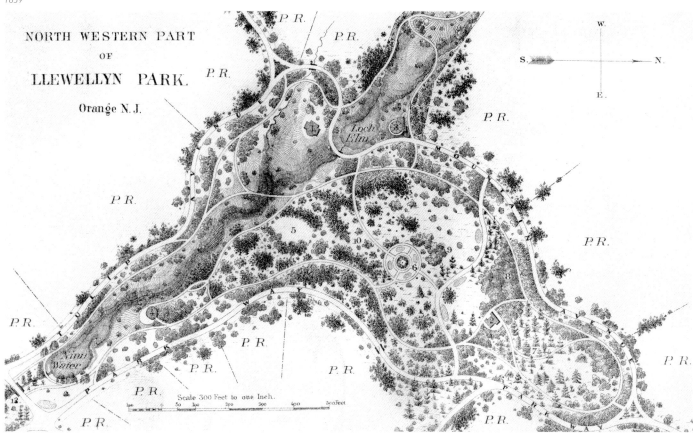

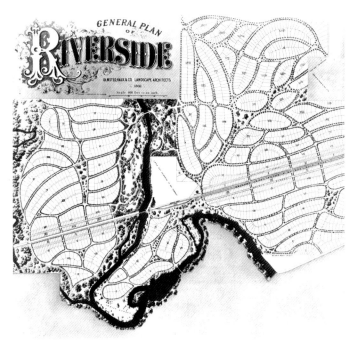

FIGS. 816, 817 *The* Naturalistic Suburb Frederick Law Olmsted and Calvert Vaux invented the naturalistic American suburb at Riverside. Their famous curvilinear community plan (Fig. 816) inspired countless later subdivisions, with curving streets and and uninterrupted flow of front lawns (Fig. 817). *Fig. 816: National Park Service, Frederick Law Olmsted National Historic Site*

ing, featureless site, notoriously, "low, flat, miry, and forlorn." Structure was established through the celebrated curvilinear street pattern (Fig. 816). More than just a design statement, Riverside provided the American model for countless subdivisions over the following century. Among Olmsted and Vaux's significant site-planning innovations was their concept of front yards as a "carpet of continuous green," in effect turning private property into linear community parklands (Fig. 817).

Tuxedo Park
1885 ff.
Pierre Lorillard, developer; **James Smith Haring, Ernest W. Bowditch**, planners; **Bruce Price**, architect
Orange County, New York, gated

This ultra-exclusive gated exurb of New York City owes much to the concepts of Downing and Olmsted. Like Llewellyn Park, Tuxedo Park was developed to enhance the natural beauty of its site. (The 7,000-acre original parcel has subsequently been reduced to about 2,000 acres.) Even more so than Llewellyn Park, Tuxedo Park is exceptionally picturesque, developed around three lakes. Unlike many subdivisions noted for their site planning or land-scapes, Tuxedo Park is also an architectural treasure trove, both its community facilities and its private mansions.

Shaker Heights FIG. 818
1905 ff.; transit line, 1916–1920; Shaker Square, 1929; Terminal Tower, 1930
Oris and Mantis Van Sweringen, developers; **William A. Pease**, planning engineer
Cuyahoga County, Ohio

"Shaker" was promoted as a model affluent suburb, leafy with gently curving streets along the lines of Riverside (opposite page), although it was also based on contemporary English Garden Cities/Suburbs. The developers even built a commuter railroad directly to downtown Cleveland. In the decade after the rail link opened in 1920, the population grew tenfold. A highly attractive ambiance has been maintained by deed restrictions and architectural guidelines.

Beverly Hills FIGS. 819, 820
1906 ff.
Wilbur Cook, Jr., planner and landscape architect; **Myron Hunt**, architect; **Olmsted & Olmsted**, landscape architects N of Sunset; **Raymond Page**, landscape architect for public landscapes
Triangle SE of Santa Monica and Wilshire Blvds.; N of Santa Monica Blvd. from Rodeo to Crescent Drives.; Lexington Rd. district N of Sunset Blvd., Los Angeles County, California

Cook's initial plan comprised only a fraction of the glittery city we now see, but included all three key environments: downtown; the gently curving, boulevarded residential blocks between Santa Monica and Sunset Boulevards; and the once semi-rural uphill slope north of Sunset.

Famous as the home of movie stars and of outrageously expensive clothing and accessories, Beverly Hills is significant as one of the first comprehensively planned communities in the LA Southland, according to Richard Longstreth. Beverly Hills was the first municipality in the region to apply commercial zoning. Neighborhoods are beautifully maintained, with block after block of impressive homes. Even so, in the studied assessment of Gebhard and Winter, ultimately, "it is the landscape architecture which makes the place."

Forest Hills Gardens FIGS. 821, 822

1909–1911 ff.

Robert de Forest, visionary for the Russell Sage Foundation; **Frederick Law Olmsted, Jr.**, planner and landscape architect; **Grosvenor Atterbury**, architect and planner

71st Ave. & Burns St., SW of Queens Blvd., Queens, New York

This 140-acre planned commuter suburb was inspired by the contemporary English Garden Cities movement. Robin Karson described Forest Hills as "distinguished by a parklike ambience, rich architectural detail, and sense of quality and permanence" (Fig. 821).

The development was undertaken by the Sage Foundation as a demonstration intended to both create a superior middle/upper-

FIGS. 821, 822 Suburban Urbanity Forest Hills Gardens provides a highly urbane residential environment, quite dense by American suburban norms.

FIG. 823 Midwestern Scale Compared to the near-contemporary Forest Hills Gardens (Fig. 821), Country Club's homesites are wildly oversized, reflecting relative land costs and, more significantly, major differences in lifestyles between New York City and Kansas City.

middle-income residential environment and to demonstrate how enlightened development could make a profit. By any measure, Forest Hills Gardens succeeded as a superior environment even if it did not break even as a real-estate investment. Sale of lots opened in 1911, and within three years more than 200 houses had been constructed, in addition to commercial and multi-unit buildings built by the developer (Fig. 822). In 1923, the foundation-developer transferred all common land and infrastructure to the property owners.

Rock Crest-Rock Glen

1911–1912 ff.

Walter Burley Griffin, Marion Mahony Griffin, planners

E. State St., Caroline, River Heights, and 1st St. S.E., Mason City, Iowa

This rugged and dramatic, though small-scale, subdivision around a rocky creek valley is the Prairie School version of the English picturesque—Humphrey Repton meets Frank Lloyd Wright. Houses encircle a wooded central open space, through which a bubbling creek flows (Regionalism chapter, Fig. 994). While the natural setting is featured, the subdivision is enhanced by houses designed by Griffin, Barry Byrne, Wright, and Curtis Besinger.

Country Club FIG. 823

1907 ff.; Country Club Plaza, 1922–1925

J. C. Nichols, developer; **Hare & Hare**, area site planners; **Edward Buehler Delk**, architect of Plaza; **Edward W. Tanner**, prewar housing architect

W city limits S of and around Ward Pkwy., Kansas City, Missouri

An initial 10-acre parcel was gradually expanded to more than 4,000 acres, and effectively into adjacent Kansas. The well-known Country Club Plaza shopping center (see Retail and Hotels chapter) establishes a strong architectural focus in Spanish Colonial Revival style. Country Club's northerly, pre–World War II residential sections contain hundreds of handsome Period Revival houses (Fig. 823).

Palos Verdes Estates/Rolling Hills

1914; master plan, 1921–1924; development of Rolling Hills, 1934 ff.

Frank Vanderlip, founder; **Olmsted and Olmsted, Charles H. Cheney**, planners; **Howard van Doren Shaw, Myron Hunt**, architects; **A. E. Hanson**, development manager

SW peninsula of Los Angeles County, California

This hilly, 16,000-acre tract was originally intended to be developed into large estates as a "Millionaire's Colony," but that elite aspiration was rendered inoperative by World War I. Development restarted in the 1920s as a "pared-down version of the original scheme," in the words of Gebhard and Winter, though still intended exclusively for high-income residents.

Although it was never accomplished on the scale of its initial plans, Palos Verdes (so named in 1932) is significant in several respects: the establishment of a required imagery, a picturesque interpretation of Mediterranean; an "art jury" to review all architectural designs; and the notion of a "guaranteed neighborhood," forever protected from encroachment by commerce and unnecessary outsiders.

Rolling Hills is located on the northerly part of the property and was developed into mini-dude ranches. Its required architectural imagery is rooted in the California board-and-batten ranch house, which evolved into a genteel, faux-rural, Western look.

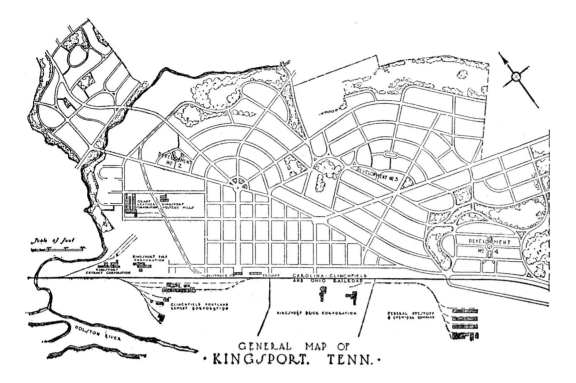

GENERAL MAP OF
· KINGSPORT. TENN. ·

FIG. 824 The Irresistible Fan Plan
John Nolen's fan-shaped street pattern for Kingsport is a favored reference for latter-day new-urbanist designers. *John Nolen*, New Towns for Old, *1927*

FIGS. 825, 826, 827 Reinventing Suburbia Radburn offered a radical planning approach for the auto age: separation of pedestrians from vehicles. Houses face landscaped courts (Fig. 825), which connect to a central green space (Fig. 826); cars are restricted to service alleys behind houses (Fig. 827), and to a few roads necessary for access and circulation.

Kingsport FIG. 824

1915–1917 ff.

John Nolen, town planner

80 mi. NE of Knoxville, Tennessee

Kingsport is probably the best known of Nolen's town plans. Its fan-shaped street grid was appropriated as a favorite motif of 1990s New Urbanists in the plans of Seaside and Celebration (Resorts chapter and later in this chapter).

Kingsport was a landmark in modern American city planning, the first opportunity for Nolen, the leading planner of his era, to devise an "ideal community pattern." Although others subsequently interpreted Nolen's plan as the community was built out, the essence of his plan was accomplished.

Other classic community plans by Nolen include Mariemont, Ohio (1921–1923) and Venice, Florida (1925).

Radburn FIGS. 825, 826, 827

1928–1931

Clarence Stein, Henry Wright Jr., Lewis Mumford, planners; **Marjorie Sewell Cautley**, landscape architect

N of Fair Lawn Ave. between Radburn and Plaza Rds., Fair Lawn, New Jersey

Of the planned community for 25,000 residents, two superblock neighborhoods housing about 1,000 were completed before development was halted by the Great Depression. Radburn was intended as, and achieved, nothing less than a comprehensive reinvention of the traditional American town in response to the automobile. Hence, the separation of pedestrians from vehicular traffic is the signature concept of Radburn's plan. Cars are parked off small service-access drives (Fig. 827), which are directly accessible to kitchens of single-family houses.

Living spaces of houses turn inward, toward linear landscaped courts (Fig. 825) leading to a central green space that provides a neighborhood focus (Fig. 826). All of this tends to give Radburn "something of the look of a secluded English village," in the words of Mumford's biographer, Donald Miller.

Architectural pretense was underplayed as community landscapes assumed prominence in establishing a singular sense of

FIG. 828 **An Island of Serenity** Superblocks—the closing of streets to make spacious, car-free parcels—was a planning concept that promised more than was usually achieved. The planners of Baldwin Hills Village beat those odds on account of the development's human scale, functional efficiency—including unobtrusive provisions for cars—and a flowing hierarchy of landscaped spaces.

FIGS. 829, 830 **Modest Dignity** Greendale new town was a federal experiment in low-cost family housing. Typically, satisfying this worthy goal has resulted in a mediocre physical environment; the standard excuse is that there wasn't enough money to do something good. By contrast, through skillful employment of efficient planning gestures, primarily in siting and landscaping, Greendale not only provided the requisite budget housing, but also a genuine town center (Fig. 829) along with pleasant neighborhoods (Fig. 830).

place. What seem at first glance to be Period Revival architectural imageries turn out to be no more than efficient gestures of texture and color—noteworthy design achievements in themselves. Mumford felt that Radburn's success was primarily due to its environmental cohesiveness and human scale.

Baldwin Hills Village FIG. 828
1938–1942
Robert Alexander, Clarence Stein, consultant site planners; **Fred Barlow, Fred Edmunson**, landscape architects; **Reginald Johnson, Wilson & Merrill**, architects
5300 Rodeo Rd./Hauser Blvd./Coliseum St./ Sycamore Ave., Los Angeles, California

Baldwin Hills Village is consistently cited as one of the best modern U.S. housing developments. Its planners thought of Baldwin Hills more as a neighborhood than as a formal design expression. The site was developed as a single superblock, with an intricate pattern of two-story apartment blocks oriented to a spatially flowing internal village green.

This green is the largest in a hierarchy of spaces. It interconnects with distinctive smaller spaces: clusters of a half-dozen apartment blocks each define smaller neighbor areas (Fig. 828); private space is provided for each unit between sidewalk and door. In this way, the plan provides open spaces ranging in scale from community to neighborhood to personal. Baldwin Hills' architecture is deliberately understated and well-maintained. The entire development is visually tied together by extensive landscaping.

Greendale FIGS. 829, 830
1935–1938; expanded, 1950
Elbert Peets, Jacob Crane, planners; **Harry H. Bentley**, architect of houses; **Walter G. Thomas**, architect of public buildings
W of Hwy. 36, 5 mi. W of Mitchell Airport, Milwaukee County, Wisconsin

Educated as a landscape architect, Peets is probably best remembered as co-author of the monumental 1922 book, *Civic Art*. He was an accomplished city planner and teacher and served on the U.S. Commission of Fine Arts. Greendale was the best-designed of the three New Deal Greenbelt towns, in the studied assessment of architect-planner Paul Spreiregen. Peets based his design on a T-plan (Fig. 829) with a pleasantly irregular street grid which departed just enough from a rigid orientation to avoid monotony, but not so much as to be too expensive (Fig. 830). As a result, this modest-income settlement established a distinct sense of identity.

The large new town of Park Forest (1946-1947), south of Chicago, was also planned by Peets.

DEVELOPMENTS AFTER WORLD WAR II

The early postwar years were marked by innovations in numerous aspects of American life, including housing and community development. Among thousands of postwar developers and subdivisions, the following four entries are especially instructive for appreciating the wide range of housing innovations underway across the United States by the 1950s.

Parkwyn Village is a small custom-home neighborhood, based on organic planning and design, buttressed by Frank Lloyd Wright's Broadacre City insights. At the other extreme, in the Levitt developments thousands of straightforward, mass-

produced homes were built at a time. These were architecturally undistinguished but provided affordable new housing for families eager for their own home.

Joseph Eichler occupied a niche that was closer to Wright than to Levitt. He developed mass-produced *designed* houses, much more expensive than those built at Levittown, with a range of modern architectural personalities responsive to informal family lifestyles, especially in California. Arapahoe Acres illustrates a superior builder's subdivision, with emphasis on the whole as much as on individual structures.

Parkwyn Village FIG. 831
1947 ff.
Frank Lloyd Wright, site planner and architect
Taliesin Drive, N of I-94, W of Oakland Dr., S of Winchell, Kalamazoo, Michigan

This modest-sized subdivision is a rare realized demonstration of Wright's suburban development ideas coming out of his visionary 1930s Broadacre City (see Frank Lloyd Wright chapter). Forty lots on a 47-acre parcel were laid out around an encircling road. On four of them, at 2662, 2806, 2816, and 2822 Taliesin Dr., were Usonian houses built to Wright's designs. By now, the subdivision's site landscaping has matured to lushness, by Midwestern standards at least, with many of the homes barely visible from the street (Fig. 831).

The nearby Galesburg Country Homes subdivision in exurban Galesburg includes four more Wright houses, at 11036, 11098, 11108, and 11185 Hawthorne Dr.

Levittown FIGS. 832, 833
1947–1950
William Levitt, developer; **Alfred Levitt**, physical planner-housing designer
Nassau County, Long Island, New York

Virtually everyone interested in American housing has heard about Levittown. As post–World War II housing shortages intensified after troops returned from overseas, the family-owned Levitt development company adopted innovative assembly-line efficiencies devised during the war to mass-produce inexpensive, standardized housing. "Levittown" soon became an American icon, its name initially expressed with admiration, later employed derisively, and just recently as a term of grudging respect among some former critics.

FIG. 831 Broadacre Neighborhood Frank Lloyd Wright's Broadacre City investigations were realized in bits and pieces after World War II. This Parkwyn Village house illustrates how Wright approached neighborhood planning as an integration of site and building.

FIGS. 832, 833 Levittown, Evolved and Matured Levitt's original Long Island subdivision (Fig. 832) offered very basic mass-produced Cape Cods. By the third Levittown, built a decade later outside of Philadelphia, three distinct models were available, adding a two-story garrison colonial and a one-story "rancher" to now-somewhat-larger capes (Fig. 833). As can be seen from these recent views, Levittown neighborhoods have long since matured out of their initial sameness, made famous/infamous by early photos.

After the original Long Island Levittown (Fig. 832) was built out, Levitt developed a second Levittown in Bucks County, northeast of Philadelphia (1951-1958), and then a third (1958-1965) nearby in New Jersey, subsequently renamed Willingboro (Fig. 833). All three have matured into pleasant, middle-class communities, looking utterly unlike the well-known construction-site photos of a sea of identical, framed houses set in a barren field.

Eichler Subdivisions FIG. 834
1947–1966
Anshen & Allen, A. Quincy Jones and Frederick Emmons, architects
San Francisco Bay Area

Builder Joseph Eichler "claimed a mission to bring good architecture to middle America," in the words of architect-planner-historian Roger Montgomery. After briefly experimenting with pre-fab houses and conventional plans, Eichler engaged architects Robert Allen and A. Quincy Jones to translate the cutting-edge residential concepts of Frank Lloyd Wright, William Wurster, and Cliff May into striking contemporary houses for somewhat-above-average-income Middle Americans.

Eichler's best-known subdivisions are located in Palo Alto and Marin County, although he developed housing across the Bay Area by 1966. In the 1950s, certainly, and probably well into the 1960s, Eichler subdivisions represented the gold standard of postwar builder's housing.

Arapahoe Acres FIG. 836
1949–1957
Edward B. Hawkins, developer-landscape architect; **Eugene Sternberg**, planner-architect
Dartmouth to Bates Aves., between Marion and Franklin Sts., Englewood, Colorado

The 30-acre, 100-house Arapahoe Acres (Fig. 836) is a disarmingly engaging postwar curvilinear subdivision based generally on the

FIGS. 834, 835 Architecture for Middle America Developer Joseph Eichler considered it his mission to offer architecturally advanced houses to a middle class not able to afford a fully custom design. Comparison of a house in Marin County, California Eichler subdivision (Fig. 834) with contemporary postwar Chicago-area tract houses (Fig. 835) reveals how advanced Eichler was for the 1950s. *Fig. 835: Jorgen Martinson*

FIG. 836 Timeless Modernism A half century after its development, Arapahoe Acres remains exceptionally attractive, and still contemporary. In this age of oversized additions and tear-downs for McMansions, it is a miracle that the subdivision's homeowners have resisted the urge to bloat.

Eichler developments (previous entry). Thomas Noel listed the development's attributes: "Careful siting maximized privacy, southern exposure, and mountain views. Lean, contemporary designs, characterized by clerestory windows and outdoor patios in cohesive landscaping, set the standard for [later housing developments elsewhere]." Arapahoe Acres is a must visit for anyone seriously interested in detached housing.

LATE-TWENTIETH-CENTURY NEW COMMUNITIES

Reston FIG. 837
1963–1965 ff.
Whittlesey, Conklin & Rossant, RTKL Associates, planners;
Sasaki Associates, landscape architects
Fairfax County, Virginia

Reston was the most prominent 1960s American new town, its fame reinforced by its highly photogenic Lake Anne Village Center (Fig. 837), designed by Conklin & Rossant. After working through the usual development reverses due to a relatively isolated regional location during its first two decades, Reston has grown into a full-fledged city of nearly 60,000 citizens and thousands of non-resident daily workers. Now deeply embedded within greater Reston, the pioneer Lake Anne Village core survives as an instructive period piece of 1960s optimism.

Arcosanti FIG. 838
1970 –
Paolo Soleri, planner and architect
3 mi. NE of I-17 Exit 262, Cordes Junction, Arizona

A singular personal vision about an ideal community, in which architecture is intended to merge seamlessly with ecology. Given

FIG. 837 The Designed Community Reston popularized the idea of a designed community, one in which design was not only evident in layout and public landscape, as from Riverside onward, but in which architectural pretense is integral with community development. Reston's photogenic Lake Anne Village Center, shown here in a recent view, was widely published and highly influential among planners and architects in the 1960s.

FIG. 838 Singular Personal Vision Paolo Soleri's Arcosanti defies pretty much every American community development convention. It seemed to be a lightning rod of inspiration in the early 1970s, when 1960s youth counterculture was evolving into Whole Earth.

this premise, Soleri's solution incorporating a dense megastructure set far out in an open desert is unexpected. On the other hand, a site visit reveals a powerful visual interplay between Arcosanti's massive concrete structures and a parallel rocky cliff just across the arroyo.

Although only a fraction of the entire plan has been constructed to date, visitors can probably understand what Soleri intended, though, of course, one cannot yet fully experience what the built-out community would be like.

FIGS. 839, 840, 841 Satisfying New Urbanism Celebration is surely the most agreeable New Urbanist community, largely free of the stiffness typical of such developments. The town center (Fig. 839) presents a relaxed mix of Main Street and subtropical references. Houses (Fig. 840) show a variety of region-appropriate imageries. The plan provides an exceptional hierarchy of of open spaces (Fig. 841).

Celebration   FIGS. 839, 840, 841, 843, 844
1987–1996 ff.

Robert A. M. Stern, Jacquelin T. Robertson, planners and architects of town center buildings; **Philip Johnson**, architect of town hall; **Michael Graves**, architect of post office; **Charles W. Moore**, architect of preview center tower; **Venturi, Scott Brown & Assocs.**, architects of bank; **William Rawn Associates**, architects of school; **Cesar Pelli & Associates**, architects of cinema; **Graham Gund Architects**, architects of hotel; **Urban Design Associates**, architectural guidelines for residential development. **EDAW**, landscape architects for town center
SE quad. of Hwy. 192 and I-4, Osceola County, Florida

Celebration is a New Urbanism-influenced planned community built within the precincts of Walt Disney World. It generally acknowledges the Seaside New Urbanism formula (see Resorts chapter), including a vestigial reference to Kingsport (Fig. 824) in its street grid.

In significant ways, however, the Celebration plan is far more knowing and nuanced than are New Urbanism exemplars like Kentlands (Fig. 842), Celebration's contemporary in suburban Washington, D.C. Stern and Robertson imaginatively synthesized—not simply mimicked—an encyclopedic array of global references and sensibilities into their plan, necessarily toned down to neighborhood scale. One might think, for instance, of Charleston's Battery when passing the line of substantial houses enfronting the golf course, of the sequence of public spaces in London's Bloomsbury District on encountering the sequence of spaces and landscapes around Greenbriar and Longmeadow (Figs. 841, 843), and of the canal extending out of Munich toward Nymphenburg Palace as a reference for the axial canal linking the town center along Market Street with the golf course. Overall, the designed qualities of Celebration's public spaces distinguish the community from American community-development norms.

New Urbanists assert that old-fashioned imageries encourage a romanticized, slow-paced lifestyle, like greeting neighbors each evening while seated on the front porch (Fig. 840). In reality, Celebration residents retreat from Florida's heat and humidity into their air-conditioned homes and watch TV, just like residents of conventional subdivisions. Initially, the major community social activity was not sitting out on front porches but organizing to protest alleged deficiencies in Celebration's schools.

Regardless, Celebration is earnestly planned, with skilled design attention given to streetscapes and the town center (Fig. 839), including an abundance of eye candy thanks to the efforts of signature architects—especially Moore's tower (Fig. 844).

FIGS. 842, 843 Designed Landscapes Make a Difference The contrast between open spaces in Kentlands (Fig. 842), a New Urbanist development near Washington, D.C., planned by Andres Duany and Elizabeth Plater-Zyberk, and Celebration (Fig. 843) is instructive. The forlorn strip of land in Kentlands is planted in a rigid line of saplings, which are apparently meant to eventually grow into a monumental *allée*

(compare with Fig. 1), ironically set right in front of these tiny houses. The appealing, residential-scale informality and the comparative maturity of Celebration's open-space landscaping illustrates an important distinction between community landscapes that are integrally *designed* and those which are simply planted as an afterthought to the development of site plans and the design of buildings.

DC Ranch FIG. 845

1995 ff.

Vernon D. Swaback, Swaback Partners, master planners-primary architects
Between N. Pima Rd. and the McDowell Mountains., at E. Thompson Peak Pkwy., Scottsdale, Arizona (single-family residential areas gated)

DC Ranch offers an environmental-focused alternative to the approach taken at Celebration. Rather than applying historical imageries within a formal street pattern, as at Celebration, the 8,300-acre DC Ranch is meant to seem to grow naturally from its desert setting. As Swaback noted, "Everything started with an understanding [of the singular local qualities] of the land." That implied more than simply developing a dusky architecture that visually complemented the rocky surroundings.

Instead, the plan recognized how desert living is unique from other environments. Swaback appreciates the ancient duality of desert living: "the joy of living openly under the sky" as well as the practical need for shade and shelter from extremes of climate. Similar to Wright's Parkwyn Village as a demonstration of the larger Broadacre vision (earlier in this chapter), Swaback's DC Ranch plan and designs can be understood as a demonstration of an environmental approach to regional development, what the architect calls the Creative Community.

FIG. 844 Celebration's Preview Tower Towns benefit from unique visual features which serve as community landmarks, offering an effective way of distinguishing one community from all others. Charles Moore's Preview Tower provides a memorable signature feature for Celebration.

FIG. 845 Expressing Desert Living The prominence of indigenous landscapes conveys the message that DC Ranch is of the desert, not just built atop its desert setting.

The City Beautiful

1893–1920

FIG. 846 Putting a Face on Reform The American City Beautiful movement paralleled the reform movements active in the United States around 1900. In concert with social reformers who worked to lessen human degradation in teeming urban wards, City Beautiful planners and architects envisioned complementing "white cities" to provide cleansed physical environments. This 1902 McMillan Plan drawing of a grandly expanded National Mall in Washington, D.C. established an ultimate City Beautiful benchmark for American planners and civic leaders. (See also Fig. 791.) *U.S. Commission of Fine Arts, rendering by F.L.V. Hoppin*

The American City Beautiful movement has always seemed easy to understand. To most people interested in urbanism, the term connotes grand groupings of white civic buildings arranged around axial spaces graced with fountains and public art. While that is indeed useful as a shorthand description, City Beautiful planning called for much more than monumental Beaux Arts environments. At its best, The City Beautiful offered a sophisticated, wide-ranging agenda intended to transform American cities from the ordinary to the extraordinary.

From our perspective, wiser in some ways a century on, that splendid goal was hopelessly utopian. Yet the City Beautiful movement had significant long-term influence for American cities, introducing the idea of *comprehensively* shaping our visual environments, an approach which has now persisted for a century as physical planning.

As it influenced so many facets of American life, the 1893 World's Columbian Exposition stimulated the City Beautiful movement. Throughout the 1890s, despite the lingering effects of financial panic, dozens of American cities founded civic art societies intended to enhance their physical settings. Their discussions and activities were summed up in two books by the writer Charles Mulford Robinson. In *The Improvement of Cities and Towns*, published in 1901, and *Modern Civic Art*, which came out two years later, Robinson in effect codified the City Beautiful movement, treating subjects as diverse as street cleaning and popular education in art as components of a cohesive philosophy of city bulding.

While these were highly influential as civic guides, the Chicago architect and planner Daniel H. Burnham, who had managed the planning and design of the 1893 fair, was the dominant figure in the movement. Burnham was a virtual force of nature, demonstrating City Beautiful planning in Cleveland, San Francisco, Manila, and Chicago, and serving as the first chairman of the U.S. Commission of Fine Arts (see The Mall chapter), implementing the McMillan Plan provisions for the National Mall that he was instrumental in formulating.

FIG. 847 **City Beautiful in the West** Axiality, a basic City Beautiful planning expression, was employed throughout the United States, especially to organize monumental groupings of public buildings, as here in Denver. This view is taken from the Capitol steps toward the 1932 City and County Building, designed by the Allied Architects Association.

FIG. 848 **Restoring Axiality** The McMillan Plan re-established axiality to the National Mall after a half-century of Romantic-era interventions like the Smithsonian Institution's "Castle" main building (1847–1855; James Renwick, architect), from which this photograph was taken. The Mall that we experience today largely reflects McMillan Plan sensibilities. *Library of Congress, Prints & Photographs, Historic American Buildings Survey*

This meant there were many nuances to the City Beautiful. It began as an outgrowth of late-1800s reform activity, and at its climax—the 1909 Chicago Plan—encompassed much more than design. Ultimately, Burnham's City Beautiful was about public order, which to him implied progressive business activity as much as the achievement of beauty, functional efficiencies as well as explicit associations with great world civilizations.

This sophisticated, comprehensive civic agenda was gradually discarded after Burnham's death in 1912, hastened by World War I and the post-Armistice "return to normalcy." A residual City Beautiful design vocabulary consisting of Classicist buildings and ordered public spaces was all that was left of the movement by the 1930s. This superficial expression was applied as a convenient master planning idiom well into the 1960s urban-renewal era (see Physical Plans chapter).

The plans cited here are among the major national City Beautiful landmarks and effectively sum up the essence of the movement. Numerous other notable City Beautiful projects were undertaken, especially in the eastern United States, although also in western cities like Denver (Fig. 847). In the succeeding period, what Mel Scott labeled the City Functional era, the strict axiality and symmetries that were characteristic of the City Beautiful gave way to a relaxed formality, in which straight axes were mixed with curvilinear patterns, as in John Nolen's fan-shaped grid for Kingsport, Tennessee, designed in 1916–1917 (Fig. 824).

World's Columbian Exposition
1892–1893
Daniel H. Burnham, chief of construction; **John Wellborn Root, Charles B. Atwood**, supervising architects; **Frederick Law Olmsted**, supervising landscape architect; **Henry "Harry" Codman**, project landscape architect
Jackson Park, Chicago, Illinois

While European classicism had already emerged in the United States (see Beaux Arts chapter), the "White City" at the Chicago fair (see Fairs and Expositions chapter) marks the symbolic beginning of American City Beautiful planning.

Senate Park Commission "McMillan" Plan
FIGS. 791, 792 846, 848
1901–1902
James McMillan, Senate sponsor; **Daniel Burnham, Charles McKim, Frederick Law Olmsted, Jr.**, planners; **Augustus Saint-Gaudens**, sculptor
National Mall, Washington, D.C.

The McMillan plan (Fig. 846) reestablished formal axiality to the Mall (Fig. 848), after L'Enfant's concept had been forsaken in the mid-1800s in favor of romantic naturalism. Due to its location and national symbolism, this plan signaled to American civic leaders and planners that The City Beautiful was the national planning vocabulary. (See The Mall chapter.)

Group Plan/Mall FIG. 849
1902–1903; last parcel cleared, 1935
Daniel Burnham, John M. Carrère, Arnold W. Brunner, planners
Area immediately NE of Public Square, to the Erie Lakefront, Cleveland, Ohio

Cleveland civic leaders had called for the creation of a formal civic center since 1895, as a competitive response to the White City at the 1893 Chicago fair—and also a practical way of eliminating squalid conditions on the edge of the city's center at Public Square.

FIG. 849 **Expressing the Modern City** Cleveland was a premier American business center in the early 1900s. Its downtown Group Plan/Mall, which extends from the lower right to the center left in this view, was meant as a demonstration of the ideal modern city characterized by civic order and beauty. (A corner of the Public Square, Fig. 802, is visible at the very bottom of this view.)

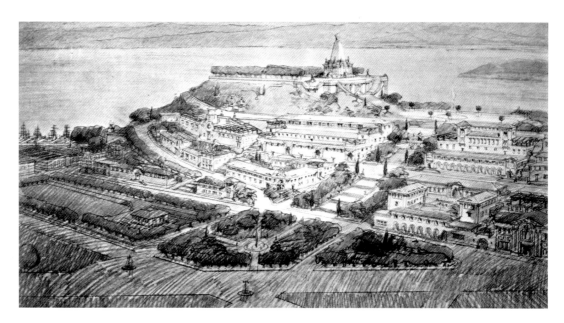

FIG. 850 **Civic Adornment** Daniel
Burnham's 1906 Plan for San
Francisco offered insights and
features in addition to the usual City
Beautiful vocabularies of axial
boulevards and grouped public
buildings. Its design provisions were
uniquely ornate in the same way
that San Francisco is a uniquely
grand American city. This drawing
from the 1906 plan illustrates an
expansive civic acropolis for
Telegraph Hill. Three decades later,
Coit Tower was built at its summit.
Plan for San Francisco, 1906

FIGS. 851, 852 **Civic Continuity**
The historic role of St. Louis as a
center of order in the wilderness
informs the continuing, century-long
development of its Gateway Mall as
a public environment (Fig. 851). The
1911 plan for a Central Parkway
connecting Downtown (Fig. 852)
to Midtown (Fig. 851) evolved into
Gateway Mall. The nascent mall is
visible near the left edge as a
block-wide island, which narrows
down to a single boulevard seven
blocks west, at Union Station,
before resolving into a Beaux Arts
plaza with a crow-foot pattern
ending at Grand Boulevard.. *Fig.
852: St. Louis Central Public Library*

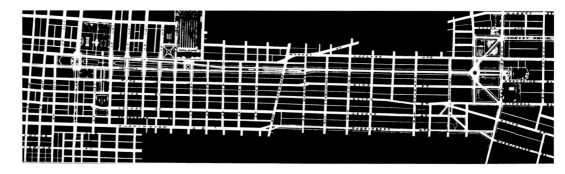

More than any other American City Beautiful plan, excepting
only Chicago's, Cleveland's was fully accomplished, with the Mall
defined by monumental buildings, including City Hall, courthouses, and later, the public auditorium (1922), main public library
(1925), and music hall (1929).

A Plan for San Francisco FIG. 850
1905–1906
Daniel H. Burnham, Edward H. Bennett, planners; **John McLaren,
Willis Polk, Arthur Brown, Jr., B. J. S. Cahill**, planning and design assistants
San Francisco, California

According to planning lore, San Francisco missed a singular opportunity to implement Burnham's proposed Beaux Arts street patterns when the 1906 earthquake and fire leveled everything just
days after the published report was released. (The plan had been
accepted late in 1905.)

The proposed new patterns somewhat recall the famed 1852–
1870 transformation of Paris by Napoleon III and Haussmann, but
owe more to Burnham's just-completed 1905 Manila plan. Of
these, only the Civic Center was accomplished as a City Beautiful
group plan.

Actually, Beaux Arts axial street patterns and formal civic groupings were only two elements of Burnham's 1905–1906 plan. Many of its conclusions and other recommendations apparently seeped into the consciousness of successive civic leaders: certainly Burnham's recurring themes of civic improvement and adornment. The plan offered more than a dozen major recommendations. Some of these emphasized design and urban beautification, while others addressed important technical matters like air pollution and the municipal water supply.

A City Plan for St. Louis FIGS. 851, 852
1907
William Trelease, chairman of the city plan committee; **Lawrence Mauran, George Kessler, Julius Pitzman, Henry Wright Jr., Wilbur Trueblood, Theodore Link, Edward Flad**, committee of design and engineering professionals
St. Louis, Missouri

In some ways, this report anticipated the later Chicago plan (next entry), including extensive background sections about the city. It also cites contemporary civic improvements in both Europe and the United States, chiefly in Chicago.

The 1907 Plan called for the establishment of more parks, provided choices among alternative schemes for a civic group, and recommended typical City Beautiful street improvements, while extolling the civic value of public art. The product of a committee structure, the plan was competent and thoughtful, but not sweeping and visionary like Burnham's Chicago plan, which was underway at the time. On the other hand, the fact that it emerged from a local committee ensured that its concepts were embedded in the community, with recommendations carried forward by later generations of civic leaders. This continuity is characteristic of St. Louis civic progress up to the present.

To cite two examples: the 1907 Plan proposed beautification of a central riverfront site, development of which was completed 60 years later with the opening of Gateway Arch (see Civic Design chapter); at larger scale, the 1907 Plan led to the development of Gateway Mall (Figs. 851, 852), which is still patiently advancing, a century later.

Plan of Chicago FIGS. 853, 854, 855, 856
1909
Charles Norton, civic visionary; **Daniel H. Burnham, Edward H. Bennett**, planners; **Jules Guerin, Fernand Janin**, delineators
Chicago, Illinois

Understandably the most famous American city plan, the Plan of Chicago was developed in 1906–1908 after Charles Norton organized support and funding from the Chicago business community.

With many exceptional attributes, the plan accomplished several objectives: it promoted a great public gesture, the open lake-

FIGS. 853, 854 Realistic Grandeur City Beautiful planning succeeded in Chicago because Burnham's planning proposals were in tune with the city's self-image. Splendid public spaces like one proposed for Michigan Avenue (Fig. 853) seemed plausible, indeed inevitable, to Chicago's business community after its triumph in staging the 1893 fair. To achieve a distinctive civic character, Burnham's 1909 Chicago Plan took full advantage of the city's physical assets, especially Lake Michigan. It was equally important that the plan integrated art with function: the proposed splendid public space was to double as a grand landscaped boulevard serving a railway station (Fig. 853). This idea of a transportation promenade along the lake eventually evolved into Lakeshore Drive and its continuous edge of public space along the lake (Fig. 854).
Fig. 853: Plan of Chicago, *1909*

front (Figs. 853, 854); it presciently recognized future inter- relationships of Chicago with its outlying environs; it endorsed and enhanced an immense regional greenbelt system (Figs. 855, 856) which had recently been proposed conceptually by Dwight Perkins and Jens Jensen; it persuasively implied that Chicago was on the threshold of becoming a great world city and must therefore consistently act like one. And there was the fine art of the plan itself. This was a singular landmark event in American city planning, where the proposer, Burnham, was equally a brilliant visionary with international experience and also a trusted local business leader.

Plan of Minneapolis FIGS. 857, 858, 859

1910–1912; published 1917

Edward H. Bennett, planner; **Daniel H. Burnham**, advisor; **Clarence E. Howard**, planning assistant; **Marcel Vilain**, design assistant; **Jules Guerin**, delineator

Minneapolis, Minnesota

Bennett's Minneapolis plan was a competent variation of its Chicago predecessor. But Minneapolis was not Chicago, and Bennett was merely an outside consultant, not a member of the local business elite, as was Burnham in Chicago. The urban grandeur that was plausible to Chicago industrialists was simply a curious pipe dream to most Minneapolitans (Fig. 857).

Nevertheless, civic leaders attempted to reshape downtown into a City Beautiful environment. In an overeagerness to demonstrate that Minneapolis was in league with Chicago and Cleveland by remaking its downtown as impressively, fragments of the ultimate plan were undertaken almost as soon as Bennett arrived in town in 1910, accelerating after Bennett's preliminary plan was issued in 1911.

But aside from a new railroad station, a Beaux Arts post office, the widening of Hennepin Avenue, and a small "Gateway Pavilion" and park—all sharing a common locality—City Beautiful improvements here were scattered about the city. Thus Minneapolis never achieved enough critical mass in any one location to establish a perceptible City Beautiful experience. Only Bennett's regional proposals were substantially accomplished (Figs. 858, 859).

THE TWILIGHTS OF CITY BEAUTIFUL

After the 1918 Armistice, the United States moved into a distinctly new era. Consequently, American social-cultural values changed radically. The City Beautiful fell out of fashion, as did progressive early twentieth-century architecture and landscape movements like the Prairie School and Craftsman (see those chapters).

To be sure, vestigial Beaux Arts axial schemes persisted through the 1930s, and occasionally well into the 1960s. But as U.S. society giddily embraced the Roaring '20s, the City Beautiful had become very much a thing of the past.

FIGS. 855, 856 Regional Vision Burnham's regional proposals reflected the expansive local view of Chicago's natural domain, "Chicagoland." The 1909 Plan proposed a series of expanding greenbelts that would both carry traffic and provide natural relief, greenery, and fresh air in densely built-up districts (Fig. 855). Much of this visionary system was accomplished as the Cook County forest preserves (Fig. 856). *Fig. 855: Plan of Chicago, 1909*

FIG. 857 Cosmetic Grandeur In contrast to Burnham's City Beautiful planning for Chicago, Edward Bennett's Minneapolis plan superficially applied generic City Beautiful planning vocabularies like spacious public plazas and diagonal boulevards. Unlike similar provisions in the Chicago plan, these were not grounded in the local civic self-image, nor did they offer additional functional value. As a consequence, while scattered civic improvements were accomplished throughout the city, Minneapolis never achieved a cohesive City Beautiful environment. *Plan of Minneapolis, 1917*

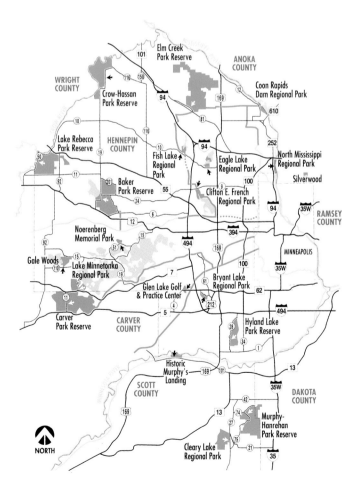

FIGS. 858, 859 Exploiting Locality Bennett's Minneapolis plan exploited regional assets. Like the Chicago plan, the Minneapolis plan proposed an expanding concentric network of regional highways (Fig. 858). These roads would connect existing lakes and streams at metropolitan scale, much as the developing Minneapolis Grand Rounds parkway system interconnected city lakes and brooks at municipal scale (see Naturalism and Roads chapters). Unlike the generic City Beautiful planning expressions of the Minneapolis plan itself, the idea of regional green interconnections was locally plausible for Minneapolis. This idea formed the basis for an extensive regional park and open space system that by today (Fig. 859)—reinforced by underlying ecological corridors not mapped here—has actually outstripped Bennett's planning concept. *Fig. 858: Plan of Minneapolis, 1917; Fig. 859: Three Rivers Park District*

Physical Plans

1949–1990

FIGS. 860, 861 Large-scale Physical Planning By the Great Depression of the 1930s, entire districts of big American cities had become noticeably blighted. As domestic issues returned to the forefront after the Second World War, federal and local authorities concluded that the problem was *structural*, meaning that dysfunction had advanced to the point that rehabilitating existing buildings would not be an effective solution. The photo of a kitchen in an inhabited St. Louis house depicts common pre-renewal physical-blight conditions (Fig. 861). Consequently, from the early 1950s, major U.S. cities undertook urban-renewal planning for their blighted districts. Sizeable areas of cities like St. Louis (Fig. 860) were largely cleared if not completely transformed through wholesale renewal, an approach that was increasingly controversial. Nevertheless, by the 1960s, the idea of large-scale, public transformation of the existing urban fabric was extended to comprehensive physical planning intended to modernize aging downtowns. *Fig. 861: St. Louis Land Clearance for Redevelopment Authority*

Most of the United States has been developed through private initiative without reference to comprehensive planning beyond basic zoning and building codes. Except in rare instances like that of San Francisco's 1905–1906 City Beautiful plan, formal municipal planning with significant design components undertaken before the New Deal of the 1930s was usually carried out by business-led civic organizations or by private development companies (see Community Development chapter).

Where municipalities did undertake city planning by writing "comprehensive" land use plans and codes, tackling transportation (meaning roads), and after 1927, setting out zoning regulations, these were normally devised by private planning consultants like Harland Bartholomew, or were based on the work of such consultants for other municipalities.

Under the Roosevelt administration of 1933–1945, the idea of national planning came to prominence, first as a direct approach to dealing with the Great Depression, and then to mobilize for and prosecute World War II. Filtered down to municipalities, prewar planning was modest. In the 1930s, big U.S. cities began to systematically assess blight and to build federally assisted public housing for low-income residents.

After the war, city and regional planning mushroomed in the United States. Norman Johnson described the late-1940s planning scene as the "emergence of great numbers of public planning agencies; of university planning curricula, their graduates, and research programs; of new private planning consulting firms; and innovations in legislation and data assembling and processing."

Reflecting this activity, a heroic age of municipal *physical* planning, emphasizing urban design and master plans, occurred between about 1950 and the early 1970s, chiefly in two formats. One was the Urban Renewal Plan, the other the 701 Comprehensive Plan. The former was employed in the urban renewal ("slum clearance") process (Figs. 860, 861); the latter, referring to a section in a federal funding law, was employed in economic development planning, chiefly meant to revitalize, if not transform, big-city downtowns. Changes in federal funding formulas in 1972 inadvertently but effectively brought this golden era of physical planning to a practical end, although physical plans were still undertaken in subsequent years under a mix of funding sources.

Urban renewal in the United States dated officially from the federal Housing Act of 1949. The act's three primary objectives were: *elimination of substandard housing* through slum clearance and removal of blight; *stimulation of housing production* to remedy the postwar housing shortage; and *achieving the goal of a decent home* and living environment for every American family.

The Housing Act employed eminent domain to acquire private properties within an urban renewal district for resale below acquisition cost to private redevelopers. This was ruled to be constitutional in 1954. Previously, eminent domain had been employed only for strictly public reuses like roads and schools.

The federal urban renewal program directly affected millions of Americans in hundreds of U.S. cities, at a public cost in the billions of dollars before the program was succeeded by a revenue-sharing approach in 1972. Over more than two decades of activity, urban renewal was increasingly controversial. Opponents contended that while the goals themselves might be admirable, they could have been accomplished much more efficiently by private enterprise; that individuals displaced by renewal rarely experienced better living conditions as a consequence; and that large areas of historic city fabric were lost to blanket clearance.

Urban renewal advocates responded that the majority of razed properties were hopelessly blighted, that realistically there was no other way of redeveloping central cities in line with modern, economically competitive patterns, and that reliance solely on private enterprise was idealistic in the extreme.

Irrespective of this controversy, every big U.S. city undertook urban renewal programs. Usually dozens of blocks were razed. In combination with concurrent freeway construction, in many cities hundreds of acres were cleared and redeveloped. The result was stunning (or shocking): an unprecedented transformation over a very short time. Thus urban renewal was a significant—if not the major—postwar change agent in big American cities.

Most municipal urban renewal officials were unknown outside of their own communities, and recognition for urban renewal plans was usually accorded to private consultants. Edward J. Logue (1921–2000), was a notable exception, charismatic as redevelopment director in New Haven, and after 1960, nationally prominent as head of the Boston Redevelopment Authority (BRA). But within many cities, redevelopment directors like Charles Farris in St. Louis were influential and locally revered figures.

Comprehensive physical planning became common in major U.S. cities by the early 1960s. Only a single city planner was as widely recognized nationally as the redevelopment official, Edward Logue. That was Edmund N. Bacon (1910–2005), executive director of Philadelphia's city planning commission. City planning directors like Charles Blessing in Detroit and Lawrence M. Irvin in Minneapolis, prominent local figures, were also well known within the national planning profession.

Government Center Master Plan
1963
Edward J. Logue, BRA director; **I. M. Pei**, principal master-planning consultant
Downtown Boston, Massachusetts

As soon as Logue arrived in Boston in 1960, he turned the BRA's attention to downtown. In the process he revitalized the three-year-old agency, already the object of some scorn, transforming central Boston in the process. Creating physical focus around a new City Hall (see Brutalism chapter) was among Logue's redevelopment goals. Some existing city fabric was cleared and replatted into larger land parcels in order to provide an adequate visual setting for the new city hall, and also make sites available for other new public and private construction.

I. M. Pei's 1963 master plan, which tied several pieces together, differed from the typical urban renewal plan in several important respects. First and foremost, the plan was based on an explicit goal, that of accomplishing a specific physical outcome. Second, a distinct spatial sequence was to be developed. Third, significant historic buildings were retained and restored. Among these, Faneuil Hall and Quincy Market were later redeveloped into a festival marketplace (see Retail and Hotels chapter). And fourth, the plan emphasized architectural quality, in preserving old buildings and in designs for new ones. All in all, Boston's was deservedly, if arguably, the preeminent U.S. urban renewal plan.

FIG. 862 Public Focus Baltimore's Inner Harbor Redevelopment largely focused on increasing tourism and entertainment venues in its public promenades, especially throughout the Rouse Company's Harborplace festival market.

Inner Harbor Redevelopment FIG. 862
1970 ff.
Wallace, Roberts & Todd, planners and landscape architects
W side of Inner Harbor, Baltimore, Maryland

Baltimore exploited its rundown conditions and proximity to federal funding agencies in Washington to effectively serve as a national demonstration site for current ideas in urban redevelopment. Over a period of three decades, Baltimore transformed its Inner Harbor district, turning the once lifeless area into a national tourism draw (Fig. 862).

Center City Planning FIGS. 863, 864
1947–1970
Edmund N. Bacon, city planning director
Delaware to Schuylkill rivers, between Spring Garden and South Streets, Philadelphia, Pennsylvania

The modern era of Philadelphia planning dates from the groundbreaking 1947 Better Philadelphia exhibition, which featured a room-sized model of an improved Center City. Although conservative in its proposals by today's standards, it was immensely significant in elevating city planning to a municipal issue in Philadelphia.

Over the ensuing two decades until his retirement in 1970, Edmund Bacon, who became executive director of the city planning commission in 1949, his staff, and architects Oskar Stonorov, Roy Larson, Louis Kahn, Vincent Kling, I.M. Pei, and others, carried out physical planning studies almost continuously. Major accomplishments included the Penn Center (Fig. 864) and Market East commercial redevelopments, Society Hill, and enhancing the Independence Mall historic district (Fig. 863). After a 1961 Comprehensive Plan, so-called continuum diagrams were published in 1963 and 1967. By the late 1960s, Bacon and his colleagues had moved from downtown to regional scale in their investigations.

Bacon was the quintessential physical planner, trained as an architect, having traveled to great cities around the world, who saw city planning as primarily a matter of structure, form, and movement, as described in his classic book, *Design of Cities* (1967).

FIGS. 863, 864 Urban Structure and Form Planner Edmund Bacon invoked classic physical planning approaches for Philadelphia's Center City, expanding the public setting around Independence Hall (Fig. 863), and redeveloping the commercial office district adjacent to City Hall (areas beyond the City Hall's tower in Fig. 864). *Library of Congress, Prints & Photographs, Historic American Buildings Survey*

Fort Worth Downtown Plan
1955–1958
Victor Gruen, Edgardo Contini, consultant planners
Central Fort Worth, Texas

Outside of Bacon's Philadelphia activities, Gruen's and Contini's Fort Worth plan was probably the best-known postwar planning among American physical planners. Even though it was not fully realized in Fort Worth, its precepts, especially the goal of reducing cars in the downtown core, influenced subsequent downtown planning throughout the United States, and as far away as the Bonifacio new city (1995 ff.) in the Philippines. The Minneapolis Metro Center '85 plan (next entry), which *was* effectively realized, adopted Gruen's basic concepts. Gruen's ideal of a modern city—that is, its downtown—seemed to be a synthesis of a medieval fortified town and Lucio Costa's functional concepts for the ultramodern Brasília, then under construction in Brazil.

Gruen's and Contini's technical innovation was downtown peripheral parking built adjacent to or over an inner-loop freeway, served by pedestrian walkways-passages within the downtown core. This idea was realized in Minneapolis, with its Skyway network (see Civic Design chapter) connected to a system of peripheral parking garages (see Transportation chapter).

Metro Center '85 FIGS. 865, 866, 867
1968–1970
Lawrence M. Irvin, city planning director; **Ronald L. Tulis**, staff project planner
Downtown Minneapolis, Minnesota

This much honored classic downtown plan built upon more than a decade of work by Irvin and his staff, especially a 1959 Central Minneapolis Plan authored by Rodney Engelen, and preliminary work in the mid-1960s by principal planner Wei-Ming Lu. The plan document was brightly colored and lavishly illustrated, organized in format in ways reminiscent of the City Beautiful plans for Chicago and Minneapolis (see The City Beautiful Chapter).

Planning recommendation were clearly set out within frameworks for land use, circulation, image, form, and environmental

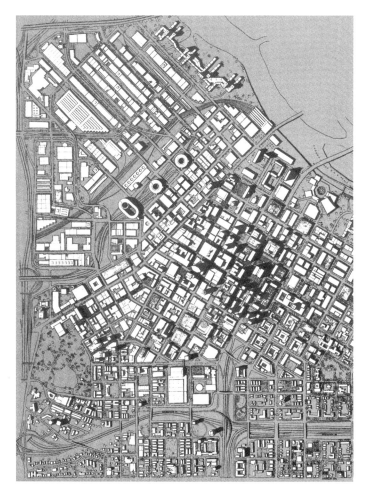

FIGS. 865, 866, 867 Successful Transformation The Minneapolis *Metro Center '85* Plan (Fig. 867) led to the conversion of a nondescript industrial zone on the downtown periphery into a civic center characterized by signature architecture. In a late-1970s bird's-eye view from the downtown core looking east (Fig. 865), Hennepin County's Government Center (1967–1973, John Carl Warnecke) rises amidst a scattering of small buildings and surface parking. The twin plazas were intended to attract private investment to surrounding parcels. As the second view, looking back toward the previous vantage shows (Fig. 866), by the mid-1990s, sites adjacent to the plazas had been filled with architecturally impressive office towers, as planned. From the left edge of this image, the building designers are Kohn Pedersen Fox, Cesar Pelli (in background), I. M. Pei & Partners, and SOM. *Fig. 867: City of Minneapolis, Metro Center '85, 1970*

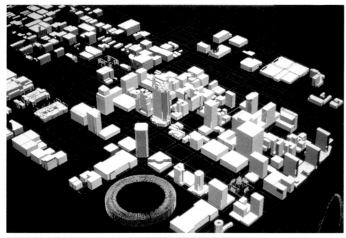

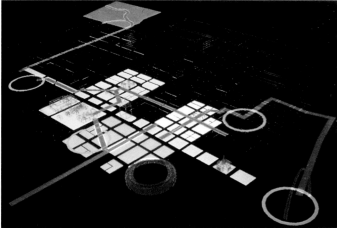

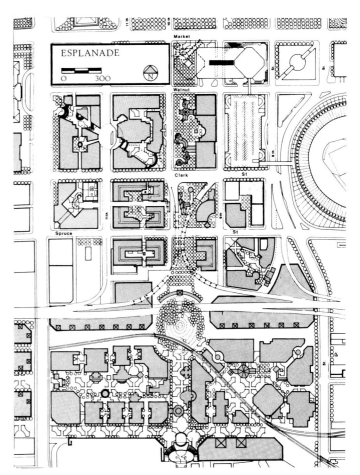

FIGS. 868, 869 Expanding the Public Realm St. Louis downtown planning places a premium on its singular public realm centered along Gateway Mall. The *1987 Plan for Downtown St. Louis* proposed extensions from the Mall at two scales (Fig. 868),

including a new Esplanade district organized around interconnected public spaces (Fig. 869). *Fig. 868: Gerardo Garcia Cepeda and W. Davis van Bakergam; Fig. 869: Charles W. Moore and Arthur Andersson, Judith P. Hoskens*

quality. *Metro Center '85* proposed an encircling peripheral parking system, à la Gruen's Fort Worth plan, which was fully operational by 1991 (see Transportation chapter). The Illustrative Site Plan of the central area (Fig. 866) functioned as the iconic image of *Metro Center '85*, and guided the successful redevelopment of downtown's Government Center district.

A Plan for Downtown St. Louis FIGS. 868, 869, 870
1986–1987
Tom Martinson, consultant project planner; **John M. Woodbridge**, planner & urban designer; **Charles W. Moore**, architect & urban designer; **Arthur Andersson**, urban designer & delineator
Downtown St. Louis, Missouri

Because of recent false starts in developing a new downtown plan, completion of the 1987 plan was symbolically important to St. Louis civic leaders. This plan integrated a number of localized technical solutions and district-wide visionary opportunities (Fig. 868) into a comprehensive and unified direction, with the expectation of future plan updates at five-year intervals.

In addition to proposing improvements in transportation and pedestrian movement, high priority was placed on area-wide landscaped interconnections with Gateway Mall (Fig. 869), thus enhancing the city's monumental public domain begun in 1907 (see The City Beautiful chapter). This was understood as essential to ensure that the city's longstanding civic traditions would be sustained.

FIG. 870 Pour Me a Cold One, Louie Breweries are prominent in the rich history of St. Louis, as are marvelous public follies. The combination inspired Charles Moore's light-hearted Biergarten as part of the 1987 Downtown Plan. *Arthur Andersson rendering*

The Strip

1916–2004

FIG. 871 Signs of Life A highway strip can be the most vibrant spot in many communities, brimming with energy. Strips typically exhibit an excess of variety, color, texture, sound, and movement, adding up to a willful disorder of barely restrained commercial zeal. Little sense of formal planning is evident along most American strips.

That is certainly the case in this Los Angeles Southland scene in the suburb of Norwalk, where only the pylon sign (1951–1954, by Styles Clements) is of any individual design interest. Regardless, many of these everyday environments are visually exhilarating.

The highway strip is one of the most "American" visual expressions (Fig. 871). From the 1920s through World War II, strips sprouted up along the highway approaches into towns across the United States. Any community without a growing highway strip was likely to be in economic decline. Prewar strips were commonly made up of small-scale, locally designed buildings with hand-painted signs. It is easy to think of these early strips, now mostly redeveloped and thus increasingly rare, as folk art (Figs. 872, 873).

After the war, franchises and chains took over most strips. In a transformation that has occurred continuously up to the present, early strips have largely been homogenized by subsequent standardized building designs. Fetching prewar sig-

nage has been eliminated by industry practice and local zoning controls. Nevertheless, the Strip is the most vibrant spot in many communities, overflowing with unchecked visual energy.

Sunset Strip
Sunset Boulevard, West Hollywood, Los Angeles County, California

The most prominent American strip in post–World War II popular culture, excepting only Las Vegas Boulevard, the Sunset Strip also flourished beyond the reach of city regulations. Yet Sunset is unique in itself. Built up with multistory buildings set hard against the sidewalk, Sunset Boulevard here has more the feel of a slightly seedy uptown, than a conventional low-rise suburban strip set back behind surface parking lots.

Woodward Avenue

Detroit, Michigan

Woodward is a great diagonal extending northwest out of downtown toward Pontiac, 25 miles distant. Woodward is primarily a civic street, beginning near the Detroit River at Cadillac Square, extending through the semicircular Grand Circus Park, while passing by architectural landmarks including the Fox Theatre, Cass Gilbert's Public Library, Paul Cret's Detroit Institute of Arts, the long-time General Motors headquarters, Shrine of the Little Flower (see Moderne chapter), and Cranbrook (See National Romanticism chapter).

Woodward is also a cultural phenomenon, locally and nationally. Between downtown and the midtown area around the historic General Motors and Fisher buildings, residential side streets were marked by elaborate gateway monuments, in recognition of the prestige of a Woodward association. From the 1940s into the 1970s, Woodward served as a national auto esplanade, a place to see and be seen in the latest Big Four/Three models.

Camp Bowie Boulevard

Fort Worth, Texas

Camp Bowie Boulevard is the symbolic main street of Fort Worth, encompassing everything from art museums designed by the likes of Louis Kahn and Philip Johnson, to a highway strip dense with the usual commercial enterprises. Much of Camp Bowie has been repaved in red brick.

FILL'ER UP!

Cars and trucks needed continuous replenishment of gasoline and oil, as well as routine repair and supplies. Soon after 1900, they were provided at what was called a bulk depot. By about 1910, these were succeeded by smaller and more numerous refueling stops, predecessors of the gas (or service) station. By about 1920, true gas-service stations were common along city streets and even rural highways.

Because this was a new building type, without architectural precedent, early gas stations were either built as rude sheds or in a quasi-domestic imagery (Fig. 874). Soon, though, gas stations were built to satisfy functional requirements as well as to beautify a location, which led to period revival expressions, especially within big cities.

After the mid-1920s, major oil companies began to upgrade and standardize their gas stations in order to distinguish their brands. Occasionally, a gas station was designed as *architecture*, like the 1928 station (next entry) located on the outskirts of Santa Barbara.

CUSTOM-DESIGNED GAS STATIONS

Barnsdall–Rio Grande Gas Station FIG. 875

1928, abandoned, deteriorating
Morgan, Walls & Clements, architects
Near W end of Hollister, the former Coast Highway, 0.5 mi E of jct. with Hwy. 101, Goleta, California

Arguably this was the most beautiful gas station in America when built. A sturdy white stucco Spanish Colonial Revival tower rises

FIGS. 872, 873 Early Strips Most prewar American strips have long since been overbuilt, leaving scattered artifacts of the 1950s and 1960s, like these roadside scenes in San Antonio, Texas (Fig. 872) and Anaheim, California (Fig. 873), as reigning auto-era antiquities.

FIG. 874 Early Service Stations Without architectural precedent on which to rely, the first U.S. service stations often looked a lot like ordinary houses. The Posey-Bonfield station, built in 1914 in suburban Washington, D.C., is an archetype. The structure is virtually unaltered since the early 1930s (6124 MacArthur Blvd., Glen Echo, Maryland). *Library of Congress, Prints & Photographs, Historic American Buildings Survey*

FIG. 875 Filling Up in Civic Glory Even in its long-abandoned, steadily worsening state, the magnificent Barnsdall–Rio Grande gas station is fully worthy of Santa Barbara. One can imagine what the station was like when immaculately maintained in the 1930s, perhaps with a chauffeured Cord fueling up at the pump.

from a blue-white checkerboard base. The facility was a perfect announcement of one's arrival at the outskirts of Santa Barbara, before the old Coast Highway was superceded by the present, slightly inland expressway.

Lindholm Phillips 66 Gas Station FIG. 876

1956–1958
Frank Lloyd Wright, architect
Corner Hwys. 33 and 45, Cloquet, Minnesota

Lindholm's boldly projecting cantilevered roof seems to have been inspired by Wright's unbuilt 1922 barge design for Lake Tahoe, a dramatic visual gesture that Wright waited 35 years to realize. Lindholm is the only Wright-designed gas station, opening just a year before the architect's death. Phillips Petroleum, which was based in Bartlesville, Oklahoma, site of Wright's Price Tower (see Frank Lloyd Wright chapter), subsequently developed a national prototype station loosely based on this design.

Exxon Service Station FIG. 877

1996
Hardy Holzman Pfeiffer Associates, architects
Buena Vista Dr., E of World Dr., Walt Disney World, Bay Lake, Florida

Amidst all of the explicit imageries of Disney World, this structure establishes a unique identity, expressed as an immense lattice truss: modern architecture. It works in this fantasy context because the canopy's visual presence and immaculate maintenance seem fantastic compared to today's mundane service stations.

FIG. 876 Rare Wright Lindholm Phillips 66 was the only Frank Lloyd Wright-designed gas station built. *Library of Congress, Prints & Photographs, Historic American Buildings Survey*

FIG. 877 Modern Fantasy Disney World's Exxon station is visually effective as architecture, without any need for *cute*.

STANDARDIZED GAS STATIONS

Wadham's Oil and Grease Company

1916–1930; no longer extant
Alexander C. Eschweiler, architect
Milwaukee based, over 100 stations

In the mid teens, gas stations were still something of an exotic building type. For this prototype, an expression of exotica resulted in an oriental imagery, a simple pavilion of stylized Chinese imagery established largely by a turned-up tile roof. The first stations were painted in red, black, and yellow; some of them had stained-glass windows.

Beacon Oil Company Respectable FIG. 878

1923–
Coolidge & Carson, architects
Main and Salem Sts., Woburn, Massachusetts

Beacon Oil built 55 of these domed stations in the Boston area. They were stately, yet scaled to fit into the close-grained neighborhoods characteristic of this area. This is the last remaining of those 55 still functioning as a gas station; two others still extant in 2004 have been converted to other uses. One hopes that residents and motorists passing through town continue to support this endangered treasure by filling up here.

Westchester Parkway Stations

1928
Penrose Stout, architect
Hutchinson River Pkwy. and other Westchester County pkwys., New York

The Westchester parkways system was the pioneer American regional parkway system (see Roads chapter). Given the superior design qualities of these roadways, it is no surprise that the Westchester stations represented an architectural high point of domestic-imagery gas stations: houselike, with stone and shingles, shutters and bay windows.

Pure Oil English Cottage

Late 1920s–1930s; a few probably remain
Carl August Peterson, designer
Multiple locations

This domestic image with a distinctive high-pitched gable roof was intended to position the Pure Oil Company as neighborly, thus trustworthy. The cottage imagery is also visually sympathetic with residential neighborhoods. A basic cottage module could be expanded with service bays which looked like suburban garages.

Standard Service Station FIG. 879

1930s; a few probably remain
SE cor. Jackson and Second Sts., Brooklyn, Iowa

One of the few extant examples of the Standard Oil Moderne prototype. This station was once highly fashionable, wirh its white glazed brick and Broadway type projecting above the cornice.

Texaco Box Prototype FIG. 880

1937; a few probably remain
Walter Dorwin Teague, designer
500 locations by 1940

Texaco took the opposite track from Pure Oil in developing a modern prototype which addressed functional matters like service-bay efficiency, product sales, and lighting. These porcelain-metal stations retained just a hint of the Moderne, but still seemed reasonably contemporary in the early post–World War II years.

FIG. 878 **The Last Respectable** Beacon Oil Company built more than 50 of these classy gas stations in the Boston area. By 2004, only three remained, just one still pumping gas.

FIG. 880 **Functional Moderne** Walter Dorwin Teague was a noted industrial designer, in an era noted for its industrial designers. Teague's 1937 Texaco Box Prototypes, illustrated by this rare remaining example in Los Angeles, introduced new levels of functional efficiencies to American gas stations.

FIG. 879 **A Little Goes a Long Way** This Standard Oil station in the small town of Brooklyn, Iowa, is basically a simple brick box. Nevertheless, its stylized graphics and colorful banding are cost-effective ways of establishing a distinctive visual identity.

FIG. 881 **Classic Moderne** Compared to Teague's Texaco prototype (Fig. 880), these Socony-Mobil Moderne stations were pure style, and of a style already going out of date at that, in the 1940s. From today's perspective, however, this seems like an elegant design. In larger cities, these Moderne stations were sheathed in porcelain metal panels, though many, like this one in Mount Pleasant, Iowa, were stucco-covered.

Socony-Mobil Moderne FIG. 881

1940s; a few probably remain
Frederick G. Frost, Jr., architect
Multiple locations

With its distinctive corner cylinder, this porcelain-metal or stucco design was a stylistic throwback to the 1930s. However the large, curving glass window wall was light and open.

Mobil Contemporary

1964; a few remain
Eliot Noyes, architect; **Tom Geismar**, graphic designer
Multiple locations

High Modernism—the gas station as abstract sculpture. Noyes played the minimalist box of the station against a bold circular canopy, evoking a space-age connotation. This design went through evolutionary adaptations continuing into the 1990s, with the participation of the Noyes firm and successor architect Alan Goldberg. With the move to self-service, larger rectangular canopies appeared, with circular lighting recesses as vestiges of the earlier geometry.

YOU WANT FRIES WITH THAT?

Diners, Drive-Ins, and Fast Food are mainstays of American popular culture, anchors of the strip. Many food service designs through the 1950s were visually unique, before chain stan-dardization homogenized the type in recent decades. On the other hand, many diners of the 1930s onward were standard models from a handful of manufacturers.

Diners appeared first, evolving out of 1870s-era food push-carts and later lunch wagons. White Castle diners, founded in 1921, are significant in several respects. Founder Billy Ingram popularized hamburgers as a mainstream food and a popular-culture staple. Ingram's innovations in standardized food serv-ice anticipated the fast-food revolution perfected a quarter-century later by the McDonald brothers.

Drive-ins began to appear as Americans took to the road in the 1920s. A Pig Stand along the Dallas–Fort Worth Highway near Dallas was apparently the first drive-in, perhaps better described as a drive-*up*, opening in 1921. Still, drive-ins were largely a California phenomenon throughout the pre–World War II era.

Drive-ins became ubiquitous in postwar America, although by the 1960s they were increasingly overshadowed by fast-food restaurants. In 1948, the McDonald brothers of San Bernardino, California converted their existing drive-in, carhop restaurant to a "Speedy Service System" approach featuring "self-service, a limited menu, and fast turnover." According to popular culture maven Michael Karl Witzel, with these innovations, the Amer-ican fast-food restaurant was born.

DINERS

White Castle FIG. 882
1921–

Billy Ingram, Walter Anderson, entrepreneurs; **Lloyd Ray**, chain
prototype designer
Wichita, Kansas, multiple national locations

White Castle's famous crenellated-castle imagery drew from the
original crude, whitewashed, rusticated concrete-block hamburger
stand, a joint venture between fry cook Anderson and Ingram, who
came from a real-estate background. Ingram built up a large chain

FIG. 882 Vanishing Urban Phenomenon Once ubiquitous in the blue-collar wards
of Midwestern cities, traditional porcelain-panel White Castles of the 1930s are, alas,
now virtually extinct. This Minneapolis Castle has been moved since this photo was
taken, and is safe for now, one hopes, in a new role as an office.

FIG. 883 The Great American Diner Classic urban diners such as Mickey's Diner
are genuine expressions of the 1930s, a time when many Americans could barely
afford a square meal. Diners like the Park West (Fig. 884) built in the affluent postwar
years did not capture the feeling of these Depression-era "greasy spoons."

of White Castles, mostly in Eastern and Midwestern locations.

White Castle System, Inc. is vertically integrated, with construction and restaurant-supply subsidiaries. Ray's classic porcelain-panel Castles of the 1930s are now largely lost, supplanted by
a modernized prototype that retains abstracted crenellations and a
vestigial tower that superficially recall the earlier stands. Among
the 1930s classics is a twice-moved 1936 stand (Fig. 882), converted into a business office, now located at 33rd and Lyndale
Avenue S., in Minneapolis. Some recent White Castles have
returned to their material origins, enclosed in crude, whitewashed,
rusticated concrete block.

Mickey's Diner FIG. 883
1937–1939

Jerry O'Mahony Company, manufacturer
36 W. Seventh St., St. Paul, Minnesota

A classic 1930s diner, with Broadway graphics and an integrated
rooftop sign, Mickey's provides a palpable, authentic connection to
an earlier era when downtown St. Paul was a mecca of the workingman.

Park West Diner FIG. 884
1990s

Kullman Corporation, manufacturer
1400 Rt. 46 W, 0.2 mi. E of Hwy. 639, Little Falls, New Jersey

Americana Diner
1990s

Kullman Corporation, manufacturer
Hwy. 35 and Shrewsbury Ave., Shrewsbury, New Jersey

Rather than expressing a unique look of our own times, today's
new diners seem to be searching for a catchy retro look by incorporating a hodge-podge of earlier diner design elements from the
1930s and the 1950s. In these two nearly identical diners, a basic
railway-car diner form is rendered baroque with a double-rolled
roof. A bulky vertical entrance tower of glass block plays off
uneasily against the horizontal mass. The interior is sleek and shiny,
with hints of the past abstracted in laminate.

DRIVE-INS

Drive-ins date either from a Dallas-area Pig Stand that opened in 1921 or, more explicitly, from a *carhop* Pig Stand at the corner of Sunset and Vermont in Hollywood, which opened in 1932. In any case, Los Angeles drive-in chains like Carpenter's and Herbert's soon followed, making the LA Southland a prewar center of drive-in innovations. John Love noted that by the early 1940s, Los Angeles entrepreneur-operators like Robert Wian, inventor of the "Big Boy" sandwich, were exporting the "carhop drive-in phenomenon throughout the United States."

Stan's Drive-In
1941, razed
Stanley Burke, entrepreneur
16th and K Sts., Sacramento, California

Burke popularized the round drive-in, which dates from Wayne McAllister's 1936 design for Herbert's drive-in in Los Angeles, and proceeded to build a chain in California during the 1940s. Stan's clean lines and fluted parapet were architecturally advanced for their time. The neon really "lit up the boulevard" at night, complemented by the streetfront pylon sign featuring a 20-foot-high flashing neon carhop. What we think of as the postwar California car culture effectively dates back to just before World War II, at Stan's.

Bob's Big Boy Drive-In FIG. 885
1949
Wayne McAllister, architect
4211 Riverside Dr., Burbank, California

McAllister was respected for his efficient circular drive-in designs. For this design, however, any operating efficiency is far overshadowed by the 35-foot-high neon sign "ensemble," which visually dominates both the restaurant and its surroundings. The entire spectacle is especially sensational at night. Little wonder that Bob's has been designated a historic landmark.

Googies FIG. 886
1949, razed
John Lautner, architect
Sunset Blvd. at Crescent Heights, West Hollywood, California

A true celebrity building, both lavishly praised and cruelly ridiculed for its uninhibited collage of forms and colors, including the bright red roof. Soon after its opening, over-the-top designs, especially if located in Southern California, began to be described as "Googie Architecture."

STANDARDIZED FAST-FOOD RESTAURANTS

In 1940, Richard and Maurice McDonald opened a drive-in at Fourteenth and E streets in San Bernardino, California. While successful, it faced increasing competition, and the presence of carhops tended to turn drive-ins into teen-age hangouts, which kept away families.

In response, the McDonalds simplified their menu, concentrating on hamburgers, and changed the format from carhops to service windows. Their changes were comprehensive, including a "fishbowl" look that highlighted gleaming stainless steel prepa-

FIG. 884 Retro Diners The Depression had receded safely into the distant past by the 1990s, and visual nostalgia powered a predictable wave of retro diners, most of them in the East. As cosmetic interpretations of a markedly different period, diners like the Park West could never seem authentic. No matter. Today's customers, lacking personal experience with the 1930s, are probably satisfied to appreciate newer diners as campy entertainment.

FIG. 885 A Blast From the Past Bob's Big Boy Drive-In authentically transports one back in time to the energetic early post–World War II years. The restaurant is a period piece in itself, though overshadowed by its signature freestanding sign.

FIG. 886 Googie Architecture This modest-scaled coffee shop attained national notoriety on account of its audacious expressiveness in an era dominated architecturally by button-down Modernism. © J. Paul Getty Trust. Used with permission. Julius Shulman Photography Archive Research Library at the Getty Research Institute

FIG. 887 Proto-Icon For this transitional McDonald's in Downey, California, Richard McDonald arrived at a diagram of the classic Golden Arches McDonald's drive-in.

FIG. 888 Iconic Golden Arches The mature expression of McDonald's classic Golden Arches drive-ins can be experienced at Des Plaines, Illinois. Notice the subtle softening of the arch radius, compared to Downey (Fig. 887), and how Downey's triangular side fascia has here evolved into a soffit.

ration areas. More important, the McDonald brothers developed a standardized assembly-line food preparation process. To maximize efficiencies, they invented new kitchen equipment and tools. John Love stated that in the late 1940s, "they had so refined their production techniques that they had discovered a unique restaurant format." That format was fast food.

McDonald's Drive-In FIG. 887
1953
SW corner Lakewood Blvd. and Florence Ave., Downey, California

There were at least two transitional McDonald's drive-ins between the McDonald brothers restaurant in San Bernardino and the classic prototype (following entry). This one was the first, followed by another built in 1954 at 563 E. Foothill Blvd. in Azusa, California. Gebhard and Winter assessed this design as "midway between popular and serious architecture."

McDonald's Classic Golden Arches FIG. 888
1955
Richard McDonald, conceptualizer; **Stanley Meston**, architect
400 N. Lee St., Des Plaines, Illinois

While the first of this classic design was built in Phoenix, opening in 1953, the McDonald's Corporation restored this first Ray Kroc–era restaurant in suburban Chicago to mint condition, adding restored vintage cars to the parking lot. This McDonald's "museum" is a must-see destination for popular culture aficionados.

McDonald's Mansard
1968
James Schindler, corporate architect
Multiple locations

In the late 1960s, McDonald's moved to an indoor-seating format, and the classic walk-up design was superceded by an earth-toned box with a double-pitch mansard roof. The iconic Golden Arches was relegated to signs and a paste-on logo applied to the walls. Variations of this prototype design were still in service four decades after its introduction.

Carl's Jr. Prototype FIG. 889
2003
RSA (Los Angeles), architects
7200 Firestone Blvd., Downey, California

Rare among fast-food chains: a stylish work of architecture, one that has also been designed to function well. Special attention has been given to the drive-through environment, because half of the customers choose the drive-through option. Clean, sweeping lines set this prototype apart from the typical fast-food norm.

Incidentally, this location is only a couple of miles from the 1953 McDonald's drive-in cited above.

INDIVIDUALIZED FAST FOOD RESTAURANTS

Consistency is the highest goal of most fast-food chains, and that usually implies standardizing design. Standardization does not have to result in mediocre buildings, as the Carl's Jr. prototype (previous entry) demonstrates, but, alas, it usually does. However, individual fast-food locations and smaller chains occasionally achieve interesting personalities.

Among the latter is Beef-a-Roo, a regional chain of nine restaurants based in Illinois. Each of the Beef-a-Roo's Rockford-area restaurants follows a distinct theme, enhanced by authentic, period artifacts displayed inside the restaurant. Visual imageries vary by neighborhood setting, intended to tie in with local history.

Beef-a-Roo, "Rock & Roll"
1991
Seigfreid, Edwards & Coady, architects
6380 E. Riverside Blvd., Loves Park, Illinois

The exterior reference to Moderne diners is symbolically appropriate for this contemporary strip setting. However, the memorable visual experience occurs on the interior, which is packed with authentic Rock & Roll–era artifacts.

Beef-a-Roo, "North Woods"
1999
Seigfreid, Edwards & Coady, architects
4601 Adamson Ln. SE corner N. Alpine Rd., Machesney Park, Illinois

Compared to the "Rock & Roll" format above, this site achieves its desired visual flavor through a combination of imagery and artifacts: the feeling of a stylized hunting lodge combined with a collection of old fishing reels, an ancient outboard motor, and plenty of game trophies.

FIG. 889 **Design Innovation** The Carl's Jr. prototype was approached as architecture, as opposed to *faux* imagery. The design emphasizes the drive-through, choice of fully half of the location's customers.

FIG. 890 **Theming** Beef-a-Roo's Train Station restaurant in Illinois was modeled after a regional landmark. While the design was necessarily modified to accommodate its program, the restaurant attains a plausible sense of authenticity through the cultural connection.

Beef-a-Roo, "Train Station" FIG. 890
2003
Seigfreid, Edwards & Coady, architects
5109 Rockrose Ct., NW corner Hwy. 251 and Hononegah Rd., Roscoe, Illinois

The chain's theming techniques continued to evolve, from primarily interior artifacts in the 1991 restaurant, to more of a balance between architectural imagery and artifacts in 1999, to primarily an architectural expression here. Based on a historic railroad station in French Lick, Indiana, this restaurant is carried visually by its architectural qualities, a deft synthesis of explicit historical references and functional accommodation.

(NO) VACANCY

As Americans took to the roads in the early 1900s, new forms of overnight lodging were required. Conventional hotels in the centers of towns usually did not provide convenient, inexpensive accommodations. Nor were there enough available rooms of any kind, as ever-increasing numbers of motorists embarked on cross-country trips.

By the teens, two kinds of auto-related lodging had sprung up along highways: houses converted to "tourist homes" (more recently known as bed-and-breakfasts), and small tourist cabins, cottages constructed so that cars could drive right up to the door and unload-reload efficiently. This latter type evolved into the motel ("motor hotel"), a term dating from the Milestone Mo-Tel (1924–1925) in San Luis Obispo, California

Only a tiny percentage of either type was of any visual distinction. At best—and this was rare—a restored historic property set in mature landscaping happened to be near a highway and provided both convenience and a handsome physical environment. Today, one reacts with predictable nostalgia when encountering pre–World War II tourist cabins, although we usually don't actually *stay* in them! A few of these tourist courts are well-maintained and colorfully painted, providing a briefly interesting visual experience.

Inevitably, the detached-cottage model was compressed into a continuous wing of side-by-side rooms, often called a tourist court; this process evolved imperceptivity into one-story motels with one or more wings of rooms. Thousands of tourist courts and early motels remain in business, especially in small-town America.

After the war, the motel model was expanded and thoroughly refined by chains like Holiday Inn, Ramada, and Howard Johnson. Without question, these newer motels were much more comfortable places in which to stay, though they were unavoidably visually homogenized in the process, if sometimes dressed up in a cardboard regional or brand imagery.

Other than the Madonna Inn, few American motels have achieved destination status as both visually unique and as desirable accommodations by contemporary standards.

The following sampling includes representatives of the anonymous early tourist courts and the postwar king of motel chains, Holiday Inn.

Fairyland Cottages FIG. 891
1937; partly demolished, 2006
410 W. Lake Dr., Detroit Lakes, Minnesota

Slightly offset from the street and crisp in their white trim and red paint, these tiny cottages represented the typical pre–World War II tourist cottages found in resort areas all over the United States.

FIG. 891 **Resort Cabins** Variations of tourist cabins based on location were offered in resort areas. Fairyland Cottages in Minnesota were located within sight of, but not directly "on" a lake. The lower land costs for properties separated from lakeshore by a busy street translated into lower rental rates, attracting budget-conscious vacationers.

FIG. 892 **Creating the Attraction** Where a motel was not located adjacent to a feature like a lake or a national park, it could be designed to become its own signature attraction. The several tepee motels, like this Wigwam Village in Holbrook, Arizona, effectively accomplished their mission as freestanding attractions.

FIG. 893 **Home on the Highways** Remarkable in the 1950s, Holiday Inns offered ideal family road-travel lodging: clean, dependable, convenient locations, and value. This first Holiday Inn, located in Memphis, included a coffee-and-donut shop offering "gifts, souvenirs, candy" in the boxy office building on the left. Drive-up rooms were provided in the low, gabled wings at the right, behind the soon-to-be famous sign. *Holiday Inn® Hotels & Resorts*

FIG. 894 **Well Beyond Mere Excess** Madonna Inn in California is mildly outrageous on the outside, becoming *seriously* over-the-top with its signature interiors like the main restaurant-dining room shown here.

FIG. 895 **Lodging as Experience** Unique lodging like the Red Caboose Motel in Pennsylvania becomes a destination in itself.

Wigwam Village Motels FIG. 892

1937
Frank Redford, owner and designer
U.S. 31 W, N of Highway 70, Cave City, Kentucky
1947
Frank Redford, owner and designer
811 W. Hopi Dr., Holbrook, Arizona

The tepee (tipi) is a familiar form in American pop culture, but Redford's seven-location chain offered perhaps the best of the tepee motels. These two remain, with vestiges of the original full-bore Western-style interiors. Individual unit-tepees are arranged in a semicircle around a larger office tepee in the Kentucky location. In Arizona, a much less gracious parking lot setting is enhanced by cars of the 1950s and 1960s parked as permanent decorative fixtures.

Blue Swallow Motel

1939; recently restored
815 E. Route 66 (old Tucumcari Blvd)., Tucumcari, New Mexico

A simple, stuccoed travel court is distinguished by a wonderful sign—splendid at night. The Blue Swallow is a reigning celebrity among connoisseurs of Route 66 signage.

Holiday Inn FIG. 893

1952; razed
Kemmons Wilson, Wallace Johnson, developers; **Eddie Bluestein**, designer; **Doll Wilson**, interiors; **William W. Bond, Jr.**, (later) corporate architect
4985 Summer Ave., Memphis, Tennessee

The Holiday Inn story is based on Wilson's being unable to find convenient, economical lodging on early post–World War II family auto trips. Thus was born the notion of a ubiquitous, moderate-cost, completely reliable motel chain. Bond was a national pioneer in standardizing and automating the production of construction documents for Holiday Inn projects. As it grew, the Holiday Inn chain developed vast numbers of urban hotels around the world.

Madonna Inn FIG. 894

1958–1969
Alex & Phyllis Madonna, designers and builders
NW corner U.S. 101 and Madonna Rd., San Luis Obispo, California

Each of the 108 guest rooms is decked out in a different theme, from Swiss Chalet to Daisy Mae. Reflecting the original Madonna family business in heavy construction, large rocks are employed everywhere. The entire extravaganza is visually tied together by a signature "Madonna Pink" color, which culminates in the glittering main dining room (Fig. 894). At Madonna Inn, popular culture has been raised to high fashion.

Red Caboose Motel FIG. 895

1970 ff.
Donald Denlinger, developer
1.4 mi. E of central Strasburg, Pennsylvania, on Rt. 741, then N 2 blocks on Paradise Ln.

Occasionally a mad personal vision becomes reality, as here, where Denlinger converted an assortment of surplus cabooses into a motel, improbably set out in a bucolic landscape.

LAS VEGAS

Las Vegas is synonymous with the ultimate strip. Founded in 1905 as a railroad camp, this remote desert settlement later managed, just barely, to survive on crumbs of federal largesse spilling over from construction of the nearby Boulder (now Hoover) Dam in the 1930s; and then from wartime military activity at what is now Nellis Air Force Base in the 1940s.

A wide-open entertainment district along Fremont Street provided the city's basic attraction in those years. It was made possible by permissive state laws and relaxed enforcement of already minimal local ordinances. Nevada re-legalized gambling in 1931.

Since the arrival of post–World War II casino culture along Highway 91 from Los Angeles, now Las Vegas Boulevard, the Las Vegas gambling-gaming industry, and hence its supporting architecture, has continuously evolved over the past half century. Today, Las Vegas provides three distinct entertainment settings. One is along the historic short stretch of Fremont Street in downtown Las Vegas (see Civic Design chapter).

The second setting is the famed Las Vegas Strip itself, subject of this section. The Strip encompasses an astonishing group of super-casinos and hotels lining Las Vegas Boulevard from Stratosphere on the north to (for now, at least) Mandalay Bay on the south. The Strip is located outside of the municipality of Las Vegas, in Clark County. That location is not accidental, since this unincorporated locale adjacent to the city of Las Vegas initially offered an absolute minimum of code restrictions to casino pioneers.

To put The Strip in perspective, early in the postwar era Las Vegas imposed truly minimal zoning restrictions, compared to

FIG. 896 Irrepressible Vegas Welcome to *Fabulous* Las Vegas sign (currently at the south end of The Strip) was designed by Betty Willis in 1959, a year after the original Stardust signs (Popular Culture chapter, Fig. 912) confirmed The Strip to be a mecca of fantastic signage. The welcome sign attracts a constant flow of people seeking to commemorate their visits by having their pictures taken with this icon.

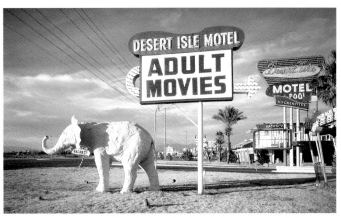

FIGS. 897, 898 Anyone Can Play Las Vegas has historically been economically egalitarian. Even considering the latest group of high-end super-casinos, a wide range of budgets is accommodated throughout the area, with modest lodgings such as the Desert Isle Motel (Fig. 897) interspersed amid mind-boggling opulence like the visually extravagant Forum (Fig. 898).

FIG. 899 Space The Strip has flourished from the 1940s Bugsy Siegel era right up to the present because of space. Although the Las Vegas region has become heavily built up, there is still plenty of vacant land right behind The Strip, as this 2005 view from east of The Strip and north of Tropicana Avenue shows. Given as well historically permissive zoning restrictions, developers are pretty much limited only by their imaginations.

FIGS. 900, 901 The Look of The Strip Has Continuously Evolved Mid-1950s casino-hotels like the Sands (Fig. 900) relied on eccentric architecture, augmented by soaring pylon signs, often with no apparent visual connection between the two. Just a decade later, the new Caesars Palace emphasized a coordinated, themed environment including clipped landscaping, fountains, and statuary (Fig. 901).

many other large U.S. cities. That it was seen as desirable to be free of even these minor requirements, hardly more stringent than guidelines, suggests just how far-out was the thinking of early casino entrepreneurs building outside city limits. Hence, modern Las Vegas, meaning the mythic Strip, began, and remains, a place utterly unlike any other in America (Figs. 897, 898).

The third Las Vegas gaming setting includes the scattering of casinos that are neither on Fremont nor The Strip. These range from mom-and-pop operations which have not yet been gobbled up by large-scale development, to the ultra-shiny McCarran airport terminal, where the merry clinking of one-armed bandits greets arriving passengers literally before they are off the jetway.

In his essential study, *Viva Las Vegas*, Alan Hess identified the first such stand-alone Las Vegas-area casino as the 1931 Meadows Club, designed by Paul Warner for a site along the Boulder Highway, an ideal location to waylay Boulder Dam workers heading toward Las Vegas for entertainment.

THE PYLON ERA
1945–early 1960s

The classic story of modern, big-time gambling in Las Vegas originates from the fabled Bugsy Siegel. It was just before World War II, in 1941, when Benjamin Siegel arrived in town. His initial attention was focused on making Mob investments in Fremont Street casinos. By war's end, however, Siegel had presciently envisioned a radically different future for Las Vegas, centered along what is now The Strip.

Siegel's 1946 Flamingo Hotel, designed by George Vernon Russell (totally remodeled in 1953 by Pereira and Luckman), was not the first Strip development: a handful of casino-resort establishments had already been opened along the Los Angeles Highway in unincorporated Clark County. Notable among these were the El Rancho Vegas (1941, razed), designed by the prolific Wayne McAllister; and the Last Frontier (1942, razed) by William Moore.

However, Siegel's Flamingo introduced an exceptionally attractive environment for a Las Vegas casino. Of course there was much more land area—raw space—than around crowded Fremont Street then and now (Fig. 899). Plenty of on-site auto parking was indispensable in luring those driving up from the LA Southland.

As significantly, the Flamingo offered a completely new visual environment: not the cowboy imageries which had characterized Las Vegas casinos up to that time, but modern and sophisticated, several years earlier than the even-more-excessive Miami Beach hotel interiors of Morris Lapidus (see Mid-Century Expressionism chapter).

With the establishment of a glamorous image at the Flamingo, the classic strip era continued with openings of the Desert Inn (1950), designed by McAllister and Hugh Taylor; Sahara (1952), by Max Meltzmann; Sands (1952, Fig. 900) by McAllister; Dunes (1955) by Robert Dorr, Jr. and John Replogle;

Tropicana (1957), by M. Tony Sherman; and Stardust (1958).

Postwar Las Vegas casinos employed architecturally extravagant interiors, textures, and colors—but most of all, spectacular pylon signs and lighting—to establish their presence. Strip signage attained its artistic peak in 1965, with the fabulous Stardust pylon (Fig. 912).

TOTAL ENVIRONMENTS
1966–mid-1980s

The 1966 opening of Caesars Palace (Fig. 901), designed by Melvin Grossman, signaled the introduction of the Strip casino as a themed total environment, no longer essentially a box with an eye-catching pylon sign in front. The Caesars pedimented sign was designed by Jack Larsen and Kermit Wayne; the 1988–1992 expansion, with an opulent sidewalk portal-pavilion (Fig. 898) and Forum shopping mall were designed by Marnell Corrao Associates.

Caesars Palace was a seamless, *designed* integration of frontage, arrival, and interior discovery. Its theme of a continuous Roman bacchanal solidified the perception that Las Vegas was fun-loving and exotic, an effective update of the national role long held by New Orleans.

Las Vegas consequently emerged as an adult Disneyland, attracting not just serious gamblers and sophisticates, but also millions of average Americans and foreign visitors who thought of themselves neither as gamblers nor as especially glamorous.

Remarkably low hotel rates and giveaway meals were attractions, casting Las Vegas as an inexpensive place for a brief visit.

DESTINATIONS
1989–present

The Strip continued its evolution with the opening of the ultra-luxurious, Joel Bergman–designed Mirage in 1989. This signaled yet another radical change in the economics of Las Vegas, toward an expensive resort destination with many upscale attractions, not just a casino-hotel with inexpensive rooms and food. The even-more-luxurious Bellagio by Jon Jerde and Butler, DeRuyter, opened nearby in 1998.

Throughout the 1990s, a series of programmatic casino-hotels opened, including the castlesque Excalibur (1990), by Veldon Simpson; the Luxor pyramid (1993) also by Veldon Simpson, and sceneographic extravaganzas like New York, New York (1997, Fig. 902) by Gaskin & Bezanski; The Venetian (1999), by The Stubbins Associates; and Paris (1999) designed by Mirage architect Joel Bergman.

This latest iteration of Las Vegas is less a cheap date and more an essential, singular travel destination, the American Bangkok. A visit costs more than in the late 1980s, but there is now much more here to experience.

For designers, the Las Vegas Strip provides unmatched demonstrations in its sheer visual energy, day and especially night, and as the international cutting edge of integrated attractions.

FIG. 902 Today's Scenographic Strip New York New York is probably the most arresting of the recent scenographic casino-hotels, in part because of its prominent, corner location, and also because of its startling plays of scale. Had this been carried out with less than brash confidence it would have been kitsch. As executed, New York New York is simply beyond words.

Popular Culture

1880–2004

FIG. 903 No Shame in Excess, Apparently American popular-culture design can be brazenly uninhibited. Celebrated freewheeling expressions like the Los Angeles pop-culture icon, Tail o' the Pup, are simply intended to gain commercial attention. Nothing deeper is at stake than having a little fun while making a buck!

American popular culture is routinely cited by both critics and admirers of the United States. Critics see attractions like, for instance, Disneyland as plastic, cheapened replicas of an authentic cultural experience. To anyone with such a sensibility, signs and programmatic structures further demonstrate the shallowness of U.S. culture.

Admirers look at the very same examples and note that Disneyland and Walt Disney World annually attract tens of millions of visitors, from all over the world. Besides, signs and programmatic structures demonstrate that creativity and freedom of expression are intrinsic to American everyday life, not just the province of high design and art.

The following sampling of American popular-culture landmarks cites Amusement Parks, Signs, and Programmatic Constructions. The time span includes a golden era of vibrant popular-culture expression, from the emergence of national mass culture after the 1880s boom until it diminished after the 1960s, as American mass-culture expressions were increasingly systematized, and thus effectively visually sanitized, despite a few noteworthy exceptions.

AMUSEMENT PARKS

Coney Island FIG. 904
Sea Lion Park, 1895; Steeplechase Park, 1897; Luna Park, 1902–1903; Dreamland, 1904
Fred Thompson, managing architect for Luna Park
Surf Ave. to the Boardwalk, between W 8th and W 19th Sts., Brooklyn, New York

Coney Island is a sandy spit of land, which as early as 1829 attracted an elite clientele drawn by its relative inaccessibility. That demographic turned completely around after public transportation reached the area in 1895. Coney Island then quickly became the leisure destination of choice for urban working families.

In addition to an ocean beach, Coney Island attractions included several self-contained amusement parks, each of which was distinctly different from the rest. In 1902, entrepreneur Fred Thompson developed Luna Park (Fig. 904), an orientalesque fantasyland which radically changed Coney Island's character, and in the process, also invented the modern American amusement park. Luna Park was at its best at night, when 250,000 lights outlined and highlighted its exotic features.

Three latter-day Coney Island amusement structures survive and have been designated official New York City landmarks: the 150-foot-high Wonder Wheel (1920); The Cyclone rollercoaster (1927); and the 262-foot-high Parachute Jump tower, relocated here after the 1939 New York World's Fair (maintained and lighted, but not operating).

The Boardwalk FIG. 905
1903 ff; Casino Arcade, 1907; Carousel, 1910–1911; Giant Dipper Roller Coaster, 1924
Fred Swanton, John Martin, promoter-developers; **Charles Looff**, Carousel; **Arthur Looff**, Giant Dipper roller coaster
Beach St., at end of Cliff St., Santa Cruz, California

This garish, visually undisciplined, and utterly charming amusement park extends along a half-mile of Pacific oceanfront. The Casino, part of which is visible in Fig. 905, provides an oasis of architectural order. Not only is The Boardwalk a true regional institution, attracting about two-million visits annually, and the only remaining beachfront amusement park on the West Coast, but as John Chase observed, it is historically valuable as "a reminder of the unsanitized pre-Disneyland amusement park."

Disneyland FIG. 906
1953–1955
Walter E. Disney, visionary, developer; **Herbert Ryman, John Hench**, Disney Imagineering, conceptual designers; **Bill Evans**, chief landscape architect
1313 S. Harbor Blvd., Anaheim, California

Disneyland was the most celebrated popular-culture development of the 1950s. The Magic Kingdom, reached through Main Street, elevated the American amusement park to new levels of order, attention to detail, and conceptual sophistication. Sleeping Beauty's castle (loosely fashioned after Mad Prince Ludwig's Neuschwanstein castle in Bavaria) and the monorail interconnecting parking, park, and hotel were instantly famous.

COMMERCIAL SIGNS

Signage is ubiquitous, and no wonder: we all depend on signs for information, and to find our way around unfamiliar places.

FIG. 904 Jam-packed Amusements Given New York City's high population and the consequent premium on beachfront property, Coney Island attractions like Luna Park were densely built up by American norms. *Library of Congress, Prints & Photographs*

FIG. 905 Regional Institution Locally cherished for a century, the Boardwalk is to many the true essence of Santa Cruz. Initially, the domed Casino, now insouciantly painted in almost-vulgar hues, served as the Boardwalk's primary visual landmark—in addition to the beach itself, of course. Today, rides are prominent. This photo of the Casino was taken off-season; throughout the summer, the Boardwalk is merrily overrun with crowds.

FIG. 906 American as Apple Pie Disneyland is virtually synonymous with "America" all over the world. This must be where the notion of an "inner child" originated, since one's inner child is lavished with unrelenting attention throughout the park.

FIG. 907 **Hollywoodland** Eye-catching promotions seem to be fundamental to American culture. That is probably why so many become visual icons. Of course it sure helps if your advertising sign is several hundred feet long and located near a mountain crest. This dramatic photo of the Hollywood sign looks north over Mount Lee into the vast San Fernando Valley. *Carol M. Highsmith / Library of Congress, Prints & Photographs*

FIG. 908 **The Flying Red Horse** By the 1950s, Socony-Mobil's "Pegasus" had become ubiquitous along America's motorways. Today small, simplified versions of this symbol can be seen at many Mobil stations, but you will probably have to make a pilgrimage to see one like this.

FIG. 909 **Roadside Nostalgia** This White Rose gas station attendant has faithfully watched over his section of what was once a busy Iowa highway. The route is now superseded by I-80, passing by a mile—and a lifetime—away.

Signs can also be controversial, especially advertising signs and billboards, if they are perceived as what some critics label "visual clutter." Whatever the take on signage, generally, the signs in this section have become local icons, visually energizing their settings.

Hollywoodland, now "Hollywood" FIG. 907
1923; "land" removed in 1945
Hollywood Hills, Los Angeles, California

Originally, this LA icon was nothing more than a temporary sign advertising a real estate development. It lost its last four letters in the process of becoming the international emblem of Movieland. Donated to the city in 1945, it was rebuilt in permanent materials in the 1970s.

Socony-Mobil "Pegasus" FIG. 908
1933
8051 Flying Cloud Dr. (Hwy. 212), Eden Prairie, Minnesota

The once-ubiquitous "Flying Red Horse," is now found at only a handful of locations nationwide, including the Gordon Smith Mobil station (Fig. 908).

White Rose Gas Station Attendant FIG. 909
1935
Old Hwy. 6 at Sherman St., Menlo, Iowa

This larger-than-life figure was probably thought of as unremarkable roadside advertising when installed, just as long-distance auto travel was becoming practical. Now this faded sign in a tiny Midwestern town provokes instant nostalgia for those simpler times.

Pedro the Big Man FIG. 910

1951

Hwy. 301, just off I-95 at North Carolina exit I, North Hamer, South Carolina

South of the Border is a 350-acre Mexican-themed tourist stop that is the East Coast equivalent of South Dakota's Wall Drug, although the programmatic construction here is far better. The star of this irrepressible complex is the 97-foot-high "Pedro," topped by the requisite sombrero.

Anheuser-Busch Flying Eagle

1950s

Westbound Hwy. 40, St. Louis, Missouri

A neon eagle based on the Anheuser-Busch corporate logo energetically flaps its wings for passing drivers. A similar sign is located atop the A-B brewery near the Newark Airport in New Jersey.

McDonald's "Golden Arches"

1952

Richard McDonald, designer; **George Dexter,** sign maker

San Bernardino, California

The idea for the squeezed parabolas to spell out an "M" was McDonald's. Dexter came up with the bright yellow color. The rest, as they say, is history.

Holiday Inn "Great Sign" FIG. 911

1952

Kemmons Wilson, Eddie Bluestein, designers

4985 Summer Ave., Memphis, Tennessee; later multiple locations

By the 1960s, Holiday Inn's Great Sign was ubiquitous throughout the United States, seemingly a permanent part of the American roadside. Alas, it was abandoned in the 1980s for an innocuous, backlit plastic panel sign. For popular-culture mavens, the world has never been the same.

Stardust Pylon Sign FIG. 912

Original façade and pylon signage, 1958; classic pylon with "Electra-jag" font, 1965; pylon simplified, with Helvetica font, 1991; casino demolished, 2007

Kermit Wayne, Young Electric Sign Co., 1958 signage designer;

Ad-Art Inc., 1965 classic pylon designer-builder

3000 Las Vegas Blvd., Las Vegas, Nevada

The very best vintage Las Vegas pylon sign. It boasted impressive statistics: 188 feet tall, 40,000 bulbs, 10,000 fluorescent tubes, 27 separate lighting sequences, and more. But its artistry and sparkling exuberance far transcended any such figures.

Wayne's original 1958 road sign was circular, with a wondrous complementing universe of starbursts and planets spread across an otherwise nondescript casino front. The 1958 sign was replaced by the classic 1965 space-age design; it lasted until a 1991 revamping. Even so diminished—it's hard not to grieve for the "Electra Jag" font—this was still pretty striking signage. Stardust was closed at the end of 2006, the property to be redeveloped.

BILLBOARDS

Coca Cola FIG. 913

1895

2 W. Main St., Cartersville, Georgia

The earliest American billboards were ad bills pasted to the walls of buildings. Soon, semi-permanent advertising was painted on the

FIG. 910 Truly The Big Man "Pedro" is the surely most memorable character you will encounter along I-95 between New York and Florida! Even better, he is surrounded by a multi-block convention of whimsical creatures.

FIG. 911 The Late, Great Sign Holiday Inn's distinctive Great Sign easily stood out from the visual cacophony of most any strip. The substitution of an innocuous plastic panel sign after 1982 was a milestone in the homogenization of American roadside culture.

FIG. 912 Signs as Art The 1965 Stardust pylon sign, now gone, was more than a classic of the Golden Age of Las Vegas pylons. Especially considering the technical complexity of such an elaborate production, Stardust was a great work of popular art.

FIG. 913 **Proto-Billboard** Painted wall advertising served as a precursor for the twentieth-century billboard. This restored 1890s sign in a small Georgia town is one of the earliest remaining commercial wall signs.

FIG. 914 **Prized Pachyderm** Like the Hollywood sign (Fig. 907) a real estate promotion that grew on its community, Lucy the Elephant is now a revered civic treasure in Margate, New Jersey.

FIG. 915 **Southland Babylon** Hands down, Los Angeles is the capital of programmatic structures. You can probably understand why, while programmatic designs are usually based on objects, Samson Tyre and Rubber Company's offices were based on a *city*.

sides. This is one of the oldest remaining painted advertisements in the United States, restored in the 1990s.

Coppertone Girl with Dog
1959, art created
Joyce Ballentyne Brand, graphic artist
SE quadrant, Golden Glades interchange, I-95 and Hwy. 836/NE. 167th St., Miami-Dade County, Florida

Post–World War II was the great era of painted-bulletin billboards, for the plethora of new products introduced after the war. Brand's Coppertone Girl was widely employed in print ads as well, but here is an original billboard, appropriately located next to a road leading straight to the beach.

Superrealism
1970s
Sunset Strip, Los Angeles and elsewhere

Billboard advertising closely follows the contemporary art scene: indeed, superstar artist James Rosenquist once painted billboards as his day job. The immense photo-realistic images of people and products of 1970s billboards reflected a synthesis of the pop-art subjects of Andy Warhol and super-realist images of painters such as Richard Estes.

DISTRICT SIGNAGE

Times Square
1904; Cityscape/Bright Lights 1976–1980; 42nd Street Development Project, 1981 ff.; Lighting & Signage Codes adopted, 1987
Roger Kennedy, Richard Weinstein, Donald Elliott, Cityscape/Bright Lights; **Cooper/Eckstut**, development guidelines; **Robert A.M. Stern, Tibor Kallman**, 42nd Street planners; **Paul Marantz**, lighting designer and signage planner
Broadway corridor between W. 42nd and W. 51st Sts., New York, New York

Times Square is the "center of the city that is the center of the world," asserted author James Traub, "the nation's capital of popular culture." There are several distinct current associations with

"Times Square," ranging from a reference to The Newspaper, to the renaissance of live theatre along 42nd Street, to the Square's national role in celebrating New Year's Eve. With the exception of Las Vegas (see The Strip chapter), the Times Square district along Broadway is without peer in the United States in demonstrating the potent visual energy of lighted advertising signage.

A 1916 Zoning Ordinance specifically allowed large signs in Times Square, and by the 1920s "Times Square"—more than just the named block between 44th and 45th—was awash in light. The first moving electric sign was installed in 1928. And soon this part of Broadway was known internationally as the Great White Way. The creative high point of advertising signage occurred with the 1941 installation of Douglas Leigh's once-famous smoking Camel cigarette sign, located between 43rd and 44th Streets.

By the 1980s, that glittering marquee era had long passed. The blocks on and around Times Square had devolved into a collection of porn shops and other cheap attractions. The city and state formed the Forty-Second Street Development Project to clean up Times Square and environs, succeeding beyond anyone's expectations. Massive new redevelopment has triggered criticism that Times Square has been sanitized—certainly true, compared to the depths of 1980, and not necessarily bad. Given its past history, the area will probably continue to evolve, endlessly.

Fortunately from a physical-visual perspective, the city had the vision to require that new district buildings include large advertising signs as part of their designs. The resulting visual environment is absolutely sensational at night. Not to be missed by visitors to Manhattan.

PROGRAMMATIC CONSTRUCTIONS

Programmatic architecture is a fancy way of describing buildings which are expressed as recognizable objects. They are meant to be eye-catching, and most of us probably understand them as fun, as long as there aren't too many in any one place!

Programmatic design is often thought of as a phenomenon of the Los Angeles Southland. Certainly, the LA area is a programmatic treasure trove. But marvelous programmatic constructions are found here and there throughout the United States, as the following sampling demonstrates. If you would like to identify more programmatic architecture, be sure to consult the publications of programmatic pioneer John Margolies.

Lucy the Elephant FIG. 914
1881; restored, 1966
William Free, designer
9200 Atlantic Ave., Margate, New Jersey

This engaging, 65-foot-high pachyderm was built to attract attention to a beachfront resort development near Atlantic City. The real estate office was located in Lucy's belly, and prospects could view the panorama of available building lots from a howdah on her back. Today, Lucy is a revered civic figure in Margate, though hemmed in a bit after her relocation in 1970.

Samson Tyre and Rubber Company FIG. 915
1929–1930
Morgan, Walls, and Clements, architects
5675 Telegraph Rd., NE frontage of the Santa Ana Fwy./I-5, City of Commerce, California

FIG. 916 **The Famous Big Duck** If you are a 20-foot-high duck and have a burning desire to be a celebrity, it's definitely a great strategy to nest in alongside the main road to Long Island's Hamptons.

One might rightfully wonder why an auto tire company would construct a block-long Babylonian temple for its factory. In the 1920s, durability of tires was of paramount concern, given the primitive condition of U.S. roads. And what could be stronger than Samson? True, the ancient city of Khorsabad, on which this extravaganza was freely based, was not exactly located in the Land of Canaan, but who's to quibble about something done this well?

The Shell Gas Station
1930–1933
J. H. Glenn, Jr., Bert L. Bennett, designers
Sprague and Peachtree Sts. NW., Winston-Salem, North Carolina

This is the only survivor among eight shells built in the early 1930s for Shell Oil filling stations in North Carolina. All were similar: a giant concrete shell, 16 feet high and 20 feet across, served as the office.

The Big Duck FIG. 916
1931
William Collins, designer; **Martin Maurer**, builder
Flanders Rd./Rt. 24 E., Riverhead vicinity, Long Island, New York

The often-moved Duck, built to sell prized Long Island duck to passing motorists, was made famous by architect Robert Venturi, whose design taxonomy includes buildings which are objects— "ducks"—or false-fronted "decorated sheds."

Tail o' the Pup FIG. 903
1938
Milton J. Black, designer
329 N. San Vicente Blvd., N of Beverly Blvd., Los Angeles, California (moved from its original LaCienega Blvd. site)

A literal image for a hot-dog stand, crudely built and almost obscene, yet perhaps for these very reasons, unforgettable.

Mammy's Cupboard FIG. 917
1939–1940
Henry Gande, builder
555 S. Hwy. 61, Natchez, Mississippi

Built as an attention-grabbing office for a filling station, Mammy has long since lost her pumps. The current home-cooking café is actually much more plausible for the Aunt Jemima imagery (the design was contemporaneous with the movie version of "Gone With the Wind"). Mammy is especially memorable for her bemused expression, and for her visual presence along this semi-rural stretch of open highway.

Randy's Donuts FIG. 918
1954
805 W. Manchester Blvd., Inglewood, California

Placing a replica of one's product on the roof of an unremarkable food stand sounds like a no-brainer. But this approach does not always come off as successfully as it does here, where the donut has achieved truly gourmand scale, and consequently asserts a monumental presence at this otherwise ordinary suburban street corner.

FIG. 917 **Song of the South** Although Los Angeles is the center of American programmatic designs, large numbers of programmatic constructions can be found throughout the South and in Florida. While most of these are crude and only momentarily interesting, Mammy's Cupboard in Natchez stands among the best, nationally.

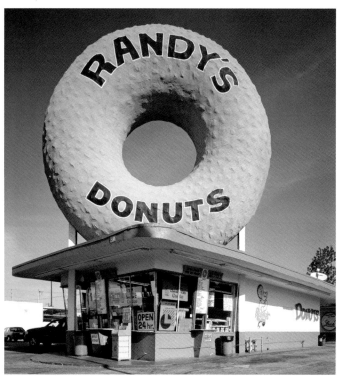

FIG. 918 **Programmatic Monumentality** Randy's Giant Donut in Southern California achieves real presence, in part because of its prominent corner site, but mostly because it is twice as high as the building it rests on. This reversal in common proportion heightens the donut's mouth-watering presence. *Carol M. Highsmith / Library of Congress, Prints & Photographs*

Hat 'n' Boots FIG. 919
1954–1955; moved and restored 2004–2005
Lewis Naysmith, designer; **Albert Donald Poe**, architect of record
E. Marginal Way S. at Corson Ave., Seattle, Washington; moved to Oxbow Park, 6400 Corson Ave. in 2003

Marginal Way was Old U.S. 99, a main drag from Seattle toward California, so this now-derelict area, bypassed by I-5 a few blocks to the east, was once a prime location for a service station. Hat 'n' Boots initially served as a fetching logo for the Frontier Shopping Center, which was built out in phases after 1947. The 22-foot-high hat with a 45-foot brim served as the gas station office, while the pair of 24-foot-high cowboy boots held the rest rooms. A six-foot-high concrete cactus enclosed the air pump.

Among the most endearing of American programmatic designs, Hat 'n' Boots was vacant and severely deteriorated by 2003, when it was moved to a city park nearby. One can only be overjoyed by its preservation, although now set on a landscaped plot, deprived of a working role at this gritty intersection, Hat 'n' Boots loses much of its once unforgettable visual impact.

Big Fish Supper Club FIG. 920
1958
Wayne Kumpula, builder
N side of U.S. Hwy. 2, 3 Mi. W of Bena, Minnesota

Fish may well be the most numerous of American programmatic figures: there must be hundreds, of widely varying visual and construction quality, throughout the United States. This 65-foot, built-from-scraps muskie stands out because of its obvious authenticity as craft.

The Gaffney Peach FIG. 7
1981
Chicago Bridge & Iron, manufacturer
NW side of I-85, Gaffney, South Carolina

Water towers have long been employed as local civic expressions, especially in smaller American towns. Up through the early post–World War II years, custom-built towers were the rule. The rose-maled Swedish Coffee Pot water tower (1902, Fig. 921) along Hwy. 8 in heavily Scandinavian Lindstrom, Minnesota, is a landmark of this genre.

In recent decades, municipal water-tower construction has typically been generic, the industry dominated by the massive HydroPillar model of Pittsburg-Des Moines Co. and CB&I's graceful Waterspheroid. Despite such widespread standardization, the basic CB&I design lent itself to a giant peach (Fig. 7), realistically toned in a spectrum from light yellow to burnt orange. Certainly, Gaffney's "Peachoid" is a delightful highlight along an otherwise visually unremarkable stretch of highway.

Longaberger Company Home Office, "The Basket" FIG. 922
1995–1997
Dave Longaberger, conceptual designer; **NBBJ,** architects;
Korda/Nemeth, structural engineers
1500 E. Main St. / S of Rt. 16, Newark, Ohio

Longaberger is renowned for its premium hand-woven baskets, its operations spread out across several small neighboring communities nestling just below the western edges of the Appalachian foothills. The company's need for efficient new office space was fulfilled by this arresting, 160x version of its signature product, the Medium Market Basket. The improbably scaled building is set back within an expansive, beautifully manicured greenscape, its replication so earnest, the whole mood so amiable that most visitors probably cannot help being completely won over.

FIG. 919 **Whoa!** In the 1950s, located on a gritty, busy intersection of a major Pacific Northwest highway, Hat 'n' Boots was a truly amazing sight for approaching motorists. But the world changes, and now we must be satisfied with preserving the hat and the boots as objects in a nearby city park.

FIG. 921 **Good Till the Very Last Drop** Lindstrom, Minnesota's, rosemaled Swedish Coffee Pot water tower is practically a sacred icon in this Scandinavian-American community of serious coffee drinkers.

FIG. 920 **Pop-Culture Ruin** Back before slick fiberglass promotions blanketed American roadsides, earnestly hand-built programmatic attractions were put together from locally available materials. Sadly, such constructions cannot last, as the gently crumbling Big Fish Supper Club in Minnesota demonstrates.

FIG. 922 **Aggressive Product Placement** It is one thing to build a programmatic food stand, another thing altogether to build a programmatic corporate office building. Longaberger Company's sheer daring fortunately paid off in this marvelous play on the company's product.

Civic Design
1845–2004

Three approaches to the visual enrichment of our built settings were prominent in the twentieth century. One of these, now commonly known as urban design, refers to the organization of buildings and open spaces over an area larger than a single building site. Usually identified with architects, this approach has given us groupings of public buildings like the Denver Civic Center (Fig. 847), the multi-block Rockefeller Center in Manhattan (see the Moderne chapter), and the district-scale, public-private Battery Park City development, also in Manhattan.

The second approach focuses on visual improvements to streetscapes. Countless American towns, suburbs, and cities have hung colorful banners from light standards or installed street

FIG. 925 **The Art of Illusion** Richard Haas established a double illusion in this Miami Beach installation on Collins Avenue. A blank wall was transformed into an exotic building, its *faux* open archway seemingly framing the Fontainebleau Hotel, located just beyond (compare with Fig. 454).

furniture like old-fashioned benches and designed newspaper kiosks. Some have also added ornamental lighting and public art. While professional consultants may be engaged for streetscape improvements, much of this activity is undertaken by public officials and local business leaders. The majority of American streetscape improvements are quite modest in scope and expectations, though a few, like the original Nicollet Mall in Minneapolis (later in this chapter) have transformed their settings.

The third approach, traditionally known as civic art, seeks to enrich the built fabric. As applied by classic physical planners, it is in effect the mirror approach to what we now call urban design. Rather than employing buildings as the prime vehicles to realize area improvements, civic art works with a broad palette of city-building techniques to strengthen the physical context. The standard for this approach is *The American Vitruvius: An Architects' Handbook of Civic Art* (1922) by Werner Hegemann and Elbert Peets. The authors presented a comprehensive analysis of how to achieve vibrant yet harmonious built environments, from downtown centers to suburban subdivisions. Leading figures in the New Urbanism movement have recently published *The New Civic Art* (2003), meant to demonstrate how these principles can be applied to contemporary residential developments.

This chapter offers an illustrative overview of enrichment activities, weighted toward representative civic art vocabularies such as monuments, public sculpture, and pedestrian environments. Settings are offered at city, town, village, and rural scale (it should be noted that the rural Ames Monument was built to commemorate the transcontinental rail linkage, an accomplishment of national civic importance). Fountains and private memorials are included in the Landscape Features chapter.

Although wall murals are barely touched on here, they can be arresting urban design features. These are becoming almost common in some U.S. cities. Two schools of mural painting are especially prominent. One includes community murals like the vivid wall murals in East Los Angeles. Another school is represented by the *tromp l'oeil* murals of Richard Haas in Miami Beach (Fig. 925), St. Louis, Boston, New York, and Washington. More on these can be found in *Richard Haas: An Architecture of Illusion* (1981).

Several approaches to the design of public monuments have proved to be especially effective. These include: designs that highlight purity of form, like the Washington Monument; that are set apart on the landscape, like the Jefferson Memorial; that demonstrate exceptional integration of design, like the Lincoln Memorial; or that employ a dramatic, emotive gesture, like the Vietnam Veterans' Memorial. Conveniently, all of these examples are grouped within the western precincts of the National Mall in Washington. (See The Mall chapter).

FIG. 926 Majestic Memorial The Washington Monument realigned L'Enfant's historic National Mall axis, as illustrated in this 1902 drawing from the McMillan Plan (see The Mall chapter). Even set among ranks of massive buildings, the slender obelisk visually dominates monumental Washington. *U.S. Commission of Fine Arts; Lee Stalworth photograph*

FIG. 927 What Might Have Been The original Washington Monument design was a romantic confection, reflecting the sensibilities of its era. The much-simplified built version (Fig. 926) which seems so admirably pure to us today was widely considered to be disappointingly sterile when completed. *Library of Congress, Prints & Photographs*

PUBLIC MONUMENTS–SHRINES

Washington Monument FIGS. 926, 927
1845–1854; 1876–1884
Robert Mills, architect; completed by **Thomas Lincoln Casey**
National Mall at the White House cross axis, Washington, D.C.

This slim, soaring obelisk (Fig. 926) is a simplification of the original design, which was to be higher, and surrounded at the base by a circular Greco-Roman temple (Fig. 927). Today, it is hard to imagine that what we appreciate as supreme visual purity was initially criticized as sterility. By now, the Washington Monument has become the very definition of a perfect memorial.

Ames Monument FIG. 928
1879–1882
Henry Hobson Richardson, architect
off I-80 exit 329, Buford, Wyoming, vic.

Set on a rugged, remote promontory, this bent granite pyramid easily manages to occupy an immense horizon (Fig. 928). Only as one draws near does the true size, 60 feet high and square, become apparent. Even for Richardson, and even set against the gigantic scale of the High Plains at the edge of the Rockies, Ames is extraordinarily powerful.

"Liberty Enlightening the World" / Statue of Liberty
FIG. 929
1886; assembled, 1889
Frédéric Auguste Bartholdi, sculptor; **Alexandre Gustave Eiffel**, engineer; **Richard Morris Hunt**, architect of base
Bedloes-Liberty Island, New York, New York

Presented to memorialize French-American friendship, thus: "Liberty Enlightening the World." The "Statue of Liberty" nickname grew after 1903, when a plaque with Emma Lazarus's timeless

FIG. 928 **Richardsonian Monumentality** To Henry Hobson Richardson, the stupendous geography of the Wyoming High Plains meeting the Front Range would probably have seemed a worthy foil for his design. When his Ames Monument was completed, it was apparent that both the natural setting and the construction gained from the other.

FIG. 929 **Hallowed by Multitudes** The Statue of Liberty's incalculable importance as a political and cultural symbol transcends its significance as public art. *Library of Congress, Prints & Photographs, Historic American Buildings Survey*

inscription, "Give me your tired, your poor. . . ." was added on site. While the Statue of Liberty offers an emotional touchstone for anyone whose family emigrated through New York, it is also a fine piece of sculpture, prominently sited in the Upper Bay of New York's harbor. Richard Morris Hunt's indispensible base rarely gets recognized for its complementary form and proportions.

Ceremonial Arch FIG. 930
1907; rebuilt 1956
E. Pine at Sacramento St., Lodi, California

A literal arch gateway into downtown. Although Lodi is miles from the Camino Real, its Mission imagery is still visually effective as a local civic landmark.

FIG. 930 **Gateway to Downtown** Lodi's Arch is a simple idea rendered effective because of its approachable scale, its immaculate state of maintenance, and the wonderful gilded California Bear at its apex.

Lincoln Memorial FIGS. 795, 931
1911–1922; Lincoln statue lighted, 1927; building lighted, 1972
Henry Bacon, architect; **Daniel Chester French**, sculptor of the Lincoln statue; **Jules Guerin**, artist for murals; **Frederick Law Olmsted, Jr.**, landscape advisor for the reflecting pool; **James Greenleaf**, landscape advisor for site plantings
W end of the National Mall, Washington, D.C.

Sometimes it is best to go literally by the book, as Bacon's design demonstrates. Here is a virtual checklist approach for this memorial, on this site. (See Fig. 793.) The necessary *parti* was almost too obvious: some kind of classicized temple to balance the Capitol at the other end of the National Mall; architectural dignity; a formal setting with reflecting pool; both subtle and explicit architectural references to the Civil War; and, of course, leading artists.

The memorial succeeds visually because Bacon assembled everything with consummate skill, without injecting his personality into the scheme. This is, after all, all about Lincoln and the Nation, and an architect's design statement would have been inappropriate in this context.

FIG. 931 **An Advanced Study in Planning and Design** The Lincoln Memorial functions as a brilliantly integrated ensemble, the major elements of which include the structure itself; Lincoln's figure within; its monumental setting, including the watergate engagement with the parkway behind (Fig. 795), the reflecting pool in front, and its axial closure of the National Mall. *Library of Congress, Prints & Photographs, Historic American Buildings Survey*

Thomas Macdonough Memorial

1914–1926

John Russell Pope, architect

Saranac riverfront, across from City Hall, Plattsburgh, New York

From a distance, the 135-foot-high obelisk reads as pure form. Close up, a wealth of decoration becomes evident, from the stepped peak to curved base panels. A semicircular retaining wall and steps lead down to the river, thus integrating the public realm, symbolized by City Hall, through the memorial, with nature.

Liberty Memorial FIGS. 932, 933

1924–1926; restored 2007

H. Van Buren Magonigle, architect; **Jules Guerin, Daniel MacMorris**, muralists; **ASAI Architecture**, architects for restoration and museum

100 W. 26th St., Kansas City, Missouri

Visitors immediately notice the 271-foot-high shaft, but that is only one element of the memorial, which also includes a 500-foot-long inscribed wall, flanking buildings for a museum and hall of memory set in a vast expanse (Fig. 933), murals, an "eternal flame" of steam and colored lights, and a block-long landscaped allée. This entire composition engages in a visual relationship with the nearby Union Station just below, and the downtown skyline beyond.

A thorough restoration of the memorial was completed in 2007, along with additional National World War I museum spaces in the undercroft beneath it (entrance seen in Fig. 932).

World War I Monument

1927–1929; relocated, 1996

Paul P. Cret, architect; **Carl P. Jennewein, Janet de Coux**, sculptors

Gardner-Jackson Park, S. Main St., Providence, R.I.

FIG. 934 Ever-changing Presence The Jefferson National Expansion Memorial's "Gateway Arch" can be seen from points all across the St. Louis region, continuously shifting in appearance with the progressions of the sun and changes in the weather. (See also Fig. 851.) *Library of Congress, Prints & Photographs, Historic American Buildings Survey*

FIGS. 932, 933 Monumental Setting From a distance, Kansas City's Liberty Memorial is marked by its 271-foot-high shaft (Fig. 932). For the visitor on site, its immense plaza-acropolis dominates perception (Fig. 933).

FIG. 935 Pastoral Monument Philip Johnson's Roofless Church is unexpected in several respects. Among them: the singular expression of the architecture itself; the enclosed precinct's sense of uncomplicated order played off against adjacent marshlands; and surprise that such a monumental work fits so well into this small Indiana town.

FIG. 936 The Wall That Speaks to a Generation Rarely has so simple a concept moved so many as has the Vietnam Veterans' Memorial on Washington's National Mall.

Cret won this commission in an open, two stage competition. The tall fluted column was widely understood at the time of its design as Greek, but today it seems to have anticipated the stripped classicism of the soon-to-emerge PWA Moderne. Indeed, Cret would design the surpassing PWA Moderne monument, the Federal Reserve Bank in Washington, D.C., in less than a decade (Fig. 369).

Jefferson Memorial
1935–1938, completed as revised in 1943
John Russell Pope, conceptual architect; **Eggers and Higgins**, architects
Tidal Basin at S end of White House cross axis, Washington, D.C.

See the National Romanticism chapter.

Jefferson National Expansion Memorial, "Gateway Arch" FIG. 934
1947–1948; 1959–1967
Eero Saarinen & Associates, planners and architects; **Severud-Elstad-Krueger Associates**, structural engineers; **Dan Kiley**, landscape architect
Mississippi riverfront, St. Louis, Missouri

A monument on this riverfront site—commemorating the vast Louisiana Purchase acquired under President Jefferson—was first proposed in 1907. St. Louis civic leaders persisted for 40 years, until a postwar competition, which Saarinen won. Another 20 years passed until the monument was completed. Now recognized around the globe as a symbol of the United States, the shimmering 630-foot-tall stainless steel arch offers an ever changing visual presence.

Roofless Church FIG. 935
1959–1960
Philip Johnson, architect; **Jacques Lipchitz**, sculptor
North St. W of Main, New Harmony, Indiana

Its grandeur is perhaps unexpected for this tiny Harmonist/Owenite historic town in rural Indiana. With his walled but "roofless"

church focused on a shingled baldachin, Johnson achieved a sense of monumentality on less than an acre, while fitting his work comfortably into the small-scale community fabric.

Vietnam Veterans' Memorial FIG. 936
1981–1984
Maya Lin, designer; **Cooper-Lecky Partnership**, executive architect; **Frederick Hart**, sculptor
S of Constitution Ave. at 21st St., Washington, D.C.

One of the great tales of twentieth-century American architecture: an underrated student project which was unappreciated by those it was to recognize becomes a site of great emotional outpouring, an immense success as a public memorial. Lin's simple, powerful gesture, a V-shaped granite retaining wall with names of those lost in the war (called a "gash" by its vehement opponents) proved to be exactly in tune with American society. The V of the wall and the walkway along it are laid out to align with the Washington Monument and the Lincoln Memorial, so that visitors leaving the memorial face one of these uplifting landmarks. (Hart's sculpture, representing American troops, was added to the memorial precincts to satisfy critics of the design.)

Christopher Columbus Monument
1988–1992
Venturi, Scott Brown & Associates, architects
SE of Christopher Columbus Blvd. and Dock St., Philadelphia, Pennsylvania

Typically for the Venturi Scott Brown practice, the design is simultaneously direct and complex. The almost cartoon-like abstraction of an Egyptian-European obelisk is merely the first level of design development, which includes lighting that shines through the simulated mortar joints.

STREETSCAPES

Even though (or perhaps because) the United States is a century deep into the automobile era, American planning doctrines elevate the pedestrian, without fail. This section provides representative examples of three types of urban pedestrian environments: Esplanades, Pedestrian Malls, and Skywalks.

ESPLANADES

Paseo del Rio, "Riverwalk" FIG. 937
1937–1941; 1962–1968; extended 1984
Robert Hugman, architect for the original WPA project; **Cyrus Wagner**,
O'Neill Ford planners for 1960s renovations
Downtown San Antonio, Texas, generally between N. St. Mary's and Soledad
Sts, and Villita and College Sts.

Surely Riverwalk is the most creative and beautiful urban flood control solution in the United States. A chronically flooding river was transformed into a singular environment and civic symbol where it wound through downtown. Typically, we bury streams out of sight when they are in the way of urban development. San Antonio turned this situation into a magnificent public feature.

Biscayne Boulevard Sidewalk Test FIG. 939
1988–1989
Roberto Burle Marx, landscape architect
Biscayne Blvd. at NE. 17th St., Miami, Florida

The peerless Burle Marx was commissioned to design a prototype sidewalk like his internationally famous Copacabana beachfront promenade in Rio de Janeiro. Miami's demonstration section was constructed on an undistinguished site, across the street from the massive Omni complex.

Copacabana (Fig. 938) and Biscayne (Fig. 939) were separated by nearly three decades, and of course these were very different physical and cultural settings. Consequently, Burle Marx's Miami

FIG. 937 **Urbane Flood Control** If only all of our cities were as creative with their infrastructure as San Antonio's marvelous Paseo del Rio, "Riverwalk."

solution was very different from his Rio expression, which recalls traditional Portuguese patterns that are culturally authentic for Brazil but not for the United States, especially in Hispanic Miami. So rather than mimicking the hypnotically graceful black-and-white waves of Rio, the Biscayne sidewalk was more agitated and geometric, predominantly colored in brown and deep red. Alas, Burle Marx's design was not extended beyond this tiny demonstration strip.

Bunker Hill Steps FIG. 940
1989–1990
Lawrence Halprin, landscape architect
5th St. between Hope and Flower, Los Angeles, California

The Southland Baroque version of Rome's Spanish Steps, though in this case energetically asymmetrical. The view upslope from 5th presents a jumbled tableau of forms and shapes, small kiosks and massive skyscrapers, with a tightly channeled watercourse bubbling merrily between the staircases. Remarkably, Halprin's design neatly ties this visually messy scene together.

DOWNTOWN PEDESTRIAN MALLS

Olvera Street
1929–1930
Within Sunset Blvd., Los Angeles, Arcadia, and Main, Los Angeles, California

The closing of Olvera Street to traffic and a concurrent restoration of colonial-era buildings was intended to establish a one-block "Hispanic Marketplace." This near-pedestrian-mall incarnation of Olvera Street has functioned as a draw for locals and tourists.

Syracuse Mall Proposal
1943
George Nelson, Henry Wright, Jr.
Eleven-block section of Erie Blvd., Syracuse, New York

Nelson and Wright proposed the prototype postwar American pedestrian mall in the May 1943 issue of *Architectural Forum*. While their proposal was not realized, it did provide a conceptual model for later pedestrian malls.

Kalamazoo Mall
1957–1958; extensions in 1970 and 1974
Victor Gruen, planner
Burdick St. between Eleanor and Lovell, Kalamazoo, Michigan

Promoted as the nation's first downtown pedestrian mall, the Burdick Mall, as it is known locally, was one part of an overall downtown strategy, including auto bypass routes and peripheral parking —a strategy only partly accomplished. If the measure of success is whether the mall "saved" downtown as the principal regional retail center, then it has failed. Yet in bringing national attention to Kalamazoo, Burdick Mall has surely succeeded as a community landmark.

Lincoln Road Mall FIG. 941
1957–1960, later alterations
Morris Lapidus, planner
Lincoln Rd., Miami Beach, Florida

Lincoln Road was the main shopping street of Miami Beach, but by the late 1950s smart shops were beginning to move up-island. Hence, this mall, like Kalamazoo's, was conceived as a way to "save" Lincoln Road as a primary shopping destination. As was

FIGS. 938, 939 A Tale of Two Waves Roberto Burle Marx was engaged to reprise his mesmerizing Copacabana beach walk in Rio de Janeiro (Fig. 938) along Miami's signature way, Biscayne Boulevard. Responding authentically to different times, settings, and cultures, Burle Marx's solution for Miami's sidewalk test (Fig. 939) was bold and angular, rather than a copy of his soft, flowing pattern for Rio. Regrettably, his concept was not extended beyond this short demonstration section.

FIG. 940 Southland Baroque For his voluptuous Bunker Hill Steps, Lawrence Halprin moved well beyond even the freewheeling norms of Los Angeles.

FIG. 941 **The Joy of Planning** The irrepressible Morris Lapidus employed predictable design vocabularies for Lincoln Road Mall: the lush, tropical plantings of upscale South Florida and classic Zoobie forms from his Architecture of Joy (see Mid-century Expressionism chapter).

FIGS. 942, 943 **Halprin's Classic Pedestrian Mall** Nicollet Mall was stylish, while still casual enough for Midwesterners to feel comfortable. Halprin recognized that this streetscape must not be overdesigned to the point of preciousness. Predictably, individual elements like the fountains (Fig. 942) were criticized by some as not elegant enough, but that entirely missed the point of Halprin's vocabulary, which was meant to be visually memorable without seeming pretentious.

the experience nationwide, the mall did not stop new retail centers, which have proliferated all over South Florida. Still, Lincoln Road Mall probably saved this district from total neglect, or worse, destruction by urban renewal.

Fulton Street Mall
1964–1965
Edgardo Contini, Victor Gruen Associates, planners; **Eckbo, Dean, Austin & Williams**, landscape architects; stabile by **Alexander Calder**
Fulton between Tuolumne and Inyo, Fresno, California

Visually, Fresno's mall is especially successful around the Court House and displays admirable public art. On the other hand, as an economic development undertaking, this mall, like most others developed in the 1960s and 1970s, has not prevented the flow of retail and commerce out of downtown.

Nicollet Mall   FIGS. 942, 943
1958–1962, preliminary studies; 1963–1968, project design and construction; totally altered
Lawrence Halprin & Associates, project planners and landscape architects; **Barton-Aschman Associates**, preliminary planning studies
Nicollet Ave. from Washington to 10th St., Minneapolis, Minnesota; later extended to Grant St.

Halprin's Nicollet Mall was almost universally admired—and widely imitated. The Minneapolis mall along with a very few others—notably Portland's 1977 Transit Mall—transformed declining downtown retail districts, the usual stated goal of a downtown pedestrian mall.

Unfortunately, it proved impossible not to meddle with success, and Nicollet Mall was lengthened, and twice rebuilt-restyled, first by the city's public works engineers and the second time by local consultants. These efforts were highly successful in obliterating Halprin's landmark design, also in spending large amounts of money, at the cost of losing the bold energy and visual creativity of Halprin's original scheme. Today, in Nicollet Mall's third iteration, one experiences a visually homogenized streetscape, tasteful and pleasant, but unremarkable.

The Fremont Street Experience   FIG. 944, 945
1993–1995
Jon Jerde Partnership, designers
Fremont between Main and 4th Sts., Las Vegas, Nevada

The Experience is the latest attempt to repackage downtown Las Vegas as a viable competitor to The Strip. Downtown's previous casino streetscape (Fig. 944) was encased under a barrel-vaulted metal space frame (Fig. 945), what Hal Rothman described as a "circular chain link fence in the sky," It is seen at its best during brief sound-and-light shows, when the canopy's two million light sources generate moving images along its 1500-foot length. At other times, since cars have been banned, the visitor's experience is more like visiting a very bright regional shopping mall with beeping slot machines.

SKYWALK SYSTEMS

Building-to-building pedestrian bridges date from no later than the c. 1595 Bridge of Sighs in Venice, and were popular futurist images for New York City and even Los Angeles in the pre–World War II years, notably in unbuilt schemes for Rockefeller Center.

FIGS. 944, 945 New (and Improved?) Streetscape The historic casino section of Fremont Street was previously known as Glitter Gulch (Fig. 944) before being repackaged as the barrel-vaulted Fremont Experience (Fig. 945).

FIG. 946 First Downtown Skywalk Apparently the earliest true downtown skywalk in the United States, a second-level pedestrian bridge connecting the Arcade Building with Broad Street Station, was built in Philadelphia in 1900. The bridge is visible at the lower left in this drawing. *Library of Congress, Prints & Photographs, Historic American Buildings Survey*

FIGS. 947, 948 Secrets of Success Second-level pedestrian circulation featuring "skyways" over the streets quickly grew into the primary pedestrian route in downtown Minneapolis. The Minneapolis Skyway System is highly successful because it interconnects almost every block in the downtown core (Fig. 948, opposite); because skyway, street, and occasional concourse levels are conveniently, directly interconnected; and because skyways are expressed as architecture, not just treated as functional infrastructure. Minneapolis skyway design standards call for transparency (Fig. 947. an IDS Center bridge), both to dematerialize the bridges and thus lessen any negative visual impacts; and also to enhance orientation for those using the skyways. *Fig. 948: (Minneapolis) Skyway News*

Rudimentary skywalks-conveyors connecting industrial buildings in Lowell, Massachusetts, were constructed some time between 1835 and 1880. Downtown connections date from no later than an 1896 covered pedestrian link designed by Louis Sullivan, which connected a department store directly to the Chicago El transit at second level. Four years later, in 1900, architect Frank Furness designed what is probably the first American skywalk, an enclosed, second-level pedestrian bridge across Market Street in Philadelphia, connecting his Arcade Building to the Broad Street Railroad Station (Fig. 946). Two decades later, Cass Gilbert's Prudential Insurance Co. complex in Newark, New Jersey, included elegant enclosed pedestrian bridges over Halsey and Bank Streets.

Downtown skywalk systems have been developed in a number of American cities since the 1960s. The experience in many of these has been mixed, at best. Among the reasons: not enough human activity to support both street- and second-level retail; a poorly worked-out circulation network; and indifferent design. The Minneapolis Skyway system is the premier national achievement of this genre.

Minneapolis "Skyway" System FIGS. 947, 948, 949, 950
1962 ff.
Edward F. Baker, architect of first skyways, over Seventh St. and Marquette Ave.
Downtown Minneapolis, Minnesota

Several North American cities have built skywalks since the 1960s, but nowhere has the concept been so refined and extensive as in the 70-plus-block Minneapolis system. One key early decision was to encourage design individuality, rather than to standardize skyway design, a course that was chosen in neighboring St. Paul.

As a result, while some Minneapolis skyway bridges are ordinary and even a bit worse, a surprising number have exceptional designs. Among the best of these are the four Philip Johnson-John Burgee skyway bridges extending from IDS Center (Fig. 947. See also Late Modernism and Interior Spaces chapters), and the skyway over Marquette between 6th and 7th Sts., a collaboration between architect Cesar Pelli and artist Siah Armajani (Fig. 950).

FIGS. 949, 950 Skywalk Evolution The first Minneapolis pedestrian bridges (Fig. 949), designed by Edward F. Baker, proved too narrow to accommodate the system's unanticipated popularity, as additional blocks were continuously added to the network. In response to high-volume patronage, later pedestrian bridges including one by architect Cesar Pelli and artist Siah Armajani (Fig. 950) were doubled in width.

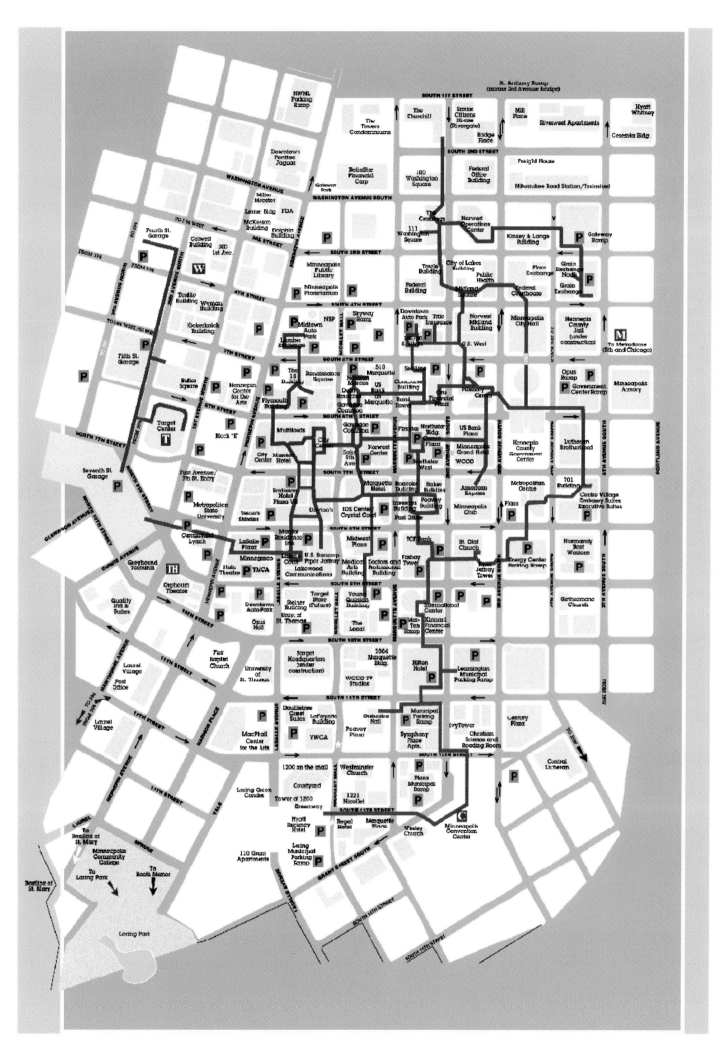

LANDSCAPE
ARCHITECTURE

1660–1800

Landscape in America

1660–1800

FIGS. 951, 952 A Yearning to Beautify Landscaping was widely employed in the colonial era. As one example, Toddsbury estate near Gloucester, Virginia, was patented about 1660, its main house built before 1743. In this view toward a later guest house (Fig. 951 and upper right of the main house in plan, Fig. 952), we can appreciate how colonial landscape beautification might involve more than plantings, commonly also including textures, colors, and studied visual relationships among structures. Early colonial landscapes were rarely developed as a piece, across an entire property at once. Rather, a formal garden layout might initially be established near the main house, as here (above the drive in plan). Other parts of the property would be landscaped separately over time, following function, fashion, or whim. (Guest house in photo open as B & B.) *Fig. 952: Library of Congress, Prints & Photographs, Historic American Buildings Survey*

Landscaping was virtually nonexistent during the initial European settlement of North America. Rather, the indiscriminate cutting down of trees and the clearing of organic understory were prominent ongoing activities among the first colonists. Understandably, then, landscape histories of the United States often begin in the early 1800s with the polymath Thomas Jefferson identified as a precursor-founder, as Jefferson was for so many disciplines. Histories may also identify early horticulturalists, contemporaries of Jefferson, before beginning a canon of American landscape architecture with Andrew Jackson Downing and his prolific activities of the 1840s, up to his untimely death in 1852.

Yet the desire to beautify through landscaping emerged within the lifetimes of some who at least figuratively stepped off Plymouth Rock. Prior to 1660, geometrical formal gardens had been

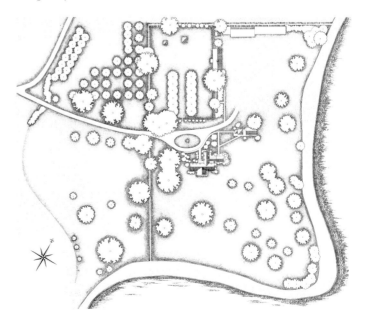

plotted along the Hudson Riverfront in Dutch New Amsterdam
—Manhattan (Fig. 953). Formal gardens were widely established
before the mid-1700s by prominent colonial planters.

Early "æsthetic" landscaping in the nascent United States
was usually expressed in formal vocabularies. Similar to the
experience in other areas of American culture, refinement in
the colonies generally began with the upper class, then was
gradually taken up by the skilled and merchants, ultimately dif-
fusing throughout society—more typically for public landscapes
than for individual private properties.

Aspiring American colonials naturally looked to England for
cultural direction, and in the late 1600s that meant Renaissance-inspired Classicism. English estates were then designed as
a stylistically consistent, house-landscape environment, so, as
Richard Bushman noted, "Renaissance houses [for the upper
class] came to America with gardens attached."

New Amsterdam Gardens FIG. 953
1660
Adriaen Cornelissen Van der Donck, municipal patron; **Gommaart
Paulusz**, gardener
Battery district of Manhattan, New York, New York

Van der Donck was a patroon who served as a visionary intermediary
between the trading post–colony of New Amsterdam and the government and sponsoring trading houses of mother country Holland.

By the 1640s, Amsterdam was undergoing a Renaissance-
inspired reordering of its Medieval fabric. Elsewhere in Holland,
the nation's judicial center was named after its distinctive
"Count's Hedge," *'s Gravenhage* (in English, The Hague). Russell
Shorto described The Hague as a planned government town with
"broad, tree-lined avenues," which must have presented a painful
contrast for the visiting Van der Donck to the "motley" built
environment of 1640s New Amsterdam. Still, Mariana Van Rensselaer noted that an herb garden located near Fort New Amsterdam, which she identified as the "earliest garden of a scientific
sort in any of the colonies," was already "falling into decay" in
1649.

When Van der Donck returned to New Amsterdam in 1653
after a lengthy stay in Holland, he brought along Paulusz, a native
of Antwerp, as personal gardener for his patroonship, which was
located up the Hudson near the later Van Cortlandt House (see
Mid-Atlantic Colonial Architecture chapter). By now, New Amsterdam was also being improved: streets paved, brick houses
replacing frame, tile roofs replacing thatch. Within the Fort itself,
space was provided for "great trees and shady groves of aboriginal
growth" . . . "encumbered by . . . gardens and orchards." Some of
the outlying Dutch settlements, like *Nieu Haerlem*, today's Harlem,
were laid out around a village green.

A 1660 drawing of New Amsterdam (Fig. 953) mapped an orderly
town layout, with carefully plotted streets and a mosaic of geometric
gardens, some of which, Van Rensselaer observed, no doubt reflected
the "draughtsman's desire to make his map as pretty as possible"
rather than precisely documenting the actual state of development.
Almost certainly, Van der Donck, who died in 1655, was a principal
guiding influence for these conceptual landscape advances in New
Amsterdam. The presence of Paulusz suggests that his knowledge of
contemporary European garden planning was material to the district
improvements that were accomplished in the colonial city.

As Shorto observed, on the eve of New Amsterdam's handover
to the English in 1664 and its renaming as New York, the town had

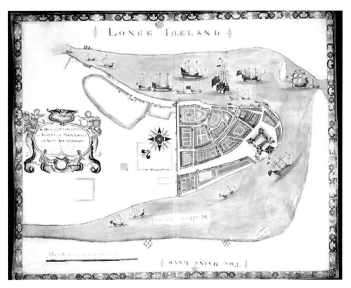

FIG. 953 Dutch Gardens By the time Holland relinquished New Amsterdam to
England in the 1660s, geometric garden plots influenced by Renaissance sensibilities
were interspersed with buildings across the tip of Manhattan Island, as illustrated by
a 1660 drawing of New Amsterdam. *Library of Congress, Prints & Photographs*

taken on "that defining Dutch characteristic: tidiness." Landscaping was fundamental to this well-ordered, early town planning.

College of William and Mary Formal Garden
1694; not extant
Anonymous King's Gardener from Hampton Court
Williamsburg, Virginia

Apparently this long lost garden was was designed by a royal gardener, hence presumably laid out according to leading contemporary English practice. It was considered by Bushman to be the
"grandest of formal gardens" in the New World at its time, implying that it was not the *only* colonial formal garden of its era.

Governor's Palace Gardens–Parterres
1712 ff.
Alexander Spotswood, William Byrd II, garden designers
Williamsburg, Virginia (open)

Governor Spotswood stimulated garden design in Virginia with his
plans based in part on the landscape layout of Stansted, in Sussex,
England.

For colonial mansions built after about 1725, Bushman noted
that "the installation of [formal] gardens became standard." Byrd
later visited many English gardens for inspiration as he developed
his father's gardens at nearby Westover plantation after 1730 (next
entry). (See also the Garden Restorations chapter.)

Westover Formal Garden FIG. 954
After 1730; reconstructed after 1900
William Byrd II, owner-gardener
25 mi. SE of Richmond off Hwy. 5, Charles City County, Virginia (open)

Westover's reconstructed formal garden (along with its signature
gates north of the main house) illustrates a handsome Colonial
Revival landscape. The conjecturally reconstructed garden at
nearby Carter's Grove (Fig. 954) offers a more accurate interpretation of an authentic colonial garden. Following known eighteenth-century practice; it is laid out in a formal box pattern, but
not fastidiously ringed in boxwood. It is planted with vegetables
and fruits, and an ornamental garden with flowers and shrubs.

FIG. 954 **Practical Order** The conjectural garden at Carter's Grove in James County, Virginia, is orderly in layout more than it is an artfully designed landscape. This twentieth-century interpretation probably approximates eighteenth-century reality. It is planted as both a kitchen garden and an ornamental landscape.

FIG. 955 **Lagging in Fashion** The Colonies were unavoidably cultural backwaters. Taste and style flowed from Europe, sometimes after a lengthy delay. In the mid-1700s, when formal gardens were still *the* landscape expression for American colonial estates, English landscape gardener Lancelot "Capability" Brown set contemporary fashion with his new informal style, illustrated here by the grounds at Blenheim. Brown's "natural" design vocabularies inspired the romantic, "naturalistic" landscapes which emerged a century later in the United States, as promoted by Andrew Jackson Downing.

Stratford Gardens

After 1730; reconstructed 1929–1940s
Thomas Lee, eighteenth-century owner; **Morley J. Williams**, principal landscape architect for the twentieth-century site reconstruction
40 mi. E of Fredericksburg, off Hwy. 3, Westmoreland County, Virginia (open)

See also the Garden Restorations chapter.

Thomas Hancock Mansion

1735
Anonymous Contract Gardener
Boston, Massachusetts (not extant)

Formal gardens as a visual context were developed as the house was built, setting a precedent for subsequent Boston mansions.

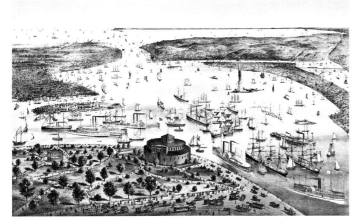

FIG. 956 **Beyond Dutch Gardens** This false-scale 1892 Currier & Ives print of the south tip of Manhattan Island depicts a well-developed romantic-era promenade near where Dutch garden plots (Fig. 953) had existed two centuries earlier. Today, Manhattan's Battery is characterized by a wooded city park. *Library of Congress, Prints & Photographs*

John Penn Estate, "Springettsbury"
1740s
Fairmount, Philadelphia, Pennsylvania (not extant)

Penn engaged a full-time gardener to enhance and maintain his grounds.

CHANGING LANDSCAPE FASHIONS

According to Bushman, most American gardens of the 1700s were Classicist and formal, with "terraces, parterres, and gravel paths laid out in straight lines among the parterres." In England, however, Lancelot "Capability" Brown (1715 or 1716–1783) was designing private estate parks in a new natural style by the mid-1700s (Fig. 955). Hence, Georgian-era American gardens were no longer up to date with current European fashion. While American gardens were thus *retardataire* stylistically, some Americans were important horticulturalists. As early as 1717, for instance, John Custis of Williamsburg routinely exchanged exotic specimens with English botanists.

MUNICIPAL AND PUBLIC LANDSCAPES

Civic gardens like those in Williamsburg were followed by installations of private estate gardens (previous entries). Eventually, municipal–public landscapes appeared, as colonial towns acquired landscaping, ranging from formal settings for civic buildings to ad-hoc plantings of street trees by individual citizens.

Pennsylvania Assembly and Courts
1732, 1784
Samuel Vaughn, gardener
Chestnut St. between Fifth and Sixth, Philadelphia, Pennsylvania

According to Bushman, the vision of a beautified public landscape setting for this site was set forth at the time the building was constructed in the early 1730s. Officials held to that vision into the 1780s, when Vaughn laid out serpentine walks in a "natural" style, planting hundreds of elms.

New York City Battery FIG. 956
Late 1780s

In the early years of the Republic, in Bushman's account, the Battery had "become a park with trees lining the paths." In 1791, Governor's Island in the harbor "was planted with a thousand trees and gardens and walks laid out." Battery Park was well developed a century later (Fig. 956).

Urban Streetscapes FIGS. 957, 958
1800

By the turn of the nineteenth century, in upper-income neighborhoods of major American cities, individual property owners planted rows of trees at the curb to enhance the visual setting of their homes.

FIGS. 957, 958 **Street Landscapes** Patchy landscaping at this Brooklyn corner (Fig. 957) adjacent to the 1824 Szold House illustrates a typical urban streetscape situation: because nineteenth-century urban neighborhoods commonly developed lot by lot, street landscaping was usually up to individual owners, as apparently here. In the twentieth century, by contrast, subdivision development was widespread across the United States. That provided an opportunity to introduce cohesive, neighborhood-scale street landscaping, like this elm-lined street (Fig. 958) planted in the 1920s Country Club subdivision in suburban Minneapolis (see Period Revivals chapter). *Fig. 957 Library of Congress, Prints & Photographs, Historic American Buildings Survey*

Formalism

1694–1961

FIGS. 959, 960 Evolutionary Formalism Gunston Hall near Lorton, Virginia, was built by George Mason IV between 1755 and 1759. Mason enhanced his property over the following three decades, achieving a far more original and dynamic landscape than was the norm for contemporary colonial estates. The main house is centered on a formal site axis, which extends outward from the façade along a 1200-foot entrance *allée* (Fig. 960). This axis terminates behind the house in a tight composition of parterres (Fig. 959). Eventually, "extensive, closely pastured lawns" connected the formal landscapes to the dense woods of a deer park. Until his death in 1792, Mason continuously improved on his original planning concept. He walked the grounds daily in reflection—and simply to enjoy the landscape. Among Mason's design innovations, the *allée*, which was composed of double ranges of cherry trees on both sides of the entrance drive, diverged slightly as it neared the main house, thus providing a subtle visual correction for the narrowing effect of perspective (open to the public). *Library of Congress, Prints & Photographs, Historic American Buildings Survey.*

As noted in the previous chapter, American landscape design began with expressions of Renaissance-inspired Formalism. Elements of Formalism appeared in gardens introduced before 1660 in Dutch Manhattan. Fully developed Formalism emerged no later than a 1694 garden at the College of William and Mary in Williamsburg.

Landscape architect and historian C. Allan Brown explained why landscape Formalism widely emerged in Virginia, before eventually spreading throughout colonial America: Foremost, the New World was still primarily wilderness, so ordered expressions of civilization, were symbolically reassuring to colonists. Virginia was the wealthiest of the British colonies, with close commercial—hence also cultural—ties to London.

It was only natural, then, that pretentious Virginians of the early 1700s would turn to the reigning Continental fashions. In landscape, that was still Formalism, since the eighteenth-century English picturesque and natural styles identified with William Kent and Lancelot Brown (Fig. 955) emerged after about 1730 and 1750, and were not widely appreciated in the New World until late in the century.

Understandably, Formalism was initially expressed less imaginatively in the culturally isolated New World than it was in Europe. American colonial mansions were generally architecturally symmetrical (see Southern Colonial Architecture chapter), facing an expansive front lawn. Occasionally, as at Gunston Hall in Virginia (Fig. 960), highly developed parterres were integral parts of an estate's site design (Fig. 959). However, New World Formalism was generally employed in the form of axiality and stiff regularity, rather than in dynamic site compositions. This was certainly true for major eighteenth-century colonial gardens, excepting Middleton Place.

Middleton Place FIGS. 961, 962

1741 ff.

Henry Middleton, George Newman, designers

4300 Ashley River Rd., NW of Charleston, South Carolina (open)

Middleton Place is the earliest monumental designed American landscape, 65 acres of gardens that, in the words of Mary Jenkins, were "conceived on a scale of grandeur that would not be attempted again [in the United States] for generations."

The Middleton plan organized around a main axis in the seventeenth-century Italian-French tradition associated with André Le Nôtre, notably at Versailles. Middleton and his English design associate introduced just a hint of the early eighteenth-century English picturesque style associated with William Kent. Twin lakes in the form of butterfly wings and a great cascade of grassy terraces descending toward the river establish the signature site features. Middleton Place is among the most memorable American designed landscapes, considered an essential destination for practitioners and mavens.

Oak Alley

mid-1700s

3645 Hwy. 18, Vacherie, Louisiana (open)

Oak Alley is one of the most widely recognized visual images of Louisiana, indeed, of the entire South. This magnificent, 800-foot axial live oak allée was planted up to a century prior to the construction of the main house, Bon Séjour, 1837–1839. The house exterior is visually defined by 28 substantial Tuscan columns, numerically matching the 28 massive oaks leading toward the front façade.

FIGS. 961, 962 Expression of Civilization The magnificent green cascade (Fig. 961) and adjacent parterres at Middleton Place must have seemed almost otherworldly in the Carolina wilderness when constructed more than 250 years ago. The experience of Middleton's signature cascade is much different on the ground (Fig. 962) than as presented in a bird's eye, as would be expected for a superscale landscape. The cascade's axis aligns with the passing Ashley River, its central lawn proportioned to visually equal the receding stream. *Fig. 961: © Middleton Place, Charleston, South Carolina*

FORMALISM REVIVED

Nineteenth-century landscape design increasingly reflected the growing influence of Romanticism in U.S. and Western European culture. By the mid-1800s, naturalistic romantic landscapes were in vogue; axiality and even regularity seemed old-fashioned to tastemakers and their designers, though due to the inherent efficiency of regular grids, formal expressions never entirely died out.

Like any style/fashion, the taste for informality eventually

FIGS. 963, 964 Monumental Landscapes Even among numerous outstanding pre–World War II estates on Long Island, the John S. Phipps estate, "Old Westbury Gardens," stands out because of its confident manipulation of space into surpassingly graceful formal landscapes. The main axis (Fig. 963) and the walled garden (Fig. 964) are seen in these views.

came to seem passé in the United States, paving the way for a national reappearance of formal landscapes. Three influences were especially effective in reintroducing Formalism in landscape design late in the 1800s. These were the formal mansions of the Gilded-Age rich (see Beaux Arts chapter), the Court of Honor at the 1893 World's Columbian Exposition (see Fairs and Expositions chapter), and the 1901–1902 McMillan Plan for the National Mall (see The Mall chapter).

As a result, landscape Formalism rapidly regained widespread favor by the early 1900s and remained popular to mid-century, especially for private estates. The impact of Formalism was not limited to traditional landscape imageries, since its symmetries influenced landscape Modernism (see that chapter).

Drumthwacket Italianate Garden
1898, 1910; restored, 1941 ff.
Daniel W. Langton, landscape designer
354 Stockton St. (Rt. 206), Princeton, New Jersey (open by reservation)

Drumthwacket is New Jersey's executive mansion. Langton, apparently a dilettante, was able to fashion a reasonably competent formal landscape without an overriding concept or obvious design skills. He simply laid out a rectangular parterre on axis behind the house, joined the two by a terrace, and added allées front and back. Existing woods and leftover spaces provided context and a modicum of visual tension. This "kit-of-parts" approach could work only with an easily understood axial system like Beaux Arts Formalism.

FIG. 965 Playful Formality Pre–World War II Miami was all about time out from the everyday grind, especially in season. Vizcaya's stylized tropical-baroque landscapes were/are perfectly in character for their situation.

John S. Phipps Estate, "Old Westbury Gardens" FIGS. 963, 964

1905-06, 1928, 1960s

George Crawley, architect

71 Old Westbury Rd., Old Westbury, Long Island, New York Exit 39 off Long Island Expwy./I-495, E on service road 1.2 mi. to first right, Old Westbury Road: 0.3 mile to garden. (open)

An Italian Renaissance garden brought to Long Island by way of a British architect. Micro-landscapes were added to the classic formal structure of long and cross axes. Crawley's Walled Garden is the landscape's visual high point (Fig. 964). It began as an austere design, but was later visually enriched by Mrs. Phipps's extensive additions of flowers. In its scale and supreme refinement, the Phipps estate offers a revealing window into the lifestyles and tastes of pre–World War II American elites.

Alfred L. du Pont Estate, "Nemours"

1909–1920s

Carrère & Hastings, architects; **Gabriel Masséna, Alfred Victor du Pont**, site planners-landscape designers

Rockland Rd. off Rt. 141, via Rt. 202 from I-95, Wilmington, Delaware (open)

Nemours illustrates an Americanized French Renaissance landscape expression, organized around a sequence of terraces cascading down a formal axis. The designers worked from a basic axiality, enriched with the usual palette of parterres, maze, pools, sculpture, and ornamental sitework, including a domed temple, the latter seemingly requisite for early twentieth-century American estates of any pretense.

Rainier Vista

1909 ff.

John Charles Olmsted and **Frederick Law Olmsted, Jr.**, landscape architects

Within Stevens Way, University of Washington campus, Seattle, Washington

Simple ideas can have great impact. Rainier Vista is a classic open-ended axial view, originally the organizing spine of the 1909 Alaska-Yukon-Pacific Exposition, then serving as the central space of this large campus. It is conventionally defined by academic buildings along at the north end; south of the impressively large and serene Drumheller Fountain, the space is defined by marvelously irregular conifer edges which convey the sense that one is indeed in the fabled Pacific Northwest. The star of this view is, of course, Mount Rainier, which if you are lucky, will be "out" the day you visit, a magnificent ghostly presence hovering above the horizon, its snowy cone just slightly off the Vista's centerline.

James Deering Estate, "Vizcaya" FIG. 965

1914–1921

Diego Suarez, landscape architect

3251 S. Miami Ave., Miami, Florida (open)

A marvelous Italian garden, though far more voluptuous than the reserved Old Westbury version (Figs. 963, 964). Vizcaya's landscape is Italian Baroque by comparison, closer in sensibility to the Orsini garden in Bomarzo. A stone barge set out in Biscayne Bay provides the memorable landscape-design feature (Fig. 322).

FIGS. 966, 967, 968 Encyclopedic Formalism Filoli offers a superb collection of formal expressions, made even more memorable by the estate's magnificent setting beneath the Coast Range. The many distinct modes of Filoli's formal landscape are illustrated in its sunken garden (Fig. 966), north vista (Fig. 967), and knot garden (Fig. 968).

FIGS. 969, 970, 971 A Kaleidoscope of Beauty Beatrix Ferrand designed Dumbarton Oaks in a relaxed, though still gracious version of formalism. If Filoli (Figs. 966, 967, 968) can be thought of as a dress-up social event, then Dumbarton Oaks is a happy afternoon conversation among friends.

William Bourn Estate, "Filoli" FIGS. 966, 967, 968

1915-1917; gardens, 1917–1921
Willis J. Polk, architect; **Bruce Porter**, garden architect; **Isabella Worn**, horticulturist
Edgewood Rd. exit off I-280, W, then N 1.2 mi to 86 Cañada Rd., Woodside, California (open)

Filoli presents a magnificent, encyclopedic demonstration of landscape Formalism. Outdoor rooms are defined by structural plantings, each expressed in a distinct formal vocabulary. After 1937, new owners enriched the original plant palette, especially by introducing flowering shrubs. A sunny day at Filoli offers a sublime experience for anyone interested in landscape design.

Dumbarton Oaks FIGS. 969, 970, 971

1921-1947; Pebble Garden, 1961
Beatrix Jones Farrand, landscape architect
3101 R St. NW., NE cor. 32nd St. NW., Washington, D.C. (open)

These expansive urban gardens represent Formalism at its most relaxed and personal (Fig. 969). The steep hillside site is carefully ordered, though not rigidly so (Fig. 970). Farrand employed a wide range of vocabularies within an overall, formal garden structure. Caroline Holmes contended, surely with sufficient reason, that Farrand combined the architectural skills of Edwin Lutyens and the gardening genius of Gertrude Jekyll.

The splashy Pebble Garden (Fig. 971) was constructed after Farrand's death in 1959.

Naturalism

FIG. 972 Landscape Naturalism Nineteenth-century American landscape architects readily surrendered to the potent spell of Romanticism. They were influenced by the eighteenth-century Picturesque, Natural, and Sublime landscape schools of England; and especially by the contemporary landscape planning of Herman Ludwig von Pückler-Muskau in Saxony (see Roads chapter). The art of American Naturalism was defined by Frederick Law Olmsted and his partner, architect Calvert Vaux. In this view at Brooklyn's Prospect Park (1866–1874), Olmsted and Vaux set a high artistic benchmark with their mysteriously undulating Long Meadow. *National Park Service, Frederick Law Olmsted National Historic Site*

For American designed landscapes, the year 1800 provides a useful threshold between eras. The formal, Italian-Renaissance-style gardens of the English Georgian period were of course politically out-of-date, and increasingly passé culturally. Jefferson would soon be completing a scheme for Monticello that integrated the surrounding natural landscapes, long views, plus working and experimental agricultural plots, into his nominally formal estate layout.

Now, too, Romanticism was taking hold in Europe, particularly in England, as exemplified by Humphrey Repton's landscape sensibility of "horrid" and "sublime" natural beauty. Such notions would soon color taste in the United States. That would eventually lead to a symbolic embrace of nature, as Naturalism in American landscape expressions.

As noted in the Landscape in America chapter, by around 1800 the idea of "æsthetic" landscaping as distinct from utilizing plantings to temper climate and provide shelter from weather had filtered down from private estates to urban neighborhoods. A space behind the statehouse in Philadelphia had matured into a handsome park. Property owners had planted boulevard trees along public streets in towns ranging in size from Philadelphia and New York to Newport and Pittsfield. Other than linear plantings of street–boulevard trees, many of these landscapes were visually informal, if not deliberately naturalistic.

A gradual transition into a naturalistic landscape imagery occurred in several, intermittent stages. These included: discarding the old formal parterres of the Georgian era; adopting informal planting patterns, especially eliminating straight lines; responding to existing natural features; and including the natural landscape—and vistas where possible—into the designed landscape composition.

The nineteenth-century American romanticization of nature in landscapes extended to architecture (see Romantic Revivals chapter), especially with regard to domestic colors. The traditional white New England frame house with green shutters remained common, if no longer fashionable as it was in the early 1800s, nearly into the 1840s. By then, Andrew Jackson Downing was popularizing naturalistic landscape expressions. Soon, fashion dictated that houses should blend into their surroundings. Architect Calvert Vaux and other tastemakers recommended earth tones so that houses would not lack sympathy with their natural surroundings.

By this point, American landscape design had arrived at Naturalism, just when refinement had triumphed in America. As Richard Bushman observed, by about 1850, "gentility had left innumerable traces on the American landscape. Fashionable houses . . . tree-lined streets . . . landscaped squares, pleasure gardens" were built to meet the needs of an increasingly genteel American population.

Mount Auburn Cemetery FIG. 973
1831–1834 ff.
Jacob Bigelow, Henry Dearborn, site planners–designers
580 Mt. Auburn St. Cambridge, Massachusetts

FIG. 973 **Poetic Landscape** Mount Auburn's celebrated Sphinx suggests the encyclopedic adventure in the Picturesque offered throughout this Boston-area cemetery.

Dedicated urban cemeteries in the U.S.—as distinct from churchyards and family grave sites—date from 1796, in New Haven. At first, these burying grounds were laid out in simple grid patterns, but with the flourishing of Romanticism, they came to be seen as ideal opportunities to devise poetic landscapes.

Mt. Auburn was initially developed as a burying ground and, equally, as both a demonstration of experimental horticulture and a picturesque community attraction, laid out in a naturalistic pattern. In order to differentiate it from rural graveyards, and to effect a high tone for the interred, slab tombstones were proscribed in favor of monuments whose imageries looked back to Classical Greece and Pharaonic Egypt (Fig. 973). This language of miniature temples and obelisks was subsequently adopted for urban cemeteries of pretense in major U.S. cities. (See landmark cemetery gates, Figs. 143, 161.) Though in no place is the American poetic romantic landscape better appreciated than here, at its origins.

Capitol Grounds FIG. 974
1850; completed by 1860; later revisions; grounds renovated 2003–2006
John Notman, designer
Between 9th and Governor Sts., Richmond, Virginia

Jefferson's Capitol (see Neoclassicism chapter) originally boasted a formal setting, Capitol Square, which was developed after an 1816 plan by Maximilian Godefroy. Notman, a Philadelphia architect known for his eclecticism, was engaged to devise a new landscape in 1850. The idea for a new plan was precipitated by the decision to locate the new Washington Monument to the west, on the side of the Capitol, rather than directly south, in front, as called for in Godefroy's plan. It is probably equally important that Formalism was well out of fashion by mid-century, and a naturalistic, romantic landscape would have been understood as up-to-date.

Notman downplayed Godefroy's bilateral symmetry and focused on establishing a naturalistic precinct to the southwest (Fig. 974), which was planted by 1852. His scheme was completely planted by 1860, becoming "the nation's first picturesque urban park," according to the Historic American Buildings Survey.

Llewellyn Park
1852–1858 ff.
Llewellyn S. Haskell, visionary developer; **Alexander Jackson Davis**, planner and architect
West Orange, New Jersey

See Community Development chapter.

Central Park, "Greensward" FIGS. 975, 976
1857–1858 ff.
N of 59th St., between 5th Ave and Central Park West, New York, New York
Frederick Law Olmsted & Calvert Vaux, planners and designers

Given its 840-acre size, location, and the professional stature of its designers, Central Park is of supreme importance in American landscape history—and urbanism. The park is composed of two distinct sections, an open, pastoral south, and a picturesque urban wilderness to the north. In addition to developing a wide range of spatial experiences (Fig. 975), and designing handsome park structures, including bridges, the Greensward scheme called for four sunken roadways employed to separate crosstown traffic from park environments (see Roads chapter).

FIG. 974 Changing Fashion The original, formal setting for Jefferson's Virginia Capitol seemed embarrassingly out of fashion by the mid-1800s. That simply *would not do* for a premier state like Virginia. So a romantic, naturalistic landscape was overplanted in the 1850s. The informal Capitol Grounds landscape that we experience today, under reconstruction in 2005, derives from this scheme.

FIGS. 975, 976 Unrivaled Romantic Landscape Because of its scale, diversity of environments, and superior design qualities, Central Park is without peer in the United States. It has strongly affected growth in adjacent areas, to which it stands in sharp contrast (Fig. 975). Among special features dispersed throughout the park according to the original plan is the lakeside Bethesda Fountain terrace (Fig. 976).

FIG. 977 **Natural Connections** Olmsted literally stitched the fabric of Boston together with the Emerald Necklace. His design is a masterpiece of visionary accommodation, alternately expressed as an urban boulevard, linear parkland, scenic landscape, and wilderness preserve. Despite what one might imagine from this sylvan view, Jamaica Pond is actually located adjacent to urbanized Boston.

FIG. 978 **Mixed Messages** Olmsted must have struggled with his Biltmore Estate commission. The vast North Carolina project was far too compelling to turn down, even as it required Olmsted to traffic in the formal design vocabularies that he abhorred. The visual upshot is a curious hodge-podge of environments, neither comprehensively formal nor satisfyingly naturalistic, especially in the developed area around the main house.

Boston Emerald Necklace FIG. 977
1880 ff.
Frederick Law Olmsted, landscape architect
Muddy River between Back Bay and Franklin Park and Arnold Arboretum

Probably America's most celebrated naturalistic landscape, Boston's Emerald Necklace provides case studies for landscape design, parkway planning, community development, and the physical and symbolic integration of city and suburbs.

Olmsted worked with a disparate array of sites extending over some ten miles of urbanized and rural lands, somehow stitching fragments into the sense of a unified whole—implausible in concept and thus especially impressive in achievement. Major parts of the Necklace occur intermittently, since Olmsted had to work partly within built-up urban neighborhoods as well as with reclaimed marshlands.

Main elements of the Emerald Necklace include Boston Common and Public Garden, the Back Bay Fens, Riverway, Leverett Pond, Olmsted Park/Jamaica Pond (Fig. 977), Franklin Park, Arnold Arboretum, and Larz Anderson Park. These are interconnected by Commonwealth Avenue, Fenway, Riverway, Jamaicaway, Arborway, Parkway Central and Pond Street.

Biltmore Estate FIG. 978
1888–1895
Frederic Law Olmsted, Warren Manning, landscape architects
Asheville, North Carolina (open)

Biltmore must be appreciated at three levels of scale. The estate originally included about 125,000 acres, equivalent to a fourteen-mile square. Within this vast area, about 8,000 acres were actively developed for agriculture and a 3-mile-long access road. Biltmore's immediate environs (see Beaux Arts chapter), the smallest-scale environment of the three, includes a formal front lawn, eight acres of formal landscapes (Fig. 978), an herb garden, and a colorful walled garden.

Continental formalism and colorful plantings were the antithesis of Olmsted's American Naturalism, which was going out of fashion among the wealthy well before Olmsted's death in 1903.

Still, the approach drive is agreeably moody, and Olmsted tucked in patches of devised wilderness around the house, wherever he could.

Minneapolis Park System FIGS. 979, 980, 981, 982
1883, 1891, 1899–1900, 1906–1930s; late 1960s
Horace Cleveland, William Watts Folwell, Warren Manning, Theodore Wirth, Garrett Eckbo
Defined by the Grand Rounds parkways encircling the city, engaging lakes Nokomis, Hiawatha, Harriet, Calhoun, Isles, Cedar; Minnehaha Creek; and the Mississippi riverfront

The basic idea for a Minneapolis park system originated with landscape architect Cleveland's proposals of the early 1880s. His street-grid plan (Fig. 979) followed a successful park referendum in 1883. Folwell's 1891 park board committee came up with the naturalistic Grand Rounds concept (Fig. 980), a complete and highly creative break from Cleveland's earlier grid scheme. The Olmsted-trained Manning apparently drew up Grand Rounds plans in 1899.

Under Wirth's three-decade leadership as Superintendent of Parks, the system matured, physically (Figs. 981, 982) and programmatically, into a powerful institution, beloved by Minnesotans and kept politically independent by generations of Minneapolis citizens. Eckbo edited and refined the parkway system in the late 1960s (Figs. 1076, 1077).

The apparent "natural" beauty of the parks and parkways was partly developed out of indifferent sites, a triumph of landscape planning, hydrology, and horticulture.

Opus 40 FIG. 983
1939–1976
Harvey Fite, sculptor-builder
50 Fite Rd., off I-87 exit 20 W of Saugerties, New York (open)

Naturalism in the most localized sense, Opus 40 is a splendid 6.5-acre, dry-laid bluestone acropolis constructed atop an abandoned quarry, which provided the rubble building material. Using hand tools, Fite built this awe-inspiring composition of "platforms,

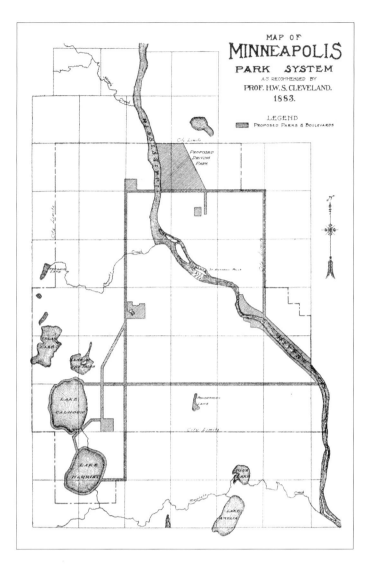

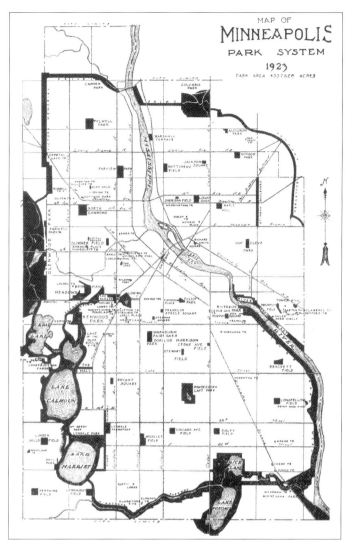

FIGS. 979, 980, 981, 982 Chain of Lakes Horace Cleveland first proposed a
Minneapolis park *system* as a network of urban boulevards (Fig. 979). His idea of a
system led to the realization of a very different planning concept, proposed and
planned by others: the Grand Rounds, a system of encircling parkways engaging the
city's lakes, streams, and parklands in a naturalistic pattern layered across the city's
USGS street grid (Fig. 980). Development of the Minneapolis Park System occurred
after 1906 (Figs. 981, 982). *Figs. 979, 980: Theodore Wirth, 1945*

FIG. 983 **Grandeur in Stone** Opus 40 is pretty much incomparable, both in the spectacular integration with its natural setting and for the sheer effort in construction, undertaken by one person over the course of nearly four decades.
Opus 40

pools, ramps, terraces, and bridges" on a splendid, wooded site set in the Catskills. Visitors can marvel equally at the astonishing effort required in construction and its superior visual qualities, which Brendan Gill described as one of "the most beguiling works of art on the entire continent."

LATTER-DAY NATURALISM

Naturalism in landscape design occurs in several guises in the United States. Much of it is grounded in Romanticism, as the previous entries in this syllabus illustrate. Currently, several versions of Environmentalism (see that chapter) are popular, ranging from reconstruction of indigenous landscapes to the poetic horticultural expressions of Oehme and van Sweden (see Environmentalism chapter).

Arthur Edwin Bye (1919–2001) also practiced a highly personal form of Naturalism. His sensibilities were in some ways closer to the idealized English natural landscapes of Lancelot Brown in the 1700s. Like Brown, Bye subtly enhanced his sites. Yet Bye's occasional employment of monumental sculptural landforms also owes much to post–World War II Modernism.

Gainesway Farm FIGS. 984, 985
1975 ff.
A. E. Bye, landscape architect
3750 Paris Pike, Lexington, Kentucky (partly open)

Bye worked on Gainesway Farm in Lexington's Bluegrass horse country throughout the 1970s. The most photogenic and thus best known of this work was the planning and setting for architect Theodore Ceraldi's stallion barns (Fig. 985). Beyond the architecture, Bye's meticulous reshaping of the fields and paddocks (Fig. 984), and his magnificent serpentine stone retaining wall/ha-ha (now fenced and inaccessible to the public) are superior achievements of contemporary American landscape design.

FIGS. 984, 985 **Polished Naturalism** A. E. Bye simplified his Gainesway Farm site through meticulous, subtle grading and understated use of materials. The highly refined finished landscape seems natural in its low swells and contemporary in its overall sense of openness.

Regionalism

1881–1951

FIG. 986 **Prairie Landscape** Surprisingly, the all-but-featureless Midwestern prairie inspired the best-known American regional landscape school. When comparing a typical prairie scene like this one in Downstate Illinois near Champaign to the Prairie Style landscapes in this chapter, it is readily apparent that the design inspiration was more philosophical than physical. Prairie School landscape architects synthesized general regional attributes and features like horizontality, rock strata, and indigenous plant species into idealized designed regional landscapes.

Regionalism in landscape architecture occurs in several distinct forms, and from several distinct perspectives about what is or is not "regional." Its creations can range from preserving a native landscape pretty much intact to creative expressions of horticultural identity, as in the work of Oehme and van Sweden (see Environmentalism chapter).

It is important to appreciate that Regionalism in landscape can apply both to design, as in the Prairie School landscape traditions, and also to treatment, as in the many installations of

FIG. 987 Regional Horticulture Devised prairie landscapes, often saturated with colorful forbs (characteristic prairie plants), are popular contemporary regional landscape expressions in the Midwest.

FIG. 988 Non-prairie Prairie Landscape Many sites of Prairie School landscape designs, such as this scene in Chicago's Graceland Cemetery, were not flat and featureless like native prairies. Prairie School landscape architects abstracted characteristic Midwestern horizontality through the prominent use of spreading native species.

FIG. 989 The Infinite Stream For Humboldt Park, Jens Jensen employed a traditional landscape visual trick by winding the shoreline of a constructed pond in order to obscure its boundaries. From most parts of the park, the pond reads as a passing stream.

prairie landscapes which have become so popular in recent years throughout the American Midwest (Fig. 987). Generally, though not always, designed regional landscapes are the province of landscape architects, while treatments are developed by nurseries and installed by individuals.

From a broad definition, Regionalism in New World landscape architecture may spring from a number of sources. These include: a native biome distinct to a particular locality; traditions brought by immigrants and applied "artificially" within a given region, like the Georgian gardens of Virginia; cues taken from regional and/or folk architecture/design; and an influential body of signature works by great designers, like the Brazilian national landscape style created by the great twentieth-century master, Roberto Burle Marx.

American Naturalism is a form of regional design, although it has been widely applied in many distinct guises across the northern tier of the United States, from New England to the Pacific Northwest. Such work is generally addressed in the Naturalism chapter. Similarly, formal European landscape approaches shaped the gardens of areas with strong ties to Europe, like Virginia and New Orleans; these are cited in the Formalism chapter.

Probably the best-known American landscape Regionalism occurred in the Midwest, especially in Chicago This was the Prairie School or Style of landscape architecture led by Jens Jensen (1860–1951) and Ossian Cole "O. C." Simonds (1855–1931). These Prairie landscape architects were influenced by the godfather of Prairie School architecture, Frank Lloyd Wright.

Characteristically, Prairie landscape designers emphasized the horizontality of the prairie (Fig. 986), employing regional specimens like dogwood and hawthorn, stratified to refer to naturally occurring plant communities. These Regionalist landscape architects might employ native rock in horizontal strata, here too to emulate its naturally occurring state.

However, many Midwestern regional landscapes were not developed in flat, prairie-like settings. David Gebhard perceptively noted that two of the finest Prairie School "regional" landscapes, Walter Burley Griffin's Rock Crest–Rock Glen development in Mason City, Iowa, and Alfred Caldwell's Eagle Point Park in Dubuque, Iowa, (both later in this chapter) were set in rocky glens, and had "far more to do with the romantic eighteenth-century English sense of the sublime than with the horizontality of the prairie."

Prairie School/Style designers like Jensen and Simonds eschewed literal restorations of prairie landscapes; they were artists more than horticulturalists. Hence the current regional interest in prairie treatments of landscape is addressed in the Environmentalism chapter.

INDIGENOUS REGIONALISM

Graceland Cemetery FIG. 988
1881–1931
O. C. Simonds, landscape architect
Clark at Irving Park Rd., Chicago, Illinois

Although Simonds featured native shrubs and trees in his Graceland schemes, his designs for several sections of the cemetery were, by necessity, densely packed, on account of the urban character of the site and its relatively small land area. Robert Grese stated that Simonds intended a rural feeling, and while that goal may have been partly achieved through an informal bushy-ness, Graceland is certainly not open and "prairie-like."

Humboldt Park FIG. 989

1907–1917
Jens Jensen, landscape architect
North Ave. between California and Kedzie, Chicago, Illinois

Jensen based his Humboldt plan on an Olmstedian naturalistic pattern, with two signature features–attributes. One is that the park is organized around an "infinite" stream or "prairie river" contrived through configuration and planting. This design technique was employed by eighteenth-century English landscape designers, notably Lancelot Brown, and in the 1940s by Roberto Burle Marx for his Pampulha development in Belo Horizonte, Brazil. Second, the horticulture emphasized native–indigenous plantings, for reasons of plant health and design expression.

Columbus Park FIG. 990

1917–1920
Jens Jensen, landscape architect
Austin and Jackson Blvds., Chicago, Illinois

Within a decade of the his initial scheme for Humboldt Park (above), Jensen had evolved from the naturalistic Olmsted patterns to a concept featuring wide-open meadows, though also incorporating a prairie river. Columbus Park has much more of a countryside feeling than does Jensen's Naturalism of a decade earlier.

Lincoln Highway "Ideal Section"

1917–1925, totally overbuilt
Jens Jensen, landscape architect
U.S. Hwy. 30, between Schererville and Dyer, Indiana

This 1.3-mile corridor was a seminal landscape design for American roadbuilding, unfortunately not widely replicated nor, alas, preserved. The scheme was based on the usual Jensen formula of native shrubs and indigenous trees with horizontal growth structure, like hawthorn and crabs. He also employed large amounts of colorful forbs, a rare expression for Jensen (see also Roads chapter).

Lilacia Park

c. 1929
Jens Jensen, landscape architect
Maple St., one block W of S. Main St., Lombard, Illinois

A mock waterfall–grotto provides the visual focus. This construction, now overgrown, is of horizontal limestone courses intended to recall natural rock cuts like those found in prairie areas along the Illinois and Rock rivers. As an example, compare the Lilacia waterfall to the exposed limestone strata along I-39 just south of Rockford, Illinois.

Lincoln Memorial Garden FIGS. 991, 992

1934–1936
Jens Jensen, landscape architect
E. Lake Shore Dr., 2.6 mi. NE of I-55 Exit 88, Springfield, Illinois

A summation of Jensen's ideas and vocabularies, undertaken in a true prairie setting. A 63-acre farm was chosen as the site by Jensen. This sparsely wooded parcel, later expanded to 100 acres and by today densely overgrown, was developed into a sequence of

FIG. 990 Opening Up Columbus Park was laid out a decade after Humboldt (Fig. 989). Jensen had by now moved away from Olmstedian naturalism. Rather than tightly controlling views as at Humboldt, he organized the Columbus landscapes around spacious meadows.

FIG. 991, 992 Finale Lincoln Memorial Garden was developed almost a generation after Prairie School expressions peaked in the mid-teens. It is by now agreeably overgrown, Jensen's council rings encircled by woods.

FIG. 993 **Home Laboratory** Jens Jensen worked out his design ideas on his ample suburban Chicago lot, the "Ravinia" house and studio, which was bordered on two sides by a wooded ravine. Jensen's first council ring, which became a signature built feature in most of his designs, was constructed on a descending point above the ravine. *Library of Congress, Prints & Photographs, Historic American Buildings Survey*

prairie meadows (Fig. 991) and wooded groves, now functioning almost as side-by-side rooms. Jensen employed his "council rings," circular stone benches (Fig. 992), for orientation and to emphasize particular spaces.

JENSEN'S HOMES

Jensen (Ravinia) Home and Studio, "The Clearing" FIG. 993
1908–1918; studio expansion 1921 or 1922; property subdivided after 1951
Jens Jensen, architect and landscape architect
950–954 Dean Ave., Highland Park, Illinois

Jensen bought this 2.5-acre property in 1908. He moved his studio here in 1918, remaining until he began residing year-around at his Wisconsin Clearing (next entry) in 1935. The site was wooded, edged by a steep ravine on two sides, in no way resembling a prairie. Nevertheless, it served as Jensen's laboratory: he cut a sun-trap opening in the oak woods, softening the cut with his now-familiar vocabulary of gray dogwoods, crabs, and stratified hawthorns. Jensen built his first council ring on a point above the ravine (Fig. 993).

After Jensen's death in 1951 the property was subdivided and is by now overgrown, although a basic outline remains.

Jensen Retreat and School, "The Clearing"
1919 ff. 1934–1951
Jens Jensen, landscape architect; **Hugh Garden, John Van Bergen**, consulting architects for the lodge–dining hall and classroom building, respectively
12171 Garrett Bay Rd., Ellison Bay, Wisconsin

After Jensen's wife died in 1934, he moved to this 129-acre summer property located right at the tip of the scenic Door County peninsula. The site is magnificent: a high, wooded overlook above Lake Michigan. In 1932 Jensen established a school combining classical studies with ecology at The Clearing, and it was here that he wrote his influential 1939 book, *Siftings*.

ROMANTIC REGIONALISM

Rock Crest–Rock Glen FIG. 994
1911–1912 ff.
Walter Burley Griffin, Marion Mahoney Griffin, planners
E. State St., Caroline, River Heights, and 1st St. S.E., Mason City, Iowa

A topographically extreme site, what English romantic gardeners would have termed "horrid and sublime," was left as an open park, with the houses arranged around the periphery, giving them, in common, a picturesque scene focused on a small stream.

Eagle Point Park FIG. 995
1934–1936
Alfred Caldwell, Wendell Reffenberger, landscape architects
NE of town along the Mississippi River bluff, off Shiras Ave., Dubuque, Iowa

Few municipal parks can boast such an inspired combination of dramatic setting, architectural quality, and integration of the built with a dynamically rolling site.

FIG. 994 **Picturesque Regionalism** Rock Crest–Rock Glen is simple in concept: handsome homes, several designed by major Prairie School architects (Fig. 271), encircle a meadow through which a small stream flows. The park-like shared space achieves a Midwestern ideal: pleasant with a minimum of pretentiousness.

FIG. 995 **Prairie Setting** Nestling snugly into its site, Alfred Caldwell's native stone pavilion forms Eagle Point Park's centerpiece "parkitecture."

Garden Restorations

1928–1941

Colonial Revival landscape design peaked in the 1930s with nationally prominent garden restorations at Williamsburg and Stratford Hall in Virginia and at the La Purísima Mission in California.

Early twentieth-century re-landscapes of historic sites had been improvisational, if not literally made up. For instance, as noted in the American Colonial Revivals chapter, the central area of Litchfield, Connecticut, served as a garbage dump and as a site for animal pens throughout the colonial era and a lifetime beyond, until the mid-1830s. That once-utilitarian space was reconstructed in 1913 as a village green (Fig. 202).

This twentieth-century village green design was highly successful, visually, a major reason why Litchfield is widely admired today as an authentic Colonial New England town even though, like its townscape, which was also reconstructed as colonial at the same time, Litchfield's community landscape was artfully devised as colonial 130 years after the end of the colonial era.

Such an openly inventive approach to historic landscapes was tested at Colonial Williamsburg. As a "restoration," this first-class undertaking would logically have been expected to be

FIGS. 996, 997 Idealized Views of the Past During the golden era of Colonial Revival landscape restorations in the 1930s, two opposing philosophies were tested. One of these, favored by historians, was strict accuracy, as much as it was possible to determine from reliable sources. Unfortunately, historic colonial settings were usually functional in the extreme, visually quite bleak. So an alternative philosophy was advanced, primarily by landscape architects. This approach emphasized presenting a beautiful picture of the past, whether or not that was historically accurate; usually it was not. By and large, idealized restorations advocated by designers won out, as these exquisitely trimmed forms at Colonial Williamsburg attest.

FIG. 998 **Pretty as a Postcard** Twentieth-century colonial revival sensibilities ensured that Williamsburg (and other restorations) would be beautiful well beyond historical accuracy. Because of its prominent location along Williamsburg's Duke of Gloucester Street, adjacent to the Palace Green, the Cole-Geddy Row was among the first to receive this characteristically enhanced restoration.

FIG. 999 **Through Rose-colored Glasses** The quintessence of 1930s colonial revival restorations, Colonial Williamsburg was rebuilt with a keen appreciation of what the American public would find attractive, even if that was not strictly historically accurate. For instance, this monumental *allée* leading to the Governor's Palace was a rough grazing pasture when governors lived here. Williamsburg's enduring popularity confirms this restoration approach.

historically accurate, or at least to be based on some plausible historical basis.

As a practical matter, however, pioneering restoration landscape architects were at some disadvantage, usually working without detailed historical and archeological evidence to guide their designs. Moreover, according to Charles Hosmer, "Administrators of historical restorations believed that visitors should see an essentially beautiful picture of the past" (Fig. 998). Since most colonial landscapes were unplanned and utterly functional in character, this dreamy goal was clearly a stretch if strict accuracy was to be achieved.

Indeed, from the outset of work on Williamsburg, benefactor John D. Rockefeller, Jr.'s, "penchant for neatness caused the Williamsburg gardens to look like picture postcards all year long," in Hosmer's description. He went on to note that Williamsburg's gardens were intended as attractive "frames" for restored structures, not as accurate restorations of landscapes of the colonial 1700s, nor even of the new Republic in the 1800s. Besides Hosmer observed, historic site managers "did not want to present something ugly to the public ... which needed refreshment, not desolation" in the depths of the Great Depression.

Such idealized views of the past colored 1930s garden-restoration efforts (Figs. 996, 997). Only recently were these Colonial Revival historic landscapes re-restored closer to everyday authenticity. Even today, these more authentic restored landscapes are maintained with much greater care and reliability than would have been the case in colonial America.

Today, historians might be more successful in forcing scruffy austerity if not outright rudeness on designers. But, by now well more than 50 years old, these embellished American Colonial Revival landscapes are authentically "historical" in their own right, and thus preservationists now have two distinct authentic interpretations of colonial landscapes from which to choose.

Litchfield Green

1719; town transformed after 1913; Congregational church reconstructed as colonial, 1919–1929
A. P. F. Adenaw, LaFarge and Morris, F. B. J. Renshaw, architects of the 1913 colonialization plans; **John Charles Olmsted, Frederick Law Olmsted, Jr.**, landscape architects; **Richard Henry Dana, Jr.**, church reconstruction architect
Litchfield, Connecticut

In colonial times, Litchfield's central space served multiple utilitarian roles, including that of town dump. After the community's sweeping twentieth-century neo-colonialization campaign, this space emerged as a beautifully manicured green, the idealized setting for the town's signature church, itself reconstructed as colonial in the 1920s. (See American Colonial Revivals chapter and Fig. 202.)

Colonial Williamsburg FIGS. 996, 997, 998, 999
1928–1937 ff.
Arthur A. Shurcliff (Shurtleff), landscape architect and area planner
James City County, Virginia (open)

Although the Williamsburg restoration was initially driven by architecture, and thus by the architects Perry, Shaw & Hepburn, Shurcliff was influential in establishing an overall direction for the restoration–reconstruction. Shurcliff did not restrict his efforts to horticultural designs, but also functioned as a preliminary area/site planner, carefully investigating early surveys and determining historically authentic lot layouts.

At the outset, Shurcliff was concerned about authenticity. He was thorough in his field research, including on-site studies of historic properties throughout the region. He particularly did not want his landscapes to seem "too good looking . . .too many flowers . . . trees, because they wouldn't be appropriate" as ambiance given the somewhat shabby communities and unpretentious houses typical of the colonial period.

Despite his stated intention to create a realistic portrayal of colonial everyday life, Shurcliff eventually succumbed to the poetic possibilities of the Williamsburg landscape-townscape. This shift in approach came at the expense of historical accuracy, even of cultural plausibility.

The handsome landscaped "park" (Fig. 999) in front of the Governor's Palace, for instance, was never anything more than a cow pasture in colonial times. Similarly, the ornamental boxwood maze was based on one at Hampton Court Palace; none could be documented in the colonies, much less in Williamsburg. This was justified by Shurcliff on the basis that if there was one in England during the colonial period, then it was okay to install one at Williamsburg, purely as a visitor attraction. All in all, Shurcliff's design enthusiasms eventually overwhelmed his earlier reticence about overdesigning the historic landscape. In the end, his spectacular visual effects won over many doubters, reportedly even among those who valued strict historical accuracy.

As a consequence, even after a toning down of its townscape in recent years in a nod toward historical accuracy, Colonial Williamsburg is still surely visually far more vibrant and interesting as a restoration than the town of Williamsburg ever was during colonial times.

Lee Plantation, "Stratford Hall" FIGS. 1000, 1001
1929–1940 ff.
Arthur A. Shurcliff (Shurtleff), preliminary planner; **Morley J. Williams**, principal landscape architect for site reconstruction
40 mi. E of Fredericksburg, off Hwy. 3, Westmoreland County, Virginia (open)

Williams was an associate of Shurcliff. And of course the foundation undertaking the restoration of the Stratford Hall house (Fiske Kimball restoration architect, see Southern Colonial Architecture

FIGS. 1000, 1001 Rebuilding from Scratch When landscape restorations at Lee Mansion, "Stratford Hall," began in 1929, little hard archeological information was available about any historic gardens around the main house. The extensive and extraordinarily attractive landscapes that we experience today date from creative restoration designs of the 1930s. Similarly, the North Vista (Fig. below) was enhanced beyond strict accuracy with the addition of ornamental plantings. *Fig. 1000: Library of Congress, Prints & Photograph, Historic American Buildings Survey*

chapter) was well aware of the contemporary restoration activities at Williamsburg.

The Stratford foundation relied on highly qualified volunteers for its historical research, which was extremely thorough, documenting the property's evolution from the 1700s right up to the 1930s. Shurcliff was involved in a 1930 archeological excavation of the site, concluding that the estate was "imposing" and "laid out with a generous hand." That provided a rationale for Williams to develop the formal East Garden alongside the house (Fig. 1000), although nothing here was as historically fanciful as were some of Williamsburg's devised landscapes.

The West Garden, originally designed by Innocenti & Webel, is a flower garden typical of the 1700s. The kitchen garden is surrounded by espaliered fruit trees. The North Vista is Stratford's

FIGS. 1002, 1003 Fanciful Restoration As in other restorations, the question of authenticity versus attractiveness emerged as a central restoration issue for Mission above). Historians documented that a "bare, dusty space" would have been authentic, but that would not have been very appealing to visitors. So landscape architects developed utterly fanciful schemes of how the grounds might have been developed. Today (Fig. below), La Purísima's site is toned down compared to the 1930s design proposals, but remains ahistorically tidy compared to its traditional bare, dusty state.
Fig. 1002: Library of Congress, Prints & Photograph, Historic American Buildings Survey

most imposing landscape element (Fig. 1001). This nearly mile-long allée extending toward the Potomac River was reopened, widened, and ahistorically enhanced by ornamental plantings of dogwood, redbud, and paulownia, resulting in a monumental space worthy of the visually powerful main house.

Mission La Purísima Concepción FIGS. 1002, 1003
1934–1941
Phillip T. Primm, landscape architect; **Ed Rowe**, landscape foreman; **Russell Ewing**, historian; **Emerson Knight, Fred Hageman**, supervisory architects
Rt. 246, Lompoc, California (open as state park)

By 1935, La Purísima mission church (1812–1823) had fallen into a state of dilapidation (Fig. 1002). The federal government and State of California jointly undertook the reconstruction of an entire mission community, not just rebuilding the mission church itself.

Compared to the proposal-and-decision structure for Stratford Hall, or even for Colonial Williamsburg, this was a highly bureaucratic undertaking. Nonetheless, when the landscape scheme was developed, the same issues of strict authenticity vs. visual effects emerged, as they had at Williamsburg.

National Park Service historians and archeologists maintained that the proposed landscape design was too elaborate, doing "certain violence" to the notion of a "working museum of mission culture." Simplicity, if not realistic austerity of plantings, was recommended.

In response, the landscape architects contended that authenticity required a "bare, dusty space" with a few scrubby trees randomly scattered across the site. This historically accurate treatment "would be of little interest to the majority of visitors."

Very much in line with Shurcliff's rationale for the maze at Williamsburg, the resulting formal layout and substantial plantings (Fig. 1003) represent what "perhaps might have happened under . . . a mission padre interested in plants," according to landscape architect Rowe.

FIG. 1004 **Practical Horticulture** As suggested by this view of Monticello's west lawn, Jefferson's gardening focused less on site aesthetics, what we now think of as "landscaping," than on experimentation with exotic species and, of course, on growing a reliable supply of food for Monticello's residents and guests. *Library of Congress, Prints & Photograph, Historic American Buildings Survey*

Monticello FIG. 1004
1939 ff.

Thomas Jefferson, naturalist and landscape gardener; **Peter J. Hatch**, late-twentieth-century garden restorer

5 mi. SE of Charlottesville, Virginia, off Hwy. 53. (open)

The incomparable Jefferson is considered to be the American "father" of numerous disciplines and interests, from architecture to wine making. Characteristically, he traveled across Europe studying gardens.

Here on his Monticello estate (Fig. 1004, see also Neoclassicism chapter), Jefferson kept careful, detailed records of his crops and botanical experiments, compiling a "collection of garden wisdom." This was finally published in 1944, well more than a century after his death in 1826.

Without Jefferson, Monticello's garden landscapes quickly disappeared. By the time the Garden Club of Virginia initiated a restoration of the grounds in 1939, no visual artifacts of Jefferson's planting beds and fields remained. Restoration of the garden and agricultural fields was necessarily more of a considered reconstruction based on excavations, records of species Jefferson sent home, and other, documented American gardens of the early 1800s.

The current emphasis of Monticello's gardens, guided by Hatch, is on a two-acre kitchen garden plot located along a 1,000-foot terrace just below the southeast ridge of the lawn. A re-creation of Jefferson's "free-spirited design," its plantings range from the routine, like Jefferson's beloved peas and tomatoes, to the exotic, reflecting his global interests.

Labyrinth FIG. 1005
1939–1941
S. Main St./Rt. 69, New Harmony, Indiana

FIG. 1005 **Beautiful Reconstruction** The luxuriant, perfectly curving hedges of New Harmony's Labyrinth attain a level of perfection which surely far surpasses the original "working" labyrinth.

A meditative labyrinth was constructed by the founding Harmonist sect sometime before 1825, when they decamped and returned to the East. Unattended, their labyrinth planting fell into disrepair; it had ceased to exist by the twentieth century.

The present labyrinth was developed on an adjacent plot. This beautiful new planting of flawlessly concentric rows of privet hedge focusing on a small stone "temple" in the center would surely dazzle the builders of the original labyrinth, which would hardly have been groomed to such perfection.

Exotic Landscapes
1910–1993

Exotic landscapes are defined here as designed expressions for U.S. sites which are not American in origin and/or in imagery. In two respects, exotic American landscapes reflect English Victorian romantic landscape traditions: the importing of non-indigenous plant species like the spectacular Andean Monkey Puzzle (*Araucaria aracauna*) colonnade at Bicton in Devon; and appropriating a distinctive national garden type/style, such as Japanese Gardens, from another part of the world.

By now, of course, many once-exotic imports of plants or styles are commonplace in the United States. For instance, palm landscapes are ubiquitous from Florida to California. Yet the palm is a tropical-equatorial family. Outside of the Florida peninsula, only five of 2,800 palm species are indigenous to the continental United States. While striking boulevard palms in communities like San Marino, California, seem truly exotic in every respect (Fig. 1006), such plantings are so widespread throughout the Sunbelt as to now seem native.

Similar observations can be made for some ubiquitous landscape compositions. For instance, the formal Georgian gardens of colonial Virginia (see Landscape in America chapter) were European in origin. By today, Beaux Arts gardens/site layouts have undergone multiple cycles of popularity and decline in the United States.

Topiary is another exotic vocabulary (Fig. 1007), now found in settings as dissimilar as Ladew Topiary Gardens (3535 Jarretsville Pike, Monkton, Maryland) and Walt Disney World (see Landscape Features chapter).

Consequently, this chapter focuses on American landscape vocabularies that have not yet been widely assimilated throughout the United States.

JAPANESE GARDENS

Japanese garden history begins no later than the Nara period (645–784). Over the next dozen centuries, Japanese gardens have been designed in a seemingly infinite number of subtle permutations, reflecting the prevailing attitudes of any given era about religion, political power, and foreign influences.

In the United States, images of Japanese gardens have been distilled down primarily to just two: the austere and abstracted dry Zen garden, and the exquisitely scenic, fully planted stroll garden.

These common (among Americans) images are necessarily a generalized synthesis of many nuanced variations of Japanese preference and expression, such as whether a beautiful garden should reflect opulence or refined poverty. For those who wish to understand the authentic design bases of Japanese gardens, a reading of Treib and Herman is highly recommended. We should also recognize that U.S. Japanese gardens, even those designed by Japanese garden masters, are inevitably—given the considerable distances of time, place, and culture—imperfect interpretations of historic exemplars.

FIG. 1007 Topiary Once considered exotic, fanciful clipped shrubbery can be found in a broad range of American settings, from the front lawns of houses in Chicago's suburbs to Disney World. This outstanding grouping is a feature of Longwood Gardens, near Philadelphia.

Japanese Hill and Pond Garden, Brooklyn Botanic Garden
1914–1915
Takeo Shiota, artist & garden master
1000 Washington Ave., Brooklyn, New York

This early (for the United States) Japanese garden includes the classic attributes of stroll gardens: an idealized landscape which employs the ancient technique of "borrowed scenery" to establish "hide and reveal" movements through the spaces. Individual design elements are also employed to express Japaneseness, as does the red *torii*-gateway rising from a pond.

Japanese Garden, Missouri Botanical Garden FIGS. 1008, 1009
1977
Koichi Kawana, garden master
4344 Shaw Blvd., St. Louis, Missouri

Japanese garden masters effectively practiced Modernism centuries before European designers. The famous abstracted *Ryoan-ji* rock garden in Kyoto was designed about 1500, a full 400 years before Modernism emerged in American landscape architecture.

This comparatively recent Japanese garden is notable for its abstracted, clipped azaleas set in broad, raked stone beds (Fig. 1008), along with other traditional settings (Fig. 1009). Although the azalea design seems to be a thoroughly modern expression, direct precedents can be found in the *Shoden-ji* and *Shisen-do* gardens in Kyoto, dating from the early 1600s.

"Garden of the Heart of Heaven"
1986–1988
Kinsaku Nakane, garden master
N of the Museum of Fine Arts, Boston, 465 Huntington Ave., Boston, Massachusetts

Less than a quarter-acre in size, the Boston garden is a fusion of fifteenth-century Japanese Zen gardens and modern American sensibilities. Its design blends the deep and subtle dry Zen garden symbolism of rocks and abstractly stylized shrubbery, the customary visual purity of which has been tempered by the introduction of color and non-traditional textures in flowering perennials.

PARADISE GARDENS

Persian/Moorish/Islamic landscapes, or "paradise gardens," are occasionally found in Period Revival designs for American estate houses. Typically, the "paradise" theme is highly abbreviated in expression, limited to a channel or trickle fountain, without the shading and distinctive four-fold patterns of a true Persian garden. Most of these are inaccessible to the public. However, Persian-inspired landscapes can be found at Walt Disney World.

Unsurprisingly, many American paradise gardens are located in South Florida and Southern California. The star-shaped fountain courtyard (Fig. 1010) in George Washington Smith's Maverick-Zachary House in the San Antonio suburbs is a notable exception.

Those who visit great American estates houses and gardens will eventually encounter some kind of paradise garden refer-

FIGS. 1008, 1009 Exotic Modernism This bed of clipped azaleas (Fig. 1008) in the Japanese Garden at the Missouri Botanical Garden in St. Louis seems thoroughly modern. Actually, this twentieth-century design is centuries late compared to the state of garden design in Japan: design precedents are found in Kyoto gardens constructed in the 1600s. The sense of modernity in the azalea planting is tempered by adjacent settings inspired by traditional Japanese stroll gardens (Fig. 1009). *Fig. 1009: Library of Congress, Prints & Photographs, Historic American Buildings Survey*

FIG. 1010 Private Paradise Gardens Moorish themes were by definition basic to pre–World War II architect-designed homes embodying Andalusian imageries. This courtyard fountain in suburban San Antonio was designed by the leading Spanish Colonial Revival architect, George Washington Smith for the Maverick-Zachary House (1928–1929).

ence. To learn more about the gardens on which these were based, those interested can consult books by Moore, Mitchell, and Turnbull and by Brookes.

ECCENTRIC LANDSCAPES

John D. Rockefeller Estate, "Kykuit" FIG. 1011
1893 ff. Japanese Tea House and Garden, 1909–1910; New Tea House, 1962; Garden expanded, 1963
William Welles Bosworth, landscape architect; **David E. Engel**, landscape architetct for the 1963 expansion; **Uyeda & Takahashi**, 1909–1910 Tea House builders, **Junzo Yoshimura**, architect of 1962 Tea House
200 Lake Rd., Pocantico Hills, Westchester County, New York (open)

With the rise of corporations in the late 1800s, and the resulting immense wealth of their owners, great country estates were built around major cities, especially New York. Exotic landscapes were sometimes included in these estates as visual counterpoints.

Kykuit's Japanese Garden is typical of the eclectic mixture that often occurred, beginning with a "Japanese" garden designed by an American landscape architect; a tea house in a Chinese-flavored imagery built by two Japanese carpenters; a later Tea House (Fig. 1011) built as a miniature replica of a great Japanese villa outside of Kyoto; the usual carefree mixture of *stroll* and *dry Zen* imageries, arranged in descending levels, like a tiny Philippine rice terrace—all enriched by Rockefeller's superb collection of Korean, Chinese, Japanese, and Tibetan lanterns. While this sounds like a stylistic mongrel, the resulting visual environment is both beautiful and believable—yet another example of a fresh American synthesis of foreign sources.

Ganna Walska Lotusland FIG. 1012
1941–1984
Ganna Walska, "peasant gardener," **Lockwood de Forest, Ralph T. Stevens, William Paylen, Oswald da Ros, Charles Glass**, consulting landscape architects
Sycamore Canyon Rd. 1 block N of Ashley Rd, Montecito, California; advance reservation required (open by appointment)

Walska's garden fantasy is about as singular a landscape experience as one could imagine. The setting is sublime: on the flanks of a mountainside in America's most exclusive suburb, along a neigh-

FIG. 1011 Estate Landscapes Exotic references, sometimes entire exotic installations, were familiar features of American country estates. The Rockefeller Westchester County estate, "Kykuit," includes an elaborate Far Eastern precinct focused on a tea house. *Library of Congress, Prints & Photographs, Historic American Buildings Survey*

FIG. 1012 Profusion The entrance pathway at Lotusland in Southern California leads intriguingly into a wonder world of exotic landscapes.

FIGS. 1013, 1014 **Diverse Exoticism** Huntington Gardens near Los Angeles offers a dozen different garden environments, including a spectacular Japanese garden (Fig. 1013) and the North Vista (Fig. 1014), where statuary arrayed along a European-style allée is played off, unconventionally, to say the least, against tropical palms.

borhood road with a scattering of upscale houses set within large lots.

The once-famous Polish diva retired here in order to develop a truly exotic home yard on 37 lushly wooded acres. Jenkins described this as a "nearly unimaginable profusion, even excess" of "bromeliads, ferns, succulents and countless hundreds" of other tropical specimens. These are employed to establish dozens of unforgettable exterior spaces and images, not the least "a pair of fantastical weeping succulent trees whose snakelike tendrils writhe up, down, and sideways."

TROPICAL LANDSCAPES

Huntington Gardens FIGS. 1013, 1014
1905 ff.; Japanese Garden, 1911
William Hertich, Wilbur David Cook, master gardeners–landscape architects
Allen Ave. at Orlando Rd., San Marino, California (open)

Several distinct landscape environments are found within the Huntington estate, notably the Shakespearean, Japanese (Fig. 1013), Rose, Desert/Cactus garden, and the North Vista (Fig. 1014). The Japanese Garden and John Russell Pope's 1933 mausoleum for the Huntingtons mark the visual extremes, both characterized by high artistic achievement.

Fairchild Tropical Garden FIG. 1015
1938 ff.
Robert Montgomery, founder; **David Fairchild**, botanist; **William Lyman Phillips**, landscape architect
10901 Old Cutler Rd., Coral Gables, Florida (open)

A glorious fusion of horticulture, design, and setting, Fairchild Gardens offers a seemingly limitless menu, with thousands of exotics: 900 species of palms alone. David Fairchild was a preeminent botanist who collected and preserved rare and endangered tropical specimens from all over the world. Phillips shaped the site into a memorable visual experience, much of which can be taken in from a slight eminence on the west (Fig. 1015), which offers a panoramic overlook of the property.

FIG. 1015 **Visual Horticulture** Fairchild Garden in Florida is a center for the scientific study of tropical specimens. In no way does that diminish its striking visual qualities. This signature vista only hints at Fairchild's cornucopia of exotic surprises.

FIG. 1016 **Expressiveness in the Extreme** Punctuated by succulents, Ralph Steven's Tremaine Garden in Southern California approaches the exotic tactility of Roberto Burle Marx's tropical landscapes. © *J. Paul Getty Trust. Used with permission. Julius Shulman Photography Archive Research Library at the Getty Research Institute*

Tremaine Garden FIG. 1016
1949
Ralph Stevens, landscape architect; **Roberto Burle Marx**, initial unrealized scheme
1636 Moore, Montecito, California (private residence)

This striking succulent garden (the 1948 house is by Richard Neutra) is plausibly tropical in its imagery, even though Santa Barbara's climate is not tropical. Although not usually accessible to the public, the Tremaine garden, located a short distance from Lotusland (above), has been widely illustrated, .

Cascade Garden
1992–1993
Roberto Burle Marx, landscape architect
Longwood Gardens, Hwy. 1, 3 mi. NE of Kennett Square, Pennsylvania (open)

A mere handful of Burle Marx designs were realized in the United States, only two of them publicly accessible. (Biscayne Boulevard in Miami is the other; see Civic Design chapter.) This is inexplicable and unforgivable, since Burle Marx (1909–1994) often traveled through the United States and was a singular world figure in landscape architecture, not just in his native Brazil. There he was designated a living national monument, like the international soccer superstar, Pele (See Fig. 1017).

Longwood Gardens engaged Burle Marx to develop a small tropical garden room in a corner of its conservatory. If one looks closely, especially at the wall treatments and bundled plant columns, one can perceive Burle Marx's art (as reference, compare with Bardi, esp. pp. 15, 35, 137).

FIG. 1017 **The Exotic Landscapes of Roberto Burle Marx** The great master was renowned for his vivid, tactile modernist designs, represented by this view at his rural estate outside of Rio de Janeiro. For those who would like to experience the flavor of a Burle Marx landscape in the United States, Longwood Gardens maintains its Cascade Garden, a small interior installation designed by Burle Marx just before his death in 1994.

Modernism

1925–2004

FIG. 1018 Landscape Modernism Thomas Church's 1958 design for the Kelham-Phillips estate in California's Napa Valley conveys the essence of post–World War II Modernist landscape sensibilities. Trees and shrubs are treated as abstracted forms, parts of a larger conceptual visual composition. The feeling of clarity and openness is characteristic of 1950s and early 1960s Modern American design.

More so than for architecture, it is possible to efficiently illustrate entire eras of landscape architecture through the work of a representative handful of practitioners. In American landscape Modernism, the seminal figures are Thomas Church (who moved, recurrently, into Modernism after the World War II), Garrett Eckbo, Dan Kiley, and James Rose. Their practices can be bracketed, at the front by Fletcher Steele, and later by Hideo Sasaki, Robert Zion, Peter Walker, and George Hargreaves.

The approaches of each of these designers differ significantly, so they do not constitute a school as much as they share common attitudes of an era.

A brief overview like this chapter must unavoidably overlook many superior landscape designers of national and regional importance. However, a number of Modernist landscape architects are cited within project teams in the architecture chapters.

Naumkeag FIG. 1019

1926 ff.; Blue Steps/Stairs, 1938
Fletcher Steele, landscape architect
Prospect Hill Rd., NW of central Stockbridge, Massachusetts (open seasonally)

Naumkeag is known for its signature Blue Steps ("stairs" in Steele's drawings), but they represent only a small part of Steele's efforts to transform a hilly site into a sculpted landscape. Born in 1885, Steele was a contemporary of Mies and Le Corbusier, and thus was well established as a practitioner when Modernism came into vogue in the late 1920s, when Modernist landscape architects like Thomas Church (b. 1902) were just beginning their careers.

Dewey Donnell Estate, "El Novillero" FIG. 1020

1947–1948
Thomas Church, Lawrence Halprin, landscape architects; **Adeline Kent**, sculptor; **George Rockrise**, architectural designer
Sonoma County, California, N end of San Pablo Bay (private estate, not visible from public roads)

Surely Donnell is the best-known Modernist landscape design in the United States. The iconic view over the exaggerated curves of the pool, past the visually floating Kent sculpture, and toward the bay (Fig. 1020) is virtually required for any book on modern landscape architecture. The Brazilian landscape architect Roberto Burle Marx had been working in expressive, curvilinear forms since the early 1940s, his famous curvilinear Monteiro Garden near Rio was also completed in 1948. But for American landscape architects, the Donnell Garden was even more influential. By the 1950s, free-form design had become a characteristic expression of the new modern era, just as glass-box office buildings became ubiquitous after Lever House.

Abby Aldrich Rockefeller Sculpture Garden, Museum of Modern Art

1953 ff.
Philip Johnson, architect; **James John Fanning**, landscape architect; **Zion, Breen & Richardson**, post-1961 landscape architects; **Yoshio Taniguchi**, architect for the 1997–2004 revisions
11 W. 53rd St., New York, New York

MoMA's signature garden has evolved over the decades. The essence of Johnson's intent was probably best experienced in the late 1960s, after plantings had matured, following Johnson's light editing as a part of a 1964 museum remodeling. The garden's current iteration benefits in many ways from Taniguchi's massive expansion, including a harmonious facing of all garden edges (Fig. 1139). The stone plaza with abstract planting cutouts remains basically true to the original scheme, and the 2004 plantings will in time mature. The garden's feeling has unavoidably changed dramatically since the early 1950s, when its surroundings were of much smaller scale.

J. Irwin Miller Garden

1953–1954
Dan Kiley, landscape architect
N. Washington St. along the Flatrock River, Columbus, Indiana (expected to be open c. 2011)

An extraordinary masterpiece of modern American landscape architecture, widely considered by those comparatively few who have actually experienced it as one of the great Modernist gardens in the United States. Kiley's landscape steals the show from the Miller's Eero Saarinen–designed house. Now more than a half-century old, the original design is still basically extant, excepting the 1973 replacement of an arborvitae privacy hedge-screen with *taxus*.

FIG. 1019 Early Modernism Dating from 1938, Fletcher Steele's Blue Steps at the Naumkeag estate in Western Massachusetts constitute a landmark of American landscape Modernism.

FIG. 1020 The Symbol of Postwar Modernism Completed in 1948, Thomas Church's sensuously curving pool for the Donnell estate in California instantly became an international icon, still the most potent image of postwar mMdern American landscape architecture.

FIG. 1021 **Pastoral Modernism** The subtly abstracted site of the John Deere office building in Illinois reads almost as a pre-existent Arcadian landscape, although Nature is never so meticulously arranged.

John Deere Headquarters FIG. 1021
1957–1964
Sasaki, Dawson, Demay/Sasaki Walker, landscape architects
John Deere Rd., East Moline, Illinois

Deere is deceptively simple in concept, sublime in execution. Approaches are carefully shaped as arrivals are presented with a classic axial view of the main building, then taken around a constructed lake and through subtly enhanced woods up to parking.

The site response was integral to architect Eero Saarinen's architectural design concept (see Modern Masters chapter). In order to preserve views out onto a beautiful site, he provided overhanging exterior louvers as sun screens, therefore rendering interior blinds or shades unnecessary.

Paley Park
1964–1968
Zion & Breen, landscape architects
5 E. 53rd St., New York, New York

This urbane space demonstrates the splendid potential of vest-pocket sites. At barely over 4,000 square feet in area, enclosed on three sides by high buildings, Paley Park has been immensely popular since its opening. Its designers seem to have done everything right, creating an attractive and serene environment in the midst of big-city activity.

Mauna Kea Beach Resort FIGS. 701, 702, 1022, 1023, 1024
1965–1968
Eckbo, Dean, Austin & Williams, landscape architects;
Robert Trent Jones, Sr., golf course architect
Kamuela, Kohala Coast, Big Island, Hawaii

A persuasive demonstration for modern landscape architecture, Mauna Kea Beach Resort is in a class by itself in terms of its very large scale, pioneering solutions (see Resorts chapter), an astonishing transformation of its existing site, a black-lava moonscape, and the sheer beauty of its wide variety of designed landscapes.

Unlike the all-too-numerous lost modern landscapes (see the next two entries, for example), this property looks better than ever today.

Harlequin Plaza FIG. 1025
1980–1982; fundamentally altere
SWA Group, landscape architects
7600 E. Orchard Rd., Greenwood Village, Englewood, Colorado

Harlequin Plaza was the sensational design that vaulted SWA designer George Hargreaves to national prominence as the signa-

FIGS. 1022, 1023, 1024 **Many Faces of Modernism** Eckbo, Dean, Austin & Williams's Mauna Kea Beach Resort landscapes are a visual delight, with expressions ranging from carefree (Fig. 1022) to lightly ordered (Fig. 1023) to firmly geometrical (Fig. 1024). © 2005 EDAW/Photography by Dixi Carrillo

ture landscape architect of his generation. There was little traditional "landscaping" in this design, if that implies emphasis on organic material. Rather, black-and-white diamond-patterned paving extended between mirrored surfaces. The plaza was bisected by red and purple walls, which were devised to visually engage the viewer by introducing ambiguity.

The space was subsequently remodeled, its signature harlequin paving replaced by muted tiles, the walls removed. The basic volume remains intact, as are the reflective surfaces. This is probably a more relaxed everyday environment for tenants taking lunch in the plaza, but of course the magic is gone.

Nations Bank Park Plaza
1984–1988; reflecting pools removed, plaza currently endangered
Dan Kiley, landscape architect; **Harry Wolf**, building architect
between Ashley Dr. and Hillsborough Riverfront, N of Kennedy Blvd., Tampa, Florida

Nations Bank (NCNB Bank when built) was a noteworthy collaboration between Kiley and Wolf, who was architect of the tower and banking hall. The 4.5-acre plaza site was shaped to acknowledge the Golden Mean/Proportion described by the Fibonacci Series.

According to Kiley's staff designer, Peter Lindsay Schardt, this guiding mathematical concept set the designers off on an integrated design of Kiley's "tartan grid" and Wolf's powerful building fenestration. The polygonal plaza was developed in rectangular grids, defined by reflecting pools, sable palms, and crepe myrtle.

All landscapes require appreciation and maintenance to survive and, sadly, both seem to be lacking under recent stewardship of this landmark environment.

Walker Art Center Sculpture Garden FIG. 1026
1986–1988
Edward L. Barnes, project architect; **Peter Rothschild**, assisting landscape architect
Vineland Place, Minneapolis, Minnesota

The Sculpture Garden is an important demonstration, in several respects. On the positive side, the museum's connoisseurship by Martin and Mildred Friedman was first-rank: this is an exceptional visual resource, with a full range of superb modern sculpture including the signature piece, "Spoonbridge and Cherry" by Claes Oldenburg and Coosje van Bruggen.

In terms of execution, everything is beautifully detailed, employing high-quality materials. Considered as urbanism, the garden completes a critical pedestrian link by connecting the Mississippi

FIG. 1025 **Sensation in the Suburbs** The Op-Art design of Harlequin Plaza brought international attention to an otherwise conventional 1980s suburban office park in Colorado. *photograph © Gerry Campbell, SWA Group*

FIG. 1026 **Architectural Landscape** A triumph of connoisseurship, Walker Art Center's Sculpture Garden also provides a critical urban design linkage between downtown and the Minneapolis Grand Rounds park system (see Naturalism and Roads chapters) via the Whitney Pedestrian Bridge (see Bridges chapter), visible at the right edge. Designed by an architect, the garden was conceptually approached as an roofless building, unintentionally providing an illuminating demonstration of how Modern architects think differently from traditional landscape architects – even when, as in this case, traditional landscape architecture is their ostensible model.

FIGS. 1027, 1028, 1029
Regional Modernism Across the vibrant, designed landscapes of Solana, between Dallas and Fort Worth, *built* and *natural* are expressed as distinct realms, a distinction enhanced by the visual abstraction of plantings and site features.

Riverfront to the Grand Rounds parks system (see Naturalism, Roads, and Bridges chapters).

Alas, similar high accolades do not apply to the design concept itself, which lacks the nuances one expects in an advanced landscape design. This was probably inevitable, as the garden was designed by an architect. Barnes had produced a brilliant design for the adjacent museum (see Brutalism chapter), but approached the landscape scheme as an outdoor building: a 20-foot fall across the site was minimized rather than exploited, arborvitae were treated as if they were brick walls, etc.

As a consequence, an approach that could have seemed pure and elegant in a building comes off as predictable, even sterile, as a land-

scape. The sculpture garden is a fine attraction, but could have been even more. A later expansion to the north by landscape architect Michael van Valkenberg largely deferred to Barnes's approach.

Solana FIGS. 1027, 1028, 1029
1991
The Office of Peter Walker and Martha Schwartz/Peter Walker and Partners, site planners and landscape architects
Along Hwy. 114, NW of Dove Rd., Westlake-Southlake, Texas

Solana was a dream team collaborative effort, aimed at creating the ultimate mixed-use suburban commercial development. Adopting a Modernist expression, they pretty much succeeded.

Walker and his associates were engaged by the design-oriented Los Angeles developer Maguire/Thomas, who also commissioned Ricardo Legorreta (Fig. 1027) and Mitchell/Giurgola as building architects. In Walker's site scheme, the initial buildings on the westerly part of this 850-acre parcel are arranged within a powerful, arcing armature, which in plan looks suspiciously like a 1960s megastructure. Instead, the on-site experience is humane and engaging—indeed, exhilarating. Given that this all occurs at the edge of an endless, lightly rolling prairie rather than within a built-up urban precinct, such a tightly controlled landscape-building-parking compositions might seem a bit overblown to those with a preference for Naturalism or indigenous landscapes. But the visitor is aware mainly of an agreeable profusion of colors, textures, and abstracted shapes (Figs. 1028, 1029) and a vibrant, ever-changing sequence of visual experiences while moving around the campus on foot or by car.

ART AND LANDSCAPE: ISAMU NOGUCHI

Modern American landscape architecture embraces an extreme range of approaches and perspectives, from horticulture to environmental art.

Among the latter: Walter de Maria's 1977 *The Lightning Field* in rural New Mexico; Robert Smithson's 1970 *Spiral Jetty*, alternately on and under the Great Salt Lake in Utah; and Robert Irwin's Getty Center garden. Such works are appreciated by most viewers as art even more than as landscape designs.

Isamu Noguchi (1904–1988) bridged the gap between environmental artists and Modernist landscape architects. Noguchi was a gifted sculptor and he also fashioned commercial and civic landscapes. In this respect, Noguchi was a singular figure in American landscape Modernism.

Chase Manhattan Bank Sunken Court FIG. 1030
1961–1964
Isamu Noguchi, artist–landscape architect
1 Chase Manhattan Plaza; Pine and William Sts., New York, New York

An oculus in the street-level plaza opens to a circular court on the lower level, where Noguchi created a stylized (now dry) Zen garden, which was originally partly filled with water to form a marvelous landscape of water and islands, energized by darting fish. It remains an unexpected island of serenity amidst the incessant din of the city, ultramodern while also timeless, almost traditional in feeling as experienced.

A California Scenario FIGS. 1031, 1032
1982
Isamu Noguchi, artist-landscape architect
SW of Anton Blvd. & Avenue of the Arts, one block NE of the Bristol St./I-405 intersection, Costa Mesa, California

One could hardly imagine a less likely site for high art: a relatively small space, enclosed by a busy freeway, office buildings, and a parking garage. Within a wide-open stone plaza (Fig. 1031), Noguchi fashioned abstracted landscapes in reference to the deserts, rivers, forests, and mountains of California (Fig. 1032).

FIG. 1030 **An Eye in the Storm** Isamu Noguchi's Chase Manhattan Bank sunken court offers a place for contemplation amid the din of Lower Manhattan. The plaza sculpture in the background is Jean Dubuffet's 1972 "Group of Four Trees."

FIGS. 1031, 1032 **California in Sculpture** Noguchi's California Scenario abstracts the Golden State's natural features, including a "volcano" fountain, on this suburban plaza hidden away between a parking garage and a freeway.

Environmentalism

1960–2004

FIG. 1033 Classic Environmental Landscape The Sea Ranch is *the* landmark environmental landscape design in the United States. Lawrence Halprin's inspired master plan for this Northern California coastal resort followed a deceptively simple concept: signature site features like the rugged oceanfront, grassy meadows, and wooded ridges would be left undeveloped, rather than subdivided into showcase building lots. New construction would be tucked back unobtrusively into hedgerows and forest, thus preserving the essential qualities which made the site attractive in the first place. That such an obvious approach seemed so radical, then and still today, says a great deal about conventional American real estate development values.

Several distinct environmental design approaches have been prominent in the United States in recent generations. These may be distilled down to four prominent directions, based on mixtures of emphasis on design and horticulture.

One is Conceptual Environmentalism. This approach was introduced by Lawrence Halprin in the early-1960s at The Sea Ranch (Figs. 712, 1033), fully developed by Ian McHarg in the early 1970s, and subsequently carried on by landscape architecture practices like Andropogon. This is a complex planning and design approach intended to better fit new large-scale development into community and regional landscapes.

Reconstructive Design is another major environmental landscape activity. This focuses on stitching back together the rup-

tures in the urban fabric caused by thoughtless development. Lawrence Halprin is also a well-known practitioner of reconstructive design.

Restoration is the suburban-rural horticultural equivalent of reconstructive design, as much the province of specialized nurseries as it is of landscape architects and designers.

The fourth direction, exemplified in the practice of Wolfgang Oehme and James van Sweden, defies easy description, much less classification, as it could be associated with Naturalism, Regionalism, and even Modernism as well as Environmentalism. For the sake of classification in this chapter, their landscape design approach may be thought of as Poetic Horticulture.

CONCEPTUAL ENVIRONMENTALISM

The Sea Ranch FIG. 712, 1033, 1034
1963–1965 ff.
Lawrence Halprin & Associates, planners and landscape architects
Hwy. 1, SE of Gualala, Sonoma County, California

Working with a windswept former sheep ranch extending along ten miles of Pacific coastline (Figs. 712, 1033), Halprin clustered homesites into existing hedgerows (Fig. 1034) or set them back into the upper woods in order to preserve the open, undeveloped feeling of the site—to be experienced more as a ranch and less like a typical built-up resort community. Halprin's visionary environmental approach was unfortunately later compromised by successor developers who reverted to a conventional land-sale mindset (see Resorts chapter).

An Ecological Study for the Twin Cities Metropolitan Area FIG. 1035
1968–1970
Ian McHarg, Wallace, McHarg, Roberts & Todd, planners
Metropolitan Minneapolis, Minnesota

McHarg carried out an ecological study of a seven-county region centered on Minneapolis, based on climate, landforms, hydrology, soils, vegetation, wildlife, and human settlement. From these sur-

FIG. 1034 Merging Into the Environment Coastal sections of The Sea Ranch site were bisected by hedgerows dating from use as a windswept sheep ranch. New houses were set into these windbreaks, which also screened access drives from view.

veys, he devised a "composite intrinsic suitability analysis," which provided a road map for future regional development based on the actual dynamics of the region.

Had McHarg's ideas been followed even generally, the Twin Cities area would have become a model of enlightened regional development. Sadly, this proved too progressive a concept for the newly formed Metropolitan Council planning agency to embrace. Instead of adopting a visionary perspective, the Council chose to regulate the ensuing three decades of regional growth on the basis of the public cost of sewer lines.

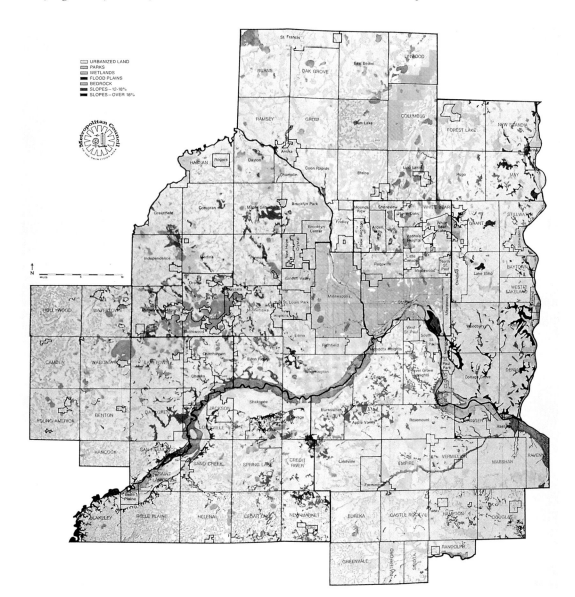

FIG. 1035 Ecological Planning In his 1970 Ecological Study for the Twin Cities Metropolitan Area, Ian McHarg proposed that regional expansion around Minneapolis be guided by the practical suitability of the land to support development. The innate sensibleness of this approach seems to have passed right over the heads of metropolitan planners *Metropolitan Council of the Twin Cities*

The Woodlands FIGS. 1036, 1037, 1038

1966, Kamrath-Pickford plan; 1971–1974, McHarg-Pereira plan, initial development, opening

George Mitchell, developer; **Ian McHarg, Wallace, McHarg, Roberts & Todd**, conceptual planners; **William Pereira**, master plan architect; **Leslie Sauer, Anne Spirn**, landscape architects
I-45, NW of Houston Intercontinental Airport, Montgomery County, Texas

Underway right after Earth Day, the timing of The Woodlands was ideal for an ecologically based, planned new town, especially for one located on the outskirts of notoriously undisciplined Houston.

FIGS. 1036, 1037, 1038 Ecological Development Ian McHarg's ideas were appreciated by a Houston developer, who built a successful new town, The Woodlands, following McHarg's ecological planning approach. Native vegetation was retained wherever possible, providing woodsy settings for architecturally conventional houses (Fig. 1037). Site utilities like this water-retention basin were turned into community landscape features (Fig. 1036). Major arterial roads were expressed as naturalistic parkways; with commercial buildings tucked back into clearings (Fig. 1038).

McHarg employed his signature comprehensive survey methods, similar to his Twin Cities study (previous entry). The critical Woodlands planning issue turned out to be storm drainage, because of the virtually impenetrable fragipan soils. In effect, the community had to be designed on the basis of hydrology.

In response, McHarg employed watercourses as his primary design vocabulary. Mundane site plumbing like retention basins (Fig. 1036) and drainage channels were transformed into landscape features; clearance of the oak-pine forest was minimized in order to maintain soil porosity.

The resulting community is visually distinctive. Although individual houses are generally similar to those built in conventional Houston subdivisions, their settings within thick forests (Fig. 1037), development of parkways (Fig. 1038) instead of arterial roads, and the numerous water features result in a community environment that is unlike anyplace else in the Houston region.

RECONSTRUCTIVE DESIGN

Freeway Park FIG. 1039

1970–1976

Lawrence Halprin Associates, landscape architects, **Angela Danadjieva Tzvetin**, designer
Bridging I-5 between University and Seneca Sts., Seattle, Washington

Seattle's downtown was physically severed from its earliest affluent neighborhood, First Hill, by 1960s freeway construction. As a partial healing of the disruptive tear in the urban fabric, this lushly landscaped park reconnects the two sides of the freeway in ways no bridge connections could. Working with the fragments of cleared land along the freeway right-of-way, Halprin incorporated appealing pedestrian routes, seating areas, and features such as fountains.

Gas Works Park FIG. 1040

1975

Richard Haag, planner-landscape architect; **Olson/Walker Architects**, architects
N end of Lake Union, off Northlake Way, Seattle, Washington

Haag's inspired concept for this polluted industrial site preserved the old gas works as an industrial ruin. The convoluted, rusty gasworks plays off visually against its relatively featureless surroundings, the grassy park and the lake. If you stand just northwest of the works-ruins on a fog-free day, it is neatly replicated in silhouette by the distant downtown skyline to the south (Fig. 1040).

Largely overlooked because of the well-deserved praise for the gas works as public sculpture is Haag's precedent-setting restoration of the entire site through phytoremediation, which employs site aeration and plants to naturally restore damaged soils.

RESTORATION

Distinct indigenous landscapes exist in every part of the country. In the course of urbanization, these have been largely erased in heavily populated regions. In dense city centers, little unbuilt or unpaved space suitable for plants and trees remains. Region-wide, there is ample room for horticulture, but open areas have often been planted in entirely new landscape vocabularies. For instance, the lush landscapes of urbanized Southern

FIG. 1039 **Urban Connective** Seattle's Freeway Park spans an interstate highway which had severed Downtown from an adjacent historic neighborhood. Planted to seem like a Pacific Northwest forest, it made a feature out of a destructive tear in Seattle's historic urban fabric.

FIG. 1040 **Industrial Sculpture** The rusty decommissioned plant of Seattle's Gas Works Park plays off dramatically against its grassy lakeshore site and the distant downtown Seattle skyline. *Ryan Giordano*

California were wholly devised, the native arid, grizzled landscape transformed through irrigation and importation.

Recently, the restoration of indigenous landscapes has become increasingly popular in the Midwest. The result of this movement is quite different from the Prairie School landscapes that flourished in the same region in the early twentieth century (see Regionalism chapter).

Rather than creating idealized regional landscapes, as was the intent of Prairie School designers like Jens Jensen, today's regionalists focus on the introduction of native plants, chiefly grasses and forbs (Fig. 1041). While there is occasionally a sense of design to these landscapes, as at the Sears campus, in general, the current emphasis is on horticulture.

FIG. 1041 **Prairie Subdivisions** Restorations of once-native prairie grasses and forbs have expanded beyond rural preserves. In this otherwise conventional suburban subdivision, prairie has replaced a conventional front lawn.

Village of Long Grove FIG. 1042

1979 ff.
Old McHenry Rd., W of Arlington Heights Rd., Lake County, Illinois

This semi-rural, upper-income Chicago exurb employs a prairie-grass vocabulary on municipal properties and encourages private property owners to do so as well. Because architecture is not considered, this occasionally results in implausible confrontations, like an American Colonial Revival bank rising from a naturalistic grass-and-forbs prairie landscape (Fig. 1042). But the overall effect is distinctive, alluding to its pre-development prairie setting.

Sears Merchandise Group Headquarters

1992
Smith Group/JJR, landscape architects; **Patricia Armstrong**, consulting botanist
3333 Beverly Rd., NW of I-90 & Hwy. 59, Hoffman Estates, Illinois

Sears moved from its landmark tower in the Chicago Loop (see Late Modernism chapter) to an 800-acre exurban campus, Prairie Stone. In keeping with its setting and name, 200 acres of the parcel were planted in a prairie mix of grass and forbs, perhaps the most extensive prairie restoration of a commercial property in the United States.

FIG. 1042 **Municipal Restorations** Long Grove, a Chicago exurb, has encouraged prairie installations since the late 1970s. This is understood locally as matter of yard landscaping, rather than as an opportunity to create an integrated ecological synthesis of building and site. As a result, one encounters contextually amusing juxtapositions like this bank with Colonial pretensions rising from a hill covered with colorful prairie forbs.

POETIC HORTICULTURE

Wolfgang Oehme and James van Sweden are, above all, horticultural artists. They are grounded in horticulture, paint in vibrant, colorful drifts, employ unexpected, exotic counterpoints, and integrate water into their landscape compositions whenever possible. Significantly for the well-populated temperate regions of the United States, Oehme and van Sweden consciously design for four seasons, and especially consider the character of their gardens in winter.

Their landscapes, widely known as The New American Garden, are at once daring and subtle, memorable and seasonally changing. Unfortunately, much of their work is not generally accessible to the public. Moreover, any landscape will degrade over years if not maintained by its owners. The major Oehme & van Sweden project loss to date has been their revolutionary (for monumental Washington, D.C.) Pennsylvania Avenue Plantings (1981 ff.), which have been lost due to lack of maintenance. If you didn't experienced these vibrant environments when they were recognizable, Oehme's and van Sweden's Pennsylvania Avenue concepts of can be appreciated by reference to their book *Bold Romantic Gardens*.

Federal Reserve Garden
1979; reconstructed for enhanced security, 2005
Oehme & van Sweden, landscape architects; **Raya Bodnarchuk, Sol Lewitt**, sculptors
Triangle bounded by C St. NW., Virginia Ave. NW., and 20th St. NW., Washington, D.C.

A richly textured landscape, almost domestic in character and scale, with just a touch of the exotic, employing then-uncommon ornamental grasses. Set within the formal precincts of Washington, the garden caused a minor sensation, given that it was anything but the "prim, pressed and starched" traditional norm for area landscapes. As such, this design introduced an entirely new landscape approach for monumental areas of the District.

German-American Friendship Garden
1987
Oehme & van Sweden, landscape architects
S of Constitution Ave., between 16th and 17th Sts. NW., Washington, D.C.

Another richly textured, human-scaled landscape worked into the immense monumental open spaces of Washington. Benches and small walk-through fountains provide a shady respite for foot-weary visitors to the National Mall.

Gardens of the Great Basin, Chicago Botanic Garden
FIG. 1043
Botanic Garden, 1965–1972 ff; Gardens of the Great Basin, 2002
John O. Simonds, Geoffrey Rausch, original master planners; **Oehme & van Sweden**, landscape architects for the Gardens of the Great Basin
1000 Lake Cook Rd., SE quad. Edens Expwy.–Hwy. 41, Glencoe, Illinois

Chicago Botanic Garden has been under development since the early 1960s, initially following the planning of John O. Simonds, son of O. C. Simonds (see Regionalism chapter), and Geoffrey Rausch. By 2004, the Garden encompassed more than two dozen distinct environments within a 385-acre site.

FIG. 1043 The New American Garden Oehme & van Sweden dramatically employed their signature horticultural palette featuring grasses and forbs for their Gardens of the Great Basin at the Chicago Botanic Garden. Plantings are enhanced by engaging site features like this marvelous serpentine bridge. *photograph by Richard Felber* © 2002 courtesy Oehme, van Sweden & Associates

Oehme & van Sweden were engaged to develop the Great Basin area, which includes the five-acre Evening Island, the Lakeside Garden, and the Water Garden. Partly funded by state and federal environmental grants, Oehme & van Sweden's technical solutions were intended as a "showcase demonstration of shoreline restoration and stabilization," as described by the Environmental Protection Agency.

Oehme & van Sweden addressed landscape design primarily at two levels. One included distinct enhancements for each environment expressed in variations of the New American Garden, with low-maintenance installations emphasizing grasses and a rich tapestry of textures. At project scale, the entire Great Basin area was visually tied together, chiefly through the employment of landscape features like pathways, terraces, overlooks, and bridges – in particular the signature serpentine bridge (Fig. 1043).

GREENING OF CHICAGO

Environmentally, Chicago, whose official motto translates as "city in a garden," occupies a singular position among big American cities. Under Mayor Richard M. Dailey, Chicago has embarked on a permanent course of reconstructive design at a scale and of a scope unmatched elsewhere in the United States. Chicago's environmental undertakings embrace multiple initiatives ranging from meat-and-potato programs like replanting the urban forest and conserving energy to highly visible initiatives like green roofs for commercial buildings and experimental programs.

Underway since the 1990s, Chicago's environmental development approach has long since passed beyond the demonstration stage and seems now to be an ingrained local sensitivity.

Landscape Features

1890–2004

FIG. 1044 Signal Construction Landscapes often include constructed elements. These range from stairs and retaining walls to elaborate designs like this splendid Mediterranean gateway to a prewar subdivision in surburban St. Louis.

Designed landscapes commonly include integral constructed elements such as stairs, walls, markers (Fig. 1044), and water features. Similar kinds of design enhancements were identified in the Civic Design chapter. Purely for convenience in organizing this book, civic design emphasizes larger-scale improvements like major public monuments and urban streetscapes.

This chapter's brief overview provides a sampling of smaller-scale landscape features: fountains, private memorials, and the personal-scale feature gardens at Walt Disney World.

As noted in the Civic Design chapter, the classic reference, for those interested, is Werner Hegemann and Elbert Peets, *The American Vitruvius: An Architects' Handbook of Civic Art* (1922). You should be able to find it in the collections of most big-city central public libraries and major university libraries.

FIG. 1045 **City of Fountains** Nichols Fountain at Country Club Plaza is a landmark among the numerous public fountains marking Kansas City as the "City of Fountains."

FIG. 1046 **Versailles in America** Chicago's Buckingham Memorial Fountain claims bragging rights for biggest and best. Its breathtaking lakefront setting is certainly a plus in advancing any such contentions.

FIG. 1047 **Intermittent Masterwork** Halprin and Moore's occasionally gushing Lovejoy Plaza Fountain in Portland is truly a joy to experience. Try to visit on a weekday, when it is turned on.

FOUNTAINS

"City of Fountains" FIG. 1045
1896 ff.
Kansas City, Missouri

While few of the city's 29 public fountains, many sited along parkways, are signature works, in the aggregate they are impressive and memorable.

Buckingham Memorial Fountain FIG. 1046
1926–1927
Bennett, Parsons & Frost, architects; **Jacques Lambert**, fountain designer
Congress St. extended, E of Michigan Ave. in Grant Park, Chicago, Illinois

Everything a public fountain should be: exuberantly splashy, with big jets of water, multicolored at night. According to local legend, Buckingham Fountain is modeled after "the one at Versailles," though Chicago's is said to be bigger, probably even the biggest fountain in the world!

Regardless of any quantitative measures or local mythmaking, its siting could not have been better. Buckingham Fountain terminates the long Congress Street–Eisenhower Expressway axis, and from its spacious Grant Park setting visitors can gaze out across Lake Michigan or take in the stunning Chicago skyline.

Orpheus Fountain
1926–1934; dedicated, 1936
Carl Milles, sculptor
Cranbrook Academy of Art, Lone Pine Rd. W of Woodward Ave., Bloomfield Hills, Michigan

Milles's fountains and sculpture represent a high point in the integrated-design ideal of Cranbrook. His Cranbrook works (for other examples there, see Figs. 388, 389) comprise the largest collection of Milles sculpture in the world outside of the artist's home in Sweden.

"Meeting of the Waters" FIG. 391
1936–1940
Carl Milles, sculptor
Aloe Plaza, Market St. between 18th and 20th Sts., St. Louis, Missouri

A wonderful composition in its own right, the fountain gains even greater civic importance by its location at one end of Gateway Mall (see City Beautiful chapter) across the street from Union Station, in a renewal district which has been revitalized by the Union Station festival marketplace (see Retail and Hotels chapter).

Fountain of Faith
1939–1952
Carl Milles, sculptor
Rts. 29/211, W of Falls Church, Virginia

Milles's characteristic figural grouping is here set off by integrated jets of water. True to its name, there is no obvious message. Rather, it is solely up to each viewer to discover deeper meaning.

War Memorial Fountain
1947–1964
Marshall Fredericks, sculptor
The Mall, Cleveland, Ohio

A single heroic figure extends upward, seemingly touching the sky. The sculpture might have seemed dated by the time it was finally installed, when abstract art had become prominent. But with time, it now reads as an expressive work of art.

FIGS. 1048, 1049 Water Theater Handsome purely as a design, Portland's Auditorium Forecourt Fountain becomes even more appealing when animated by visitors.

FIGS. 1050, 1051 Just Add Greenery Fort Worth's Water Garden landscapes have matured nicely over the past three decades.

Lovejoy Plaza Fountain FIG. 1047

1961–1968

Lawrence Halprin, landscape architect; **Charles W. Moore**, project designer

S.W. Hall, between 3rd and 4th, Portland, Oregon (You can hike in from Harrison, which does not have an identifying street sign nearby, but is the street with the embedded light-rail tracks.)

Water gushes (on weekdays) down abstracted steps, invigorating an otherwise typical 1960s urban renewal superblock redevelopment. Lovejoy is a major civic work by designers of superior talent; too bad that it is buried away from street view. Unlike the highly visible Auditorium Forecourt Fountain nearby (next entry), this fountain is largely unknown to visitors, perhaps even to some Portlanders.

Auditorium Forecourt Fountain FIGS. 1048, 1049

1970

Lawrence Halprin Associates, landscape architects; **Angela Danadjieva Tzvetin**, project designer

SW. 3rd and 4th Aves. between Clay and Market Sts., Portland, Oregon

Auditorium Forecourt is arguably the best contemporary urban fountain in the United States. Powerful sheets of water flow over blocky masses (Fig. 1049), providing a wondrous rushing sound. Since people are able to walk freely throughout the fountain, this landscape design really functions, beautifully, as public theater (Fig. 1048).

Water Garden FIGS. 1050, 1051

1974

Philip Johnson & John Burgee, architects; **Zion & Breen**, landscape architects

1300 Houston St., Fort Worth, Texas

A merrily splashing walk-through fountain (Fig. 1050) complements an adjacent spray fountain (Fig. 1051). Fort Worth's Water Garden was built to function as a symbolic public feature, intended to visually anchor the redevelopment of a convention district at the south end of downtown.

FIGS. 1052, 1053 Fantasy on Antiquity Only Charles Moore possessed the combination of scholarship, design talent, delight with water, and unbridled imagination to have come up with Piazza d'Italia in New Orleans. The fountain is seen from behind (Fig. 1052), with its complementary clocktower across the plaza. Moore's colleagues memorialized the achievement by placing his likeness on twin medallions (Fig. 1053).

When it opened, there seemed to be way too much concrete, especially considering the brutally hot Texas summers. Fortunately, as the plantings have matured the Water Garden has evolved into a serene, green refuge from the surrounding urban hardscape.

Piazza d'Italia Fountain FIGS. 1052, 1053
1976–1979
Charles W. Moore, Urban Innovations Group, design architects; **Perez Associates**, executive architects

The guiding concept behind this fountain celebrating Italian-American heritage seems all too easy: water trickles down a relief map of Italy, with bubblers marking the locations of Rome and probably Florence, into a pool defined by "Sicily" and "Sardinia" meant to represent the Tyrrhenian Sea.

But such things are easier imagined than accomplished, and the execution of this idea was creative in the extreme: Moore know-

ingly and gleefully broke just about every rule of Classical architecture, while making up a few new ones—all to joyful effect on viewers, who become willing participants.

Don't miss the medallions-gargoyles of Moore, created and inserted by his design associates without Moore's knowledge (Fig. 1053).

PRIVATE MEMORIALS

Adams Memorial, "Grief" FIG. 1054
1886–1891
Augustus Saint-Gaudens, sculptor; **Stanford White**, architect
Section E, Rock Creek cemetery; enter at Webster St. and Rock Creek Church Rd., Washington, D.C.

Two of the greatest design talents of the era collaborated to create this emotionally charged, artistically powerful monument.

Dodge Memorial, "Angel of Death" FIG. 1055
1916–1918
Daniel Chester French, sculptor
N. 2nd at Lafayette St., Council Bluffs, Iowa

One of the finest American private memorials, this work offers evocative sculpture, a simple but effective approach-forecourt sequence, and a bluff-top site affording a stupendous panorama across the limitless Great Plains.

Eklutna Cemetery FIG. 1056
Early 1900s
NW of Glenn Hwy., 25 mi. NE of Anchorage, Alaska, at Hwy. 1 Mile 26.3

Despite the presence of a rare log Russian Orthodox church, a group of brightly painted spirit houses is the visual treasure of this indigenous village. According to Alison Hoagland, these reflect neither Orthodox nor Athapaskan burial traditions, but rather "seem

FIG. 1054 **Contemplating Loss** Superb as sculpture, the Adams Memorial, "Grief," gains additional emotive power through its meditative, sylvan setting in a Washington's romantic-era Rock Creek cemetery. *Library of Congress, Prints & Photographs, Historic American Buildings Survey*

FIG. 1056 **Indigenous Beauty** Powerful visual impact is sometimes realized through simple means. The colorful, earnestly hand-built spirit houses in Eklutna Cemetery in Alaska remain vividly in memory long after a visit.

FIG. 1055 **The Limitless Panorama of Life** Unlike the introspective siting of "Grief" (Fig. 1054), the Dodge Memorial, "Angel of Death," in Iowa faces out over an infinite view, providing another perspective on life and death.

FIG. 1057 **Feature Gardens** Walt Disney World Gardens offer a wide spectrum of happy landscapes, ingeniously planned and immaculately maintained. As these dying palms suggest, complex plantings at such immense scale require constant renewal across the development.

to be an original product of the collision of two belief systems." Whatever the cultural basis, a visit to this colorful, fragile cemetery offers a wondrous experience, even in this state boasting an over-abundance of awesome visual settings.

FEATURE GARDENS

Walt Disney World Gardens FIG. 1057
1969–1971 ff.
Bill Evans, chief landscape architect; **Morgan Evans**, project landscape architect; **Tony Virginia**, director of horticulture
Walt Disney World, Orange and Osceola Counties, Florida

Raw numbers are impressive: 300 staff gardeners tend a half-million square feet of annuals within EPCOT alone. However, the Dis-

ney World gardens are even more impressive in the remarkable attention given to perfecting the garden as a show setting.

Disney employs a wide typology of gardens: "Flower Gardens For All Seasons," the underlying resort landscape; "Gardens In The Rough," existing and created natural environments; "Gardens Of Yesteryear," for Americana attractions; "Old World Gardens," to support European World Showcase settings; "Gardens Within Gardens," roughly based on Persian water-pleasure gardens; "Gardens of the Exotic," to evoke a sense of tropical paradise; "Interior Gardens," to bring horticulture into buildings; "Gardens With A Purpose," featuring edibles like bananas and cabbages; "Gardens Of Tomorrow," stylized landscapes for futuristic settings; and "Gardens of Fantasy," chiefly topiary.

These imaginative custom landscapes, which must remain perfect every day, are extraordinary conceptual and horticultural achievements.

CIVIL
ENGINEERING

1000s–2004

Public Works

1564–2004

FIG. 1058 Public Structure Is Everywhere This view along the Mississippi riverfront in Minneapolis encompasses a lock and dam, a power plant, a historic railroad bridge preserved and converted to pedestrian use through public action; power lines and lighting. The river supplies the city's water, and some years it requires flood control. Roads are not visible in this view but present. Storm and sanitary sewers, plus electrical, telephone, cable, and natural gas lines lie just beneath the surface. Trees mark the location of regional parklands. Perhaps because public infrastructure is ubiquitous, it falls beneath the notice of most of us. If so, that might explain why little of our infrastructure is esthetically superior. The following chapters identify some of the relatively few civil engineering constructions that have been culturally or visually significant, in addition to fulfilling vital functional roles.

Public works in what became the United States date from 1564, with the construction of a French fort near Jacksonville (see the Spanish Colonial Architecture chapter). The earliest European public works in the New World took the forms of crude docks, temporary fortifications, and sanitary areas.

Of course, Aboriginal American city builders had constructed sophisticated irrigation canals nearly two millennia

FIG. 1059 **Sublime Engineering** Great works of engineering like San Francisco's Golden Gate Bridge transcend mere function.

earlier (see the Aboriginal Cultures chapter). As a practical matter, rudimentary public works date from Day One of human settlement.

A complete extent of public works in the United States is probably beyond realistic tabulation. However, the American Public Works Association published a magisterial, 1976 Bicentennial history of public works in the United States. This survey addressed public works with respect to:

Waterways
Roads, Streets, and Highways
Railroads
Urban Mass Transportation
Airways and Airports
Community Water Supply
Flood Control and Drainage
Irrigation
Light and Power
Sewers and Wastewater Treatment
Solid Wastes
Public Buildings
Educational Facilities
Public Housing
Parks and Recreation
Military Installations
Aerospace

Considered at this scope, the staggering scale of public works in the United States is apparent. By now, the nationwide public infrastructure investment is valued in trillions of dollars.

Since public works are omnipresent (Fig. 1058)—in the United States one can often be out of sight of buildings and people, but rarely is anyone very far from some kind of infrastructure—the visual impacts and potentials of public works should be of paramount importance. Unfortunately, that seldom seems to be the case. Public works undertakings are subject to budgets, while being scrutinized and mitigated for environmental impacts. But few of us express opinions about the visual qualities of infrastructure, as we do for architecture. It is as if we think that engineering is solely a matter of calculations, and can only manifest in a certain preordained form.

That would be ironic, since engineering has given us some of our most sublime constructions. Infrastructure, especially when united with its setting, can be visually engaging. One need only to think of the dramatic visual poetry created by San Francisco's Golden Gate Bridge, the ever-shifting fog, and the City's skyline beyond (Fig. 1059).

Nor is superior design necessarily a matter of cost. Some of the great works of engineering are beautiful because of their functional clarity. For instance, the surpassingly beautiful early twentieth-century bridges in Switzerland by Robert Maillart were built not because of their superior esthetic qualities, but because they were the least expensive among alternative designs. So we should appreciate the considerable visual potentials of public works, as the representative examples in the following chapters demonstrate.

Roads

1000s–1984

FIG. 1060 The Timeless Presence of Roads Roads, represented in this view of the Appian Way on the outskirts of Rome (the asphalt paving is recent, of course), have been essential features of Western civilization for millennia—in this case since 312 B.C. Roads interconnect cities and nations, supporting trade and personal travel. Understandably then, roads—surface routes, from trails to expressways – occupy a central role in American life, both functionally and in numberless national myths.

Roads are essential to modern life. Several long-distance transportation modes have been prominent at one time or another in U.S. history. These include canoes, ocean-going ships, interior vessels from flatboats to steamboats, trains, and airplanes. Yet roads of varying scale, ranging from wilderness paths and pioneer trails to city streets and rural super-highways, have always supported transportation for Americans on foot or on horse, riding in carriages, wagons, taxis, or buses, or driving their own cars.

Three types of roads have been especially prominent in American culture. These are: national roads, which served as landmarks of their eras; parkways, designed to high visual standards; and expressways, which radically transformed post–World War II American life and its built environments.

NATIONAL ROADS

Great Warriors' Path

Pre-Columbian
Approximately along the route of I-81, from the Carolinas to central New York State

We know from archeology that Americans traded widely by 1000 BCE (see Aboriginal Cultures chapter). This travel took place over semi-permanent path networks. A scouting party sent by Virginia's colonial governor Alexander Spotswood chanced across one such well-traveled route in 1716, while exploring the Shenandoah Valley.

The route was clearly marked by hatchet chops on trees and extended from the Carolinas through the Shenandoah Valley up through western Maryland and central Pennsylvania, ending in the Iroquois tribal lands of central New York State. Historian Walter McDougall commented that this "Great Warriors' Path" functioned as the first interstate highway in the eastern United States, and "had served the Indians in war and commerce for centuries."

Royal Roads, Los Caminos Reales

1500s–1600s
New Spain, connecting to San Francisco, to Santa Fe, and to St. Augustine.

The Spanish government for New Spain, based in Mexico City, constructed a network of "Royal Roads" beginning in the 1500s. By the 1600s, these "high ways" extended into the far provinces, including Alta California (today's state of California), the upper Rio Grande valley, and northern Florida.

Boston Post Road FIGS. 1061, 1062

1673, for designated mail routes
Boston to New York along multiple routes.

The Boston Post Road was the first important national colonial road. It began informally along dirt Indian trails, to be upgraded, piecemeal, into a wood-planked highway. Extended southward from Boston to New York, Philadelphia and beyond, the Post Road evolved into the major north-south pre-Interstate highway along the Eastern Seaboard, U.S. Highway 1. The exact route was continually adjusted as road and bridge building techniques advanced. Many portions are still known—officially or unofficially—as Boston Post Road or by shortened versions such as Boston Road or simply "the Post Road."

Wilderness Road

1775
Daniel Boone, trail blazer
Across Cumberland Gap, Hwy. 25E, Middlesboro, Kentucky, vicinity

George Caleb Bingham's iconic painting, *Daniel Boone Escorting Settlers Through the Cumberland Gap* documented the exceptional symbolic power of this road on American culture. As a reliable, trans-Appalachian connection to the West, the Wilderness Road trail opened up the United States to manifest-destiny expansion.

National Road FIG. 1063

1806; 1811–1839, sections uncompleted
Albert Gallatin, visionary
Cumberland, Maryland to Vandalia, Illinois, via Columbus and Indianapolis, generally following the route of U.S. Hwy. 40; 591 mi.

Stirred by the explorations of Lewis and Clark, Congress authorized a national road in 1806. Improvements to and a lengthening of existing trails began five years later. Initially, the National Road extended from Cumberland, the head of navigation on the Potomac, to Wheeling, West Virginia, on the Ohio River. In effect,

FIGS. 1061, 1062 Road to the Republic Boston Post Road evolved from a rutty trail (Fig. 1061) into a vital highway interconnecting the centers of colonial America: Boston, New York, and Philadelphia. Post Road mile stones dating from the early 1700s can still be found in the Boston suburbs (Fig. 1062). *Fig. 1061 by Carl Rakeman, Federal Highway Administration; Fig. 1062: Library of Congress, Prints & Photographs, Historic American Buildings Survey*

FIG. 1063 Western Expansion Although it provided passage for innumerable travelers, the National Road was in places little more than a well-worn path. Passing this historic toll house near Sharpsburg, Maryland, the National Road seems to have been barely a dozen feet wide. *Library of Congress, Prints & Photographs, Historic American Engineering Record*

the National Road functioned as a portage for water-borne transportation. Road improvements gradually ground to a halt before mid-century, as railroads increasingly supplanted frontier roads for long-distance travel until well into the twentieth century.

Santa Fe Trail FIG. 1064
1821
Independence, Missouri, to Santa Fe, New Mexico, through Kansas, Colorado or Oklahoma, and New Mexico; 780 mi.

As the principal nineteenth-century overland route to the Southwest, the Santa Fe Trail accommodated as many as 5,000 wagons annually until 1880, when railroad service was finally extended to Santa Fe.

Oregon Trail FIG. 1065
1842
Independence, Missouri, to the Columbia River in Oregon via Kearny, Laramie, and Boise; approx. 2,000 mi.

Sections of what became the Oregon Trail had been used by trappers as early as 1742. Lewis and Clark followed parts of these routes in 1804–1806. The first emigrant wagon train to follow the entire trail crossed in 1842. By mid-century, the Oregon Trail had become the main overland route to the Pacific Northwest.

Lincoln Highway FIGS. 1066, 1067
1912–1925; 1931
Carl Fisher, **Henry Joy**, proponents; **Jens Jensen**, landscape architect for a 1.3 mi. "Ideal Section" demonstration (1917–1925) constructed between Schererville and Dyer, Indiana (see Regionalism chapter). From New York to San Francisco via Newark, Philadelphia, Pittsburgh, Fort Wayne, Clinton, Omaha, Cheyenne, Salt Lake City, Ely, Reno, Sacramento, and Oakland; generally along the route corridor of present-day U.S. 30/I-80; 3,143 mi

The Lincoln Highway Association promoted the construction of a Coast to Coast Rock Highway, "the first toll-free, all-weather road in America." The road was not intended to connect big cities but rather planned to follow a "natural" alignment which provided the most direct cross-continent route and easiest terrain. Construction of the Lincoln Highway began in 1916 (Fig. 1066); the route was largely passable by the early 1920s (Fig. 1067) and almost totally paved by 1931. When a 1925 federal law decertified named highways, the Lincoln Highway was incorporated into several numbered routes, primarily as U.S. Hwy. 30.

U.S. Route 66 FIG. 1068
1926–1938
Cyrus Avery, **John Woodruff**, originators of the idea of a route linking Chicago with Los Angeles

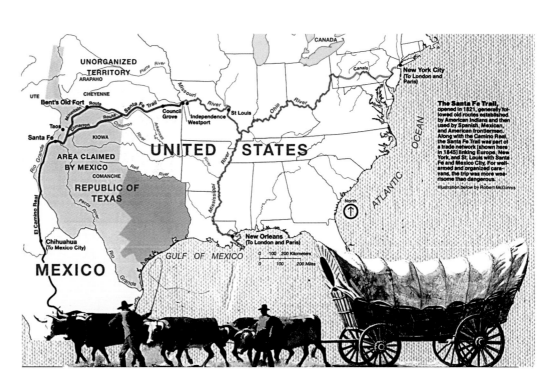

FIG. 1064 To the American Southwest The Santa Fe Trail served as Main Street for nineteenth-century settlement of the southern Plains, New Mexico, and beyond. *University of Texas Libraries*

FIG. 1065 To the Pacific Northwest Together with the Santa Fe Trail, the Oregon Trail formed a wishbone of routes for nineteenth-century overland expansion across the Great Plains and the mountain West. *University of Texas Libraries*

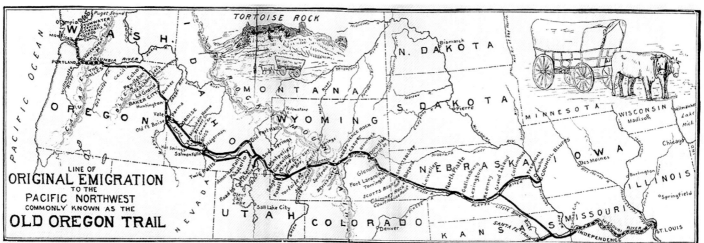

FIGS. 1066, 1067 The Coast-to-Coast Rock Highway Automobiles transformed the use of American roads. Up through the early 1900s, roads were used primarily for short, horse-drawn trips, "farm-to-market." As auto ownership increased, long-distance travel by road became popular among the adventuresome and desirable by countless others. That is why the Lincoln Highway captured the imaginations of Americans when proposed, in 1913, to cross the entire nation on an all-weather surface. While the painting depicts a broad, concrete roadway (Fig. 1066), in reality, well into the 1920s, much of the Lincoln Highway was made up of narrow, graveled lanes like this remnant in Utah, located parallel to a later paved highway (Fig. 1067). *Fig. 1066 by Carl Rakeman, Federal Highway Administration; Fig. 1067: Library of Congress, Prints & Photographs, Historic American Engineering Record*

Chicago to Los Angeles via Springfield, St. Louis, Tulsa, Oklahoma City, Amarillo, Albuquerque, Flagstaff, San Bernardino, ending at the Pacific Ocean as Santa Monica Boulevard.

Route 66 has taken on a mythic standing in American social history. In popular-culture iconography, Route 66 is associated with roadside architecture: filling stations, diners, tourist-courts-motels, and signs. Even so, the highway is neither first nor best with respect to date, extent, or visual character.

Rather, Route 66 attained lasting celebrity status largely through John Steinbeck's characterization as the "Mother Road" in The Grapes of Wrath. Nat "King" Cole's recording made "Get your kicks on Route 66" a national catch-phrase, and the popular 1960s TV series, "Route 66" further enhanced the road's pop-cultural allure. Today, many if not most communities along the historic route emphasize their Route 66 heritage.

Alaska "Alcan" Highway FIGS. 1069, 1070
1942 ff.
**Staff engineers, U.S. Army Corps of Engineers,
U.S. Bureau of Public Roads**
Dawson Creek, British Columbia to Delta Junction, Alaska; 1,422 mi.

The last mythical American highway (1,220 miles of which are actually in Canada), the Alcan was constructed as a passable mil-

FIG. 1068 The Mother Road U.S. Route 66 was an ordinary highway, connecting mostly ordinary towns, within which were relatively ordinary roadside strips like this one in Holbrook, Arizona. Nevertheless, Route 66 has by now assumed a mythic status in American popular culture. Indeed, drivers crossing Arizona on I-40 will come across an exit (139) in the middle of nowhere, built specifically to allow motorists to get off the interstate and drive a remote fragment of the original Route 66 roadway.

FIGS. 1069, 1070 The Legendary Alaska Highway Despite being passing mostly through Canada, the Alaskan "Alcan" Highway is the stuff of American myth. Built to supply Alaska after the outbreak of World War II, the highway initially consisted of "corduroy," logs and brush laid side-by-side to provide a crude driving surface (Fig. 1069). Even jeeps needed chains to pass. By 1943, a graded, gravel-surfaced road was open to trucks (Fig. 1070). *Library of Congress, Prints & Photographs*

FIG. 1071 **Vehicular Separation** Grade separations for busy highways can be traced back to Olmsted and Vaux's Greensward plan for Manhattan's Central Park (see Naturalism chapter), which separated crosstown traffic, pleasure drives, horse-riding trails, and pedestrians by employing a network of bridges and sunken roads. *Library of Congress, Prints & Photographs, Historic American Engineering Record*

itary road in just eight months under seemingly impossible conditions. After World War II, driving the Alcan Highway, most of which was still gravel-surfaced and hundreds of miles from help, was considered an act of bravado in American popular culture.

URBAN PARKWAYS

The idea of parkways dates back to the mid-1800s, first in Germany, then eventually in the United States. Parkways were initially understood to be naturalistic pleasure drives. By the late 1800s, "parkway" connoted a landscaped road connecting two or more parks. Three distinct types of parkways have been prominent in the United States.

One of these is the urban parkway, found in large cities and their nearby suburbs. These are intended and engineered for slow-moving local traffic, and indeed they often interconnect municipal parklands.

The second type is the regional parkway, which is designed for higher speeds and longer distances within a metropolitan area. At their best, regional parkways are beautifully landscaped and serve as agreeable alternatives to arterial-road and freeway commutes.

The third type is the scenic parkway. These are located in areas of exceptional environmental value, intended to fit into and showcase the natural landscape and significant built environments and/or to provide access to recreational sites.

Central Park, "Greensward" FIG. 1071
1858–1863, 1865–1878
Frederick Law Olmsted, landscape architect; **Calvert Vaux**, architect
New York, New York

Among several design innovations in their competition-winning "Greenward" plan, Olmsted and Vaux separated pedestrians from pleasure carriages by providing footbridges (Fig. 1071) and from crosstown traffic by building sunken roads designed to move traffic efficiently between the east and west sides of Manhattan. At the large scale of this 840-acre park, Olmsted and Vaux's naturalistic interior roadways not only minimize impact of other traffic on pedestrians, but persuasively demonstrated the potentials of grade-separated urban parkways.

Buffalo Parkways FIG. 1072
1868–1872; partly altered
Frederick Law Olmsted, landscape architect; **Calvert Vaux**, architect
Extending outward from Delaware Park, Front, and Parade

As in their Greensward scheme for Central Park (above), Olmsted and Vaux separated pedestrian and vehicular traffic within Buffalo's parklands. And while they were including wide boulevards as parts of their 1868 plan for Brooklyn's Prospect Park (see Naturalism chapter), they also planned several broad, landscaped parkways and streets for Buffalo, not only to interconnect parks, but also to extend outward, physically engaging with the rest of the city.

Olmsted scholar Charles Beveridge identified the ways these 200-foot-wide parkways differed from earlier major streets and boulevards: ". . . a central, smoothly paved road for the sole use of private carriages. This carriage drive was lined on each side by a median of trees, grass, and walks outside of which were streets for carts and wagons. The four parkways connecting surrounding neighborhoods to Delaware Park were the first true American parkways."

Boston Emerald Necklace
1880 ff.
Frederick Law Olmsted, landscape architect
Muddy River between Back Bay and Franklin Park, Boston, Massachusetts

See Naturalism chapter

Euclid Avenue FIGS. 1073, 1074, 1075
1882–1883
George and **William Chaffey**, real-estate developers
Ontario–Upland, California

The Chaffeys were the developers of a model agricultural community, Ontario, and eventually of its northerly extension, Upland. They devised Euclid Avenue as a privately constructed civic expression, a "beautiful enhancement." Euclid appeared as a 200-foot-wide corridor which extended seven miles, from the Ontario train station directly toward the looming San Gabriel Mountains above nascent Upland. Seen from a rise at the avenue's southerly origin, the Euclid corridor presented a magnificent vista. The center median of Euclid Avenue was planted with two rows of pepper trees, with enough space for a horse-drawn rail car—early light-rail transit. The boulevard was planted in majestic, straight rows of silk oaks.

Minneapolis Grand Rounds FIGS. 1076, 1077, 1078
1883, 1891, 1899–1900, 1906–1930s, 1960s
Horace Cleveland, William Watts Folwell, Warren Manning, Theodore Wirth, Garrett Eckbo
System of parkways and boulevards encircling the city, engaging Lakes Nokomis, Hiawatha, Harriet, Calhoun, Isles, Cedar, and Brownie, Minnehaha Creek, and the Mississippi riverfront.

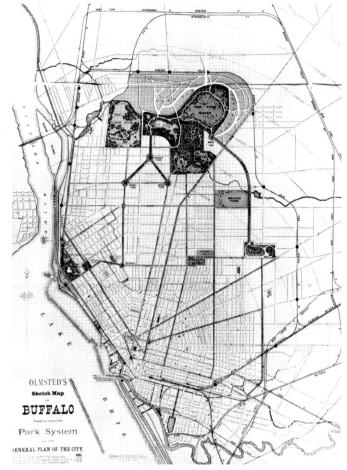

FIG. 1072 Urban Landscape Expanding on their Greensward concept for New York City, Olmsted and Vaux extended parklike boulevards-parkways out into the community in Buffalo. Their concept of a citywide park *system* was visionary at a time when many up-and-coming American cities did not yet have individual landscaped parks. *U.S. Department of the Interior*

The Minneapolis Grand Rounds represents a high point in American naturalistic urban parkway planning. Landscape architect Cleveland proposed the general idea of a parkway system in 1883, though his scheme relied primarily on widening and landscaping the city's existing street grid. A successful parks referendum in 1883 led to the establishment of a municipal park board.

In 1891, a committee of park board commissioners chaired by William Watts Folwell proposed a continuous encircling band of naturalistic parkways to be called the Grand Rounds (Fig. 1078). In 1899 the Board hired Boston landscape architect Warren Manning to devise Grand Rounds designs, which were carried out by

FIGS. 1073, 1074, 1075 Developer's Streetscape Euclid Avenue in Ontario, California, is one of the grandest monumental public spaces in the United States. Surprisingly, then, it is not the product of public vision. Rather, it was built by real estate developers to improve the economic viability of their isolated property. *Library of Congress, Prints & Photographs, Historic American Engineering Record*

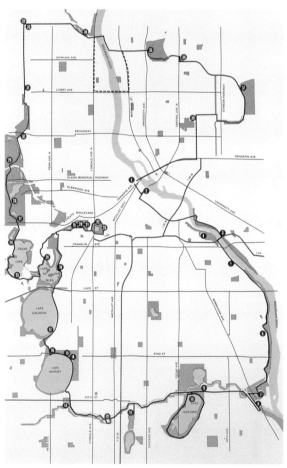

FIGS. 1076, 1077, 1078 Public Parkways Minneapolis Grand Rounds settings achieve their civic character because the city's celebrated water features are within the public domain: housing and commercial structures do not encircle lakeshores and wall off streams, because private buildings are sited outside of the encircling Grand Rounds parkways. Grand Rounds circulation was refined by Garrett Eckbo in the late 1960s, with additional separation of vehicles, cycles, and pedestrians (Fig. 1077). *Fig. 1078: Minneapolis Board of Park Commissioners*

FIGS. 1079, 1080 **Civic Boulevards** Kansas City's park system developed around landscaped boulevards like The Paseo (Fig. 1079). Unlike the Boston Emerald Necklace and Minneapolis Grand Rounds, these parklike roadways largely coincide with the underlying city street grid (Fig. 1080). As eventually extended beyond George Kessler's original plan, Kansas City park roadways intermittently strayed off the grid to engage natural features. *Fig. 1080: Kansas City Public Library*

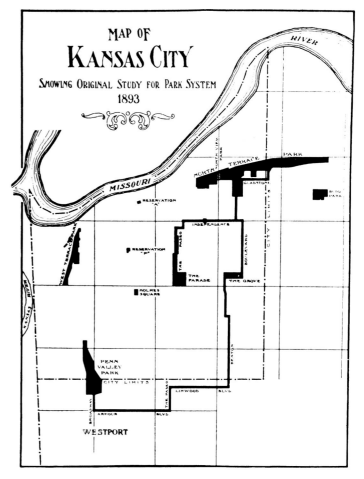

parks superintendent Theodore Wirth between 1906 and the mid-1930s. The Grand Rounds was revitalized and lightly altered by landscape architect Garrett Eckbo in the late 1960s (Figs. 1076, 1077). See also Naturalism chapter.

Kansas City Boulevards FIGS. 1079, 1080
1890–1893; 1900–1915
George E. Kessler, park system planner
Major city boulevards and parkways, especially The Paseo, Kansas City, Missouri

Kessler, who had worked briefly under Olmsted, was not yet out of his twenties when asked, in 1890, to devise a park system. Three years later, he issued a report. Mel Scott noted that this was much more than simply a parks plan, rather "a detailed and comprehensive look at Kansas City's topography and traffic patterns, population density and growth, its industrial and residential sections, and its prospects for future development . . . in a word, [city] planning."

The timing was unfortunate, coinciding with the Great Panic of 1893, but the parks idea was kept alive through a private donation, in 1896, of two square miles of land for a park. Development began in earnest in 1900 and was substantially completed by 1915.

The Kansas City system is similar to Horace Cleveland's unexecuted 1883 Minneapolis park system proposal in that it emphasized the enhancement of major city grid streets (Fig. 1080), with a secondary incorporation of natural features. One outgrowth of the Kansas City park system has been the citywide installation of 29 fountains in prominent locations, thereby establishing its self-image as "The City of Fountains" (Fig. 1045)

Monument Avenue FIG. 1081
1886–1929; 1993–1996
C. P. E. Burgwyn, planning engineer; **Frederick Moynihan**, **Jean Antonin Mercie**, **Edward Valentine**, **F. William Sievers**, **Paul DiPasquale**, sculptors
W from Lombardy St., Richmond, Virginia

Monument Avenue is more than a grand boulevard along the lines of Commonwealth Avenue in Boston or the Beaux Arts streets of Europe. Like Euclid Avenue (above entry), this mile-and-a-half-long streetscape was built to promote private real estate development and to establish a distinctive image, both for the development and for Richmond. *(Continued on following page)*

FIG. 1081 **Private Enhancement** Like Euclid Avenue (Figs. 1073–1075), Monument Avenue in Richmond, Virginia, is a majestic public streetscape that was conceived and constructed as part of a private real estate development. *Richmond Renaissance*

FIG. 1082 Integrated Design Rock Creek and Potomac Parkway in Washington, D.C., was not only a very early motor parkway, but also set high design benchmarks for the skillful integration of roadway and setting, as here at the monumental Watergate behind the Lincoln Memorial (See also Fig. 795). *Library of Congress, Prints & Photographs, Historic American Engineering Record*

The distinguishing planning concept is a sequence of traffic circles, each focused on a monumental sculpture of a Confederate military hero. That has understandably been a source of both pride and uneasiness on the parts of many Richmonders. To a great extent, the balance shifted toward pride with the 1996 installation of a final monumental sculpture, of an African-American native son of Richmond, tennis superstar Arthur Ashe.

Rock Creek and Potomac Parkway FIG. 1082
1901–1902; 1923–1936
Frederick Law Olmsted, Jr., concept planner; **William Partridge**, **James Langdon**, **Irving Payne**, **Thomas Jeffers**, landscape architects; the **Rock Creek and Potomac Parkway Commission** and the **U.S. Army Corps of Engineers**
Along Rock Creek valley from the National Zoo to West Potomac Park; 2.5 mi.

According to the National Park Service, Historic American Engineering Record, this parkway is "one of the best-preserved examples of the earliest stage of motor parkway development [and significant] for its physical design, which combines landscape architecture, engineering, and architecture to provide an attractive and useful local park and commuter artery."

REGIONAL PARKWAYS

The nineteenth-century German prince Herman Ludwig von Pückler-Muskau was the progenitor of the twentieth-century American motor parkway. While improving his large, scattered estate throughout Saxony, Pückler demonstrated two planning approaches which would be widely followed by road designers in the United States for more than a century.

One of these was the simple device of interconnecting isolated land parcels by romantic, winding roads. That idea was adopted by Olmsted for Boston's Emerald Necklace, employed by civic leaders for the Minneapolis Grand Rounds,(both earlier in this chapter) and developed at regional scale in the extensive Long Island parkway system of Robert Moses (below).

Pückler's other idea was valuable as a universal design insight. This was the realization that naturalistic landscapes could be either developed authentically or merely contrived—stylized. According to landscape historian Norman Newton, Pückler distained, as contrived, the "so-called English style"

where "straight roads are then curved into corkscrew forms in the most tedious manner."

Pückler's alternative was to manipulate the land with the intention of enhancing its most picturesque qualities, within which roads would be fitted in response to the landforms and the desired scenic effect (Fig. 1083). While an authentic landscape as so defined by Pückler was not always possible or desirable—much raw land, alas, is not particularly appealing or endowed with superior intrinsic visual qualities—this is certainly an effective approach wherever some potential exists.

Among the best American examples of "authentic" naturalistic roads, cited in the following section, are the Westchester County parkways and the later Merritt Parkway in Connecticut.

Bronx River Parkway Reservation FIG. 1084
1907–1925; numerous later modifications
Leslie G. Holleran, principal engineer; **Hermann W. Merkel**, landscape architect
Westchester County, New York

The Bronx River Parkway was America's first limited-access, divided automobile parkway, the "first acknowledged modern motor parkway" in the United States, according to the Historic American Engineering Record.

The American motor parkway concept did not emerge fully formed overnight, of course. Bronx River reservation was in effect a linear pleasure ground (Fig. 1084), a then-common aesthetic expression for public parklands. Just as moving pictures were initially offered as one act of a larger vaudeville show, so, too, was the landscaped motorway initially understood simply as one recreational feature of the Bronx River park reservation.

Where conventional pleasure grounds included romantically twisting carriageways for Sunday drives, now the auto roadway was less contorted, in response to the auto's higher speeds. The resulting gently curving roadways evolved into the signature expression of American regional parkways of the 1920s and 1930s.

Westchester County Parkways
1913–1932 ff.
Jay Downer, chief engineer; **Gilmore Clarke**, landscape architect
Westchester County, New York

The popular and aesthetic successes of Bronx River Parkway motivated Westchester County to undertake a county-wide parkway system. Major routes include the Hutchinson River Parkway (opened in 1928), the Saw Mill (1929), and the Cross County (1931).

These parkways were typically two lanes each way, with protective rights-of-way of from 200 feet up to 1,700 feet in width. Recreational areas were incorporated into the Westchester parkways where possible, although these routes were soon heavily used by commuter traffic.

Taconic State Parkway FIGS. 1085, 1086
1923–1932; 1925–1963
Jay Downer, **Leslie Holleran**, principal engineers; **Gilmore Clarke**, **Herman W. Merkel**, principal landscape architects, all for Westchester sections; **E. J. Howe**, **James W. Bradner, Jr.**, **James Bixby**, chief engineers for state sections; **Charles Baker**, chief staff engineer; **Theodore Bowman**, chief landscape architect for state sections
Westchester, Putnam, Dutchess, and Columbia Counties, New York; 105 mi.

Taconic marked the zenith in the design of regional parkways: broadly curving roadways with wide, wildflower-filled meadows

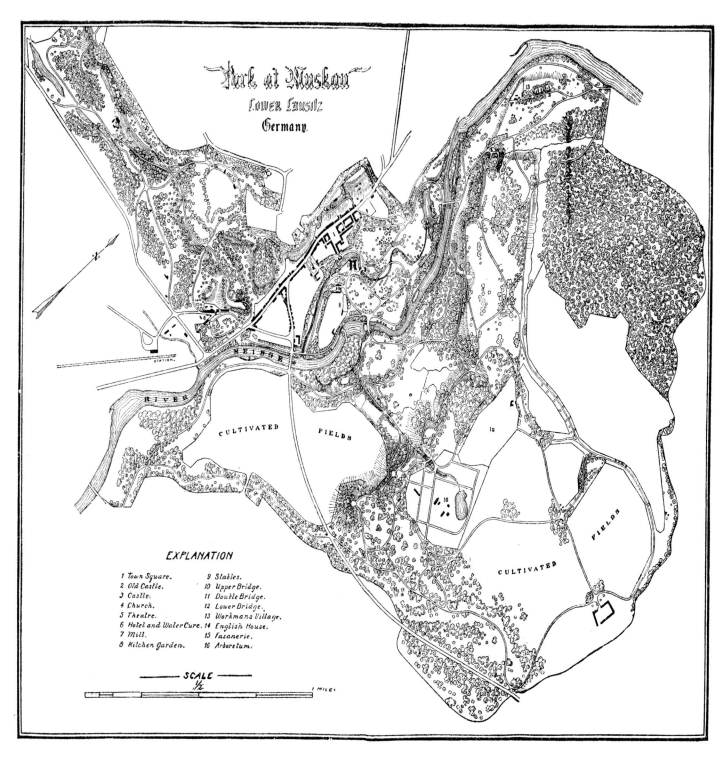

FIG. 1083 The Fountainhead Prince Herman's Muskau estate planning provided an essential source for nineteenth-century American romantic landscapes and strongly influenced the design of twentieth-century American motor parkways. *Charles Eliot, Landscape Architect, 1902*

FIG. 1084 Automobile Pleasure Grounds Motor parkways did not suddenly emerge, fully developed, when autos became generally available to the public. Rather, they evolved from then-current expressions of public park landscapes. As this 1919 view illustrates, the pioneering Bronx River Parkway Reservation was in effect a larger linear variation of late-nineteenth-century public park pleasure grounds, providing swimming and canoeing, horseback riding, skating, settings for festivals, picnicking, "scouting," and just sitting out in a beautiful landscape. And yes, also a gently winding auto roadway, a necessary modification, because of the increased scale and speed of auto travel, of the twisting carriage paths of earlier pedestrian-oriented pleasure grounds. *Library of Congress, Prints & Photographs, Historic American Engineering Record*

FIGS. 1085, 1086 **The Ultimate Motor Parkway** Taconic State Parkway is widely considered to be a supreme visual achievement among early motor parkways. Its planners exploited natural features, chiefly rock outcroppings (Fig. 1085), while introducing designed landscapes and bridges (Fig. 1086). *Library of Congress, Prints & Photographs, Historic American Engineering Record*

FIG. 1087 **The Nation's Parkway** Mount Vernon Memorial Highway and its northern complement, the George Washington Memorial Parkway, offer a singular mix of national sites, monumental views of the capital city, the bordering Potomac River, and superior landscaping. *Library of Congress, Prints & Photographs, Historic American Engineering Record*

as medians and landscaping that, in Phil Patton's description, could have been "taken from a Constable painting." Lewis Mumford, no apologist for highways, called Taconic a "consummate work of art."

The Taconic was eventually extended northward through four counties and was completed after World War II. Alas, by the post-war years, Taconic was already a wonderful and unattainable anachronism, as national highway design sharply slanted toward functional freeways.

Mount Vernon Memorial Highway FIG. 1087
1928–1932
George Washington Memorial Parkway
1930–1935, completed 1965
R. E. Toms, principal highway engineer; **Gilmore Clarke**, landscape design consultant; **Jay Downer**, engineering consultant; **Frederick Law Olmsted, Jr.**, **Charles W. Eliot II**, concept planners; **Wilbur Simonson**, project landscape architect; **J. V. McNary**, project design engineer; **J. W. Johnson**, construction engineer; postwar sections designed by the **U.S. Bureau of Public Roads** and its successor, the **Public Roads Administration**, in association with staff

architects and landscape architects of the **National Park Service**
Fairfax and Arlington Counties, Virginia; 15.2 mi. from the gates of Mount Vernon to
the Arlington Memorial Bridge, excepting within the city of Alexandria; from the
Arlington bridge to the Capital Beltway (I-495), another 9.7 mi. as the George
Washington Memorial Pkwy.

This limited-access parkway along the west bank of the Potomac
River is among the best landscaped urban roadways in the United
States. It interconnects major historical and national sites, develops
a sequence of vistas over the Potomac, and offers panoramic views
of monumental Washington, D.C., and Georgetown.

SCENIC PARKWAYS

Columbia River Highway FIGS. 1088, 1089
1913–1915; extended to The Dalles in 1922
Samuel Hill, visionary; **Samuel Lancaster**, design engineer
Columbia River Gorge, between Troutdale and The Dalles, Oregon; designated
U.S. Hwy. 30 in 1925; 75 mi.

The Gorge's extraordinary natural beauty was respected, if not almost
matched, by this superb civil engineering design, known as the "poem
in stone." Inspired by alpine roads in Europe, Lancaster's concept
showcased views of natural wonders at nearly every turn (Fig. 1089).
Each of dozens of bridges was singular in design, as was the stunning
Vista House overlook (Fig. 1088), built 1916–1918 at the Crown Point
promontory, more than 700 feet above the river. The roadway was
partly overbuilt by I-84 in the mid-1960s, but the original Lancaster
design is currently being restored, with completion anticipated by 2010.

Long Island Parkways
1926–1928 ff.
Robert Moses, conceptual planner and project director; **Gilmore Clarke**,
Clarke and Rapuano, **Clarence Combs**, landscape architects
Southern State Parkway and Jones Beach Causeway, Nassau County, New York

The larger-than-life story of Robert Moses (1888–1981) and the
Long Island parks-parkways system cannot be adequately recounted
here. If you are interested in the absorbing background, be sure to
consult Robert Caro's *The Power Broker*, especially pp. 143–240.

Moses had seriously thought about parks and recreation since
1922, and through a bolt of inspiration, realized that it would be
possible to economically piece together a series of never-utilized
Brooklyn suburban water-supply properties, thus launching what
grew over subsequent decades into a continuous parks-parkways
network extending across Long Island and linked to parkways inside
the New York city limits. The work was accomplished in the late
1920s with the essential political support of New York Governor Al
Smith, and later governors continued to back the popular system.

The entire undertaking provided a classic case study—today,
realistically, an unapproachable benchmark—for subsequent generations of public officials and planners, with respect to conception,
acquisition, funding, integration of movement with attractions,
design, and system-wide consistency.

Colonial National Historical Parkway FIG. 1090
1931–1937, 1940–1949, 1954–1957
Oliver G. Taylor, engineer-in-charge; **Stanley W. Abbott**, chief designer;
Charles E. Peterson, landscape architect-in-charge; **William H. Smith**,
associate highway engineer; **William Robinson, Jr.**, park superintendent;
Bureau of Public Roads, project supervision; **National Park Service**,
design review and approvals; coordination with **Arthur Shurcliff**, landscape
architect and area planner for Colonial Williamsburg.
James City and York Counties, Virginia; a three-lane roadway beginning at the
site of Jamestown, following the James River before turning north and

FIGS. 1088, 1089 Poem in Stone Columbia River Highway is an American
transliteration of European alpine roads. On a clear day—an iffy occurrence in this
climate—the drive is especially magnificent. *Library of Congress, Prints & Photographs,
Historic American Engineering Record*

FIG. 1090 A Paradigm of Balance Colonial National Historical Parkway is an
exceptionally beautiful drive. Its design secret is balance: individual elements like
bridges and plantings do not stand out from other elements. Instead, the entire
corridor is almost flawlessly harmonious.

tunneling under Colonial Williamsburg, then turning eastward along the York River to the Yorktown battlefield, 23.24 mi.

Colonial Parkway is surely one of the most engaging scenic parkways in the United States, small-scaled and closely interrelated with its adjacent context. It interconnects three major colonial-revolutionary war sites: Jamestown, Williamsburg, and Yorktown.

Blue Ridge Parkway FIG. 1091

1935–1987

Stanley Abbott, conceptual planner and superintendent; **Jay Downer**, consulting engineer; **Gilmore Clarke**, consulting landscape architect; **Hendrick van Gelder** and **Edward Abbuchl**, project landscape architects; **Harold J. Spellman**, supervising engineer; **William Austin** and **W. I. Lee**, project engineers; staff planners and designers of the Bureau of Public Roads and the **National Park Service**.

From Shenandoah National Park, Virginia, to Great Smoky Mountains National Park, North Carolina; 469 mi.

As succinctly described by the Historic American Engineering Record, "Blue Ridge Parkway was the first long-distance rural parkway developed by the National Park Service. Its designers adopted parkway strategies originating in suburban commuter routes and metropolitan park systems, and expanded them to regional scale. . . . The parkway was conceived as a multiple-purpose corridor that would fulfill a variety of social, recreational, environmental and programmatic functions . . . [and] display the traditional cultural landscapes of the southern Appalachian highlands, providing visitors with an idealized vision of America's rural heritage."

FIG. 1091 *The* **Scenic Parkway** Winding elegantly for nearly 500 miles through surpassingly beautiful sections of the Appalachians, Blue Ridge Parkway has understandably garnered glowing accolades since the moment it opened. *Library of Congress, Prints & Photographs, Historic American Engineering Record*

FIG. 1092 **Access** Of course, not all scenic highways are handsome in themselves. The majority of such roads have nondescript designs. They are "scenic" in the sense of providing human access to remote sites of natural beauty, as is this unremarkable two-lane road passing through the spectacular formations of Arches National Park near Moab, Utah. *Library of Congress, Prints & Photographs, Historic American Engineering Record*

LANDSCAPED EXPRESSWAYS

Early motor parkways like the Bronx River were conceived of as pleasure drives carefully landscaped to enhance the natural beauty of their corridors. This preoccupation with nature, design, and beauty carried on into the 1930s with the Long Island parkways developed by Robert Moses. His Southern State and Meadowbrook parkways leading to Jones Beach demonstrated an ultimate integration of natural features, roadway landscaping, and architecture. (See entries earlier in this chapter.)

However, as more and more people bought cars, and demand built incessantly, road builders increasingly focused on capacity over beauty, and on workday commutes over weekend recreational trips. This shift in highway emphasis from natural beauty to functionality—from parkways to expressways—accelerated in large part on account of the highly influential General Motors Futurama exhibit at the 1939 New York World's Fair (See the Fairs and Expositions chapter). Created by the famed industrial designer Norman Bel Geddes, Futurama demonstrated how a national highway system could be developed across—as opposed to sympathetically working with—"every type of terrain."

Bel Geddes promoted a truly modern expression of the road. Like the newly emerging European strains of modern architecture, these new superhighways were intended to overcome, rather than to fit into, their existing context: "never deviating from a direct course." Bel Geddes referred to "the four basic principles of highway design: safety, comfort, speed, and economy" as if these were universally acknowledged, immutable laws. And, indeed, soon only token attention was accorded to highway landscaping and beauty. At about this time, a new term, the freeway, gained popularity. Compared to the visual experience of the parkway, the freeway was all about efficient movement of vehicles.

Initially, these new expressways were similar to the previous parkways: the Merritt Parkway offered higher-speed capacity along with beautiful landscaping. But its California contemporary, the Arroyo Seco Parkway, later rechristened the Pasadena Freeway, was already more utilitarian in character than were the classic Eastern motor parkways of the 1920s and 1930s.

Functional expressways proliferated in the post–World War II years, beginning with the Pennsylvania Turnpike. Freeways expanded in the West, along with mostly limited-access toll highways, primarily east of the Mississippi, that followed the Pennsylvania example. Since then, the beautifully landscaped highway has been very much the exception throughout the United States.

Here and there, as along U.S. Hwy. 101 through the exclusive Santa Barbara suburb of Montecito (Fig. 1093) or I-90 east of Lake Washington in suburban Seattle, major American highways are still lushly landscaped. Colorful median flower beds are effective along North Carolina freeways.

Where highways cut through beautiful natural landscapes highway planners could achieve a kind of indigenous beauty by accommodating existing copses or rock formations (Fig. 1092), such as the monumental median rock formations along I-89 near Montpelier, Vermont. Yet sophisticated landscaping like that along a 40-mile stretch of I-24 in southeastern Illinois (Fig. 1103), or the park-like plantings along Highway 8 southeast of Litchfield, Connecticut (Fig. 1094), have been rare since World War II.

Broadacre City Road System FIG. 1095

1930s; Model, 1934–1935
Frank Lloyd Wright, planner
Broadacre Model located in the Dana Gallery, Hillside Home School, Taliesin Estate, Spring Green, Wisconsin

After a decade of intensive thought about the emerging American regional city, Wright developed an integrated set of "experimental micro-environments," as Taliesin-trained architect Vernon Swaback described this famous study, in a giant, 12-by-13-foot model unveiled in New York City in April, 1935 (Fig. 250).

Broadacre featured a systematic, integrated hierarchy of movement, from walkways to freeways. Freeways were composed of five side-by-side corridors divided by continuous boulevard landscaping. These provided separate, multiple lanes in each direction for cars and for trucks, plus a transit lane down the center intended, ultimately, for a monorail.

Anticipating the practice of post–World War II motel chains, Wright located an "automobile inn" off the freeway interchange, buffered from highway noise by industrial buildings set along the

FIGS. 1093, 1094 **Highway Landscapes** Post–World War II American highways have occasionally been well landscaped. The lush plantings along U.S. 101 in Santa Barbara (Fig. 1093) and the park-like median along Highway 8 near Litchfield, Connecticut (Fig. 1094) are exemplars.

FIG. 1095 **Integrated Roadways** Frank Lloyd Wright's Broadacre City was organized around a carefully considered hierarchy of roads, from local streets to superhighways. Wright's road system especially differed from American norms in its design qualities and in its functional interconnections between the local economy, land use, and transportation. This detail of an "athletic" bridge illustrates the level of Wright's engineering explorations. *Published with the permission of the Frank Lloyd Wright Foundation*

FIG. 1096 **Prewar Swan Song** Merritt Parkway represents a culmination of the American motor parkway. A beautiful designed environment in itself, the parkway fits into adjacent communities by highlighting pre-existent landforms and natural views, thus enhancing a sense of locality.

FIGS. 1097, 1098 **Classic California Freeway** The Arroyo Seco "Pasadena" Freeway was originally conceived as a pleasant driving experience along an uncrowded, landscaped roadway. That Arcadian ideal soon evolved into the Pasadena Freeway, and reality, of course, became much different, as traffic volumes soared. Cramped by its necessarily twisty alignment through hilly terrain, with additional lanes later squeezed in to augment capacity, the Pasadena Freeway is today anything but a sublime drive. Extremely tight on-off ramps are reminders of the highway's early date (Fig. 1098). *Library of Congress, Prints & Photographs, Historic American Engineering Record*

freeway edge. A shopping mall dramatically bridged a connecting arterial.

Main roads led to a central civic parkway, within which cultural facilities including an arboretum, a zoo, and an aquarium were sited in the median. This predated the similar concept employed by Roberto Burle Marx in the early 1950s for his highly advanced Gloria-Flamingo park-expressway in Rio de Janeiro.

Wright's concept of "great architectural roads" was illustrated in Broadacre by "athletic" suspension bridges, one of which crossed over both an arterial and a stream in a single span (Fig. 1095). Both conceptually and in individual demonstrations, Broadacre provided a potent pattern for postwar American road builders.

Merritt Parkway FIG. 1096
1934–1940
George L. Dunkelberger, bridge designer; **W. Thayer Chase**, landscape architect; staff design engineers, **Connecticut Bureau of Engineering and Construction**
SW Connecticut; parallel, inland, to the U.S. Hwy. 1 / I-95 corridor, connecting with the Hutchinson River Pkwy. in Westchester County, New York, and to the Wilbur Cross Pkwy. W of New Haven; 37 mi.

The Merritt Parkway represents the 1930s state of the art in highway design and construction, including the stylistic influence of the Moderne in many of the bridges, along with emerging construction technologies. Freed of agreements that required stone facing on New York State parkways (Fig. 1086), the Merritt bridge-overpass designer exploited the sculptural and ornamental potentials of exposed concrete, making each span unique. A remarkable synthesis of romantic parkway sensibilities with the need to accommodate modern levels of regional traffic, the Merritt is, in effect, an ultimate mature expression of the landscaped American expressway.

Yet even before World War II, expressway design was moving away from such high aesthetics and into pure functionalism. The Arroyo Seco freeway (next entry) marked the transition toward this sensibility, which was demonstrated in full by the Pennsylvania Turnpike toll road (following section). Remarkably, this radical transition in American highway design norms occurred simultaneously, when all three of these highways opened in 1940.

Arroyo Seco "Pasadena" Freeway FIGS. 1097, 1098
1938–1940
Fwy. 110 from Downtown Los Angeles to Pasadena, California

The Arroyo Seco was the first increment of what was to have been a 600-mile system of regional parkways proposed in 1939, near the closing stages of the classic motor parkway era in the United States. Indeed, by the mid-1940s the notion of parkways had already evolved into one of utilitarian freeways, and in 1947 the next increment of the LA regional highway system opened as the serviceable, visually unremarkable Hollywood Freeway.

Garden State Parkway FIG. 1099
1945–1957
Michael Rapuano, **Clarke & Rapuano**, planners and landscape architects
Nanuet, New York, to Cape May, New Jersey; 172.4 mi.

The Garden State proved to be a last hurrah for the 1920s and 1930s landscaped parkway ideal, since it was built in the post–World War II era of utilitarian expressways. This design was intended as a "hybrid," combining the efficiency of the Pennsylvania Turnpike with the beauty of Merritt Parkway, and it largely succeeded, especially along the sections south of Atlantic City.

The parkway was built with a central median, which was typically about 100 feet wide, occasionally as much as 200 feet. This was landscaped in a gentle, undulating pattern. Clusters of colum-

FIG. 1099 **Postwar Holdover** Garden State Parkway was intended as a hybrid of prewar beauty and postwar functionality. Thus while it is generally straighter and wider than Merritt Parkway, especially the southern section of the Garden State is quite handsome.

FIG. 1100 **The Precipitous Decline of Beauty** A spectacular transportation success, the Pennsylvania Turnpike was also a precursor of the post–World War II emphasis on functionality in American highway engineering. *Library of Congress, Prints & Photographs*

FIGS. 1101, 1102 **Interstate Expressways** The 1956 Interstate system introduced an entirely new scale to American highways, as suggested by an immense interchange outside of Fort Lauderdale (Fig. 1101). The interstate network of limited-access roadways sharply decreased long-distance travel times, while reducing congestion on the older trunk highways that ran through the centers of towns. The system's economic value is incalculable. Among the negatives, expressways shower adjacent neighborhoods—some of which they irreparably divided—with noise and polluted air. Because of an emphasis on functionality, many urban freeways are truly dismal, as a scene along the Davison Freeway in Detroit attests (Fig. 1102). *Fig 1102: Library of Congress, Prints & Photographs, Historic American Engineering Record*

nar evergreens were set within the existing deciduous forest, providing a subtle rhythm along both sides of the roadways (Fig. 1099). Among subsequent changes to the original concept, additional lanes have been added in the central and northern sections, and incidental evergreen plantings that do not reinforce Rapuano's landscape scheme have been added in the south and central sections. Nevertheless, drivers can still experience the essence of the original design.

FUNCTIONAL EXPRESSWAYS

Pennsylvania Turnpike FIG. 1100
1938–1940
Samuel W. Marshall, chief engineer, Pennsylvania Department of Highways
Pittsburgh to Harrisburg, Pennsylvania, now incorporated into I-76; 160 mi.

Built over an abandoned railroad right-of-way, the Turnpike was inspired by the German Autobahns of the mid-1930s. It became "an immediate sensation" when opened, attracting 10,000 toll-paying cars daily over the first two weeks This was stunning to almost everyone, since the federal Bureau of Public Roads had predicted a daily volume of 715 cars.

Highway historian Phil Patton identified the Turnpike as America's first superhighway, in that it caught the national attention, demonstrating the expressway as a practical, everyday concept for the United States, even when economically weakened by a decade of Depression. The Pennsylvania Turnpike became the first segment of the post–World War II Interstate Highway system.

National System of Interstate and Defense Highways
FIGS. 1101, 1102
1956–1978, 1984
Frank Turner, U.S. Federal Highway Administrator
41,000-mi., nationwide; about 47,000 mi. by 2004

The idea of a national interstate highway system drew to a significant extent upon the Dream Highways exhibit by Norman Bel Geddes for the General Motors Futurama pavilion at the 1939 New York World's Fair (see Fairs & Expositions chapter). However, as early as 1937 President Franklin D. Roosevelt had diagrammed his own scheme, which consisted of six cross-country superhighways, three each running north-south and east-west.

In 1940, the U.S. Bureau of Public Roads outlined a concept for a 29,300-mile superhighway system. By 1944 that preliminary concept had been refined into a close approximation of the 41,000-mile Interstate Highway system approved by Congress in 1956 under Public Law 627. According to Patton, the final section of Interstate opened in 1978. The last stoplight on the Interstate system was removed in 1984, less than 30 years after enabling legislation was passed. The subsequent two decades have largely been marked by small expansions to the system.

Interstate Highway 24 FIG. 1103
1963 ff; construction 1974–1976
Illinois Department of Transportation; Wilbur Smith Associates, consultants
SE Illinois; 38-mi. segment extending from 11 mi. S of Marion to the Ohio River near Metropolis.

The Illinois segment of I-24, especially its central and northerly sections, is among the most visually sophisticated of the post–World War II non-scenic expressways. Four attributes especially contribute to its superior visual qualities.

One of these is its mostly rural setting, with significant roadside development only occasionally visible from the highway.

Second, the roadside corridor has been artfully brushed, so that the edges of tree stands vary irregularly and thus are plausibly "natural," compared to the typical straight-edge roadway-landscape definition.

Third, new plantings, chiefly of evergreens, have been selectively introduced as visual accents.

And fourth, a dramatic rock cut was exposed along the northerly section of the highway, with a spectacular display of evergreens growing out of near-vertical rock walls (Fig. 1103). This occurs in both directions, although the best visual situation occurs on a sunny afternoon for northbound traffic immediately south of milepost 11. All highways should be so expressive!

FIG. 1103 Picturesque Freeway Few post–World War II expressways were developed as beautiful landscapes like the prewar motorway corridors. Interstate-24 in Illinois is among the most arresting among postwar freeway designs, especially its dramatic rock cut.

Bridges

1800–2004

FIGS. 1104, 1105 The Dramatic Visual Potentials of Bridges Chicago is one of a handful of American cities which consistently exploits the visual qualities of its bridges. Elsewhere, bridges are usually thought of simply in functional terms, as necessary transportation infrastructure. Bascule bridges (Fig. 1105) over the Chicago River put on a impressive ensemble performance with every sequence of lifts. Sections of each bridge engage in a constantly changing visual play when opening and closing, while adjacent bascules are performing similar theatrics at different points in the cycle. Enhancing the effect is a rich, reddish-brown color custom-developed for the downtown Chicago River bridges (Fig. 1104). Since bridge steel has to be periodically repainted, this signature visual enhancement over the previous battleship gray color is gained at negligible cost. *Fig. 1105: Library of Congress, Prints & Photographs, Historic American Engineering Record*

Bridges are everywhere. Over a half-million street and highway bridges are in use throughout the United States, more than 2,000 in New York City alone. Even so, we seem barely to notice bridges. Rarely is there any public out-cry when yet another banal, utilitarian bridge is constructed. No doubt that is because little civic expectation is normally attached to bridges. They are considered to be infrastructure,

FIG. 1107 Technological Art The Eads Bridge at St. Louis is a spectacular nineteenth-century engineering achievement, from numerous technical innovations to its majestic beauty

and thus largely a matter of engineering calculations, best left to technical specialists.

Most of the relatively few prominent American bridges are cited for their specifications: longest, greatest span, and so forth. Thus the Chesapeake Bay Bridge/Tunnel in Virginia is more than 17 miles long; the Mackinac Bridge in Michigan is suspended over 8,600 feet; the Verrazano Narrows Bridge in New York has the longest main span, 4,200 feet, and towers nearly 700 feet high. All well and good, but to what end?

By contrast, the following bridges offer special character. They are handsome or at least interesting, aside from any quantifiable attributes such as longest, tallest, or earliest. These bridges are memorable creative additions to their communities —and to the nation.

PEDESTRIAN BRIDGES

Wheeling Suspension Bridge FIG. 1106
1847–1849; collapsed, 1854; reopened, 1856
Charles Ellet, Jr., design engineer and builder
U.S. Hwy. 40 over the Ohio River, Wheeling, West Virginia

Behind the Wheeling bridge lies a marvelous story of the resolve of a remote community with little backing from the distant centers of state power in then undivided Virginia, facing a potent civic rivalry with larger Pittsburgh. A competition to design it took place between two great bridge builders, John Roebling and Ellet, who got the job.

A daunting 1,000-foot span was built in a single year, 1848–1849, although it succumbed to wind-generated oscillation only five years after completion. Immediately rebuilt and stiffened with sway bracing, Wheeling is the oldest continuously operating vehicular suspension bridge in the world.

On opening, the Wheeling bridge served as a literal gateway to the West, carrying the National Road (see Roads chapter) as it descended out of the Appalachians. After a jarring, over-mountain trip to the comparative wilderness of Ohio, travelers must have been reassured by the ruggedly handsome stone towers and majestic cable span, presenting an unexpected scene of civic grandeur.

Eads Bridge FIG. 1107
1867–1874
James B. Eads, engineer; **Charles Pfeifer**, **William Chauvenet**, structural consultants
Washington Ave. at the Mississippi River, St. Louis, Missouri

The Eads Bridge defined technical cutting edges in underwater construction, utilization of materials, and various structural innovations, in addition to establishing the longest crossing. Yet even these impressive achievements pale in the face of the extraordinary, tactile handsomeness of this structure, a creative triumph of function and form.

Brooklyn Bridge FIG. 1108
1869–1883
John Augustus Roebling, Washington Roebling, Emily Roebling, engineers
SE of New York City Hall, Manhattan to Brooklyn, New York

The Roeblings must be credited with superior achievements in engineering, architecture, and in providing crossing pedestrians with an exhilarating visual experience. The Brooklyn Bridge is so rooted in American cultural history that detailed description here is unnecessary.

Smithfield Street Bridge FIG. 1109
1882–1883, 1889
Gustav Lindenthal, design engineer
Monongahela River, downtown Pittsburgh, Pennsylvania

Smithfield is considered to be the most elegant among Pittsburgh's signature bridges, and surely one of the most graceful bridges in the nation. The double-lenticular truss design is beautiful, and strikingly architectonic.

Lincoln Highway Bridge FIG. 1110
1915
1100 block of E. 5th Street, Tama, Iowa

This small municipal highway bridge is of no intrinsic engineering or design importance when compared to others in this chap-

FIG. 1108 **The Urban Bridge** Most of the great American bridges are located in big cities, but the Brooklyn Bridge is especially associated with city life, both in literature and because of its startling juxtaposition with the neighborhoods below at its bridgeheads in Brooklyn (shown here) and Manhattan. *Library of Congress, Prints & Photographs, Historic American Engineering Record*

FIG. 1109 **Graceful, Defined** Pittsburgh's Smithfield Street Bridge illustrates the inherent gracefulness of lens-shaped—lenticular—trusses.

FIG. 1110 **Roadside Identity** The Lincoln Highway Association assiduously branded its transcontinental route, wherever and however possible. Several early bridges were cast with "Lincoln Highway" as a structural support. You can still see this one in Tama, Iowa.

FIG. 1111 **Workhorses of the Bridge World** Concrete-arch bridges like the Tunkhannock Creek Viaduct in Nicholson, Pennsylvania, handle long reaches, while accommodating steep changes in topography. *Library of Congress, Prints & Photographs, Historic American Engineering Record*

ter. But it is significant as one of the few remaining bridges of the culturally influential "Coast-to-Coast Rock Highway," as the Lincoln Highway was originally billed (see Roads chapter). The Tama bridge is especially notable among this handful of holdovers because the words "Lincoln Highway" form the side balustrades.

Tunkhannock Creek Viaduct FIG. 1111
1912–1915
Abraham Cohen, design engineer
Nicholson, Pennsylvania

Concrete-arch bridges are widely employed over long reaches, as the Tunkhannock extends over 2,375 feet. Concrete arches of the Lincoln Highway/U.S. 30 George Westinghouse Memorial Bridge (Fig. 1112) accommodate a precipitous 200-foot drop.

Bayonne Bridge FIG. 1113
1931
Othmar Ammann, design engineer; **Cass Gilbert**, consulting architect; **George Goethals**, consulting engineer
Kill van Kull between Bayonne, New Jersey, and Staten Island, New York

Ammann's design captured the elemental engineering clarity of a bowstring truss. Reduced to its essential structural elements, this bridge is abstracted to the point that it is almost a diagram of forces. In this instance, less is definitely more.

Golden Gate Bridge FIG. 1059
1933–1937
Joseph B. Strauss, chief engineer; **Othmar Ammann, Leon Moisseiff, Charles Derlith, Jr.**, consulting engineers; **Irving Morrow**, consulting architect
U.S. Hwy. 101 between San Francisco and Marin County, California

An impossibly picturesque setting was enhanced by the visual interplay between this gorgeous reddish structure and the surrounding greenery—green in season, at least. During summer, the constant shifting of fog adds to the high drama of this spectacular man-nature composition, further amplified by San Francisco's picturesque skyline in the distance. Understandably, Golden Gate is the most famous bridge in the United States.

6th Street Viaduct FIG. 1114
1995–2002
David Kahler, concept architect; **Michael Brush**, design architect
N. 6th St. over the Menomonee River, downtown Milwaukee, Wisconsin

Infrastructure intended, and succeeding, as public art. Dramatic slanted pylons support cable stays, suggesting an influence from Santiago Calatrava's nearby art museum pedestrian bridge (see Deconstruction chapter). The bare-bones beauty of this design reminds one of the poetic yet economical Swiss bridges of the 1920s and 1930s by Robert Maillart.

Frank Lloyd Wright Bridge FIG. 1115
1999–2002
Evan Mauer, civic visionary; **Anthony Puttnam**, (**Taliesin Architects**) architect
Third Ave. S. crossing I-94, Minneapolis, Minnesota

The idea for a signature bridge with palpable regional roots came from Mauer, director of the nearby Minneapolis Institute of Arts, which includes the William Purcell House (see Prairie School chapter) and a hallway from Frank Lloyd Wright's razed 1912 Francis W. Little House among its collections. Target Corporation, headquartered a few blocks away, paid the difference between the cost of the usual mundane, standardized bridge and this singular design by a senior architect at the successor practice, after Wright.

Puttnam's scheme is marked by multiple curves, in plan and section. This is a visually graceful departure from highway-bridge norms, and also functionally innovative in subtly accommodating the need for widening traffic lanes at the bridge's downtown end.

PEDESTRIAN BRIDGES

Irene Hixon Whitney Pedestrian Bridge FIG. 1116
1987–1988
Siah Armajani, artist-designer; **Ericksen Roed & Associates**, structural engineers
Hennepin-Lyndale Aves., N of W. 15th St., Minneapolis, Minnesota

Truss-as-bridge-as-sculpture. Virtually no part of this arresting pedestrian bridge over I-94 is superfluous to its functional requirements, save the pale yellow and blue paint. Armajani provided a persuasive demonstration of the high artistic potentials of structural engineering.

FIG. 1112 Negotiating Extreme Terrain The George Westinghouse Memorial Bridge in East Pittsburgh, Pennsylvania carries U.S. 30, the old Lincoln Highway, over Turtle Creek with seeming ease—from the perspectives of motorists. In reality, it was America's longest concrete-arch bridge, extending 1,560 feet, when it opened in 1932. Designed by the Allegheny County Department of Public Works, the bridge soars 200 feet above the valley floor. *Library of Congress, Prints & Photographs, Historic American Engineering Record*

FIG. 1113 Diagram of Forces The Bayonne Bridge linking New Jersey and New York is essentially a structural skeleton, an exquisite expression of pure engineering. *Library of Congress, Prints & Photographs, Historic American Engineering Record*

FIG. 1114 Civic Infrastructure Milwaukee's 6th Street Viaduct is a bridge you will look at twice—and again and again. A distinctive downtown gateway.

FIG. 1115 Regional Imagery Tony Puttnam's homage to Frank Lloyd Wright in Minneapolis introduced a distinctive, regional reference that is missing in conventional, standardized spans.

FIG. 1116 Engineering as Art
Artist Siah Armajani intended his Whitney pedestrian bridge to enhance Walker Art Center's adjacent sculpture garden in Minneapolis (see Modernism chapter). His design demonstrates inherent interrelationships between art and engineering.

Sundial Bridge FIG. 1117

1997–2004

Santiago Calatrava, architect-engineer

Turtle Bay Exploration Park, Redding, California, from I-5 exit 678, W on Rt. 44, Exit 1 N on Auditorium Dr.

A surpassingly graceful cable-stay design, Sundial looks like a harp for mythological gods—perhaps not that much of a metaphorical stretch, given that a local company, Red River Forests, promoted the Paul Bunyan myth in its 1920s advertising.

The bridge's exquisite visual qualities play off magnificently with the Sacramento River below and against distant views of the Cascade and Trinity ranges. Moreover, the bridge's pylon functions as a sundial, in three ways on sunny days. The pylon casts shadows along ceramic markers on the ground; these shadows shorten or lengthen with changing seasons. Continuous seasonal change is amplified by shadow patterns on the pylon itself. And at local solar noon, the dark reveal along the pylon edge lights up with a glow. Thus this man-made construction ingeniously engages with the eternal cycles of nature.

BP Pedestrian Bridge FIG. 1118

2004

Frank Gehry, Gehry Partners, architects

E side of Millennium Park, crossing Columbus Dr. at Washington Blvd. Ext., Chicago, Illinois

FIG. 1117 Beyond Astonishing Santiago Calatrava is justly famous for his bridges. Even so, his Sundial Bridge in California radiates an extraordinary physical presence that is only barely suggested in photographs, all the more remarkable in that it is only a footbridge.

As if his Pritzker Pavilion in Millennium Park (see the Late Modernism chapter) wasn't amazing enough, Gehry provided an equally unexpected reprise with this serpentine, metal-sheathed footbridge.

COVERED BRIDGES

If Americans barely acknowledge their bridges, as contended here, the same cannot be said about covered bridges. In sharp contrast, covered bridges are widely revered as rare, treasured links to a vanished past.

Actually, thousands of covered bridges were built coast-to-coast, dozens each in some single counties of Pennsylvania and Ohio. Hundreds remain, nationwide. Most were built in the 1800s. The first scheme for an American covered bridge dates from 1787, intended to span the Schuylkill River at Philadelphia; actual construction, with a new design, began in 1800.

A large majority of American covered bridges were shabby and utilitarian. As noted by covered-bridge authority Richard Sanders Allen, human comfort and safety were not the motivation for covered bridges. Rather, bridges were enclosed to prolong their structural life.

Covered bridges are especially "American" in two respects. One is in their no-nonsense functionality. The other is in their almost endless design innovations. Although outwardly similar, usually sheathed in crude barn planking, they frequently embodied structural innovations and engineering adaptations. The basic Warren truss was augmented with patented variations such as the Howe, Burr, Brown, and Wernwag trusses, various lattice systems, and iron catenaries.

Smith's Bridge

1839; restored, 1955; reconstructed 2002

Smith's Bridge Rd., NE of Granogue, New Castle County, Delaware, spanning Brandywine Creek

Few American covered bridges assert any pretense of style, but here the ends are finished in a Greek Revival motif that would have been very fashionable in 1839. While the bridge was earlier painted white, it is now red, with crisp, white trim.

Montague City Bridge FIG. 1119

1870; reinforced 1901; destroyed by flood, 1936

Spanning the Connecticut River at Montague City, Massachusetts

Smith's Bridge (above), notwithstanding, most American covered bridges were functional in the extreme, without a touch of style. This double-deck bridge accommodated horse-and-buggy traffic on its main platform, and a railroad on the roof. As rail rolling stock grew heavier, additional structure was scabbed on in order to handle the increased loads.

Cabin Run Covered Bridge FIG. 1120

1871

David Sutton, builder

Schlentz Hill Rd., E of Pipersville, Bucks County, Pennsylvania

Both the first (1800) and last (1956) American covered bridges were built in Pennsylvania. This one is architecturally a cut above the covered-bridge norm, with framed openings and stone approach walls.

FIG. 1118 **Extreme Serpentine** Frank Gehry's sinuously winding BP Pedestrian Bridge in Chicago is, like his architecture, unexpected and unique.

FIG. 1119 **Characteristic Lack of Pretense** As is typical for bridges, especially for American covered bridges, the Montague City Bridge in Massachusetts was functional in the extreme. As loads increased, additional structure was scabbed on, resulting in a hybrid (or mongrel, if you are an engineer) of truss- and laminated-arch construction. *Library of Congress, Prints & Photographs, Historic American Buildings Survey*

FIG. 1120 **Straightforward and Satisfying** Cabin Run covered bridge in Pennsylvania is handsome without pretense. It is simple in form, well-built, and gains a pleasant architectonic effect on the inside from its structural latticework. *Library of Congress, Prints & Photographs, Historic American Engineering Record*

Dams

1890–1945

FIG. 1121 Industrial Majesty This view toward Boulder (now Hoover) Dam from beyond a service tower reminds us that dams are industrial structures, first and foremost. Even so, the combination of a striking natural setting, heroic scale, powerful forms, and crisp architectural detailing has resulted here in a functional construction of awesome beauty.

Dams are built for several purposes, including flood control, impounding of water for irrigation and municipal water supplies, and for the generation of electricity (Fig. 1121). Since major dam construction requires a large labor force of relatively unskilled workers, dam projects were espe-cially prominent in the United States during the 1930s, when unemployment was extremely high, and the New Deal sought to create jobs for the unemployed.

An uncountable number of dams has been constructed throughout the United States. Dams range from simple agri-

FIG. 1122 **National Flagship Projects** Muscular structures like the Fort Peck Dam in Montana were widely employed as powerful symbols of progress, and thus of hope, during the depths of the Great Depression. Impressive images were likely to be published as soon as possible. This carefully cropped construction photo made the cover of the nation's leading weekly magazine four years *before* the project was completed. *U.S. Army Corps of Engineers*

cultural weirs and earthen dams, dozens of which might be built and then removed, seasonally, on any single farm, to a few internationally famous dams of significant visual quality, chiefly those built by the TVA in the East, and by the Bureau of Reclamation in the West.

The dams cited in this chapter are among the best-known to the American public for their visual qualities. These structures are highly photogenic and sufficiently heroic in scale to have found their way onto the covers of national magazines like *Life* (Fig. 1122).

New Croton Dam FIG. 1123
1892–1907
Alphonse Fteley, design engineer; **W. R. Hill**, **J. Waldo Smith**, **W. H. Sears**, successive chief engineers.
Rt. 129, 2.5 mi. NE of Croton-on-Hudson, New York

New Croton Dam and its reservoir are part of the New York City water supply system. The dam is often couched in superlatives: at a maximum height of 297 feet, the tallest dam in the world at the time of its construction; more than 2,200 feet long; the second-largest hewn-stone structure in the world after the Great Pyramid, etc.

None of these statistics is necessary to assure New Croton Dam's eminence, since it is exceptional in four respects. One is the dam's sheer visual mass, especially apparent from below. A second is the singular cascading spillway. Third, the handsome granite texture. And fourth, the reservoir itself, encircled by low wooded hills. A roadway leading up alongside the spillway and across the dam,

Croton Dam Road, has been intermittently closed for security purposes since 9/11/2001, but simply passing by below is sufficient to experience the structure's striking presence.

Boulder (Hoover) Dam FIGS. 1121, 1124
1931–1936
Gordon Kaufmann, architect; **John Lucian Savage**, chief engineer; U.S. Bureau of Reclamation staff engineers; **Oskar J. W. Hansen**, sculptor; **Allan True**, artist
U.S. Hwy. 93 at the Nevada-Arizona border, E of Boulder City, Nevada

Boulder Dam offers one of the most striking interrelationships, anywhere, between construction and nature, engineering and art. The nearly sheer, curving, 700-foot face of the dam is wedged within a scenographic setting of rocky hills (Fig. 1121). Topside architectural details are quite handsome (Fig. 1124), if unavoidably trivial within a context of such scale and visual power.

FIG. 1123 **Visual Resourses** Dams can offer more than just utility. New Croton Dam near New York City is an architectural landmark, its splashing spillway an attraction, as is its reservoir lake. *Library of Congress, Prints & Photographs, Historic American Engineering Record*

FIG. 1124 **King of the Colorado** Boulder Dam more than holds its own visually against its rugged natural setting, the exhilaratingly arid moonscape around the Nevada-Arizona border. Visitors experience an extreme range of scale, from the delicate topside sculpture seen here, to the dam's massive face (Fig. 1121).

Norris Dam FIG. 1125

1933–1936

Tennessee Valley Authority, engineers; **Arthur Morgan**, chief TVA engineer; **Roland Wank**, chief TVA architect

Hwy. 441, Norris, Tennessee, 20 mi. NE of Knoxville, Tennessee

Norris Dam was the first Tennessee Valley Authority dam to be built, serving as a model for later TVA facilities. Wank, designer of the Cincinnati rail terminal (see Moderne and Transportation chapters), established the spare Moderne vocabulary which distinguished much of TVA design. Norris Dam is often cited for its austere, functional beauty.

Bonneville Dam FIG. 1126

1933–1937

C. I. Grimm, chief engineer; **H. C. Gerdes**, dam engineer, U.S. Army Corps of Engineers; **D. C. Henny, L. C. Hill**, principal engineering advisors

I-84 exit 40, Multnomah County, Oregon

This Army Corps of Engineers dam in the Pacific Northwest differs in several ways from the other dams in this chapter. Chief among them is its spread-out configuration, required because of a relatively weak rock foundation, and the need to pass large flows of floodwater without a sharp fluctuation in the headwater elevation.

Visually, the dam is much less of an architectural statement than are Wank's TVA dams (preceding and following entries), reflecting functional engineering considerations more than architectural pretense. Ancillary buildings were rendered with a flavor of American Colonial Revival instead of the insistently contemporary Moderne favored by the TVA.

Kentucky Dam FIG. 1127

1938–1944

Arthur Morgan, chief TVA engineer; **Roland Wank**, chief TVA architect

Hwy. 641, SE of Paducah, Kentucky

The immense, highly photogenic traveling gantry cranes (Fig. 1127) atop Kentucky Dam provided a signature design image for the TVA. Visitors traversing the dam walk or drive right beneath these towering machines, which might remind Star Wars buffs of the Walkers at the beginning of "The Empire Strikes Back."

Don't miss the marvelous lake view in the other direction when you drive past, gaping at the cranes!

FIG. 1126 **Functional Engineering** Not all 1930s dams were dramatic architectural statements. Poor underlying soil conditions at the Bonneville Dam site on the Columbia River in Oregon required a spread-out scheme which diluted potential architectural effects. This aerial view shows the powerhouse section (center) separate from spillways (lower right edge), the latter providing the primary visual interest.
Library of Congress, Prints & Photographs, Historic American Engineering Record

FIG. 1127 **Photogenic to the Max** Traveling gantry cranes atop Kentucky Dam near Paducah served as potent visual icons for the TVA, even overshadowing the up-to-date Moderne architecture that was identified with the authority.

Public Engineering

1800–1945

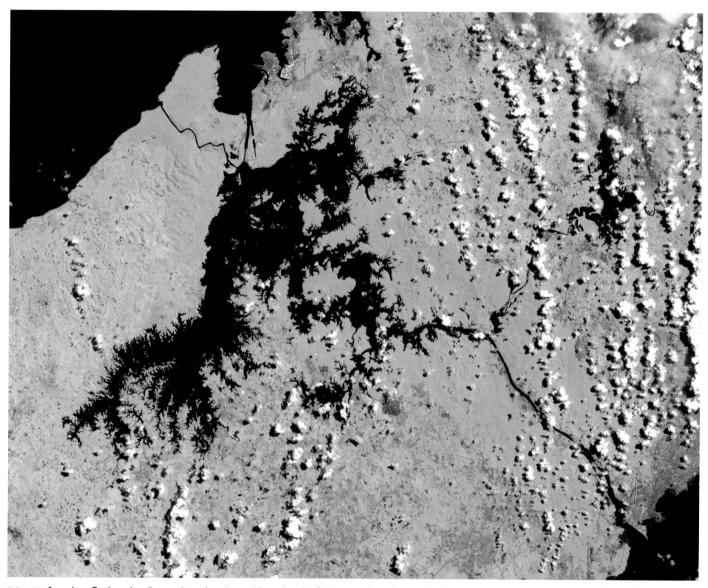

FIG. 1128 American Engineering Extraordinary American public engineering feats include the Panama Canal, seen here is a view from space. The canal extends from the Pacific Ocean at Panama City (light-purple patch at lower right) northwest along the famed Gaillard Cut (thin blue line) into Gatún Lake and then through Limon Bay at Colón (rose-colored peninsula) into the Gulf of Mexico at the top of the image. Local geography places the Gulf end farther west than the Pacific end. *Earth Observatory, NASA*

America is a monumental achievement in numerous respects: as an ongoing political and social experiment, in its varied and vibrant culture, and in its complex physical infrastructure. The extraordinary is almost ordinary for the United States.

Even set within this remarkable context, however, several epic engineering undertakings tower far above national norms. These public engineering projects are often closely identified with charismatic advocates who, through personal vision and sheer force of will, accomplished the seemingly impossible. As both demonstrations and inspirations, these projects have transformed American society.

The post–World War II U.S. interstate highway system is the most expansive and influential of American public engineering achievements. That program is cited in the Roads chapter.

Erie Canal FIGS. 1129, 1130, 1131

1817–1825; subsequent improvements and recent upgrading

Elkanah Watson, visionary; **De Witt Clinton**, proponent and Governor; **Benjamin Wright, James Geddes, Charles Broadhead**, district administrators; **Nathan Roberts**, chief engineer

Connecting the Hudson River near Albany, New York, to Lake Erie near Buffalo, 340 mi.

FIGS. 1129, 1130, 1131 **Human Scale in Public Engineering** Prominent national projects like the Erie Canal, illustrated by an aerial photograph at Lockport (Fig. 1129), near the canal's western end, are not necessarily overwhelming as experienced. Indeed, the accompanying views of a long-abandoned Erie Canal lock (Fig. 1130) and viaduct (Fig. 1131) illustrate the generally intimate scale of what was, at completion, the major commercial transportation route to the American interior. *Library of Congress, Prints & Photographs, Historic American Engineering Record*

Watson's visionary canal concept was inspired by Dutch canals he had visited in the early 1780s. In 1806, he made a canal presentation to President Jefferson, who pronounced it a "splendid" project, one that might be possible to carry out about a century hence. This polite rejection did not apparently discourage Watson, who continued to promote the idea of the canal. By 1815, Watson had won over Clinton, who ran for Governor of New York in 1817 partly in order to build it.

Even today the canal would be a substantial engineering challenge, requiring 82 locks with a total lift of 690 feet. The canal was about 40 feet wide by 4 feet deep, and the route also employed a stretch of the Mohawk River.

Despite the Erie Canal's success, the American canal era was brief. By the mid-1800s, railroads had supplanted water as the preferred long-distance mode for passengers and freight. Nevertheless, the Erie Canal opened up New York State to development. It also "sharply accelerated the growth of the Upper Midwest," according to historian Walter McDougall, directly contributing to the ensuing dominance of Chicago as the nation's major mid-continent transportation hub (see National Expansion chapter).

While parts of the canal have fallen into a degree of disrepair (Figs. 1130, 1131), it is handsomely restored at Pittsford, and portions are functioning across the state as parts of the New York State Barge Canal System. If you are in the vicinity of Buffalo–Niagara Falls, be sure to see the canal, including functioning locks, in nearby Lockport (Fig. 1129).

Transcontinental Railroads FIGS. 1132, 1133, 1134

1829–1916

Robert L. Stevens and others, innovators; **James J. Hill, Edward H. Harriman, and others**, entrepreneurs

Railways evolved rapidly in the early 1800s, initially in England. At first, railways were considered to be an industrial conveyance, combining the traditional horse-drawn rail wagon with the modern steam locomotive invented by George Stephenson in 1814. The world's first steam-powered passenger train, also by Stephenson, began service in 1825. This "railroad" concept was a sensation, soon to be adopted outside of England.

The first American railway, initially a horse-drawn line, was organized in 1827 as the Baltimore & Ohio Railroad. The first American train ran only two years later, in 1829, and U.S. rail building soon took off. By 1850, 9,000 route-miles were in operation, and as Freeman Allen noted, in the 1850s "Americans were laying down as much new track as the rest of the world combined."

The 1869 completion of a transcontinental connection was one of the great national achievements of the nineteenth century, symbolically and functionally (Fig. 1133). At peak length in 1916, just as highways began to supplant rail, nearly 250,000 route-miles were in operation within the United States.

Panama Canal FIGS. 1128, 1135

1904–1914

George W. Goethals, chief engineer, U.S. Army Corps of Engineers; **William Gorgas**, U.S. Army medical officer

Previous attempts by the French to build a canal across the Panamanian isthmus had been defeated by terrain, climate, disease, and a lack of labor. However, after the Spanish-American War of 1898 and the consequent rise of an American global presence, a newly pressing need for efficient naval mobility led the United States to undertake construction of a cross-isthmus canal.

A 40-mile sequence of locks, channels, and artificial lakes raises and lowers ships by 85 feet. Endless construction superlatives, like

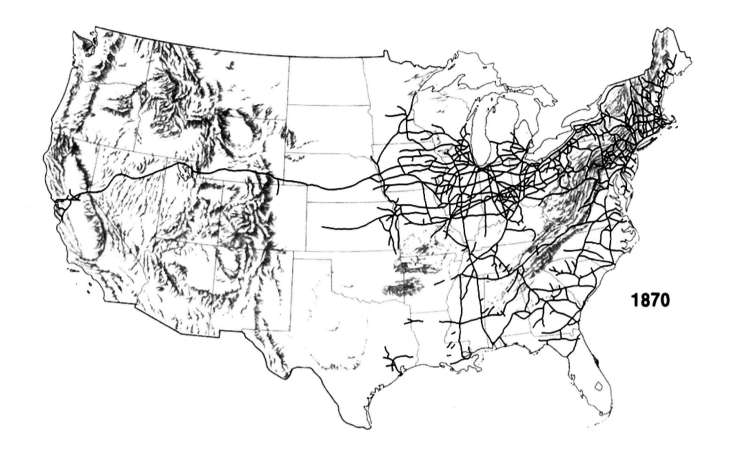

1870

FIGS. 1132, 1133 Linking the Nation Completion of the first transcontinental rail line in 1869 (Fig. 1132) was a momentous event in American history. The achievement was memorialized in a famous Harper's magazine engraving depicting the ceremony when the symbolic final "golden" spike was driven at Promontory Summit in the (then) Utah Territory (Fig. 1133). *Library of Congress, Prints & Photographs*

FIG. 1134 Railroads Shaped National Developoment In the American Midwest and West, rail-line alignment was a life-or-death matter for the success of nineteenth-century settlements. Where no settlements existed within a planned rail corridor, railroads would build refueling stations at regular intervals determined by the water requirements of steam engines. These sites commonly developed into towns. This railroad-determined settlement pattern is still apparent in the communities that line up across southern Wyoming along the later routes of the Lincoln Highway and I-80. The railroad-built Rock Creek station (Fig. 1134) was the equivalent of today's highway truck stop, with the all-important water tower surrounded by a bunk house and a general store. *Library of Congress, Prints & Photographs, Historic American Buildings Survey*

FIG. 1135 Monumental Undertaking An epic feat of organization, engineering, and construction, the Panama Canal linked two oceans across a torrid, pestilential jungle (Fig. 1128). As can be appreciated from this period photo, canal construction required staggering effort. *Library of Congress, Prints & Photographs*

250 million cubic yards of excavation (Fig. 1135) and building the world's largest locks and dam, and the success of Gorgas in eradicating tropical diseases, or at least keeping sufficiently at bay, rank as monumental achievements.

Tennessee Valley Authority, "TVA" FIG. 1136
1932–1941 ff.
George Norris, Senate sponsor; **Arthur Morgan**, chief TVA engineer; **Roland Wank**, chief TVA architect; **Earle Draper**, head of TVA regional planning
Tennessee River Valley, especially in Tennessee, Alabama, and Kentucky

TVA was intended to transform the rural Tennessee River Valley: to provide renewable water power and flood control through a series of dams; to encourage new industry; and to expand public recreation, especially on reservoir lakes created by the dams. (See also Norris and Kentucky Dam entries, Dams chapter.)

As a massive governmental program it was unavoidably controversial, but TVA did effect a radical transformation of its largely rural domain, just as intended. Wank's signature Moderne designs established TVA projects as design-oriented and up-to-date. The confident, relentless sense of progress projected by the TVA in the 1930s was an especially important symbol of hope for millions of Americans trapped in the Great Depression.

The Pentagon FIG. 1137
1941–1943; renovated, 1997–2002; partly rebuilt, 2001–2002
U.S. Army: **Brehon B. Somervell,** chief of construction; **Hugh J. Casey**, chief of design, **George Edwin Bergstrom**, chief architect (initial); **David J. Witmer**, chief architect (completion); **Robert D. Farquhar, Pierpont Davis**, architects
Jefferson Davis Hwy. at I-395, Arlington, Virginia

Development of the Pentagon was unprecedented in three respects. First, with a program of five million square feet, with offices for 40,000 people, it was the largest building in the world (as built, the Pentagon enclosed 6.24 million square feet). Second, the basic design concept, for a program which was itself without any real precedent, was devised over a single weekend. Third, initial occupancy occurred just eight months after the start of construction. Built to accommodate the burgeoning staff of the U.S. War Department, it is now the headquarters of the Department of Defense.

Despite major change orders, including adding a fifth floor after construction was well underway, the entire project was fully completed 17 months after groundbreaking. Fifteen thousand workers on around-the-clock shifts were effectively organized and supervised. The building was constructed in five sections in order to speed occupancy.

In an impressive symbolic reprise, the section damaged by 9/11/2001 terrorists was completely rebuilt in less than one year.

Manhattan Project FIG. 1138
1942–1945
Leslie R. Groves, head of the Manhattan Project; **Willard C. Krueger Associates**, architects-engineers for Los Alamos; **Stone & Webster**, industrial planner, **Skidmore, Owings & Merrill**, community planner for Oak Ridge; **E. I. Du Pont de Nemours Co.**, designer-builder of the Hanford facilities
Los Alamos, New Mexico; Oak Ridge, Tennessee; Hanford (Richland vic.), Washington

The vision, leadership, political skills, and administrative abilities of General Groves dwarfed even the monumental career accomplishments of Robert Moses (see Roads chapter). For the Manhattan Project, an entire infrastructure of plants, new towns (Fig. 1138), and top-secret sites had to be developed overnight in order to support the highest-priority development of the atom bomb.

Groves's biographer Robert Norris observed that for the vast effort to succeed, Groves "planned the project, ran his own construction, his own science, his own army, his own State Department and his own Treasury Department."

The procedures and practices developed for the Manhattan Project not only probably shortened World War II, but also led directly to the postwar military-industrial complex and the national-security state. Among many engineering innovations, development of the Hanford site demonstrated the value of Critical Path (CPM) construction scheduling for very complex, large-scale, time-sensitive facilities.

FIG. 1136 A Relentless Sense of Progress The Tennessee Valley Authority consummately nurtured the support of citizens, rarely failing to suggest that since the TVA was chartered by Congress, its actions were in the public good, "because TVA is owned by the public." The photo shows a group tour at Norris Dam (Fig. 1125), a centerpiece of TVA's charter to transform the Tennessee Valley. *Library of Congress, Prints & Photographs*

FIG. 1137 A Wonder of Construction At the time of its construction the largest building in the world, the Pentagon in Arlington, Virginia, was conceptually designed over a weekend and constructed at extraordinary speed to meet war-time demands. *U.S. Department of Defense, ARPA*

FIG. 1138 The Look of Efficiency Oak Ridge in Tennessee was built almost literally overnight to accommodate Manhattan Project engineering. Planning necessarily emphasized clarity and utility. Houses and dormitories, shown here, were functional in the extreme.

Postscript

2004

FIG. 1139 The Modern Is Still Modern This view toward Manhattan's Museum of Modern Art Sculpture Garden was taken just after MoMA reopened in 2004. *Photograph © Timothy Hursley*

The year 2004 offered a convenient ending for this survey. The big story in American architecture for 2004, if not as apparent in the related fields encompassed in this book, was a return to Modernism.

Three prominent landmarks signaled a powerful resurgence of Modernism, similar to the landmarks marking the architectural profession's swerve toward Postmodernism three decades earlier (see Postmodernism chapter).

The first of these, chronologically, was the annual April Record Houses issue in the leading national architectural periodical, *Architectural Record*. Had one just awakened from a 30-

year, Rip van Winkle slumber, she or he would never have suspected from reading the Record Houses section that Postmodernism had ever occurred in the United States.

Seemingly meant to drive home this point beyond any doubt, the issue began with a short feature about radical alterations to a picturesque little bungalow in the German countryside. Undertaken by the once–New Brutalist architect Peter Smithson, the resulting Modernist overbuilding was praised by Record as reflecting "unremitting rigor, honesty, and puritanical expressions of materials, structure, and function." So much, it would seem, for architectural Postmodernism, and for related passing planning fashions like New Urbanism!

The expanded and refined Museum of Modern Art in New York City (see Neomodernism chapter; galleries reopened in 2004, an education building in 2006) provided a second potent symbol of Modernism's resurgence in the United States (Fig. 1139). MoMA is the high temple of American visual Modernism, located in America's cultural epicenter, Manhattan. Hence, the project's accolades amount to an establishment imprimatur for Modernist architecture.

In addition, MoMA demonstrates that modern architecture can enhance urbanism, specifically in terms of its potential compatibility with adjacent historic fabric. Architect Yoshio Taniguchi carefully stitched together his site, encompassing existing buildings, creating spaces, capturing views, while celebrating human movement. His accomplishment deflates arguments by those who insist that historic preservation requires that new buildings be rendered as deferential cartoons of old styles.

The William J. Clinton Presidential Center (Fig. 1140) in Little Rock, Arkansas (2001-2004; Polshek Partnership, architects; Leslie E. Robertson, structural engineer; Hargreaves Associates, landscape architects) provided a third 2004 symbolic milestone in the resurgence of Modernism in American architecture.

Clinton was the first American president since Franklin D. Roosevelt with an informed interest in architecture. He chose the Polshek office largely on the basis of its design for the Rose Center for Earth and Space (2000) at the American Museum of National History in Manhattan. As a Rhodes scholar at Oxford, Clinton was well aware of the glories of traditional architecture. So his knowing embrace of Modernism, and his insistence that the Center be "an environmentally responsible building," was especially significant.

How much are we to make of this apparent Return of Modernism to the forefront of American architecture? After all, pre-dictions of the future are as unreliable as they are irresistible to make.

Even so, a re-emphasis on Modernism should not be surprising. American architecture follows a continuous ebb-and-flow, closely mirroring the cycles of American society. In the past, when Americans sensed that their contemporary society was out of balance, as it has been over the past two decades, many looked back to "better times," to an imagined Golden Age, for reassurance. This social nostalgia was inevitably reflected in a flourishing of historic architectural styles, like the Romantic Revivals of the nineteenth century and the Period Revivals of the twentieth.

In sharp contrast, during eras marked by either crisis or confidence, Americans have tended to look forward. Of course, the stimulus for looking forward differed between crisis and confidence eras. Modern design expressions have become especially prominent at such times.

Today, the apparent resurgence in Modernism seems more like an echo of dissatisfaction. This is not the bold, inventive, making-the-world-better, everyday Modernism of the 1950s, but rather an elite artistic critique from outside the American mainstream, similar to the International Style Modernism of the 1920s. Indeed, as in the 1920s, much of today's Modernist design leadership comes from Europeans, and now also from leading Japanese architects, who did not discard modern principles in the late twentieth century.

If the past is indeed prologue, Modernism will once again flourish in the United States, colored by the time-honored American qualities of locality, innovation, and common sense. In whatever forms modern design takes in the future, built America will surely continue to offer a landscape of remarkable variety and vivid interest.

FIG. 1140 **A Resurgence of Modernism** The William J. Clinton Presidential Center in Little Rock dramatically symbolizes the recent revival of modernist architectural design in the United States. *Photograph © Timothy Hursley*

Acknowledgments

Friends sometimes ask, "How did you ever find out about all of these places?" Good question. I suppose the simple answer, surely true for all of us, is that when you are interested in something, you'll naturally pick up on references to that something, wherever and whenever they occur.

Even so, a survey like this especially relies on three kinds of sources. Books are an important resource; as you can imagine for an appraisal on this scale, hundreds of books. Publications which are particularly relevant to any given chapter are cited in Sources by Chapter. My sincere thanks to all of these outstanding authors. And my endless gratitude to the Hennepin County Library, especially to its resourceful Edina Branch librarians.

Field visits are another indispensable source. Although I haven't (yet!) visited every site included in this book, I've been to more than ninety percent of them at least once, and to thousands of others that were not included. Like the old saw about "practice makes perfect," the more environments that you consciously experience, the better the feel you'll have for all structures, sites, and landscapes. If something in this book really appeals to you, almost certainly you'll enjoy it even more in person. Be sure to take that as a hint.

Insights of teachers and colleagues are a third essential source. Among many esteemed teachers at the University of Minnesota, John R. Borchert, Frederick Koeper, John Sterling Myers, Donald Torbert, Dimitri Tselos, and George Winterowd introduced me to built America.

Among scores of stimulating colleagues, several have especially influenced my views about what has been built in the United States. Within days of college graduation, I was taken under the collective wings of Charles H. Atherton and Donald B. Myer at the U. S. Commission of Fine Arts; James C. Massey, Russell Keune, and John Poppeliers of the Historic American Buildings Survey; and J. P. Noffsinger of the University of Kentucky. Fondly looking back, I realize that this book really began during that formative summer in Washington, D.C.

Over the ensuing four decades, I have benefited beyond measure from the scholarship and insights of many. I especially wish to acknowledge Marc Treib and Spiro Kostof of the University of California, Berkeley; Carol Herselle Krinsky of New York University; Robert Winter of Occidental College; and Eileen Manning Michels of the University of St. Thomas.

Numerous practitioner-colleagues have offered perceptive critiques about our built environment, in particular, Catherine R. Brown, Sean Chiao, Michael Cronin, Dorothée Imbert, Malcolm Holzman, Charles W. Moore, William Morrish, Denise Scott Brown, Douglas Suisman, Vernon D. Swaback, Ronald L. Tulis, Robert Venturi, and John M. Woodbridge.

David Gebhard of the University of California, Santa Barbara, has been the greatest influence of all. Over more than two inspiring decades, David and I traveled to the far corners of America, looking at everything from Indian mounds to skyscrapers. David's achievements as a teacher, mentor, researcher, author, lecturer, preservationist, and civic visionary set a very high benchmark for all who knew him.

Many people helped this book through their arrangements, information, and support. My deepest gratitude to Arthur Andersson, Martha Andresen, Diana Apalategui, Nicole Apple, Ryan Apple, Hilda Bakke, Martine Bellen, Liz Bentley, Anne Blecksmith, Jessica Blum, Russ Bodnar, Bronwyn Griffith Brommare, Dixi Carrillo, Kate Christianson, Christine Cordazzo, Jim Cox, Wendy Cox, Regina Curtis, Walter Declerck, Hoyt Fields, Tom Fox, Diane Dodson Galt, Scott Gillson, Patricia Gebhard, and Anne Giffen.

Also, to Allan Greenberg, David Griffith, Katherine Griffith, Kathy Gustafson, George Hansen, Keri Hansen, John C. Harkness, Beverly Hart, Ryan Hewson, Arlene Hicks, Tim Hursley, Rachel Jacobson, Dave Jonah, Christine Kelley, Pat Kennedy, Julie Lally, Andrea Landsman, Paul A. Latham, Faye LeDoux, Ken LeDoux, Peter Leyden, Frank Edgerton Martin, Ryan Martin, and Lynn Martinson.

And to Bryan McDaniel, Brad Minor, Barbara Mitchell, Dale Mulfinger, Karyn Osterman, Jacqueline Pidlubny, Alfred Pinot, Mike Plotnick, Susan Raposa, Stacey Ray, Gary Schuster, Mohammad Shafi, Rhonda Winchell Sharp, John P. Sheehy, Julio Sims, Keith W. Stokes, Erica Stoller, Ellen Thompson, James van Sweden, Alex Vertikoff, Jean Vitale, Elaine Walker, Lena Watanabe, Jeff Whetzel, Richard Wills, Alexa Griffith Winton, and Carol Wyllie.

While I'd love to take credit for *The Atlas of American Architecture*, what you hold in your hands is really the work of five gifted creators. Based on a few pages of manuscript and a handful of images, David Morton of Rizzoli envisioned this book. When several boxes containing the full text and all of the images arrived at Rizzoli, Douglas Curran organized everything into sufficient order so that editing and production could begin, and provided continuing technical assurance. Rizzoli's publisher, Charles Miers, encouraged enhancements to what was already a splendid design.

Abigail Sturges not only had to interrelate hundreds of pages of texts, entries, and captions with more than 1,100 images, but necessarily invented a graphic format for my hybrid guide. John Morris Dixon edited and managed *The Atlas of American Architecture* with such sensitivity, thoroughness, and knowledge that I was constantly both grateful and humbled. If you enjoyed this book, these are the people to thank.

My wife, Joyce, inspired this book, encouraged my research, spent countless hours on the road visiting obscure sites when she would rather have been birding, worked up graphics, and photoshopped 2,000 images—all the while never missing a beat in our everyday life. Amazing. As usual.

Illustrations

I still recall the 1969 Aspen Design Conference. Its theme was "The Rest of Our Lives," with a focus on the future. One of the presentations, by Hudson Institute president Tony Wiener, got right into imagining how our lives might be different in the distant future—like the 1990s.

Among his way-out scenarios, some of which turned out to be uncannily accurate, I remember Wiener predicting that geography would be much less of a barrier, that people living in, say, Montana would be able to research the Library of Congress from their homes. "Terrific, if unlikely," I thought. But if you change Montana to Minnesota, that is just how this book became possible.

We all know that the Library of Congress is unmatched as source of American documents. Its Prints and Photographs division contains millions of images. While library staff is invariably efficient and helpful, there was always the practical problem of identifying which images were available. And even when you knew an image and its code, if you needed the hundreds of LOC images you've seen here, despite the Library's modest charges, prints would cost tens of thousands of dollars.

Everything changed with Internet access and downloads. For the price of one's time and a few sparks of electricity, anyone—worldwide—can now conveniently review any of millions LOC documents, easily downloading selected ones.

That efficiently opens the priceless photo and drawing archives of the Historic American Buildings Survey and the Historic American Engineering Record of the Interior Department's National Park Service. The address to get you into Prints and Photographs is www.loc.gov/rr/print/catalog.html. HABS and HAER are located alphabetically down the menu of collections. Specifically, the link provides access to thousands of additional illustrations of *The Atlas of American Architecture* entries—plans, sections, interiors, and much more—that we could not include in this book for practical reasons.

Other excellent sources are also available. The University of Texas Libraries offers downloading of its historical maps at www.lib.utexas.edu/maps/historical. The Society of Architectural Historians provides an index of download resources at www.sah.org/netresources.html. And Google Images ® sources images located outside of the Library of Congress.

The rest of the illustrations you've seen come primarily from three other sources. One of these is images licensed from professional photographers. Also, several design professionals/practices have provided images of their work, at my request. Both of these sources are identified in the captions. Finally, many of the photos were taken over the years by me.

Alas, few graphic images are technically perfect. So I cannot overemphasize the value of Adobe Photoshop ® as orchestrated by my wife, Joyce. Most of the illustrations in this book have been Photoshop-improved, sometimes markedly. I hope you've enjoyed them.

Sources by Chapter

ABORIGINAL CULTURES
Spencer Wells, *The Journey of Man*, 2002; James Shreeve, "The Greatest Journey," *National Geographic*, March, 2006; Michael D. Lemonick and Andrea Dorfman, "Who Were the First Americans?" *Time*, March 13, 2006, pp. 44-52; Charles C. Mann, *1491: New Revelations of the Americas Before Columbus*, 2005; Francis Jennings, *The Founders of America*, 1993; Maria Longhena, *Ancient Mexico: The History and Culture of the Maya, Aztecs, and Other Pre-Columbian Peoples*, 1998; Janine M. Benyus, Biomimicry (Chapter 2), 1997, 2002; Marko Pogačnik, *Nature Spirits and Elemental Beings*, 1995, 1996; Béatrice Caseau, "Sacred Landscapes," in G. W. Bowersock, Peter Brown, and Oleg Grabar, eds., *Late Antiquity: A Guide to the Postclassical World*, 1999; Earl H. Swanson, *The Ancient Americas*, 1989; Frank Waters, *Book of the Hopi*, 1963; National Park Service, "Mesa Verde," 2005; the PBS TV program, "The Mystery of Chaco Canyon," 1999; Brian Fagan, "Chaco Canyon," 2005; National Park Service, "Chaco Culture," 2004; Miriam Horn, "Where the Moon Stood Still, And the Ancients Watched [Chimney Rock]," *The New York Times*, September 29, 2006, p. D1; Jon L. Gibson, Poverty Point, 1999; National Park Service, "Hopewell Culture," 2001; Karen Kingsley, *Buildings of Louisiana*, 2003; City of Phoenix Parks and Recreation Department, Archaeology Section; and the Historic American Buildings Survey

INDIGENOUS CULTURES
Marc Treib, *Sanctuaries of Spanish New Mexico*, 1993; Bainbridge Bunting, *Early Architecture in New Mexico*, 1976; Francis Jennings, *The Founders of America*, 1993; Charles C. Mann, *1491: New Revelations of the Americas Before Columbus*, 2005; Gerald McMaster and Clifford E. Trafzer, eds., *Native Universe*, 2004; Clinton A. Weslager, *The Log Cabin in America*, 1969; G. E. Kidder Smith, *Source Book of American Architecture*, 1996; and the Historic American Buildings Survey

SPANISH COLONIAL ARCHITECTURE
Hugh Morrison, *Early American Architecture*, 1952; Marc Treib, *Sanctuaries of Spanish New Mexico*, 1993; George Kubler, *The Religious Architecture of New Mexico* (1940), 1972; National Park Service pamphlet, "San Antonio Missions," 1998; David Gebhard and Robert Winter, *A Guide to Architecture in Los Angeles and Southern California*, 1977; David Gebhard et. al., *A Guide to Architecture in San Francisco and Northern California*, 1985; Edward Deakin, *The Missions of California*, 1902; G. E. Kidder Smith, *Source Book of American Architecture*, 1996; Manuel Toussaint, Elizabeth Wilder Weisman, trans., *Colonial Art in Mexico*, 1967; Hugh Thomas, *Rivers of Gold*, 2003; and the Historic American Buildings Survey

FRENCH COLONIAL ARCHITECTURE
Hugh Morrison, *Early American Architecture*, 1952; Karen Kingsley, *Buildings of Louisiana*, 2003; G. E. Kidder Smith, *Source Book of American Architecture*, 1996; David Gebhard and Tom Martinson, *A Guide to the Architecture of Minnesota*, 1977; and the Historic American Buildings Survey

SOUTHERN COLONIAL ARCHITECTURE
Hugh Morrison, *Early American Architecture*, 1952; William Pierson, *American Building and Their Architects*, 1976; Richard Bushman, *The Refinement of America*, 1992; Marcus Whiffen and Frederick Koeper, *American Architecture 1607–1976*, 1981; G. E. Kidder Smith, *Source Book of American Architecture*, 1996; William B. O'Neal, *Architecture in Virginia*, 1968; Richard Guy Wilson, ed., *Buildings of Virginia*, 2002; Allan Greenberg, *George Washington Architect*, 1999; Allan Greenberg, *The Architecture of Democracy*, 2006; and the Historic American Buildings Survey

NEW ENGLAND COLONIAL ARCHITECTURE
Hugh Morrison, *Early American Architecture*, 1952; William H. Pierson, Jr., *American Buildings and Their Architects: The Colonial and Neo-Classical Styles*, 1976; Antoinette F. Downing and Vincent J. Scully, Jr., *The Architectural Heritage of Newport Rhode Island* (1952), 1967; William H. Jordy, et. al., *Buildings of Rhode Island*, 2004; Stanley Schuler, *Saltbox and Cape Cod Houses*, 1988; G. E. Kidder Smith, *Source Book of American Architecture*, 1996; and the Historic American Buildings Survey

MID-ATLANTIC COLONIAL ARCHITECTURE
Hugh Morrison, *Early American Architecture*, 1952; William H. Pierson, Jr., *American Building and Their Architects: The Colonial and Neo-Classical Styles*, 1976; G. E. Kidder Smith, *Source Book of American Architecture*, 1996; Russell Shorto, *The Island in the Center of the World*, 2004; and the Historic American Buildings Survey

NEOCLASSICISM
William H. Pierson, Jr., *American Buildings and their Architects: The Colonial and Neo-Classical Styles*, 1976; Talbot Hamlin, *Greek Revival Architecture in America*, 1944; Allan Greenberg, *The Architecture of Democracy*, 2006; Hugh Howard, *Thomas Jefferson, Architect*, 2003; William B. O'Neal, *Architecture in Virginia*, 1968; Garry Wills, *Mr. Jefferson's University*, 2002; Edward Teitelman and Richard W. Longstreth, *Architecture in Philadelphia: A Guide*, 1974; Wayne Andrews, *Architecture in Michigan*, 1967; Kathryn Bishop Eckert, *Buildings of Michigan*, 1993; Karen Kingsley, *Buildings of Louisiana*, 2003; David Gebhard and Gerald Mansheim, *Buildings of Iowa*, 1993; John Summerson, *Architecture in Britain 1530–1830* (1953), 1977; G. E. Kidder Smith, *Source Book of American Architecture*, 1996; and the Historic American Buildings Survey

ROMANTIC REVIVALS AND ECLECTICISM
William H. Pierson, Jr., *American Architects and Their Buildings: The Corporate and Early Gothic Styles*, 1980; G. E. Kidder Smith, *Source Book of American Architecture*, 1996; Kathleen Mahoney, *Gothic Style*, 1995; Henry Winthrop Sargent, [Downing's] *Landscape Gardening*, 1859; Wayne Andrews, *Architecture in Michigan*, 1967; David Gebhard and Gerald Mansheim, *Buildings of Iowa*, 1993; Kathryn Bishop Eckert, *Buildings of Michigan*, 1993; Richard Carrot, *The Egyptian Revival*, 1978; Pamela Scott and Antoinette J. Lee, *Buildings of the District of Columbia*, 1993; Richard Guy Wilson, ed., *Buildings of Virginia*, 2002; James F. O'Gorman, *The Architecture of Frank Furness*, 1973; David Gebhard, Eric Sandweiss, and Robert Winter, *A Guide to Architecture in San Francisco and Northern California*, 1985; Wayne Andrews, *Architecture in Michigan*, 1982; Rosalind L. Clark, *Architecture Oregon Style*, 1983; Charles L. Eastlake, *Hints on Household Taste in Furniture, Upholstery & Other Details*, 1872; and the Historic American Buildings Survey

VICTORIAN GOTHIC
Kathleen Mahoney, *Gothic Style*, 1995; Robert Furneaux Jordan, *Victorian Architecture*, 1966; John Steegman, *Victorian Taste* (1950), 1970; Calder Loth and Julius Trousdale Sadler, Jr., *The Only Proper Style*, 1975; Jeffrey I. Richman, *Brooklyn's Green-Wood Cemetery*, 1993; Norval White and Elliot Willensky, *AIA Guide to New York City*, 1978; Robert A. M. Stern, Thomas Mellins, and David Fishman, *New York 1880*, 1999; Jorg Brockmann and Bill Harris, *One Thousand New York Buildings*, 2002; Pamela Scott and Antoinette J. Lee, *Buildings of the District of Columbia*, 1993; G. E. Kidder Smith, *Source Book of American Architecture*, 1996; and the Historic American Buildings Survey

BEAUX ARTS
Arthur Drexler, ed., *The Architecture of the Ecole Des Beaux Arts*, 1977; Paul R. Baker, Richard Morris Hunt, 1980; Samuel G. White, *The Houses of McKim, Mead & White*, 1998; Richard Guy Wilson, *McKim, Mead & White Architects*, 1983; Antoinette F. Downing and Vincent J. Scully, Jr., *The Architectural Heritage of Newport Rhode Island* (1952), 1967; Steven McLeod Bedford, *John Russell Pope*, 1998; Barbara S. Christen and Steven Flanders, eds., *Cass Gilbert, Life and Work*, 2001; David Gebhard and Tom Martinson, *A Guide to the Architecture of Minnesota*, 1977; Pamela Scott and Antoinette J. Lee, *Buildings of the District of Columbia*, 1993; Robert A. M. Stern, Thomas Mellins, and David Fishman, *New York 1880*, 1999; Sue A. Kohler, *The Commission of Fine Arts: A Brief History, 1910–1995*, 1996; G. E. Kidder Smith, *Source Book of American Architecture*, 1996; and the Historic American Buildings Survey

AMERICAN COLONIAL REVIVALS
William B. Rhoads, *The Colonial Revival* (1974), 1977; Alan Axelrod, ed., *The Colonial Revival in America*, 1985, esp. William Butler, "Another City

upon a Hill: Litchfield Connecticut and the Colonial Revival," Charles B. Hosmer, Jr., "The Colonial Revival in the Public Eye: Williamsburg and Early Garden Restorations," and Catherine M. Howett, "A Georgian Renascence in Georgia: The Residential Architecture of Neel Reed"; David Gebhard, "The American Colonial Revival in the 1930s, *Winterthur Portfolio*, Summer/Autumn 1987; David Gebhard, "Royal Barry Wills and the American Colonial Revival, *Winterthur Portfolio*, Spring, 1992; Royal Barry Wills, *Houses for Good Living*, 1940; Royal Barry Wills, *Living on the Level*, 1955; Richard Guy Wilson, *The Colonial Revival House*, 2004; Steven McLeod Bedford, *John Russell Pope*, 1998; Mac Griswold and Eleanor Weller, *The Golden Age of American Gardens*, 1991; Samuel G. White, *The Houses of McKim, Mead & White*, 1998; Richard Guy Wilson, *McKim, Mead & White Architects*, 1983; Antoinette F. Downing and Vincent J. Scully, Jr., *The Architectural Heritage of Newport, Rhode Island* (1952), 1967; David Gebhard and Tom Martinson, *A Guide to the Architecture of Minnesota*, 1977; David Gebhard, Robert Sandweiss, and Robert Winter, *Architecture in San Francisco and Northern California*, 1985; Clive Aslet, *The American Country House*, 1990; Robert B. MacKay, Anthony K. Baker, and Carol A. Traynor, *Long Island Country Houses and the Architects, 1860–1940*, 1997; David Gebhard and Gerald Mansheim, *Buildings of Iowa*, 1993; Herb Andree and Noel Young, *Santa Barbara Architecture*, 1980; David Gebhard and Robert Winter, *Architecture in Los Angeles*, 1985; David Gebhard and Robert Winter, *A Guide to the Architecture of Los Angeles & Southern California*, 1977; Paul C. Johnson, *Western Ranch Houses by Cliff May*, 1958; Alan Hess, *The Ranch House*, 2004; Montgomery Schuyler, "A History of Old Colonial Architecture," Architectural Record, January-March, 1895; and the Historic American Buildings Survey

PROGRESSIVES

James F. O'Gorman, *The Architecture of Frank Furness*, 1973; George E. Thomas, Michael J. Lewis and Jeffrey A Cohen, *Frank Furness*, 1996; Michael Lewis, *Frank Furness: Architect and the Violent Mind*, 2001; Jeffrey Karl Ochsner, *H. H. Richardson*, 1982; Eileen Manning Michels, *Reconfiguring Harvey Ellis*, 2004; David Gebhard, Robert Winter and Eric Sandweiss, *A Guide to Architecture in San Francisco and Northern California*, 1985; Sally B. Woodbridge, John M. Woodbridge, and Chuck Byrne, *San Francisco Architecture*, 2005; David Gebhard and Gerald Mansheim, Buildings of Iowa, 1993; Robert Twombly, *Louis Sullivan*, 1986; G. E. Kidder Smith, *Source Book of American Architecture*, 1996; and Kenneth Frampton, *Modern Architecture 1851–1945*, 1983

THE CHICAGO SCHOOL

Kenneth Frampton, *Modern Architecture*, 1851–1945, 1983; and Oswald W. Grube, Peter C. Pran, Franz Schulze, *100 Years of Architecture in Chicago*, 1973; Katherine Solomonson, *The Chicago Tribune Competition*, 2001; and Nicholas Adams, *Skidmore, Owings & Merrill: SOM Since 1936*, 2006

FRANK LLOYD WRIGHT

William Allin Storrer, *The Architecture of Frank Lloyd Wright*, 2002; Neil Levine, *The Architecture of Frank Lloyd Wright*, 1996; Henry Russell Hitchcock, *In the Nature of Materials*, 1941; Grant Carpenter Manson, *Frank Lloyd Wright to 1910*,1958; John Sergeant, *Frank Lloyd Wright's Usonian Houses*, 1976; Franklin Toker, *Fallingwater Rising*, 2003; Ada Louise Huxtable, *Frank Lloyd Wright*, 2004; David Gebhard and Robert Winter, *Architecture in Los Angeles & Southern California*, 1977; David Gebhard and Tom Martinson, *A Guide to the Architecture of Minnesota*, 1977; David Gebhard, Eric Sandweiss, and Robert Winter, *A Guide to Architecture in San Francisco and Northern California*, 1985; David Gebhard and Gerald Mansheim, *Buildings of Iowa*, 1993; and the Historic American Buildings Survey

PRAIRIE SCHOOL

Many of the insights in this chapter are based on numerous discussions with William Purcell's biographer and confidant, David Gebhard. Also: H. Allen Brooks, *The Prairie School*, 1972; Mati Maldre and Paul Kruty, *Walter Burley Griffin in America*, 1996; David Gebhard and Tom Martinson, *A Guide to the Architecture of Minnesota*, 1977; David Gebhard and Gerald Mansheim, *Buildings of Iowa*, 1993; David Gebhard, *Charles F. A. Voysey Architect*, 1975; and Mark Hammons' Prairie website, www.organica.org

CRAFTSMAN

Robert Winter and Alexander Vertikoff, *Craftsman Style*, 2004; Robert Winter and Alexander Vertikoff, *American Bungalow Style*, 1996; Robert Winter, *The California Bungalow*, 1980; Adrian Tinniswood, *The Arts &*

Crafts House, 1999; Randell L. Makinson, *Greene & Greene*, 1977; David Gebhard and Robert Winter, *Los Angeles, An Architectural Guide*, 1994; David Gebhard and Tom Martinson, *A Guide to the Architecture of Minnesota*, 1977; Stefanos Polyzoides, et. al., *Courtyard Housing in Los Angeles*, 1982; and David Gebhard and Robert Winter, *An Architectural Guidebook to Los Angeles*, 2003

CALIFORNIA

Esther McCoy, *Five California Architects*, 1960; David Gebhard and Robert Winter, *A Guide to Architecture in Los Angeles & Southern California*, 1977; David Gebhard and Robert Winter, *Los Angeles, An Architectural Guide*, 1994; David Gebhard and Robert Winter, *An Architectural Guidebook to Los Angeles*, 2003; David Gebhard, Eric Sandweiss, and Robert Winter, *A Guide to Architecture in San Francisco and Northern California*, 1985; Sally B. Woodbridge, John M. Woodbridge, and Chuck Byrne, *San Francisco Architecture*, 2005; Paul C. Johnson, ed., *Western Ranch Houses by Cliff May*, 1958; Alan Hess, *The Ranch House*, 2004; Alexander Vertikoff and Robert Winter, *Hidden LA*, 1998; G. E. Kidder Smith, *Source Book of American Architecture*, 1996; and Kenneth Frampton, *Modern Architecture 1851–1945*, 1983

PERIOD REVIVALS

Herb Andree & Noel Young, *Santa Barbara Architecture*, 1980; Karen J. Weitze, *California's Mission Revival*, 1984; Sally B. Woodbridge and Richard Barnes, *Bernard Maybeck Visionary Architect*, 1992; Kenneth H. Cardwell, *Bernard Maybeck*, 1977; Steven McLeod Bedford, *John Russell Pope*, 1998; Robert A. M. Stern, *George Howe*, 1975; Donald Miller, *The Architecture of Benno Janssen*, 1997; Elizabeth Meredith Dowling, *American Classicist The Architecture of Philip Trammell Shutze*, 1989; Patricia Gebhard, *George Washington Smith*, 2005; Donald W. Curl, *Mizner's Florida*, 1984; David Gebhard, *Robert Stacy-Judd*, 1993; Dale Mulfinger, *The Architecture of Edwin Lundie*, 1995; *The Work of Cram and Ferguson Architects*, 1929; Ethan Anthony, *The Architecture of Ralph Adams Cram and His Office*, 2007; Aaron Betsky, *James Gamble Rogers and the Architecture of Pragmatism*, 1994; The Tribune Company, *Tribune Tower Competition*, 1923; Katherine Solomonson, *The Chicago Tribune Competition*, 2001; Patricia Gebhard and Kathryn Masson, *The Santa Barbara County Courthouse*, 2001; David Gebhard and Tom Martinson, *A Guide to the Architecture of Minnesota*, 1977; David Gebhard and Robert Winter, *Architecture in Los Angeles*, 1985; David Gebhard and Robert Winter, *Los Angeles, an Architectural Guide*, 1994; Kansas City Chapter, AIA, *Kansas City*, 1979; Norval White and Elliot Willensky, *AIA Guide to New York City*, 1978; Robert Winter and Alexander Vertikoff, *The Architecture of Entertainment: LA in the Twenties*, 2006; G. E. Kidder Smith, *Source Book of American Architecture*, 1996; Franklin Toker, *Fallingwater Rising*, 2003; Clive Aslet, *The American Country House*, 1990; Robert B. MacKay, Anthony K. Baker, and Carol A. Traynor, *Long Island Country Houses and the Architects, 1860–1940*, 1997; Mac Griswold and Eleanor Weller, *The Golden Age of American Gardens*, 1991; Henry Wiencek, *America's Great Houses*, 1999; Martha Thorne, ed., *David Adler, Architect*, 2002; and the Historic American Buildings Survey

MODERNE

David Gebhard, *The National Trust Guide to Art Deco in America*, 1996; Barbara Capitman, Michael D. Kinerk, Dennis W. Wilhelm, with Randy Juster, *Rediscovering Art Deco USA*, 1994; Robert Winter and Alexander Vertikoff, *The Architecture of Entertainment: LA in the Twenties*, 2006; David Gebhard and Robert Winter, *A Guide to Architecture in Los Angeles and Southern California*, 1977; Kathryn Bishop Eckert, *Buildings of Michigan*, 1993; David Gebhard and Tom Martinson, *A Guide to the Architecture of Minnesota*, 1977; Walter Creese, *TVA's Public Planning*, 1990; Steven McLeod Bedford, *John Russell Pope*, 1998; Carol Herselle Krinsky, *Rockefeller Center*, 1978; Daniel Okrent, *Great Fortune: The Epic of Rockefeller Center*, 2003; David A. Hanks with Jennifer Toher, *Donald Deskey*, 1987; Junior League of Tulsa, *Tulsa Art Deco*, 1980; David Gebhard and Gerald Mansheim, *Buildings of Iowa*, 1993; G. E. Kidder Smith, *Source Book of American Architecture*, 1996; and Robert Caro, *The Power Broker*, 1975

NATIONAL ROMANTICISM

Markku Komonen, *Saarinen in Finland*, 1984; Eileen Manning Michels, *Reconfiguring Harvey Ellis*, 2004; Charles Whitaker, *Bertram Grosvenor Goodhue*, 1925; Richard Oliver, *Bertram Grosvenor Goodhue*, 1983; Steven McLeod Bedford, *John Russell Pope*, 1998; Robert Judson Clark, *Design in America*, 1983; Wayne Andrews, *Architecture in Michigan*, 1967; George McCue, *Artist in Bronze, Water, and Space: Carl Milles and His*

Sculpture, 1985; Meyric R. Rogers, *Carl Milles: An Interpretation of His Work*, 1940; and Claes Caldenby and Olof Hultin, *Asplund 1985*, 1986

THE INTERNATIONAL STYLE
Dennis Sharp, *Twentieth Century Architecture: A Visual History*, 2002; Henry-Russell Hitchcock and Philip Johnson, *The International Style*, 1932; Sigfried Giedion, *Space, Time and Architecture*, 1941; G. E. Kidder Smith, *Source Book of American Architecture*, 1996; David Gebhard and Robert Winter, *A Guide to Architecture in Los Angeles and Southern California*, 1977; David Gebhard, *Schindler*, 1971; Edward Durell Stone, *The Evolution Of An Architect*, 1962; Jorg Brockmann and Bill Harris, *One Thousand New York Buildings*, 2002; and the Historic American Buildings Survey

POSTWAR MODERNISM
Alexandra Griffith Winton, "'A Man's House is his Art'" [Walker Idea Houses] *Journal of Design History*, Vol. 17, No. 4, 2004, pp. 377–396; Franklin Toker, *Fallingwater Rising*, 2003; Esther McCoy, *Richard Neutra*, 1960; Philip Johnson, *The Architecture of Philip Johnson*, 2002; John Howey, *The Sarasota School of Architecture*, 1995; Christopher Domin and Joseph King, *Paul Rudolph: The Florida Houses*, 2002; *Marcel Breuer Buildings and Projects 1921–1961*, 1962; Elizabeth A. T. Smith, ed., *Blueprints for Modern Living*, 1989; David Gebhard and Robert Winter, *A Complete Guide to Architecture in Los Angeles*, 1985; Franz Schulze, *Mies Van Der Rohe*, 1985; Carol Herselle Krinsky, *Gordon Bunshaft of Skidmore, Owings & Merrill*, 1988; Nicholas Adams, *Skidmore, Owings & Merrill: SOM Since 1936*, 2006; Dennis Sharp, *Twentieth Century Architecture: A Visual History*, 2002; and G. E. Kidder Smith, *Source Book of American Architecture*, 1996

MODERN MASTERS
Vincent Scully Jr., *Louis I. Kahn*, 1962; Aline B. Sarinen, ed., *Eero Saarinen On His Work*, 1962; Antonio Román, *Eero Saarinen: An Architecture of Multiplicity*, 2003; Donlyn Lyndon, *Houses by MLTW*, 1975; Eugene J. Johnson, ed., *Charles Moore: Buildings and Projects, 1949–1986*; Kevin M. Keim, *An Architectural Life: Memoirs & Memories of Charles W. Moore*, 1996; Charles Moore, Gerald Allen, Donlyn Lyndon, *The Place of Houses*, 1974; Stanislaus von Moos, *Venturi, Scott Brown & Associates, 1986–1998*, 1999; David Gebhard and Robert Winter, *A Guide to Architecture in Los Angeles & Southern California*, 1977; David Gebhard, Eric Sandweiss, and Robert Winter, *Architecture in San Francisco and Northern California*, 1985; David Gebhard and Robert Winter, *Los Angeles: An Architectural Guide*, 1994; and G. E. Kidder Smith, *Source Book of American Architecture*, 1996

MID-CENTURY EXPRESSIONISM
Sidney K. Robinson, *The Architecture of Alden B. Dow*, 1983; Dow House website, www.abdow.org; Wayne Andrews, *Architecture in Michigan*, 1967; Morris Lapidus, *Too Much is Never Enough*, 1996; Bruce Harold Schaefer, *The Writings and Sketches of Matthew Nowicki*, 1973; Edward Durell Stone, *Evolution Of An Architect*, 1962; Colin Faber, *Candela/The Shell Builder*, 1963; John Howey, *The Sarasota School of Architecture*, 1995; Christopher Domin and Joseph King, *Paul Rudolph: The Florida Houses*, 2002; Norval White and Elliot Willensky, *AIA Guide to New York City*, 1967, 1968; David Gebhard and Tom Martinson, *A Guide to the Architecture of Minnesota*, 1977; Jeffrey Cook, *The Architecture of Bruce Goff*, 1978; Robert Adams Ivy, Jr., *Fay Jones*, 1992; David Gebhard and Robert Winter, *Los Angeles, An Architectural Guide*, 1994; and Alan Weintraub and Alan Hess, *The Architecture of John Lautner*, 1999

BRUTALISM
Marcel Breuer, *Buildings and Projects 1921–1961*, 1962; Rupert Spade, *Paul Rudolph*, 1971; G. E. Kidder Smith, *Source Book of American Architecture*, 1996; Norval White and Elliot Willensky, *AIA Guide to New York City*, 1978; and David Gebhard and Tom Martinson, *A Guide to the Architecture of Minnesota*, 1977

LATE MODERNISM
Dennis Sharp, *Twentieth Century Architecture: A Visual History*, 2002; Robert A. M. Stern, David Fishman, and Jacob Tilove, *New York 2000*, 2006; G. E. Kidder Smith, *Source Book of American Architecture*, 1996; Colin Rowe, Kenneth Frampton, and Arthur Drexler, *Five Architects*, 1972; David Gebhard and Robert Winter, *Los Angeles, An Architectural Guide*, 1994; Oswald W. Grube, Peter C. Pran, and Franz Schulze, *100 Years of Architecture in Chicago*, 1976; Nicholas Adams, *Skidmore, Owings & Merrill: SOM Since 1936*, 2006; David Gebhard and Tom Martinson, *A Guide to the Architecture of Minnesota*, 1977; and Philip Johnson, *The Architec-*

ture of Philip Johnson, 2002; Michael Sorkin, *Hardy Holzman Pfeiffer*, 1981; Michael Sorkin and Mildred F. Schmertz, *Hardy Holzman Pfeiffer Associates Buildings and Projects 1967–1992*, 1992; Mildred Friedman and Glenn M. Andres, *Hardy Holzman Pfeiffer Associates Buildings and Projects 1993–1998*, 1999; Hardy Holzman Pfeiffer Associates, *Theaters*, 2000; Malcolm Holzman, *Stone Work*, 2001; Mason Andrews, *Frank Gehry Buildings and Projects*, 1985; Walker Art Center, *The Architecture of Frank Gehry*, 1986; David Gebhard and Robert Winter, *Los Angeles, An Architectural Guide*, 1994; David Gebhard and Robert Winter, *An Architectural Guidebook to Los Angeles*, 2003; and James S. Russell, "Project Diary…Walt Disney Concert Hall," *Architectural Record*, November 2003: 134–151; Timothy J. Gilfoyle, *Millennium Park*, 2006

POSTMODERNISM
Charles Jencks, *Post-Modernism*, 1987; Robert A. M. Stern, *Modern Classicism*, 1988; David Gebhard and Robert Winter, *A Guide to Architecture in Los Angeles & Southern California*, 1977; Clifford A. Pearson, ""Getty Villa," *Architectural Record*, May, 2006:106–115; Philip Johnson, *The Architecture of Philip Johnson*, 2002; and Beth Dunlop, *Building a Dream, The Art of Disney Architecture*, 1996

NEOTRADITIONALISM
David Gebhard and Robert Winter, *Los Angeles, An Architectural Guide*, 1994; Clifford A. Pearson, "Getty Villa," *Architectural Record*, May, 2006: 106–115; *An Architectural Design Profile: Contemporary Architecture*, 1988; Allan Greenberg, *The Architecture of Democracy*, 2006; Robert A. M. Stern, *Modern Classicism*, 1988; Rebecca Conrad and Christopher H. Nelson, *Santa Barbara, A Guide to El Pueblo Viejo*, 1986; Philip Johnson, *The Architecture of Philip Johnson*, 2002; Mary Miers, *American Houses: The Architecture of Fairfax & Sammons*, 2006; and David Colman, "Mid-18th-Century Modern: The Classicists Strike Back," *The New York Times*, February 10, 2005, p. D1

DECONSTRUCTION
Bernard Tschumi, *Cinerama Folie Le Parc De La Villette*, 1987; Philip Jodidio, *New Forms: Architecture in the 1990s*, 1997; David Gebhard and Robert Winter, *Los Angeles, An Architectural Guide*, 1994; David Gebhard and Robert Winter, *An Architectural Guidebook to Los Angeles*, 2003; Philip Johnson, *The Architecture of Philip Johnson*, 2002; John M. Broder, "New Los Angeles Cathedral Evokes Survival in Adversity," *The New York Times*, August 30, 2002; Carol Herselle Krinsky, "And Architecture of Washington's Newest Museum," *Wall Street Journal*, November 28, 2004; Sheri Olson, "Seattle's Central Library Kindles Book Lust," *Architectural Record*, July, 2004:88–101

NEOMODERNISM
Sigfried Giedion, *Space, Time and Architecture*, 1941; David Gebhard and Robert Winter, *Los Angeles, An Architectural Guide*, 1994; Stephen Kinzer, "Deep in the Heart of Modernity," *The New York Times*, January 29, 2003, p. B1; David Dillon, "Modern Art Museum of Fort Worth," *Architectural Record*, March, 2003: 98–113; Lola Gómez and Cristina Montes, *The Next House*, 2002; Sarah Boxer, "The Modern's Cool New Box: Displaying Art, Not Fighting It," *The New York Times*, May 5, 2004, p. B1; Nicolai Ouroussoff, "Art Fuses With Urbanity in an Aesthetically Pure Redesign of the Modern," *The New York Times*, November, 15, 2004, p. B1; Suzanne Stephens, "New York's Museum of Modern Art finally becomes what it wanted to be all along," *Architectural Record* 01:2005 (January), pp. 94–109; Thom Mayne, *Morphosis Volume IV*, 2006; Gwenda Blair, "In Traditional Chicago, The Politics of Fitting In," *The New York Times*, November 6, 2003, p. D8; and Robert A. M. Stern, David Fishman, and Jacob Tilove, *New York 2000*, 2006

RURAL STRUCTURES
Hugh Morrison, *Early American Architecture*, 1952; Samuel Chamberlain, *The New England Image* (1962), 1994; Joe Sherman, *The House at Shelburne Farms*, 1986, 1992; David Gebhard and Tom Martinson, *A Guide to the Architecture of Minnesota*, 1977; David Gebhard, Eric Sandweiss, and Robert Winter, *A Guide to Architecture in San Francisco and Northern California*, 1985; David Gebhard and Gerald Mansheim, *Buildings of Iowa*, 1993; Julie Nicoletta, *The Architecture of the Shakers*, 1995; Herbert Schiffer, *Shaker Architecture*, 1979; Clive Aslet, *The American Country Estate House*, 1990; Mac Griswold and Eleanor Weller, *The Golden Age of American Gardens*, 1991; William Allin Storer, *The Architecture of Frank Lloyd Wright*, 1974; Andrea Oppenheimer Dean, *Rural Studio*, 2002; Alan Hess, *Rancho Deluxe*, 2000; and the Historic American Buildings Survey

INDUSTRIAL STRUCTURES

Sigfried Giedion, *Space, Time and Architecture*, (1941) 1962; Betsy Hunter Bradley, *The Works: The Industrial Architecture of the United States*, 1999; Margot Gale and Carol Gale, *Cast-Iron Architecture in America: The Significance of James Bogardus*, 1998; Grant Hildebrand, *Designing for Industry: The Architecture of Albert Kahn*, 1974; Steven Watts, *The People's Tycoon: Henry Ford and the American Century*, 2005 [chapters Eight and Fourteen]; David Gebhard and Gerald Mansheim, *Buildings of Iowa*, 1993; Norval White and Elliot Willensky, *AIA Guide to New York City*, 1978; Jorg Brockmann and Bill Harris, *One Thousand New York Buildings*, 2002; W. Barksdale Maynard, *Architecture in the United States, 1800–1850*, 2002; Wayne Andrews, *Architecture in Michigan*, 1982; Kathryn Bishop Eckert, *Buildings of Michigan*, 1993; and the Historic American Buildings Survey and the Historic American Engineering Record

TRANSPORTATION

Barbara Capitman, Michael D. Kinerk, Dennis W. Wilhelm, with Randy Juster, *Rediscovering Art Deco USA*, 1994; David Gebhard and Gerald Mansheim, *Buildings of Iowa*, 1993; Herb Andree and Noel Young, *Santa Barbara Architecture*, 1980; David Gebhard and Robert Winter, *Los Angeles, An Architectural Guide*, 1994; Richard Longstreth, *City Center to Regional Mall*, 1997; Alice Sinkevitch, *AIA Guide to Chicago*, 1993; Rupert Spade, *Paul Rudolph*, 1971; Ronald L. Tulis, *Metro Center '85* (City of Minneapolis), 1970; and G. E. Kidder Smith, *Source Book of American Architecture*, 1996

RETAIL AND HOTELS

Richard Longstreth, *City Center to Regional Mall*, 1997; Richard Longstreth, *The Drive-In, The Supermarket, and the Transformation of Commercial Space in Los Angeles*, 1999; M. Jeffrey Hardwick, *Mall Maker: Victor Gruen, Architect of an American Dream*, 2004; Sally B. Woodbridge and Roger Montgomery, *A Guide to Architecture in Washington State*, 1980; Virginia A. Greene, *The Architecture of Howard Van Doren Shaw*, 1998; Joan L. Michalak/Kansas City Chapter AIA, *Kansas City*, 1979; James W. Elmore, ed., *A Guide to the Architecture of Metro Phoenix*, 1983; Joseph L. Eldridge, *Architecture Boston*, 1976; Frank Peters and George McCue, *A Guide to the Architecture of St. Louis*, 1989; David Gebhard and Robert Winter, *Los Angeles, An Architectural Guide*, 1994; Arnold Berke and Alexander Vertikoff, *Mary Colter: Architect of the Southwest*, 2002; and Norval White and Elliot Willensky, *AIA Guide to New York City*, 1978

INTERIOR SPACES

Johann Friedrich Geist, *Arcades*, 1983; Lawrence N. Powell, *Louisiana's Capitols*, 1995; Karen Kingsley, *Buildings of Louisiana*, 2003; Deborah Slaton, "Burnham and Root and the Rookery," in the *Midwest in American Architecture*, 1991; Daniel Okrent, *Great Fortune: The Epic of Rockefeller Center*, 2003; Philip Johnson, *The Architecture of Philip Johnson*, 2002; and David Gebhard and Tom Martinson, *A Guide to the Architecture of Minnesota*, 1977

MOVIE THEATERS

Maggie Valentine, *The Show Starts on the Sidewalk: An Architectural History of the Movie Theater, Starring S. Charles Lee*, 1994; David Naylor, *Great American Movie Theaters*, 1987; Q. David Bowers, *Nickelodeon Theatres*, 1986; Barbara Capitman, Michael D. Kinerk, Dennis W. Wilhelm, with Randy Juster, *Rediscovering Art Deco USA*, 1994; Mary Strauss, *The Fabulous Fox*, 1985; David Gebhard and Robert Winter, *Los Angeles: An Architectural Guide*, 1994; David Gebhard and Tom Martinson, *A Guide to the Architecture of Minnesota*, 1977; Kathryn Bishop Eckert, *Buildings of Michigan*, 1993; and the Historic American Buildings Survey

RESORTS

Christine Barnes, Fred Pflughoft, and David Morris, *Great Lodges of the National Parks*, 2002; Christine Barnes, *Great Lodges of the West*, 1997; Kathleen Mahoney, *Gothic Style*, 1995; Arnold Berke and Alexander Vertikoff, *Mary Colter: Architect of the Southwest*, 2002; David Gebhard and Tom Martinson, *A Guide to the Architecture of Minnesota*, 1977; S. Allen Chambers, Jr., *Buildings of West Virginia*, 2004; David Gebhard and Robert Winter, *A Guide to Architecture in Los Angeles and Southern California*, 1977; David Gebhard, et. al., *A Guide to Architecture in San Francisco and Northern California*, 1973; Kathryn Bishop Eckert, *Buildings of Michigan*, 1993; Sarah Milstein, "Back to the Beach for a Blast of 50s Cool," *The New York Times*, June 28, 2002; James Laabs, *The Wisconsin Dells*, 1999; Beth Dunlop, *Building a Dream, The Art of Disney Architecture*, 1996; Stephen M. Fjellman, *Vinyl Leaves*, 1992; City of Cape May website; the City of Aspen & Pitkin County Colorado website; Charles A. Birnbaum and Robin Karson, *Pioneers of American Landscape Design*, 2000; G. E. Kidder Smith, *Source Book of American Architecture*, 1996; and the Historic American Buildings Survey

FOLLIES

David Gebhard and Tom Martinson, *A Guide to the Architecture of Minnesota*, 1977; David Gebhard and Gerald Mansheim, *Buildings of Iowa*, 1993; David Gebhard and Robert Winter, *A Guide to Architecture in Los Angeles and Southern California*, 1977; Richard Guy Wilson, *The Colonial Revival House*, 2004; Karen Kingsley, *Buildings of Louisiana*, 2003; David Gebhard, Eric Sandweiss, and Robert Winter, *A Guide to Architecture in San Francisco and Northern California*, 1985; John Maas, *The Victorian Home in America*, 1972; Deidi von Schaewen and John Maizels, *Fantasy Worlds*, 1999; Samuel Chamberlain, *The New England Image*, 1962; Susan Piedmont-Palladino, *Devil's Workshop: 25 Years of Jersey Devil Architecture*, 1997; William L. Hamilton, "Paradise Regrouted," *The New York Times*, June 26, 2003, p. D1; Frank Peters and George McCue, *A Guide to the Architecture of St. Louis*, 1989; David Edwin Harrell, Jr., *Oral Roberts: An American Life*, 1985; Timothy K. Beal, *Roadside Religion*, 2005; G. E. Kidder Smith, *Source Book of American Architecture*, 1996; and the Historic American Buildings Survey

FAIRS AND EXPOSITIONS

Alfred Heller, *World's Fairs and the End of Progress*, 1999; Erik Larson, *The Devil in the White City*, 2003; Jim Zwick, *World's Fairs & Expositions* website, 2003; Mel Scott, *American City Planning Since 1890*, 1971; SanFranciscoMemories website, 2003; Sally B. Woodbridge, John M. Woodbridge, and Chuck Byrne, *San Francisco Architecture*, 1992; David Gebhard, Eric Sandweiss, and Robert Winter, *A Guide to Architecture in San Francisco and Northern California*, 1985; David Gebhard and Robert Winter, *A Guide to Architecture in Los Angeles and Southern California*, 1977; Bertram Grosvenor Goodhue, *The Architecture and the Gardens of the San Diego Exposition*, 1916; Richard Amero, "A History of the Exposition," on the San Diego Historical Society website; Sally B. Woodbridge and Roger Montgomery, *A Guide to Architecture in Washington State*, 1980; William B. Rhoads, *The Colonial Revival* (1974), 1977; Robert Hughes, *American Visions*, 1997; Sigfried Giedion, *Space, Time and Architecture* (1941), 1962; Robert A. Caro, *The Power Broker*, 1974; Eugene J. Johnson, *Charles Moore, Buildings and Projects 1949–1986*, 1986; and Woody Register, *The Kid of Coney Island*, 2001

ORDERING THE LAND

Andro Linklater, *Measuring America*, 2002; Andro Linklater, *The Fabric of America*, 2007; Hildegard Binder Johnson, *Order Upon the Land*, 1976; Dora Crouch et. al., *Spanish City Planning in North America*, 1982; Hugh Thomas, *Rivers of Gold*, 2003; Phil Patton, Open Road, 1986; Abel Buell, "A New and correct Map of the United States of American Layed down from the latest Observations and best Authority agreeable to the Peace of 1783," 1784 (at The New Jersey Historical Society); and Hernando de Soto, *The Mystery of Capital* (Chapter Five), 2000.

EUROPEAN NEW WORLD TOWN PLANS

John W. Reps, *The Making of Urban America*, 1965; John W. Reps, *Cities of the American West*, 1979; Richard Bushman, *The Refinement of America*, 1992; Elizabeth Barlow Rogers, *Landscape Design: A Cultural and Architectural History*, 2001, G. E. Kidder Smith, *Source Book of American Architecture*, 1996; Dora Crouch, Daniel Garr, and Axel Mundigo, *Spanish City Planning in North America*, 1982; Hugh Morrison, *Early American Architecture*, 1952; and Don Metz, *New Architecture in New Haven*, 1973

THE MALL

Richard Longstreth, ed., *The Mall in Washington, 1791–1991*, 1991, including the following essays: Norma Evenson, "Monumental Spaces;" Pamela Scott, "This Vast Empire;" Therese O'Malley, "A Public Museum of Trees;" Thomas S. Hines, "The Imperial Mall;" Jon S. Peterson, "The Mall, the McMillan Plan, and the Origins of American City Planning;" David C. Streatfield, "The Olmsteds and the Landscape of the Mall;" Richard Guy Wilson, "High Noon on the Mall"; and J. Carter Brown, "The Mall and the Commission of Fine Arts;" Sue A. Kohler and Pamela Scott. eds., *Designing the Nation's Capital The 1901 Plan for Washington, D.C.*; 2006; Andro Linklater, *The Fabric of America*, 2007; Architect of the Capitol, *Master Plan*, 1981; Sue A. Kohler, *The Commission of Fine Arts, A Brief History, 1910–1995*, 1996; Howard Saalman, *Haussmann: Paris Transformed*, 1971; Colin Jones, *Paris: Biography of a City*, 2004 (Chapters 6 & 9); and the Historic American Buildings Survey

NATIONAL EXPANSION

John W. Reps, *The Making of Urban American*, 1965; John W. Reps, *Cities of the American West*, 1979; Andro Linklater, *Measuring America*, 2002; Carol Poh Miller and Robert Wheeler, *Cleveland: A Concise History*, 1990; the Historic American Buildings Survey; and the Historic American Engineering Record

COMMUNITY DEVELOPMENT

Werner Hegemann and Elbert Peets, *The American Vitruvius: An Architects' Handbook of Civic Art*, 1922; Henry Winthrop Sargent, *Landscape Gardening*, 1859; Robert A. M. Stern, ed., "The Anglo-American Suburb," *Architectural Design* 51, 10/11 1981; Charles E. Birnbaum and Robin Karson, eds., *Pioneers of American Landscape Design*, 2000; Rex Beach, *The Miracle of Coral Gables*, 1926; Carol Poh Miller and Robert Wheeler, *Cleveland: A Concise History*, 1990; David Gebhard and Robert Winter, *A Compleat Guide to Architecture in Los Angeles*, 1985; David Gebhard and Robert Winter, *Los Angeles, An Architectural Guide*, 1994; David Gebhard and Gerald Mansheim, *Buildings of Iowa*, 1993; John Nolen, *New Towns for Old*, 1927; John L. Hancock, *John Nolen and the American City Planning Movement*, 1964 diss.; Clarence S. Stein, *Toward New Towns for America*, 1957; Elizabeth A. T. Smith, ed., *Blueprints for Modern Living*, 1989; Susan L. Klaus, *A Modern Arcadia*, 2002; David Gebhard, Eric Sandweiss, and Robert Winter, *A Guide to Architecture in San Francisco and Northern California*, 1985; Greg Hise, *Magnetic Los Angeles*, 1997; Richard Longstreth, *City Center to Regional Mall*, 1997; Donald Miller, *Lewis Mumford*, 1989; William Allin Storrer, *The Architecture of Frank Lloyd Wright*, 1974; Herbert J. Gans, *The Levittowners*, 1967; Roger Montgomery, "Mass Producing Bay Area Architecture" [Eichler], in Sally Woodbridge, ed., *Bay Area Houses*, 1988; Paul Adamson and Marty Arbunich, *Eichler / Modernism Rebuilds the American Dream*, 2002; Cory Buckner, *A. Quincy Jones* [Eichler], 2002; A. Quincy Jones and Frederick E. Emmons, *Builders' Homes for Better Living*, 1957; Thomas J. Noel, *Buildings of Colorado*, 1997; www.arapahoeacres.org; Douglas Frantz and Catherine Collins, *Celebration USA*, 1999; Andrew Ross, *The Celebration Chronicles*, 1999; Todd Bressi, ed., *The Seaside Debates: A Critique of New Urbanism*, 2002; Vernon D. Swaback, *The Creative Community*, 2003; Vernon D. Swaback, *Designing With Nature*, 2005; G. E. Kidder Smith, *Source Book of American Architecture*, 1996; William H. Tishler, ed., *American Landscape Architecture*, 1989; and Witold Rybczynski, *Last Harvest*, 2007

THE CITY BEAUTIFUL

Charles Mulford Robinson, *Modern Civic Art*, 1903; Werner Hegemann and Elbert Peets, *The American Vitruvius: An Architects' Handbook of Civic Art*, 1922; Howard Saalman, *Haussmann: Paris Transformed*, 1971; Mel Scott, *American City Planning Since 1890*, 1969; Kristen Schaffer, *Daniel H. Burnham: Visionary Architect and Planner*, 2003; Carol Poh Miller and Robert Wheeler, *Cleveland: A Concise History*, 1990; Edward F. O'Day, ed., Sue A. Kohler and Pamela Scott. eds., *Designing the Nation's Capital The 1901 Plan for Washington, D.C.*, 2006; *Report on a Plan for San Francisco*, 1906; The Civic League of Saint Louis, *A City Plan for Saint Louis*, 1907; Charles Moore, ed., for The Commercial Club, *Plan of Chicago*, 1909; David A. Johnson, *Planning the Great Metropolis*, 1996; The Civic Commission of Minneapolis, Minnesota, *Preliminary Plan of Minneapolis*, 1911; and Andrew Wright Crawford, ed., for The Civic Commission, *Plan of Minneapolis*, 1917

PHYSICAL PLANS

Martin Anderson, *The Federal Bulldozer*, 1964; Mel Scott, *American City Planning Since 1890*, 1969; Norman John Johnston, *Harland Bartholomew: His Comprehensive Plans and Science of Planning*, 1964 diss.; Greg Hise and William Deverell, *Eden By Design*, 2000; John Guinther, *Direction of Cities*, 1996; Victor Gruen, *The Heart of Our Cities*, 1964; M. Jeffrey Hardwick, *Mall Maker: Victor Gruen, Architect of an American Dream*, 2004; Edmund N. Bacon, *Design of Cities*, 1967; Robin Pogrebin, Edmund Bacon obituary, *The New York Times*, October 18, 2005; and Tom Martinson, "The Persistence of Vision: A Century of Civic Progress in St. Louis," *Places: A Quarterly Journal of Urban Design*, Summer, 1990, pp. 22-33

THE STRIP

John Margolies, *The End of the Road*, 1981; Alan Hess, *Googie*, 1985; Daniel I. Vieyra, *Fill 'er Up*, 1979; Michael Karl Witzel, *The American Gas Station*, 1992; John A. Jakle and Keith A. Sculle, *The Gas Station in America*, 1994; Michael Karl Witzel, *The American Diner*, 1999; Michael Karl Witzel, *The American Drive-In*, 1994; Richard Longstreth, *The Drive-In, The Supermarket, and the Transformation of Commercial Space in Los Angeles*, 1999; Philip Langdon, *Orange Roofs, Golden Arches*, 1986; John F. Love, *McDonald's Behind the Arches*, 1986; Jeffrey Tennyson, *Hamburger Heaven*, 1993; David Gerard Hogan, *Selling 'em by the Sack*, 1997; Ingrid Whitehead, "A California fast-food restaurant supersizes its design vision," *Architectural Record*, November 2003:87–88; Lorraine B. Diehl and Marianne Hardart, *The Automat*, 2002; Michael Karl Witzel, *The American Motel*, 2000; Robert Venturi, Denise Scott Brown, Steven Izenour, *Learning From Las Vegas*, 1972; Alan Hess, *Viva Las Vegas*, 1993; Hal Rothman, *Neon Metropolis*, 2002; www.library.unlv.edu/arch/lasvegas/index.html; David Gebhard and Robert Winter, *A Guide to Architecture in Los Angeles and Southern California*, 1977; David Gebhard and Robert Winter, *Los Angeles: An Architectural Guide*, 1994; David Gebhard and Robert Winter, *An Architectural Guidebook to Los Angeles*, 2003; David Gebhard and Tom Martinson, *A Guide to the Architecture of Minnesota*, 1977; David Gebhard and Gerald Mansheim, *Buildings of Iowa*, 1993

POPULAR CULTURE

Woody Register, *The Kid of Coney Island*, 2001; John Chase, *The Sidewalk Companion to Santa Cruz Architecture*, 1975; Beth Dunlop, *Building a Dream, The Art of Disney Architecture*, 1996; Jim Cullen, *The Art of Democracy*, 1996; David Gebhard and Gerald Mansheim, *Buildings of Iowa*, 1993; Sally Henderson & Robert Landau, *Billboard Art*, 1980; Tom Martinson, *Signs of the City*, 1996; Fred E. Basten, *Great American Billboards*, 2007; Alan Hess, *Viva Las Vegas*, 1993; Norval White and Elliot Willensky, *AIA Guide to New York City*, 2000; James Traub, *The Devil's Playground, A Century of Pleasure and Profit in Time Square*, 2004; J. J. C. Andrews, *The Well-Built Elephant*, 1984; Sally B. Woodbridge and Roger Montgomery, *A Guide to Architecture in Washington State*, 1980; Alan Hess, *Googie*, 1985; Michael Karl Witzel, *The American Drive-In*, 1994; John F. Love, *McDonald's Behind the Arches*, 1986; David Gebhard and Robert Winter, *A Guide to Architecture in Los Angeles and Southern California*, 1977; John Margolies, The End of the Road, 1977; Jim Heiman and Rip Georges, *California Crazy*, 1980; Lisa Mahar, *American Signs*, 2002; Peter Korda and Nick Constantine, "The First Basket Building in the World," *Structure*, Spring, 1998; Phil (Peter) Berg, *Ultimate Garages*, 2003; www.scripophily.net; www.roadsideamerica.com, and www.agilitynut.com/roadside2.html

CIVIC DESIGN

Werner Hegemann and Elbert Peets, *The American Vitruvius: An Architects' Handbook of Civic Art*, 1922; Edmund N. Bacon, *Design of Cities*, 1967; Norval White and Elliott Willensky, *AIA Guide to New York City*, 1978; David Gebhard and Robert Winter, *A Guide to Architecture in Los Angeles and Southern California*, 1977; David Gebhard and Robert Winter, *Los Angeles, An Architectural Guide*, 1994; Sue A. Kohler, *The Commission of Fine Arts: A Brief History*, 1910–1995, 1996; Aline Saarinen, *Eero Saarinen On His Work*, 1962; Wayne Andrews, *Architecture in Michigan*, 1967; Richard Longstreth, *City Center to Regional Mall*, 1997; Morris Lapidus, *Too Much is Never Enough*, 1996; Kathryn Bishop Eckert, *Buildings of Michigan*, 1993; Pamela Scott and Antoinette J. Lee, *Buildings of the District of Columbia*, 1993; Hal Rothman, *Neon Metropolis*, 2002; Robert Twombly, *Louis Sullivan*, 1986; James F. O'Gorman, *The Architecture of Frank Furness*, 1973; and the Historic American Buildings Survey

LANDSCAPE IN AMERICA

Richard Bushman, *The Refinement of America*, 1992; Russell Shorto, *The Island at the Center of the World*, 2004; Mariana Griswold (Mrs. Schuyler) Van Rensselaer, *History of the City of New York in the Seventeenth Century*, 1909 [Vol. 1, chapter XIV; Vol. 2, chapter XVIII]; and Roger Turner, *Capability Brown*, 1985

FORMALISM

Elizabeth Barlow Rogers, *Landscape Design*, 2001; Therese O'Malley and Marc Treib, eds., *Regional Garden Design in the United States*, 1995; Caroline Holmes, *Icons of Garden Design*, 2001; Mary Zuazua Jenkins, *America's Public Gardens*, 1998; Mac Griswold and Eleanor Weller, *The Golden Age of American Gardens*, 1991; Karen Kingsley, *Buildings of Louisiana*, 2003; and the Historic American Buildings Survey

NATURALISM

Richard Bushman, *The Refinement of America*, 1992; Elizabeth Barlow Rogers, *Landscape Design*, 2001; Norval White and Elliot Willensky, *AIA Guide to New York City*, 1978; Paul Wade and Kathy Arnold, *Boston & Environs*, 2001; Theodore Wirth, *Minneapolis Park System*, 1945; David Wallis, "A Monumental Vision of Half a Lifetime" [Opus 40], in *The New*

York Times, June 2, 2006, p. D9; A. E. Bye, *Art into Landscape into Art*, 1983; Andrew Jackson Downing and Henry Winthrop Sargent, *Downing's Landscape Gardening*, 1859; and the Historic American Buildings Survey

REGIONALISM
Therese O'Malley and Marc Treib, eds., *Regional Garden Design in the United States*, 1995; David Gebhard and Gerald Mansheim, *Buildings of Iowa*, 1993; Jens Jensen, *Siftings*, 1939; Robert E. Grese, *Jens Jensen: Maker of Parks*, 1992; *The Complete Official Guide of the Lincoln Highway* (1924), 1993, including the chapter by Jens Jensen, "Roadside Beautification;" and Charles A. Birnbaum and Robin Karson, eds., *Pioneers of American Landscape Design*, 2000

GARDEN RESTORATIONS
Charles B. Hosmer, Jr., "The Colonial Revival in the Public Eye: Williamsburg and Early Garden Restoration," in Alan Axelrod, ed., *The Colonial Revival in America*, 1985; M. Kent Brinkley and Gordon W. Chappell, *The Gardens of Colonial Williamsburg*, 1996; Stratford Hall Plantation, *Stratford Gardens and Grounds*, 2002; David Gebhard and Robert Winter, *A Guide to Architecture in Los Angeles & Southern California*, 1977; Ann Raver, "Thomas Jefferson Weeded Here," *The New York Times*, March 18, 2004, p. D1; and Mary Zuazua Jenkins, *America's Public Gardens*, 1998

EXOTIC LANDSCAPES
Marc Treib and Ron Herman, *A Guide to the Gardens of Kyoto*, 1980; revised and expanded edition, 2003; Mary Zuazua Jenkins, *America's Public Gardens*, 1998; Charles W. Moore, William J. Mitchell, William Turnbull, Jr., *The Poetics of Gardens*, 1988; John Brookes, *Gardens of Paradise*, 1987; The Walt Disney Company, *Gardens of the Walt Disney World Resort*, 1988; Elizabeth B. Kassler, *Modern Gardens and the Landscape*, 1984; Patricia Gebhard, *George Washington Smith*, 2005; David Gebhard and Robert Winter, *Los Angeles, An Architectural Guide*, 1994; David Gebhard and Robert Winter, *A Guide to Architecture in Los Angeles & Southern California*, 1977; P.M. Bardi, *The Tropical Gardens of Burle Marx*, 1964; Alec Blombery and Tony Rodd, *Palms*, 1982; and the Historic American Buildings Survey

MODERNISM
Marc Treib, "Aspects of Regionality and the Modern(ist) Garden in California," 1995; Marc Treib, ed., *Thomas Church Landscape Architect*, 2003; Marc Treib and Dorothée Imbert, *Garrett Eckbo, Modern Landscapes for Living*, 1997; Elizabeth B. Kassler, *Modern Gardens and the Landscape*, 1984; Gary R. Hilderbrand, *The Miller Garden*, 1999; Linda Mack, "The Minneapolis Sculpture Garden," *Architecture Minnesota*, September/ October, 1988; Leah Levy, *Peter Walker Minimalist Gardens*, 1997; "The Landscapes of Noguchi," *Landscape Architecture*, April, 1990; Ana Maria Torres, *Isamu Noguchi: A Study of Space*, 2000; Marc Treib, *Noguchi in Paris: The UNESCO Garden*, 2003; G. E. Kidder Smith, *Source Book of American Architecture*, 1996; and Robert Hughes, *American Visions*, 1997

ENVIRONMENTALISM
Donlyn Lyndon and Jim Alinder, *The Sea Ranch*, 2004; Ian McHarg, *Design With Nature*, 1969; Ian McHarg, *A Quest for Life*, 1996; Ann Forsythe, *Reforming Suburbia* [The Woodlands], 2005; Janine M. Benyus, *Biomimicry* (Chapter 7) (1997), 2002; Sally B. Woodbridge and Roger Montgomery, *A Guide to Architecture in Washington State*, 1980; Anne Raver, "From Ruin and Artifice, Landscape Reborn," *The New York Times*, February 24, 2005, p. D6; Sally Wasowski, *Gardening With Prairie Plants*, 2002; Wolfgang Oehme and James van Sweden, *Bold Romantic Gardens* (1991), 1998; James van Sweden, *Gardening With Water*, 1995; James van Sweden, *Gardening With Nature*, 1997; James van Sweden, Thomas Christopher and Penelope Hobhouse, *Architecture in the Garden*, 2002; Richard Louv, *Last Child in the Woods: Saving Our Children From Nature-Deficit Disorder*, 2005; and Stephen R. Kellert, *The Value of Life: Biological Diversity and Human Society*, 1996

LANDSCAPE FEATURES
Werner Hegemann and Elbert Peets, *The American Vitruvius: An Architects' Handbook of Civic Art*, 1922; George McCue, *Artist in Bronze, Water, and Space: Carl Milles and His Sculpture*, 1985; Meyric R. Rogers, *Carl Milles: An Interpretation of His Work*, 1940; George Plumptre, *The Water Garden*, 1993; William B. O'Neal, *Architecture in Virginia*, 1968; Eugene J. Johnson, ed., *Charles Moore, Buildings and Projects 1949–1986*,

1986; David Gebhard and Gerald Mansheim, *Buildings of Iowa*, 1993; Alison K. Hoagland, *Buildings of Alaska*, 1993; The Walt Disney Company, *Gardens of the Walt Disney World Resort*, 1988; Beth Dunlop, *Building a Dream, The Art of Disney Architecture*, 1996; Stephen M. Fjellman, *Vinyl Leaves*, 1992; and G. E. Kidder Smith, *Source Book of American Architecture*, 1996

PUBLIC WORKS
Ellis L. Armstrong, ed., *A History of Public Works in the United States, 1776–1976*, 1976; David P. Billington, *Robert Maillart's Bridges: The Art of Engineering*, 1979; and the Historic American Engineering Record

ROADS
The Historic American Engineering Record and the Historic American Buildings Survey, both of the National Park Service; Walter A. McDougal, *Freedom Just Around the Corner*, 2004; Tim Blanning, *The Pursuit of Glory*, 2007, pp. 3–18; Karl Raitz, ed., *A Guide to the National Road*, 1996; Archer Butler Hulbert, *The Cumberland Road*, 1904; George R. Stewart, *U.S. 40: Cross Section of the United States* (1953), 1973; Dayton Duncan and Ken Burns, *Horatio's Drive*, 2003 [Also: PBS DVD, Ken Burns, "Horatio's Drive," 2003]; Phil Patton, *Open Road*, 1986; Charles Beveridge, "Buffalo's Park and Parkway System," in *Buffalo Architecture: A Guide*, 1981; Theodore Wirth, *Minneapolis Park System: 1883–1944*, 1945; Mel Scott, *American City Planning Since 1890*, 1969; Drake Hokanson, *The Lincoln Highway*, 1988; Michael Wallis and Michael S. Williamson, *The Lincoln Highway: Coast to Coast from Times Square to the Golden Gate*, 2007; *The Complete Official Road Guide of the Lincoln Highway* (1924), 1993; Robert Caro, *The Power Broker* (1974), 1975; General Motors Corporation, *Futurama: Memento of the New York World's Fair Exhibit*, "Highways and Horizons," 1939; Norman Bel Geddes, *Magic Motorways*, 1940; Bernd Polster, Phil Patton, and Jeff Brouws, *Highway*, 1997; Warren Stuart and Brian Litt, *Moon Handbooks: Columbia River Gorge*, 2002; Paul Gleye, *The Architecture of Los Angeles*, 1981; Kansas City Chapter, AIA, *Kansas City*, 1979; David A. Remley, *Crooked Road: The Story of the Alaska Highway*, 1976; Microsoft *Encarta* 2001; Elizabeth Barlow Rogers, *Landscape Design*, 2001; Jan Cigliano and Sarah Bradford Landau, *The Grand American Avenue: 1850–1920*, 1994; Charles A. Birnbaum and Robin Karson, *Pioneers of American Landscape Design*, 2000; www.nycroads.com; and the Division of Highways, Illinois Department of Transportation

BRIDGES
The Historic American Engineering Record and the Historic American Buildings Survey; David Outerbridge and Graeme Outerbridge, *Bridges*, 1989; Charles S. Whitney, *Bridges of the World* (1929), 2003; Billy Joe Peyton, "Surveying and Building the Road," in Karl Raitz, ed., *The National Road*, 1996; G. E. Kidder Smith, *Source Book of American Architecture*, 1996; S. Allen Chambers, Jr., *Buildings of West Virginia*, 2004; David Gebhard and Gerald Mansheim, *Buildings of Iowa*, 1993; Patricia Leigh Brown, "Bridge Out of Nowhere," *The New York Times*, February, 19, 2004, p. D1; Richard Sanders Allen, *Covered Bridges of the Middle Atlantic States*, 1959; *Covered Bridges of the Middle West*, 1970; and other volumes by Allen surveying covered bridges of the South and the Northeast

DAMS
Walter Creese, *TVA's Public Planning*, 1990; and the Historic American Engineering Record

PUBLIC ENGINEERING
Walter A. McDougall, *Freedom Just Around the Corner*, 2004; Ronald E. Shaw, *Canals for a Nation*, 1990; G. Freeman Allen, *Railways: Past, Present & Future*, 1987; David McCullough, *The Path Between the Seas: The Creation of the Panama Canal*, 1977; Walter Creese, *TVA's Public Planning*, 1990; Steve Vogel, *The Pentagon*, 2007; Robert S. Norris, *Racing for the Bomb*, 2002; and the Historic American Engineering Record

POSTSCRIPT
Architectural Record 04:2004 (April); Suzanne Stephens, "New York's Museum of Modern Art finally becomes what it wanted to be all along," *Architectural Record* 01:2005 (January) pp. 94–109; and Clifford A. Pearson, "Polshek Partnership's Clinton Library connects with Little Rock and the body politic," *Architectural Record* 01:2005 (January), pp. 110–119

Places Index

Page numbers in *italics* indicate illustrations

Creators Index

Page numbers in *italics* indicate illustrations

Bebb, Charles
Seattle Art Museum, Seattle WA *179*, 179–180
Becker, William
Lambert–St. Louis Airport Terminal, St. Louis, MO 215, *215*, 287
Becket, Welton & Associates (*see also* Wurdman & Becket)
Palace of Fine Arts, San Francisco, CA 155
Beckhard, Herbert
Starkey House, Duluth, MN 197, *197*
Bedell, James and Jotham
Shadows-on-the-Teche, New Iberia, LA 78, *78*
Beissel, Johann Konrad
Ephrata Cloister, Ephrata, PA 274
Bel Geddes, Norman
New York World's Fair (1939–1940), Queens, NY 334–335
GM Futurama 334, 484
Bell, Robert E.
Camp Snoopy, Bloomington, MN 293, *293*
Belluschi, Pietro
Equitable Building, Portland, OR 198, *198*
Bennett, Bert L.
The Shell Gas Station, Winston-Salem NC 405
Bennett, Edward H.
Plan of Chicago, Chicago, IL 379–380, *379–380*
Plan of Minneapolis, Minneapolis, MN 380, *381*
Plan for San Francisco, San Francisco, CA *378*, 378–379
Bennett, Parsons & Frost
Buckingham Memorial Fountain, Chicago, IL 2–3, 464, *464*
Bentley, Harry
Houses, Greendale, WI 370, *370*
Bentley, Percy D.
Bartl House, La Crosse, WI 148
Chase House, La Crosse, WI 148
Salzer House, La Cross, WI 148, *148*
Scott House, La Cross, WI 148, *148*
Benton, Arthur B.
Glenwood Mission Inn, Riverside, CA 170, *170*
Bergman, Joel / Atlandia Design / Bergman, Walls & Youngblood
Mirage Casino & Hotel, Las Vegas, NV 399
Paris Casino & Hotel, Las Vegas, NV 399
Bergstrom, George Edwin
The Pentagon, Arlington, VA 502, *503*
Berry, Parker N.
Merchants National Bank, Grinnell, IA 124, *124*
Berry, Scott R.
Centennial Ice Palace, St. Paul, MN *13*
Minnetonka Municipal Building, Minnetonka, MN 230, *230*
Bertoia, Harry
Chapel, MIT campus, Cambridge, MA *201*, 204, *204*
General Motors Technical Center, Warren, MI 204, *205*
Manufacturers Trust Company Bank, New York, NY 199
Northwestern National Life Insurance, Minneapolis, MN *217*, 217–218
Southdale, Edina, MN 293, *293*
Bettenberg, P. C.
Minneapolis Armory, Minneapolis, MN 178, *178*
Bigelow, Jacob
Mount Auburn Cemetery, Cambridge, MA 432, *432*
Birch, Stephen
Kennecott Mines, McCarthy vic. AK *280*, 280–281
Birkerts, Gunnar
Federal Reserve Bank, Minneapolis, MN 220, 221
Bishop, Wayne

Dakota County Government Center, Hastings, MN 230, *230*
Bitter, Karl
Panama-Pacific International Exposition, San Francisco, CA *332*, 332–333
Bixby, James
Taconic State Parkway, Westchester, Putnam, Dutchess and Columbia counties, NY 480, 482, *482*
Black, Milton J.
Tail o' the Pup, Los Angeles, CA *400*, 405
Blaisse, Petra
Seattle Central Library, Seattle, WA 263, *263*
Blake, Edward
Pinecote Pavilion, Picayune, MS 223
Blanchfield, Emmett
Timberline Lodge, Mt. Hood National Forest, OR *315*, 315–316
Bland, Theodorick
Planning of Williamsburg, VA 350, *351*
Blessing, Charles
City Planning Director, Detroit, MI 383
Bloomer, Kent
Wonderwall, Louisiana World Exposition, New Orleans, LA 336–337, 337
Bluestein, Eddie
Holiday Inn, Memphis, TN 396, *396*
Holiday Inn "Great Sign," Memphis, TN 403, *403*
Bodnarchuk, Raya
Federal Reserve Garden, Washington, D.C. 462
Bogardus, James
Cast-iron skeletal construction 281, *281*
Fire Watch towers, New York, NY 281–282, *282*
Laing Stores, New York, NY 281, *281*
Bojourquez, Pedro
San Xavier del Bac, Tucson, AZ 39, *40*
Bond, William W. Jr.
Holiday Inn Motels, multiple locations 396
Boone, Daniel
Wilderness Road, vic. Middlesboro, KY 473
Bosworth, William Welles
Rockefeller Estate, "Kykuit," Westchester County, NY 449
Boullée, Etienne-Louis
Early Modern forms 73
Modern precursor 264
Bourne, George
Bourne "Wedding Cake" House, Kennebunk, ME 322, *322*
Bowditch, Ernest W.
Tuxedo Park, Orange County, NY 367
Bowman, Dean
Hopperstad Stave Church, Moorhead, MN 326, *326*
Bowman, Theodore
Taconic State Parkway, Westchester, Putnam, Dutchess and Columbia counties, NY 480, 482, *482*
Boyington, William W.
Allen House, "Terrace Hill," Des Moines, IA 87, *87*
Water Tower, Chicago, IL *125*
Bower, Lewis & Thrower
Philadelphia Savings Fund Society, Philadelphia, PA 193, *193*
Bradner, James W. Jr.
Taconic State Parkway, Westchester, Putnam, Dutchess and Columbia counties, NY 480, 482, *482*
Brand, Joyce Ballentyne
Coppertone Girl, Miami-Dade County, FL *397*, 404
Breuer, Marcel
Convent of the Assumption, Bismarck, ND 226, 227
St. John's University, Collegeville, MN

Abbey Church *226*, 227
Alcuin Library *225*
Dormitories *225*
Starkey House, Duluth, MN 197, *197*
UNESCO Headquarters, Paris, France 227
University Heights Campus, New York University, The Bronx, NY 227
Whitney Museum of American Art, New York, NY 228, *228*
Broadhead, Charles
Erie Canal, Hudson River to Lake Erie, NY 500, *500*
Brockett, John
Plan of New Haven, CT 349, *349*
Brooks, James
Marine Air Terminal murals, Queens, NY 287
Brown, A. Page
California Pavilion, World's Columbian Exposition, Chicago, IL 170
Crocker Row, Santa Barbara, CA 161, *161*
Brown, Arthur Jr.
Plan for San Francisco, San Francisco, CA *378*, 378–379
Brown, Lancelot, "Capability"
Blenheim Palace grounds–landscape, Oxford-shire, England *424*, 425
Brown, Timothy
Brown "Spirit" House 322–323, *323*
Bruder, Will
Barr Central Library, Phoenix, AZ 262, *262*
Bruner/Cott
Crown and Eagle Mills conversion, North Uxbridge, MA *279*, 279–280
Brunner, Arnold
Group Plan/Mall, Cleveland, OH 338–339, 377, 377–378
Brush, Michael
6th Street Viaduct, Milwaukee, WI 492, *493*
Buck, William L.
Pratt "Honolulu" House, Marshall, MI 88, *89*
Bucklin, J. C.
Arcade, Providence, RI 299, *299*
Buelna, Felix
Buelna's Roadhouse, Portola Valley, CA 273, *273*
Buffington, Leroy S.
Pillsbury Hall, University of Minnesota, Minneapolis, MN *182*
Tainter Memorial, Menomonie, WI *119*, 119–120
Bulfinch, Charles
Bulfinch Scheme (Mall plan), Washington, D.C. 355
Faneuil Hall, Boston, MA 294, *294*
First Church of Christ, Lancaster, MA 71
Massachusetts State House, Boston, MA 71
Otis House (First), Boston, MA 71, *71*
United States Capitol, Washington, D.C. 76
Bunshaft, Gordon (SOM)
Chase Manhattan Bank, New York, NY 200, *200*
Connecticut General Life Insurance, Bloomfield, CT 199
Lever House, New York, NY *198*, 199
Manufacturers Trust Company, New York, NY 199
New York World's Fair (1964–1965), Queens, NY 336, *336*
Buonarroti, Michelangelo
Campidoglio, Rome, Italy 408
Burgwyn, C. P. E
Monument Avenue, Richmond, VA *479*, 479–480
Burke, Stanley
Stan's Drive-In, Sacramento, CA 393
Burle Marx, Roberto
Biscayne Boulevard Sidewalk Test, Miami, FL 414, *415*
Brazilian national style 451

Lambert–St. Louis Airport Terminal, St. Louis, MO 215, *215*, 287

Cook, Wilbur David Jr.
Beverly Hills, Los Angeles County, CA 367, *367*
Huntington Gardens, San Marino, CA 450, *450*

Coolidge & Carson
Beacon Oil Company Respectable, Woburn, MA 390, *391*

Coolidge, Charles Allerton (*see* Shepley, Rutan & Coolidge)
Stanford Memorial Church, Palo Alto, CA 120, *121*

Cooper/Eckstut
Times Square development guidelines, New York, NY 404

Cooper/Lecky Partnership
Vietnam Veterans' Memorial, Washington, D.C. 413, *413*

Cope & Lippincott
Guild House, Philadelphia, PA *210*, 211

Copeland, Robert Morris
Oak Bluffs, Martha's Vineyard, MA 317

Corbett, Harvey Wiley
Century of Progress Exposition, Chicago, IL 334
Rockefeller Center, New York, NY 178

Cortés, Hernán (Hernando)
1518–1521 Rebuilding of Tenochtitlan, Mexico City, Mexico 341

Cossutta & Ponte
Christian Science Center, Boston, MA 220

Costa, Lucio
National Capital Plan, Brasília, Brazil 385

Cox, Kenyon
Minnesota State Capitol, St. Paul, MN 100, *100*

Coxhead, Ernest
3200 Block of Pacific Avenue, San Francisco, CA 104, *105*
Waybur townhouse, San Francisco, CA 104, *105*

Craig, James Osborne
El Paseo shopping arcade, Santa Barbara, CA 42, *42*
Casa de la Guerra, Santa Barbara, CA, 42, *42*
Street of Spain, Santa Barbara, CA 42

Cram, Ralph Adams / Cram, Goodhue & Ferguson / Cram & Ferguson
Gothicist, partner of Bertram Goodhue 183
Graduate College, Princeton University, Princeton, NJ *160*
St. Thomas Church, New York, NY 171, *171*
United States Military Academy, West Point, NY *183*

Crane, C. Howard
Fox Theatre, Detroit, MI 307
Fox Theatre, St. Louis, MO 307–308, *308*
Leading designer of movie theaters 306

Crane, Jacob
Plan of Greendale, WI 370, *370*

Crawley, George
Phipps Estate, "Old Westbury Gardens," Old Westbury, NY *428*, 429

Cret, Paul Philippe
Federal Reserve Bank, Washington, D.C. 180, *180*
Cincinnati Union Terminal, Cincinnati, OH 178, 285, *285*–286
World War I Monument, Providence, RI 412–413

Crowther, Richard
Cooper Cinerama Theaters *312*
Denver, CO 312
Omaha, NE 312
St. Louis Park, MN 312

Cuningham Group
Stratosphere Casino & Hotel, Las Vegas, NV 397

Curtis, Glenn
Fantasy real-estate development, Opa Locka, FL *321*

Custus, George Washington Parke
Custus-Lee Mansion, Arlington National Cemetery, VA 76, *76*

Custus, John
Botanical specimens 425

Dailey, Richard M.
Chicago's environmental mayor 462

Dakin, James
Bank of Louisville, Louisville, KY 79, *79*
Old State Capitol, Baton Rouge, LA 299, *299*

Daly, Leo A. Company
National World War II Memorial, Washington, D.C. 359

Dana, Richard Henry
Church reconstruction, Litchfield, CT 113, *113*

Danadjieva Tzvetin, Angela
Auditorium Forecourt Fountain, Portland, OR 465, *465*
Freeway Park, Seattle, WA 460, *461*

Darby, Abraham III
Iron Bridge, Coalbrookdale, England 281

Daroff Design
Philadelphia Savings Fund Society, Philadelphia, PA 193, *193*

da Ros, Oswald
Walska Lotusland, Montecito, CA *449*, 449–450

Davis, Alexander Jackson / Town & Davis
Custom House, New York, NY 77
Delamater House, Rhinebeck, NY 83
Llewellyn Park, West Orange, NJ 365–366, *366*
Lyndhurst, Tarrytown, NY *82*, 83
Rotch House, New Bedford, MA 83, *83*
Rustic cottages 82

Davis, Pierpont
The Pentagon, Arlington, VA *502*, *503*

Davis, Robert
Seaside, Walton County, FL 320, *320*

Davis, Stuart
Radio City Music Hall, New York, NY 303

Dayton's Department Store
Southdale, Edina, MN 293, *293*

Daza, Ignacio
Castillo San Marcos, St. Augustine, FL 37, *37*

Dearborn, Henry
Mount Auburn Cemetery, Cambridge, MA 432, *432*

de Bretteville and Polyzoides
Gartz Court, Pasadena, CA 153, *153*

de Coux, Janet
World War I Monument, Providence, RI 412–413

de Forest, Lockwood
Steedman House, "Casa del Herrero," Montecito, CA *165*, 165–166
Walska Lotusland, Montecito, CA *449*, 449–450

de Forest, Robert
Forest Hills Gardens, Queens, NY 368, *368*

de la Guerra, Jose
Casa de la Guerra, Santa Barbara, CA 42, *42*

Delano & Aldrich
Beaux Arts practitioners 97
Dinner Key Pan-Am base, Miami, Fl 287
Marine Air Terminal, Queens, NY *286*, 287

de la Tour, LeBlond
Nouvelle Orléans, New Orleans, LA 349, *349*

Delk, Edward Bueler
Country Club Plaza, Kansas City, MO 292, *292*, 368, *368*

De Maria, Walter
"The Lightning Field," Catron County, NM 457

Denlinger, Donald
Red Caboose Motel, vic., Strasburg, PA 396, *396*

de Pauger, Adrien
Nouvelle Orléans, New Orleans, LA 349, *349*

Derlith, Charles Jr.
Golden Gate Bridge, San Francisco, CA *471*, 492

Derrah, Robert V.
Coca Cola Bottling Plant, Los Angeles, CA 158–159, *159*

Deskey, Donald
Radio City Music Hall, New York, NY 178, 303

Despont, Thierry W.
Getty Center, Los Angeles, CA 260, 261

de Portzamparc, Christian
LVMH Tower, New York, NY 262

de Wolfe, Elise
Deering Estate, "Vizcaya," Miami, FL 163–164, *164*

Dexter, George
McDonald's Golden Arches sign, San Bernardino, CA 403

Dietrich, William
Dorton Arena, Raleigh, NC 215, *215*

Diman, Joanna
Connecticut General Life Insurance Company Headquarters 199

Dine, Jim
Biltmore Hotel, Los Angeles, CA 297

Dinkeloo, John, Eero Saarinen & Associates / Roche, Dinkeloo & Associates
CBS Building, New York, NY 205
Deere Headquarters, East Moline, IL 205, *205*

DiPasquale, Paul
Monument Avenue, Richmond, VA 479, *479*–480

Disney, Walter Elias
Disneyland, Anaheim, CA 401, *401*
Sleeping Beauty's Castle 401
Monorail 401
Disney World, Orange and Osceola counties, FL 318–319, *319*

DMJM Harris
World Trade Center PATH Terminal, New York, NY 286

Dobberson, Paul M.
Grotto of the Redemption, West Bend, IA 324, *325*

Dodds, Chamberlin
Kaufmann House, "La Tourelle," Fox Chapel, PA 163, *163*

Dominy, Nathanial V
Gardiner's Mill, East Hampton, Long Island, NY 279
Hook Windmill, East Hampton, Long Island, NY 279, *279*

Dorr, Robert Jr.
Dunes Casino & Hotel, Las Vegas, NV 398

Doullut, Milton Paul
Doullut "Steamboat" Houses, New Orleans, LA 324, *324*

Dow, Alden B.
Dow Home & Studio, Midland, MI 214, *214*

Downer, Jay
Blue Ridge Parkway, Virginia and North Carolina 484, *484*
Mount Vernon Memorial Highway/George Washington Memorial Parkway, Fairfax and Arlington counties, VA *482*, 482–483
Taconic State Parkway, Westchester, Putnam, Dutchess and Columbia counties, NY 480, 482, *482*
Westchester County Parkways, Westchester County, NY 480

Downing, Andrew Jackson
Downing Plan (National Mall plan), Washington, D.C. 356, *356*
First national figure in landscape architecture 356, 422, 432
Llewellyn Park, West Orange, NJ 365, 432
Rustic cottages 82

Draper, Earle S.

Hunt House, Woodland, MN 163, *163*

Fort–Brescia, Bernardo / Arquitectonica
Spear House, Miami Shores, FL 232, *234*
The Atlantis, Miami, FL 237, *237*

Foster, Richard
New York World's Fair (1964–1965), Queens, NY 336, *336*
New York State Pavilion 336

Fowler, Joe
Disney World, Walt, Orange and Osceola counties, FL 318–319, *319*

Franklin, George B.
Forum Cafeteria, Minneapolis, MN 177

Franzen, Ulrich
Bradford-Emerson Halls, Ithaca, NY 229–230, *230*
Boyce Thompson Institute, Ithaca, NY 229–230
Veterinary Research Laboratory, Ithaca, NY 229–230, *230*
Veterinary Research Tower, Ithaca, NY 229–230

Frawley, Henry J.
Frawley Ranch, Spearfish, SD 272

Frazee, John
Custom House, New York, NY 77

Fredericks, Marshall
War Memorial Fountain, Cleveland, OH 464

Free, William
Lucy the Elephant, Margate, NJ 404, 405

Freed, James Ingo (Pei Cobb Freed)
United States Holocaust Memorial Museum, Washington, D.C. 359

French, Daniel Chester
Boston Public Library, Boston, MA 98, *98*
Dodge Memorial, "Angel of Death," Council Bluffs, IA 466, *467*
Lincoln Memorial, Washington, D.C. 101, 411, *411*
Louisiana Purchase Exposition, St. Louis, MO 332, *332*
Minnesota State Capitol, St. Paul, MN 100, 100
Old Post Office, St. Louis, MO 88, *88*

French, Fred B. Co.
Tudor City, New York NY 172

Freret, Douglass
Burnside Plantation, "The Houmas," Burnside, LA 80

Freret, William A.
Old State Capitol, Baton Rouge, LA 299, *299*

Friedman, Martin, and Mildred "Mickey" Friedman
Walker Art Center, Minneapolis, MN 230, 230
Sculpture Garden *455*, 455–456

Friedman, William
Walker Art Center Idea House II, Minneapolis, MN 195

Fries, John
Alamo, San Antonio, TX 38, *38*
Frost, Frederick G. Jr.
Socony–Mobil Moderne, multiple locations 391, *391*

Fteley, Alphonse
New Croton Dam, vic. Croton-on-Hudson, NY 497, *497*

Fuller, Richard Buckminster
American Pavilion, Expo '67, Montreal, Québec, Canada 20
Dymaxion Car 20
Dymaxion House, Greenfield Village, Dearborn, MI 20

Furness, Frank / Furness, Evans & Company
Arcade Building–Broad Street pedestrian skywalk, Philadelphia, PA 418, *418*
Centennial National Bank, Philadelphia, PA 116, *116*
Pennsylvania Academy of Fine Arts, Philadelphia, PA *114–115*, 115
Physick House (attributed) Cape May, NJ 90, 91
Provident Life and Trust Company, Philadelphia,

PA 116, *116*
Undine Barge Club, Philadelphia, PA *116*, 117
University of Pennsylvania Library, "Furness Building," Philadelphia, PA *116*, 117

Gabriel, Romano
The Wooden Garden, Eureka, CA 324–325, *325*

Gallatin, Albert
National Road, Cumberland MD to Vandalia, IL 473, *473*

Gallen-Kallela, Akseli
National Romantic painter 181

Gande, Henry
Mammy's Cupboard, Natchez, MS 405–406, *406*

Gano, Ward
Timberline Lodge, Mt. Hood National Forest, OR *315*, 315–316

García Bravo, Alonso
1518–1521 City Plan, rebuilding of Tenochtitlan, Mexico City, Mexico 341

Garcia Cepeda, Gerardo
Plan for Downtown St. Louis, St. Louis, MO 387, *387*

Gaona, Ignacio
San Xavier del Bac, vic. Tucson, AZ 39, *40*

Garrett, Stephen
Getty Museum, "Getty Villa," Malibu, CA *249*, 249–250, 255, *255*

Garrison, Robert
Boston Avenue Methodist Church, Tulsa, OK 176, *176*, 222

Gaskin, Neal / Gaskin & Bezanski
New York, New York Casino & Hotel, Las Vegas, NV 399, *399*

Gatje, Robert
Starkey House, Duluth, MN 197, *197*

Gaynor, John
Haughwout Building, New York, NY 282, *282*

Geddes, James
Erie Canal, Hudson River to Lake Erie, NY 500, *500*

Gehry, Frank / Frank O. Gehry & Associates / Gehry Partners
BP Pedestrian Bridge, Chicago, IL 494, *495*
Chiat/Day Headquarters, Los Angeles, CA 245, *245*
Davis House/Studio, Malibu, CA 242
Disney Concert Hall, Los Angeles, CA 246, *247*
Gehry House, Santa Monica, CA *243*, 243–244
Gemini G.E.L., Los Angeles, CA 243, *243*
Guggenheim Museum, Bilbao, Spain 242
Lewis Building, Case Western Reserve University, Cleveland, OH 246, *246*
Loyola University Law School, Los Angeles, CA *244*, 245
Norton Beach House, Los Angeles, CA 244, 245
O'Neill Hay Barn, San Juan Capistrano, CA 242
Pritzker Pavilion, Chicago, IL 246, *247*
UCLA Student Placement Center, Los Angeles, CA 243
Weisman Art Museum, University of Minnesota, Minneapolis, MN 245–246, *246*
Winton Guest House, Orono–Owatonna, MN *244*, 245

Geismar, Tom
Mobil Contemporary, multiple locations 391

Gerdes, H. C.
Bonneville Dam, Multnomah County, OR 498, *498*

Geren/CRS Sirrine
River Crest Country Club, Fort Worth, TX 251–252, *252*

Gibbs, Charles
La Cuesta Encantada, "Hearst Castle," San Simeon, CA *154*, 156, *157*

Gilbert, Cass
Allen Art Museum, Oberlin, OH 492, *493*
Bayonne Bridge, Bayonne NJ to Staten Island,

NY 492, *493*
Eight-story skyscraper, Butte, MT 364
Fine Arts Building, Louisiana Purchase Exposition, St. Louis, MO 332
Minnesota State Capitol, St. Paul, MN 100, *100*
Prudential pedestrian skywalks, Newark, NJ 418
United States Supreme Court, Washington, D.C. 101, *101*
Woolworth Building, New York, NY 171

Gilbertson, Victor C. / Hills, Gilbertson & Hayes
Christ Church Lutheran, Minneapolis, MN 188, *188*

Gill, Irving
Dodge House, Los Angeles, CA 156, 191, *191*
Horatio West Court, Santa Monica, CA 156, *156*
La Jolla Women's Club, La Jolla–San Diego, CA 155–156, *156*

Gillies, George H.
Field Estate, "Caumsett," West Neck, Long Island, NY 109

Girard, Alexander
Mauna Kea Beach Hotel, Kamuela, Big Island, HI 316, *316*

Glaser Associates
Cincinnati Union Terminal, Cincinnati, OH 178, *285*, 285–286

Glass, Charles
Walska Lotusland, Montecito, CA *449*, 449–450

Glatter-Götz Orgelbau
Disney Concert Hall, Los Angeles, CA 246, *247*

Glenn, J. H. Jr.
The Shell Gas Station, Winston–Salem NC 405

Godefroy, Maximilian
Capitol Square plan, Richmond, VA 73

Goethals, George W.
Bayonne Bridge, Bayonne NJ to Staten Island, NY 492, *493*
Panama Canal, Panama 499, 500, *501*, 502

Goff, Bruce
Bavinger House, Norman, OK, 221
Boston Avenue Methodist Church, Tulsa, OK 176, *176*, 221, 222
Harder House (Glen and Luetta) vic. Mountain Lake, MN 222, *222*
Harder House (Jacob and Anna), Mountain Lake, MN *222*, 223

Goldberg, Bertrand
Marina City, Chicago, IL 218, *218*

Goodhue, Bertram Grosvenor / Cram, Goodhue & Ferguson / Bertram G. Goodhue
Hartley Office Building, Duluth, MN 172, *172*
Kitchi Gammi Club, Duluth, MN 172
Los Angeles Public Library, Los Angeles, CA *184*, 184–185
Nebraska State Capitol, Lincoln, NE *184*, 185
Panama-California Exposition, San Diego, CA 156, 333, *333*
St. Bartholomew's Church, New York, NY 184, *184*
St. Thomas Church, New York, NY 171, *171*, 183
U.S. Military Academy, West Point, NY 183

Goodwin, John
Pike Place Market, Seattle, WA 291, *291*

Goodwin, Philip L.
Museum of Modern Art (MoMA), New York, NY 193, *193*

Gordon, J. Riely
Ellis County Courthouse, Waxahachie, TX 120, *121*

Gorgas, William
Panama Canal, Panama 499, 500, *501*, 502

Goufee, Antoine
Naniboujou Lodge, vic., Grand Marais, MN 315, *315*

Gould, Carl
Seattle Art Museum, Seattle WA *179*, 179–180

Graff, Frederick C.

Mexico 39

KKE
Mall of America, Bloomington, MN 293, *293*

Klai Juba Architects
Mandalay Bay Casino & Hotel, Las Vegas, NV 399

Kling, Vincent
Center City Planning, Philadelphia, PA 384

Klipstein & Rathmann
Bevo Mill, St. Louis, MO 325, *325*

Knight, Emerson
Mission La Purísima Concepción, Lompoc, CA 444, *444*

Knight, Fraser
U.S. Post Office, Miami Beach, FL 180, *180*

Knight, Lester B.
Thompson State of Illinois Center, Chicago, IL *238*, 238–239

Knor, Jacob
Cliveden, Philadelphia, PA *64*, *65*, 67

Knowles, William
3200 Block of Pacific Avenue, San Francisco, CA 104, *105*

Koenig, Pierre
Stahl House/Case Study House #22, Los Angeles, CA 198, *198*

Kohn Pedersen Fox Associates
Museum of Modern Art (MoMA), New York, NY 266–267, *504*, *505*
Proctor & Gamble Headquarters, Cincinnati, OH 252, *252*
333 Wacker Drive, Chicago, IL 238, *238*

Komendant, August
Kimbell Art Museum, Fort Worth, TX 203, *203*
Richards Medical Research Building, University of Pennsylvania, Philadelphia, PA *202*, 203
Salk Institute, La Jolla, San Diego, CA *202*, 203

Koolhaas, Rem / Office of Metropolitan Architecture (OMA)
Seattle Central Library, Seattle, WA 263, *263*
Spear House, Miami Shores, FL 232, *234*

Korda/Nemeth
Longaberger Co. Home Office, "The Basket," Newark, OH 406, *407*

Korn Randolph
Getty Villa, Malibu, CA *249*, 249–250, 255, *255*

Kraetsch & Kraetsch
Butler House, Des Moines, IA 179, *179*

Kroehl, Julius B.
Fire Watch Tower, New York, NY 281–281, *282*

Krueger, Willard C. Associates
Jefferson National Expansion Memorial, "Gateway Arch," St. Louis, MO 204, *412*, 413
Manhattan Project, Los Alamos, NM 502–503, *503*

Kuhn, Denis, Ehrenkrantz, Eckstut & Kuhn
Custom House restoration, New York, NY 77

Kullman Corporation
Americana Diner, Shrewsbury, NJ 392
Park West Diner, Little Falls, NJ 392, *393*

Kumpula, Wayne
Big Fish Supper Club, Bena, MN 406, *407*

Kurutz, Denis L.
Getty Villa, Malibu, CA *249*, 249–250, 255, *255*

KZF
Rosenthal Center for Contemporary Art, Cincinnati, OH 266, *266*

Labatut, Jean
Beaux Arts–trained Princeton professor 248

Labrouste, Henri
French modernist, technologist 264

LaFarge, John
Minnesota State Capitol, St. Paul, MN 100, *100*
Trinity Church interior, Boston, MA 117, 117, 300, *300*

LaFarge and Morris

Colonial Revival transformation, Litchfield, CT 113, *113*, 442

Lafever, Minard
Whaler's Church, Sag Harbor, Long Island, NY 85, 85

Lamb, Thomas
Lake Theater, Oak Park, IL 310–311, *311*
Leading designer of movie theaters 306
Ohio Theatre, Columbus, OH 307, *307*

Lambert, Jacques
Buckingham Memorial Fountain, Chicago, IL 2–3, 464, *464*

Lambert, Phyllis
Biltmore Hotel, Los Angeles, CA 296–297

Lancaster, Samuel
Columbia River Highway, Troutdale to The Dalles, OR 483, *483*

Landrum, Charles
TWA Idlewild Terminal, Queens, NY 204

Langdon & Wilson
Getty Museum, "Getty Villa," Malibu, CA *249*, 249–250, 255, *255*

Langton, Daniel W.
Drumthwacket Italianate Garden, Princeton, NJ 428

Langdon, James
Rock Creek and Potomac Parkway, Washington, D.C. 480, *480*

Lapidus, Morris
Americana Hotel, Miami Beach, FL 215
Armstrong's interior, New York, NY 214
Eden Roc Hotel, Miami Beach, FL 215
Fontainebleau Hotel, Miami Beach, FL *214*, 215
Jetsons vocabulary 214
Las Vegas, relationship 398
Lincoln Road Mall, Miami Beach, FL 414, 416, *416*

Larkin, Thomas Oliver
Larkin House, Monterey, CA 42, *42*

Larsen, Jack
Caesars Pylon Sign, Las Vegas, NV 399

Larson, Roy
Center City Planning, Philadelphia, PA 384

Latrobe, Benjamin Henry
Biddle Mansion, "Andalusia," Andalusia, PA 79
Cathedral of Baltimore, Baltimore, MD 76, 76
Fairmount Water Works, Philadelphia, PA 77, 78
Latrobe Scheme (Mall plan), Washington, D.C. *354*, 355
University of Virginia, "Academical Village," Charlottesville, VA 74–75, *75*
United States Capitol, Washington, D.C. 76

Lautner, John
Arango House, Acapulco, Mexico 223
Bell House, Los Angeles, CA 223, 224
Carling House, Los Angeles, CA 223–224, *224*
Googie's, Los Angeles, CA 223, 393, *393*
Malin House, "Chemosphere," Los Angeles, CA 224, *224*
Reiner House, "Silvertop," Los Angeles, CA 224, *224*

Lawrie, Lee
Harkness Memorial Quadrangle, Yale University, New Haven, CT 171
Los Angeles Public Library, Los Angeles, CA 184, *184*
Nebraska State Capitol, Lincoln, NE *184*, 185
Rockefeller Center, New York, NY 178
St. Thomas Church, New York, NY 171, *171*

Layman, T. W.
Platt Office Building, Los Angeles, CA 258, *258*

LeBrun, Napoleon
Mohonk Mountain House, New Paltz, NY *313*, 313–314

Le Corbusier (Charles Edouard Jeanneret)
Carpenter Center for the Visual Arts, Harvard University, Cambridge, MA 227
Government buildings, Chandigarh, India 226

La Tourette Monastery, vic. Lyon, France 226
Villa Savoye, Poissy-sur-Seine, France *190*, 191
Unité d'Habitation, Marseilles, France 226

Le Doux, Claude-Nicholas
Early Modern forms 73
Modern precursor 264
1770 Axial scheme 208
Toll House, Paris, France *264*

Lee, S. Charles
Academy Theater, Inglewood, CA 311, *311*
Fremont Theater, San Luis Obispo, CA 311, *311*
Leading designer of movie theaters 306
Los Angeles Theatre, Los Angeles, CA 308

Lee, Thomas
Lee Mansion, "Stratford Hall," Westmoreland County, VA 48, *48*
Gardens 424, *443*, 443–444

Lee, Tom
Villard Houses/Helmsley Palace Hotel, New York, NY 297

Legorreta, Ricardo
Solana, Westlake–Southlake, TX *456*, 456–457

Leigh, Douglas
Smoking camel sign, Times Square, New York, NY 405

Lein, Malcolm, and Miriam Lein
Idea House I, Minneapolis, MN 195
Idea House II, Minneapolis, MN 195

L'Enfant, Pierre Charles
Plan of Washington, D.C. 352–359, *352–359*, 410

LeMessurier Associates
City Hall, Boston, MA 228, *228*

Le Moyne, Jean Baptiste, Sieur de Bienville
Founder of New Orleans, LA 349

Le Nôtre, André
Seventeenth-century French landscapes 354

Lenny, Henry
Commercial Office Building, Santa Barbara, CA 258, *258*

Levitt, William and Alfred Levitt
Levittown, Nassau County, LI *371*, 371–372
Levittown, Bucks County, PA 372
Levittown, Willingboro, NJ *371*, 372
Postwar housing innovators 371

Lewis, Sydney and Frances
Best Products Company, Richmond, VA 241

Lewis & Valentine
Post Mansion, "Mar-a-Lago," Palm Beach, FL 166, *166*

Lewitt, Sol
Federal Reserve Garden, Washington, D.C. 462

Liebenberg & Kaplan
Country Club houses, Edina, MN 169, *169*
Maco Theater, Virginia, MN 312, *312*
Regional leader in movie-theater design 306

Lin, Maya
Vietnam Veterans' Memorial, Washington, D.C. 413, *413*

Lindeberg, Harrie T.
Beaux Arts practitioner 97

Lindenthal, Gustav
Smithfield Street Bridge, Pittsburgh, PA 491, *491*

Link, Theodore
City Plan for St. Louis, St. Louis, MO *378*, 379
St. Louis Union Station, St. Louis, MO 295, *295*

Linn, Karl
Seagram Building, New York, NY 199, 199, 304

Lipchiz, Jacques
Roofless Church, New Harmony, IN *412*, 413

Lippold, Richard
General Motors Technical Center, Warren, MI 204, *205*
Inland Steel Building, Chicago, IL 128
The Four Seasons, New York, NY 304

LMN
Seattle Central Library, Seattle, WA 263, *263*

ML ¹/₁₀